MW01234122

POWERBUILDER DEVELOPER'S JOURNAL

POWERBUILDER 4.0
SECRETS OF THE
POWERBUILDER MASTERS

Edited By

Michael MacDonald
&
Steve Benfield

SYS-CON Publications
Jersey City, NJ 07305

PowerBuilder Developer's Journal
PowerBuilder 4.0: Secrets Of The PowerBuilder Masters
1st Edition
A SYS-CON Book/April 1995

ISBN 1-886141-00-2

Published and printed in the United States of America

0 9 8 7 6 5 4 3 2

Credits

Editors
>Michael MacDonald
>Steve Benfield

Authors
>Bruce Armstrong
>Derek Ball
>Rey Bango
>Steve Benfield
>Breck Carter
>Ramesh Chandak
>Henry Cortinas
>Tom Flynn
>Barry Gervin
>William Green
>Michael Griffith
>Judah Holstein
>Randy Hompesch
>Peter Horwood
>Al Lucas
>Michael MacDonald
>Kent Marsh
>John Olson
>Mike Pflieger
>Sean Rhody
>Jonathan Sayles
>Scott Virtue
>Terry Voth
>Daniel Worden
>Robert Zenobia

Managing Editor
>Rabia Terri Harris

Copy Editors
>Rabia Terri Harris
>Jane Roseen
>Elinor Holland

Art Director
>John Smith

Production Editor
>Scott Davison

Cover Design & Illustration
>Jim Morgan/Applied Image

Dedications

To my wife Patricia, and my children Amanda and Peter, all of whom I love very much.

Michael MacDonald

To my wife LeAnne: thanks for always supporting me even when I'm in my last minute panic before deadlines. Also, thanks for teaching me how not to write English like a programmer.

Steve Benfield

Introduction

I sit here on a foggy, raw New England night in late November contemplating the remainder of this volume. This book is meant to provide an in-depth overview of the features of PowerBuilder 4.0 – a product that has yet to even be finalized– a daunting task indeed. However, SYS-CON Publications, co-editor Steve Benfield, and I have assembled a cast of the very best in PowerBuilder talent in North America to help. Further, in these pages you will not only get a glimpse into the very latest release of PowerBuilder but also the advanced and very powerful techniques that have made these writers tops in their field. Such a multitude of talent and such a collection of authoritative advice is simply not available anywhere else.

I urge you to read the following pages carefully, setting aside what you may have learned in class at Powersoft, disregarding what your COBOL or dBase or C backgrounds tell you, and learn from the experts: learn the Secrets of the PowerBuilder Masters.

Michael MacDonald
Editor
PowerProgrammer Magazine

Forward

I'd like you to think of this book as a conversation between developers. When software developers get together, they swap ideas and techniques. PowerBuilder has so many features, it is impossible to learn every single function and feature of the product. The need for developers to interact and challenge each other's thinking is critical to growth. I believe this book is such an interaction. As you read this, you'll hear from many of today's top developers discussion techniques and ideas that they have. You won't find a tutorial on how to build your first PowerBuilder application and you won't find a rehash of the PowerBuilder documentation. What I hope you'll find is value-added information that only comes from talking with experienced developers, teachers, and consultants. I know that I've learned quite a bit from working on this project and I hope that you will too.

Steve Benfield
Editor
PowerBuilder Developer's Journal

Table Of Contents

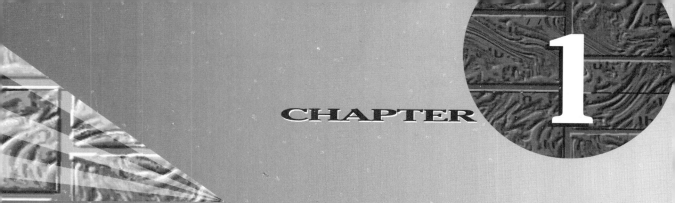

Introducing
PowerBuilder 4.0

By Michael MacDonald

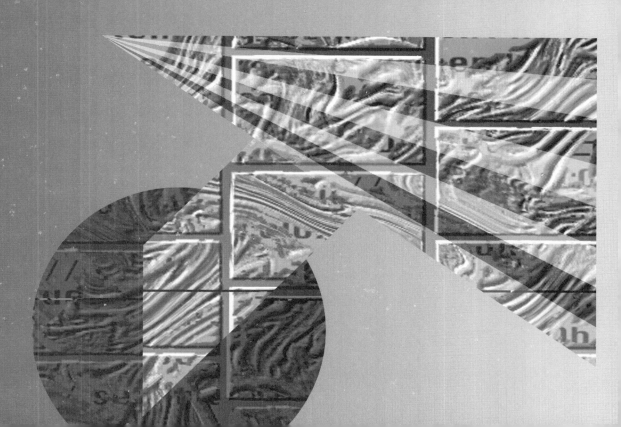

Introducing PowerBuilder 4.0

by **Michael MacDonald**

The best way to lead off the series of advanced topics in PowerBuilder–and the in-depth examination of most of the new features of PowerBuilder 4.0–that you will find in this book, is to give you a survey of the changes from PowerBuilder version 3.0. To take advantage of this overview, read on.

The most significant and yet least visible change in PB 4 is its newfound ***portability across multiple platforms***. Powersoft has successfully reengineered their entire code base to be PBL portable to Windows NT, Macintosh, and unix Motif. An OS/2 version, however, is not available and is not in the works at this time (see my related comments in "PowerBuilder Version 5.0 and Beyond").

Also noteworthy but not immediately visible is the fact that ***applications*** created under any prior version of PowerBuilder ***will port directly*** to 4.0. This means that present 2.0 shops— and there are still a significant number—need not upgrade incrementally. As in 3.0, applications may be migrated by going into the library painter and selecting Migrate Application from the Utilities menu, or by merely attempting to open the application in the application painter.

Many ***functions*** have undergone ***name changes***. For instance, dwModify has been changed to simply Modify (though PB 4.0 will still continue to support the old naming conventions). This affects mainly DataWindow and graph functions, which have had the "dw" and "gr" stripped off. The functions are now more polymorphic, with the object name telling the compiler what form of action to take. For instance, grSaveAs becomes simply SaveAs, as in *gr_1.SaveAs* versus the DataWindow form, dw_1.SaveAs.

A very exciting new feature is the ***nested report***. A nested report is a DataWindow (or report) placed in the detail band of another DataWindow (or report). Reports can be nested to any level deep, and all these can be printed *on the same page*. Any style of report may be nested. The most typical use of these nested reports will be in traditional master/detail layouts, where a DataWindow displaying an invoice header may have a nested dw showing associated line items. (To do this, create your master data window as usual. Then, while editing the detail band of the report, click on the new Report icon; then click on the place on the detail band where you want to place the nested report. Next select a second DataWindow that you have previously created (such as a list of line items) and link the two together by selecting the relationship (such as Retrieval Arguments) that you want established. Alternatively, there is a Criteria painter where you may relate columns on the nested DataWindow to columns on the master. However, the nested report need not be related to the master report at all.)

The ***new GetChild function*** works with nested reports. In a script, this function returns the handle of a nested DataWindow, allowing you to dynamically retrieve and edit the information shown in it.

Another new feature relating to DataWindows is ***sliding columns***. You may specify that any given column slide left, directly above, or all the way up. The "slide left" feature is useful when you need to print a first and last name next to each other. In PowerBuilder 3.0 you had to create a computed column to get the desired result. In 4.0, you only need specify that the last name will slide left, thus removing any excess spaces between the two names at report time. Sliding columns "directly above" and "all the way up" are similar in concept, with the most obvious application being address labels. In the former case, columns will slide up one row to fill an empty spot, while with the latter, they will slide as far up as possible. Imagine an address label where the second and third lines of some addresses might be blank. In that circumstance you would want the City field to slide "all the way up" to fill any dead space on the label..

Another hot new feature relating to DataWindows is ***newspaper columns***, which produces a report similar to the multiple column feature of Microsoft Word for Windows. A DataWindow with this option chosen will snake the data down the left of the page and then return to the top of a second display column. This differs from the PowerBuilder 3.0 N-Up report, which runs rows across the page first. You can specify the number of columns for the report (the default is 1) and the width of each column.

Crosstab reporting has been enhanced. The definition dialog has been enhanced to include drag and drop of the selected columns to the Rows, Columns, and Values areas. Crosstabs now include column, row, and value headings as well as grand-total fields for each row and column. Crosstab reports may be altered dynamically at runtime; this gives your users the ability to change the data that is displayed on a Crosstab without much programming on your part!

Graphs have also seen enhancements. In Categories, in addition to strings, Numbers, Dates, DateTimes, and Times are also now supported. Scatter graphs support Number, Date,

DateTime, and Time datatypes, as well as Double. Similarly, in addition to Double, Values may now also be Number, Date, DateTime, and Time. For DataWindows, the type defaults to that which is on the table. For Round Maximum, you may round to (Date) years, months, days; (DateTime) years, months, days, hours, minutes, seconds; (Time) hours, minutes, seconds, or microseconds. The new function grSetDataExplode (graphcontrol, series, datapoint, percentage) explodes the pie slice for series and datapoint by the percentage supplied. grDataPieExplode (graphcontrol, series, datapoint, percentage) returns the percentage, into percentage, for the pie slice specified by series and datapoint. A Modify Expression Dialog is provided to allow text to include calculated expressions for attributes such as tittle. Series and Category data may be sorted.

There is a new ***Multi-Table Quick Select*** for tables which have a primary for foreign key relationship. In 3.0, Quick Select only allowed you to select columns in one table. Under the new version, the user will get to choose from all the tables that have a foreign key relationship to the current one.

Many ***DataWindow dialogs*** have been enhanced. The Sort, Group, and Suppress Repeating Values painters now sport a sculpted, drag and drop feel. There is a ***new DataWindow print dialog***. The user may now specify page range as well as odd and even pages. The number of copies may be specified, as well as printing to a file, collation, printer setup, and changing the printer. There is a new ***Print Preview*** functionality allowing horizontal and vertical scrolling and margin adjustment by dragging the margins. This triggers the new pbmdwn-printmartginchange user event.

Another new DataWindow related function is ***Save Report as File***. In design mode, open the report and choose the Save As File option from the file menu. In Preview mode, select Save Rows as an option from the File Menu and choose one of the supplied report formats (Excel, etc.–also see *SaveAs below*), or a straight Report. This allows reports to be shared, sent via e-mail, etc.

There are ***new options in Crosstab and Grid reports.*** An aesthetic improvement on grid reports is that when the Suppress Repeating Values option is turned on, the grid lines are suppressed. In both types of reports, you can now specify whether the user can perform column moving, mouse selection, or row resizing.

There is a new ***Wrap Height*** option on ***freeform DataWindows.*** This option specifies in inches how high the detail band of the report should be. Any data that would extend below this height now wraps to the right of the other data.

The ***DataWindow Select Painter*** has been updated featuring new tabbed dialogs for Sort, Where, Group, Having, Computed Columns, and Syntax display. ***Computed fields*** can be referenced in DataWindow functions and in other computed fields. In addition, ***retrieval arguments*** can also be referenced in the computed columns on your DataWindow..

There are ***new DataWindow control functions***.

dwCopyRows (startrow, endrow, copybuffer, targetdw, beforerow, targetbuffer) copies rows from one DataWindow buffer into another, beginning with startrow and ending with endrow. dwRowsMove (startrow, endrow, movebuffer, targetdw, beforerow, targetbuffer) moves rows from one DataWindow buffer into another.

dwRowsDiscard (startrow, endrow, buffer) deletes rows from a DataWindow buffer.

There are also *new DataWindow aggregate functions*. Each of the following can be specified for all rows on the DataWindow, a particular group, a crosstab, a page, or a graph.

Large returns the nth largest data value in your data range.
Small returns the nth smallest data value in your data range.
Median returns the median value of your data range.
Mode returns the value that occurs most frequently in your data range.

There have been two new formats added to the *SaveAs* function. The enumerated data type **PSREPORT!** saves the DataWindow or report as a Powersoft Report in a .psr file. **WMF!** saves the DataWindow or report as a Windows MetaFile. The Header option is ignored in both types.

There are *new DataWindow object attributes* for dwModify and dwDescribe:

```
DataWindow.printer                Printer currently selected.
DataWindow.print.filename         Filename to print to.
DataWindow.print.page.range       Page numbers to include.
DataWindow.print.page.rangeinclude  Include all, even, or odd pages.
DataWindow.print.collate          Whether to collate output
DataWindow.print.duplex           Whether to print duplex or simplex
```

Performance in Laserjet printing and in DataWindow *sorting* operations has been improved. Significant performance improvements have also been achieved in the *execution of Power-Script* and *window instantiation*. *Bitmap printing* is now much sharper than it was in 3.0.

There is a new *OLE 2.0 control* that can be placed on a window, making PowerBuilder a Window Container: for example, you can embed a Microsoft Word for Windows document into a PowerBuilder window. A *PowerScript utility* provides the ability to write script to drive an OLE 2.0 server application using automation. Clicking on the object (such as the Word document) causes the target's menus appear in the application.

PowerTips have been added so that your application can display microtext as the mouse pointer is moved over the toolbar icons in your application when ShowText is off.

When creating a new application, you are presented the option to *generate the shell of an MDI application*. This option may be used an MDI frame, sheet, menu, toolbars, and even an About... window.

A *Project Painter* has been added to allow the creation and maintenance of *project objects*. These objects contain information for building executable files by providing the name of the executable file and, optionally, a resource file. You may specify that all objects be regenerated prior to compilation and choose whether each library in the search path is to be an EXE or a PBD. This project object has a new icon that is displayed in the Library Painter just below your application object.

The 3.0a *power panel* has been replaced by an enhanced 4.0 power panel. Access is provided to all global options such as the DOS text editor and the DBA Notepad. When no toolbar or power panel is active, a *Toolbars option* on the File menu displays the Toolbars window.

The ***object control status window*** has been replaced by cues placed on the microhelp. Displayed is the object name, x and y coordinates, and width and height of the control. This is available in the window, DataWindow, report, form and user object painters.

Undo and ***Redo*** support is available for Cut, Copy, Paste, Clear, Move, and Size operations available from the edit menu. Cut, Copy, Paste, and Clear do not use the Windows Clipboard. These functions are available in the window, DataWindow, report, user object, and function painters.

Clipboard support is provided in the window, DataWindow, and report painters using traditional Windows key combinations such as <CTL-C> for Copy and <CTL-X> for Cut. You can now copy objects from one object to another using the Clipboard.

The ***PowerScript Painter*** now sports a ***Browse Object*** option by pressing <CTL-O> or selecting it in the Edit Menu. ENTER and ESC keys are supported in the drop-down listboxes under Select Event; Paste Object; Paste Global; and Paste Instance.

The ***Debugger*** has seen a couple of enhancements. Attempts to exit the debugger while an application is running will result in a warning message that continuing will cause the application to become unstable. Also, ***watch variables*** will now be saved between sessions.

There are a number of ***PowerScript*** enhancements. ***New print functions*** include PrintScreen (printjobnumber, x, y) and objectname.Print (printjobnumber, x, y). ***New MDI functions*** include window.GetFirstSheet(), and window1.GetNextSheet(window2) which returns the sheet that follows window2 in the Z-order of sheets in window1.

Many new ***user events*** have been added for ***pen windows, combobox notifications, joystick, MCI messages, waveform input/output,*** and ***MIDI input/output.***

PSR files can now be added to ***DataWindow controls***. Assigning a PSR (Powersoft Report) file to a DataWindow does not require calling SetTransObject or Retrieve. PSR files need to be added to the PBR file when compiling the program. A PSR contains both the DataWindow definition and its data. You can use PBR to e-mail reports between users.

The ***text of RMB menu items*** can now be changed dynamically using the new application attribute toolbarpopmenutext.

The ***Function Painter*** now includes File Import and File Export dialogs.

The ***UserObject Painter*** has been enhanced to allow the creation of a number of non-standard visual objects: DynamicDescriptionArea; DynamicStagingArea; Error; MailSession; Message; OleStorage; OleStream; Pipeline (see below); and, Transaction. To do so, in the UserObject Painter, select New. Select Standard and select the object type from the list.

The ***Application Painter*** has a new Edit Menu option. ***Default Global Variables*** allows you to change variable types for SQLCA; SQLDA; SQLSA; Error; and, Message. You can change the default objects and add your own custom functions to them.

There is a *new INI variable* for the [PowerBuilder] section of the *win.ini*. If you run Power-Builder 4.0 at the same time as 3.0, add *initpath040=d:\pb4\pb.ini* where d:\pb4 is your fully qualified PowerBuilder 4.0 path.

The *Data pipeline* is a significant enhancement which provides the ability to move data from one database to another. To use it, click the Database Painter icon, select a destination profile (the "from" profile being the current database), select the tables to copy, create the SQL Select statements using one of the new tabbed dialog boxes, and click the Pipeline icon to return to the workspace. A series of defaults is then presented, including how many errors to tolerate, "from" and "to" datatypes, how many records to commit after, and so on. Extended attribute information may also be copied at this time. After completing this information, click Execute. The pipeline profile may be saved. The *pipeline object* may be used in your application. It has three events: PipeEnd; PipeMeter; and, PipeStart. There are five object attributes: RowsRead; RowsWritten; RowsInError; DataObject; and, Syntax.

Bind variable support in PowerScript: embedded SQL and DataWindow updates improve performance and eliminate the limitation of 255 characters for quoted strings. Bind variable support is provided for ODBC drivers that support the SQLDescribeParm API (currently Watcom and RDB). *Cached statement support* in DataWindows-generated SQL improves performance of frequently executed statements. A new *dbParm* variable, SQLCache=n, controls the number of cursors that may be opened in a script. Other *database support* enhancements includes RPC (Remote Procedure Call) support in Oracle, sybase, Informix and ODBC DBMSes that support stored procedures (i.e. Watcom 4.0), as well as new support for sybase System 10 CTLIB.

Remote procedure support has been enhanced. Use of a new object.function notation has been added and will provide increased performance. Support for Oracle PL/SQL tables and parameters defined as both input and output is provided. The syntax for declaring an RPC is much like that for external functions.

The *Library Painter* will now show visually which objects are currently checked out.

There have been a number of *CODE enhancements* to include Intersolv's PVCS. Enhancements here include ease of use, support for multiple application development, performance, version labeling, enhanced reporting, enhanced viewing of check-out status, support for multiple release development, and an application configuration object.

The PowerBuilder tool kit includes *improved versions of tools* available in prior releases (the cross-reference tool, etc.) as well as two exciting *new utilities*. SPUD stands for Stored Procedure Update for DataWindows. It generates PowerScript statements that override default DataWindow behavior, so that you can update the database through the use of stored procedures. The PBSetUp utility is a very good Windows install utility that allows you to set up install diskettes for your programs.

This enumeration has certainly not exhausted all of the changes in PowerBuilder 4.0, but it has touched upon most. When you install Version 4.0, bring up the Help screen and press the "About 4.0" button for a complete listing. And have fun!

CHAPTER **2**

Calling Borland Pascal DLLs

By Breck Carter

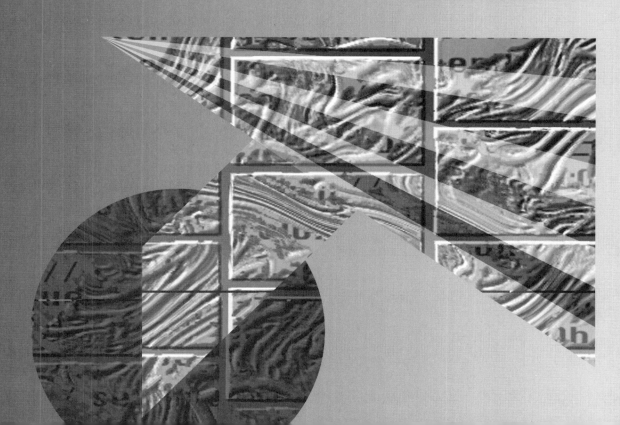

Calling Borland
Pascal DLLs

by **Breck Carter**

A Dynamic Link Library (DLL) is a file containing executable Windows code. This code can be called from a PowerBuilder program even though it is written in another language such as C or Pascal. DLLs are dynamically loaded and linked at runtime, and the code can be shared among several applications.

Depending on the options used, DLLs can also be moveable or fixed in memory, preloaded or loaded on demand, and discardable or permanently loaded. Usually, however, the dynamic nature of DLLs isn't of much interest to the application developer. The real value comes with extending PowerBuilder in new directions:

Reusing existing C and Pascal code that has been developed at great expense;
Getting closer to the operating system to do low-level DOS and Windows functions;
Building a protective layer between PowerScript and weird APIs;
Replacing glacial script loops and functions with blindingly fast compiled code.

Borland Pascal 7 for Windows (BPW) was introduced in 1992. It has a sophisticated Integrated Development Environment (IDE), complete with syntax highlighting, and provides a very simple structure for creating Windows DLLs.

This chapter concentrates on the "boundary layer" between PowerScript and Borland Pascal 7: how to declare functions and call them, and how to pass data back and forth. Any deep discussion of what you might actually code inside your Pascal functions has been omitted. It is assumed that you know what you want to do and that you have a basic familiarity with programming in PowerBuilder and Pascal.

Hello, World: Coding and Calling a Simple DLL

Figure 2-1 shows a task modal MessageBox produced by a Pascal DLL called from a Power-Builder application. The DLL is 1,536 bytes in size, and the .exe is about 13K.

Figure 2-2 shows the source code in pashello.pas. To compile it, click on "Compile"–"Primary File" in Borland Pascal for Windows (BPW) and specify the source file, then check "Compile" - "Target" - "Windows Application", and finally click on "Compile" - "Build" to produce pashello.dll. The last step takes less than a second on most machines, and there's no separate link step required.

Listing 1: Calling ef_HelloWorld() from pashello.pbl.

```
subroutine ef_HelloWorld() &
   library "pashello.dll"

ef_HelloWorld()
```

Declaring External Functions and Subroutines

Listing 2: Function and subroutine declarations.

```
Subroutine        <sName> ([[Ref] <aType> <aName>,...]) Library "file"
Function <fType> <fName> ([[Ref] <aType> <aName>,...]) Library "file"
Procedure <sName> [([Var] <aName>:<aType>;...)]            ; export;
Function  <fName> [([Var] <aName>:<aType>;...)]:<fType>; export;
```

Comparing Pascal and PowerBuilder Datatypes

```
Array             Array, if the base type is supported
Blob              Probably safest to convert to and from strings
Boolean           WordBool
Character         Char
Date              N/A, convert to and from strings instead
DateTime          N/A, convert to and from strings instead
Decimal           Probably safest to convert to and from strings
Double            Probably safest to convert to and from strings
DragObject        N/A
Enumerated Types  N/A, they're not at all the same in Pascal
Integer           Integer
Long              Longint
PowerObject       N/A
```

```
Real               Probably safest to convert to and from strings
String             PChar, but be careful
Structure          Record, if the base types are supported
Time               N/A, convert to and from strings instead
UnsignedInteger    Word
UnsignedLong       Longint might work, but probably safest to use strings

Array              Array, if the base type is supported
Assembler Types    N/A
Boolean            N/A, use Pascal WordBool instead
Byte               N/A, use Pascal Char instead
ByteBool           N/A, use Pascal WordBool instead
Char               Character
Comp               N/A, convert to and from strings instead
Double             Probably safest to convert to and from strings
Enumerated Types   N/A, they're not at all the same in PowerBuilder
Extended           N/A, convert to and from strings instead
File               N/A
Integer            Integer
LongBool           N/A, use Pascal WordBool instead
Longint            Long
Object Types       N/A
PChar              String, but be careful
Pointer Types      N/A, but used implicitly
Procedural Types   N/A
Real               Probably safest to convert to and from strings
Record             Structure, if the base types are supported
Set                N/A
Shortint           N/A, use Pascal Integer instead
Single             N/A, convert to and from strings instead
String             N/A, use Pascal PChar instead
Subrange Types     N/A
Windows Types      Use equivalent base types or structures where possible
Word               UnsignedInteger
WordBool           Boolean
```

Simple Functions

Boolean to WordBool

Listing 3: Passing and returning Booleans.

```
function Boolean ef_Boolean &
   ( Ref Boolean abTest1 ) &
   library "pascalls.dll"
 Boolean bTest1, bTest2
bTest1 = True
bTest2 = ef_Boolean ( bTest1 )

 function ef_Boolean
   ( var abTest1 : WordBool )
   : WordBool; export;
begin
   abTest1     := False;
   ef_Boolean := True;
end; {ef_Boolean}
Character to Char
```

Listing 4: Passing and returning Characters.

```
function Character ef_Character &
    ( Ref Character achTest1 ) &
    library "pascalls.dll"
 Character chTest1, chTest2
chTest1 = "A"
chTest2 = ef_Character ( chTest1 )
```

Function in pascalls.pas

```
function ef_Character
    ( var achTest1 : Char )
    : Char; export;
begin
    achTest1     := 'X';
    ef_Character := 'Y';
end; {ef_Character}
```

Integer to Integer

Listing 5: Passing and returning Integers.

```
function Integer ef_Integer &
    ( Ref Integer aiTest1 ) &
    library "pascalls.dll"
 Integer iTest1, iTest2
iTest1 = 1
iTest2 = ef_Integer ( iTest1 )

  function ef_Integer
    ( var aiTest1 : Integer )
    : Integer; export;
begin
    aiTest1 := -MaxInt;
    dec ( aiTest1 );        {smallest}
    ef_Integer := MaxInt; {largest}
end; {ef_Integer}
```

Long to Longint

Listing 6: Passing and returning Longs.

```
function Long ef_Long &
    ( Ref Long alTest1 ) &
    library "pascalls.dll"
 Long lTest1, lTest2
lTest1 = 1
lTest2 = ef_Long ( lTest1 )

  function ef_Long
    ( var alTest1 : Longint )
    : Longint; export;
begin
    alTest1 := -MaxLongint;
    dec ( alTest1 );          {smallest}
```

```
    ef_Long := MaxLongint; {largest}
end; {ef_Long}
```

UnsignedInteger to Word

Listing7: *Passing and returning Unsigned Integers*

```
function UnsignedInteger ef_UnsignedInteger &
    ( Ref UnsignedInteger auiTest1 ) &
    library "pascalls.dll"
 UnsignedInteger uiTest1, uiTest2
uiTest1 = 1
uiTest2 = ef_UnsignedInteger ( uiTest1 )

  function ef_UnsignedInteger
    ( var auiTest1 : Word )
    : Word; export;
begin
    auiTest1 := 65535;        {largest}
    ef_UnsignedInteger ·= 0; {smallest}
end; {ef_UnsignedInteger}
```

Special Problems

String to PChar

Listing 8: *Passing and returning Strings.*

```
function String ef_String &
    ( Ref String asTest1 ) &
    library "pascalls.dll"
 String sTest1, sTest2
sTest1 = "1234567" // make room
sTest2 = ef_String ( sTest1 )
MessageBox ( "ef_String", sTest1 + sTest2 )

  function ef_String
    ( asTest1 : PChar ) {don't use var}
    : PChar; export;
const sWorld : PChar = 'World!';
begin
(* asTest1 := 'Hello, '; {don't change the pointer} *)
    StrPCopy ( asTest1, 'Hello, ' );
    ef_String := sWorld; {not a stack variable}
end; {ef_String}
```

Listing 9: *Checking string length, returning error codes.*

```
function Integer ef_KeepItSimple &
    ( Ref String asTest1 ) &
    library "pascalls.dll"

 String  sTest1
Integer iRC
sTest1 = Space ( 13 ) // make room
```

```
iRC = ef_KeepItSimple ( sTest1 )
if iRC = 1 then
   MessageBox &
      ( "ef_KeepItSimple Test 1 OK", &
         "'" + sTest1 + "'" )
else
   MessageBox &
      ( "ef_KeepItSimple Test 1 Failed", &
         String ( iRC ) )
end if

 function ef_KeepItSimple
    ( asTest1 : PChar )
    : Integer; export;
const sHelloWorld = 'Hello, World!';
begin
   if StrLen ( asTest1 )
      >= Length ( sHelloWorld )
   then begin
      StrPCopy ( asTest1, sHelloWorld );
      ef_KeepItSimple := 1;
   end
   else ef_KeepItSimple := -1;
end; {ef_KeepItSimple}
```

Structures and Records

Listing 10: A simple structure.

```
global type s_simple from structure
    boolean bfield
    char chfield
    int ifield
    long lfield
    string sfield
    uint uifield
end type

 type s_Simple = record
  bField  : WordBool;
  chField : Char;
  iField  : Integer;
  lField  : Longint;
  sField  : PChar;
  uiField : Word;
end;
```

Listing 11: Passing structures to records.

```
function Integer ef_Structure &
   ( Ref s_Simple astrTest1 ) &
   library "pascalls.dll"

 s_Simple strTest1
Integer  iRC
```

```
strTest1.bField  = False
strTest1.chField = "A"
strTest1.iField  = 1
strTest1.lField  = 1
strTest1.sField  = Space ( 13 )
strTest1.uiField = 1
iRC = ef_Structure ( strTest1 )
if iRC = 1 then ok...

 function ef_Structure
    ( var astrTest1 : s_Simple )
    : Integer; export;
const sHelloWorld = 'Hello, World!';
begin
   if StrLen ( astrTest1.sField )
      >= Length ( sHelloWorld )
   then begin
      astrTest1.bField  := True;
      astrTest1.chField := 'X';
      astrTest1.iField  := MaxInt;
      astrTest1.lField  := MaxLongint;
      StrPCopy
         ( astrTest1.sfield, sHelloWorld );
      astrTest1.uiField := 65535;
      ef_Structure := 1;
   end
   else ef_Structure := -1;
end; {ef_Structure}
```

Arrays

Listing 12: Passing and returning simple arrays.

```
function Integer ef_Array &
   ( Ref Boolean    abArray1[], &
     Ref Character achArray1[], &
     Ref Integer    aiArray1[], &
     Ref Long       alArray1[], &
     Ref String     asArray1[], &
     Ref UInt      auiArray1[] ) &
   library "pascalls.dll"

Boolean    bArray1[]
Character chArray1[]
Integer    iArray1[]
Long       lArray1[]
String     sArray1[]
UInt      uiArray1[]
Integer    iRC
bArray1  [ 5 ] = False
chArray1 [ 5 ] = "A"
iArray1  [ 5 ] = 1
lArray1  [ 5 ] = 1
sArray1  [ 5 ] = Space ( 13 )
uiArray1 [ 5 ] = 1
iRC = ef_Array &
        ( bArray1, &
```

```
            chArray1, &
            iArray1, &
            lArray1, &
            sArray1, &
            uiArray1 )
if iRC = 1 then ok...

type tbArray1   = array [ 1 .. 5 ] of WordBool;
type tchArray1  = array [ 1 .. 5 ] of Char;
type tiArray1   = array [ 1 .. 5 ] of Integer;
type tlArray1   = array [ 1 .. 5 ] of Longint;
type tsArray1   = array [ 1 .. 5 ] of PChar;
type ptsArray1  = ^tsArray1;
type tuiArray1  = array [ 1 .. 5 ] of Word;

function ef_Array
   ( var abArray1  : tbArray1;
     var achArray1 : tchArray1;
     var aiArray1  : tiArray1;
     var alArray1  : tlArray1;
         asArray1  : ptsArray1; {don't use var}
     var auiArray1 : tuiArray1 )
   : Integer; export;
const sHelloWorld = 'Hello, World!';

begin
   if StrLen ( asArray1^ [ 5 ] )
      >= Length ( sHelloWorld )
   then begin
      abArray1  [ 5 ] := True;
      achArray1 [ 5 ] := 'X';
      aiArray1  [ 5 ] := MaxInt;
      alArray1  [ 5 ] := MaxLongInt;
      StrPCopy
         ( asArray1^ [ 5 ], sHelloWorld );
      auiArray1 [ 5 ] := 65535;
      ef_Array := 1;
   end
   else ef_Array := -1;
end; {ef_Array}
```

Structures of Arrays

Listing 13: Passing and returning structures of arrays.

```
global type s_structurearray from structure
    int ifield[]
    string sfield[]
end type

function Integer ef_StructureArray &
   ( Ref s_StructureArray astrTest1 ) &
   library "pascalls.dll"
 s_StructureArray strTest1
Integer          iRC
strTest1.iField [ 5 ] = 1
```

```
strTest1.sField [ 5 ] = Space ( 13 )
iRC = ef_StructureArray ( strTest1 )
if iRC = 1 then ok...

 type s_StructureArray = record
  iField : tiArray1;
  sField : tsArray1;
end;
function ef_StructureArray
   ( var astrTest1 : s_StructureArray )
   : Integer; export;
const sHelloWorld = 'Hello, World!';

begin
   if StrLen ( astrTest1.sField [ 5 ] )
      >= Length ( sHelloWorld )
   then begin
      astrTest1.iField [ 5 ] := MaxInt;
      StrPCopy
          ( astrTest1.sField [ 5 ],
            sHelloWorld );
      ef_StructureArray := 1;
   end
   else ef_StructureArray := -1;
end; {ef_StructureArray}
```

Arrays of Structures

Listing 14: Passing and returning arrays of structures.

```
global type s_arraystructure from structure
    integer ifield
    string sfield
end type

function Integer ef_ArrayStructure &
   ( Ref s_ArrayStructure astrTest1[] ) &
   library "pascalls.dll"
 s_ArrayStructure strTest1[]
Integer           iRC
strTest1 [ 5 ].iField = 1
strTest1 [ 5 ].sField = Space ( 13 )
iRC = ef_ArrayStructure ( strTest1 )
if iRC = 1 then ok...

 type s_ArrayStructure = record
  iField : Integer;
  sField : PChar;
end;

type ts_ArrayStructure
   = array [ 1 .. 5 ] of s_ArrayStructure;
function ef_ArrayStructure
   ( var astrTest1 : ts_ArrayStructure )
   : Integer; export;
const sHelloWorld = 'Hello, World!';
```

```
begin
   if StrLen ( astrTest1 [ 5 ].sField )
      >= Length ( sHelloWorld )
   then begin
      astrTest1 [ 5 ].iField := MaxInt;
      StrPCopy
         ( astrTest1 [ 5 ].sField,
           sHelloWorld );
      ef_ArrayStructure := 1;
   end
   else ef_ArrayStructure := -1;
end; {ef_ArrayStructure}
```

Nested Structures

Listing 15: Passing and returning nested structures.

```
global type s_nestedstructure from structure
    int ifield
    string sfield
end type

global type s_masterstructure from structure
    int ifield
    s_nestedstructure strnested
    string sfield
end type

function Integer ef_NestedStructure &
   ( Ref s_MasterStructure astrTest1 ) &
   library "pascalls.dll"
 s_MasterStructure strTest1
Integer            iRC
strTest1.iField           = 1
strTest1.strNested.iField = 1
strTest1.strNested.sField = Space ( 13 )
strTest1.sField           = Space ( 13 )
iRC = ef_NestedStructure ( strTest1 )
if iRC = 1 then ok...

 type s_NestedStructure = record
  iField : Integer;
  sField : PChar;
end;

type s_MasterStructure = record
  iField   : Integer;
  strNested : s_NestedStructure;
  sField    : PChar;
end;

function ef_NestedStructure
   ( var astrTest1 : s_MasterStructure )
   : Integer; export;
const sHelloWorld   = 'Hello, World!';
const sGoodbyeWorld = 'Goodbye, World!';
```

```
begin
   if  ( StrLen ( astrTest1.strNested.sField )
          >= Length ( sHelloWorld ) )
   and ( StrLen ( astrTest1.sField )
          >= Length ( sGoodbyeWorld ) )
   then begin
       astrTest1.iField              := 2;
       astrTest1.strNested.iField := 3;
       StrPCopy
          ( astrTest1.strNested.sField,
            sHelloWorld );
       StrPCopy
          ( astrTest1.sField,
            sGoodbyeWorld );
       ef_NestedStructure := 1;
   end
   else ef_NestedStructure := -1;
end; {ef_NestedStructure}
```

Some Debugging Tips

Listing 16: pascalls.map.

```
Start          Length   Name                Class
0001:0002      01C8H    PasCalls            CODE
0002:0002      0035H    Strings             CODE
0003:0002      01B5H    System              CODE
0004:0000      0076H    DATA                DATA
Address                 Publics by Value
0001:0002               ef_Boolean
0001:0034               ef_Character
...
0001:0161               ef_KeepItSimple
0001:01B5               @
0002:0002               StrLen
0002:0019               StrPCopy
0004:002A               HPrevInst
...
Line numbers for PasCalls(d:\pascalls.pas) segment PasCalls
   30 0001:0002    34 0001:0019    35 0001:0021    36 0001:0026
   50 0001:0034    51 0001:004B    52 0001:0052    53 0001:0056
   ...
Program entry point at 0001:01B5
```

SQL: A Quick Tutorial

By Kent Marsh

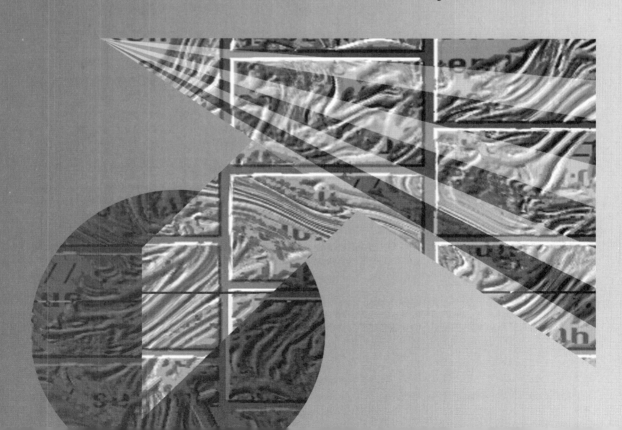

SQL: A Quick Tutorial

by **Kent Marsh**

SQL (pronounced "sequel") is an acronym for Structured Query Language. It is generally accepted as the industry-standard database access language. SQL provides a wide variety of commands for querying data, manipulating data, maintaining data objects, managing database security, and enforcing data integrity. SQL is not exactly the same on every DBMS platform, but is becoming more consistent as ANSI standards are adopted. Still, not all DBMS systems have the same set of features, so in any event you should become particularly aware of the syntax and features of your chosen DBMS platform. The following sections will present the logical structure of relational databases and then focus on the statements that query and manipulate data using Watcom SQL syntax.

Any serious PowerBuilder developer will need to be very familiar with SQL because it is the language used to communicate with all PowerBuilder-supported DBMS platforms. SQL Selects are the fundamental way DataWindows are populated with data. When you issue a DataWindow Update() function call, the DataWindow will automatically generate the SQL Insert, Update and/or Delete statements required to maintain the data. The "dialect" of SQL generated by DataWindows is dependent upon your "native" database. When you set the Transaction object for the DataWindow (using SetTrans() or SetTransObject()), the DBMS attribute will tell the DataWindow which dialect of SQL to use.

Beyond DataWindows, PowerBuilder allows you to enter SQL statements as Embedded SQL and as "Declarative" SQL. PowerBuilder's Embedded SQL is what you are using when you type SQL statements right in your PowerScript. It is still DBMS-dependent. For the most part, the Embedded SQL allowed is a subset of SQL commands that is common to all DBMSes, but the actual syntax will be checked against your database when compiling.

Declarative SQL is used when you want to build the SQL statement dynamically and pass it to the database as a string. Using PowerBuilder's "Dynamic SQL" also allows you to build any SQL statement allowed by your DBMS. The syntax cannot be checked until runtime because it is a string which is often unknown until then.

The Database Objects

A *Relational Database Management System* (RDBMS) contains many different types of objects which make up the RDBMS logical structure. All SQL statements work on data from these objects and organize them into sets of data called tables. Similarly to a spreadsheet, a RDBMS table arranges data in columns and rows (or records). Unlike a spreadsheet, in which any cell can handle any sort of data or formula, each column of a table is restricted to a consistent type of data (i.e., each row will have the same structure). Tables in multi-user databases in turn are associated with an owner. (An owner's group of tables is sometimes called a schema). Objects are organized in a hierarchical structure:

Databases (or DBMS instances, applicable in some DBMS cases) contain
Objects (Tables) which contain
Attributes (Columns or individual data elements)

When you reference a database object you can qualify it by one or more of each of these elements so that you determine which object is used. If you don't qualify it completely, then the DBMS will try at runtime to resolve exactly which object your are using. Suppose your database has two objects. In general, we reference objects according to the following format:

```
<Database>.<Owner>.<Object>.<Attribute>
```

Suppose you had a database that contained two owners (Owner_A and Owner_B) each of which had an Employee table. Because both of these tables are in the same database, don't need to qualify the database. If we are not presently connected to one of the owners, then we will need to qualify which owner's Employee table is to be used. We could reference the table as follows:

```
<Owner>.<Object>
Owner_A.Employee
```

When you do not qualify the owner, then the default OwnerName will be the login name you are currently using. Say you owned an Employee table and you are logged in as yourself. You do not need to qualify the table owner because you are connected as the owner. You could use the following command.

```
SELECT EMPLOYEE.EMP_ID,
       EMPLOYEE.EMP_FNAME,
       EMPLOYEE.EMP_LNAME
   FROM EMPLOYEE  ;
```

Tip: When PowerBuilder generates a SQL statement it will automatically add double quotes to the names of every database object in it. The double quotes **are not necessary** and can be deleted. (Unfortunately, this "feature" cannot be turned off on every platform.) In fact, because the DBMS has no problem resolving which table owns these columns, you could use the following syntax;

```
SELECT  EMP_ID,
            EMP_FNAME,
            EMP_LNAME
FROM EMPLOYEE;
```

Tip: In PowerBuilder, once you qualify a column in a SQL statement, then every column owned by that table in the SQL statement will have to be qualified as well. You will either have to qualify each employee column or not qualify any of them. Even though this should be a valid SQL statement, PowerBuilder will not accept the following:

```
SELECT EMP_ID,
            EMPLOYEE.EMP_FNAME,
            EMP_LNAME
FROM EMPLOYEE  ;
```

Tip: When you need to qualify columns by their table name, create a short table alias to save typing and make a more legible script. Below is an example of using "e" and "d" as table aliases for the Employee and Department tables respectively.

```
SELECT  e.emp_id,
            e.emp_fname,
            e.emp_lname,
            d.dept_name
  FROM employee    e,
        department d
 WHERE e.dept_id = d.dept_id;
```

Tip: It gets confusing and complicated when you repeatedly have to reference objects requiring long qualifications. Some databases support an object called a SYNONYM which is just an alias for a database object. Using a SYNONYM adds flexibility to the DBA by "hiding" where the actual object is stored.

For example, in Oracle you could create a SYNONYM "emp" for an Employee table owned by the user "personnel" with the following statement;

```
CREATE SYNONYM emp FOR personnel.Employee;
```

Datatypes

Each column in a table has a datatype the specifies what kind of data it will hold and how the DBMS will store it. Each database has its own set of datatypes. Most of the types will map across between databases. The exceptions tend to be in the Date-Time area, numeric precision, and unique datatypes peculiar to a given platform.

Table 1: WATCOM SQL Datatypes

Datatype	Description
Numbers:	
DOUBLE	A double precision floating point number. Range 2.2250738585070160e-308 to 1.79769313486231560e+308
FLOAT	A single precision floating point number. Range 1.175494351e-38 to 3.402823466e+38.
INTEGER{size}	Signed integer, maximum size 2,147,483,647. Abbreviated form is INT.
NUMERIC{precision{,scale}}	A decimal number with precision total digits and with scale of the digits after the decimal point. The default for precision is 30 and for scale is 6.
SMALLINT	Signed integer of maximum value 32,767.
String:	
CHAR{size}	Character of maximum length size. The default size is 1. The maximum size is 32,767.
LONG VARCHAR	Character of maximum length 2 gigabytes.
VARCHAR{size}	Character of maximum length size. The default size is 1. The maximum size is 32,767.
Date and Time:	
DATE	A calendar date (year, month, and day). A date column can contain a time but you should use TIMESTAMP for anything with a date, hours, and minutes.
TIME	A time of day, containing hour, minute, second, and a fraction of a second. The fraction is stored to 6 decimal places.
TIMESTAMP	A point in time, containing year, month, day, hour, minute, second, and a fraction of a second. The fraction is stored to 6 decimal places.

Binary:	
BINARY{size}	Binary data of maximum length size. The default size is 1. The maximum size is 32,767. The binary data type is identical to the CHAR data type except when used in comparisons. Binary character are compared exactly; CHAR values are not case sensitive.
LONG BINARY	Binary data of maximum length 2 gigabytes. The binary data type is identical to the CHAR data type except when used in comparisons. Binary character are compared exactly. CHAR values are not case-sensitive.

When you create a table, you need to specify the datatype for each column. Once a table has been created, you cannot change any of the column datatypes with out "dropping" the table (deleting it). However, you can easily add columns and make existing columns longer.

```
CREATE TABLE DEPARTMENT
        (DEPT_ID         INT NOT NULL,
         DEPT_NAME       CHAR(40) NOT NULL,
         DEPT_HEAD_ID    INT );
```

Delete the table by:

```
DROP TABLE DEPARTMENT;
```

SQL Statements

The four major commands in SQL that deal with manipulating data in tables are: SELECT, INSERT, UPDATE, and DELETE. These four commands are all that DataWindows require to do their processing. These commands can also be used as Embedded SQL in your Power-Script code.

SELECTs

In these examples we will use the Employee table from the PowerBuilder 4.0 demo database:

Simple SELECTs

SELECT is used to retrieve data. It is the only command which, on its own, cannot modify data. The simplest kind of SELECT would be:

```
SELECT <Column List> FROM <Table Name>;
```

A SELECT command must always have the keywords SELECT and FROM in it. The following statement will retrieve the columns listed from the Employee table:

```
SELECT emp_id,
       emp_fname,
       emp_lname,
       dept_id,
       start_date
  FROM employee  ;
```

The results of this statement would be:

Emp Id	First Name	Last Name	Dept Id	Start Date
105	Alan	Chamberlain	100	01/01/85 00:00:00
247	John	Spellman	100	07/01/83 00:00:00
318	Peter	Ciccone	100	12/23/88 00:00:00
479	Mary	Houston	100	07/23/80 00:00:00
501	Linda	Watson	100	08/04/75 00:00:00
667	Ronald	Garcia	200	11/22/89 00:00:00
703	Michael	Stanley	200	12/01/80 00:00:00
855	Richard	McMahon	200	06/01/86 00:00:00
902	Edward	Fitzgerald	200	10/01/79 00:00:00
1090	Susan	Smith	100	06/14/87 00:00:00
1142	Alice	Clark	200	07/21/82 00:00:00
1293	Howard	Barclay	300	09/01/75 00:00:00
1336	Janet	Bigelow	300	02/25/84 00:00:00
1482	Jack	Sussman	300	01/08/79 00:00:00
1576	Thomas	Sinclair	400	07/01/85 00:00:00

For quick and dirty ad-hoc SELECT statements where you don't care about specific column names but just want to see all of the data, use the asterisk ("*****") character instead of the column list. The asterisk will return all of the columns in the table in the order that they were created. You should not use the "*" in production software because actual column names and creation orders may change over time and give unexpected results.

```
SELECT * FROM employee;
```

We can also sort the result set of information by using the ORDER BY clause like this:

```
SELECT EMP_ID,
       EMP_FNAME,
       EMP_LNAME,
       DEPT_ID,
       START_DATE
  FROM EMPLOYEE   ;
 ORDER BY EMP_LNAME ASC, EMP_FNAME ASC;
```

Emp Id	First Name	Last Name	Dept Id	Start Date
1293	Howard	Barclay	300	09/01/75 00:00:00
1336	Janet	Bigelow	300	02/25/84 00:00:00
105	Alan	Chamberlain	100	01/01/85 00:00:00
318	Peter	Ciccone	100	12/23/88 00:00:00
1142	Alice	Clark	200	07/21/82 00:00:00
902	Edward	Fitzgerald	200	10/01/79 00:00:00
667	Ronald	Garcia	200	11/22/89 00:00:00
479	Mary	Houston	100	07/23/80 00:00:00
855	Richard	McMahon	200	06/01/86 00:00:00
1576	Thomas	Sinclair	400	07/01/85 00:00:00
1090	Susan	Smith	100	06/14/87 00:00:00
247	John	Spellman	100	07/01/83 00:00:00
703	Michael	Stanley	200	12/01/80 00:00:00
1482	Jack	Sussman	300	01/08/79 00:00:00
501	Linda	Watson	100	08/04/75 00:00:00

The ORDER BY clause is usually the last clause in a SQL statement . (An exception to this would be in PowerScript Embedded SQL, where you specify which transaction object for the SQL statement to use by including the qualification "USING <Transaction>.") ASC in the ORDER BY clause stands for "ascending." To sort in reverse order use DESC, which stands for "descending." ASC is the default, so you do not have so specify this clause if you want the rows returned in ascending order.

> **Tip**: When using PowerBuilder DataWindows, use the SQL sort option so that data is sorted in the database server before it is returned to the client. The server sorts faster and avoids the visual flash that occurs as the client sorts the data. Use the DataWindow Sort when you need to re-sort already retrieved data.

Comparison Operators

Most of the time you do not want to retrieve all of the possible rows of data. To narrow down the result set, you can add conditional phrases in the WHERE clause. The phrases are usually built by using a comparison operator to compare one expression to another. Here is a list of the most common. Others follow.

Operator	Test
=	equal to
>	greater than
<	less than
>=	greater than or equal to
<=	less than or equal to
!=, <>	not equal to
!>	not greater than
!<	not less than
LIKE	Wild Card '%' , Pattern Matching
IS NULL	test for NULL value
BETWEEN	range of values
IN	set of values
EXISTS	True if a subquery returns 1 or more rows

NOT	Negative comparison qualifier, as in **NOT** LIKE IS **NOT** NULL **NOT** BETWEEN **NOT** IN **NOT** EXISTS
ALL	Totally Inclusive Comparison Qualifier
ANY	Partially Inclusive Comparison Qualifier

The datatypes of all expressions being compared must be the same. For dates and times, "<" means earlier and ">" means later. For strings, "<" means earlier in the alphabet. Character sort orders can be specified for individual databases, so sort results may differ. For example, in some database sorts upper case characters are sorted prior to lower case, while in others they aren't. In your database are numeric characters less than alpha characters?

The WHERE clause follows the FROM clause in the SELECT command.

```
SELECT SelectList
FROM TableName
WHERE Expression1 ComparisonOperator Expression2;
```

Using our sample data, we could retrieve the names of the employees in Dept. 200 by:

```
SELECT EMP_FNAME,
       EMP_LNAME
  FROM EMPLOYEE
 WHERE DEPT_ID = 200;
```

Ronald	Garcia
Michael	Stanley
Richard	McMahon
Edward	Fitzgerald
Alice	Clark

LIKE

The LIKE comparison operator is very powerful. It does–for strings only–much what an "=" clause does. In addition, it allows the use of wild cards and pattern matching. ANSI standard

SQL languages support the "%" symbol and a similar set of pattern matching characters.

%	matches any string of zero or more characters
_	matches any single character
[ ]	a list of characters to be matched
[^]	matches any single character not specified

All other characters in the match string must be matched exactly. The "%" can be used at the beginning and the end of a string to match a substring '%FRED%'. The following example would return all the last names that began with the letter "B":

```
SELECT emp_fname,
       emp_lname
  FROM employee
 WHERE emp_lname LIKE 'B%';
```
Returns:
```
Howard Barclay
Janet Bigelow
```

IS NULL

NULL is the value stored in a column that has not been assigned a value. NULL, by definition, is not equal to anything. NULL is not the same as zero or an empty string. Comparisons of NULL values to zero or empty string will fail. In order to compare NULL values you must use the IS NULL or IS NOT NULL comparison operators. The following statement finds all of the employees who have a NULL termination date.

```
SELECT * FROM employee
WHERE terminate_date Is NULL ;
```

Tip: Using NULLs allows three-way logic. A column used in a comparison may be TRUE, FALSE or NULL. If you tried to find all of the "employee.termination_date" values greater then 1/1/1990 using the > operator, any null values would not be selected. If a NULL date is considered a MAX date, then you will need to doubly qualify the comparison.

```
WHERE ( terminate_date > '1/1/1990' OR terminate_date
IS NULL )
```

BETWEEN

The BETWEEN operator is used to inclusively select a range of values. Using BETWEEN is a simpler way of writing x >= *From value* AND x <= *Thru Value*.

```
SELECT * FROM employee
WHERE salary BETWEEN 50000 AND 60000;
```

IN

Use **IN** to compare a value to a set of values. The set of values may be specified or can be the result set of a nested SELECT statement. The logical opposite of **IN** is **NOT IN**.:

```
SELECT * FROM employee
WHERE dept_id IN (100, 200 ) ;
```

OR

```
SELECT * FROM employee
WHERE dept_id IN (
  SELECT dept_id
  FROM    department
  WHERE   dept_id < 300 ) ;
```

HAVING

In the same way that the WHERE clause limits the rows displayed, the HAVING clause limits the groups displayed (see GROUP BY later in this chapter). The HAVING clause eliminates groups. Because the HAVING clause eliminates groups, the columns or functions listed in the having clause must be legal columns that could be listed in the group by clause. This includes aggregate functions.

```
SELECT dept_name, Count(*)
FROM employee, department
WHERE employee.dept_id = department.dept_id
GROUP BY dept_name
HAVING Count(*) > 3;
```

EXISTS

EXISTS tests for the results of subqueries. EXISTS test true if the subquery returns at least one row. A subquery is a SELECT statement inside of a SQL statement. It allows you to use a list of values that is the result of another SELECT statement. Only one column should be returned in a "nested" SELECT. For example, you can find all of the departments that have employees by using:

```
SELECT dept_name
FROM department d
WHERE exists
  (SELECT *
   FROM employee e
   WHERE e.dept_id = d.dept_id );
```

The SQL engine will first execute a selection of all the department dept_id values so it can build a temporary list of dept_id's. Then for each department.dept_id it will execute the nested SELECT statement:

```
( SELECT *
FROM employee e
WHERE e.dept_id = d.dept_id )
```

Because we are only using an EXISTS clause, there is no need to select all of the possible answers, so most SQL engines will optimize the SELECT and stop processing the nested select as soon as one value is found. If the EXISTS phrase is the only phrase in the WHERE clause and an employee is found, then the row for that department will be included in the result.

You could use the same SELECT to find departments that had no employees by using the SQL shown below. This kind of SQL statement is great for finding data that's not being used.

```
SELECT dept_name
FROM department d
WHERE NOT exists
  (SELECT *
   FROM employee e
   WHERE e.dept_id = d.dept_id );
```

Tip: Use the following syntax to find orphan records or resolve why a foreign key Create statement is failing. (Orphan records are those that should reference a foreign key. but a row with that key is missing. For *foreign key*, see "Referential Integrity," below.) You could find all of the employees that reference an invalid dept_id by the following statement:

```
SELECT emp_id, emp_lname, emp_fname
FROM employee e
WHERE NOT exists
  (SELECT *
   FROM department d
   WHERE e.dept_id = d.dept_id );
```

Other Operators

To complete our discussion on JOINs we need two more types of operators, logical and set-related. Logical operators combine two or more conditions into a single outcome, TRUE or FALSE. You have seen these before in other languages. They are:

AND

AND returns a TRUE if the expressions on both sides of the AND are TRUE; otherwise it returns a FALSE.

OR

OR returns a TRUE if either of the expressions on the sides of the OR are TRUE;

otherwise it returns a FALSE.

NOT

NOT returns a TRUE if the expression following it is FALSE; otherwise it returns a FALSE.

Set operators combine the outcomes of two SELECTs into a single result. Not all RDBMSes support these, and some only support one of them. Again, check your RDBMS.

UNION, UNION ALL

The UNION operator is used to combine the result sets of two or more SELECT statements. The source of the data can vary between SELECT statements, but each SELECT statement in the UNION must return the same number of columns having the same datatypes in each position. There are two forms of UNION statement:

```
UNION          returns only unique rows
UNION ALL      returns all rows including duplicates
```

INTERSECT (Oracle 7)

SELECT only the rows common to both queries.

MINUS (Oracle 7)

SELECT only the rows in the leading SELECT but not the second.

INTERSECT example:

```
SELECT DISTINCT dept_id
FROM department
INTERSECT
SELECT DISTINCT dept_id
FROM employee;
```

Results in:

MINUS example:

```
SELECT Flavor
FROM Pies
MINUS
SELECT Flavor
```

```
        FROM IceCream;
```
Results in:

Blueberry
Cherry

Sophisticated SELECTs

GROUP BY

One of the ways people manage large amounts of information is by grouping and categorizing: placing like items together and treating them as a whole. This is done by using a GROUP BY clause. The GROUP BY clause commands the RDBMS to search through the specified rows and treat all the rows in which the contents of the specified column is identical as one row. As a result, only the contents of the specified rows and aggregate functions can be included in the select list for a SQL command using the GROUP BY clause.

Aggregate Functions

Before actually using the GROUP BY clause, aggregate functions must be introduced. Aggregate functions are functions that work on groups of information. The following aggregate functions are supported by most DBMSes:

COUNT()	The number of rows in the set
MAX()	The maximum value in the set
MIN()	The minimum value in the set
AVG()	The average of a numerical value
SUM()	The numeric sum of values in the set

Note that in all of the above the keywords DISTINCT or ALL may be used inside the parenthesis, and that an expression may be used in the first three. Harking back to set theory, ALL will bring back all values and DISTINCT will bring back only distinct values. ALL is the default.

Count all of the employee records:

```
    Select count(*) FROM employee;
```

Count the number of employee records (same as previous because emp_id is unique):

```
    Select count(emp_id) FROM employee;
```

Count the number of departments referenced by employee records (The DISTINCT operator is required so that each department is only counted once.):

```
Select count( DISTINCT dept_id ) FROM employee;
```

The next example combines the aggregate function Count() with a GROUP BY clause, so that we can select the department id's and the count of employees in each department. (The uses of COUNT(emp_id) and Count(*) are interchangeable in this case.)

```
SELECT dept_id, Count(emp_id)
FROM employee
GROUP BY dept_id
ORDER BY dept_id;
```

dept_id	Count(emp_id)
100	6
200	5
300	3
400	1

VIEWS

A VIEW is simply a select statement that has been stored in the database. VIEWs are an important method of limiting the access of users to data. VIEWs are also a nice tool for organizing data into prearranged sets so that the user doesn't have to go through the effort of building complex SELECT statements. VIEWs will perform faster than ad hoc SELECT statements because the SQL syntax is already checked, parsed, and optimized when they are stored.

VIEWs are database objects, so you can grant user access permissions to them. Say you had users who were not allowed to see the "employee.salary" column. You could create an employee VIEW that included all of the permissible columns, grant access to the VIEW, and deny access to the Employee table as a whole.

Most relational databases are designed for the normalized storage of data. Users who are not familiar with all of the table relationships find it difficult to create SELECT statements that return the desired results. Developers can help users by creating VIEWs specifically designed to present data in an organized fashion that lends itself to end user ad hoc queries and reports.

The syntax for creating a VIEW is simply entering the CREATE VIEW clause in front of a valid SELECT statement.

```
CREATE VIEW <View Name> AS
<SQL Select Statement>;
```

For example, we could create a VIEW of the Employee table that includes the department name and a concatenated employee name called "usr_employee". The VIEW uses column aliases "emp_Name" and "Emp_Dept" to make the column names more recognizable. Table aliases "e" and "d" have been substituted for the table names to simplify the syntax.:

```
CREATE VIEW usr_employee AS
  SELECT
        e.emp_lname || ', ' || e.emp_fname emp_name,
        d.dept_name dept_name
   FROM department d, employee e
  WHERE e.dept_id = d.dept_id;
```

A selection from the VIEW usr_employee might return;

```
SELECT * FROM usr_employee;
```

emp_name	dept_name
Barclay, Howard	Corporate Management
Bigelow, Janet	Corporate Management
Chamberlain, Alan	Software Development
Ciccone, Peter	Software Development
Clark, Alice	Business Services
Fitzgerald, Edward	Business Services
Garcia, Ronald	Business Services
Houston, Mary	Software Development
McMahon, Richard	Business Services
Sinclair, Thomas	Marketing
Smith, Susan	Software Development
Spellman, John	Software Development
Stanley, Michael	Business Services
Sussman, Jack	Corporate Management
Watson, Linda	Software Development

Joins

One of the marks of a relational database is the ability to *join* information located in more than one table into a single result set. The joining of data usually occurs in tables that are related to each other through reference columns. Often the reference columns are related as primary keys and foreign keys (see "Referential Integrity," below). The primary key/foreign key relationships are usually the most efficient means of joining two tables together, but even when columns are not foreign keys, a relational database can use similar columns as a means of tying tables together in a SELECT statement. Performance efficiency in joining tables has more to do with relative table sizes and available indexes than it does with whether or not the columns are keys. Typically, primary keys will be indexed and will be the columns involved in a join, but it is not a requirement. You create a join in a SQL statement by including the tables to be joined in the FROM clause. Then you should specify the column(s) that these tables will use to reference each other. The structure of a simple SELECT with a join becomes:

```
SELECT select-list
FROM table1, table2
WHERE table1.col_ref1 = table2.col_ref2;
```

Whenever two or more tables are listed in a FROM clause, a Cartesian product is performed on the tables. A Cartesian product is all the possible combinations of the rows from each of the tables. If we ran the following query, which is actually three in one, we would see the count of rows in the Department and Employee tables plus the Cartesian product when they are joined.

```
SELECT count(*) FROM department
UNION
SELECT count(*) FROM employee
UNION
SELECT count(*)
FROM department, employee;
```

The results of the query are displayed below:

```
Count(*)
   5
  75
 375
```

When selecting information from two tables it is important to limit the possible return values. You can see in the example above that even two relatively small tables can have a sizable Cartesian product. Imagine doing this on two large tables! The Department and Employee tables can be joined in several ways depending on the information we wish to display. If we want to list department names and the names of employees that are members, then we would join the Department table dept_id with the Employee table dept_id.

```
SELECT    department.dept_name,
          employee.emp_lname,
          employee.emp_fname
```

```
      FROM employee, department
WHERE (department.dept_id = employee.dept_id);
```

In Watcom SQL the order of the columns in a WHERE clause will determine the order that the tables are searched. In the example above the Department table is the "driver" table because it is on the left side of the equals sign. Watcom will search for all of the employees for each department. The result set is automatically ordered by Department.dept_id. If the employee.dept_id column were on the left side of the equals sign in the WHERE clause, then the Employee table would be the "driver" table. When the example below is executed, the result set will automatically be sorted by employee.emp_id.

```
SELECT    department.dept_name,
          employee.emp_lname,
          employee.emp_fname
    FROM employee, department
WHERE (employee.dept_id=department.dept_id);
```

> **Tip**: **For Watcom SQL**: When searching for a small set of rows within a larger table (e.g. to select all of the employees in Dept 100) it is usually more efficient to put the smaller table on the left hand side of the equals sign. When selecting more than fifteen percent from a large table and joining with a smaller table, put the larger table on the left. In more complex queries the rules get much more difficult, and the optimizer should resolve the query plan adequately if the major joins are done on columns with indexes.

It is important to note that in a join operation a computer will first create a Cartesian product, and then remove the columns that do not meet the WHERE criteria. A computer can handle queries with a small number of tables quickly. However as the size and number of tables increases, the Cartesian product will increase exponentially. Since he number of rows to be compared is equal to the number of rows in each table multiplied together, a join of three or four large tables will be a difficult task for a DBMS to handle. Unless you have a very fast DBMS, you should avoid joins of more than four large tables.

Left Outer Joins

Not all RDBMSes support outer joins. The *left outer join* refers to a SELECT statement where two of the tables involved have a relationship such that a column in the first table references a column in the second table, but the corresponding value in the second table may not exist. The "driver" table's column is on the left side of the equals sign in the WHERE clause–thus the name "left outer join".

For example, the Employee table we have been using includes a column "dept_id" which references the dept_id column in the Department table.

Say we wanted to list all of the departments in the Department table along with the names of their employees. If a Department record has no associated employees, in a normal join it will not be displayed. The left outer join will allow us to list all the Department records regardless of whether they have employees or not. The Department table is on the left- hand side of the equals sign and is the "driver" table. All of the Department records will be scanned. The

Employee records will be searched for each Department record scanned. When an employee record is not found, a NULL will be used for any of its selected columns (in this case the emp_fname and emp_lname).

In Watcom SQL:

```
SELECT department.dept_name,
        employee.emp_fname,
        employee.emp_lname
FROM {oj department LEFT OUTER JOIN employee ON
department.dept_id = employee.dept_id};
```

In Oracle 7 SQL:

```
SELECT department.dept_name,
        employee.emp_fname,
        employee.emp_lname
   FROM employee, department
 WHERE department.dept_id (+)=employee.dept_id;
```

In Sybase/SQL Server:

```
SELECT department.dept_name,
        employee.emp_fname,
        employee.emp_lname
   FROM employee, department
 WHERE department.dept_id *= employee.dept_id;
```

UPDATEs

The UPDATE command is used to modify columns of existing data. This clause will only update data in one table at a time. You can UPDATE one or more columns in one or more rows within the table. You specify the column(s) to be updated in the SET clause (e.g. "SET col1=value1, col2=value2, col3=value3"). If you do not include a WHERE clause, then all of the rows in the table will be updated.

```
UPDATE TableName
SET column = ValueToBeAssigned
WHERE WhereClause;
```

In the example below, all of the employees in Department 100 will have their salaries raised twenty-five percent:

```
UPDATE employee
   SET salary = salary * 1.25
 WHERE dept_id = 100;
```

In the example below, all of the employees in departments other than 100 will have their salaries raised twenty-five percent.

```
UPDATE employee
   SET salary = salary * 1.25
```

```
    WHERE dept_id in (
SELECT department.dept_id
  FROM department
 WHERE department.dept_id <> 100 );
```

DELETEs

The DELETE clause is used to delete sets of rows from a table based on the criteria specified in a WHERE clause. Any rows that satisfy the WHERE clause will be deleted. If you do not include a WHERE clause then *all* of the rows in the table will be deleted.

```
DELETE FROM TableName
WHERE WhereClause;
```

If you want to delete a specific row, use the column(s) of the primary key.

```
DELETE FROM employee
  WHERE emp_id = 501;
```

If you wanted to delete all of the employees in the sales department, but didn't know the dept_id, you could use the following statement with a "nested" SELECT statement.

```
DELETE FROM employee
  WHERE dept_id = (
SELECT department.dept_id
  FROM department
 WHERE department.dept_name = 'Sales' );
```

Whenever you do a DELETE statement such as the one above, it is a good idea to test the SELECT statement by itself before you execute the DELETE, to make sure you are going to delete what you intend!

INSERTs

INSERT clause is used to insert rows of data into a table. When inserting rows you must be sure to include all of the required column values, other wise the statement will fail. Likewise, any column constraints that exist for the table must be satisfied. There are two basic formats of the INSERT statement. In the first format the column values are stated in a VALUES clause. In the second format the column values are selected in a SELECT statement.:

```
INSERT INTO TableName
(ColumnList)
VALUES (ValueList);
```

We can INSERT a row into the Employee table using the following statement. (These statements can get fairly large, especially when working with tables having lots of columns.)

```
INSERT INTO employee
      ( emp_id, manager_id, emp_fname, emp_lname,  dept_id,
```

```
                 street, city, state, zip_code, phone,
                 status, ss_number, salary, start_date, termination_date,
                 birth_date, bene_health_ins, bene_life_ins, bene_day_care )
   VALUES ( 999, null, 'New', 'Guy',     300,
'            111 Beacon Street', 'Boston', 'MA', '02135',
'            617-789-1234',
             null, '123-45-6789', 20000, '1991-01-01', null,
'            1932-01-31', 'N', 'N', 'N' );
```

The value-list may also be expressed as a SELECT statement. The VALUES (<value-list>) is replaced with a SELECT statement. If you wanted to copy an employee row of data with only minor changes you could use a statement like the one below:

```
INSERT INTO employee
          ( emp_id, manager_id, emp_fname, emp_lname,  dept_id,
            street, city, state, zip_code, phone,
            status, ss_number, salary, start_date, termination_date,
            birth_date, bene_health_ins, bene_life_ins, bene_day_care )
SELECT 998, manager_id, 'New Twin', emp_lname,   400,
            street, city, state, zip_code, phone,
            status, ss_number, salary, start_date, termination_date,
            birth_date, bene_health_ins, bene_life_ins, bene_day_care
FROM Employee
WHERE emp_id = 999;
```

IF you don't include a column list, then the column list will be defaulted to include all of the table's columns. The column positions will be the same as that in the table's CREATE statement. It can be dangerous to assume the column order when inserting rows. In some cases, however, this is a nice feature.

> **Tip**: To copy all of the data from one table (TableA) to another (TableB) having the identical structure, you could execute the following INSERT:
>
> ```
> INSERT INTO TableA SELECT * FROM TableB;
> ```

> **Tip**: Some database platforms allow you to create tables with an INSERT statement. The following example works in Oracle:
>
> ```
> CREATE TABLE emp_Copy  as select * from employee;
> ```

Transactions

A database transaction is one or more SQL statements that form a logical unit of work: if one portion of the logical unit fails, then the whole may be invalid. Whenever there is an error condition that violates the logical transaction, the whole transaction should be undone. Databases do not actually write data manipulation changes to the database until a COMMIT is received. If a logical transaction fails along the way, you can "undo" any pending data manipulations that have not yet been COMMITted by issuing a ROLLBACK. The amount of control available in COMMITs and ROLLBACKs varies with the database platform, so you should check your specific platforms manual in this area.

```
.. transactions ..
COMMIT;

..transactions..
ROLLBACK;
```

When using databases, such as Oracle, which support record locking, you should check the user's manual to see the affects of issuing a COMMIT. In most databases, a COMMIT or a ROLLBACK statement will release all locks. On some platforms, ROLLBACKs can be limited to a portion of the transaction. In that case, if you want to limit how far back into the transaction a ROLLBACK will go, you can set a SAVEPOINT and then limit the ROLLBACK by using a statement like "ROLLBACK TO SAVEPOINT;" This kind of logic is very database-specific.

Integrity Constraints

Integrity constraints limit the values a column may have so that business rules and data integrity are enforced. When designing a database, the values intended to be stored in columns should be defined and then enforced as well as is possible through the use of integrity constraints. You should check your particular database platform's user's manual for the constraints available.

PowerBuilder developers should be aware of the integrity constraints placed on the tables they are using. If their application allows data that violates any one of these constraints to be sent to the database, then a database error will occur. Developers should design their windows to minimize the possibility of violating integrity constraints. Using default values coupled with window controls like CheckBoxes, RadioButtons and DropDownListBoxes, which allow only valid values, will dramatically limit the possibility of integrity errors.

The integrity constraints allowed in a table definition vary from database to database. Some databases allow column values to be limited to ranges of values and/or sets of values. One of the most common constraints is the "NOT NULL." The NOT NULL constraint means that a value must be entered in the column so that the result is NOT NULL.

NULL
>   means that a column may be empty; i.e. may contain a NULL.

NOT NULL
>   means a column may NOT be empty; it requires a value.

CHECK (Some platforms)
>   means that a column must satisfy a condition of some sort. The most common use of this would be a switch value, as mentioned above, or a not-negative value. A not-negative value might be useful for things like not having a negative wage amount in a payroll application (no matter how much it feels like at the time).

UNIQUE (Some platforms)

forces a distinct value to be entered. This usually creates an index on the column or columns involved. The same effect can be achieved by creating a unique index on the columns involved.

Integrity constraints can also be expanded by the use of "triggers" on column INSERT, UPDATE and/or DELETE (see "Stored Procedures and Triggers," below). In the trigger you can include a great deal of logic for enforcing business rules that goes beyond what can be declared in a TABLE CREATE statement. Think of triggers used for integrity constraints as extensions of the table definition and enforcers of business rules.

Referential integrity

In relational databases, columns will often refer to data in other tables. When that reference is to a *primary key* in another table, you can declare the column as a *foreign key*. Columns that are foreign keys can only contain values that are already stored in the related primary key. For example, let's say the dept_id column in the Employee table was defined as a foreign key for the dept_id in the Department table. When you enter a value in the Employee.dept_id column, the database will check to see if there is a corresponding Department.dept_*id* value. If there isn't, then a database error will occur. Likewise, if you try to delete a Department record and there are Employee records that contain a reference to the record's dept_id, a database error will occur. In this way, the database insures that there is integrity in the data. Otherwise, you would need to constantly check and validate values as you manipulated data.

PRIMARY KEY is a unique column or columns, of which no part should be NULL. A table has only one primary key. If a key is made up of more than one column, it is also known as a *composite* or *compound* key.

FOREIGN KEY is a column or columns in one table (often called the child table) which is the same as the primary key in another table (called the parent table) and references that table. (In today's databases, the parent and child tables are usually in the same database.)

In the PowerBuilder demo database there is a common pairing of Department and Employee tables. The Department table is a parent of the Employee table. In other words, the Department table holds a key value that must exist before an Employee record can be added (i.e. the dept_id). Below is a definition of the Department table.

```
CREATE TABLE "dba"."department"
               ("dept_id" integer NOT NULL,
                "dept_name" char(40) NOT NULL,
                "dept_head_id" integer
          , PRIMARY KEY (dept_id)
       , FOREIGN KEY ky_dept_head (dept_head_id)
       ) REFERENCES "dba"."employee"
       ON DELETE  SET NULL
       );
```

The primary key of the Department table is declared as dept_id in the phrase

```
PRIMARY KEY (dept_id)
```

Notice also that the column "dept_head_id" is a foreign key of the Employee table through the phrase

```
FOREIGN KEY ky_dept_head (dept_head_id)
REFERENCES "dba"."employee"
ON DELETE   SET NULL
```

Watcom SQL now allows for some referential integrity extensions for managing dependent rows when the primary key (the Department.dept_id) is deleted. These options can be set through the radio buttons in the "On Delete of Primary Table Row" group box in the "Foreign Key Definition" dialog box available from the Alter Table dialog in the PowerBuilder Database Painter. In this case the option is set to "ON DELETE SET NULL." Now when a department record is deleted, any columns in other tables that reference the deleted department's dept_id will be set to NULL automatically. If one of those columns has a constraint of NOT NULL, a database error will occur. The Employee table actually has a NOT NULL constraint on its dept_id column. Whenever a Department row is deleted, Watcom will see if there are any dependent Employee rows. If any exist, then the DELETE will fail.

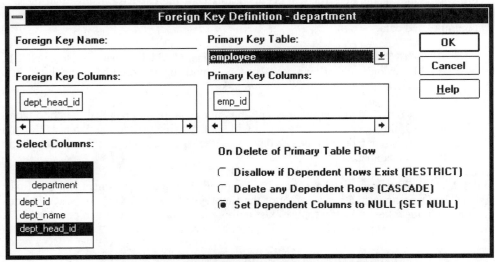

Figure 3-1: Foreign key definition in PowerBuilder.

The three options available in Watcom SQL for extending the referential integrity constraints on DELETE are as follows:

> **RESTRICT** Do not allow delete if any dependent rows exist. (The NOT NULL constraint is not required on the dependent rows.)

> **CASCADE** Delete along with any dependent rows that may exist. (These rows

may in turn have dependent rows that could trigger additional deletes. Any failure in any part of the transaction will cause the entire transaction to fail.)

SET NULL Set dependent columns to NULL. (The delete will fail if any dependent column uses the NOT NULL constraint.)

The Employee table dept_id column is a foreign key of the Department dept_id column. The Employee dept_id column also has the NOT NULL constraint. This means that for a record to be added to the Employee table, an existing department must be entered for that employee. The Department dept_head_id column is a foreign key back to the Employee table. Fortunately, the Department dept_head_id column does not have the NOT NULL constraint. This definition will allow you to add a department record without specifying the department head. If the Department dept_head_id column had the NOT NULL constraint, then adding the first department would be impossible, and subsequent adds would be difficult at best.

Stored Procedures and Triggers

Stored procedures are blocks of SQL code which have been compiled and stored on the server. Stored Procedures may be called from client processes or from within *triggers*. The RDBMSes which allow stored procedures use a procedural language to logically control the sequence of SQL commands. Triggers and stored procedures together allow for sophisticated processing to occur on the server. A stored procedure may return no result or one or more result sets. Arguments can be used when calling stored procedures. In the Client/Server architecture, stored procedures are useful for minimizing the amount of network traffic required to send a long series of SQL commands to the server. Stored procedures are "preparsed" when they are stored, so they take very little time to load and do not require syntax checking or optimization. The performance effect of this is noticeable on very complex SQL statements or when stored procedures are used for repetitive processing.

Triggers are SQL scripts that automatically execute when a row is inserted, updated, or deleted in a table. A trigger may fire before or after a row is inserted, updated. or deleted. It may fire one time for each row that is being operated on, or it may fire once per SQL statement. In some RDBMSes it may also fire on the update of a particular column.

Triggers are event-driven, whereas stored procedures are called. Think of the differences between PowerBuilder events and functions. Triggers, like events, cannot be passed any arguments and do not return any values. They are executed in response to some action. Stored procedures, on the other hand, can be passed arguments and can return values. They are executed as the result of being called in SQL scripts.

Triggers will cause additional overhead during data manipulations. Usually this is not a concern, but in cases of high volume transactions, this additional overhead is multiplied and may cause problems. Triggers that perform data manipulations (INSERT, UPDATE, or DELETE)–in the table being modified or other tables–may fire additional triggers. The database designer should be careful not to add too many triggers that could cause conflicting actions.

Triggers and stored procedures may also call other stored procedures. Their actions in turn may also fire triggers. When constructing triggers and stored procedures it is best to add them incrementally and test them thoroughly.

> **Tip: Enforcing business rules.** Whenever possible, use column constraints, referential integrity, and triggers as the primary methods of enforcing the business rules of the database. These are automatic. Do not use stored procedures as the primary means of checking business rules because the rule will not be enforced unless the procedure is called. Triggers, however, may call stored procedures as functions and subroutines.

SQL Performance

SQL SELECT statements in your DataWindows and in Embedded SQL should be written in a way that will produce the optimum performance for your database platform. The PowerBuilder SQL Painter makes no attempt to optimize queries. The effect of this may be that your application will have many slow-performing SELECT statements. A few will present obvious major bottlenecks. The others will just make everything more sluggish. You should learn what SQL syntax is best for your platform and habitually use that as you build applications. Overall performance of the application will be better, and you will be able to limit performance tuning to those few bottlenecks.

Often an RDBMS will have a set of syntax rules that, when applied to the statement, result in a "query plan.. The query plan is the method a database engine will use to get the results from the database. For example, in Watcom SQL the order of the columns in a WHERE clause will determine the order that the data is searched. You should also refer to your SQL manual for tips on constructing the SELECT statements that will perform most efficiently.

If you are joining a long table with a short table, the table used as the "driver" will affect performance. If you are only selecting a few rows out of the long table then you should drive through the short table. If you are selecting lots of rows out of the long table, then you should drive through the long table.

When you join two tables, PowerBuilder will look for primary key/foreign key relationships, or two commonly named columns in both tables and base joins over these columns. The result is not always the best method for selecting the data. The biggest performance boosts usually involve adding an index or changing a WHERE clause.

When the columns in a SELECT statement are all contained in an index, then the data needs can be satisfied by just looking at the index. Knowing this, sometimes you can construct indexes on commonly retrieved columns so that just the index will be used and the actual table will not have to be queried.

The fastest join is to compare a constant value against a unique clustered index. If the column value has to be manipulated in order to be compared, then the index will not be used. For example, if you have an index on employee name and are converting it to upper case in a WHERE clause, then any index on employee name will not be used. If this is a common SELECT, in order to optimize it you may want to add a column that stores the upper case of the name, and index it. The example below would not be able to use an index on the "emp_lname" column.

```
SELECT * from Employee
       WHERE  Upper(emp_lname) = 'SMITH';
```

SQL Quick Reference

Item	Purpose	Example
DELETE	Delete existing data	DELETE FROM employee WHERE dept_id = 100;

INSERT	Add new data	INSERT INTO department
		VALUES (100, 'Sales', 111);
		1'
		INSERT INTO department
		    (dept_id, dept_name, dept_head_id)
		VALUES (100, 'Sales', 111);
		
		INSERT INTO department
		    (dept_id, dept_name, dept_head_id)
		  SELECT 100, 'Sales', emp_id
		  FROM Employee
		  WHERE emp_lname = 'Barclay';

UPDATE	Modify existing data	UPDATE employee SET salary = salary * 1.25 WHERE dept_id = 100;
SELECT	Retrieve a set of data	SELECT * FROM employee WHERE salary >= 41000;
	IN- find all the employees in the list of departments.	SELECT * from employee WHERE dept_id IN (100, 200, 300);

	EXISTS - return any emp records where the department does not exist.	SELECT * from employee
		  WHERE dept_id NOT EXISTS (
		    SELECT dept_id
		      FROM department);

	BETWEEN - return all emps with a salary between $41,000 and $80,000.	SELECT * FROM employee WHERE salary BETWEEN 41000 AND 80000;
	IS NULL - find all depts that do not have a head.	SELECT * FROM department WHERE dept_head_id IS NULL;

	ALL - find all employees who are in one of the departments where the department head has employee id 501.	SELECT * FROM employee WHERE dept_id = ALL (SELECT dept_id FROM department WHERE dept_head_id = 501);
	ANY - Return any employee that is a department head.	SELECT * FROM employee WHERE emp_id = ANY (SELECT dept_head_id FROM department);
	AND, OR, NOT	SELECT * FROM employee WHERE (salary > 80000) AND (emp_lname LIKE '%B' OR emp_fname = 'Howard') AND NOT (dept_id = 100);
	UNION, UNION ALL	SELECT * FROM employee WHERE (salary > 80000) AND (emp_lname LIKE '%B' OR emp_fname = 'Howard') AND NOT (dept_id = 100) UNION SELECT * FROM employee WHERE (salary < 80000) AND (dept_id = 100);

	INTERSECT	SELECT * FROM employee
		  WHERE (salary > 80000)
		INTERSECT
		SELECT * FROM employee
		WHERE (salary < 80000)
		  AND (dept_id = 100);

	MINUS	SELECT * FROM employee MINUS SELECT * FROM employee WHERE (salary > 80000) AND (emp_lname LIKE '%B' OR emp_fname = 'Howard') AND NOT (dept_id = 100);

	GROUP BY - list department names and the total count of employees in each department.	SELECT dept_name, Count(*)
		  FROM employee, department
		WHERE employee.dept_id =
		    department.dept_id
		  GROUP BY dept_name;

	ORDER BY	

	HAVING	
	COUNT(), MAX(), MIN(), AVG(),SUM()	SELECT dept_id, Count(emp_id) FROM employee GROUP BY dept_id ORDER BY dept_id;

CHAPTER 4

The PowerBuilder System Catalog

By Kent Marsh

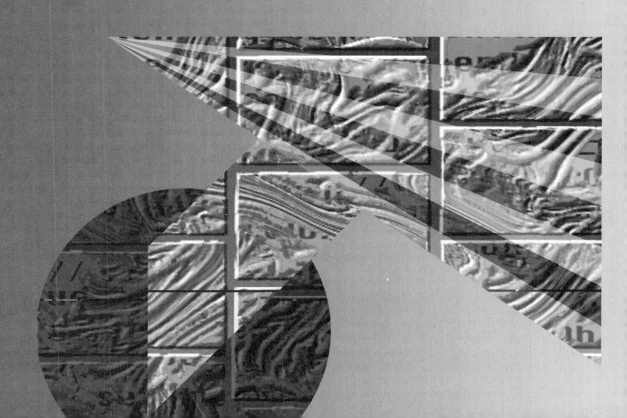

The PowerBuilder System Catalog

by **Kent Marsh**

PowerBuilder utilizes a set of five tables to extend the attributes of data objects when creating a PowerBuilder application. These five tables comprise what is sometimes referred to as the PowerBuilder System Catalog or the System Catalog for short. The System Catalog is created automatically in the database platform you use while working in the PowerBuilder development environment. When you create a Watcom SQL database in PowerBuilder's Database Administrator, PowerBuilder automatically creates the System Catalog tables in the new database instance.

> **Tip**: If you are installing PowerBuilder for the very first time on a platform other than Watcom SQL then you should connect as a user who has DBA permissions. PowerBuilder will attempt to create the System Catalog tables in an area owned by the "system administrator" of the database. This will of course vary, depending on the database platform.

The System Catalog tables need to be available to any PowerBuilder developer working on that database platform. These tables do not distinguish between application developers or even applications: the tables will commingle information for any PowerBuilder application built by any developer using that database. You can help simplify some of the confusion by using some simple rules of nomenclature that you should standardize in your shop.

The "Group of Five" System Catalog tables are comprised of the following:

```
pbcattbl       Table attributes
pbcatcol       Column attributes
pbcatfm        Display formats
pbcatedt       Edit styles
pbcatvld       Validations
```

These tables are updated through the various activities you perform in the Database Painter. The Create Table and Alter Table dialogs are used to maintain tables, columns, and their attributes. Some of the information you are maintaining will go into database object definitions. However "extended" attribute information will be stored in the PowerBuilder System Catalog tables **pbcattbl** and **pbcatcol** (which store table and column attributes respectively). Some databases support table and column comments, and some do not. PowerBuilder used to store table and column comments according to the facilities available in the native database. Since Version 3.0, PowerBuilder stores table and column comments in **pbcattbl** and **pbcatcol.**

The Database Painter gives you dialogs to create display formats, edit styles, and validations which can be used as extended column attributes in the Create Table and Alter Table dialogs, as well as in the DataWindow Painter. When you add any of these extended attributes to a column, PowerBuilder will automatically utilize them when creating DataWindows. It is important to note that these attributes form only the default attributes for new DataWindow columns. In other words, no DataWindow column attributes will be updated when you maintain extended column attributes, nor when you maintain a display format, edit style, or validation. When you edit one of these, keep in mind that you may also have to make a pass through any related DataWindows.

As you create your database schema, you should be building and loading extended attributes. Do not start creating DataWindows until after your schema is fairly stable and all known extended attributes have been created and assigned to columns. Otherwise you will not get the benefits of their defaults.

> **Tip**: If you need to change column attributes based on the current extended attribute stored in one of the System Catalog tables, you can query the appropriate Catalog table and then use dwModify() to change the column attribute, at runtime, to the value selected.

The Data Manipulation window that is part of the Database Painter will utilize all of the extended attributes defined for tables and columns in the Create Table and/or Alter Table dialog. This is a quick and easy testing tool for editing display formats, edit styles, validations, and even default field sizes. If you select the Data Manipulation window from the Database Painter menu, you will also get a choice of the presentation style to be used.

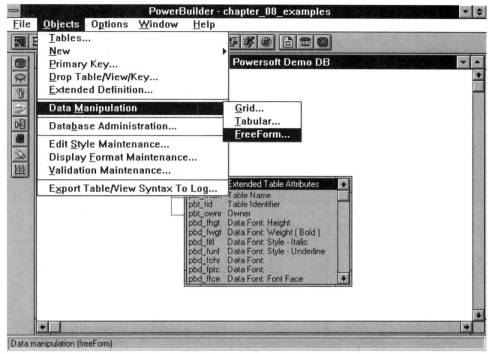

Figure 4-1: Data Manipulation window.

Table Attributes Catalog

The extended table attributes catalog is stored in the table **pbcattbl**. Below is a listing of the create statement for the table. The primary key of the table uses the columns (pbt_tnam, pbt_ownr).

PBCATTBL: Table Attributes

Column	Data Type	Description
pbt_tnam	char(129)	Table Name
pbt_tid	integer	Table Identifier
pbt_ownr	char(129)	Table Owner
pbd_fhgt	smallint	Data Font: height

pbd_fwgt	smallint	Data Font: weight (Bold)
pbd_fitl	char(1)	Data Font: Italic
pbd_funl	char(1)	Data Font: Underline
pbd_fchr	smallint	Data Font:
pbd_fptc	smallint	Data Font:
pbd_ffce	char(18)	Data Font: Font Face
pbh_fhgt	smallint	Header Font: height
pbh_fwgt	smallint	Header Font: weight (Bold)
pbh_fitl	char(1)	Header Font: Italic
pbh_funl	char(1)	Header Font: Underline
pbh_fchr	smallint	Header Font:
pbh_fptc	smallint	Header Font:
pbh_ffce	char(18)	Header Font: Font Face
pbl_fhgt	smallint	Label Font: height
pbl_fwgt	smallint	Label Font: weight (Bold)
pbl_fitl	char(1)	Label Font: Italic
pbl_funl	char(1)	Label Font: Underline
pbl_fchr	smallint	Label Font:
pbl_fptc	smallint	Label Font:
pbl_ffce	char(18)	Label Font: Font Face
pbt_cmnt	varchar(254)	Comment

The default character font and style attributes for the table are stored for data, headings, and labels. In this case data refers to the field used to display a column of data retrieved from the database in a DataWindow. Headings are the DataWindow text fields associated with each column in a tabular presentation style. These text fields will appear in the Header band of the DataWindow directly above the data field. Labels are the DataWindow text fields associated with each column in a freeform presentation style. These text fields will appear in the Detail band of the DataWindow to the left of the data field.

The **pbcattbl** table uses a column prefix of "pbd_" for the data attributes, and "pbh_" and "pbl_" for headings and labels respectively. The following default character fonts and styles for data, headings, and labels attributes can be defined as shown in the data attribute example below.

```
// Data Font / Style attributes
pbd_fhgt    Font Height
pbd_fwgt    Font Weight (Bold)
pbd_fitl    Style Italic
pbd_funl    Style UnderLine
pbd_ffce    Font Face ("Arial", "Courier" )
```

You can store descriptive table comments of up to 254 characters in length. While you are in the Database Painter you can add comments to tables displayed in on the screen by using the right mouse button and clicking on the table title bar. A pop-up menu will give you a number of options, including Comments.

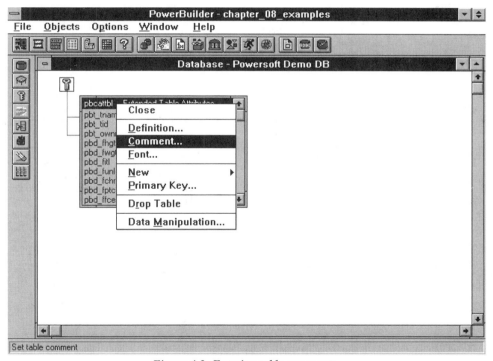

Figure 4-2: Entering table comments.

The table comments you enter will be stored in the pbcattbl.cmnt column. PowerBuilder will then display the comment to the right of the table name whenever the table is opened in the Database Painter.

Column Attributes Catalog

The extended column attributes catalog is stored in the table **pbcatcol**. Below is a listing of the create statement for the table. The primary key of the table uses the columns (bc_tnam, pbc_ownr, pbc_cnam.) Although there is not a declared foreign key constraint, each row of the **pbcatcol** table should have a row in the **pbcattbl** table with a matching (pbc_tnam, pbc_ownr) concatenated primary key.

PBCATCOL: Column Attributes Catalog

Column	Data Type	Description
pbc_tnam	char(129)	Table Name
pbc_tid	integer	Table ID
pbc_ownr	char(129)	Table Owner
pbc_cnam	char(129)	Column Name
pbc_cid	smallint	Column ID
pbc_labl	varchar(254)	Label Text
pbc_lpos	smallint	Label Position on side of data(23=**Left** or 24=Right)
pbc_hdr	varchar(254)	Header Text
pbc_hpos	smallint	Header Position (23=Left, 24=Right, 25=Center)
pbc_jtfy	smallint	Justify Data (23=Left, 24=Right, 25=Center)
pbc_mask	varchar(31)	Display Format Name Reference to pbcatfmt.pbf_name
pbc_case	smallint	Display Text Case (26=any, 27=Upper, 28=lower)
pbc_hght	smallint	Data Field Height
pbc_wdth	smallint	Data Field Width
pbc_ptrn	varchar(31)	Validation Name Reference to pbcatvld.pbv_name

pbc_bmap	char(1)	Display as Bitmap Flag ('Y'=Yes, 'N'=No)
pbc_init	varchar(254)	Initial Value
pbc_cmnt	varchar(254)	Column Comment Text
pbc_edit	varchar(31)	Edit Style Name Reference to pbcatedt.pbe_name
pbc_tag	varchar(254)	Tag (Unused?)

Most of the column attribute values are entered in while editing a table definition in the Create Table or Alter Table dialog. Some of these are also available for editing with in the Database Painter. If the table is open, click on the column to be edited using the right mouse button. A pop-up menu will allow you to edit the comment, display format, edit style, and validation. The "Definition..." selection will open the Alter Table dialog. The "Header..." will open a dialog that will allow you to edit the column label and header text attributes.

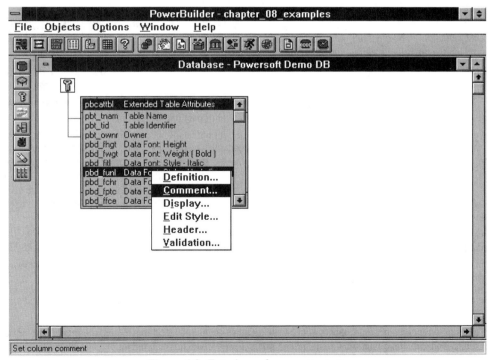

Figure 4-3: Entering column comments.

The most common way to edit extended column attributes is through the Alter Table dialog. This dialog can be opened in numerous ways, some already mentioned above. A simple way is to just double-click on an open table in the Database Painter. Using this dialog you can add columns and maintain their extended attributes. Most of the columns in the **pbcatcol** table map to fields in the extended attributes section of this window.

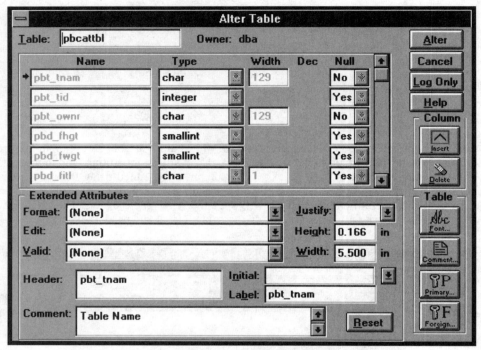

Figure 4-4: Alter Table dialog box.

Like the table attributes catalog, the column comments stored in the column pbc_cmnt will be displayed to the right of each column name whenever a table is opened in the Database Painter. It is very helpful to fill in the column comments attribute to help you remember what columns are to be used for. Column comments are only 254 characters long, so you are limited in the detail of what can be stored. Store very brief but informative text as a quick reference.

The pbc_mask column is a reference to the display format associated with the column. The name entered should match a format name stored in pbcatfmt.pbf_name.

The pbc_ptrn column is a reference to the validation rule associated with the column. The name entered should match a validation name stored in pbcatvld.pbv_name.

The pbc_edit column is a reference to the edit style associated with the column. The name entered should match an edit style name stored in pbcatedt.pbe_name.

There is not a database foreign key constraint on the columns pbc_Mask, pbc_Ptrn, or pbc_Edit, so you can manually put in values that do not have a corresponding value in **pbcatfmt, pbcatvld,** or **pbcatedt**. PowerBuilder will limit the entries in the Alter Table dialog to those that are currently available, but there is nothing to keep you from deleting the corresponding value later.

There is a new dialog box available only by clicking on the column name displayed in an open table in the Database Painter. Select the menu item "Display..." in the pop-up menu.

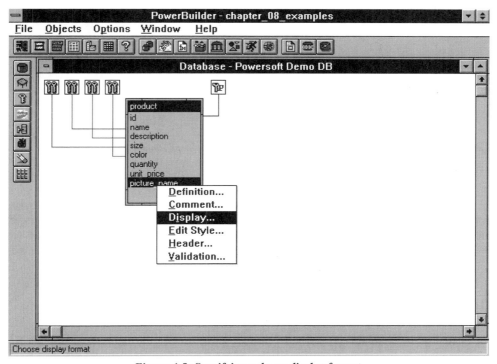

Figure 4-5: Specifying column display format.

When the Column Display Format dialog is displayed, you can set a number of attributes not available in any other place. There is a **Picture:** CheckBox for setting whether the column should be displayed as a picture. You can store a string containing the file name of a bitmap in the column data. PowerBuilder will automatically display the column as the bitmap the data string is referencing.

If you don't select the **Picture:,** then the dialog will make visible the option of setting the **Case:** of the text as "any," "Upper," or "lower." You can also set the justification of the text in the **Justify:** DropDownListBox.

```
Picture:    pbc_bmap    Y = Yes,    N = No
Justify:    pbc_jtfy   23 = Left,  24 = Right, 25 = Center
Case:       pbc_case   26 = any,   27 = Upper, 28 = lower
```

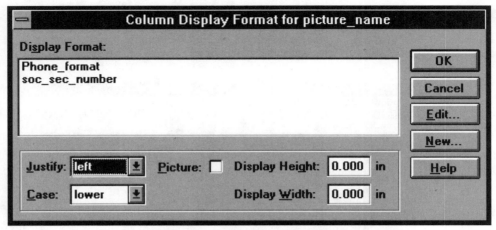

Figure 4-6: Selecting a display format.

The pbc_tag column doesn't appear to be used any where. It would be nice if it defaulted to the column tag value when creating DataWindows. Some developers like using the DataWindow tags, along with the windowcontrol tag attributes, to hold the text used to display micro help when the column has focus. Others use the tag value as a means of context-sensitive help. At least it is a place where you can store text on a column level.

Display Format Catalog

The display format catalog stores display format information in the table **pbcatfmt**. The format name (pbf_name) is also the primary key of the table. Because display formats for several applications may be stored in the same table, you may decide to distinguish formats for various applications by adding a prefix to the format name. For example, if you have a general ledger application, you could name all of its formats beginning with a **GL_**: you could have GL_Dollars, GL_Debit, GL_Credit, GL_Date, GL_TotalAmt.

The actual format used is stored in the column pbf_frmt. The format syntax is much like Microsoft Excel. (See the *PowerBuilder User's Guide* for more detail on format syntax). PBCATFMT: Display Format Catalog

Column	Data Type	Description
pbf_name	varchar(30)	Format Name (Primary Key)
pbf_frmt	varchar(254)	Display Format Syntax

pbf_type	smallint	Data Type: 80 = String 81 = Number 82 = Date 83 = Time 84 = DateTime
pbf_cntr	integer	Change Counter

If you don't care for all of the formats provided by PowerBuilder, go ahead and delete them. They are easily recovered and it will reduce the number of wrong assignments.

The change counter pbf_cntr is used to track versions of formats. It is incremented whenever an edit change is made to a format. Counters of this type are useful for tables being maintained in a multi-user environment. If the change counter has changed between the time you read it and the time you try to write your changes back, then you know that someone else has updated the record in the meantime.

Edit Style Catalog

The edit style catalog stores edit styles in the table **pbcatedt**. The edit style name (pbe_name) is also the primary key of the table. Because edit styles for several applications may be stored in the same table, you may decide to distinguish formats for various applications by adding a prefix to the edit style name. Managing edit styles is not a trivial task.

Edit styles will often reference PowerBuilder objects stored in PowerBuilder libraries. If these objects are not in the application library path when you try to use them, then the edit style will not work. For example, a DropDownDataWindow edit style obviously references a PowerBuilder DataWindow object. PowerBuilder will sometimes give a GPF if you try to edit an edit style containing a reference to an object that is not in the current library path! At runtime, in this case, the edit style will simply not function. So if you decide to use edit styles in your application, remember that you will need to manage the objects they reference as well. Because the edit styles are stored in a system-level database, you may want to put the PowerBuilder objects used by edit styles in a library to be used by any application using that database as well.

PBCATEDT: Edit Style Catalog

Column	Data Type	Description
pbe_name	varchar(30)	Edit Style Name
pbe_edit	varchar(254)	Attribute Value

pbe_type	smallint	edit style Type 85 = CheckBox 86 = RadioButton 87 = DropDownListBox 88 = DropDownDataWindow 89 = Edit 90 = Edit Mask
pbe_cntr	integer	Change Counter
pbe_seqn	smallint	Attribute Sequence
pbe_flag	integer	Changes use with Type
pbe_work	char(32)	Changes use with type

Creating edit styles outside of PowerBuilder's dialog boxes is very difficult. Each edit style type will store information differently. The table is not normalized, so each attribute gets its own row. Some edit styles only require one or two rows. Others, such as a DropDownList-Box, will require many rows. In the case of the DropDownListBox, aside from some of the other attributes, there are at least two rows for each DropDown row; i.e. one for the data value and one for the display.

Every time a change is made to an edit style, the numeric value in the column pbe_cntr is incremented for all of the rows associated with that edit style. PowerBuilder uses this counter to keep track of what rows belong to which versions. As the versions change, the older version rows are deleted.

The pbe_seqn attribute is used by PowerBuilder to order the rows of the edit style in a particular way so that the various edit style attributes can be deciphered. For example, in the CheckBox edit style, the row where pbe_seqn = 2 is the row that will store the "ON" value, and the row where pbe_seqn = 3 is the row that will store the "OFF" value. It is really difficult to think of a reason for trying to programmatically build these items. By far the easiest way is through the PowerBuilder dialogs.

Validation Catalog

The validation catalog stores DataWindow column validation rules in the table **pbcatvld**. The validation name (pbv_name) is also the primary key of the table. As is the case with edit styles, validation rules for several applications may be stored in the same table. Consequently you may decide to distinguish formats for various applications by adding a prefix to the validation name.

Validation rules can also reference PowerBuilder objects stored in PowerBuilder libraries. Here too, if these objects are not in the application library path when you try to use them, the

validation will not work. For example, you can include your own function calls in validations. These functions are "global" functions created in the Function Painter and stored in a PowerBuilder library. If the function used in the validation is not in the current application library path, then the validation will fail. So when using custom functions in validations, remember that you will need to manage the functions along with the validations. If you are going to use a lot of custom functions, its a good idea to create a special library of validation functions used by any application, and one for those unique to each specific application.
PBCATVLD: Validation Rule Catalog

Column	Data Type	Description
pbv_name	varchar(30)	validation Name (Primary Key)
pbv_vald	varchar(254)	validation Rule
pbv_type	smallint	Data Type of Column to be tested
pbv_cntr	integer	Change Counter
pbv_msg	varchar(254)	Error Message

The change counter pbf_cntr is used to track versions of formats. It is incremented whenever a edit change is made to a format.

If a column entry violates the validation rule associated with it, then PowerBuilder will display an error message. The error message to be displayed is stored in the column pbv_msg. If you leave this field blank, then PowerBuilder will insert a default error message for you.

> **Tip**: Basic validations can only have one error message. If you need to have more control over the error messages displayed and/or want to have more complex validation logic, use a custom function in the validation rule. If you are clever, you can override the error message stored in the DataWindow column validation from within your custom function by using

```
<DataWindow>.dwModify(l_col + ".validationMsg=~'" + &
l_Msg + "~'" )
```

Where **l_col** = current column name,
and **l_Msg** = error message text.

Example validation rule: Customized date validation.

```
f_IsDate()
```

Within the function **f_IsDate()** you can perform multiple edits and tests on the data. If you can also pass the function a reference to the current DataWindow, then you will be able to get the text entered (**GetText()**), override the error message, and basically do anything you want with the DataWindow from the function code. Validation functions used like this should return a boolean True or False for validation pass or fail respectively.

Moving System Catalogs

If you move your development software from one database to another, you will need to move any System Catalog data associated with that application. It is easy if you can just copy the entire set of System Catalog tables. If there is already a set of System Catalog tables on the destination system, then you will want to update that set with the additional catalog entries desired. This task can be made easier if you have been consistent in your nomenclature and used some kind of prefix for all of the System Catalog table entries.

Controlling System Catalog Access

As your reliance on the System Catalog tables' data grows, you may want to limit the access to those tables. There are a number of standard methods used in any database for protecting data that can be employed, and a couple of unique ones. Developers will need access to these tables while developing the PowerBuilder application, but not necessarily at other times.

Different databases have varying capabilities and facilities for protecting access. Your strategy will depend on the database being used. Sorry, there aren't any sure-fire, foolproof solutions here. If it seems worth the effort, here are some suggestions.

If you are using a multi-user database such as Oracle or sybase, and you have several application development projects using the same set of System Catalog tables simultaneously, there will be some conflicts. Separating the data through views is possible, but has its problems. Another method is to create a unique set of System Catalog tables for each development team, and use synonyms or views of these tables utilizing the standard PowerBuilder names. As far as PowerBuilder is concerned, they are the same tables. Using separate tables is nice, because the number of rows of Catalog items is limited to just one application. You may decide to create a special user id, or perhaps an Oracle 7 ROLE, for developers to use while developing. Then when users who are not developing log in, they will use another id.

Controlling ODBC system catalog access

You can control database and Catalog access to Watcom and other ODBC databases in the development environment by setting the read-only variable in pb.ini or pbodb040.ini. Settings in pbodb040.ini take precedence over those in pb.ini. The chart below gives examples.

When the PBNoCatalog variable is turned on (1 in pb.ini or Yes in pbodb040.ini), DDL and DML (INSERT, UPDATE, and DELETE) statements are allowed. However, the Powersoft repository tables will not be created if they do not exist; and if they exist, they will not be referenced. The DataWindow and Report painters will always use the appropriate default values for extended attributes. (This feature, when tested, did not appear to be fully implemented in the release of PowerBuilder 4 available. Updates to the System Catalog tables were prevented, but only after wading through a number of error message boxes. Hopefully by the time you read this things will be resolved.)

	PB.INI	PBODB040.INI
No-catalog access	[Database] PBNoCatalog=1	[WATCOM SQL] PBNoCatalog="NO" [EXCEL] PBNoCatalog="NO'
Allow-catalog access	[Database] PBNoCatalog=0	[WATCOM SQL] PBNoCatalog="YES" [EXCEL] PBNoCatalog="YES'

Summary

We have seen that using the PowerBuilder System Catalog is useful for creating defaults in DataWindow columns. To make the most of your efforts, you should enter as many extended attributes as possible before creating your DataWindows. It is not uncommon to display a column in more than one format, so you should pick the one that will be used most often. You should definitely take advantage of the table and column comments. These will help you, and any other developers using the data files, to better understand what the intent is behind the use of these objects.

Use a standard nomenclature when creating objects stored in PowerBuilder System Catalog so that

Objects are listed by application.
Object usage is clear for developers.
Management of objects is easier.
Moving objects' System Catalogs is easier.

Using edit styles and validations can help standardize how columns are used and simplify the effort of catching business rule violations before the data hits the database. However, when edit styles and validations reference objects stored in PowerBuilder libraries (i.e. DataWindow objects and functions) then you need to pay more attention to their management.

The tables in the PowerBuilder System Catalog should be protected against modification by non-developers. PowerBuilder offers some ways to help through .ini file settings. It is far more secure to have your DBA devise a permission scheme that follows the capabilities of the particular DBMS where the tables are stored. If possible, your DBA should also try to separate the PowerBuilder System Catalog into different sets for each development group that may be sharing the same DBMS.

CHAPTER **5**

Stored Procedures

By Ramesh Chandak

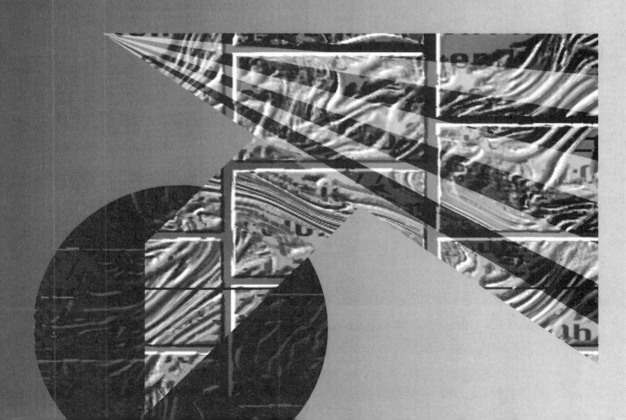

Stored Procedures

by **Ramesh Chandak**

Introduction

When you are building a PowerBuilder application, a variety of data sources are available for your DataWindows. The data source specifies where the data to be used in the DataWindow object will comes from (see Figure 5-1). You can choose from the following data sources:

Quick Select
SQL Select
Query
Stored Procedure
External

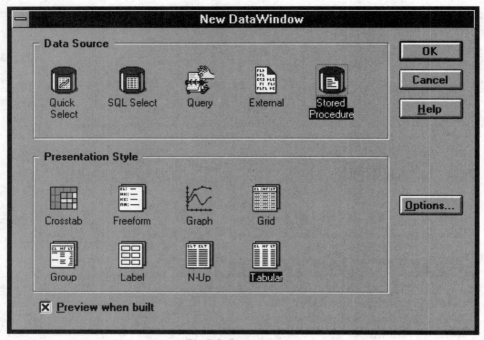

Fig 5-1: Data sources.

If the data is being retrieved from a database, you may choose Quick Select, SQL Select, Query, or Stored Procedure. If the data is not coming from a database, you must select External.

This chapter introduces the concept of stored procedures. Not all DBMSes support stored procedures. Although there are a number that do, the examples below refer particularly to Sybase SQL Server.

What are Stored Procedures?

A stored procedure is a group of sequentially executed SQL statements. Stored procedures can:

> accept parameters
> call other procedures
> return status values indicating success or failure
> return values of parameters to a calling procedure
> be executed on remote servers

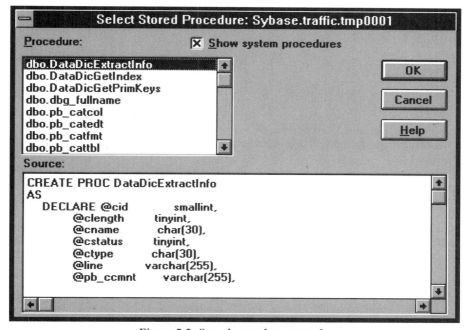

Figure 5-2: Stored procedure example.

Differences between stored procedures and embedded SQL

Stored procedures are pre-compiled. The first time any stored procedure is executed, the server creates an execution plan and stores it in the system table. Subsequently, the stored procedure is executed per the execution plan. Therefore stored procedures execute almost instantaneously.

How to Create a Stored Procedure

You use the CREATE PROCEDURE command to create a stored procedure. The syntax for the CREATE PROCEDURE command, without using any parameters, is:

```
create procedure <procedure_name>
as <SQL statements>
```

For instance, use the following CREATE PROCEDURE command to select all the last names from an address table:

```
create procedure lastnames
as select last_name from address
```

The complete syntax for CREATE PROCEDURE is:

```
create procedure [owner.]procedure_name[;number]
  [[(]@parameters_name datatype [=default][output]
  [,@parameter_name datatype [=default]
  [output]]...[)]] [with recompile]
as sql_statements
```

Using parameters

You can also declare stored procedures with one or more parameters. (A parameter is an argument to a stored procedure.) You must pass the values for these parameters when calling the procedure.

Parameter names are local to the procedure. They must be preceded by the @ symbol. The maximum length for a parameter name, including the "@" symbol, is 30 bytes. The maximum number of parameters in a stored procedure is 255.

For instance, use the following stored procedure to retrieve a loan from the loan database, given the loan number.

```
create proc loan_info @loan_id char(10) as
select bank_name, branch_name, loan_type, closing_place
from loan
where loan.loan_id = @loan_id
```

You may also specify default parameters. A default parameter can be any constant, and is taken as the argument to the procedure when the user does not provide one. For instance, if no argument value is provided to the following procedure, a default value of 1 is assumed.

```
create proc loan_info @loan_id char(10) = "1" as
select bank_name, branch_name, loan_type, closing_place
from loan
where loan.loan_id = @loan_id
```

Nesting procedures

You can nest procedures within procedures. A maximum of sixteen nesting levels is allowed with SQL Server. If you execute a procedure that calls another procedure, the called procedure can access objects created by the calling procedure.

Using temporary tables in stored procedures

You can create temporary tables in your stored procedures. Such tables exist only for the duration of the stored procedure. When the execution of the procedure is completed, the temporary tables are dropped automatically. The following example demonstrates creation and use of a temporary table within a stored procedure.

```
create proc loan_info as
create table #temptable
(bank_name char(30), branch_name char(20), loan_type
```

```
char(10), closing_place char(30))

insert #temptable
sselect bank_name, branch_name, loan_type,
closing_place
from loan
where loan.loan_id  = @loan_id

exec loan_info
```

How to Execute a Stored Procedure

Use the keyword EXECUTE to execute a stored procedure. The complete syntax for EXECUTE is:

```
[execute] [@return_status = ]
[[[server.]database.]owner.]procedure_name[;number]
[[@parameter_name =] value |
[@parameter_name =] @variable[output]
[,[@parameter_name =] value |
[@parameter_name =] @variable [output]...]]
[with recompile]
```

The complete syntax for executing a procedure on a remote server is:

```
execute
server_name.[database_name].[owner].procedure_name
```

Dropping Stored Procedures

Use the DROP PROCEDURE command to remove procedures. The complete syntax for DROP PROCEDURE is:

```
drop procedure [owner.]procedure_name
[, [owner.]procedure_name]...
```

Renaming Stored Procedures

Use the system procedure sp_rename to rename a stored procedure. The complete syntax for the rename procedure is:

```
spname <old name>, <new name>
```

Return Status and Information

Stored procedures return a status flag indicating success and failure. They can also return information to the calling procedure through return parameters. Such parameters are designated as return parameters in the CREATE PROCEDURE and EXECUTE procedure commands. Remote procedure calls also return both status flag and return parameters.

SQL Server has a predefined set of return status values. A 0 indicates success, and negative values in the range of -1 to -99 indicate different reasons for failure. Numbers 0 and -1 to -14 are currently in use.

Value	Meaning
0	procedure executed without error
-1	missing object
-2	datatype error
-3	process was chosen as deadlock victim
-4	permission error
-5	syntax error
-6	miscellaneous user error
-7	resource error, such as out of space
-8	non-fatal internal problem
-9	system limit was reached
-10	fatal internal inconsistency
-11	fatal internal inconsistency
-12	table or index is corrupt
-13	database is corrupt
-14	hardware error

User-generated return values

You can generate your own custom return values by adding parameters to the return statement. You can use conditional clauses to check the return status, and display your own messages.

System procedures

System procedures operate on system tables. They can be used to retrieve information from system tables, or to perform database administration tasks involving system tables. The names of all system procedures begin with "sp_".

Several system procedures can be used to obtain information about stored procedures from the system tables. For instance, sp_help generates a report on a given stored procedure. Such a report includes information about the procedure's type, its name, and its owner and date of creation. The procedure sp_helptext displays the text of the CREATE PROCEDURE statement for the given stored procedure. The system procedure sp_depends lists all the procedures that reference the stored procedure you specify.

User-defined messages

You can use system procedures to add your own messages to the sysusermessages table in a user database. Such procedures include sp_addmessage, sp_dropmessage, and sp_getmessage.

Summary

This chapter provided a basic understanding of stored procedures. We discussed how to create, execute, drop, and rename stored procedures. We further discussed how to use temporary tables and execute stored procedures. Since stored procedures are compiled and executed, they help improve the performance of the server. You can use the return status within your conditional clauses, and display your own messages for your PowerBuilder application. You can use system procedures to obtain information from system tables, or perform database administration tasks involving system tables.

CHAPTER 6

An Introduction to ODBC

By Randy Hompesch

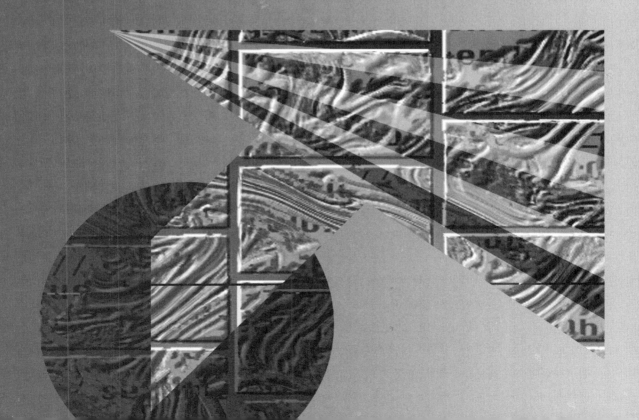

An Introduction to ODBC

by **Randy Hompesch**

While many standards have been proposed to address the needs of multi-DBMS access, ODBC has emerged as the de facto standard for the MS Windows platform and is a component of Microsoft's Windows Open Services Architecture (WOSA). Proposed by Microsoft, it has taken center stage and supplanted competing standards such as IDAPI, DRDA and SQL/RA. Essentially all modern commercial RDBMS products support this standard, either as their sole interface to the outside world or in addition to their own proprietary interface. The Powersoft desktop series, as well as most other development tools and query front ends, supports ODBC as its database access standard and hence the development tools (Power-Builder, PowerMaker and PowerViewer) can be utilized against any DBMS that supports the ODBC standard. But before we examine the ODBC standard and its components, let's first examine some of the historical factors that led to the need for such a standard.

The Evolution towards ODBC

In the early days of data processing technology, there was no such thing as a database management system. Each vendor's hardware came with one or more proprietary file access systems that was unique to that machine's hardware and operating system. The file access systems were implemented primarily in software, though some vendors provided firmware routines that increased the data storage performance. All were record oriented–read and write operations were performed on a single record at a time. Code developed for one environment could not be migrated to another, even if they were written in the same language, without major revisions to the source code, the file access routines, and the operating system interface components of the application. Applications were developed exclusively for each hardware platform and seamless portability and interoperability were only a dream.

Each of these early file access systems had varying retrieval and record writing capabilities. The simplest supported only sequential file access; data could only be read back record by record in the same order that it was written out to the file, and all writes were appended to the end. Most commercial implementations also supported key or indexed access where a record could be retrieved on the basis of a value supplied by the programmer for its key field. Indexed retrieval schemes came in many flavors from the most rudimentary to those supporting multiple columns, multiple sets of indexes and partial key retrieval. Other file systems supplied relative record retrieval as either an addition to indexed or as the sole retrieval mechanism. Vendors attempting to provide software products for multiple host environments were forced to program to a "least common denominator," using only those file system features provided by all of the file systems on the platforms they wished to support.

These file systems provided two basic services to the programmer. The first was an interface, a set of proprietary commands and functions invocable from a host language, that allowed the programmer to read and write the desired record. The second was the data storage and retrieval component. This component took the human- (or at least programmer!) readable interface statements from the host language and translated them into operating system instructions that told the host computer where physically to look on the disk for each piece of information required to meet the programmer's request. The two components were very closely tied together. The programmer had to know the capabilities of the specific file system and use the appropriate commands from its proprietary interface to read or write data into variables, which could be acted upon by their program code. Similarly, the host language compiler had to be aware of the file systems it could support so that the compile step could translate the interface commands into machine-readable format.

Of course each file system's programming interface was different, consisting of different commands and parameters available for those commands, and returning different codes indicating the success or failure of the requested operation. Similarly, there was no standardization among the datatypes supported by each file system, and translations from one to another kept many programmers gainfully employed during the 1980s. The abilities of applications programmers were often determined by how many of these proprietary file system interfaces they knew. Large shops were forced either to retain individual programmers skilled with each file access system or to train their staff on each file system in use within the shop.

Into this world of incompatible file systems came the database management system. In file access systems, each file was treated as a separate, stand-alone entity, with no inherent relationships to any other files. There was also no central place where information about that file was retained. It was up to the programmers to tell the file access system what a record in each file looked like by providing a record definition section in their programs. Gradually DBMSes evolved to address both of these two major flaws of file system implementations. System files or tables were maintained by the DBMS that described all data elements (tables, indexes, columns, etc.) and the relationships among them. This information about the data is referred to as metadata, and it paved the way for the implementation of some of the basic data integrity assurances that we take for granted today. Referential integrity constraints, for example, were not available in early file systems, as each file was a separate unit unconnected with the outside world. The metadata maintained by DBMS treated many tables as

interrelated units, with their relationships identifiable through primary and foreign key linkages.

But early DBMSes were not relational. They were based mainly on the competing network
and hierarchical data models. As such, they still required programmers to be skilled in the
navigation schemes used by the DBMS engine. It was not sufficient to specify what information you wished; you also had to specify the access method that the DBMS should use to
retrieve that information. This still necessitated highly skilled programmers for each DBMS
interface, and the difficulties of the DBMS interface language made end user access to information impossible without the intervention of the programming staff.

The codification of the rules of relational theory by Dr. E.F. Codd in the late 1970s laid the
groundwork for the evolution to the relational databases which are the industry standard
today. The mathematical foundation of relational algebra and calculus provided the framework upon which a structured query language (SQL) could be developed that would put the
burden of figuring out how to retrieve the data into the software of the RDBMS, freeing programmers to worry only about what information they needed, not how to get it. The simplicity of the row/column model made set-oriented operations possible and freed programmers
from the record-at-a-time retrieval paradigm. RDBMSes provided a simplified view of the
data for end users, and, through the introduction of triggers and stored procedures, maintained many of the business rules and data integrity constraints that were formerly handled
by application programs. The RDBMS engines began to be offered on multiple platforms,
freeing a business from reliance on a single vendor. Programmers were given a single common DBMS interface when SQL was accepted by all RDBMS vendors. Why then the need
for any further standardization?

But compatibility and proprietary interface problems continued to plague the industry,
largely because of the advent of client/server computing and the necessity to interface the
RDBMS to the application via a proprietary network operating system (e.g. Novell, Vines).
In the RDBMS world of the late eighties and early nineties, each application continued to be
developed to perform a specific task and to work with a single database engine. For example
an organization might have a payroll application that runs against a sybase database, a general ledger that uses Oracle, an order processing application that uses IMS, and a host of legacy applications tied to the file system on the host platform (e.g. ISAM, VSAM). Each
RDBMS vendor had developed its own interface or API that had to be adhered to in order
for the application to communicate to the data store through each network operating system,
and each vendor had to supply a different API for each network operating system being supported. The addition of this extra component introduced a new level of interface that had not
bee seen in the host-based applications development environment.

Additionally SQL, though indeed an industry standard, was not complete enough that the
RDBMS vendors could use it without their own proprietary extensions. In the rush to distinguish its products by the addition of advanced features, each vendor expanded the basic SQL
"standard" with its own proprietary enhancements to support the capabilities offered by its
products. ODBC emerged as an attempt to address the new interface component introduced
by the network operating system and to resolve incompatibilities between the SQL dialects
offered by competing vendors. It is an attempt finally to capitalize on the promise of
RDBMS independence, or interoperability, for applications development.

Anatomy of an RDBMS Interface

RDBMS engines are used almost exclusively in client/server applications, so that will be the model referenced throughout the remainder of this chapter. In this architecture, far more complex than that of a host-based implementation, there are four different components on the client and an additional four on the database server.

The client side consists of the application, the database network API, the network operating system interface, and the client operating system. The application may be a custom-developed program to perform a specialized task, or a front-end query tool designed for end user reporting. It formulates the SQL queries which are then passed to the database network API–which is unique to the combination of the RDBMS engine and network operating system. This software layer provides the interface to the network operating system, splitting the SQL request into packets utilizing the formats and protocols of the network operating system. The network operating system interface then routes these packets to the appropriate destination on the local area network (LAN)–the server machine in this case–performing error detection and retransmission as required.

The server machine consists of the RDBMS engine, the database network API, the network operating system interface, and the server operating system. The server receives the packetized request through the network operating system interface. The request is then processed by the database network API into a format that is presented to the RDBMS engine. The RDBMS engine selects the appropriate rows or performs the desired processing and returns the result set and return codes, through the database network API, to the network operating system interface. The network operating system then passes these results over the network to the client machine, where the results are passed back up through these software layers until finally the application program has access to the information. The first portion of this process, the transmission of the SQL request, is illustrated in below.

In the application component, SQL access requests are embedded in the host language. The host language source code actually consists of code from two different languages: the host language itself and SQL. The source code is first precompiled, where the SQL statements are translated into calls and statements of the host language, then passed through the host language compiler. Each RDBMS vendor supplies its own precompiler, supporting its own SQL dialect, to perform this task. Embedded SQL is not conducive to database interoperability. Imagine an application like Excel, which has database access extensions. Using embedded SQL, there would have to be several versions of the software, each precompiled with a specific RDBMS vendor's precompiler. If five RDBMSes were to be accessible, there would be five different versions of Excel, each precompiled using a different precompiler.

The second source of incompatibility occurs at the database network API level. This component handles the interface between a specific network operating system and a specific RDBMS. Each RDBMS vendor's product must be constructed specifically to work with the network operating system being used on the client and server machines. sybase for example offers its Open Client product in several flavors: one for Novell Netware, one for Banyan Vines, etc. If a client machine wants to access, through different applications, data in Oracle and sybase, it must have two API's installed–one from Oracle and one from sybase, both specific to the network operating system being utilized.

The ODBC Standard

To address incompatibility issues at both the SQL and the database network API level, Microsoft introduced its Open Database Connectivity (ODBC) standard. The current version of this standard is 2.0,[1] and it will be the one discussed for the rest of this chapter. It should be reaffirmed that ODBC is not the only such standard addressing database interoperability. It is, however, the one most commercially successful to date and has become the de facto standard in the industry.

There are two basic methods to assure interoperability between application programs and RDBMS engines:

1. All clients and data sources adhere to a standard interface.
2. All clients adhere to a standard interface and software performs translations to each RDBMS.

ODBC uses the latter philosophy. It provides the standard interface to which the client must adhere, a set of drivers to handle the conversion from the standard client interface to each individual RDBMS, and the driver manager program necessary to call the correct driver for any given RDBMS. The client side interface is neither very interesting nor demanding from a technical standpoint. Since virtually all front end tools with any significant market share are ODBC-compatible, I won't spend any time on that interface here. Each of the remaining components of the ODBC standard will be discussed in more detail in the next section.

ODBC is implemented as a Call Level Interface (CLI) for SQL. A CLI is a library of function calls. The CLI for SQL is the set of function calls that can be used by application programmers to invoke SQL statements and return their result sets. The CLI for SQL is defined by both the X/Open and SQL Access Group (SAG) of ANSI, and so in itself constitutes a standard.

The ODBC interface defines:

A library of function calls that allow an application to connect to a data source[2], execute SQL statements and retrieve results, and return codes. There are two levels of these functions. Core functions are based on the X/Open and SAG specifications. Extended functions are defined by Microsoft to support the extended functionality present in some engines (e.g. scrollable cursors) yet not covered by the X/Open and SAG standards. An SQL syntax based on the X/Open and SAG (SQL-92) specifications. The syntax also includes standard representations of data types that must be supported by the data source. A set of standard return codes for SQL calls.

A standard mechanism for connecting to and logging on to any data source.

1. Be aware that each driver conforms to a version of the ODBC standard, and some features have changed classification between versions 1.0 and 2.0.
2. A data source is typically an RDBMS, but many non-relational database engines have had drivers written for them that enable them to mimic RDBMS functionality to some degree.

However, neither all drivers nor the RDBMS engines which they support are created equal. In order to give the applications programmer some idea of the capabilities of the different drivers available for each data source, the library of function calls (the ODBC API) and the SQL syntax both define various conformance levels. Any driver supplied for a data source should specify the level of conformance to which it adheres for both the ODBC API and the SQL syntax. This is critical information for programmers attempting to construct a set of data sources which will be supported by their application. If the application requires a certain level of conformance in both of these areas (and all will), then only data sources with available drivers conforming to both these required levels will allow the application to use the data source for which the driver was written. To put it more simply, if the application functionality requires Level 2 conformance for the ODBC API component, it will not support any data source for which drivers at Level 2 conformance are not available.

The ODBC API (which consists of the functions which the application programmer uses to connect to the data source, execute SQL statements, retrieve result sets and return codes, and log off) specifies three distinct level of conformance. Each additional level is additive, with Level 2 containing all of the features of Level 1 and the Core. Summarized below are the major functions defined for each of these levels[1].

Core API

Perform housekeeping processes (such as allocation of storage for handles) necessary to work with data sources and SQL statements. Connect to data sources and use multiple SQL statements on a single connection[2]. Execute SQL statements, retrieve results sets, return codes and information about the result set (e.g. number of columns, datatype of each). Commit and rollback transactions.

Level 1 API

Connect to data sources using dialog boxes specific to each data source.
Retrieve information about connection options, driver capabilities, and data source capabilities. Retrieve catalog information (the metadata).

Level 2 API

Browse connection information and list available data sources. Send and receive arrays as parameter values and as result set columns. Retrieve information about supplied parameters. Support scrollable cursors.

Each function in the ODBC API conforms to one of these levels. The highest level used by any function in the application program will determine the ODBC API conformance level

---

1. The definitive source of information for this topic, as well as most in this chapter, is Microsoft's *ODBC 2.0 Programmer's Reference and SDK Guide*, available from Microsoft Press.
2. This is similar to the advantage of PowerBuilder's SetTransObject over Set-Trans functions.

that must be required of any data source driver in order for its target data source to be used by the application program.

The SQL syntax is divided into three conformance levels, each additive, as follows.

Minimum

CREATE TABLE and DROP TABLE statements.
SELECT (with limited functionality), INSERT, UPDATE, SEARCH and DELETE SEARCHED statements. CHAR, VARCHAR and LONG VARCHAR datatypes.

Core

ALTER TABLE, CREATE INDEX, DROP INDEX, CREATE VIEW, DROP VIEW, GRANT, and REVOKE statements. Full support for the SELECT statement allowing for all capabilities as defined by SQL-92. Subquery and set-oriented functions such as SUM, MIN, MAX, AVG. DECIMAL, NUMERIC, SMALLINT, INTEGER, REAL, FLOAT, and DOUBLE PRECISION data types.

Extended

Support for advanced data manipulation statements such as those providing outer join capability, the union operator, positioned UPDATE and DELETE, and SELECT FOR UPDATE.

Obviously, the minimum SQL conformance level will be sufficient for only the most rudimentary application. Most of the capabilities that we associate with a "good" RDBMS engine are found in the Core level and continue on into the extended. In the adoption of Version 2.0 of the standard, certain core functions were moved into the extended level, thus making it less difficult for a driver manufacturer to claim adherence to the core level of functionality. It also points out that ODBC does not completely eliminate the need for a least-common-denominator approach.

The ODBC Products

Standards are great, but until products are available that comply to them, they're nothing more than paper documents–notoriously difficult to use to construct a working application! In the case of ODBC, there are a host of products available both from Microsoft and from third-party vendors than provide working real world solutions using the ODBC standard. Let's examine the software components that are used to implement the ODBC interface.

The Microsoft ODBC 2.0 Programmer's Reference defines the following four components of the ODBC architecture, shown graphically in Figure 6-2.

Application

Either custom-built or provided by third-party vendors, this is the component that actually addresses the business problem. It uses ODBC function calls to allow it to use SQL against one or more ODBC-compliant data sources.

Driver manager

Supplied by Microsoft, it loads the specific data source driver requested by an ODBC function call request from the application. It is implemented as a dynamic-link library (DLL).

Drivers

Provided by both Microsoft and various third-party vendors, these are also DLLs, each specific to a data source. They actually perform the processing of the ODBC function call submitted by the application. This processing includes establishment of the connection, the transmission of SQL statements, and the provision of the result set and return codes to the application (in response to other ODBC function calls from the application). Each driver also has the task of modifying the SQL request, passed as a parameter of the ODBC function call, as necessary to comply with the specific SQL dialect of the data source which it supports. It also performs any requisite datatype translations to convert the data source datatype to one compliant with the SQL syntax supported by the ODBC interface, and handles transaction control and cursor maintenance if required.

Data source

The actual data store, normally an RDBMS engine. It is a specific instance of a combination of an SQL RDBMS, the operating system on which the RDBMS engine resides, and the network operating system used to connect it to the client application. It is normally (though not in the case of single tier drivers discussed below) the destination of the SQL statements, and the component necessary for performing the requested action on the stored data.

There is also a fifth component, also supplied by Microsoft, which is the ODBC Data Source Administrator. Implemented as an executable (odbcadm.exe). This component controls the definition of ODBC data sources, mapping the data source name to the specific driver necessary to access the data. More on that later.

Additionally, there are two types of drivers: single and multiple tier. In multiple tier drivers, which are more common, the SQL request is actually processed by the RDBMS. With single tier drivers the SQL statements are actually processed by the driver, which maps the SQL to the proprietary file system access interface of the DBMS. Single tier drivers thus provide some of the functionality that is achieved by the RDBMS engine in a multiple tier configuration. Single tier drivers are frequently used with older DBMS systems (such as xBase and Paradox) which do not natively support SQL, and are often more limited in functionality.

Drivers are available from a variety of vendors. Microsoft provides a set–with both its ODBC Software Development Kit (SDK) and Desktop Database Drivers package–that contains specific drivers for MS Access, MS Excel, Btrieve, Borland's Paradox, MS FoxPro, and text files. Intersolv offers a set of twenty-five drivers, supporting a variety of DBMSes, via its acquisition of Q+E. Consult the particular vendor for more information on product availability, content, licensing and pricing. Additionally many vendors offer a single driver for more esoteric DBMSes. These include drivers that connect to MDI Gateways and to IBM's AS/400, among others. Although it is beyond the scope of this chapter to provide a full discussion of available products (which would be outdated by the time it went to print!), the point is that there is a large base of third-party vendors providing products to support the

ODBC standard, and you can probably find one already on the market that will give you the capabilities you need.

Defining an ODBC Data Source

While ODBC allows applications to be developed that are not specific to a single database engine, before any connections can be established the data source must first be registered to ODBC. And before a data source can be registered, the driver which it uses must be installed. Although the data source registrations can be done programmatically, it is normally accomplished by using the ODBC Data Source Administrator program, referred to as the ODBC Administrator for short.

Normally whenever you purchase a product that provides ODBC drivers, you are given the option during the setup procedure to install all of them, or just specific ones. PowerBuilder, for example, provides the ODBC driver needed by Watcom SQL, and all necessary driver-related files are automatically copied over to the appropriate destination[1] and the driver is registered. To install a data source, invoke the ODBC Administrator. The panel shown in Figure 6-3 will then appear. It lists all currently defined ODBC data sources present on your machine.

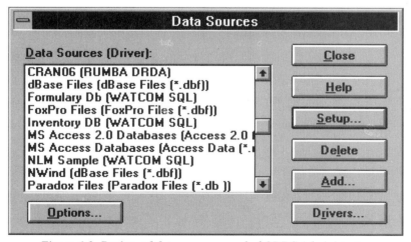

Figure 6-3: Registered data sources panel of ODBC Administrator.

As you can see, the machine which I am using has quite a few different data sources defined, for a variety of different drivers. The data source name (which is used in the ODBC Connect function calls) is listed and, following in parenthesis, the driver which the data source uses (i.e. the one the driver manager will load in response to a request to connect to that data

---

1. It's also not uncommon for the tool vendor to provide a copy of the odbcadm.exe and .hlp files. At one point I had three different renditions of this program on my hard drive; who knows from whence each came!

source). But let's concentrate on the drivers first. Pressing the "Drivers..." button will provide a similar panel that displays all of the registered drivers. An example of the one I'm using is shown in Figure 6-4.

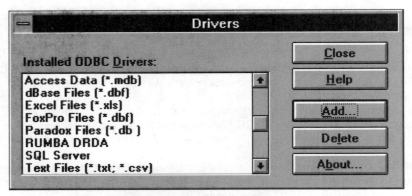

Figure 6-4: Registered driver panel of ODBC Administrator.

To add a new driver, if not done by the setup program, you must have the disk containing the driver related files. Pressing the "Add..." button prompts you to insert the appropriate driver disk into A:\ and proceeds with the installation. The "About..." button is more interesting as it provides information on the driver manufacturer, the name of the DLL it uses, and other information that may (or may not) be pertinent. Information about the installed drivers is contained in the file odbcinst.ini, normally in the Windows directory. The following is an portion of this file:

```
[ODBC Drivers]
WATCOM SQL=Installed
Access Data (*.mdb)=Installed
Excel Files (*.xls)=Installed
Text Files (*.txt; *.csv)=Installed
MS Access V2.0 (*.mdb) = Installed

[WATCOM SQL]
Driver=c:\windows\system\wsqlodbc.dll
Setup=c:\windows\system\wsqlodbc.dll

[Access Data (*.mdb)]
Driver=c:\windows\system\simba.dll
Setup=c:\windows\system\simadmin.dll
```

The first lists each installed driver. Each then has its own section that defines two DLLs. The first DLL is to be loaded by the driver manager when actually connecting to a data source defined on the driver. The second is the program that controls the setup of a data source for that driver. In the Watcom SQL section you can see that one program performs both functions. But for MS Access (which is version 1.1 here) the simadmin.dll controls data source setup while simba.dll is the actual driver.

Once the desired driver has been installed, you can begin to define ODBC data sources that use it. From the Data Source panel (Figure 6-3) pressing the "Add..." button brings up a panel displaying all installed drivers and requests you to select the one on which you wish to base the new data source. Selecting one and pressing "OK" will invoke the DLL specified as the setup program for that driver. Since each driver connects to a different database engine, the parameters will be different for each. Each setup program is aware of the information which needs to be provided in order to start the desired database engine and begin using the data source. For example, with MS Excel drivers, all that is needed is the name and location of the file. MS Access v1.1 asks for the file name and location too, but also allows you to specify Exclusive access, a system database to be used, page size, and buffering values. Figure 6-5 below shows the information prompted for by a request to set up a data source using the Watcom SQL driver.

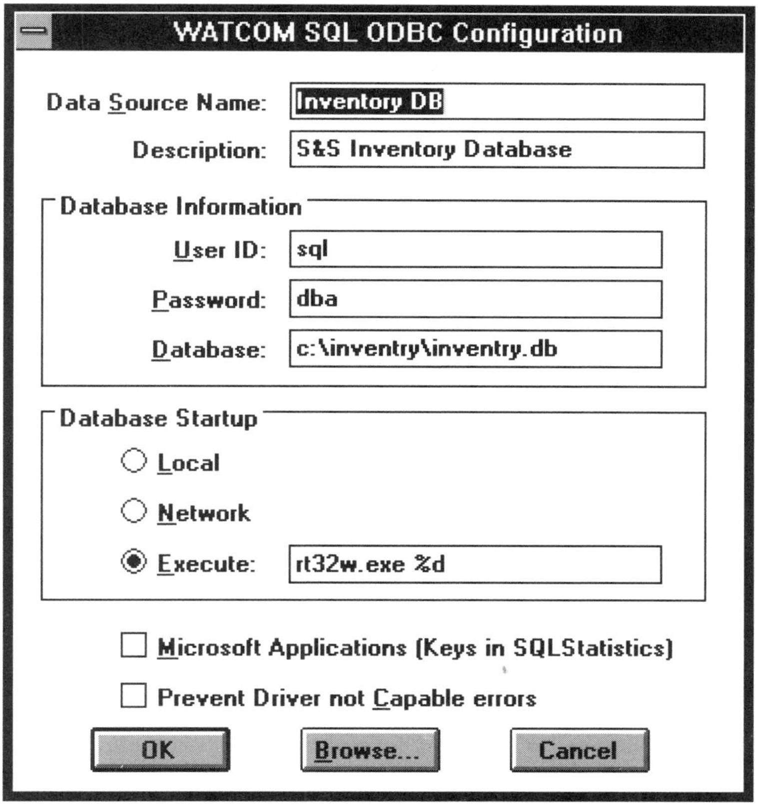

Figure 6-5: Data source setup parameters for the Watcom driver.

Once these parameters for the data source have been captured, they are stored in a second file in the Windows directory. It is called odbc.ini, and hold connection information for all registered data sources. The following is a portion of this file.

```
[ODBC Data Sources]
PowerBuilder Demo DB=WATCOM SQL
Formulary DB=WATCOM SQL
Inventory DB=WATCOM SQL
PowerMaker Demo DB=WATCOM SQL
```

```
Repository DB=WATCOM SQL
CeisLocl=MS Access V2.0 (*.mdb)

[PowerBuilder Demo DB]
Database=c:\pb3\pbdemodb.db
UID=dba
PWD=sql
Driver=c:\windows\system\wsqlodbc.dll
Description=PowerBuilder Demo Database
Start=db32w %d
```

[Editor's Note: By default, Watcom uses two megabytes of memory for its database cache, so you'll lose almost 2 megs of memory if you don't specify something different. The command line parameter for cache memory is -c. To specify only 256K of cache, use the following Start line in your odbc.ini:

Start=db32w -c256K %d]

Understanding the entire contents of this file is beyond the scope of this chapter, and would in any case require a different examination for the ODBC drivers available on each machine. Suffice it to say that these are two of the prime areas to check for connectivity problems to ODBC databases. I've even had success adding the necessary lines to both of these files using PowerBuilder's SetProfile() function to alleviate the difficulty of having to manually define ODBC data sources on remote machines. A quick glance at the drivers and data sources which you have installed would be well worth the effort.

Conclusion

While this chapter has not been intended to provide either an exhaustive discussion of the technical issues involved in ODBC nor of PowerBuilder's front-end interface to the driver manager,I hope it has at least laid the foundation for you to understand some of the reasons behind the development and popularity of ODBC and how it actually functions from an applications standpoint. Let's now discuss the relative benefits of using ODBC.

I have used PowerBuilder, Visual Basic, and MS Access as front ends to ODBC data sources. Data sources I've used include Watcom SQL, MS Access, and IBM's OS/400. On the plus side, ODBC is here, is supported by both Microsoft and a variety of third party driver vendors, and does indeed work...to an extent. I have one application for example, though it is read-only, that runs in a client/server mode via both LAN and WAN connections using OS/400 files on an IBM AS/400 as the data source. The same application runs in a stand-alone mode on laptop computers against a local MS Access database. There is only one version of the source code, and the only allowance made for the different data sources is in the data source connect, disconnect, and connection option function calls. Obviously this a big advantage over having two separate versions of the same code that must be maintained and tested independently, yet still kept in sync. And it really wasn't very difficult to accomplish once I understood some of the differences in the driver capabilities. Thus one at least of the historical problems has been addressed–a standard data access mechanism (SQL) can be used against a variety of disparate DBMSes.

Another positive is that the other major historical problem targeted by ODBC has been alleviated, although not eliminated. While programmers still need to code to least common denominator capabilities, at least it is easier to identify which drivers will support that functional subset. In other words it is now simpler for programmers to determine what drivers will support their functional needs. Once they determine they need Level 1 ODBC API functionality and Core SQL conformance, it is now easy to identify driver products which supply these levels of compliance. This is much better than when each function used by the application had to be researched to see if it was supported by each RDBMS.

Another major benefit for ODBC is that some legacy file systems will only allow themselves to be accessed as servers in a client/server environment through ODBC. The current release of IBM's AS/400, V2R3, falls into this category–without third-party drivers that translate the ODBC standard to the DRDA specification which IBM uses on this platform, the only other option for connectivity is a gateway. The ODBC solution is far less costly and easier to maintain.

On the minus side are the many issues of longevity and compatibility that may make the ODBC solution undesirable. As far as longevity goes, although Microsoft's ODBC 3.0 standard is due for release next year, several articles in the trade journals[1] have made reference to Microsoft moving away from ODBC in favor of an OLE-based solution for interoperability. While this might provide an even better solution in the long run, it doesn't give me a warm and fuzzy feeling right now.

From a compatibility standpoint, at the very least the addition of a third-party ODBC driver adds one additional vendor to the problems of software compatibility (see "Randy's Rules of Software Compatibility" in the "Introducing Client/Server Technology to Your Organization" chapter for a synopsis of my experiences with making various products work together). And chances are, if you're using ODBC, you're going to be using a third-party driver at some point.

Here is a real-world example of compatibility issues: I had PowerBuilder, Visual Basic, and MS Access all happily utilizing the AS/400 as a data source using a third party ODBC driver. Then IBM supplied a PTF for OS/400 and the driver vendor supplied an update. Now MS Access can't attach any new tables (though it can still use ones previously attached?!?) and PowerBuilder is getting wildly erroneous results (though no error messages) on retrieved summary fields. I'm awaiting a PTF from the ODBC vendor to see if this will solve the problem.

I also found that while MS Access will read a Watcom database built in PowerBuilder, it is impossible to update certain tables, apparently because the primary key on the tables is not being recognized by MS Access. Another current problem I have is that with the release of MS Access 2.0, there apparently is no ODBC driver that is fully compatible with the standard. Microsoft claims to be developing one, but for now, at least, PowerBuilder cannot use MS Access 2.0 as a data source. I have been forced to revert to the older version, 1.1, to continue deployment of the application.

The end result of problems like these can be as large as forcing major revisions to applica-

---

1. One such is the Sept 5, 1994 *InfoWorld* article entitled, "Microsoft Leans Toward OLE for Database Links."

tions or delaying releases until products are delivered. Normally all it takes it a great deal of time and effort–time and effort that could more productively be spent developing solutions for the business.

Although these compatibility issues are product-related and not directly attributable to the ODBC standard or necessarily to any of the Microsoft-supplied components, they are very real and costly issues that have forced me to reevaluate the place ODBC has in my development projects. Although I can attest that ODBC works and has provided me with solutions to some very difficult technical and management issues, I would now only recommend ODBC if one of the following is true: Interoperability against a large variety of DBMSes is a critical success factor for the application, or ODBC is the only cost-effective means of accessing a legacy data store.

If neither of these conditions is met–and I'd try hard to find a work-around if either one is– I'd stick with the native API supplied by the RDBMS vendor every time. When developing for sybase's SQL Server on a unix machine, I elected to go with their proprietary Open Client API, even though I was using ODBC for a number of other applications for this same customer. ODBC is a great idea, but for my money the compatibility issues are too costly to be ignored.

CHAPTER 7

Transaction Management

By Judah Holstein

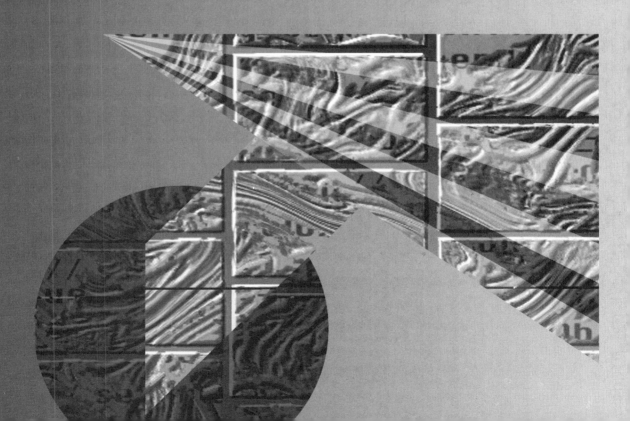

Transaction Management

by **Judah Holstein**

What is a Transaction? An Overview

A transaction is defined as a logical unit of work. You start a transaction; then you do some database updates; then you can either commit the updates, saving your changes permanently; or you can roll back, ignoring the updates and restoring your database to the state it was in when you started the transaction. In addition, some databases support transaction savepoints–intermediate moments at which you can save your current state, making it possible to roll back to it instead of all the way to the start of the transaction. That way, if you have certain sets of related updates, you can define a savepoint between each set. Then if you need to roll back any particular set of updates, you won't be losing the entire transaction's worth of data.

By properly managing your transactions you can ensure the integrity of your database. You can make sure that no changes are really saved to the database until they are complete and verified.

Let's take an example. Say that you have a system in which the user is allowed to update a customer record. The customer record is not really just one record in one table, though. It is made up of records from two different tables. The first table holds personal information, such as name, address, and phone number. The other table holds order history information, such as balance due, orders pending, etc. When the user updates the customer record on the screen, multiple update statements are required to properly alter all the relevant data. Now if a record is inserted in the history table, but the update of the matching personal information record fails, the values in the history table will have to be restored to what they were before the whole update process began. Otherwise the database is out of synch, and its information is incorrect.

Providing safeguards like this can require a fair amount of effort, including storage of multiple sets of data for each update, and extensive logging and tracking to ensure that restores occur in the proper order if there are multiple updates to the same record. Most databases, however, do all of this for you inside a transaction.

We can choose to begin a transaction before we update the first customer record. Then the updates are submitted to the two component records within this transaction. If the second update fails, we can roll back all the changes, and it is as if we had not even updated the first record. Otherwise, we can commit the changes, and instantaneously both component updates are saved to the database, almost as if they were a single action.

In a multi-user environment, there is another serious reason for good transaction management. That has to do with the locks that occur when you perform updates to your database. When you change a record in the database, a lock is placed on the record (or the page, depending what DBMS you are using) to prevent anyone from interrupting your update. If someone else during that time attempts to perform an update on your record, the DBMS will either wait until the lock is released before performing its update, or will simply fail the update and return an error (again depending on which DBMS you are using and the type of lock on the record). In general, though, protection is provided so that you will not have two people updating the same record at any time.

Most DBMSes include different types of locks. There are read locks, or shared locks, and there are write locks, or exclusive locks. In a read lock, when one person is reading a record, other users can read but not write to it until the read is complete. Write locks, however, occur when someone is updating a record. They prevent anyone else from reading *or* writing that record until the write is complete. Thus different locks can have different effects on the end users of a multi-user system.

The reason this is important is that in general, locks that occur outside of a transaction last only as long as the SELECT, UPDATE, INSERT, or DELETE statement itself. However, locks that occur inside a transaction are held until the transaction is completed–that is, either committed or rolled back. Because of this, multiple updates within a transaction may stack up a set of locks that can eventually grow very large, causing a system-slowing traffic jam as people queue up to retrieve the same locked data.

This phenomenon makes efficient transaction management critical. Related updates must be encapsulated within the smallest transactions possible so that users aren't spending more time waiting to get access to their data than they are getting the data itself! The first rule of good transaction management is to keep the amount of time (i.e.: processing) between the start of a lock and the commit or rollback of that transaction to a bare minimum.

(Incidentally, I should point out that in most DBMSes, SELECT statements don't hold the lock after they are complete, even within a transaction, unless you specifically ask them to. In Sybase, you can place the statement WITH HOLDLOCK at the end of your SELECT statement to do this. In Oracle, you would say FOR UPDATE. If you perform a SELECT statement inside a transaction without specifying that you want the lock to be held, then the read lock will disappear immediately after the SELECT statement completes, just as if it were not inside a transaction. This is important to realize because it means that SELECT statements usually *won't* cause a backup of retrievals unless there is a lock specifically requested. Check your DBMS for details.)

This chapter will survey techniques that you can use inside PowerBuilder to manage your transactions properly. It will also demonstrate a Transaction Manager user object that you can incorporate into your applications to manage your database transactions for you!

The AutoCommit Attribute

PowerBuilder attempts to make transaction management simple for the developer through a feature called AutoCommit. You control this feature by setting the value of the AutoCommit attribute of your transaction object to TRUE or FALSE. When the AutoCommit feature is on, or TRUE, PowerBuilder passes your SQL statements directly to the server, without any additional interaction. Each statement is then automatically committed to the database as soon as it is executed. (You can also perform your own transaction management using database transaction commands when the AutoCommit setting is set to TRUE. We'll talk more about this in the next section.)

Alternatively, however, you can set the AutoCommit flag to FALSE. With this setting, PowerBuilder requires that you use the COMMIT and ROLLBACK keywords to commit and roll back your transactions when you are finished with them. In addition, it invisibly begins your transactions for you so that you don't have to be bothered to do it yourself. It begins a transaction as soon as you connect, and then again after each COMMIT or ROLLBACK statement that it encounters.

The advantage here is obviously convenience. It's very convenient to not have to think about your transactions and just commit or roll back any changes you make. However, convenience and control generally are inversely related. For one thing, there is no savepoint or transaction nesting allowed with the PowerBuilder AutoCommit feature–even if your DBMS supports them, you are limited to the support that PowerBuilder offers. However, for most applications this is sufficient, and nesting of transactions and/or savepoints are not necessary.

The other disadvantage to using the AutoCommit feature has to do with readability. Since you don't actually code the start of a transaction, it can be difficult to debug problems with transactions and locks, since you may have trouble figuring out where the transaction actually started. And, of course, if you would like to perform some update outside of any transaction, you cannot do this very easily. Although this is a less serious problem, it gives us one more reason that it may be more desirable to explicitly specify the start of a transaction.

There is a way in which you can explicitly specify the start of your transaction and still use the internal PowerBuilder AutoCommit feature. Remember that as long as the AutoCommit attribute is set to FALSE, the start of the transaction will occur automatically. However, if you set the AutoCommit flag back to TRUE, the system will cancel the transaction. (Though it is not clearly documented, I believe this is implemented as if there were a COMMIT issued, as opposed to a ROLLBACK. It may depend on your DBMS.) Therefor you can leave AutoCommit set to TRUE until you would like explicitly to start a transaction. Then, you can explicitly set AutoCommit to FALSE, which will begin the transaction at that point.

However, be sure to remember to set AutoCommit back to TRUE immediately after your COMMIT or ROLLBACK statement!

If you want to make the code more readable (since remembering AutoCommit settings can sometimes get confusing) you can create functions that will do this for you. The following code illustrates how you might begin, update, and complete a transaction:

```
SQLCA.AutoCommit=FALSE  // This Begins the Transaction
IF Update( dw_history) > 0 THEN
 IF Update( dw_main) > 0 THEN
 COMMIT;  // Both updates succeeded, COMMIT the changes.
ELSE
ROLLBACK;  // Update of dw_main failed, ROLLBACK the changes;
END IF
 ELSE
 ROLLBACK;  // Update of dw_history failed, ROLLBACK the changes;
END IF
SQLCA.AutoCommit = TRUE  // Clean up AutoCommit after Commit/Rollback
                         // To Prevent
                         // Another transaction from beginning.
```

Complete Control: Using Database Transaction Commands

The above method for handling your transactions is a very simple, convenient, yet powerful way of getting "the best of both worlds"–internal PowerBuilder transaction management, and a fair amount of control and readability as well. However in some DBMSes, and in some applications, you may want to take advantage of features like nested transactions and save-points. The internal PowerBuilder transaction management does not provide enough power to do this. Instead, you must do it on your own.

Doing transaction management on your own involves using the database transaction commands of your DBMS. Of course, if you are going to do your own transaction management, you must tell PowerBuilder not to do it for you! So, when managing your own transactions with database transaction commands, you must always set AutoCommit to TRUE. Then PowerBuilder will not build transaction commands for you behind the scenes, and you can create your own commands without worrying about PowerBuilder messing up your transaction count.

Let's talk about the specific commands that are required to implement your own transaction management.

The key to using your own database commands is the EXECUTE IMMEDIATE command of PowerBuilder. The EXECUTE IMMEDIATE command allows you to execute *any* database command that you would like, even if it is not internally supported by PowerBuilder. All you have to do is place the command into a string. You can use EXECUTE IMMEDIATE to do DDL–that is to create tables, keys, procedures, and indexes; to do SET commands that set variables and states inside of your DBMS; and even to do transaction management. The command to begin a transaction is

```
BEGIN TRANSACTION name
```

Where *name* is an optional name for the transaction.

The command to commit a transaction is

```
COMMIT TRANSACTION name
```

Where again, *name* is the name of the transaction that you would like to commit, if it was specified in the beginning of the transaction. The rollback statement is

```
ROLLBACK TRANSACTION name
```

Where *name* is the name of the transaction or savepoint that you would like to roll back to, if specified. Finally, the savepoint command is

```
SAVE TRANSACTION name
```

In this case the name is required, and is the name of the savepoint which you may decide to roll back to later.

Although this usage is the SQL standard, many DBMSes allow you to abbreviate, even though some abbreviate it differently. For example, in Sybase you can abbreviate TRANS-ACTION to TRAN. In Oracle, you can use the word TRANS. However, all DBMSes that follow the SQL standard will support the full word, TRANSACTION. So if you would like to be consistent and generic in your implementation of this feature, use the full word, TRANSACTION.

Let's take a look at how you might implement the same code that we cited in the section above using this new method of transaction management.

```
EXECUTE IMMEDIATE "BEGIN TRANSACTION t_1"; // This Begins the Transaction
IF Update( dw_history) > 0 THEN
IF Update( dw_main) > 0 THEN
// Both updates succeeded, COMMIT the changes.
EXECUTE IMMEDIATE "COMMIT TRANSACTION t_1";
ELSE
// Update of dw_main failed, ROLLBACK the changes;
EXECUTE IMMEDIATE "ROLLBACK TRANSACTION t_1";
END IF
ELSE
// Update of dw_history failed, ROLLBACK the changes;
EXECUTE IMMEDIATE "COMMIT TRANSACTION t_1";
END IF
```

This code segment looks very similar to the previous code segment. The obvious difference is that the begin, commit, and rollback of the transactions are even clearer than before. They are in real database syntax instead of being based on AutoCommit settings, and have names associated with them, so that you can match a COMMIT or ROLLBACK to its proper BEGIN.

However, there is also a danger here. I have found that developers using this method forget to put in their rollbacks or commits more often than they do when using other methods. (Perhaps this is because it is not the way they learned to do it in the PowerBuilder courses.) The result, of course, is lockups. Updates occur, and locks are held because someone forgot a COMMIT. Then a queue of users waiting to perform an update on the same table builds up, and people start rebooting their machines instead of waiting. Time-outs get reached a few minutes later, and people think that the performance of the application is miserable. All this trouble boils down to a single missing COMMIT statement. It happens more often than you might think, and it's a very difficult problem to debug if you are not using the right tools, or aware of why the problem is occurring.

One way to minimize this kind of problem is to have a good Transaction Manager class. If you implement a Transaction Manager you help make the code more readable, since begins, commits, saves, and rollbacks will all be encapsulated inside a function call, which should be easier to read. Additionally, you can implement functionality inside your Transaction Manager class that can help you debug problems with your transactions and locks. You can set up something as simple as a transaction logging mechanism, or something as complex as a detection mechanism for transactions that have never been closed, perhaps after a specific time period or some other event.

A Transaction Manager Class

Let's go ahead and build a relatively simple, yet effective, Transaction Manager class. In fact, let's extend the PowerBuilder transaction object itself to support our transaction management functions.

First, create a standard class user object. Open the User Object Painter by pressing <Shift>-<F11> or clicking on the User Object Painter button on the PowerBar. Now click on the "New" button on the Select User Object dialog. Then, click on the "Standard Class" icon. If you selected the "Standard Visual Object" icon by accident, just close up and start over.

Now you will be presented with an empty User Object screen. Let's create the first function, which we'll call f_begin().

Select User Object Function from the Declare menu. Then, click the "New" button to create a new function. Enter the function name, f_begin, into the proper edit box. The function will return a boolean TRUE if it succeeds, and a boolean FALSE if it fails, and therefore the return type should be *Boolean*. Since this function will be called from outside of the object, we will allow *Public* access to this function. Since it is not yet clear what parameters to the function we will need, let's not even place any in it for now. We'll come back to them later. Instead, click on the "OK" button, and begin creation of your Transaction Manager Begin Transaction function.

Let's first create a Transaction Manager object that uses the first of the two methods discussed above to handle transaction management– toggling the AutoCommit flag. Using this method, the f_begin function should turn on the transaction simply by setting AutoCommit to FALSE. So we enter the following two lines of code into the f_begin function:

```
AutoCommit = FALSE
RETURN TRUE
```

Remember that since this is an extension of the transaction object, the AutoCommit that you are turning off is your own AutoCommit. If you want to be more explicit, you could say

```
THIS.AutoCommit = FALSE
```

But that's up to you, since the THIS is implied. That's all there is to the f_begin function. Save and close the function, and let's move on to the close of the transaction.

After the database actions are complete, the developer will need to be able to either commit or roll back his database commands. Since we are using the internal method of database transaction management, we can simply use the internal COMMIT and ROLLBACK statements that PowerBuilder supports. For the user, we'll create a function called f_commit() to handle a commit to the database, and another function called f_rollback() to handle a rollback. However, internally, they both perform in much the same way, and so we'll first create a function called f_end() to handle the close of a transaction.

Create a new user object function called f_end(). The function this time will return a *long* value, representing a database error if there is one, or a 0 if the function succeeds. The access to the function will be private, since it will only be called from the f_commit and f_rollback functions, and not directly from the outside world. Finally, there will be one parameter, a string parameter called *ps_end_type*, which we'll use as a quasi-enumerated type. If the parameter passed is the word "COMMIT," we will perform a database COMMIT. If the parameter passed is the word "ROLLBACK," we will perform a database ROLLBACK.

Now let's code the function. The following code will first check the value of the parameter, then perform the proper database command, then check for errors, and finally reset the Auto-Commit setting.

```
CHOOSE CASE Upper( ps_end_type)
  CASE"COMMIT"
  COMMIT USING THIS;
  CASE"ROLLBACK"
  ROLLBACK USING THIS;
  CASEELSE   // Invalid function call. Abort the function.
```

```
      MessageBox(ClassName(), "Invalid Parameter Passed")
      RETURN -1
END CHOOSE
IF SQLCode < 0 THEN
            // An error occured, put up a messagebox and
            // return the error code.
      MessageBox( "Database Error #: " + String( SQLDBCode), SQLErrText)
ELSE
            // No error occured. Set AutoCommit back to TRUE
            // to turn off transactions
            // Until the next begin call.
      THIS.AutoCommit=TRUE
END IF
            // Return the contents of SQLDBCode,
            // which will be the error number if there was one, or
            // 0 if there wasn't any.
RETURN SQLDBCode
```

Finally, we can then simply create two functions, f_commit and f_rollback, that each call this function with the proper parameter, and return the result to the caller. Create the f_commit function as a public function, which returns a long, and has no parameters. The code inside the function will appear as follows:

```
      RETURN f_end( "COMMIT")
```

Create the f_rollback function as a public function, which also returns a long, and has no parameters. The code inside the f_rollback function will appear as follows:

```
      RETURN f_end( "ROLLBACK")
```

It's just that simple. If you wanted to, you could even put in checks to enforce that the proper sequence of calls is being made. In the f_begin function, simply place the following code at the beginning of the function (before the other line that is in there).

```
IF AutoCommit = FALSE THEN
// AutoCommit is already false, already inside a transaction.
  MessageBox( ClassName(), "Illegal Attempt To Begin a Transaction")
  RETURN FALSE
// (This is why I made the function a boolean, and not a void)
END IF
```

You could update the f_end function to validate the call in the same manner by performing a similar check prior to the first line of code in the function, as follows:

```
IF AutoCommit = TRUE THEN
// AutoCommit is true, not inside a transaction.
  MessageBox(ClassName(), "Illegal Attempt To End a Transaction")
  RETURN -1
END IF
```

Save this transaction object as *scut1001_xact_mgr_int*, with the comment, "Transaction Manager Standard Transaction User Object With Internal PowerBuilder Transaction Management."

Now let's make a Transaction Manager that uses the second method of management, where we explicitly request the start and end of a transaction directly from the database, using database syntax calls.

In reality, the structure for this Transaction manager is not much different from the structure for our first one. Therefore, rather than start from scratch, let's save the current Transaction Manager object with a new name, and make the changes to the code there. Select Save A*s* from the File menu, and save this Transaction Manager with the name *scut1002_xact_mgr_db*, and the comment, "Transaction Manager Standard Transaction User Object with Explicit Database Syntax Calls." Realize that until we actually make any changes, this is a duplicate of the *scut1001_xact_mgr_int* object. But also realize that this will prevent us from accidentally overwriting the other object, too.

First, let's go in and change the f_begin function to use database calls. Open up the f_begin function and delete the entire set of code that is in there now. Replace it with the following code.

```
String  ls_sql
ls_sql  = "BEGIN TRANSACTION " + ps_name
// Begin a transaction
EXECUTE IMMEDIATE :ls_sql USING this;
IF SQLCODE < 0 THEN
  MessageBox( "Database Error #: " + String( SQLDBCode), SQLErrText)
  RETURN FALSE
END IF
RETURN TRUE
```

Before you can save this function, though, you will need to modify the function declaration so that the function accepts a string parameter, *ps_name*, which will be the name of the transaction that you would like to use. Once you do this, save the function.

Now let's fix the close functions f_end, f_commit, and f_rollbac*k*, so that they also work with the database call method, and accept a name parameter as well. First, open the f_end function and replace its code with the following:

```
String  ls_sql
ls_sql  = ps_end_type + " TRANSACTION " + ps_name
IF Upper( ps_end_type) <> "COMMIT" AND Upper( ps_end_type) <> "ROLLBACK" THEN

// Invalid function call. Abort the function.
  MessageBox(ClassName(), "Invalid Parameter Passed")
  RETURN -1
END IF
EXECUTE IMMEDIATE :ls_sql USING This;
IF SQLCode < 0 THEN
// An error occured, put up a messagebox and return the error code.

  MessageBox( "Database Error #: " + String( SQLDBCode), SQLErrText)
END IF
// Return the contents of SQLDBCode,
// which will be the error number if there was one, or
// 0 if there wasn't any.
RETURN  SQLDBCode
```

In addition, add the *ps_name* parameter to the function declaration. Finally, update the f_commi*t* and f_rollback functions to also include a *ps_name* parameter, and pass that parameter as the second parameter to the f_end function. For example, the code in the f_commi*t* function should now read

```
f_end( "COMMIT", ps_name)
```

That's really all there is to it. Whether you use the first or second method of transaction management, or improvise with a method of your own, all you now need to do to manage your transactions is to start and end them with a function call. Let's say you have created an "OK" button in a window that contains a DataWindow called dw_data. The "OK" button calls a validation function to validate the data that was updated in dw_data *prior to starting the transaction*. Then it starts the transaction, updates the DataWindow, and commits if the update is successful, or rolls back if it is not. The code inside the "OK" button would probably look something like this:

```
IF f_validate() THEN
  SQLCA.f_begin( "dw_data")
  IF dw_data.Update() < 0 THEN
  SQLCA.f_rollback( "dw_data")
  ELSE
  SQLCA.f_commit( "dw_data")
  Close( Parent)
  END IF
END IF
```

Incidentally, there is no reason that we could not have taken this a step or two further. You could have your Transaction Manager validate that the user is still logged on during a BEGIN TRANSACTION request, and reconnect to the database if he is not. You could implement this in the BEGIN TRANSACTION function by having it attempt to select some constant from the database, or to select something from the system catalog tables. If the select succeeds, the user is still connected. However, if the select fails, you can detect the reason for failure and reconnect if it has to do with a disconnect.

You could have your Transaction Manager respond to a PROFILE FILE setting to log BEGIN and END TRANSACTIONs, with their names, to a file on the user's machine for debugging or accounting purposes.

You could have your Transaction Manager figure out its error state on its own, and determine whether it will perform a commit or rollback, without the developer having to perform additional code to do it manually (being careful, of course, not to prevent the developer from being able to deal with multiple DataWindows inside a single transaction).

You could even have your Transaction Manager deal with multiple transaction objects if you want to offer each of your users more than one connection to the database with asynchronous communications. Of course, in this case, you might not extend the PowerBuilder transaction object itself, but instead would create a custom class that would hold an array of transaction objects.

There really is no limit to the features that you can implement in your Transaction Manager except your own creativity...and perhaps your time and budget!

Other Tips and Techniques

Notice that in the last example care was taken to start the transaction *after* the validation of the DataWindow data. The reason that we did this was to minimize the amount of code between the start and end of a transaction. The goal here is to keep your locks as short as possible. As already mentioned, longer locks mean longer waits and more collisions, which eventually translate to unhappy users. In general, performance problems caused by locks that are held too long increase exponentially as you increase the number of users connected to the database. So while your code may run really nicely when you are testing it by yourself, as soon as you jump into the real world with fifteen or twenty users, your system will start crawling. Then hopes and dreams of fifty, sixty, or a hundred users will quickly fade away, only to be replaced by long hours of meetings with hardware specialists trying to figure out how much RAM they can fit into a server–when all it really comes down to is taking a few precautions to ensure that the amount of time spent inside a transaction is as short as can be.

The first step in doing this, of course, is keeping the actual code in the transaction to a bare minimum, as we demonstrated just above. Keep in mind, also, that you may sometimes have to update multiple DataWindows inside a single transaction. If this is the case, you'll want to perform validations on *all* of the DataWindows *outside* of the transaction itself, so that only database commands are within the transaction. Imagine spending seconds or minutes validating a second DataWindow after you began the locks on the first! I've seen more than one application run into concurrency problems because of this.

It is especially important to watch out for validations that are being performed inside of events like UpdateStart when working with multiple DataWindows, since the UpdateStart event will *only* get triggered inside a transaction. It won't cause problems for a single DataWindow update, since the locks won't be created until the first update actually occurs, after the UpdateStart event is complete. However, if you have two DataWindows being updated, and the second one has code in the UpdateStart event, the first DataWindow will update, creating locks on the database. Then the second DataWindow will run its UpdateStart event, potentially causing excessive lock lag time. The moral of the story: watch out for code that occurs in events that might interrupt the expected flow of control and allow pauses between the start and finish of a transaction.

Another way you can help minimize this kind of problem is by keeping transaction starts and finishes in the same function or script. That way you can easily eyeball your scripts and see the start and end of each transaction, ensuring that there is no wasteful logic in between. If you keep your transactions as tight as possible, you minimize the risk of lock lag.

Of course if your SQL is just plain slow, it won't matter all that much when your transactions are started and finished anyway! If users have to wait five minutes to complete a single retrieve or update, they will get stuck waiting in queue, and a queue of twelve people with five minutes per request will take as much as an hour. SQL statements that are taking too long should be optimized. In general, most DBMSes allow you to take certain measures to optimize your SQL and your table structure for speed. The right indexes will be critical, and in some cases you may find the need to break your SQL statements into sets of smaller statements to help improve performance. Allocate a fair amount of effort to optimizing your SQL; you will find that the effort is worthwhile. Most of the bottlenecks in a client/server application will be with the database.

The last tip that I can offer in dealing with transactions and locks is to talk to your DBA, or any expert with your DBMS. Each DBMS has specific exceptions and extensions to the standard SQL language that will probably be important to making the most of your transaction management procedures. Some DBMSes allow you to control how and when locks will be held for certain SQL statements. Others allow you to use special commands to monitor your locks, usage, and other activities on the database. Others can show you details about how specific SQL commands will be executed by the server, what indexes will be used, and how the disks will be accessed. Most DBMSes give you tools you can use to figure out what is happening when you run your SQL. They are mostly designed to help you optimize your SQL, but they can also be used to help you optimize your transactions–after all, optimizing and monitoring your SQL is half the battle in transaction management anyway.

Manage your transactions as best you can. You will find your system to be much more robust and effective if you do. You'll probably save your company or client thousands of dollars in hardware, too!

CHAPTER 8

Accessing
Your Mainframe Data
with PowerBuilder

By Daniel Worden

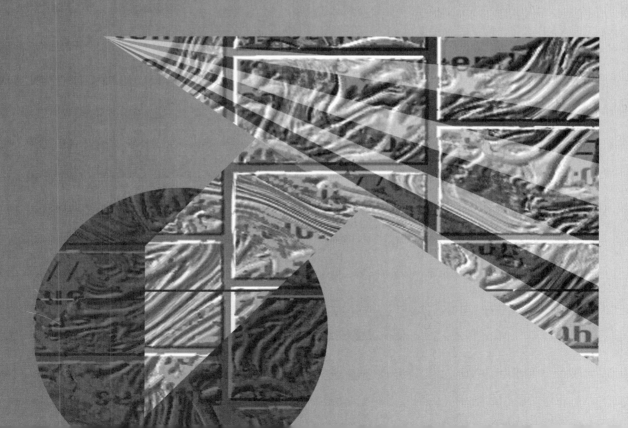

Accessing Your Mainframe Data with PowerBuilder

by **Daniel Worden**

Introduction

If you do not have to integrate your PB applications with any legacy data or "big iron" systems, count yourself lucky–and skip this chapter. On second thought, stick with it and you will gain a better appreciation for where PowerBuilder can fit in the overall scheme of systems architectures.

This chapter covers integration of PowerBuilder and existing data stores, usually held on mainframe systems. To a lesser extent, we'll also look at how you can use PowerBuilder to move data between database environments–and why you would want to do so.

Increasingly, PowerBuilder is being accepted as a serious development tool to be used for the creation of more than simple prototypes or departmental applications. Third-party products built with PB, such as Dun & Bradstreet's Smart Stream and Financial Stream applications, are also being marketed and implemented at the organizational level.

With this higher profile and wider scope frequently comes a requirement to fit into an existing systems architecture. In some shops, PowerBuilder is used extensively for decision-support applications rather than for the development of mission-critical production systems. If any of these development considerations apply in your environment, you should gain something from this chapter.

We will focus on the key methods of gaining access to mainframe data. Whether your data is kept on the mainframe and accessed across a network, or replicated to different database servers, this chapter will provide you with an appropriate description and useful techniques for incorporating legacy data into your PowerBuilder applications.

Acknowledging the Host

The first step in any client/server development effort, including one using PowerBuilder, is to understand the architecture within which you will be developing. When you hear systems people, typically consultants, describing architectures, sometimes the underlying idea is not properly conveyed. There is not really a single architecture for systems within an organization, but rather three distinct architectures. These include:

Hardware & Communications
Applications
Data

You might argue that h/w and networks are really separate architectures in their own right, but in terms of accessing mainframe data from your PowerBuilder applications they can be addressed at the same time. For the purposes of network designers and capacity planners they might well be broken out into distinct architectures and defined to great levels of detail. From our perspective, it is only important to understand what databases servers are out there and how we can connect to them.

In larger shops, or in organizations where mainframe processing has been outsourced, the traditional mainframe is still a very important component of the systems architecture. In other words, you are not going to replace it. You have to incorporate it.

At the same time, mainframe processing is expensive and laborious. After all, that is part of the reason systems management has decided to migrate many applications to a client/server environment. It is most important to understand the continuing role of the mainframe in your particular organization before designing an application in PowerBuilder to integrate with it.

For some companies, the mainframe is the only way to consolidate and validate data gleaned from widely distributed branch offices. In one multi-billion dollar insurance organization, they use fifty-five distributed PowerBuilder/SQL Server systems to feed sales and branch management data into a centralized mainframe application which is used to crunch and validate the numbers for the company as a whole.

This is an architectural level consideration, inasmuch as the company is publicly traded on the stock market and must pay significant fees to have its books audited by independent accounting firms. To move all of its systems off the mainframe would require systems audit procedures that are simply not ready nor proven effective for an organization of that size and scale.

The key point here is that in many cases, it is actually a good idea to KEEP the mainframe, for reasons which go beyond technology, flexibility, or accessibility of data. If you have a clear picture of your organization's systems architecture and the reasons why it was chosen, it will be much easier to develop maintainable applications within that framework.

In other companies there may be a published strategy to move off the mainframe by outsourcing first, and then developing replacement applications. In such situations there is typically a reasonably long-term contract signed between the outsourcing service provider and your company. This means that at some point in the distant future you will be expected to pull the plug on the mainframe with nary a bump or wrinkle. However, in the meantime, the organization is still paying for mainframe services and generally expects to receive some value for its money. This provides a competing pressure, as outsourced mainframe service providers typically charge significant sums for reports, program changes, etc. In these cases, you may be expected to integrate with the mainframe to access existing reports or applications and use those to feed your PowerBuilder applications, where the data can be more flexibly manipulated.

Last, the role played by your host may be more than one of feeding data down to PowerBuilder-based client/server applications. You may actually have to update your mainframe data store through your applications. This is usually a bit more problematic (read harder), than pulling data off the mainframe, and it too must be understood within the context of the systems architecture of your organization. You may have to identify data entry applications and validation routines on the mainframe to which you must submit the output of your application as a batch. Of course, you will need to duplicate, and likely expand on, the data checking routines run by the mainframe within your application. You will not want to have data that has been validated by your application ending up rejected by the host, thus leaving your users to sort through the data to determine the problem.

The point here is that to integrate your application with the mainframe it is not only necessary to determine which data will be moved down to or up from your application, but also to understand the functions performed by the legacy applications. Especially for updates to mainframe data stores, it is not just a question of moving data but of integrating applications as well. The bottom line? The mainframe host is alive and well in many organizations and you must fit in or flock off with your client/server friends.

Application Integration

Let's start at the highest level at which we can integrate your mainframe system with PowerBuilder. Assuming that you have not only data on the mainframe, but applications with which you must peacefully coexist, there are several options open to you.

First, we should acknowledge that in too many cases, the move to client/server and other PowerBuilder-related toolsets is being driven less by real requirements and more by a desire to see pretty applications. Heads down data entry people, who normally rarely take their eyes off their input sheets, want Windows and related applications. In fact, to many managers out there, client/server simply means having a Windows-based application with which to work.

Of course, there are real-world advantages to working with graphical user interfaces, and certainly no one is accusing PowerBuilder of being simply a fad. The point to consider here is simply that in some cases, the most appropriate thing to do is provide your users with access to their mainframe data by way of a "face-lift". Products known as *screenscrapers* are designed to do just that.

By using the High Level Language Application Programming Interface (HLLAPI), it is possible to present users with an apparently Windows-based application which is directly mapped to a TSO or other mainframe terminal screen. The users never see the older mainframe application, other than where its behavior, rather than its appearance, is consistent with terminal sessions.

Since this only gives you the look of a GUI-based application, without much of the client side processing you take can advantage of with PowerBuilder, you might wonder why anyone would do this.

There are several reasons:

Users are given the opportunity to get familiar with their old applications under the graphical interface. A screenscraped application can be incorporated into PowerBuilder as a user object, allowing data to be moved from the mainframe to the PB application and thence out to another database.

Logins and passwords can be automated as part of the PowerBuilder application, relieving users of the necessity to manage multiple profiles–and more importantly, allowing you to give them a single view of all their applications while taking your time to redesign, develop, and release the older mainframe apps. Tools such as Easel and Rumba have been used for these purposes for several years. They support a variety of mainframe environments and have been successfully incorporated into larger PowerBuilder applications and projects.

As you might expect, performance is very much a problem with this type of access. The screenscraper has a great deal of work to do, mapping fields and user actions from the GUI to the terminal environment. Also, maintenance of the mainframe applications can become a major headache. This approach can work for applications which have been frozen and are not being redesigned or developed themselves. Should the screen of the application change for any reason, the matching screenscraped version must be changed as well.

However, there is a role for this technique to play in migration to client/server projects, especially where the mainframe applications are being phased out over time and all new development is to be done in a GUI tool like PowerBuilder.

Data Replication

When we talk about replication of data, people often think we are simply referring to the copying of data from one source to another. At one level this is true, but replication carries with it a requirement to synchronize data to ensure that applications which use it do not misconstrue the accuracy or timeliness of the data. In other words, replication means not only copying data from system to another, but making sure that one copy is designated and remains the master copy. Data may be replicated from one database to another on the basis of time (month end for instance) or on the basis of a changed value. For replication services with a high degree of synchronization, the transaction logs of the master database will be applied to replicated databases at some designated interval after the transaction completes on the master. This ensures that, although there is a delay in updates recorded on the replicated database, the two are essentially mirror images of each other, to the transaction level.

From the standpoint of a PowerBuilder developer this is of interest for two reasons: access and performance. In some cases, it is simply not possible to gain access to data which is needed for your application. This may be a question of permissions and security, or it may have more to do with the location of the data. If the source of your data is located far enough away, you will probably consider replicating it.

Many mainframe applications are built around 9,600 baud dial-up lines. The data is located in another building, or across the country. Whatever the case, it is still difficult to build solidly performing PowerBuilder applications which incorporate links at this speed. So, you may choose to replicate your data instead.

In the comments made about systems architecture earlier in the chapter, we referred to data architecture. Beyond logical data modeling, complete with entity-relationship and data flow diagrams, the data architecture needs to designate ownership of the data. As companies integrate departmental and divisional systems into a corporation-wide or enterprise systems architecture, the originator of the data must be clearly identified and accountability for data integrity designed into the data architecture.

This is an important step for anyone who wants to move data into a local database for processing purposes rather than decision support. If all you want to do is analyze and report on data from another source, there is very little difficulty. File transfer applications abound for every platform, and protocol conversion is also well established in readily available products. The real issues arise when you want to move data off the mainframe and update it or add to it, then write it back. Then you are making a statement not unlike the sign you read at the gas station: In case of disagreement, this register will be taken to be correct.

Take a practical example of this process. We worked on one PowerBuilder project that automated an organization's salesmen. They needed to connect to the corporate database while in the office, move relevant rows of data down to their PCs, disconnect their machines from the network, and take them with them when they met with prospects and clients. During the course of those meetings they would complete screen forms using a custom application written in PowerBuilder–taking full advantage of validations and calculations, of course. At the beginning of the next day they would come into their offices, connect with the corporate system, and synchronize their data with the centralized server. All of this processing was written by the development team, based on reviewing the data and flagging questionable data for confirmation by a supervisor.

Database replication does not have to be an expensive service offered by a database vendor. It might help to take advantage of some of that expertise, of course, but you can choose to implement it yourself. The key point is that in some cases you will choose to access your mainframe data by copying it down to a local database or some other accessible data store. You may decide to do this for performance reasons; simply to have the data locally; or you may need to move large chunks of data from one server to another location where it can be massaged more cheaply by your applications. Of course, it may also be necessary to take advantage of this technique due to sheer volume of data.

Some larger client/server shops using PowerBuilder applications and relational databases are finding that moving approved departmental or divisional data from the corporate server down to a local box can only be handled as a batch process. Transferring a gigabyte of data from one platform to another, populating a database, and rebuilding indexes requires hours. It is usually set up to chug away during the wee hours of the morning. The process used is a simple, cheap and effective one.

First, COBOL programs are created which extract the records from the mainframe databases according to the relevant business criteria–for example, the transactions of that particular day for a financial system. Using one of the third-party communications programs which can attach to mainframe hosts as well as UNIX minicomputers, Novell file servers, and various other systems, the extracted files are moved from the host to the relational database server using the file transfer protocol (ftp). The files are then located on the UNIX platform as a text file. As part of the successful transfer, the files on the mainframe are deleted. An operating systems script, scheduled to wake up and look for the existence of the name of the downloaded file, discovers that the file is in fact present and launches a database script to load the text data into the database. In the vernacular: a chron job wakes up and kicks off an SQL script. The next morning, the data awaits the users.

Even from the perspective of a PowerBuilder developer all this is handled in the background. You look for data in the format you need and at the source you want. The fact that your source is replenished from a designated master copy somewhere in the organization does not have to be of all that much concern.

Given that departments, branches, regional offices–and let's not forget corporate headquarters–all have a legitimate claim to ownership and origination of some data, you can see how important a clear and comprehensive data architecture becomes, if you want to allow your PB applications to take advantage of data generated elsewhere in the organization.

Gateways and Middleware

A new (and quite expensive) approach to linking PowerBuilder applications to legacy and other sources of data can be lumped under the heading of middleware. Often taken to mean the communications wiring, conduits, and switches over which the network connects client applications to servers, middleware is beginning to emerge as a service provider in its own right.

The primary function provided by middleware is to broker or translate data between otherwise incompatible systems. From an architectural standpoint, these gateways allow developers to treat servers as though they were familiar local data sources. At one level, ODBC can be consider to provide this service, as ODBC presents the common interface to multiple data providers, without having to configure the client workstation to manage the multiple protocols and linkages necessary to gain access to the data. Products such as Open Server and

OmniSQL Gateway from Sybase also provide this kind of service. However, instead of allowing access to Paradox, dBase and Access databases, the higher end middleware products allow you to treat DB/2, IMS, Oracle and VSAM files as though they were SQL Server resources.

This provides several key advantages. Not only does it do away with the need to wait for Powersoft to develop an interface kit to VSAM (and we probably shouldn't hold our breath for that), but it means that the same tool, the same configuration, and the same techniques can be used to connect PowerBuilder applications to a wide variety of data sources, including the mainframe. Additionally, as a PowerBuilder developer, you need not be all that concerned about the host side of the equation. If you can open a transaction object which accesses the server, you can deal with the data in the same manner as you would any other relational database. The fact that the data resides in a flat file on a big iron host does not have to affect you.

Of course, there is a penalty to pay for all of these wonderful services. Along with price, performance is cited as the key reason against using this approach. To be fair, many of these products are in Version One of their commercial life. The entire approach is new, and (like many of the individual products) will mature rapidly as the marketplace dictates its requirements—and as vendors stabilize on what works, and address those things which do not quite work as advertised.

A practical example of how this sort of middleware can be incorporated into a PowerBuilder application and allow access to your mainframe data is Sybase's Open Server from Sybase. Here's how it works:

As indicated, Open Server libraries can allow a client to access data sources such as DB/2 or VSAM files as if those files were database objects within an SQL Server. This is achieved by loading the libraries—a collection of C programs—onto the target platform, and configuring them to run as an ongoing process. If you wish to access a mainframe-based program which retrieves data from various filesets, you can use Open Server to treat the application as a stored procedure. The Open Server libraries act as a wrapper around the data, and through stored procedures, that wrapper can include applications.

From a client perspective, this process has a name and can be addressed as if it were a complete SQL Server installation. PowerBuilder DataWindows can be built using these stored procedures, thereby allowing you to connect your PB applications to existing mainframe applications and data.

The disadvantage of Open Server is inherent in the way it works. To allow any client to connect to the target data source, the target has to be aware of how to interpret the SQL commands issued to it. This means that the Open Server implementation has to trap the commands from Sybase-compliant T-SQL and translate them into commands that can be interpreted by the host running the Open Server. In many cases this might be reasonably straightforward—in the case of selects or deletes, for example. However, there are many constructs which do not translate from one environment to another. Take the Sybase datatype DATETIME. On many systems, relational and otherwise, two distinct datatypes for date and time are supported. To manage this in Open Server, whoever installs and configures the product must predict and accommodate these details.

On the other hand, why reinvent the wheel? Using Open Server technology, Sybase itself has created OmniSQL Gateway. The functions provided are a superset of Open Server, presented in the format of a shrink-wrapped, supported product. The key advantage to a turnkey gateway is that it is no longer necessary to handle these translations yourself. They have already been programmed into the gateway product using the Open Server functions.

There are many other vendors of effective and reliable gateways to mainframe data. These examples have been offered here simply as a means to explain what the technology can do in general terms. Naturally, you will have to evaluate the best solution to solving your mainframe access requirements based on the specifics of your applications and environment.

Unquestionably, the most commonly used method of accessing data from the mainframe is to periodically port it to a local relational database. Gateways and other middleware products are making serious inroads into this market, and you can look for increasingly sophisticated access and improved performance as these products mature.

Summary

As you can see, there are many viable methods to incorporate your mainframe data into your PowerBuilder applications. True, these methods are often based on systems integration technologies, requiring the cooperation of database and systems administrators to set up. But the upside is your ability to create transparent paths to data stored on the mainframe, whether directly accessed through middleware or on local servers fed by data replication.

You should also now have a better appreciation for the reasons why your mainframe applications may need to soldier on, and how you could use screenscrapers to help you migrate your users over to a GUI environment and start the learning process. The key is to understand how your hardware, network, data, and applications architectures can allow you to successfully integrate your PowerBuilder development environment, resulting in high value GUI applications which leverage your users and let them get on with the business of your business.

By sheer market momentum and quality of results, PowerBuilder developers are showing that their applications and technology will be a force for the future. But there is a danger in thinking that wholesale replacement of existing mainframe systems is always the best alternative. Large data volumes and processing requirements have been the traditional mainstay of big iron. Until client/server technology has stabilized and proven itself beyond any doubt, one critical success factor for PB developers will continue to be how well our PowerBuilder applications allow us to access our mainframe data.

CHAPTER 9

Accessing COBOL
From PowerBuilder

By Jonathan Sayles

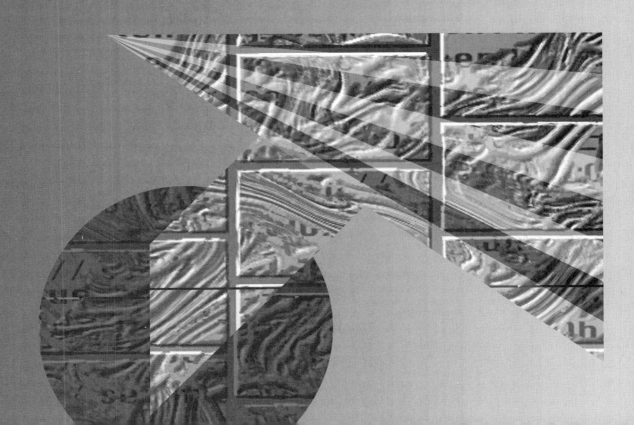

Accessing COBOL From PowerBuilder:

Exploiting legacy application assets through Client/Server computing

by **Jonathan Sayles**

Client/Server "Generations"

The Windows-Client/Server computing model is evolving and expanding. It's moving from a personal and departmental application solution towards large-scale interdepartmental and enterprise-wide computing. Applications are moving from read-only database access to full OLTP and traditional production systems. Moreover, they're evolving from applications of smaller scope and scale to large and complex systems. Meeting the challenges introduced by this evolution will not be easy for client/server architects, designers, and developers. New strategies, operations, tools, and procedures must be introduced into the project life cycle in order to avoid the chaos and learning curve that inevitably accompany any technology rising to meet increasing challenges.

Reuse versus Rewrite

Consider this simple question (just one among many faced by the new generation of client/server developers): "What components should I use in building a client/server application that replicates existing legacy functionality?" Should you build such an application entirely from within your chosen 4GL-Windows development toolset (reverse-engineer, and rewrite the existing legacy functionality)? Or, through reuse, should you develop the majority of the application using the 4GL-Windows toolset, "externalize" calls to existing legacy-asset functions as necessary, when appropriate, *and when possible,* thus saving the time and money required to reverse-engineer large, complex, and fully-tested production code? Before answering this question, we should probably take a minute to ask; "Just how often can we/would we reuse existing legacy assets in a client/server world?"

Gartner Group, in its *Client/Server Computing in the 1990s, Part 5,* states, "The huge installed base of legacy applications and data volumes mandates that only in rare cases can an entirely new processing model be implemented. Therefore, client/server computing can become mainstream during the five-year planning period only if *coexistence with,* and migration from, legacy applications is achieved." Further, Gartner Group, in a technical research paper (T-525-1071), states unequivocally that "...there is an increased requirement for the integration of the mainframe COBOL-based systems with the new Client/Server applications...", and "Organizations should use COBOL when there is a high investment in staff, support systems, methodologies, and business applications–*particularly organizations that want to minimize their technology risk.*"

Recently, other industry spokespersons have been joining the choir. Max Hopper, chairman of the SABRE Group, says, "Our existing systems may be our greatest asset. Client/server can be used to give those systems new life." Lee Morgan of the Lotus Consulting Services Group states, "We need a new breed of applications that integrate operational and strategic considerations, focusing on distributed and extended-enterprise systems." And finally, at the DCI Conference in April, 1994, Christine Comaford said, "Find a way to reuse COBOL/ CICS executables. It's the only way to go."

In my own personal experience, as a PowerBuilder instructor and consultant, in over eighty percent of the classes I taught from 1993 through 1995 at least one student, often a project leader or manager, would ask me to teach them how to write external function calls to COBOL programs. They planned on reusing portions of existing COBOL production applications. And in the many client/server presentations I've attended at PowerBuilder and Micro Focus User Groups, as well as DCI and DBExpo seminars, COBOL reuse from a Windows-client/server application architecture was always a popular topic, typically playing to full rooms and enthusiastic crowds.

Interoperability needs and requirements for access to legacy computing assets come up often. Further, in the debate as to whether to reuse versus rewrite, "reuse" wins hands down. This will come as no surprise to readers who have attempted to reverse engineer the functionality of 100,000+ lines of COBOL code into C or C++. COBOL applications with 100,000+ lines of code are *small* by mainframe application standards. Technical "impedance mismatches" (which are differences in the data and language semantics between COBOL and C), application size, logical complexity, testing ,and a host of other issues, have proved this point time and time again. It is; however, unfortunate that not enough attention has been paid to the reuse-beats-rewrite verdict in the popular press. Indeed, this entire chapter introduction might well be a true introduction to this topic for many readers...quite unfortunately.

What It Is, Versus How to Do It

Industry analysts often present their findings as summarizations of *what* to do, without too much *why* and even less *how*. We'll leave the whys and whats to the Gartner Group. For "inquiring technical minds that want to know," in the remainder of this chapter we'll take a look at the how-to of COBOL reuse, and specifically, at the means of accessing legacy computing assets from PowerBuilder applications.

Reusable Components

Conventional wisdom holds that the two components of legacy assets which are candidates for reuse are *process* and *data*. Process includes business logic, generally in the form of production COBOL code or production COBOL code plus called procedures such as IBM mainframe assembly language (ALC) subroutines, FORTRAN subroutines, utilities, etc. Data includes production MVS-staged data. What kind of data? If the industry analysts are to be believed, only twenty percent (or less in many studies)of this data is relational. The remaining eighty percent of production data is staged in non-relational files and databases–VSAM and QSAM files, IMS and IDMS databases, etc. Because so much production data is in non-relational format, real questions about the *meaning* of this data, if accessed independently of the processes which maintain it, must be asked.

The problem of unnormalized data reuse

As a general rule, before the days of formalized data modeling, data normalization, etc., meaningful production information only resulted from business logic in the form of 3GL code acting upon data. In other words, there is a distinct difference between raw data files in a pre-relational format and *meaningful information*. Merely giving users–and even developers–who don't understand the concepts of normalization, data integrity, or consistency, access to production data sources, does not ensure the delivery of applications which produce accurate business information upon which informed decisions can be based. This is not the fault of the developers or users, but the overly optimistic judgment of just what the data in a production file represents. Business facts or valid *semantics* can rarely be found in QSAM/VSAM files, or IMS or IDMS databases designed in the 70's and 80's. Business facts are derived from the execution of application logic reading from and writing to these data sources. This is an important point, and must be understood by everyone attempting to forge links to production data from client/server applications. The obvious implication of this point is that legacy application *process* is reusable, *process+data* is reusable...but unnormalized legacy data alone is not directly reusable from a 4GL-Windows application. A VSAM file server will be more trouble than it's worth.

Reusable components revisited

From an architectural or application-level perspective, an expedient breakdown of reusable legacy application components is described below in Figure 9-1. While the list in Figure 9-1 is not complete, it will suffice to allow you to conceptualize the reuse of these components within a PowerBuilder client/server architecture.

* Access to an entire COBOL application (application *rehosting*)
* Access to one or more COBOL subroutines
* Access to an entire DB/DC (TPNS) transaction (application *rehosting*)
* Access to a portion of a DB/DC transaction
* Access to COBOL "batch" procedures:
   - Reports
   - File and/or Database processing *(esp. non-relational data)*
   - Utilities

Rehosting and applications

In terms of reusable components, access from a PowerBuilder application to an entire COBOL application or database/data communications (DB/DC) transaction, really represents *rehosting* of the COBOL application on a networked platform. Typical examples of rehosting projects that would port existing production applications from the mainframe include data collections, batch reporting, batch file updating, etc. These projects could be fired off from a PowerBuilder application as custom events or synchronous functions from a command button or toolbar option. Such rehosting projects, while not trivial efforts, do not represent a high degree of technical difficulty or risk, and have proven to deliver a quick return on investment. Companies such as Micro Focus, Inc., provide mainframe emulation runtimes and emulation workbenches on 16 and 32-bit Windows (including NT), unix, OS/2, and DOS. Add-ons are also available which support CICS, ALC, IMS DB/DC, DB2, etc.

Reusing application components

It is nice to know that you can rehost an entire mainframe application on a server-based platform. Many companies are doing just that as a transition strategy. But of broader appeal and relevance to PowerBuilder application developers is *access to one or more COBOL subroutines* and access to a *portion* of a DB/DC transaction. This "slicing into" a COBOL legacy application to interface with a single program or small number of programs which encapsulate an important business procedure or a business logic routine, represents a more granular, low-cost, and often more critical requirement. Selective application component-level reuse characterizes the majority of client/server-COBOL interface requirements.

Application component reuse—the big picture

To make COBOL application components available for reuse within a PowerBuilder client/server architecture, several steps must be taken.

Identify the COBOL programs that you wish to call from PowerBuilder, and analyze their interface requirements. Batch COBOL programs interface through the Linkage Section data elements as declared in the PROCEDURE DIVISION or ENTRY USING statements in the COBOL program. CICS programs interface through the fields of the CICS COMMAREA or Basic Mapping Support (BMS) screens.

Download those programs and all related elements (copybooks, test files, databases, etc.) to the PC.

Prepare the programs for execution on the PC using the Micro Focus Workbench.

Generate a call to the programs from PowerBuilder through the PowerScript "external function" statement(s).

If you do not understand COBOL and have never written and tested a production program, you will need assistance in analyzing, downloading, and preparing the COBOL programs. The COBOL technical world is vast, and experience is usually the key to success in working with it. Once the COBOL programs are established, it is time to jump back into Power-Builder and generate the external call interface to your COBOL application.

Generating External Function Scripts for COBOL Programs

There are many different options and approaches you can take to generate external function scripts for your PowerBuilder applications. Covering all options is well beyond the scope of this chapter. However, there are two basic methods of generating external function calls:

Code the external function script manually, in a one-to-one way, for each COBOL program.

Use a third-party tool, such as PowerBridge, to generate the external function script.

PowerBridge is a product from Micro Focus which automates the process of external function script generation (see Figure 9-2). In this chapter we will describe the procedures and functions common for both approaches to script generation. At the end of the chapter there is a short description of PowerBridge.

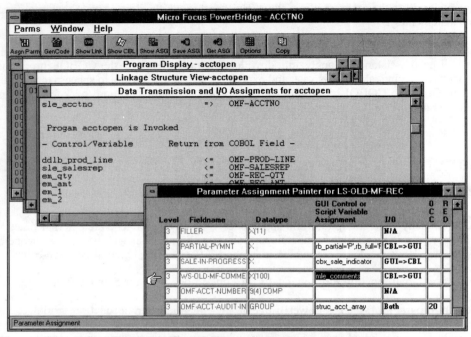

Figure 9-2: PowerBridge code construction painter.

External function interface to COBOL .dlls from PowerBuilder

To access each COBOL program you must:

Compile and link the program into a dynamic link library (.dll). Note that one-to-many individual COBOL programs can be linked to a single .dll. Declare a PowerBuilder global external function for that *.DLL* (unless using PowerBridge). Call the COBOL .dll from within the appropriate PowerBuilder event script using a PowerScript external function call. Different steps, requirements, and tools apply when using PowerBridge as opposed to non-PowerBridge (or manual)coding. So throughout the remainder of this chapter we will refer specifically to *manual* writing, coding, compiling, and linking, so that you can distinguish the steps and procedures from PowerBridge generation and application administration.

Compiling and linking COBOL .dlls

Dynamic link libraries (.dlls), are similar to COBOL "load libraries." Load libraries are a collection of compiled and executable functions or procedures (COBOL programs), each with its own unique entry point and parameter list. To create a COBOL .dll manually, compile the program from a DOS prompt using the Micro Focus COBOL compiler, with a statement such as:

```
cobol <programname.cbl> omf"obj" LitLink deffile deffiletype"win";
```

The COBOL "directives," also called compiler parms, deffile, and deffiletype "win," tell the compiler to generate a "definition" file, which is basically a "make" file that is suitable for use with Windows. By default the compiler names the definition file <programname.def>.

Once the program is successfully compiled, you link the program's object language file (.obj), which is output from the compile, with the Micro Focus Windows runtime libraries. A generic DOS command prompt statement to do this is:

```
link <programname.obj>+Libinit+cblwinl,<programname.dll>,,Lcobolw+
Lcobol+cobw+<programname.def > /NOE/NOD;
```

The above statement will link your program into a COBOL .dll, thus making it available for calling from within a PowerBuilder application through the PowerScript external function construct.

There are many different approaches to the design, creation and management of production COBOL .dlls. For more information on these issues, please consult the Micro Focus COBOL User Guide reference manual.

Once the COBOL .dlls have been created, you are ready to declare and write external function calls to them. To compile and link the programs with PowerBridge, use the Power-Bridge administration system (Figure 9-3). The administration system provides a graphical point-and-click approach to identifying programs, documenting their use from Power-Builder, combining, compiling and linking them into .dlls.

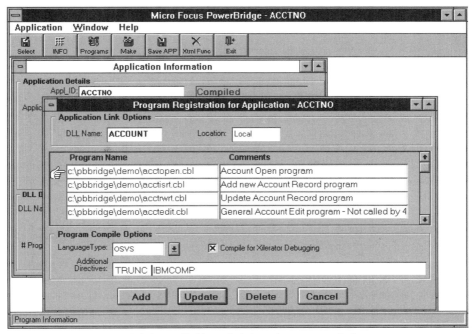

Figure 9-3: PowerBridge administration system windows.

Application prerequisite: Declare external function calls

When coding manually, a separate PowerScript external function call declaration must be entered into the PowerBuilder Global External Function Declaration Window or in the Local External Function Declaration Window in the User Object/Window Painter. An external function call declaration defines the external .dll object name and specifies its input/output parameter list. You can think of the external function call declaration as defining the "programmatic interface" between your PowerBuilder calling application and the COBOL called module. The following is an example of an external function declaration syntax structure:

```
FUNCTION int <program_entry_point> (REF <datatype> <data-itemname>,
  REF <datatype> <data-itemname>, REF <datatype> <data-itemname>...)
  library "<dllname.DLL>"
```

where:

FUNCTION   is a required/reserved word
int is the datatype of the return code (like a PowerScript function return code)
REF is a required/reserved word marking a parameter list
<datatype> is the PowerBuilder datatype of a Linkage Section 01 parameter
<data-itemname> is the PowerBuilder declared name of a Linkage Section 01 parameter
library is a required/reserved word
"<dllname.DLL>" is the name of the COBOL .dll.

Manually-coded external function calls

A separate external function declaration, customized to each COBOL program's PROCE-DURE DIVISION USING ... or ENTRY USING ... statement in the .dll, must be made for each and every COBOL program to be accessed from your PowerBuilder application. A complete example of an external function declaration would be:

```
FUNCTION int ACCTREC(REF string acctkey, REF string acctdate,
      REF string acctacty, REF int acctnbr, REF string acctstatus,
      REF dec{2} acctdue, REF dec{2} acctoverdue,
      REF string action_ind) library "ACCT.DLL"
```

About your COBOL program (considerations for manual coding)

When you are coding external function calls to COBOL manually, your external function call REF items must correspond to COBOL USING 01s as coded in your program's Linkage Section. In other words, there must be a one-for-one *positional* correspondence with the PowerBuilder declaration, the PowerBuilder external function call, and your COBOL program's USING clause. The parameters must match POSITION, SIZE, and DATATYPE. Further, if your COBOL program contains COBOL data *structures,* which are COBOL Linkage items containing 05 and 10 level data items within the 01s–*and this is very common*–you will have to recode the COBOL Linkage Section so it contains only 01 level data items. In addition, you will have to analyze the impact these code changes have on your Procedure Division logic such as the USING statement, group MOVE statements, etc. This will often turn out to be a non-trivial effort, as most legacy applications contain one or more complex data structures passed in Linkage. Reengineering these data structures can be time-consuming and difficult.

Finally, if you are reusing mainframe COBOL applications which do sorting or searching on alphanumeric values, and you need to maintain the integrity of the original EBCDIC alphanumeric collating sequence so that file updates, report production, etc. match the original mainframe outputs, you will need to translate the ASCII fields passed to the COBOL program into EBCDIC. This can also turn out to be a non-trivial effort.

PowerBridge external function declaration

If you are using PowerBridge, which acts as an "application server," you only need to declare three external functions for access to any and all COBOL programs. The three external function declarations are shown below:

```
FUNCTION int MF_SUB_REQUEST(REF int status, REF string reserved,
    REF string progname, REF char array_mask[ ]) library "MFLOCAL.DLL"
FUNCTION boolean _MFDLLSTOP() LIBRARY "mflocal.dll"
FUNCTION int MF_STRNG_REQ(REF int status,REF int IN,
    REF int OUT) LIBRARY "mflocal.dll"
```

About your COBOL program (considerations for PowerBridge construction)

If you are using PowerBridge, you will not have to make any changes to Linkage or Procedure Division code. That is, you will not have to reengineer complex Linkage Section data structures. PowerBridge, as an application server, handles all PowerBuilder-to-COBOL-to-PowerBuilder datatype assignments/transformations, considerations, etc., between PowerBuilder and COBOL–including ASCII-to-EBCDIC conversion issues.

Coding and testing the external function

Once you have compiled and linked your .dlls, and declared your PowerBuilder external function, you may begin writing the external function call to the COBOL program. As with many aspects of data processing technology, coding the actual call and writing the statement to invoke the external function request is not a difficult matter. The issue(s) for consideration consist of choosing the appropriate event script from which to fire off the request analyzing and understanding the COBOL program you are intending to reuse utilizing the elements of the COBOL program intelligently.

These issues are discussed at length in the next section.

In the beginning, there were event scripts

Before you generate an external function call using PowerBridge, you must first decide from which event script you intend to invoke the COBOL program. Generally this is an easy decision. You invoke the COBOL program from within the PowerBuilder event script just prior to the event time where process or data is required by your application logic. This can be some action-oriented event script like the Clicked! event from a command button or menu option, the DoubleClicked! event from a Listbox, the Open! event of a window, etc. Occasionally (and this happens more frequently when doing massive COBOL reengineering as opposed to reuse or rehosting) you might want to split and/or combine elements of a COBOL program along very different lines from their original mainframe executable sequence. In cases where a one-to-one relationship between a COBOL program and a given event script does not exist, you may need to invoke the program *in advance* of where the data is actually used. For instance, you may want to populate a group of window or global variables–PowerScript structures–with COBOL values at the beginning of your application, or before a window opens or a custom user-event occurs in your script, etc. In this case, you would choose a more global event script, such as the Application Open! event script or Window Construct! event script, from which to populate PowerScript variables or structures. In general, decisions about where to place the external function calls which invoke COBOL programs under PowerBridge, while not irrevocable, should be carefully thought out and analyzed.

Once you've determined where in your application you wish to invoke the COBOL program, you can enter the PowerBuilder object painter (Window Painter, User-Object Painter, Function Painter, Menu Painter, etc.), and either code the external function call manually, or invoke PowerBridge to generate the external function call. Before we tackle the external function call itself, it is useful to consider the various alternatives to COBOL data reuse.

Development Techniques: Mapping PowerBuilder Fields to COBOL Data Items

The different methods and alternative assignment possibilities supported through manual coding efforts, and by PowerBridge, for mapping PowerBuilder application and graphical objects to COBOL fields are listed below in Figure 9-4. Details on the specific techniques follow in the next section. Note for Figure 9-4, an "X" denotes PowerBridge-automated code generation as well as manual code construction availability. An "*" denotes only manual code construction availability.

```
COBOL Data-Items
Elmnt Group  Expl. All  2-Dim Complex
Mapping Techniques/PowerBuilder Var./CntrlsField  FieldOccursOccurs Table
Occurs
     Assignment to local, instance,              X   X  X  X  X   X
     shared and global variables

     Assignment to custom-coded local window  X   X  X  X  X   X
     or global PowerBuilder structures

     Direct assignment to the text portion of a      X   X  X  *   *    *
     Window control

     Direct assignment to a specific attribute of X  X   X       *   *    *
     a specific Window control

     Assignment as a single element of a ListBox  X   X
     or DropDownListBox (ADDITEM)

     Assignment of all elements to a ListBox  X
     or DropDownListBox (ADDITEM)

      ".checked" logic for option     X  X   X
     controls (rb_, cbx_, etc.)

     Single field map to edit cell of an existing   X  X  X
```

```
DataWindow control

Elementary or complex OCCURS to an  X   X
existing DataWindow Control

Elementary or complex OCCURS to a   X
PowerBridge-generated DataWindow Control

Complex OCCURS to an existing graphics   X
control (row/column coordinates)
```

Figure 9-4: External function mapping techniques for COBOL-to-GUI assignments.

Assignment to PowerScript Variables: Overview

By either using the PowerBridge-generated local variables or by assigning COBOL Linkage fields to your own custom PowerScript variables, you may make use of the data passed from COBOL to your PowerBuilder application in the most flexible manner. You may reuse COBOL values within different event scripts and, for global variables, even across different windows in your PowerBuilder application. As Figure 9-5 (below) shows, there are no restrictions on the supported COBOL datatypes for assignment to variables. Note that when you assign COBOL values to custom PowerScript variables, you will have to code your own window control assignment statements. You are also responsible for other aspects of presentation logic coding, such as math precision, datatyping, etc. There are two different approaches you can take with PowerScript variable assignments: assign COBOL fields to your own custom-coded variables whether local, instance, or global; or use the Power-Bridge-generated local variables for COBOL fields.

COBOL data-item to PowerBuilder script: PowerBridge considerations

PowerBridge automatically generates a local PowerScript variable for each elementary COBOL data field in the Linkage Section of your program named in the USING clause. In fact, PowerBridge communicates with the COBOL program exclusively through the use of these local variables. This is an important point to understand if you are thinking about using PowerBridge and either modifying the PowerBridge-generated code, or creating your own local or window instance variables. PowerBridge-generated code references only its automatically generated local variables at the point in the event script of the external function call to the COBOL program. This means that if you declare your own variables on top of those automatically generated and used by PowerBridge, you might be redundantly and unnecessarily defining excess local storage. Besides generating the local variables, Power-Bridge generates all necessary conversion statements and syntax requirements. Local variables are a storage-efficient means of utilizing values temporarily. If you are using PowerBridge and not intending to display a variable in a GUI control, and you do not need to access the COBOL value beyond the scope of the current event script from which the external function call was made, we recommend that you use the local PowerScript variable generated by default for your field.

```
COBOL Datatype    PowerBuilder Equivalent Datatype
PIC X String-absolute field sizes handled with Left(string, PIC_size)
 ...or char_array(PIC_size) - (preferable, as the data item is fixed-length)

    PIC 9          Decimal
    PIC S9         Decimal
    PIC 9(4) COMP  Integer
```

```
PIC 9(5)    COMP        Long
PIC 9(n)    COMP-3      Decimal
PIC S9(4)   COMP        Integer
PIC S9(5)   COMP        Decimal
PIC S9(n)   COMP-3      Long
OCCURS                  PowerScript arrays of the same datatype
PIC 9 COMP-1            Real (Floating Point)
PIC 9 COMP-2            Double (Floating Point)
```

Figure 9-5: COBOL-PowerBuilder datatype equivalents in PowerBridge.

PowerScript/COBOL variable naming conventions

We recommend that you generate with a unique name based on the original COBOL data-item Linkage Section name. This is what PowerBridge does, and it seems to work well in terms of reinforcing the data-item usage and association between your PowerBuilder script and the COBOL Linkage Section. Example:

```
01 LS-AF-ACCTNO     PIC X(21)
...in COBOL becomes...
String      LS-AF-ACCTNO
```

In case of COBOL variables with duplicate names, code (or generate using PowerBridge) a unique PowerScript name for each variable, possibly utilizing a naming convention as follows:

```
First elementary field name found: COBOL_elementary_field_name
Second elementary field name found:
ancestor_fieldname_COBOL_elementary_fieldname
Subsequent elementary field names found:
ancestor_fieldname_COBOL_elementary_fieldname_#n
Where:
```

ancestor_fieldname is the name of the group level directly above the elementary_fieldname. _#n represents a generated sequence number used by PowerBridge to guarantee unique field names.

You may decide to choose a different naming convention; however, we recommend that you consider the above when determining your coding standards.

External function call event script: Manual coding considerations

Consider each event script external function call as being composed of, at a minimum, five separate logical sections:

Variable declarations, where you define your work areas prior to the call.

Input from GUI section, where you assign PowerBuilder control.text fields to the variables you are passing through the external function call.

The *external function call* itself.

Error and exception condition handling, where you test the external function call return code for mission success/failure.

Output to the GUI, where you reassign the values from the COBOL program to other Power-Script variables or directly to GUI controls.

These five areas of the external function call are coded using PowerScript statements, edits, functions, and so forth. If you use the PowerBridge product, all of the above is generated automatically based on the Linkage Section data fields found in the COBOL program. A skeleton event script is described in Figure 9-6.

```
(original external function declaration - currently in the Global External
Function Declaration Painter)
------------------------------------------------------------------------+
FUNCTION int ACCTREC(REF string acctkey, REF string acctdate,           |
     REF string acctacty, REF int acctnbr, REF string acctstatus,       |
     REF dec{2} acctdue, REF dec{2} acctoverdue,                        |
     REF string action_ind) library "ACCT.DLL"                          |
------------------------------------------------------------------------+

//Variable declarations
int   acctkey, acctdate, acctacty, acctstatus, action_ind
dec{2} acctdue, acctoverdue
int   acctnbr
...

//Input from GUI
acctdue=INT(sle_acctdue.text)
acctkey=sle_acctkey.text
...

//The external function call
ACCTREC(status,acctkey, acctdate, acctacty, acctnbr, acctstatus, acctdue,
acctoverdue, action_ind)

//Check return code
If action_ind = 'Accept' Then
...
ElseIf action_ind - 'Reject' Then
...
EndIf

//Output to GUI
If action_ind='Accept' Then
 rb_accept.checked=true
ElseIf action_ind='Reject' Then
 rb_accept.reject=true
EndIf
...
```

Figure 9-6: Sections of manually-coded external function scripts.

External function call event script: PowerBridge considerations

When using PowerBridge-generated local variables to map PowerBuilder applications to COBOL fields, PowerBridge generates the following in response to the PowerBuilder COBOL mapping:

PowerScript definitions for the local variables

PowerScript statements to assign graphical controls or PowerScript variables to COBOL fields

PowerScript statements to populate a char_array with the local variables

PowerScript external function call to MF_Sub_Request
(entry point in PowerBridge local .dll)

PowerScript statements to check the return-code from the external function call

PowerScript statements to "unstring" the char_array back into the local variables

PowerScript statements to assign COBOL fields to graphical controls or PowerScript variables

If you are using PowerBridge and you wish to make use of the PowerBridge-generated local variable outside of the external function call in other areas of your event script, it is your responsibility to ensure that the necessary and sufficient user values are assigned to the generated PowerScript definition before the call to MF_Sub_Request takes place. And it is your responsibility to process the returned values correctly after the external function call finishes.

COBOL data item mapping techniques: Detailed discussion

Now that you've seen a basic external function request, it is time to turn our attention once again to the topic of COBOL data item usage in a PowerBuilder GUI application. This section details the various methods and alternatives for COBOL data item mapping in depth, and gives specific examples of ways to map COBOL to GUI. In this section you will be able to see–from the PowerBuilder application's point of view–different methods of COBOL data item utilization and mapping, as well as what is required to complete these tasks.

We will be approaching these techniques by discussing general characteristics of the method, and by listing an example of both PowerBridge-generated code and the manual declarations and assignments necessary to code the PowerScript manually. The listing will follow this format:

```
PowerBridge
COBOL Specification      ParmAssign Spec. Resulting generated code
05 LS-ACCTNO            _____ Definition:_____
Input Assign: _____
Call to Module: _____
Unstring:_____
Output Assign: _____
```

Figure 9-7: Example of assignment specifications.

As listed in Figure 9-7, the COBOL specification relates to the original COBOL Linkage Field. Recall that if you are not using PowerBridge, you will have to recode all complex COBOL records in the USING clause, as a series of 01 fields. The PowerBridge ParmAssign Spec column relates to the window shown in Figure 9-8, and can be ignored if you are coding manually. The resulting generated code refers to what must be written or PowerBridge-generated to complete the technique.

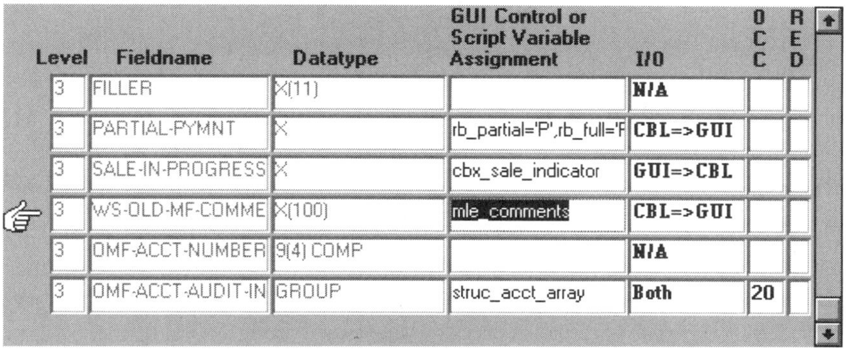

Level	Fieldname	Datatype	GUI Control or Script Variable Assignment	I/O	OCC	RED
3	FILLER	X(11)		N/A		
3	PARTIAL-PYMNT	X	rb_partial='P',rb_full='F'	CBL=>GUI		
3	SALE-IN-PROGRESS	X	cbx_sale_indicator	GUI=>CBL		
3	WS-OLD-MF-COMME	X(100)	mle_comments	CBL=>GUI		
3	OMF-ACCT-NUMBER	9(4) COMP		N/A		
3	OMF-ACCT-AUDIT-IN	GROUP	struc_acct_array	Both	20	

Figure 9-8: PowerBridge ParmAssign Window (used for relating COBOL
fields to PowerScript variables, object attributes, or window controls).

Mapping technique: Assignment to *custom-coded* local, window or global PowerScript variable

Sometimes you will need to store the values returned by your external function call to a COBOL program beyond the scope of the current event script. To do this, you declare the custom variables in your event script. (See Figure 9-5 for help in choosing a PowerScript variable type.) Then manually code the assignment–or using the PowerBridge ParmAssign window as shown in Figure 9-8, assign the COBOL field to a PowerScript global or instance variable in the ParmAssign Window's GUI Control or Script Variable Assignment cell.

Note that for custom-coded variable assignments, whether using PowerBridge or coding manually, it is your responsibility to *match datatypes* correctly between COBOL fields and PowerBuilder variables. See the chart in Figure 9-5 for assistance in doing this. Finally, it is important to remember that COBOL math truncates to the significant digits specified in the COBOL data item Picture clause, while PowerScript decimal math always rounds up. This can make math results between parallel mainframe/PowerBuilder testing runs difficult to reconcile. To avoid this problem, you may add the PowerScript Trunc function to any custom-coded assignment statements you hand-write. Example:

```
custom_variable=Trunc(PowerBridge_generated_variable,COBOL PIC size)
loc_var=Trunc(ls-avg-acctno-amt,2)
```

See the PowerBuilder Function Reference manual or on-line help for more details on the Trunc function.

Mapping technique: Assignment to custom-coded window or global PowerScript structure

To assign a COBOL variable to a field within an existing local, window, or global Power-Script structure, key in the structure name followed by the elementary variable name.

```
PowerBridge
COBOL Specification    ParmAssign Spec. Resulting generated code
05 LS-ACCTNO          struc.win_inst_acctnoDefinition: Local Variable LS-ACCTNO
Input Assign: LS-ACCTNO= struc.win_inst_acctno
Call to MF_Sub_Request: Yes
Unstring: Yes
Output Assign:struc.win_inst_acctno=LS-ACCTNO
```

Figure 9-9: Custom-coded variable mapping chart.

Direct COBOL assignment to PowerBuilder window controls: Value assignment versus attribute assignment

COBOL data values can be integrated and mapped to PowerBuilder windows and window controls in two ways:

Assignment to PowerScript variables/window control .text, etc. Direct assignment to other attributes of the PowerBuilder GUI, such as a window or DataWindow title, menu text, etc. COBOL assignment to window control text is the most direct method of reusing COBOL and integrating COBOL data fields graphically into your PowerBuilder application. We continue our discussion of COBOL mapping techniques with a section on this approach.

Mapping technique: Direct COBOL data-item to GUI control assignment

Often you will want to display the results of a COBOL program's processing directly in a window control, or send the controlname.text data from the GUI into a COBOL program. You may manually assign the fields in the Input Section of your external function request from the event script by coding **variable_to_be_passed = control.text** on the input side, and **control.text = variable_to_be_passed** on the output side (see Figure 9-7). You can also use PowerBridge to generate the assignments by typing the name of the control in the ParmAssign window's GUI Control or Script Variable Assignment cell, or selecting the control name from the DropDownListBox of window controls provided (see the ParmAssign Window in Figure 9-8).

Using PowerBridge to assign fields directly

Upon input to the COBOL program, PowerBridge assigns the text portion of your window control to the PowerBridge-generated local variables before passing the data to the COBOL Linkage fields. Example:

```
ls_af_acctno=Left(sle_acctno.text,21) ** length determined by original
PIC(xx)
```

Upon output from the COBOL program, PowerBridge assigns the text portion of your window control to the COBOL Linkage field as passed through the PowerBridge-generated local variable. Example:

```
sle_acctno.text=ls-af-acctno
```

```
PowerBridge
COBOL Specification      ParmAssign Spec. Resulting generated code
05 LS-ACCTNO             sle_acctnoDefinition: Local Variable LS-ACCTNO
Input Assign: LS-ACCTNO= LEFT(sle_acctno.text,21)Call to MF_Sub_Request: Yes
Unstring: Yes
Output Assign: sle_acctno.text=LS-ACCTNO
```

Figure 9-10: GUI control assignment mapping chart.

Mapping technique: Direct attribute assignment

As mentioned previously, COBOL data values may be integrated into other aspects of your GUI application by assigning COBOL Linkage Section values directly to object control attributes. This allows you to generate x/y window-control-coordinate placement, window-control labels, window titles, and other presentation logic options dynamically from COBOL program Linkage values.

All PowerBuilder window controls may have their attributes modified using the above technique. However, not all PowerBuilder controls are supported by COBOL due to unsupported PowerBuilder datatypes such as boolean and graphic. Figure 9-11 lists the supported window controls and PowerBridge processing. It also describes the types of PowerScript statements commonly used to assign values to these objects.

```
Window control type  Support Prefix Specification PowerScript code
Checkbox   Value   cbx_  cbx_name='literal'  if COBOL-field='literal'
cbx_controlname.checked=true

Attrib   cbx_ cbx_name.attr                    cbx_name.attr=COBOL-field
CommandButton Attrib  cb_  cb_name.attr         cb_name.attr=COBOL-field
DataWindowControl  Value  dwc_  dwc_name,columnname  INSERTROW(current row)an
SET/GETITEMxxxx(row,columnname)
Attrib  dwc_  dwc_name.attr                     dwc_name.attr=COBOL-field
DropDownListBox Value ddlb_ ddlb_name              ADDITEM(COBOL-field
Attrib ddlb_ ddlb_name.attr                     ddlb_name.attr=COBOL-field
EditMask Value em_ em_name                       em_name.text=COBOL-field
Attrib em_ em_name.attr                          em_name.attr=COBOL-field
Graph Value gr_ gr_name=X/Y For/Next & X/Y coordinate script
Attrib gr_ gr_name.attr                          gr_name.attr=COBOL-field
GroupBox Attrib g_ g_name.attr                     g_name.attr=COBOL-field
HScrollBar Attrib hsb_ hsb_name.attr             hsb_name.attr=COBOL-field
ListBox Value lb_ lb_name                           ADDITEM(COBOL-field
  Attrib lb_ lb_name.attr                        lb_name.attr=COBOL-field
MultiLineEdit Value mle_ mle_name               mle_name.text=COBOL-field
  Attrib mle_ mle_name.attr                      mle_name.attr=COBOL-field
Oval Attrib oval_ oval_name.attr                oval_name.attr=COBOL-field
Picture Attrib p_ p_name.attr                     p_name.attr=COBOL-field
PictureButton Attrib pb_ pb_name.attr            pb_name.attr=COBOL-field
RadioButton Value rb_ rb_name='literal'       if COBOL-field='literal'
 rb_controlname.checked=true
Attrib rb_ rb_name.attr                          rb_name.attr=COBOL-field
Rectangle Attrib r_ r_name.attr                    r_name.attr=COBOL-field
RoundRectangle Attrib rr_ rr_name.attr           rr_name.attr=COBOL-field
SingleLineEdit Value sle_ sle_name              sle_name.text=COBOL-field
  Attrib sle_ sle_name.attr                      sle_name.attr=COBOL-field
StaticText Value st_ st_name                     st_name.text=COBOL-field
  Attrib st_ st_name.attr                        st_name.attr=COBOL-field
UserObject  Attrib uo_ uo_name.attr              uo_name.attr=COBOL-field
```

```
VScrollBar  Attrib vsb_ vsb_name.attr       vsb_name.attr=COBOL-field
```

Figure 9-11: GUI control attribute assignments.

A list of PowerBuilder object attributes, which can be modified by COBOL program values, is shown below in Figure 9-12. You may assign string values from your COBOL program's Linkage Section to any of these attributes. See the PowerBuilder Objects and Controls Reference Manual for more information on the object attributes described below.

```
PowerBuilder Object  PowerBridge Supported Attributes
Application  dwMessageTitle
  AppName
  MicroHelpDefault

Window  Icon
  MenuName
  Pointer
  Tag
  Title
  ToolbarTitle

Menu    MicroHelp
  Tag
  Text/ToolbarItemText

Standard Controls DragIcon
  CheckBox FaceName
  CommandButton Pointer
  GroupBox Tag
  MultiLineEdit Text
  RadioButton
  SingleLineEdit/StaticText

DataWindow Control DataObject
& Graph Control DragIcon
  Icon
  Tag
  Title

List Controls  DragIcon
  ListBox   FaceName
  DropDownListBox  Item[n] - note, must be explicit array occurrence
  Pointer
  Tag
  Text

Extended Controls  DisplayData
  EditMask DragIcon
  FaceName
  Mask
  Spin
  Pointer
  Tag
  Text

Scrollbar Controls  DragIcon
  HScrollbar Pointer
  VScrollbar Tag
```

```
Picture Controls    DragIcon
  Picture FaceName
  PictureButton PictureName
  Pointer
  Tag
  Text - PictureButton only

UserObject ClassName
  DragIcon
  Pointer
  Tag/Text
```

Figure 9-12: String-defined attribute assignments by PowerBuilder object.

PowerBuilder object assignment: PowerBridge considerations

When you enter an attribute along with a PowerBuilder object in the ParmAssign window (Figure 9-8), the entire specification is used "verbatim" during the code generation process. PowerBridge makes no attempt to determine if what you have typed is logically correct or incorrect, spelled correctly, or whether the PowerBuilder object indeed even exists. If you make a typo, the PowerBuilder compiler will catch it. But, of course, this is after code generation has completed and you have inserted the generated script into your PowerScript event script and tried to save or compile your code.

```
PowerBridge
COBOL Specification      ParmAssign Spec. Resulting generated code
05 LS-ACCTNO            w_acct.title Definition: Local Variable w_acct_title
  Input Assign: w_acct_title=w_acct.title
  Call to MF_Sub_Request: Yes
  Unstring: Yes
  Output Assign: w_acct.title=w_acct_title
```

Figure 9-13: Direct COBOL-GUI-attribute assignment mapping chart.

Mapping technique: COBOL group item processing techniques

Most PowerBuilder-to-COBOL data mapping is done on an elementary field-for-field basis. That is, each COBOL field with a Picture clause is mapped directly to a single variable or GUI control. But what if you know that all of the fields in a Linkage Section group are related and can be utilized intelligently by a single PowerScript variable or GUI control? To specify COBOL Group item processing, code PowerScript assignment statements that concatenate the elementary fields (see PowerBridge-generated example below). Or if you are using PowerBridge, enter the name of a PowerScript variable or PowerBuilder window control in the Group area (a COBOL field without a Picture clause), in the GUI Control or in the Script Variable Assignment cell on the ParmAssign window. When PowerBridge receives such a specification in the ParmAssign window, it concatenates all lower-level elementary field assignments into a single text processing operation as shown below.

```
COBOL specification:

05 DATE-WS.
10 DATE-MM  PIC X(2).
10 DATE-DD  PIC X(2).
10 DATE-YY  PIC X(2).

Assignment specification:
```

```
PowerBridge
COBOL Specification ParmAssign Spec. Resulting generated code
05 DATE-WS  sle_date  Definition: Local Variables: date-mm, date-dd, date-yy
  Input Assign: date_ws = mid(sle_date.text,1,2)+
     mid(sle_date.text,3,2)+
     mid(sle_date.text,5,2)
  Call to MF_Sub_Request: Yes
  Unstring: Yes
  Output Assign: sle_date.text=
  sle_date-mm+sle_date_dd+date-date-yy
```

Figure 9-14: COBOL group data-item mapping chart.

Mapping Technique: Listbox processing techniques

You may assign COBOL table values, as specified in the OCCURS statement, to Power-Builder graphical controls in one of two ways: single elementary fields or specific occurrences within a table may be assigned directly to GUI controls, or the entire contents of a COBOL table may be used to populate a listbox or DropDownListBox. By writing your own FOR/NEXT or DO loops you may code for this technique. Or, if you are using PowerBridge, simply enter an **lb_** or **ddlb_** control name in the ParmAssign Window control (Figure 9-8).

```
PowerBridge
COBOL Specification     ParmAssign Spec. Resulting generated code
05 ACCT-NBR           lb_acctnoDefinition: Local Variable: acct-nbr[20]
    OCCURS 20Input Assign: acct-nbr[1]=lb_acctno.SelectedItem()
    (if Listbox)
Input Assign: acct-nbr[1]=ddlb_acctno.text
    (if DropDownList)
  Call to MF_Sub_Request: Yes
  Unstring: Yes
  Output Assign: For I = 1 to 20
  lb_acctno(I)=acct-nbr[I]
  Next
```

Figure 9-15: COBOL OCCURS data-item mapping chart.

Note that on input to the COBOL program, you will most likely use the *selected item* from the listbox (or ddlb_name.text) portion of the control, which can be assigned to a Linkage Section data item. That is, mapping the entire contents of a listbox or DropDownListBox into a COBOL OCCURS table upon input into the COBOL program is a technique with little real-world-applicability. Few GUI applications utilize listboxes and DropDownListBoxes in this manner. They are almost exclusively built programmatically for output user selection.

In the unlikely event that you do need to pass the entire contents of a listbox to a COBOL program that is accessed using PowerBridge, you can always script your own FOR/NEXT processing to assign arrays to any combination of fields prior to the call of the COBOL program. To do so, simply find the area in the generated script documented as *//*** Window Control Input Assignments ****, and place code to loop through the default-declared local variable group, assigning fields from the listbox. For example:

```
For I = 1 to ListBoxname.TotalItems()
COBOL_field_name[I]=ListBoxname(I)
Next
```

Mapping technique: Generated *.checked* logic for window "option" controls (radio buttons and check boxes)

Most GUI applications present the user with decision options graphically, in the form of check boxes or radio buttons, depending on the exclusivity of choices (see the PowerBuilder User Guide, Chapter 7, "Working with Controls," for more information on this topic). You can either write your own custom code, or have PowerBridge generate the required Power-Script *.checked* logic upon output processing. Then map the necessary literal values automatically on input processing by simply entering the control name followed by an equal sign (=) and the literal value you wish assigned or tested for. As an example:

```
GUI_controlname='literal value'.
```

Reengineering COBOL 88-levels

Creating and assigning radio buttons and check boxes to COBOL 88-level data-item conditionals is a particularly effective technique for mapping the semantic equivalent of COBOL 88-level fields to GUIs. 88-levels in COBOL are conditional statements coded as part of the Linkage Section data-item definition.

The reengineering technique for *multiple 88-levels* is to assign each 88-level under a data-item to a different radio button, and surround the entire set with a GroupBox control. This isolates the scope of the radio button exclusivity to radio buttons within the groupbox (see the PowerBuilder User Guide, Chapter 7, for more information on radio button behavior). The reengineering technique *for single conditional 88-levels* (one 88 per data-item) is to map each 88 to its own CheckBox control.

```
PowerBridge
COBOL Specification     ParmAssign Spec. Resulting generated code
05 PAYMENT-IND     rb_a=`Y',rb_b=`F'  Definition: Local Variable: PAYMENT-IND
 Input Assign: If rb_a.checked = true then
PAYMENT-IND=`Y'
elseif rb_b.checked = true then
PAYMENT-IND=`F'
  End if
Call to MF_Sub_Request: Yes
Unstring: Yes
Output Assign: If PAYMENT-IND=`Y' then
  rb_a.checked = true
elseif PAYMENT-IND=`F' then
   rb_b.checked = true
End if
```

Figure 9-16:COBOL 88-level (GUI option-control) mapping chart.

Mapping complex controls

COBOL Group-level OCCURS, which is a group field that both OCCURS some number of times and contains elementary items, can logically be mapped to a PowerBuilder DataWindow. You may either code the necessary GETITEMxxx/SETITEMxxx statements, or use the IMPORTFILE DataWindow function to populate a previously defined DataWindow and DataWindow control with COBOL elements. It must be noted here that you will need to define the DataWindow as an *External*-type DataWindow in order to access non-relational data sources (see chapter 14 in the PowerBuilder User Guide for information on how to define External-type DataWindows).

Specifying Input/Output, Both, or Not/Applicable (ParmAssign Window)

For each field, you should consider specifying an "input/output assignment direction." The assignment direction dictates whether the window control and script variable assignments to the default local variables occurs before or after the call to the COBOL program. You may specify that the data gets passed using one of the following four choices:

upon input to the COBOL program (**GUI=>>COBOL**),
upon output from the COBOL program back to the PowerBuilder GUI (**COBOL=>>GUI**),
upon both input and output (**Both**), or
not assign values (**Not Applicable - N/A**).

Note that the perspective used in these examples to view the data assignment I/O direction is taken from the COBOL program (Input to the program, Output from the program, Input to/ Output from the program, etc.). Note also that in the absence of a clear understanding of whether to pass data in a given direction, you should default to passing in **Both** directions. Specifying Input/Output or Not Applicable is primarily a performance decision. This is because your PowerBuilder application must send the COBOL program, at a minimum, a data value "placeholder" for each elementary field within an 01-level Linkage item, refer-enced in the Procedure Division USING clause. PowerBridge defaults to assigning a single space, for PIC X fields, and a single zero, for numeric fields, to the local variables passed to your COBOL program using the char_array. Passing a single byte/field is obviously more efficient than transmitting multiple bytes, in terms of network I/O and data manipulation (pre- and post-call). The key to using I/O assignment direction is an understanding of the I/O processing needs of your COBOL logic, at the field level, in order to take advantage of the performance benefits of specifying GUI=>>COBOL, COBOL=>>GUI, or N/A.

One way to analyze I/O processing in COBOL Linkage fields, is to use the CSI facility of the Micro Focus Workbench. CSI allows you to analyze the use of all COBOL variables, including Linkage elements, and generate a report which documents the way a data-item is used throughout a COBOL program (see Figure 9-9). To generate such an analysis report, compile your program with the CSI directive (CSI is almost always a default directive for COBOL language dialects). Enter the Workbench, and load your program into the editor. Using the *Character-based* Workbench Editor:

Press F2-COBOL
Place your cursor on the field you wish to analyze
Press F6-CSI-at-cursor
Press F4-compress

```
 ─                           COBOL Workbench                        ▼ ◆
   38  _    05  OMF-ACCTNO                         PIC   X(21).      ◄═══Defn
   85   '   MOVE LS-AF-ACCTNO TO OMF-ACCTNO.                         ◄═══Mod
   94       IF  OMF-ACCTNO > '400' AND < '500'          AND          ◄═══Test
  103     . IF· OMF-ACCTNO > '400'·AND < '500'          AND          ◄═══Test
  112       IF  OMF-ACCTNO > '100' AND < '200'          AND          ◄═══Test
  121       IF  OMF-ACCTNO > '900' AND < '994'          AND          ◄═══Test
  130       IF  OMF-ACCTNO > '999' AND < '1500'         AND          ◄═══Test
  139  ·    IF  OMF-ACCTNO > '000' AND < '120'          AND          ◄═══Test




                                          ┌Data─────────────────size─refs┐
                                          │OMF-ACCTNO PIC X(21)      21  .8m│
                                          │Working-Storage               │
CSI: OMF-ACCTNO──────────────Executes Exec-from──────────All─────
F1=help F2=posn-exit F4=expand    F5=enter F6=csr F7/F8=prev/next F9/F10 <‹/›> Esc
exec-From eXecutes Window Hide Locate/Return Tag Options Query Display
```

Figure 9-17: CSI data analysis and usage report.

You will see a report similar to the one shown in Figure 9-17.

Lines that show a usage attribute of "mod" describe where a field is being written over by some other field or literal. Lines that show a usage attribute of "use" describe where a field is being moved to some other field. Lines that show a usage attribute of "test" describe where a field is being compared. Lines that show a usage attribute of "def" describe where a field is defined (Data Division).

You can make use of the information in this report by double-clicking on each field in Linkage from within CSI, and viewing a compressed (F4) report showing only the program lines which reference the field. If, throughout the entire program, a Linkage data field is only defined (Def), you can specify N/A as its PowerBridge I/O attribute. If, throughout the entire program, a Linkage data field is defined and only used or tested (Use, Test), you can specify GUI=>>COBOL as its PowerBridge I/O attribute. If the Linkage field is defined and only modified (Mod), you can specify COBOL=>>GUI as its PowerBridge I/O attribute. However if a field is defined, used/tested, and modified, you will need to transmit the data in Both directions (Both).

OCCURS: COBOL table handling options

COBOL Linkage fields with OCCURS clauses, commonly known as COBOL tables, are normally displayed as listboxes or DropDownListBoxes in PowerBuilder. As shown in previous examples, you can assign these tables to listboxes/DropDownListBoxes directly by coding the ADDITEM() statements manually, or by using PowerBridge, you can automatically generate the code. If PowerBridge finds an OCCURS clause attached to a data item, it places a number in the OCC column of the ParmAssign Window (Figure 9-8). The number displayed corresponds to the number of occurrences designated on the field in the Linkage Section definition. PowerBridge allows you to reuse COBOL OCCURS in several different ways. Before we look at these options, let's define some terms surrounding the use of COBOL table handling in the context of PowerBuilder access.

OCCURS: Terms and concepts

Like most third generation languages, COBOL supports a wide variety of table definitions and table-handling facilities. PowerBridge does not support, through automated code generation, all possible COBOL table-handling options and semantics. Figure 9-11 lists COBOL OCCURS definitions and PowerBridge's support. In addition to the information in Figure 9-11, some terms and vocabulary should be established before continuing:

Single-dimension elementary OCCURS

A single-dimension elementary OCCURS is a single COBOL elementary field with a single OCCURS clause attached, that is not part of some other OCCURS structure. No higher-level data item to which this elementary field belongs has an OCCURS clause.

Single-dimension elementary OCCURS fields are referenced using a single subscript or single index (the COBOL "INDEXED BY" clause).

```
05 PROD-LINE-TABLE  OCCURS 20 TIMES PIC X(2).
   ...
      MOVE 'AL' TO PROD-LINE-TABLE(SUB).
```

PowerBuilder access to single-dimension elementary OCCURS is available as follows:

1. Through local variable arrays

Single-dimension elementary COBOL OCCURS fields can be processed through PowerBuilder single-dimension fixed-size arrays.

```
05 PROD-LINE-TABLE  OCCURS 20 TIMES PIC X(2).
...becomes...
string PROD-LINE-TABLE[20]
```

2. Through direct assignment to PowerBuilder listbox and DropDownListBox controls.

You may assign a single-dimension elementary OCCURS field directly to a PowerBuilder listbox or DropDownListBox graphical control through manual coding using the ADDITEM()/SELECTEDITEM() statements. Or the statements can be generated with PowerBridge by entering the control name in the ParmAssign screen (Figure 9-8). Note that in either case, a single-dimension array is used to interface the COBOL program to your PowerBuilder application.

```
For I = 1 to 20
ddlb_prod_line.AddItem(prod-line-table[I])
Next
```

Also, recall from a previous discussion that the options to populate listboxes from single-dimension elementary OCCURS, are generally used in *Output processing* (data transmitted from COBOL and assigned to GUI controls). Input processing options are usually limited to assigning the first occurrence of a table to the SelectedItem(), from a listbox or .text attribute of a DropDownListBox.

Elementary occurrences of a table

You may also assign specific occurrences of a COBOL table to specific controls or Power-Script variables. To do this, code the statements manually, referencing the specific array element occurrence you wish to access (PROD-LINE-TABLE[4] or PROD-LINE-TABLE[SUB]).

Multi-dimension elementary OCCURS

Multi-dimension elementary OCCURS are COBOL elementary fields with a single OCCURS clause attached, that are part of some other OCCURS structure. This means a higher-level data item to which the elementary fields belong also has an OCCURS clause. Multi-dimension elementary OCCURS fields are referenced using the same number of subscripts as make up the table dimensions. PowerBridge supports tables with a maximum of two dimensions in the current release; that is, structures that "OCCUR within an OCCURS" are supported. Three levels of table nesting or more are not supported. However, three- and greater- dimensioned tables are supported using PowerScript arrays, so you may be able to use manual coding techniques to handle situations where a program's Linkage Section contains three-level tables. It should be noted that few instances of three- or higher-dimensioned COBOL tables exist in the Linkage Section of production applications.

Below is an example of a two-dimension COBOL table and reference to a specific field with a two-level subscript.

```
03 REC-HIGHER-LEVEL   OCCURS 30 TIMES.
05 PROD-LINE-TABLE   OCCURS 20 TIMES PIC X(2).
   . . .
MOVE `AL' TO PROD-LINE-TABLE(SUB-1, SUB-2).
```

You may manually code PowerScript to manipulate two-dimensional tables, which are fixed-size, in any way you wish. PowerBridge code generation supports multi-dimension elementary OCCURS data-items only through automated local array variables and declarations. For each multi-dimensional elementary field encountered in your COBOL program, PowerBridge will generate a PowerScript array of the same dimension. Example:

```
03 REC-HIGHER-LEVEL   OCCURS 30 TIMES.
05 PROD-LINE-TABLE   OCCURS 20 TIMES PIC X(2).
...becomes...
string   REC-HIGHER-LEVEL.PROD-LINE-TABLE[30, 20]
```

There is no PowerBridge-generated direct assignment of two-dimensional COBOL tables to GUI controls, or detailed assignments of specific occurrences within a two-dimensional COBOL table to GUI controls or custom Script variables. In terms of the ParmAssign screen, this means that the Window Control Assignment field must be left blank for two-dimension elementary OCCURS data-items.

Single-dimension complex OCCURS

Single-dimension complex OCCURS are COBOL elementary fields that are part of a group which has a single OCCURS clause attached, but are not part of some other OCCURS structure. No higher-level data item to which the elementary fields belong has an OCCURS clause. Think of single-dimension complex OCCURS fields as similar to PowerScript "structure-arrays." Example:

```
05 PROD-LINE-TABLE  OCCURS 20 TIMES.
10 PROD-NBR  PIC X(2).
10 PROD-DESC  PIC X(20).
  ...
MOVE 'AL' TO PROD-NBR(SUB-1).
MOVE 'CARRIAGE BOLT' TO PROD-DESC(SUB-1).
```

PowerBridge supports single-dimensional complex OCCURS through automated local array variable generation and declarations, listbox processing, and DataWindow generation (see examples and discussion in previous sections of this chapter).

Local array variable declarations

For each elementary field that is part of a single-dimensional complex OCCURS, manually code (or generate through PowerBridge) a PowerScript array of the same size, datatype, dimension, and name.

```
05 PROD-LINE-TABLE  OCCURS 20 TIMES.
10 PROD-NBR  PIC X(2).
10 PROD-DESC  PIC X(20).
...generates...
string PROD-NBR[20]
string PROD-DESC[20]
```

It should be noted that you may also code and utilize PowerScript "array-structures" for single-dimension complex OCCURS processing.

Listbox and DropDownListBox Support

Like the single-dimension elementary OCCURS options, you may assign each elementary field that is part of a single-dimension complex OCCURS directly to a PowerBuilder listbox or DropDownListBox graphical control. To code this technique manually, write the necessary ADDITEM() statements referencing your array-variables or array-structures. To specify this process using PowerBridge, simply type the name of the listbox or DropDownListBox control in the ParmAssign window (Figure 9-8) control area.

DataWindows support

Because a single-dimension complex OCCURS data item so closely resembles a PowerBuilder DataWindow object, where each occurrence represents a row and each field represents a column, you may consider assigning values from such complex COBOL tables directly to PowerBuilder DataWindows. If you are manually coding, create the necessary GETITEMxxx and/or SETITEMxxx PowerScript functions to assign local array-variables or array-structures to the DataWindows. Using PowerBridge, this technique is supported on two levels:

Direct assignment to existing DataWindow objects. You specify the DataWindow control name followed by a comma and the DataWindow column name where you wish to place the

COBOL field values. Then PowerBridge generates GetItem() functions on input processing, or InsertRow() and SetItem() functions on output processing. Automated DataWindow generation. PowerBridge generates the DataWindow object and imports it into a dynamically-created PowerBuilder library (.pbl).

Multi-dimension complex record OCCURS

Multi-dimension complex record OCCURS are tables which contain tables (two-dimensional tables), along with the one-dimensional occurrences. Multi-dimensional complex record OCCURS are extremely complex data structures, and are best handled through local array variable manipulation. Consider the following complex COBOL record definition:

```
03 REC-HIGHER-LEVEL  OCCURS 30 TIMES.
05 ACCT-NBR          PIC X(75).
05 ACCT-VALUE        PIC S9(12)V99 COMP-3.
05 ACCT-TERRITORIES PIC X(08) OCCURS 12 TIMES.
05 PROD-LINE-TABLE   OCCURS 20 TIMES.
10 PROD-NBR          PIC X(2).
10 PROD-DESC         PIC X(20).
```

Note that this COBOL record portion begins with a group field that OCCURS 30 times (REC-HIGHER-LEVEL). Within this group field there are two elementary fields (ACCT-NBR, and ACCT-VALUE). Two tables–an elementary table, ACCT-TERRITORIES, and a complex table, PROD-LINE-TABLE– follow.

Local array variable declarations

For each field that is part of a multi-dimension complex OCCURS, code variables and arrays to match the COBOL structure definition. PowerBridge generates PowerScript arrays of the same size, datatype, and name. For the above complex record portion, PowerBridge would generate the following:

```
string ACCT-NBR[30]
dec{2} ACCT-VALUE[30]
string ACCT-TERRITORIES[30, 12]
string PROD-NBR[30, 20]
string PROD-DESC[30, 20]
```

Listbox and DropDownListBox Support

Like the single-dimension elementary OCCURS options, you could consider assigning each elementary field that is part of a multi-dimensional complex OCCURS, *that is referenced by a single subscript,* directly to a PowerBuilder listbox or DropDownListBox graphical control. Code the necessary ADDITEM() statements–or for PowerBridge users, utilize the ParmAssign screen in the Window Control or Variable field to type in the name of the listbox. Consider carefully the *meaning* of the data passed in the arrays that are embedded in complex structures. Often low-level tables with two or three dimensions do not represent atomic and/or normalized lists, and should not be assigned to separate and distinguishable graphical objects.

Summary: COBOL table handling in PowerBridge

While not directly supporting all available COBOL table-handling constructs and facilities, PowerBuilder datatypes and structures offer many different options for COBOL table handling. The options available depend on whether the COBOL table is one or two-dimensional. It also depends if the table is simple; where the OCCURS is coded on the field with the Picture clause, or complex; in which the OCCURS is part of the group item containing the field with the Picture clause. Figure 9-18 below shows a list of the available options for COBOL handling in the current release of PowerBridge.

```
COBOL Table Definition             Array Variables  ListBox DataWindow
  - Simple table, one dimension        X              X
  - Simple table, two dimensions       X
  - Complex table, one dimension       X              X        X
  - Complex table, two dimensions      X
```

Figure 9-18: Support for COBOL table handling.

RED: Handling COBOL data redefinitions

The Redefines clause allows COBOL developers to assign a given area of storage to different datatypes, field definitions, and so forth. For example, a storage area used to hold a string PIC X(100) could be redefined, for a given record type, to be used as ten 10-byte numeric fields, or as four 25-byte table occurrences. Redefines use evolved from a period of mainframe technology when storage was scarce.

Redefines presents an interesting dilemma to PowerBuilder access developers. In COBOL, redefinition of storage is used for a given process and is determined dynamically at runtime by instructions inserted by the COBOL compiler. In defining an interface to a particular storage area, whether using PowerBridge or coding manually, you will have to choose one, and only one, redefinition for each external function call. Or you may simplify matters by choosing the most basic string-defined redefinition and map, probably through concatenation of data elements into the string, and passing them into the COBOL program.

If you are coding manual interfaces to COBOL programs, watch out for Redefined storage, and follow the instructions above. Either choose a given redefinition and stick with it throughout your event script, or code PowerScript statements to handle multiple redefinitions inside your event script before the external function call. If you are using PowerBridge and a Linkage Section data-item has a REDEFINES clause, a red "R" is displayed in the ParmAssign Window column indicating that additional redefinitions of the field may be selected. Double-click your cursor on the field which is Redefined, and you will be presented with a list of the COBOL redefinitions for your field taken from the Linkage Section. Select the redefinition you want for the COBOL data-item by double-clicking over the field. After selecting a Redefinition for a field, your ParmAssign screen is updated to reflect the data-item selected in the Redefine menu.

Considerations for redefined fields

It must be pointed out that OSVS COBOL allows you to redefine a field with a shorter total picture length than the original data-item. A longer redefined length is not allowed, but a shorter length is. While this practice might be considered poor programming, it probably does occur in some applications. PowerBridge does not support this COBOL practice. All redefines must be the same length as all other redefines, and the same length as the original defined field. Microsoft Windows GPFs may occur if redefined fields of shorter length are passed to COBOL programs through PowerBridge.

This completes our section on mapping techniques and assigning PowerBuilder objects to COBOL Linkage fields. We end this chapter with a short description of PowerBridge.

Micro Focus® Bridge Technology™ Version 1.0

Micro Focus Bridge Technology is Microsoft Windows™-based client/sever *code-construction middleware*. It allows developers to generate distributed external function calls, including all .dlls necessary for client Windows applications running on the desktop. This allows Windows applications to interoperate and communicate with COBOL and CICS application components running (on the desktop) in a networked architecture, or on the mainframe. Bridge Technology developer components integrate into the PowerBuilder development toolset, and from a developer's perspective, are indistinguishable from the base PowerBuilder product. This means that a PowerBuilder developer using Bridge to access COBOL components can maintain the high standards of productivity and ease-of-use facilitated by the underlying toolset. All of the COBOL access routines are generated in a simple point-and-click process, with little to no 4GL script writing or COBOL reengineering necessary.

Bridge Technology provides an extended range of distributed computing environments and architectures. Client/server developers using Bridge Technology™ in conjunction with existing production Micro Focus® runtime environments and add-on software products can place COBOL/CICS processes or data quite literally anywhere; running standalone (local), running remote-networked, and running from the mainframe. Data can be separated from process, providing three-tier architecture solutions as well as the ability to rightsize your COBOL and CICS procedures and non-relational data to the platform and operating system of your choice.

Examples of application architectures made possible include: 16-bit Windows client to 16-bit Windows COBOL or CICS routine running locally; 16-bit Windows client to 16- *or 32-* bit server-based COBOL or CICS routine running on any of the supported platforms and protocol; 16-bit Windows client to mainframe server COBOL or CICS routine running on any of the supported platforms and protocols. All of the above COBOL subroutines or CICS transactions, running in any of the above mentioned platforms, may in turn be reading and/or updating relational *and non-relational* data sources such as: VSAM files, QSAM files, IMS databases, and DB2 databases. If the mainframe server architecture is chosen, Windows client applications may even access legacy databases such as CA-IDMS™, ADABAS, CA-Datacom/DB™, etc.

Testing of cross-platform distributed applications is facilitated through the use of the Micro Focus debugging tools Animator and Xilerator, and Bridge's own administration and built-in trace facilities. Using existing Micro Focus production runtime systems, Bridge facilitates nearly all combinations of local-/remote-/mainframe-based process and data distribution.

Bridge Technology™ supported platforms and required software:

Development environment

Windows client:
- Micro Focus *Workbench*™ 3.2 (or later) license:
* COBOL compiler, Link support
* Xilerator - Source level Debugger
* External File Handling
MCOV3 Thin client

Micro Focus Business Server

OS/2 16 bit
- Workbench with MCO v3
OS/2 32 bit
- COBOL SDK with MCO v3.2 (beta)
Win/NT
- None

Unix Versions

- SCO Unix 3.2 v4.2
- Unix System V Rel 3.0
- Unix System V Rel 4.0
- IBM AIX V3.2.5
- OSF/1
- Novell UnixWare
- Sun Solaris 2.3

Communications protocols supported:

Windows client to OS/2 server

- IPX,
- NetBios
- NamedPipes
- TCP/IP

Windows client to unix server

- TCP/IP

Server to MVS host connectivity

- LU6.2 APPC

Remote file support:

Bridge support remote file support through FileShare

- FileShare - OS/2
- FileShare NLM/3.x Novell
- FileShare/CICS MVS/ESA APPC support

CHAPTER 10

Using PowerBuilder with Multiple Data Sources in a Distributed Client/Server Environment

By Al Lucas

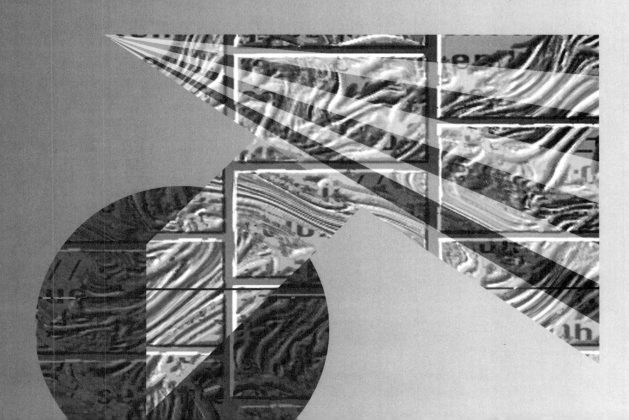

Using PowerBuilder with Multiple Data Sources in a Distributed Client/Server Environment

by **Al Lucas**

In a distributed client/server environment, one can no longer assume a single connection to a data source. More and more circumstances arise where data may have to be retrieved from either more than one database on a server, more than one server, or even more than one network. It is even possible that data may be accessed from RPCs or other distributed sources.

For example, many organizations are entering the client/server world while still maintaining a large amount of data on mainframe systems. Often referred to as "legacy data", this information is often the critical underlying superstructure of any client/server deployment. Within these systems are long running tracking and management, personnel, and accounting systems. Client/server is well suited to the Decision Support access to this information. Timely access to legacy data, in addition to local server information, is often critically necessary. Otherwise, massive amounts of data might have to be replicated across the enterprise.

Another "opportunity" arises when multiple client/server systems must interact. Information in a variety of servers may need to be combined into reports and analyses. PowerBuilder may be used to facilitate this access.

It is even conceivable that the server from which a table is accessed may change, depending on the context of a transaction. For example, local personnel information may be accessible from a table (using server.database.owner.object syntax):

localserver1.employee.dbo.employee

and on a company–wide basis from headquarters:

companyserver.allemps.dbo.employee

A variety of techniques may be used to hide the differences in the data sources, allowing the developer and user to concentrate on the analysis of the data returned, and not from whence the data has come.

PowerBuilder Facilities for Transaction and Multiple Connections

PowerBuilder provides a variety of tools for operating in a multiple database client/server environment. Transaction objects, embedded SQL commands with the "using" verb, and DataWindow mapping all provide useful capabilities.

A transaction object is a PowerBuilder data type used to store connection information for a particular server. Information in the object is used for the initial connection, and the messages from the server are returned to the application through the object. This object is fundamental to maintaining connections to multiple data sources.

A particular application may have multiple connections to a server by maintaining multiple transaction objects. A single connection is often maintained through the predefined Power-Builder variable, SQLCA. Multiple connections often name their transaction objects in a standardized manner, such as gtr_connect1 (for global transaction connection 1).

Embedded SQL may use multiple transaction objects by making use of the "using" clause of most embedded SQL operations:

```
// single transaction
connect;
if sqlca.sqlcode < 0 then return;
select count(*) from table1;
commit;

// multiple transaction
transaction ltr_1,ltr_2

// init the transactions
ltr_1 = create transaction // use create to alloc objects
ltr_2 = create transaction
f_init_xacts(ltr_1,ltr_2)// call function to set DBMS, etc

connect using ltr_1; // do the connects
if ltr_1.sqlcode < 0 then return;

connect using ltr_2;
if ltr_2.sqlcode < 0 then return;

// actually get something
select count(*) into :ll_cnt1 from table1 using ltr_1;
select count(*) into :ll_cnt2 from table1 using ltr_2;
commit using ltr_1; // not necessary but nice, releases resources
commit using ltr_2;
```

In the case of DataWindows, any DataWindow may connect to variety of databases, assuming that the necessary tables and views are available in the underlying databases, and the syntax underlying the DataWindow, i.e. joins, aggregates, etc. are all consistent with both underlying database engines. (In most cases, ANSI SQL is a minimal set from which to build generic SQL statements.)

Scripts, fired by the retrieve_start event, may be used to dynamically associate a DataWindow with a particular data source.

```
// if data is local, connect locally else connect to the enterprise db
string ls_src

ls_src = f_get_data_source(dw_1) // determine the table locs for this dw
if ls_src = 'L' then // local data source
dw_1.setTransObject(gtr_local)
else // enterprise data source
dw_1.setTransObject(gtr_enterprise)
end if
```

SQL differences

Differences in how SQL is used on different platforms contributes to the problem encountered when trying to build applications using data from multiple sources. Differences in object naming, facilities available on a server, implementation, syntax, data definition language, commenting, and system table technique differences, are some of the issues you should be aware of.

Object naming

A fundamental difference in vendor SQL syntaxes exists in naming objects. Two predominant approaches exist:

server.user.object: (Examples: DB2, Oracle, Gupta)

server.database.owner.object: (Example: SYBASE)

Usually this can be overcome by authenticating the owner of the objects in the database, allowing the objects to be referenced simply as "objectname.column". Sometimes though, this may be difficult, particularly if multiple users must access data objects.

Some vendors, such as SYBASE, provide aliasing abilities which allow a user or member of a group to be aliased to a particular user id. This makes all objects owned by the alias appear to be "local" objects.

Facilities available on a particular server

SQL engines may differ in the fundamental range of services they provide. For example, from a Relational Integrity (RI) standpoint, the ability to manipulate triggers can have a profound effect on the SQL used by the server. If triggers are available, RI may be handled by the server; if not, all RI may need to be handled by the client.

Stored Procedures (SP) are another useful facility which can be used for purposes such as maintaining the Unit of Work or accessing tables permitted to the Stored Procedure, but not the specific user. These capabilities are used through the execute SQL facilities of Power-Builder.

In addition, dynamic SQL may be used to issue any type of Data Definition Language (DDL) or Data Manipulation Language (DML) statements to a server. The fundamental differences in servers are most noticeable when using non–generic facilities such as Data Definition or resource statements.

SQL Implementation differences

Implementation differences refer to effects, such as default data population issues. For example, populating a table would work differently in DB2 and SYBASE. The following commands work in DB2 because DB2 packs to the right with blanks on character fields.

```
// create a table, insert a row, and access
create table user(name char(10));
insert into user(name) values ('dave');
select * from user where name = 'dave        ';
```

Such issues include handling nulls, either in comparisons, arithmetic, or aggregation, and computation precision, particularly in DB2 can overflow or underflow in precision. In addition, differences in naming including sizes, permitted characters, etc. can affect implementation. Furthermore, differences in supported data types, such as char vs. varchar, blobs, and other more exotic types, and differences in object widths, such as the number of columns permitted in tables, views, etc. can all cause problems.

Syntactical Differences

Syntactical issues involve the datatypes used, the available keywords, operators, and functions. Issues in the syntactic area including datatypes and default data lengths, such as floats, integer lengths and timestamps, all tend to differ. In addition, scalar functions, which are such things as character/numeric conversions and time and data manipulation, all tend to vary dramatically between databases. Often, the name, number of parameters, and values returned are dissimilar for such simple functions as "substring()" and "dateToChar()".

Data Definition Language differences

Databases become more dramatically different when Data Definition Language (DDL) comes into play. Many databases support a generic ANSI subset of DDL (views, tables, etc.), but tend to vary when resources and security permissions are involved.

For example, adding a user using SYBASE isql involves:

```
1>sp_addlogin username,password
2>go

login added

1>use dbname1
```

```
2>go

1>sp_adduser   username
2>go

1>grant select, update on table1 to username
2>go
```

where using Oracle SQLDBA commands include:

grant connect to username identified by password;

create table dbname1.test1 (name char(40));

grant select, update on dbname1.test1 to username;

Comment differences

Even something as subtle as comments can cause problems. For example, –

DB2 accepts '—' as a comment specifier,–
Gupta and SYBASE accept '//'–
Oracle likes '/* */'

System table differences

All RDBMS servers store data about their internal state in a set of tables, often referred to as the system catalogs. As with everything else, the system tables and prefix extensions to access them, tend to differ from server to server.

For example, the DB2 system tables are prefixed with "sysibm", and include:

```
syscatalog - tables and views on the server, found by name
sysviews - views and their creation syntax, found by name
syscolumns - columns on tables and views, found by name and tbname
sysindexes - columns indexed, found by ixname
```

On WATCOM, those same tables:

```
syscatalog - objects on server, found by tname
sysviews - views and syntax, found by viewname
syscolumns - columns on tables and views, found by cname and tname
sysindexes -join of indexes and columns, found by iname
```

In general, one can expect to find systables, sysviews, syscolumns, and sysindexes on any particular SQL server. The internal format, names of columns, and meaning of the information, may differ from vendor to vendor, and generally does.

Handling Differences

There is no easy way to handle all the differences between such varied data sources. In extreme cases, code may need to recognize which server an application is connected to, and dynamically create the appropriate code for data access using dynamic SQL.

The most obvious approach is to only allow the subset of SQL which is recognized by all data sources in the enterprise. The problem is this often means significantly more work to get information which should be readily available.

Another possibility is to define a set of stored procedures or views on each database server, defining an interface layer between your application and the multiple servers. For instance, in the case of catalog differences, one might create stored procedures to return catalog information, or create views to allow access to the columns of system catalog tables in a generically defined manner.

For example:

```
// db2 using systables
create view gen_catalog
(name,
 creator,
 ncols)
as
select name,tbcreator,colct) from sysibm.systables;

// in WATCOM using syscatalog view
create view gen_catalog
(name,
 creator,
 ncols)
as
select tname,creator,ncols) from sys.syscatalog;
```

Note that the maintenance of multiple views at each server may become an issue.

Connections and validation

Another consideration is the need to connect and authenticate to the various data sources prior to accessing information. There are a number of important issues to be considered, not the least of which isthe issue of remembering multiple passwords and of using "good passwords".

One possibility is to keep all IDs and passwords the same for any user on all servers. The problem here is the compromise of the ID and password on any one server implies the failure on all servers.

Another approach is to use a security server (SS), which validates and provides sets of passwords for all servers. This also suffers from the problem of "single point of failure", but the SS can be built more formidably (requiring better passwords, using state information, etc.), and only provide authenticated access to applications which can communicate with the SS.

The Athena Project at Cambridge uses "Kerberos", a distributed security server, to provide access to system services through the use of "tickets". Tickets are stamped for service, user, and time, and may only be used for the service at the defined time. This provides a single login source and access to a wide variety of data sources. The Kerberos approach has been adopted as the security mechanism of the Distributed Computing Environment (DCE)

Most systems allow users to be considered as members of groups for granting privileges. Using groups can vastly reduce the number of access rights that must be processed for an enterprise–scale project.

For example, access to a stored procedure or view might be allocated according to groups:

```
create group admin,payroll;
grant select,update,delete on emp_view to admin;
grant select on emp_view to payroll;
```

Administrative users have access to change or remove employee data, and payroll may access the same data to find out the employee salary grade.

An extension of this idea is to associate groups with logins to data sources. For example, once authenticated to an application, the connection to another data source may be associated with the application, not the user of the application. In this way, the application logs into the data source as a single user. The drawback here is that individual user behavior tracking on the data source is lost; all users look like the application! The advantage of this method is security maintenance at the data source is for one user only, vastly reducing the administrative burden.

Gateways and Interfaces

The use of gateways may allow access to a variety of resources in a defined manner. This is done by coding "intelligence" in front of a server to allow it to pre–process the data stream prior to its submission to a DB engine.

Several vendors provide facilities for front–ending other servers with applications, which make those external applications appear the same to their server. SYBASE OpenServer and IDI EDALink are examples of such applications.

In some cases it is possible to manipulate the SQL being passed to the server. OpenServer can be programmed to parse incoming SQL and handle inconsistencies between vendors. EDA, on the other hand, passes the SQL syntax straight through, so all SQL must be legal DB2. Be sure to consider such issues when connecting to multiple SQL parsers.

Other services are becoming available which allow access to data through RPCs. These calls allow access to information in a generic manner. An application registers with a service. Once registered, the application can access information by sending messages to a service, receiving a data packet with the result set in response.

Such services generally use Brokers, which determine the location of a service and its accessibility. Brokers often monitor the state of services, redirecting and restarting requests if a server is down. Access to these kinds of processes may be through external source DataWindows or result set mappings to tables on SQL servers.

Server Routing

Another important issue in handling multiple data sources is the concept of routing. This involves deciding which data source contains the required data and accessing that source. This may be handled by maintaining tables that point to the most current or appropriate source servers for tables, and maintaining the connections to access those tables. Various methods for maintaining the table locations exist, including maintaining a "table" of tables on a server (centralized) or storing data locations on a directory service, e.g. X.500 (distributed).

Coordinating updates

This kind of routing process also facilitates the coordination of updates on multiple servers. By defining the business rules of changing enterprise information into the routing schema of the application, the order of changes, and thus the Unit of Work, is handled by business management, not software developers.

Limitations of SQL in multiple routing

The main limitation in routing is the requirement that the SQL syntaxes be acceptable to all routed sources. Using gateways, ANSI SQL, and preprocessing engines all help to reduce these problems; however, there are still many pitfalls to be handled depending on the combination of data sources being used.

As mentioned before, mapping DataWindows to views, which may differ from data source to data source but look the same to DataWindows, often helps to generalize the interface.

Conclusion

The problems in handling multiple source connections are complex and often difficult to anticipate. A basic strategy must be adopted to avoid differences between systems by using only ANSI SQL, and to mask differences by mapping to views, different DtaWindows, or generating dynamic SQL.

In any case, a thorough study of the candidate data sources, their similarities and their differences, is a critical component of any consideration when deciding to develop in a multiple data base and multiple vendor or server environment. Believe no promises about what and when capabilities will be available. Make sure your application can be written in the environment now, or you may be in for a great deal of grief.

CHAPTER 11

Programming in a Multi-Programmer Environment

By Judah Holstein

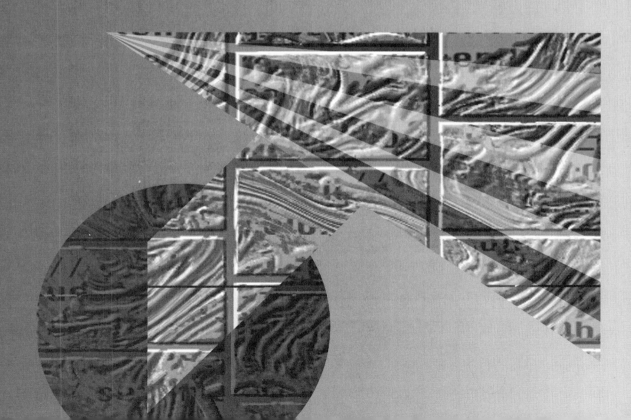

Programming in a Multi-Programmer Environment

By **Judah Holstein**

What's So Different?

It's late at night. You're home alone. You're building your own little PowerBuilder application. You've been building every evening and every weekend for the last three months. "This is going to be the most awesome accounting application there is on the market today," you think to yourself...again. You're really chugging along on this receivables window. "But wait," you exclaim. "I forgot that I need to deal with the receipt date in the income statement, too!"

It's okay. You quickly open up a copy of the DataWindow painter, pop open the income statement DataWindow, and fix the formula so that it excludes pending receivables. You then open the income statement window and touch up the code for ten minutes. Whew! That was easy! You're all set now. Nothing to it. The day is saved.

That's perfectly fine when you are the only one working on the accounting program. But let's say that you have made this change to the accounting program in a large, corporate, multi–programmer environment. You took the pending accounts receivables out of the income statement, but the income statement was assigned to me! I knew that the income statement included the pending receivables, because I was subtracting it out in a separate line at the bottom! I wasted three days trying to figure out why all of a sudden the income statement and balance sheets all started coming up wrong. I've needlessly modified thousands of lines of correct code to try to accommodate for this error that you caused, simply by changing something that you're not supposed to! Geez! It will take me two days just to change everything back! Now the project is going to be a week late, and we'll all get fired! Thanks a lot!

Well, perhaps this is a little bit of an exaggeration, but not much. Programming in a multi–programmer environment requires teamwork, organization, and discipline. Without it, a team is just a bunch of disjointed programmers, each working in his or her own world, each stepping on the others' toes, and generally moving the project backward instead of forward.

In a multi-programmer environment, standards and communication are essential. You can't just change any code you want without evaluating the effects of that change. You need to establish defined interfaces before you start, so other programmers can write their code and expect your code to be available and properly working where they need it. Other programmers will need to depend on your code reacting in a predictable manner–the manner that you have told them you will be making your code work.

If you change what the other developers expect from your code, or the manner in which they expect to call it, you need to inform them of your changes. Otherwise they will be making invalid assumptions, and the system will stop working.

In a single-programmer environment, you are in complete control. If you don't like the way something works, you can change it, and that's the end of it. In a multi–programmer environment, though, every line of code that you write may have an impact on other developers in the environment. There are certain changes that you simply cannot make without informing the rest of the team. And in the same light, any change that someone else on the team makes, may make an impact on you. And so much more effort goes into maintaining the proper communication channels and organization in a multi-developer environment than when you are programming by yourself.

A Team Project Recipe

As simple as it may seem, the secret to a successful multi-developer project comes down to five main ingredients. As with a cake, the recipe may differ slightly. Here, too, it is possible to have a tasty, successful team project even if some of the ingredients are substituted or missing. However, following this recipe will give you the best chances for success. The recipe involves a thorough application design, good communication, capable teamwork, effective organization, and sufficient discipline.

Design

There are many excellent design methodologies available on the market today. If you are responsible for building a system using PowerBuilder, I recommend an object-oriented design methodology, with clear and concise representation of the PowerBuilder objects that need to be developed. Personally, I prefer Grady Booch's design method, which can be studied in his book, *Object-Oriented Design with Applications*. Additionally, there are a couple of case tools that support his method, including Rational's *Rose*, which will make your life much easier if you decide to use his method. Still, there's nothing wrong with the other OOD methodologies; I just personally prefer Booch and have used it with much success in large, multi-developer PowerBuilder projects, as well as smaller personal projects.

If your design is good, it will be easy to task out objects to individuals. You will be able to evaluate how much time and effort will be required for each object and what the interfaces for all of the objects are. Consequently, your team will be able to properly determine who should build each of the objects, and in what order. Then, you can start the building process by stubbing each of the interface functions out, and allowing one of the team members to build the application shell.

In other words, let's say you have a binary tree object in your application that maintains a set of data as a binary tree. Let's say this binary tree object has a function called f_get_sql() to traverse the tree and return a SQL statement. It doesn't really matter to callers of the function what happens inside the function. They don't really care when they call the function whether the SQL statement they get is part of the binary tree, or is just a SQL statement that is hard-coded right into the function; they just know that when they call the function they need a SQL statement. Ultimately, of course, the function will need to work properly before the system as a whole will work correctly. However, in order to allow other team members to use your object even before the object is complete, you could temporarily hard-code a SQL statement in the function, and have it return that statement when it is called. Then, when it's time to build this function properly, you can build it and integrate it seamlessly into the application, since all of the objects that need the SQL statement are already calling your function. And all of a sudden, instead of them getting this hard-coded SQL statement, they will start getting the SQL statement that is built from the binary tree.

As members of the team complete the functions they are responsible for, remove the stub code, and replace it with real functionality, the system as a whole will start to work. In fact, using this method, your team will be able to minimize their overall integration effort, since essentially the functions are integrated from the start, and all that needs to be re-integrated is changes and oversights in the design. That is why a good design is so critical in a large project. Don't allow your large project to start without one.

Communication

It should be relatively simple to see how a good design will allow each team member to move forward on the project nearly independently and without having to worry too much about what the other team members are doing. However, this can also be disastrous if no one on the team talks to anyone else.

In general, no design is perfect. No design will truly be a hundred percent complete before the application itself is nearly a hundred percent complete. This is especially true when there are deadlines involved. And so, it is likely that as individual team members find they are encountering shortcomings in the design of their own pieces, or other pieces that they interact with, they will expand upon or modify the design to meet their needs. In some cases, this will not be a problem. If the interface between objects is left unchanged, then what happens inside a particular object will generally have little or no effect on anyone else on the team. But if a change in the interface between objects is required, additional members of the team will need to be informed.

Whenever there is a change to *anything* that has an effect on someone else, there must be a method of communicating that fact to the person who is affected. If you do not disperse this type of information among the appropriate members of the team, the team as a whole will probably fail. The project will slip because people will be unable to integrate their components. There will be a plethora of recoding and redesigning at the end of the project instead of during the project cycle, as people work frantically to make everything fit. This generally means that the last ten percent of the project will take as long as the first ninety percent did. Then new issues will arise, new changes will need to be made, and the next seven percent will take as long as the last ten percent did. Then, the process will repeat again, and the next five percent will take as much time as the last seven percent did. Finally, the process will repeat at least one last time, and so the final three percent will take as long as the previous five percent. The total project work will add up to 115%, and the actual duration will be as much as three to four times the original plan.

These numbers are only slightly tongue-in-cheek. That's pretty much the way it actually does happen when you don't communicate effectively. I've worked on more than one project that went over 200% overrun because of "scope creep" (115%), and poor communication . I've heard of other projects that were canceled around the 400% mark. These projects became critical because of the same types of problems.

Effective channels of communication for a project are critical. The team members need to be able to keep in touch. This doesn't mean that they have to sit in the same room, though. Obviously, you won't succeed with team members who sit on different floors or in different buildings and never answer their telephones or show up for meetings. And communication will be most easily achievable if you have all of your team members working together in a single lab. But there is no reason that you can't have team members working on different floors, in separate offices, or even at home once the design is accepted and distributed, as long as they can be reached when they are needed, can receive their memos, mail, and notices, and be available in the office for meetings. But communication has to be there, or the project will fail. It's that simple.

Communication manifests itself in a couple of ways. Verbal communication is a very effective mode of communication. However, written communication, even with diagrams, is often much clearer. If you have a situation where you are on a large team, it is always best to communicate important information via a memo or a document (even e-mail is acceptable), rather than by voice mail or in person. It's a lot easier to refer back at a later date to a memo or document, than to try to remember what exactly you said last week or last month.

Teamwork

Of course, you can write memos and documents all day and night and still have your project fail if people don't actually read them. Or if they do read them, and then ignore what they say. The members of your team must be able to work together to achieve their common goals. In a team environment, any single member who is not helping the team move forward is probably holding the team back.

In the beginning of a team project, you will probably find differences of approach and opinion, or even personality clashes. But the team has to be able to work together to make progress, and members of the team have to learn to accept each other. These issues must be nipped in the bud before they become a problem later on. People who refuse to listen to new ideas from their team members can effectively sabotage a project. By the same token, people who feel the need to dispute every statement that comes out of anyone's mouth but their own, can also cause team problems. Spend time to work out the differences among the team members. It will save you from disaster in the end.

Teamwork also means that the members of a team need to help each other when they are having trouble. If one of your team members asks you a question, don't blow him off. Answer the question as best you can, or if you are too busy, nicely ask him to let you finish with what you're in the middle of and then speak to him afterward. By the same token, if you have a question, be sensitive to the work habits of your teammates. If they look extremely busy or in the middle of a meeting or a thought, start off by telling them you have a question and ask if now is a good time. If they ask you to come back later, ask someone else on the team, or come back when they are not busy. Don't be insulted if they can't help you right away, even if they don't actually look busy. Programming is a form of creativity, and creative thought manifests itself in any number of ways. Even if your associate looks like he's just daydreaming, or even playing Minesweeper, he may be in deep thought working out a complex algorithm. (Although if he's playing Solitaire, he's probably just playing. That game takes too much concentration!)

The most important lesson here, though, is that a team works together to meet its common goals. After several weeks of positive teamwork, the members of the team will support and help each other, establish mentors, determine roles, and even begin to bond. That is the proper way for a team to evolve. If your team grows in this way, you will find that it is very strong and very successful. If there is dissension among team members; however, failure is likely to occur.

Organization

Once the design has been completed and communicated, and the team roles and responsibilities have been established, you will need to organize your team to achieve your goals. The first step in organizing the team is to build a project plan listing each of the responsibilities of the team as a task, evaluating how long each task will take, and assigning each task to a single member of the team.

The project plan is not a bible. The moment you create or update it, the project plan will probably already be somewhat outdated. However, the project plan is intended as a tool from which you and your team members can get direction.

In general, individual team members are not familiar with the "big picture" of the project. There are probably a number of relationships with other teams who have responsibilities that tie into the responsibilities of your team. For example, there might be another team that is sharing the data from your database. Perhaps more realistically, there is probably a dedicated team of system administrators who are building and managing your network and have dependencies on your project in that manner. In any case, there are very few projects that run in complete isolation from other teams in the company.

If each team were to have a project plan that reflects accurate task lists with realistic targets and dependencies, quite a number of stalled projects would suddenly succeed! In any case, you can help your own team build an accurate project plan by cooperating with the team leader and building it with him.

Don't blow off the project plan, it is very important. It may take you an extra hour or two a week to update it, but it will save your team a lot of time in the long run. Planning and designing aren't always fun, and aren't always directly relevant to your job, but you will absolutely be more effective if you discipline yourself and be sure to plan properly.

Good organization comes down to much more than the project plan, however. The plan itself is a set of guidelines as to how to organize your project–the who, what, and when of how to get your project done. However, if the project plan is chucked onto a voluminous stack of documents, memos, bug reports, coffee cups, newspapers, etc., as soon as it is printed out, then it will probably not be very effective. In fact, it will probably go unnoticed. In order to make effective use of your project plans and other documents, you need a good filing system for them.

I am a slob, and I am the first to admit it. (Well, maybe the second if you count my dear wife–she tends to remind me quite a bit.) Anyone who has worked near me has seen the stacks of papers strewn across my desk. But at the same time, I also have a filing system, and it doesn't actually sit on my desk–it's usually in one of my drawers. Certain things are important enough that they don't belong on the desk.

Notes, ideas, doodles–these are all things that are not critical enough for me to worry whether they are filed properly or not. After all, my notes will all get retyped into memos, my ideas will all get stuck into an "ideas" file that I will look at periodically, and my doodles will eventually be filed in the infamous "File 13." The serious files are meant to be organized and neat. Memos, documents, project plans, and other important papers that are related to the project should go into your files, and be easily accessible. Pretty pictures that you might have doodled during a design meeting belong on your wall or in a frame or something.

In general, there will be one person on the team who is more organized than the others. Take advantage of that fact as a team. Invite the team to vote that person "most organized document keeper," and ask him or her to manage all of the documents and memos. Keep your own files as well, in case there are memos that are sent to you personally that the document keeper doesn't get. But at least you and the other members of the team have someone you can count on to have the documents you need if you can't find your own copy. If everyone on the team has a fair filing system, the team as a whole will be more productive and will be able to find reference information when they need it, even if a single individual lost his or her copy. Do your part to make that happen, too.

Since this is a development team, you will probably also need to deal with computer files. A good directory structure will be critical in managing your on-line files and documents, including your libraries, etc. We will talk in more detail about the directory structure later. Additionally, you will need release procedures for releasing new versions of your data, application, documents, and so forth. Since as a team you will be working on different pieces of all of these, you need to evaluate and establish how you will release updates without causing difficulties for other members of the team. This is another common failure in team environments.

Finally, you will need to establish standards for pretty much everything anyone does. As a team, each of you will be writing documents, writing code, building objects, etc. The team must have standards for how to do each of these things, and more. There should standards for reporting bugs and errors, requesting changes to the design, and even complaining about a problem.

Many people don't like standards, but I think it is because they are annoyed at having to learn something new. After a few weeks of having to follow a standard, you will find yourself being less and less annoyed. Instead, using the standards will become a trivial matter, and you will find them most helpful when you have something to communicate to others on the team. If everyone has a standard for writing code, you will all find it easier to read each other's code. If there is a standard for documenting, you will all be able to understand the team's documents.

Standards really are a good thing once you get used to them. And in general, they are pretty easy to get used to. We will spend some more time talking about standards later.

Discipline

So now you have a team with a project plan, a design document, a directory structure, even some code. Things are looking great. All of a sudden, one of the team members decides that he is not going to write his code using your standards, but instead is going to follow the standards from his last company, since they are easier for him to remember. Seeing this, two other team members decide to use their old standards as well. Before long, everyone is using different standards, following different rules, and the entire team is in anarchy. Of course, this is a slight exaggeration. But it is important for all team members to recognize that these rules, plans, designs, and standards are all made for a reason. Using them will, in fact, help achieve success in your project. Each member of the team must have the self-discipline to adhere to the rules. Otherwise it places the entire team in jeopardy.

Additionally, the team should work together to protect itself from interests that attempt to sabotage the team. This includes team members who refuse to play by the rules, of course. But it also includes managers who continuously commit the team to unrealistic deadlines. It includes database administrators who continuously change data structures without proper communication and release procedures. It includes network administrators who can never get around to connecting your computer to the LAN.

In order to protect your team you should be sure to create an issue list, document each issue, and communicate them all to management.

Discipline requires courage. It takes courage to tell a manager that the requested deadline is too aggressive. It takes courage to tell a manager that the project is running late because you had to rebuild code on account of a design flaw. It takes courage to tell a manager that you cannot proceed until the LAN administrator sets up your machine. But if you do not have that courage, you will fail. And if you fail, all other team members, who are dependent upon your success, will also fail. The chain will continue, and the entire team will fail. Discipline is required to keep the chain connected.

Standards and Procedures

Throughout the life of your project, you will create many documents that will be used by the members of your team. The major documents you need will be the requirements document (sometimes referred to as the scope document); architecture and design and system documents; test plans and test cases; standards and procedures documents; and a system manual or user's guide. There will probably also be operations run books, bug reports, issue lists, and other interesting pieces of paper to be created during the life of your project. You will find; therefore, that it would be prudent to create documentation standards prior to creating any of the documents that you plan on delivering.

If you are using a word processor that allows for styles or templates, create a documentation template and distribute it to team members with samples and instructions. Do the best you can to communicate the importance of using a standard document template for your documents so that they all look consistent and can be integrated. Most of your documents, especially the design and system documents, will probably be written by individual members of the team. If you all use the same document template, integrating these individual pieces will be much easier. If you don't, you may need a team member to spend time editing it.

Additional documentation standards have to do with defining the kinds of things that you will describe in your documents. For example, you may decide that in your design documents, the programmer must list each object in style "heading 2," followed by the title Functions in "heading 3," followed by the list of all of the functions in the "function" style, and then the word Attributes in style "heading 3," followed by a list of all of the attributes in the "attribute" style. As simple as this standard may seem, it not only communicates the styles of the components of the document, but it also dictates which components in the document you are interested in. Team members who follow this guideline will be sure to have all of the required components, and they will be using the right styles.

Standards are also required for coding. Coding standards should include things like naming conventions for libraries, objects, events, functions, and variables, as well as naming conventions for tables, stored procedures, columns, etc. It should include information on where to store your files within the directory structure. Although it is not "required," I generally find it useful to include a "Tiny Tidbits" or "Helpful Hints" section. In this section, team members can include a sentence or two about problems, workarounds, or ideas for effective coding techniques that they might want to share with other members of the team.

You may find it helpful to publish your documents in Windows Help format. This way, team members can quickly find what they need in the document. If they need to look up a naming convention, they can find it much more quickly with the Windows Help engine than by flipping through mounds of paper. Look into using a help authoring tool like Wextech's Doc-To-Help or Blue Sky Software's RoboHelp to make it easy to create your on-line documents.

The next standard you will want to define is your directory structure. We will talk more about this in the next section. Suffice it to say; however, you will want to define a directory structure that allows your team to easily find the files they are looking for. You will need to establish and communicate the directory structure early so your team members can save their documents in the right place.

Next, you will need to define the different team procedures. For example, you will want to define procedures for bringing up and shutting down the system. You will need backup, release, communications, issue tracking, support, and enhancement request procedures. You will also need procedures for expanding the scope and for changing the design. You will need procedures for creating new documents, new objects, and for submitting bug reports.

Basically, anything you do that affects the team or others outside of the team will probably require a set of procedures. The above list is a good start, but there will surely be additional needs. We even had one project where we had a documented procedure for how to respond to requests for new features from the user.

Procedures and guidelines let team members know what to do when a situation arises. After you have documented these once, each person can be independently responsible for following them. However if you never document your procedures, your people will waste a lot of time trying to figure out how to do things, and step on each others' toes trying to do them their own way.

All a procedure document really needs to do is explain step-by-step how to do something. Whatever the procedure that you are trying to document is, the clearer and simpler you make it, the easier it will be to follow. Introduce the procedure with a sentence or two, and then simply list the steps to perform the procedure.

In order for the development team to effectively track issues, we have assigned Joe Shmoe as the issue track manager. He will be collecting all issues and formalizing them into a document for weekly review by the team. More urgent issues will still be tracked in the same manner and reviewed weekly, but will be directed to the appropriate person as soon as possible for immediate attention.

When submitting a new issue for tracking, use the following steps to ensure that the issue is accepted and received:

1. Pick up a copy of the New Issue Form from the Lab.

2. Fill out the New Issue Form, using clear and concise terminology. We will not be able to resolve issues that we cannot understand.

3. Be sure that you have filled out all questions on the form. Be sure that your name, extension, and the date are on the form.

4. Make a copy of the form for your records. (Mail sometimes does get lost.)

5. Send the form via InterOffice Mail to Joe Shmoe, Technology Center location 2-

221, or drop it in the "New Issues" mailbox outside the lab.

6. If your issue is urgent, you may also send your message via e-mail to shmoej@tech.bus.com, or you can call Joe at x4567. However, even if you do this, you should be sure to send a copy via InterOffice Mail for record keeping purposes.

7. When your issue is assigned, you will be notified via InterOffice Mail. If there are any questions regarding your issue, we will try to call you for more information.

As you can see, the procedure for submitting an issue to the development team includes clear, concise steps that anyone should be able to follow.

Documenting your procedures in this way also helps ensure order and organization within your environment. After all, in the above example, you prevent external members from hounding your developers with issues, and you give the developers a document to refer people to if they try to ignore the rules. Document and publish your procedures. It will allow your team to concentrate more on their jobs, and less on their political savvy. It can also prevent disasters, like loss of data because everyone thought someone else was backing up the data.

Creating a Good Directory Structure

I am sure that on your personal computer you do not store all of your files in a single directory, but instead have a well-organized directory structure. And I am also sure that if you are working on a team, each team member probably has a different directory structure on his or her home computer. In fact, I wouldn't be surprised to find out that all members even has a different directory structures on their office machines. But when you are working as a team, you need to build a common directory structure to store the files that the team needs to share, so that each team member can quickly and easily find the files he or she needs to work with.

For starters, you should define all of the types of files that your team is likely to require. Generally, it is a good idea to organize your files based on purpose or target. For example, you don't want to create a directory to store all Word documents, and a different directory to store all spreadsheet documents. Before long you would probably have a lot of files in your directory, and it would be very difficult to decipher a file's contents. Instead, think about the different types of Word documents that you will need.

You will surely need a directory to store your standards and procedures documents. You will need a directory to store your scope document, and another one for your design documents. You'll need directories to store your PowerBuilder libraries. In fact, you will need directories to store different releases of your libraries. You may need a production directory, a beta directory, a testing directory, and a development directory, each of which contain subdirectories to hold the proper set of source code, SQL scripts, data, and executables.

A release procedure might dictate that you copy your development directory to the next test directory when you freeze your development. Then, when testing is complete, you rename the test directory to a beta directory. When beta testing is complete, you rename the directory to production directory, and so forth.

If you have created .dll files or other external files, you will need to store them somewhere too. You'll want a directory to store all of your issues, and to store all of your bug reports. You'll want directories to store important memos and letters. You'll want directories to store just about anything else that you may save on your disk.

A good directory structure is self-documenting, and makes an easy-to-use file system for the entire team to share. A poor directory structure makes for toe-stomping, lost files, and wasted time because it's impossible to find documents. And when you do find them, you may be looking at the wrong ones–or worse yet, even overwriting the right ones.

Another issue with regard to team directory structure has to do with networking. If your network is relatively small and is disconnected from the backbone, then you may want to consider creating an application server for use by your team members. An application server allows your team members to run their applications (like Windows and PowerBuilder) from the server instead of installing a version of each application on each member's machine. Although this may mean applications will run slightly slower, the speed decrease will probably be negligible if your application server is isolated from other network traffic (either via a router or simply by being disconnected from the backbone, and instead being private to the team members).

I am a strong supporter of doing whatever it takes to get a team on an application server. Personally, I feel it helps ensure the team is working as a unit even further, and offers other major conveniences, especially when developing in a PowerBuilder environment. After all, if you change the IP address of your database server, or upgrade to a new version of Windows or PowerBuilder, instead of having to run around to update fifteen different machines, you can generally update the changes right from your machine to all of the team members in one shot. Even installing new software for the team to use becomes a breeze when you are working with an application server, and it is set up properly. Additionally, if you are using an application server with a proper setup, a team member should be able to sit down at any machine on the network, login as himself, and be working in a comfortable, familiar, standard environment, with all of his files right where he left them.

The methodology that I am about to describe stems from a Novell Netware topology that I have used since before there was such a thing as PowerBuilder and client/server development. Novell offers certain features that facilitate this topology. However, I have successfully implemented it in several different network environments, including Novell Netware, LANtastic, Microsoft LAN Manager (with an OS/2 server), Microsoft NetBEUI (with a Windows NT server), and even using TCP/IP itself with PCNFS mounts to a Unix file server. So regardless of what networking environment you are using, you should be able to build the same kind of structure, even if it means taking a few extra steps to do it. I think that if you do, you will be very happily rewarded.

If you are going to use an application server, I recommend creating a master subdirectory where all application directories will reside. Even if the application server is separate from the development server, I think this is worth doing, since servers generally don't remain "dedicated" throughout their lifetime. Additionally, each team member should have a *home* directory, where he can store all of his personal files. All of the home directories should be inside a separate directory on the server. Separate drives should be mapped to the development directories, application directories, and the home directory.

After logging into the server, each machine on the network should call a startup batch file that will set up its environment for the network. This includes mapping to the appropriate drives, setting up the path, etc. If you are using a Novell network, this is done for you using login scripts. In that case, set up the mappings in the system login script instead of the startup batch file.

As far as setting up each individual machine, that should be all that is necessary. The machine logs in to a login directory and calls this single batch file (or login script), which maps the drives and sets up the path. Unfortunately, with DOS, there is no way to install drivers in config.sys after logging into a network. You will need to update the config.sys file on each machine to load whatever device drivers the user may need for the network and for the protocol you are using to connect to your database server, e.g.: TCP/IP.

Next you will want to set up the application server to contain all of the applications your team members will be sharing. I would recommend that before you do this, you strip your autoexec.bat and config.sys files to contain only exactly what is needed to connect to the network. This way, you will be able to use these files as a template for your users' startup batch files later.

The first thing that you should install is Microsoft Windows itself. To install Windows on a network, put the /A parameter on the command line when you run Setup. Install Windows to the network using the command line parameter, SETUP /A. This will install **all** Windows files to your network server. You can then install Windows for each individual team member's machine using the command line parameter, SETUP /N.

Install Windows to a WIN subdirectory of the user's home directory. That way the Windows .ini files are on the network, and you can access them to update things like new IP addresses and PowerBuilder InitPaths.

After you have installed Windows, create a new Program Manager group to hold all of the network applications. You may want multiple groups. For example, you can have a Documentation Tools group to hold documentation tools like Word, Excel, and any CASE tools you may be using. Then you can have a separate Development Tools group for development tools like PowerBuilder, and help, standards, and procedures documents.

Install each program on the application server into a directory under the APPLICATIONS directory. Move the icons for the applications to their appropriate icon groups. When you are done, look in your Windows directory for the group files you just created. They will have the .grp extension. Copy these files to the main shared Windows directory, and make them read-only. Now, when you set up each individual machine to run Windows, you can also create a group that points to the shared group, and will automatically appear on each machine. Later, if you add new shared software, you can place the icon into the shared group and it will automatically appear on each team member's machine the next time he or she restarts Windows.

Create templates for each of the .ini files, including the pb.ini and win.ini files, and place them in a TEMPLATES directory under the shared Windows directory. Update the pb.ini template to include a pointer to a shared pbshare.ini file that will contain database profiles for all of the database connections that you will have. Place the following two lines in the win.ini template file:

```
[PowerBuilder]
InitPath=W:\PB.INI
```

Be sure to put the proper path in for the InitPath. I used W:\ assuming that you will follow my instruction (below) to include W: as a root mapping to the user's Windows directory. But if you didn't, be sure to put the proper path there in its place. Also, you should be sure to create a pbshare.ini file shared in the PowerBuilder directory that includes all of the database profile connections you will be using. That way, when a new database release is cut, it will be simple to update everyone's database profiles in one pass.

After you are done installing all of the shared files, you can set up the shared startup batch file (or system login script) to include whatever files need to be included in the path. Take care to create a separate drive mapping for each user's personal Windows directory. I generally recommend using easy-to-remember drive letters for these things. For example, make drive W: a root mapping to the user's Windows directory (which is a subdirectory of his home directory). Test the process with your own login connection by relogging into the system a couple of times, and making sure everything works.

You can then go to each machine and install its Windows system from the network. Then you can set up its shared batch file, shared group files, and win.ini file to point to the right IP addresses and PowerBuilder Profile file by copying them from the TEMPLATES directory. All users will need their own pb.ini files in their own home directories, which are pointed to by the win.ini file but copied from a template as well.

Keep in mind that even though you are only installing a single physical copy of each application on your server, most license agreements require that a separate license be purchased for each concurrently running copy of the software, even if only one copy is physically installed. You should contact the software manufacturer for license information if you have questions. There are software license monitoring programs that you can use to ensure that there are no license violations on your network, in case you don't want to purchase one license for each team member. For example, even if you have ten team members, you may only want to buy three licenses of a program because only three members will be using it a time. In this case, you can also purchase a monitoring program that will enforce your license by preventing more than three team members from running the program concurrently.

Although every project is slightly different, most projects will, at a minimum, require the above listed items to be saved in their directories. Listing 2 demonstrates an effective directory structure for the different file servers that should prove to be a simple-to-navigate filing system.

Listing 3 is a sample shared setup batch file for a LAN Manager or LANtastic network. After running the batch files in Listing 3, your system will have logged into the network and set environment variables for the user's name and current development directory. Then, it will use those variables to map the user's drive G: to the home directory of the user; drive H: to the development directories; drive I: to the documents directory; drive J: to the applications directory; drive V: to the user's personal Windows directory; drive W: to the shared Windows directory; and drive X: to the PowerBuilder directory. Then it updates the PATH to include the Windows directories and the PowerBuilder directories. Finally, it runs Windows.

Listing 2: An effective directory structure.

Application Server

```
ROOT Directory             C:\
Login Script Directory     C:\LOGIN
Applications               C:\APPS
MS Windows                 C:\APPS\WINDOWS
Templates                  C:\APPS\TEMPLATES
PowerBuilder               C:\APPS\PB3
MS Word                    C:\APPS\WINWORD
MS Excel                   C:\APPS\EXCEL
Home Directories           C:\HOME\<login name> (eg: C:\HOME\JSHMOE)
Individual Windows Files   C:\HOME\<login name>\WIN31
                             (eg: C:\HOME\JSHMOE\WIN31)
```

Development Server

```
Root Directory             C:\
Documents                  C:\DOCS
Scope Documents            C:\DOCS\SCOPE
Design Documents           C:\DOCS\DESIGN
Standards Documents        C:\DOCS\STDS
Procedures Documents       C:\DOCS\PROCS
Memos                      C:\DOCS\MEMOS
Issues                     C:\DOCS\ISSUES
Development Files          C:\DEVnn(nn is the version,
                             eg: C:\DEV01, C:\DEV02)
Production Files           C:\PRODnn
Test Files                 C:\TESTnn
Beta Files                 C:\BETAnn
PowerBuilder .PBLs         C:\DEVnn\LIBS
                             (This will be duplicated for each of the
SQL Scripts                C:\DEVnn\SQL
                             different subdirectories as needed ie:
Data Files                 C:\DEVnn\DATAC:\PRODnn\LIBS,
                             C:\TESTnn\LIBS, C:\BETAnn\LIBS, etc.)
Executables & .PBD Files   C:\DEVnn\EXEC
.DLL Source Code           C:\DEVnn\DLL\<dll name>
                             (Each DLL should have its own directory)
```

Listing 3. Sample batch files.

```
AUTOEXEC.BAT (on user's machine)
REM Put the basic autoexec.bat here. Just end it with...
CALL LOGIN <username>
LOGIN.BAT (on user's machine)
IF "%1"=="" THEN GOTO ERROR
REM Create a User environment variable for user later...
SET USER=%1
NET LOGON %1 %2
IF ERRORLEVEL==1 THEN GOTO :END
NET USE F:=\\APPSVR\LOGIN
CALL F:\STARTUP.BAT
GOTO END

:ERROR
ECHO Format:
ECHO LOGIN <username> [<password>]
GOTO END
```

```
:END
STARTUP.BAT (on Login Server in C:\LOGIN)
SET DEVDIR=DEV02
NET USE G:\=\\APPSRVR\HOME\%USER%
NET USE H:\=\\DEVSRVR\%DEVDIR%
NET USE I:\=\\DEVSRVR\DOCS
NET USE J:\=\\APPSRVR\APPS
NET USE V:\=\\APPSRVR\HOME\%USER%\WIN31
NET USE W:\=\\APPSRVR\APPS\WINDOWS
NET USE X:\=\\APPSRVR\APPS\PB3

SET PATH=%PATH%;V:\;W:\;X:\;
WIN
```

Using this configuration, you can easily manage your network, share your files, and find the things that you are looking for. Everything is well-organized and self-explanatory, so the system works like an efficient file system. It's easy to learn, easy to use, and easy to maintain. Using this directory structure will allow your team to spend more time working and less time searching, overwriting, and restoring.

Organizing your PowerBuilder Libraries

Once you have set up your directory structure, you now need to create libraries to store the PowerBuilder objects that you and your team will create. In the PowerBuilder sample application, the libraries are organized by object type. There is a library for windows (actually, there are two of them), a different library for DataWindows, another one for menus, another for functions, and yet a different one for user objects. I've seen some development teams model their libraries after this style. This method is effective for a sample application, because users can quickly find the things that they are looking for. But when you are developing a real application, using this type of library organization is going to be very annoying and will be very limiting.

Instead, you should organize your libraries by object group. For example, let's say that your design calls for objects to communicate with the database, different objects to manage your queries, and yet different objects to handle reports. Each of these object types would go into its own set of libraries.

In general, you will have assigned a single set of objects to an individual team member. So by organizing your libraries to hold only those objects that are related, you permit several things to happen. First, you allow each member to become an expert in his or her own object. This minimizes the amount of toe-stepping by members of the team, since each member is responsible for the things in a single clearly defined set of libraries. If you were to organize the objects based on whether they are a menus or windows, you would run more risk of people touching other people's objects, since they are all working in the same library.

Using the object-oriented organization methodology also makes it easier to distribute updates to your application. You can create .pbd files for all of your libraries to distribute with your application. Then, you can easily upgrade your application when you make changes to just one object group by simply redistributing a single .pbd file instead of an entire new application. Since most changes to an existing application will probably occur within a specific object or set of objects anyway, now you will only have to redistribute the libraries that contain modified objects.

In other words, if you have to make a change to the query object, it is highly likely that you will need to change some of its menus, functions, DataWindows, and windows. If you organize your libraries so the objects related to the query object all reside in the same library, you can simply redistribute the query library as a .pbd. However, if you had organized your libraries by PowerBuilder object type, you would have to redistribute the window, menu, function, and DataWindow libraries. In other words, you would pretty much have to redistribute the entire application. This is both wasteful and costly.

To help keep you organized, you should be sure to always create comments for your libraries, as well as for the objects inside them. The library comments you create should be useful and describe what object the library represents. As a rule, you shouldn't put more than thirty objects into a library if you can avoid it. And make sure that your libraries don't get larger than about 1 MB in size, even if there are fewer than thirty objects inside. To keep to these limits, it is possible you will need more than one library. Use sequence numbers in your library names to protect you from confusion. Reserve the last one or two digits for a sequence number, e.g.: qcrprt01.pbl.

Checking In and Out

In addition to your application object libraries, you will need checkout libraries for all of the members of your team. Checking your objects in and out of your library allows you to make changes to your components, test them, debug them, and adjust them without any effect on anyone else working on the application.

Imagine you just created a new feature for the system. In creating this new feature, you inadvertently messed up some return code of a function that is needed to start the application. Now the function fails during application startup and goes into an endless loop. All of a sudden, ten people on your team are locked into an endless loop because of your little mistake. And now no one can run the application and get any work done on their own components, until you fix this bug.

Although check in and check out don't actually cure this problem, they make it possible for you and your teammates to work on your pieces independently. You can test and debug your code with the rest of the application before anyone else on the team can see it. Of course, there is always one smart guy who makes a change without checking out the object into his library, thinking it's a teeny-weeny change no one will notice. It holds everyone up anyway. But at least if your team uses check in and check out, this will be limited to a few incidents, and not be a regular occurrence.

By and large I find it easiest to work with objects in the Library Painter, and among the other developers I have known this seems to be a common perception. So you should probably already be familiar with the Library Painter. Let's say you are about to modify your main query window. You need to add a new type of query clause to your engine. The first thing you will need to do is check out your library entry. To do this, highlight the entry and select

Check Out from the Source menu or click on the "Check Out" button on the toolbar. If you have never checked any library entries out before, a window will appear asking you your User ID. Enter your login name, so it will be unique and easily recognizable. The User ID will be stored in your pb.ini file in the [Library] section, with the keyword UserID. You will be able to see it in the Preferences Painter as well. Once it is stored in the pb.ini file, you won't need to change it again, unless you change your login name for some reason or sit down at someone else's desk.

Once you have entered your User ID, you will be asked which library you would like to check your entry into. You should choose your checkout library. It will create a copy of the object in your checkout library and lock the first object in the original library, preventing anyone else from updating it. If you are using the version control interface with a version control vendor such as PVCS, it will retrieve a copy of the file for you to edit. In the meantime, you have now checked out your PowerBuilder library entry.

Now two things will happen. First, you will be the only one allowed to edit your checked out object. Second, all other team members will still be running against the original unchanged library entry until you check yours back in. Why? Because of the library path. All team members should include their own checkout libraries as the very first–and only–entry in their library paths. You should not include anyone else's checkout library in your library path at all. That way, if you have something checked out into your checkout library, you will see it and its changes as part of your application. But if other people have something checked out into their own checkout libraries, you won't see their changes until they check it back in, since their checkout library is not in your library path.

After you have checked out your library entry, you can make whatever changes you need. Since you surely followed my instructions previously and started off by building stub functions for all of your objects, you will simply be adding in the real functionality in your checkout library. When you are finished making your changes or updating your code, you can run the application as if your library entry was part of the application. Even though there are two copies of the object in your library path, since your checkout library appears first, PowerBuilder only looks at the one in the checkout library and ignores the second one that everyone else sees. So you can now test all of your changes without any adverse effects on anyone else.

When you are satisfied your changes work properly and do not mess anything else up, you can check your library entry back in by either selecting Check In from the Source or Right Mouse menu, or clicking on the "Check In" button on the toolbar. Once it is checked in, it will overwrite the old version and automatically become part of everyone else's application. PowerBuilder will unlock the entry as well, allowing you or anyone else to check it out again to make further changes. In other words, once you check it back in, it is public property again.

While you are working on a team project, members of the team will need to check items in and out for various reasons, primarily to make changes to their code. You can see a list of all of the checked out objects by selecting the View Check Out Status menu item from the Source Menu. This will bring up the View Check Out Status window (Figure 11-1), which shows a list of all of the items that you have checked out, where they are, and where their originals are. You can also see the entire list of checked out objects in your library path by clicking on the "Show All Users" checkbox.

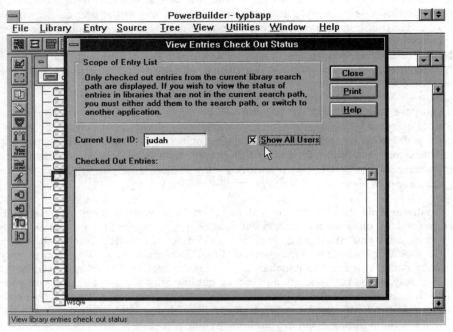

Figure 11-1. The View Check Out Status window.

there is also a menu item in the Source menu that allows you to clear the checkout status of a checked out object. I recommend against using this menu item for any reason, except in an emergency. When you are developing in a team environment, you will often be tempted to do this when someone tells you about a bug in the original version of an object that you have checked out for other reasons, and are still working on, but is not ready for release. You will probably figure that the easiest thing to do is to clear the checkout status of the object, fix the bug in the old version quickly, and then continue working on your version. And while this is not necessarily a disaster in itself, it is very risky. After all, you won't be able to re-lock the original entry, so no one will know that you have it checked out. It is possible that someone else will come along and check out the object, make changes, and check it back in before you copy your version over it. Then the other person's changes will be lost, and potentially other components of the application will get out of synch. Additionally, if you are using version control software, your version control mechanism will probably get out of synch.

The best way to handle a problem like the one described above includes clearing the check-out status, but in addition requires some additional steps. First, copy your mid-update object to a backup library (or export it to a flat file). Then clear the checkout status of the object and delete it. Check out the old object, make the changes, and test them. When you are done, check it back in. Then, check the object out again. Copy the backed up object (that you were updating in the beginning) over the checked out object in your checkout library. Believe it or not, the system will still know that the object is checked out, and not allow anyone else to change it. Then you can continue to work on your object from where you left off, and no one else will be able to put you out of synch.

Keep in mind, though, that you will probably need to duplicate the "quick fix" in the new object that you backed up. If it is a small change, you can do it again in the other object by hand. If it is more serious, you can export the old object with a different name, and copy and paste the changes using a text editor. Then, you can re-import the new merged object back into your checkout library. Incidentally, the re-merging of the different changes will be the most difficult, accident-prone part of making this type of change. But if you must do it, you should be sure to at least take the precautions that I have just described. This will prevent any serious loss of data and synchronization problems because of multiple people working on the same object. Additionally, you should make a few extra backups of basically everything before you take on an endeavor like this.

If you follow the above development procedures, your team environment will run smoothly. You will be able to check out your library entries, make whatever changes you need, test them to make sure they don't adversely affect anyone else, and check them back in when you are comfortable they are ready. Check in and check out are a required effort for successful team development. Without them, editing objects in a team environment will be chaos.

A Hundred and Twenty Thousand People for Five Minutes

If you are developing applications as a team, you are probably working in a corporate environment. The project executives have probably budgeted a given amount of time, money, and resources for the project. Generally, it won't be enough. It doesn't really matter what the project is, who is leading it, who is responsible for it. There are almost certainly not enough time, money, and resources to finish the project. You will have to either cut scope, get more people, extend the project deadline, spend more money, or some combination of all of the above. And so there is a likelihood that you will find new members being added to the team, as managers decide that more team members will make the project run faster. The further behind you are, the more people will be added, and the longer it will take to bring those people up to speed. Most managers feel that the more people they add, the faster they will be able to deliver. They somehow think that the end result will be the same whether they have five people for 120,000 minutes or 120,000 people for five minutes. They try to throw people at the project to bring the delivery closer to five minutes than a year.

In fact, a rule of management called the Law of Diminishing Returns says that a point exists beyond which adding people will proportionally decrease productivity. In general, I have found that teams larger than five or six people need to be broken up into smaller units, or they begin to lose effectiveness. Communication becomes a bigger problem, and more time is spent getting the team organized than getting any actual work done.

If you have a team of more than five or six people, subdivide it. Make each unit responsible for a particular group of objects in the application. For example, one team might be responsible for the front end, and another for the back. Or one team might be responsible for communications, another for business logic technology, and another for user interface. But each team should have a logical set of responsibilities with clearly defined boundaries and clearly defined deliverables. A smaller team will work very effectively. I've had success breaking larger teams up into groups of two and three, especially if you can match up individual strengths and weaknesses so that they complement each other.

The Hit By a Truck Theory (And How to Replace the Victims)

Perhaps you've heard of the "Hit By a Truck" theory before. It is based on the fact that over one million people each year get hit by trucks, cars, buses, trains, and other high-speed moving vehicles. It presumes that some percentage of these victims are computer programmers. The theory states that although each individual programmer's chances of being hit by a moving vehicle are difficult to predict, it is likely that at some point one or more of the annual victims will be developers working on your team. It additionally states that when this occurs, even if the victim is not actually killed, there is a likelihood he or she will be unable to continue working for some period of time. During this period of time, someone else on the team will have to take over those responsibilities and finish developing those components. It could even be you.

Of course, there are many reasons that a team member may become unavailable for an extended period of time that don't necessarily involve moving vehicles. These include termination of employment, leave of absence, department transfer, illness, disability, retirement, etc. And as mentioned before, a new team member may be added for reasons other than replacement. Regardless of the reason for the team adjustment, this situation is probably one of the best tests of your team recipe. If the documentation is good, the standards are adhered to, the files are easily found, and the plan is being maintained, then integration of the new team member or of new responsibilities will be very smooth, and probably only put the project back a short time. However, if all of the functional knowledge of the project is now literally buried with the team member who was lost, it is unlikely that the project will be able to get back on track for a very long time. In fact, you will probably find yourself doing quite a bit of rebuilding.

The moral of the story is to follow the recipe for team success. If you do, the rewards will be great, the project will most likely succeed, and all the team members will learn from each other and enjoy the experience. If you ignore the team recipe, your apple pie will probably turn out quite sour.

CHAPTER 12

Nested Reports

By John Olson

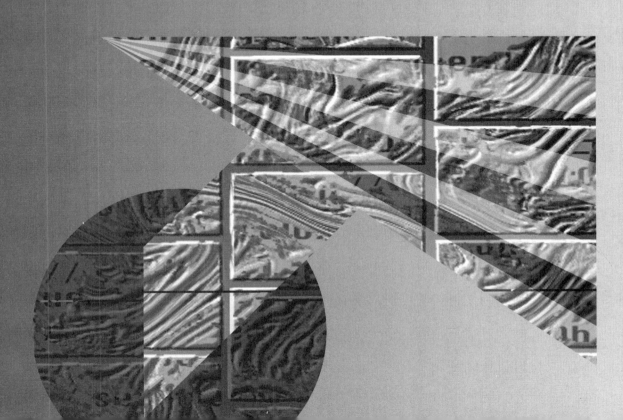

Nested Reports

by **John Olson**

Introduction

With the release of PowerBuilder 4.0 come some exciting new features, including the Project Painter, the link to Watcom C for class development, the DataPipeline, DataWindow column sliding, and more. However, in my opinion the most exciting new feature is the ability to nest DataWindows within DataWindows. This new feature greatly enhances the broad reporting functionality which PowerBuilder 3 already possessed. Using PowerBuilder 3, developers often had to resort to scripting to apply behaviors to DataWindow reports. Now, with PowerBuilder 4.0 those same behaviors and many more can be applied with no scripting. There were also some limitations in reporting which have been eliminated. In this chapter we will explore the uses of nesting reports and perform step by step development of some DataWindows which use Nested Report objects.

The power of nesting reports lies in its ability to allow fully functional DataWindows to be placed within other DataWindows. A nearly unlimited number of DataWindows can be nested, with each nested DataWindow having its own DataWindow type, columns, arguments, formatting, fonts, colors, etc. Also, a DataWindow which has a nested report on it can itself be used as a nested report, with no limit to the number of levels of nesting. However, because a nested report can potentially be retrieved for each row in the DataWindow in which it is nested, the time required for retrieval can increase somewhat with each additional nested report, and dramatically with each new level of report nesting.

Nested Reports are not treated as standard DataWindow columns. Since a Nested Report doesn't have a value (it may in fact have several rows of values) it can't be treated like a column. You can't group on a Nested Report, use one in a comparison expression, filter on one, sort on one, specify formats or validation expressions, specify "suppress repeating values," etc. No "value-based" features or functions can be applied to Nested Reports. However, you can reference Nested Reports from PowerScript in the same way as you reference Drop-DownDataWindows. Later in this chapter I'll demonstrate manipulating Nested Reports using PowerScript.

The example for this chapter will be based on the simple purchase order tracking system developed in the "Data Driven Architecture" chapter of this book.

Creating the Basic Report

Supposing that we need to develop a report which lists purchase orders by cost center for a specified range of quarters. We'll develop a few simple DataWindows and nest them on another DataWindow.

First, we need to create a report which will display cost center information. We'll call it d_cost_center_with_po, because it will eventually list all purchase orders for each cost center. Initially, this dw will contain only 2 columns, cost_center_id and cost_center_desc.

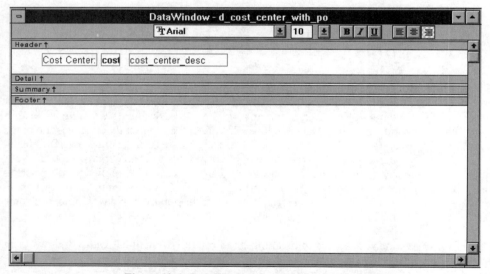

Figure 12-1: DataWindow d_cost_center_with_po.

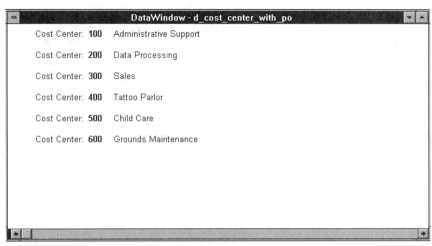

Figure 12-2: Print Preview for d_cost_center_with_po.

Next we need to create a DataWindow which will display purchase order information and allow the user to specify a starting quarter and year and an ending quarter and year. The data should be sorted by cost center, purchase order date and finally by purchase order number. The DataWindow will be named d_po_for_cc.

The following SQL Select will be used for d_po_for_cc. By creating SQL computed columns for quarter and year we can allow the user to specify quarter and year selection criteria.

```
SELECT
cost_center_id,
po_date,
po_no,
po_desc,
project_id,
amount,
(((month(po_date)-1)/3)+1) "qtr",
year(po_date) "yr"
FROM
purchase_order
WHERE
( "qtr" >= :Start_Qtr ) AND
( "yr" >= :Start_Year ) AND
( "qtr" <= :End_Qtr ) AND
( "yr" <= :End_Year )
ORDER BY
cost_center_id ASC,
po_date ASC,
po_no ASC
```

The DataWindow will accept four arguments which will define the date range for the purchase orders to be retrieved: Start_Qtr, Start_Year, End_Qtr, and End_Year.

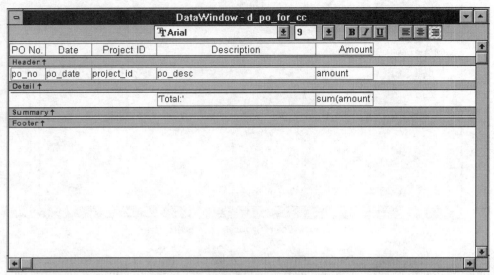

Figure 12-3: DataWindow d_po_for_cc.

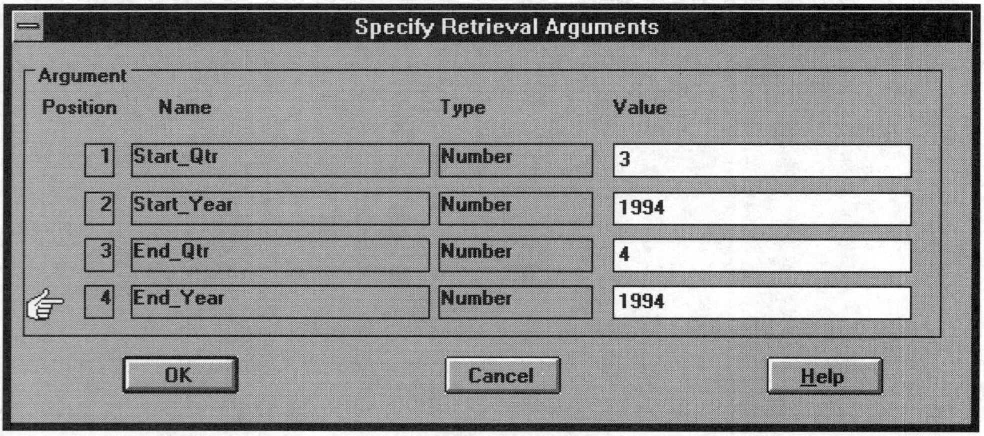

Position	Name	Type	Value
1	Start_Qtr	Number	3
2	Start_Year	Number	1994
3	End_Qtr	Number	4
4	End_Year	Number	1994

Figure 12-4: Retrieval arguments specified for d_po_for_cc.

DataWindow - d_po_for_cc

PO No.	Date	Project ID	Description	Amount
13638	09/03/94	9240	Black Thumb Landscape Service	$4,265.00
13639	09/05/94	1664	Chalk board	$456.50
13640	09/10/94	5500	Company Car - used BMW	$5,500.00
13641	09/12/94	4300	VCR for tattoo parlor	$645.10
13642	09/20/94	1664	Extra close haircut for Gregg	$25.00
13643	09/25/94	1110	6 dongles	$987.20
13644	10/05/94	1664	New model 2000 abacus	$454.10
13645	10/05/94	1090	WordStart upgrade CPM to DOS	$495.00
13646	10/06/94	4300	Retainer for lawsuit #14234	$10,000.00
13647	10/06/94	2300	10 rack cd player for bus	$995.00
13648	10/07/94	5500	Mr Mens' Hawaii trip	$4,900.00
13649	10/07/94	3000	Check out potential hire	$95.00
13650	10/08/94	1110	Computer Dr. fixed WordStart	$495.00
13651	10/08/94	8800	Mitchell's moisturizer	$5.50
			Total:	$53,953.79

Figure 12-5: Records retrieved for d_po_for_cc.

Now we'll add an argument for column cost_center_id so that for each row in d_cost_center_with_po, only those purchase orders for the specified cost center will be displayed. After adding argument Cost_Center_ID, we must add a condition to the WHERE clause. The final WHERE clause is:

```
WHERE
( cost_center_id = :Cost_Center_ID ) AND
( "qtr" >= :Start_Qtr ) AND
( "yr" >= :Start_Year ) AND
( "qtr" <= :End_Qtr ) AND
( "yr" <= :End_Year )
```

With the addition of argument Cost_Center_ID, d_po_for_cc is ready to be used as a Nested Report on d_cost_center_with_po.

Note: All DataWindows, regardless of type, can be used as Nested Reports.

Placing a Nested Report on a DataWindow

To place a Nested Report on a DataWindow, click the "Nested Report" icon on the DataWindow PainterBar, then point to the location you want it to be placed and click your left mouse button. The Select Report dialog will prompt you to select a DataWindow for your Nested Report object. You must select a DataWindow; the DataWindow painter will not allow you to place a Nested Report object which does not have a DataWindow assigned to it. For the example, select d_po_for_cc and place it on d_cost_center_with_po.

Note: Nested Reports can't be placed on cross-tabular DataWindows.

Figure 12-6: DataWindow PainterBar Nested Report icon.

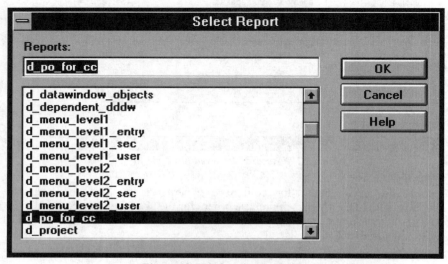

Figure 12-7: Select Report dialog.

Like a DataWindow control, a DataWindow object is associated with a Nested Report object; but unlike the DataWindow control, the DataWindow is not visible within the Nested Report object. This is unfortunate; it would be beneficial to be able to see the DataWindow object within the Nested Report object. However, while it would be a nice feature, it certainly isn't critical to using Nested Report objects.

After selecting a DataWindow, the Nested Report object will automatically be sized according to the width of the DataWindow selected. The width will reflect the width of the selected DataWindow (with a small padding), while the height will be a standard default value.

In our example, since the x coordinate of the column Amount is 1861, and it is 343 units wide, it extends to x coordinate 2204. When d_po_for_cc is placed as a Nested Report object on d_cost_center_with_po, the width of the Nested Report object automatically sizes to 2241. In this case, that is the width of d_po_for_cc + 37 PB units.

After the Nested Report object is placed on the DataWindow you can resize the height and width to your specifications. If the width of the Nested Report object is reduced below the actual width of the Nested Report DataWindow, the contents of the Nested Report will be cropped when data is retrieved. The height of the Nested Report object will be covered in the

Autosize Height section later in this chapter.

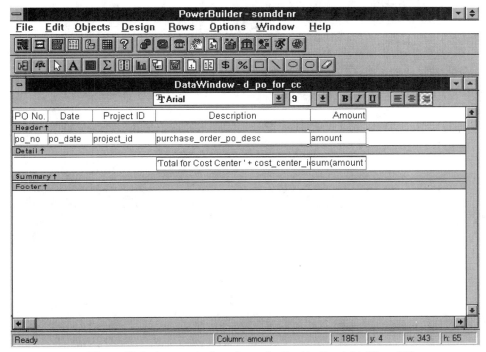

Figure 12-8: Amount is the column farthest to the right. The width of d_po_for_cc = the x coordinate of Amount + the width of Amount.

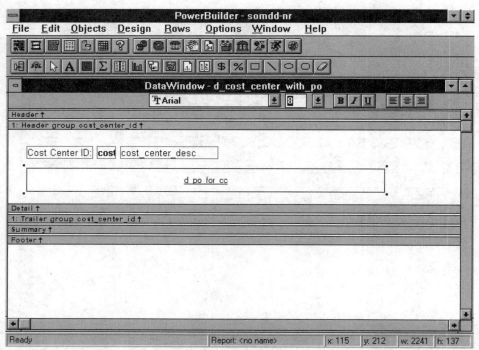

Figure 12-9: The default width of the Nested Report object is based on the width of the DataWindow selected for that object.

Once the Nested Report is placed on your DataWindow you can specify its graphical and behavioral settings. There are no settings which are specific only to Nested Reports; instead the Nested Report settings are a combination of those for DataWindow controls (on a window) and DataWindow columns. The settings can be changed by placing your pointer over the Nested Report and pressing your right mouse button.

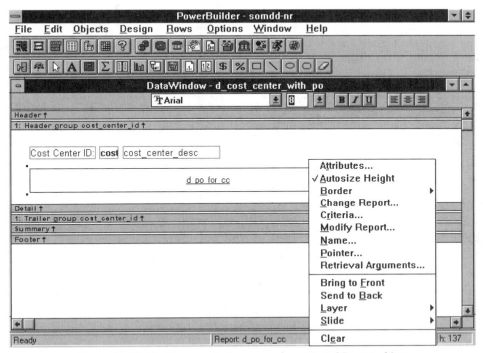

Figure 12-10: Right mouse button menu for a Nested Report object.

Note: A DataWindow with a Nested Report on it is not updatable.

Attributes

New to PB4 is the Attributes right mouse button menu option for all objects on the DataWindow. Values and expressions for object attributes can be directly entered in the DataWindow painter, thereby reducing the amount of scripting needed to define the behavior of a DataWindow control. This provides the ability to encapsulate the expressions in the DataWindow object itself, and allows for a broader range of behaviors to be previewed in the DataWindow Painter's Print Preview mode. Developers will no longer have to use dwModify to set expressions into object attributes.

When Attributes is selected, the Attribute Conditional Expressions dialog pops up. This dialog allows values or expressions to be entered for several attributes. To illustrate the use of a conditional expression for a Nested Report attribute, suppose you only want to display the Nested Report if a particular condition exists for the current row. Assuming there is a DataWindow column ("show_nr") which will act as a flag for this case, the following expression could be used for the "height" attribute.

```
if ( show_nr = 'Yes', 200, 0 )
```

If the Autosize Height attribute for the Nested Report is turned off, when the report is run the height of the Nested Report would be 200 for each row in which show_nr = Yes. If show_nr = No, the Nested Report would not appear for that row. For a similar effect the expression could be put in the "visible" attribute, but even though the column wouldn't be visible it would exist with a height > 0. This could cause undesired effects if there were "sliding" columns below the Nested Report: they wouldn't slide up into the space where the invisible Nested Report was. Column sliding is another new feature to PB4 which I'll cover later in this chapter.

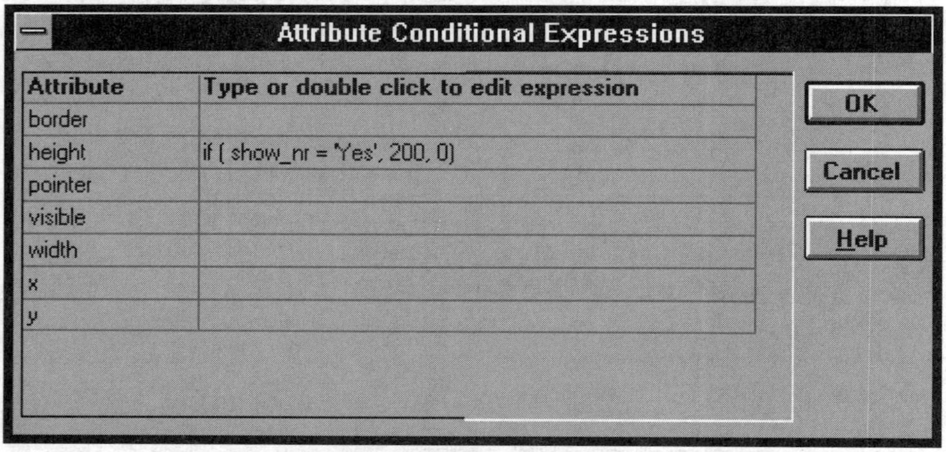

Attribute	Type or double click to edit expression
border	
height	if (show_nr = 'Yes', 200, 0)
pointer	
visible	
width	
x	
y	

Figure 12-11: Attributes Conditional Expressions dialog box.

Autosize Height

Autosize Height, a feature which was new in PowerBuilder 3, can be applied to all columns and Nested Reports. If an object has Autosize Height turned off, it will always occupy the exact amount of vertical space specified for that object in the DataWindow Painter. If an object has Autosize Height turned on, it will have a vertical height as small as 0 units and as large as is necessary to display its contents. For Nested Reports, the Autosize Height feature ensures that the report object will be tall enough to display all data retrieved into the Nested Reports, including header and footer bands. This option is available for all DataWindow columns.

The Autosize Height feature is currently only available for the detail band. If a Nested Report object is placed in a band other than the detail band (summary, trailer for group, etc.) the maximum height of the Nested Report will be the static height of the band. So if the height of the Nested Report is likely to vary, you must either size the band tall enough to contain the largest possible Nested Report, or allow some Nested Reports to be cropped at the height of the band.

For our example, since the Nested Report is in the detail band, the Autosize Height feature is available for the band. The Nested Report should be tall enough to display all purchase order records for the current cost center. Therefore, we want Autosize Height turned on for the Nested Report object and the detail band.

Note: The default Autosize Height setting for a Nested Report object is On.

Border

Select a border type for the Nested Report. The border options are the same as were available in PowerBuilder 3. This option is available for most objects on a DataWindow.

Change Report

This option allows you to change your DataWindow selection. A list of all DataWindows from all .pbl files used in your application will be displayed.

Criteria

In the DataWindow Painter, the Prompt For Criteria menu option allows you to indicate for which columns you would like to prompt the user to enter retrieval criteria. The Nested Report Criteria feature allows you to enter column retrieval criteria values and expressions for the DataWindow used by the Nested Report. Criteria can be used interchangeably with DataWindow retrieval arguments, but for some RDBMSes, using retrieval arguments may be more efficient than using Criteria.

The DataWindow to be nested can't use Prompt For Criteria. If Prompt For Criteria columns are specified, upon retrieval of the Nested Report records a DataWindow error message will display, and retrieval of the Nested Report will be aborted.

An example of using Criteria for a Nested Report would be if you wanted only to show purchase order records with purchase order numbers within the range 13500 to 14000. To do this you would enter ">=13500" and "and <=14000" in the po_no column of the Specify Retrieval Criteria dialog. The entered criteria are included in the WHERE clause of the SQL statement generated for retrieval of the Nested Report. In this case the following conditions would be added to the WHERE clause of the Nested Report:

```
po_no >= 13500 AND po_no <= 14000
```

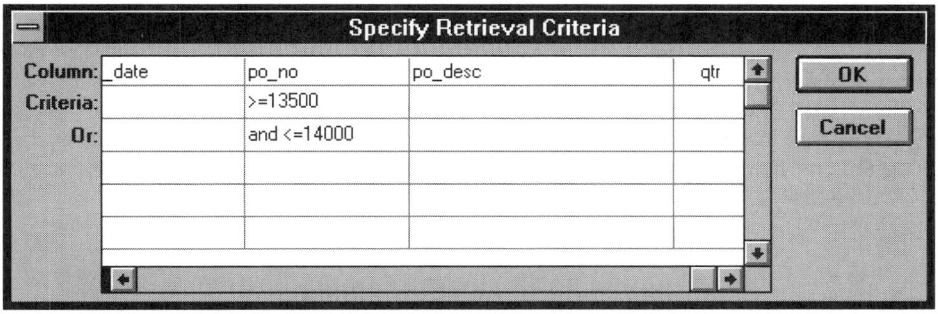

Figure 12-12: Specify Retrieval Criteria dialog.

Modify Report

This option, when selected, launches the DataWindow Painter for the DataWindow which was selected for the Nested Report. If the DataWindow used for the Nested Report is modified and saved, upon return to the main DataWindow the width of the Nested Report object will automatically be resized to reflect the new width of that DataWindow.

Name

Specify a name for the Nested Report object. This option is available for all DataWindow columns.

> **Note:** Until you specify a name for the Nested Report, the name used is the name of the DataWindow selected for the Nested Report.

Pointer

Specify the pointer to be displayed when the mouse is positioned over the Nested Report. This option is available for all objects on a DataWindow.

Retrieval Arguments

If the DataWindow selected for the Nested Report has retrieval arguments, argument values to be used for retrieval can be specified. For each Nested Report argument, you can enter a string or numeric literal, the name of a column or argument from the main DataWindow, or an expression. The value used must match the datatype of the Nested Report argument. Functions can be used in the expressions for datatype conversion.

If the DataWindow used by the Nested Report object has arguments specified for it, but the Nested Report object does not have values assigned to the arguments, the user will be prompted for arguments each time the Nested Report is retrieved. This could happen for every row in the DataWindow! If a literal or a DataWindow argument is used, then every time the SQL Select for the Nested Report is executed the identical condition will be included in the WHERE clause. If a DataWindow column is specified or is used in an expression, the current value of that column or the result of the expression will be used in a condition in the WHERE clause of the SQL Select.

To enter a value, column, argument, or expression for a Nested Report argument, select the Arguments option from the right mouse button menu. The Nested Report Arguments dialog will provide an editable DropDownListBox for selection of a DataWindow column or argument. An expression or value may be typed directly into the edit box. Alternately, double clicking the edit box will bring up the Modify Expression dialog for entry of long or complex expressions.

Note: If the Nested Report is in a group summary band, and if a DataWindow column is referenced in a Nested Report argument expression, the value returned for that column will be the value for the last row in the group.

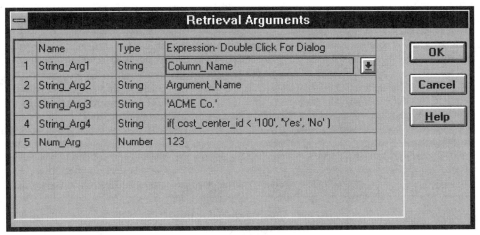

Figure 12-13: Column names, argument names, literals, and expressions can be used in the Retrieval Arguments dialog.

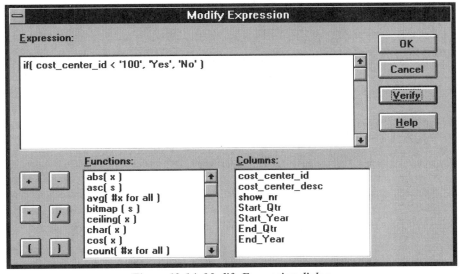

Figure 12-14: Modify Expression dialog.

Argument Syntax	###	Where # is numeric.
String Literal	'xxx'	Where x is alphanumeric.
DataWindow Column	\<column name\>	Select the column from the DropDownListBox.
DataWindow Argument	\<argument name\>	Select the argument from the DropDownListBox. Argument names are not preceded with a colon as is done when using an argument in the SQL painter.
Expression	\<expression\>	Expressions may contain column names, argument names, literals, and computed column functions.

Figure 12-15:Argument syntax.

For our example, we need to associate the 5 d_po_for_cc arguments with values from d_cost_center_with_po. Since the Nested Report will be retrieved for each row in d_cost_center_with_po, only those purchase order records which have the same cost_center_id value as the current row will be retrieved. Therefore, the first Nested Report argument, Cost_Center_ID, should be associated with the cost_center_id column.

Unless we want the user to enter the quarter ranges for each Nested Report retrieved, we have to assign some values to those arguments. The best thing to do in this case is to add the four quarter range arguments to d_cost_center_with_po, and associate those arguments to the respective Nested Report arguments. Basically, the four arguments will just be passed through to the Nested Report.

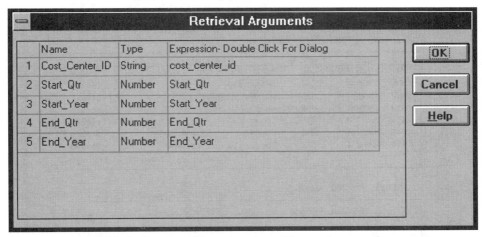

Figure 12-16: Assignment of d_cost_center_with_po columns and arguments to the arguments for the Nested Report d_po_for_cc.

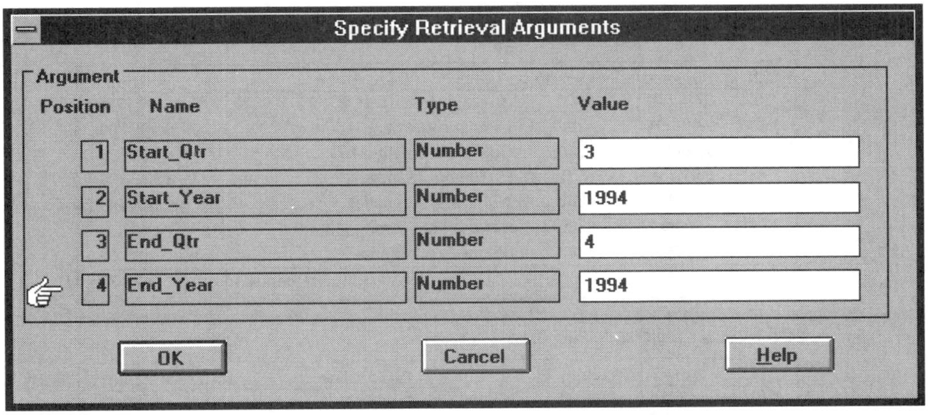

Figure 12-17: Retrieval arguments for d_cost_center_with_po.

Figure 12-18: First page of d_cost_center_with_po report.

Cost Center ID: 100   Administrative Support

PO No.	Date	Project ID	Description	Amount
13609	07/05/94	1050	Programmable Calculator	$446.50
13612	07/20/94	1665	Extra close haircut for Gregg	$15.00
13614	08/05/94	1665	Premium pencil erasers	$444.10
13621	08/08/94	1664	David's hair creme	$44.50
13622	08/10/94	1050	Temp hire	$350.00
13639	09/05/94	1664	Chalk board	$456.50
13642	09/20/94	1664	Extra close haircut for Gregg	$25.00
13644	10/05/94	1664	New model 2000 abacus	$454.10
			Total for Cost Center 100:	$2,235.70

Cost Center ID: 200   Data Processing

PO No.	Date	Project ID	Description	Amount
13613	07/25/94	1090	Donuts for LAN support staff	$977.20
13615	08/05/94	1090	CPM upgrade	$485.00
13620	08/08/94	1320	Montly support call fee	$485.00
13623	08/12/94	500	WordStart Training class	$800.00
13643	09/25/94	1110	6 dongles	$987.20
13645	10/05/94	1090	WordStart upgrade CPM to DOS	$495.00
13650	10/08/94	1110	Computer Dr. fixed WordStart	$495.00
			Total for Cost Center 200:	$4,724.40

Cost Center ID: 300   Sales

PO No.	Date	Project ID	Description	Amount
13610	07/10/94	5660	Model 9000 Super Phone	$5,490.00
13618	08/07/94	5660	Mr Mens' Key Largo trip	$4,890.00
13624	08/15/94	600	Retainer	$1,000.00
13640	09/10/94	5500	Company Car - used BMW	$5,500.00
13648	10/07/94	5500	Mr Mens' Hawaii trip	$4,900.00
			Total for Cost Center 300:	$21,780.00

Cost Center ID: 400   Tattoo Parlor

PO No.	Date	Project ID	Description	Amount
13611	07/12/94	8800	Gauze pads and first aid kit	$535.10
13616	08/06/94	4208	Lawsuit settlement - scarring	$9,990.00
13619	08/07/94	4300	Check out potential hire	$85.00
13625	08/16/94	700	P. Prescot relapse	$2,200.00
13641	09/12/94	4300	VCR for tattoo parlor	$645.10
13646	10/06/94	4300	Retainer for lawsuit #14234	$10,000.00
13651	10/08/94	8800	Mitchell's moisturizer	$5.50
			Total for Cost Center 400:	$23,460.70

Cost Center ID: 500   Child Care

PO No.	Date	Project ID	Description	Amount
13617	08/06/94	3000	Magnum P.I. contract	$985.00
13626	08/18/94	800	Cafeteria expansion	$13.45
13647	10/06/94	2300	10 rack cd player for bus	$995.00
13649	10/07/94	3000	Check out potential hire	$95.00

Note: If a Nested Report is placed in the detail band of an N-Up type DataWindow, the Nested Report will not be retrieved for each record in the DataWindow, but only once for each horizontally adjacent set of rows. If an N-Up column is used as Nested Report argument, the value from the first record of each set will be used for that row.

Bring to Front

When objects on a DataWindow overlap, you can specify how you want to graphically layer the objects on top of each other. When selected, this option displays the Nested Report on top of all objects it overlaps. This option is available for all objects on a DataWindow.

Send to Back

When selected, this option displays the Nested Report behind all objects it overlaps. This option is available for all objects on a DataWindow.

Layer

Since Nested Reports are "band" objects, it is not possible to specify a Nested Report as a foreground or background layer object. Although the layer options appear on the right mouse button menu, the selection is permanently set to Band. This option is available for all objects on a DataWindow.

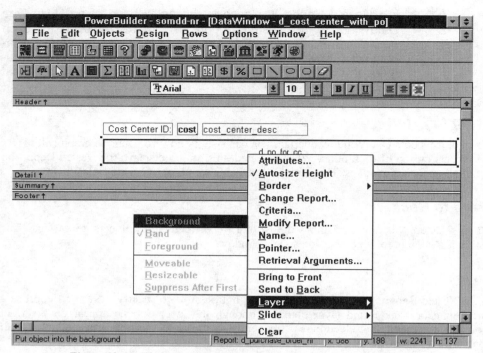

Figure 12-19: The Layer selection is always Band for a Nested Report.

Slide

A prominent new feature of PowerBuilder 4 is sliding. This new feature applies to all objects which can be placed on a DataWindow. Sliding allows columns to move left if the adjacent column in that direction vacates space, and vertically if the adjacent columns above vacate space or push downward.

Slide Left

If you have a DataWindow with three columns on it, col_a, col_b, and col_c, and col_c has Slide Left turned on. you can expect the following behaviors:

> If col_b has Slide Left turned off and the contents in col_b fills the entire width of the col_b column object, then col_c will not slide left.

> If col_b has Slide Left turned off and the contents of col_b do not fill the column object, col_c will slide left an amount equal to the empty space in col_b. For example, if col_b is 300 units wide and the string within it fills it only fifty percent, col_c will slide left 150 units (fifty percent of 300). If there is space between col_b and col_c, that space will be preserved even if col_c

slides left.

If col_b has Slide Left turned on, is only fifty percent full, and it slides left 100 units (because col_a isn't completely full), then col_c will slide left 100 units (following col_b to the left) and an additional 150 units (because col_b is only fifty percent full) for a total of 250 units.

A common use for Sliding Left would be when printing names which are composed of more than one column. The menu security feature for the purchase order system uses table User to store user security information for the application. The User table has user_id, first_name, middle_name, and last_name columns. Using PowerBuilder 3, if you were to build a simple DataWindow to display the records in User, you would display the first, last, and middle names in blocked columns. Alternatively, you could have created a computed column to concatenate the strings so that they displayed in a contiguous manner. With PowerBuilder 4 you simply check the Slide Left attribute on the middle_name and last_name columns to display the names in a contiguous manner.

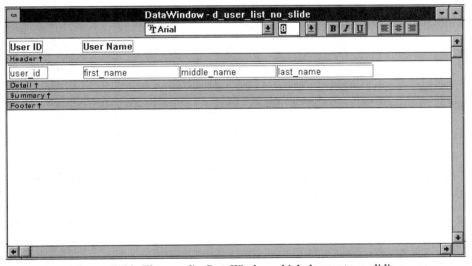

Figure 12-20: The user list DataWindow which does not use sliding.

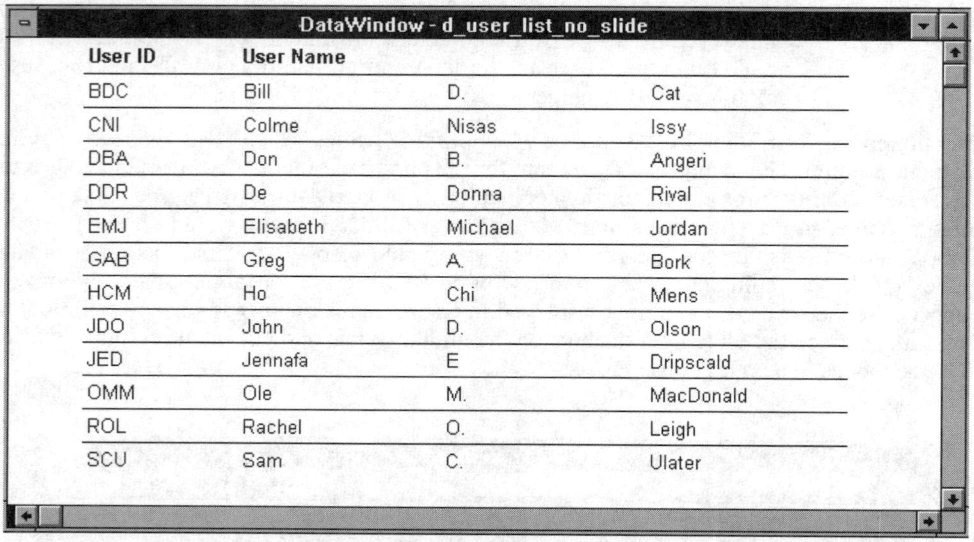

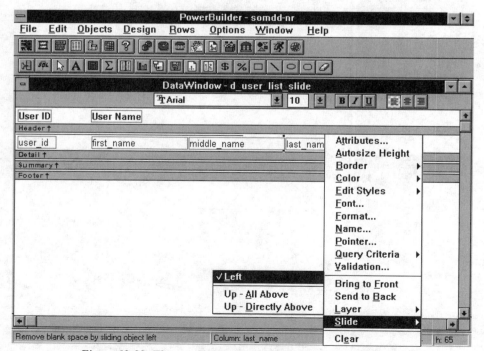

Figure 12-21: Print Preview for the user list DataWindow which does not use sliding.

Figure 12-22: The user list DataWindow which does use sliding.

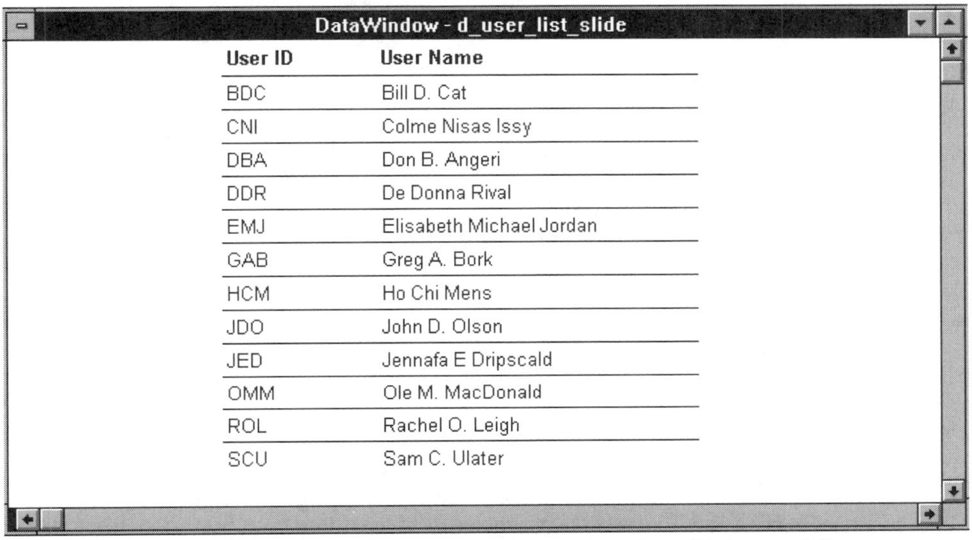

DataWindow - d_user_list_slide	
User ID	**User Name**
BDC	Bill D. Cat
CNI	Colme Nisas Issy
DBA	Don B. Angeri
DDR	De Donna Rival
EMJ	Elisabeth Michael Jordan
GAB	Greg A. Bork
HCM	Ho Chi Mens
JDO	John D. Olson
JED	Jennafa E Dripscald
OMM	Ole M. MacDonald
ROL	Rachel O. Leigh
SCU	Sam C. Ulater

Figure 12-23: Print Preview for the user list DataWindow which uses sliding.

Slide Up

The term Slide Up is a slight misnomer. Instead, it should be Slide Vertical, because it allows objects to slide up *and* down. Slide Up for a column works in a similar manner to Slide Left, except that it is dependent on the Autosize Height and Slide Up settings of the columns in the horizontal plane above it. If the Autosize Height settings are turned on for those columns, they may vacate space or push downward, thereby causing the lower column to slide vertically. (I use the term "push" because the higher columns can either expand into the space or slide down into the space.) Likewise, if Slide Up settings are turned on, then those columns may vacate space or push downward.

For example, if a column (col_b) has Slide Up turned on and the column above it (col_a) has Autosize Height turned on, and if col_a expands downward, then col_b will slide downward. If col_b has Slide Up turned off, col_b will not move when col_a expands, potentially resulting in col_a occupying the same space as col_b.

Up– Directly Above

If Directly Above is turned on for a column, that column will slide down only if at least one of the columns directly above it pushes downward. The amount it will be pushed down is dependent on how far into its space the higher column expands. The original amount of vertical space between the column and all columns above it will be preserved.

If Directly Above is turned on for a column, that column will slide up only if columns directly above it vacate space. The amount it will slide up is dependent on how much space is vacated by those columns immediately above it. The original amount of vertical space between the column and all columns directly above it will be preserved.

Note:Slide Up–Directly Above is the default setting for Nested Reports.

Up–All Above

If All Above is turned on for a column, that column will slide down only if any objects occupying the same horizontal plane as the closest object above it push downward, or if any objects at all push into that horizontal plane.

For example, if col_a and col_b are in the horizontal plane above col_c and if both col_a and col_b occupy space in at least one common y coordinate, then col_c (which has Slide Up - All Above turned on) won't slide downward unless at least one of col_a and col_b push downward. The original amount of vertical space between the column and all columns occupying the horizontal plane above it will be preserved.

If All Above is turned on for a column, that column will slide up only if *all* objects occupying the same horizontal plane as the closest object above it, vacate space.

For example, if col_a and col_b are in the horizontal plane above col_c and if both col_a and col_b occupy space in at least one common y coordinate, then col_c (which has Slide Up– All Above turned on) won't slide upward unless both col_a and col_b vacate space. The original amount of vertical space between the column and all columns occupying the horizontal plane above it will be preserved.

For our example, let's nest another report to graphically display the breakdown of purchase orders by project. Each cost center row will have a table of purchase orders and a graph. For the graph we'll use DataWindow d_po_gr, which displays the project breakdown of purchase orders for a cost center over a specified date range. It has the same arguments as d_po_for_cc. Since we'll be placing d_po_gr below d_po_for_cc we need to turn sliding on for the graph, so that the purchase order table and the graph don't overlap. Also, we need to assign the appropriate d_cost_center_with_po arguments and columns to the d_po_gr arguments.

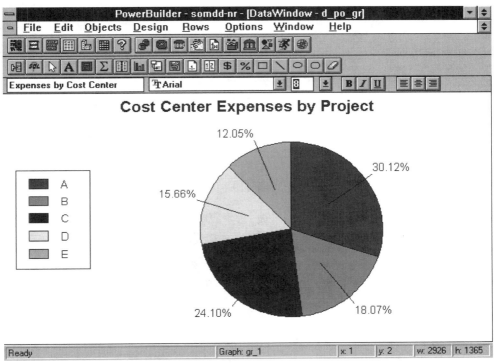

Figure 12-24: d_po_gr shows the breakdown of purchase orders by project for a cost center.

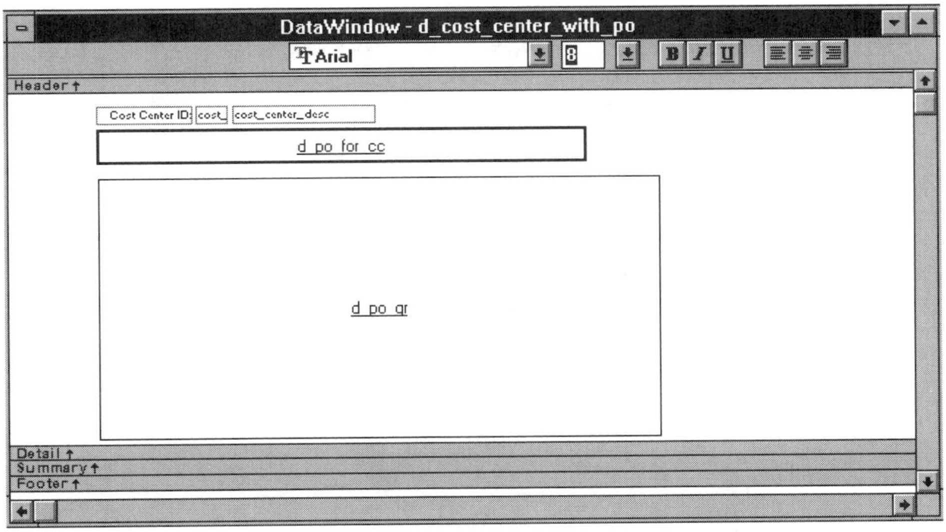

Figure 12-25: d_cost_center_with_po with a purchase order report and a graph nested on

it.

Cost Center ID: 100   Administrative Support

PO No.	Date	Project ID	Description	Amount
13609	07/05/94	1050	Programmable Calculator	$446.50
13612	07/20/94	1665	Extra close haircut for Gregg	$15.00
13614	08/05/94	1665	Premium pencil erasers	$444.10
13621	08/08/94	1664	David's hair creme	$44.50
13622	08/10/94	1050	Temp hire	$350.00
13639	09/05/94	1664	Chalk board	$456.50
13642	09/20/94	1664	Extra close haircut for Gregg	$25.00
13644	10/05/94	1664	New model 2000 abacus	$454.10
			Total for Cost Center 100:	$2,235.70

Cost Center Expenses by Project

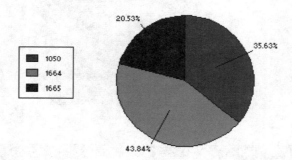

Cost Center ID: 200   Data Processing

PO No.	Date	Project ID	Description	Amount
13613	07/25/94	1090	Donuts for LAN support staff	$977.20
13615	08/05/94	1090	CPM upgrade	$485.00
13620	08/08/94	1320	Montly support call fee	$485.00
13623	08/12/94	500	WordStart Training class	$800.00
13643	09/25/94	1110	6 dongles	$987.20
13645	10/05/94	1090	WordStart upgrade CPM to DOS	$495.00
13650	10/08/94	1110	Computer Dr. fixed WordStart	$495.00
			Total for Cost Center 200:	$4,724.40

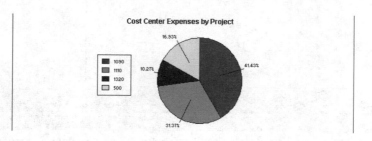

Cost Center Expenses by Project

Figure 12-26: First page of d_cost_center_with_po report.

Note: Sliding is a welcome feature for reporting. However, it can also be used on updatable DataWindows and therefore during data entry. Use it sparingly in data entry, as it could easily confuse users.

Clear

Delete the Nested Report object from the DataWindow. This option is available for all objects on a DataWindow. In PowerBuilder 3.0 this option was called Delete.

Composite DataWindow type

A frequently asked question on Powersoft's CompuServe forum has been, "How do I print more than one DataWindow in a single print job?" There are some PowerBuilder 3 techniques which could accomplish this, but only with limited flexibility. Nested Reports make it an easy task. More specifically, PowerBuilder 4 provides a new "Composite" DataWindow type which makes it possible to print multiple unrelated DataWindows in a single print run.

The Composite DataWindow type is simply a shell in which Nested Reports and other graphic DataWindow objects can be placed. There is no data associated with a Composite DataWindow. It doesn't have a data source, and therefore it has no columns and no SQL Select. Because of this, a large portion of the menu options are disabled, including all menu options under Rows. However, as with all other DataWindow types, settings can be specified for DataWindow Style, Print Specifications, and more. In addition, several types of objects can be placed on the DataWindow, including static text objects, drawing objects, pictures, computed columns, and Nested Reports.

Creating a Composite DataWindow

To create a Composite DataWindow, open the DataWindow Painter and from the Select DataWindow dialog click on "New." In the New DataWindow dialog select the Composite type and click "OK." (Notice that when you select Composite, the data sources all become disabled.) At this point the Select Reports dialog will prompt you to select 0, 1, or several existing DataWindows to nest in the Composite DataWindow. If you select one or more DataWindows, when you click "OK" the DataWindow will be created with the Nested Report objects placed in alphabetical order, left to right on the page, wrapping to a new row of Nested Report objects whenever the right margin is reached. Once the DataWindow is created you can add additional Nested Reports and other objects.

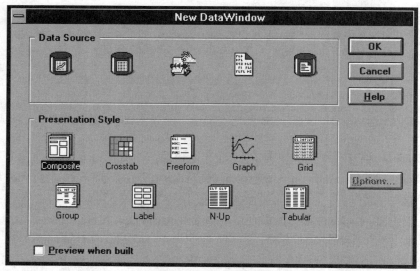

Figure 12-27: New DataWindow dialog.

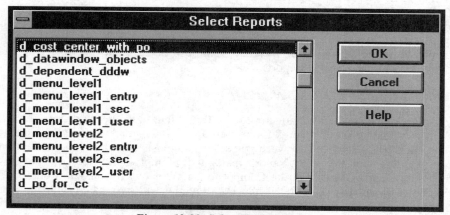

Figure 12-28: Select Reports dialog.

There are two right mouse button menu options which are available for Nested Report objects on Composite DataWindows which are not available for Nested Report objects on other DataWindow types. The two settings, Start On New Page and Trail the Footer, define how the report will look when previewed and printed.

Start On New Page

This option allows you to specify that a Nested Report always begin at the top of a new page. This is similar to the New Page on Group Break option which was new to PowerBuilder 3. The default setting for this option is Off.

Trail the Footer

Normally the footer always appears at the bottom of each page on a report. However, if Trail the Footer is turned on, the footer will appear immediately following the end of the Nested Report. The default setting for this option is On.

Composite settings

The right mouse button menu for a Composite report includes the three options which are standard to most other DataWindow types: Color, Pointer, and Units. There is an additional setting, Arguments, which is specific to the Composite DataWindow type. This menu option allows you to enter DataWindow arguments, which can be used to pass data to the Nested Report arguments.

For our example, let's assume that we need to print a summary graph which shows cost center expenses broken down by project for a specified range of quarters. In addition, we want that summary graph to print immediately after d_cost_center_with_po and as part of the same print job. First we need to develop the graph DataWindow, then we can create a composite DataWindow and nest both reports on it.

The graph DataWindow, d_cost_center_gr, will use the same arguments as those used by d_po_for_cc.

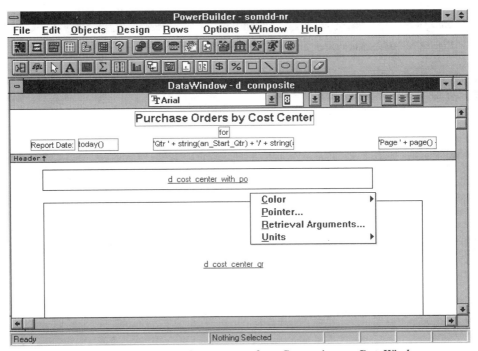

Figure 12-29: Right mouse button menu for a Composite type DataWindow.

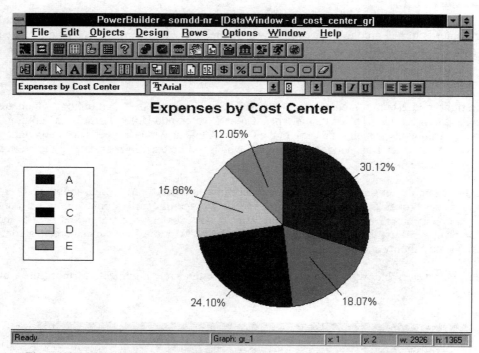

Figure 12-30: d_cost_center_gr shows the breakdown of purchase orders by cost center.

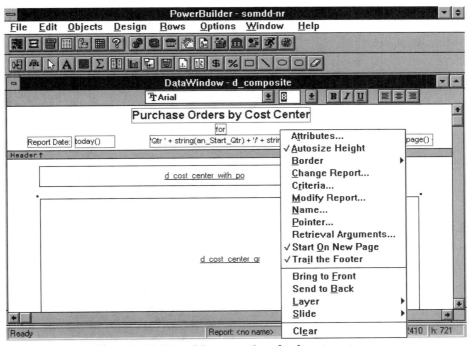

Figure 12-31: Nested Report settings for d_cost_center_gr.

The composite, d_composite, will have two nested reports on it–one for d_cost_center_with_po and the other for d_cost_center_gr. AutoSize Height must be turned on for d_cost_center_with_po, so that the entire contents of the nested report will be displayed. Sliding Up (either option) must be turned on for the graph, so that it slides vertically based on the size of d_cost_center_with_po. The four arguments used by the Nested Reports must be defined as arguments for d_composite. Once defined, those arguments must be assigned to the respective Nested Report arguments. We'll turn on Start On New Page for the graph so that it doesn't have a page break in it. Also, we'll turn Trail the Footer off for d_cost_center_with_po, but turn it on for the graph since it is at the end of the report.

Another new feature in PB4 is the ability to reference DataWindow arguments in column expressions. For our report this will come in handy since we should display the date range at the top of the report (d_composite). The expression for the computed column will be:

```
'Qtr ' + string(Start_Qtr ) + '/' + string(Start_Year )
+ ' thru Qtr ' + string(End_Qtr ) + '/' +
string(End_Year )
```

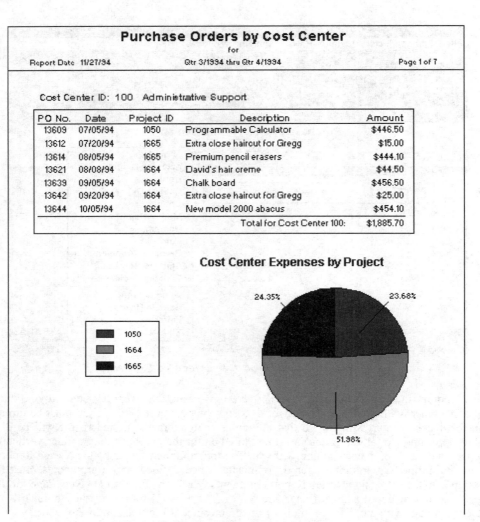

Purchase Orders by Cost Center

for

Report Date 11/27/94   Qtr 3/1994 thru Qtr 4/1994   Page 2 of 7

Cost Center ID: 200   Data Processing

PO No.	Date	Project ID	Description	Amount
13613	07/25/94	1090	Donuts for LAN support staff	$977.20
13615	08/05/94	1090	CPM upgrade	$485.00
13620	08/08/94	1320	Computer Dr. fixed WordStart	$485.00
13643	09/25/94	1110	6 dongles	$987.20
13645	10/05/94	1090	WordStart upgrade CPM to DOS	$495.00
13650	10/08/94	1110	Computer Dr. fixed WordStart	$495.00
			Total for Cost Center 200:	$3,924.40

Cost Center Expenses by Project

Figure 12-33: Second page of d_composite report.

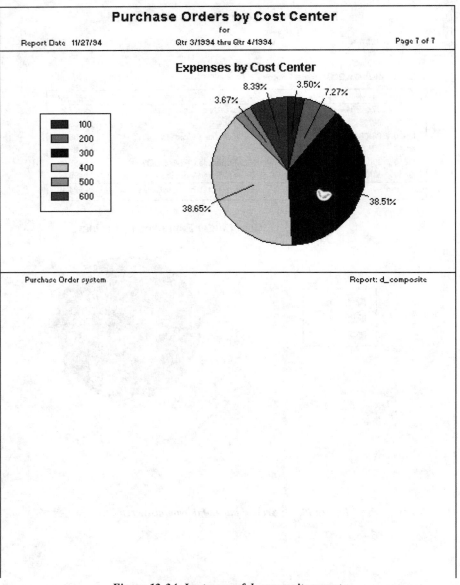

Figure 12-34: Last page of d_composite report.

Referencing Nested Reports in PowerScript

Since placing a Nested Report on a DataWindow makes that DataWindow non-updatable, Nested Reports can be used for reporting only. Combine that with the greater reporting power of PowerBuilder 4.0, and the need to manipulate Nested Reports from PowerScript may be very rare. However, when the need arises to reference a Nested Report from Power-Script, the ability to do so exists. Nested Report objects can be referenced in the same manner as DropDownDataWindows. Using the function GetChild (formerly dwGetChild), a reference to the Nested Report DataWindow can be obtained. Once obtained, DataWindow functions can be applied to the dwChild reference to manipulate the Nested Report.

> **Note:** Function names have been changed to decouple the functions from specific object types. For example, the "dw" has been dropped from all functions which previously began with that prefix. Although a large number of function names have changed, PowerBuilder 4 will still support the former names, even though they will no longer appear in the product documentation.

The function Describe (formerly dwDescribe) can be used to determine if a DataWindow has a Nested Report object on it. The following line will return a Yes or No, indicating whether a Nested Report object is on dw_1.

```
ls_return_val = dw_1.Describe( "DataWindow.Nested" )
```

The following code shows how to get a dwChild reference for a Nested Report. For this example, the Nested Report object is named nro and the DataWindow it is on is dw_1.

```
DataWindowChild ldwc_nested_report
integer li_return_code

li_return_code = dw_1.GetChild( 'nro' , ldwc_nested_report )

IF li_return_code = -1 THEN  // GetChild error
MessageBox("Error", "Error Getting Reference To dwChild ")
Return
ELSE // GetChild worked
  // do something with ldwc_nested_report
END IF
```

Once the dwChild reference is obtained, functions can be applied to the Nested Report. For example, to manually force retrieval of nro, the script would be:

```
// Set a transaction object for the nested report
li_return_code = ldwc_nested_report.SetTransObject( SQLCA )

IF li_return_code = -1 THEN
 MessageBox( 'ERROR', 'Failure Setting Transaction!' )
 Return
ELSE
// Retrieve the nested report, supply retrieval arguments if necessary
 li_return_code = ldwc_nested_report.Retrieve()
 IF li_return_code = -1 THEN
```

```
MessageBox( 'ERROR', 'Failure During Retrieval of Nested Report!' )
Return
END IF
END IF
```

As is commonly done with DropDownDataWindows, it may be beneficial for a Nested Report to share DataWindow buffers with another DataWindow. The following shows the syntax for sharing DataWindow buffers between nro and dw_2, where dw_2 is the primary DataWindow.

```
dw_2.ShareData( ldwc_nested_report )
```

Chapter Summary

The ability to nest reports is indeed one of the most exciting new features of PowerBuilder 4.0. By combining column sliding with the ability to nest fully functional DataWindows, PowerBuilder becomes an even more powerful tool for creating slick reports. Not only do these new features broaden PowerBuilder's reporting ability, but they remove some previous limitations and the need to script data-dependent behaviors. Also, Nested Reports can be referenced from PowerScript in the same manner as DropDownDataWindows. As a dwChild, Nested Reports can be manipulated by several functions, giving the developer more control over its behavior. The new Composite DataWindow type provides a data-independent shell for Nested Reports, giving developers the ability to combine unrelated DataWindows into a single report. In addition, with the ability to specify arguments, Composite DataWindows allow users to specify criteria for all Nested Reports.

Not only do these new features empower us to meet the ever-changing needs of our clients, they also give us a good indication that Powersoft is staying at the forefront of technology.

CHAPTER **13**

Applications Design
Overview from A to Z

By Terry Voth

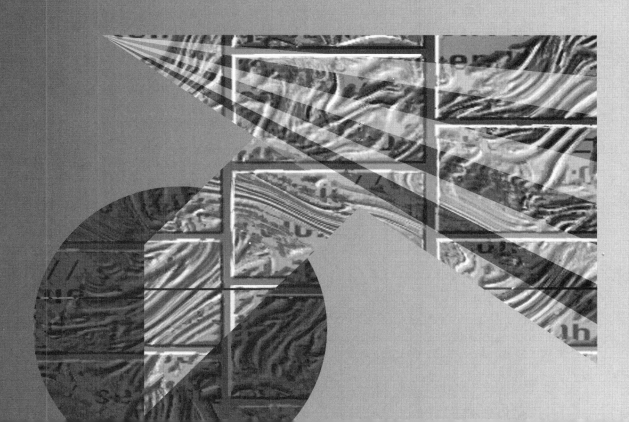

Applications Design Overview from A to Z

by **Terry Voth**

Programmers have their own kind of machismo. It is not born out of old Clint Eastwood or John Wayne movies. No one quite knows where it came from. It combines several factors: a disdain for producing documentation (perhaps because most programmers can't write graffiti without making a grammatical error); a self-reliance that claims that all you need is the language manuals (as a last resort) to produce a good application; and a belief that RAD (Rapid Application Design) is all-good and is measured in hours. What results is an avoidance of standard software life cycle development methodologies. Can you spell "disaster," boys and girls?

This chapter is not intended to be an exhaustive treatment of the topic. It gives an overview of life cycle development with a special eye to PowerBuilder and some related infrastructure issues. While assumptions include a large organization and an IS or external group providing services to a client organization, scenarios can be adapted for other situations. The common attributes that should apply are a desire to please the client, and either limited resources or a desire to limit resources spent on the project.

Who Needs All This Analysis and Design?

Design methodology is not torture to punish programmers who make too much money. It doesn't exist to kill trees. The considerable time and effort invested must provide some return. Some benefits of life cycle development methodologies are communication, scoping, control, and continuity.

The biggest challenge facing almost all aspects of business is communication. Communication failure can cost big-time. Airliners get shot down, protected wetlands get turned to oil fields, and cocker spaniels get shaved like poodles, all because of miscommunication. Software development is no exception. "That's not what I asked for" is not something you want to hear after months of development. What is it they want? Say it once. Say it again. Present it in a presentation, in a report, in a prototype. The more times and the more ways it is said, the more likely misinterpretations will come out. Risks won't be eliminated, but significantly reduced. If clients understand their software will be based on the documents they are signing off, and that the commitment to pay for the software has been made based on those documents, then you're likely to get their attention.

Black is black, right?

And then, of course, there is the ominous phrase that every developer dreads: "That's what I asked for, but not what I want." They asked for black. You programmed black. But what they really meant was a darker shade of gray. Or, they assumed that you would implicitly understand that they meant user-configurable colors. I mean, all Windows applications have user-configurable colors, don't they? (At this point you should realize that your client's exposure to Windows has been limited to the cheesiest shareware possible, so take nothing for granted anymore.) Now unless you have old family money and program only for the sheer pleasure of it, you should be getting the sinking feeling that your client is about to ask you to "fix" this "bug." For free. And if it is not money directly out of your pocket, it means that something else will have to be put off, or that you'll get to put in some overtime instead of leading a normal life. Unless, of course, you have "black" in writing. With their signature. And when it's their signature, it becomes their responsibility. This is what you asked for. This is what you got. You want something different? Can I introduce you to the concept of change management? New requirements; new money. You'd be surprised how many "implied" features get dropped when money comes into the picture.

How many developers are still working on their first system? The number may not reflect just developers new to PowerBuilder. The system starts as a simple single-document interface system with a few fields and a couple of calculations. Now it's a multiple-document interface with 1,500 distinct sheets; it's an OLE client and server, which will seek out all applications available to the current workstation and interface with each in a distinct manner; it's a disk defragmenter during its idle event; and it brews a mean cup of coffee. The scope has grown to monstrous proportions. How did this happen? "Requirements creep"– and it comes in two flavors: push and pull.

Requirements creep

You are meeting with the client to review the prototype. Conversation is going quite nicely. The client is pleased. Then you hear, "Couldn't you just add...." It sounds innocuous enough. Probably take just an hour or two. And, besides, deep down you're really a nice person! The moment the word "Sure" passes your lips, you have the push. You get back to your desk, go over your notes. Maybe you realize that you've just agreed to fifty of these "innocuous" one hour changes. Maybe once you try out this "easy fix," you discover it's not quite as straightforward as you think. Or maybe it causes problems in twenty other places. And, of course, the new version of the prototype is due tomorrow. Requirements creep has pushed right over you and left the mangled wreckage of your body and mind in its wake.

The other flavor of requirements creep, just as dangerous, starts with a similar phrase: "I could just add...." The developer is given a task to do and left alone. One day, a problem appears. A little investigation finds that the cause is two different versions of rst.dll on the workstation's path. Well, that's easy enough to fix, but what if it happens again on another workstation? Or with another DLL? It certainly wouldn't be hard to automatically check out the workstation configuration and check for duplicates of the required DLLs. Maybe even check for the right version! Soon, our hero is off researching the required files, checking API calls, making the DupDLL() function quite slick. Time passes and the deadline arrives. Manager comes by to pick up the deliverable. Not much has been done on the original specification, but check out this DupDLL()! Red-faced, the manager has to go to the client and beg for more time. Looking to pin the blame elsewhere, the Workstation Configuration group is nailed for allowing this duplicate DLL situation to crop up in the first place. Defensive, the Workstation Configuration group marches en masse to the original offending workstation of our now slightly tarnished hero. It turns out that the situation was originally created by the installation of a pirated version of "Carnage and Havoc," a game that's been occupying our former hero's lunch time. Now, people have been offended, the client is fuming over delays, and the manager, between apologizing and rescheduling, has been dropping the "Help Wanted" section on the developer's desk every day. Requirements creep might have pulled the developer right out of a job.

Requirements creep needs a firm definition of requirements scope. If requirements are written, the client has a responsibility to keep expectations within that scope. As well, written requirements delineate very clearly the developer's responsibilities. A written requirement also gives us a starting point to define "change" (remember, more features will affect money, schedule, or quality) and to teach the elusive concept of "change management."

Programmers are free-spirited types. Hackers are the ultimate personification of this, ignoring rules and claiming whatever ground they can break into. The thought of a programmer voluntarily participating in development life cycle activities that would enforce corporate control seems a little far-fetched. But consider some advantages of this control.

Not too long ago, PCs implied character-based applications. Macintoshes, already set up in the GUI world, sparked fierce debate between allies of the two machines. When the arguments raged, the Mac fanatics' most potent argument had nothing to do with this odd rodent-thing they had sitting on their desks. It wasn't the pretty pictures or the funny sounds. It was the consistency of user interface between applications. Once you learned the basics on one program, you had the basics for all the programs (or, at least, all programs that conformed to the Apple standards). Open and Save were usually under the File menu. You knew how to switch between windows and tasks. The character-based world couldn't compete. Shift-F10 in one program could mean Save, while in another it could open up a user configuration screen. Even when character-based applications introduced their version of pull-down menus, finding a particular function was either luck or familiarity with that specific application. Microsoft Windows promised to change that for all of us, provided developers followed the defined standards. Of course, you know what the free-spirited programmers started to do.

Today, application suites are still trying to make their user interface consistent throughout the different applications within the suite. The promise of increased user productivity is coming, slowly. Those who don't learn from history are doomed to repeat it. So, you're planning to put six new in-house-built applications on the users' desktops over the next two years. Going to let super-hacker implement his "better than the rest" user interface on his application? I don't think so. You want to make all six applications at least consistent with each other, if not also consistent with the off-the-shelf packages the user is already using. The time to stop super-hacker is not after his application has been installed on 2,000 desktops. The time to implement corporate standards is early, during the design phase. The later in software development the change gets made, the more expensive it is to implement. So make sure the application you're getting is the one you want before the programmer has written one line of code.

They say that no man is an island unto himself. Today, neither is any application. Interfacing with other systems is commonplace; the thought of re-keying output from one system into another is abhorrent. And then there's the executive information system, where someone with a corner office wants to grab data from every system and put it together in some insightful but as yet unimagined of way ("Let's plot the ratio of commissioned sales to the number of damaged wing nuts on the shop floor, grouped by final destination customer, against the phases of the moon!"). What happens if everyone plans the data by himself? Chaos. The customer code for Flanges Inc. is different in each system. Bridging tables matching codes between systems become more difficult to manage than the code tables themselves. Naming, data access standards, and normalization are so different, no one can use any data in anyone else's system. Use of common tables and corporate data standards will not happen by accident. Life cycle methodologies allow control over these.

In the circles I travel in, a request for documentation is usually followed by the phrase, "...just in case you get hit by a bus." Not that anyone was wishing harm on me. (At least, not that I know of.) The point was, if I had to leave the project unexpectedly tomorrow, is there sufficient documentation that others could pick up where I left off? I constantly see situations where the person with all the vital information got a better job offer, and left with all that vital information. Someone doesn't document something, expecting to be back for the next phase of the project, and gets reassigned. Life cycle methodology documents provide a vehicle of knowledge transfer. They provide a justification of why things were done the way they were. And they provide this in a way that will likely outlive your connection to any given project.

While producing documentation and interim deliverables for the life cycle methodology may not be completely enjoyable for someone who lives to code, it is far from torture. Expectation management is a vital part of any software project that involves a third party. And while methodology techniques may seem to slow final delivery, the primary objective is to identify problems as early in the life cycle as possible, thereby minimizing time and cost to fix them. For instance, a change in a validation rule identified during the design stage might cost fifteen minutes and a reprinted page. Identified after implementation, it may cost coding time, re-testing time, second rollout time, and, perhaps most crucially, hundreds of hours of end user time–because violated data integrity may mean that all data must be destroyed and re-entered. That may cost end user confidence in the application, and in all other in-house applications. While the perfect application is still a topic for textbooks, life cycle methodology should bring that idea closer to reality for you and your project.

System Conversions

While most life cycle methodologies focus on new construction efforts, keep in mind that these principles could and should be applied to an area where PowerBuilder has been booming: conversion of character-based PC and mainframe legacy systems to GUI, and conversion of single-user systems to client/server. The concept of "converting" a system is deceptively simple, and may not seem to require such a methodology. Let me illustrate from personal experience why life cycle methodology should not be ignored in a conversion.

I was brought in halfway through a project: the conversion of a Clipper system to PowerBuilder/Windows/sybase. It was determined by the project manager that analysis should consist of a two-hour application walkthrough of the Clipper system and handover of the Clipper code. Design was to be copied directly from the original system. This started the slide toward disaster. The Clipper code used an add-on library that no one on the team had the documentation for and no one on the team understood. The only person who spent time trying to analyze the Clipper code to discover its underlying functionality was dismissed for not producing windows quickly enough. Significant functionality hidden behind function keys was discovered missing from the new system at handover. Since the character-based design was copied directly, no GUI features were implemented properly, making the user interface awkward. Also, because design was bypassed, use of inheritance was not properly planned for. Once people realized the shortcomings in the approach to inheritance, they tried to reverse-engineer existing windows to use inheritance, only days before a major delivery. This major coding effort caused many all-nighters and a delivery delay. To add to the confusion, the Clipper system continued to be developed without our knowledge by the client. Since there was no documentation of expectations of what our system would contain, the client of course expected our system to match the current functionality of their system. Naturally, I would not classify this as a high point in my career. Life cycle methodology could have prevented many gray hairs and saved many pounds of antacid.

I would strongly recommend some form (perhaps limited, if circumstances justify) of both an analysis and a design stage before construction. Analysis should at least determine if the legacy system is still valid for the users' requirements, and document what functionality is in the legacy system that should be converted to the new one. Design should at least produce some kind of prototype so that the method of converting to GUI can be agreed upon. For example, if in the legacy character-based system pressing F2 in a field opened a screen that listed available codes, converting that field to a drop-down list box (or drop-down DataWindow) would be appropriate from a GUI perspective. However, that should be agreed to in the design stage, not argued over after final delivery. As you go through the description of each life cycle stage, evaluate for yourself which other elements might be useful in a conversion project.

Life Cycle Overview

Although numbers can vary between specific life cycle methodologies, the software development life cycle is broken into three stages: Analysis, Design, and Construction. I will define each of these stages, list some possible deliverables associated with each, and itemize some infrastructure items required, all with client/server and PowerBuilder in mind.

Analysis stage

Analysis is a high-level study of the planned project. It should cover an examination of corporate directions and issues as well as client departmental directions. High-level analysis of the client's business procedures and data, objectives of the project, and a decision to proceed with the project should be the results of the analysis stage.

While your client may be only one department in a large organization, it is important to understand the organization and the issues that face it, both now and in the future. For example, if a record company plans to go with only digital products within a year, spending $500,000 to deliver a system in eight months to automate the business processes of the Vinyl Products Division would be inappropriate. If a research department is about to undergo a merger with a development department, consideration of the business processes of both departments is important if a project management system is going to be useful after the merger. And, if Shipping is not going to be replacing its mainframe system for another five years, notes that interfacing into this system need to be given attention should be carried forward into the design stage.

One of the hardest things to do is to get someone to describe, in detail, what they do from day to day. After several years in a position, business processes and information flows are taken for granted. "Things just happen" and "things just get done." Getting people beyond this is the biggest challenge in defining the business or process model. Another challenge is to get people to describe the entire department's business flows, not just the portions they believe are to be automated. In defining the entire department's business model, you might identify previously unrecognized business functions that should be automated with this project. Conversely, a full discussion of a given business function may remove it from the list of candidate functions for automation. The business model may also identify other issues, such as potential interfaces to other systems inside or outside the department.

The most important output of the analysis stage is deciding which, if any, business functions to automate. When analysis begins, clients usually have a preconceived notion of what should be automated. The IS representative will tend to believe that the more that can be automated, the better. Therefore, turning the client down seems out of the question–in fact, it is more likely that a technically oriented person will want to raise a client's expectations by proposing more automation than originally anticipated. This can be the downfall of an IS organization. What is required here is brutal honesty and professional integrity. The objective of automating a business function is not to bring the client to the leading edge of technology. If there is no cost-benefit, or if the automation does not facilitate the corporation to compete more effectively, the business function should not be automated.

While this sounds defeatist to the IS organization, it in fact prolongs its life. For years technologists have promised management improved productivity and competitiveness out of automation. Organizations that have provided it have been given much slack and have been well funded. For those that haven't, the leash is tightening and the fist of punishment is constantly overhead. Integrity breeds trust. Perhaps integrity will drive us to new methods and tools to make us more effective, lowering cost and allowing more to be automated efficiently.

Closely related to the process of producing a business model is the process of producing a logical data model. This is a high-level description of both internal and external (i.e. to and from other systems) data requirements. Entities, attributes, and relations should be documented. While the logical data model will be direct input for the database definition, it should not be expected that entities and attributes will map directly to tables and columns. The logical data model should not be normalized. That step is left until the database design stage.

Once data and functions are defined, ballpark volumetrics should be created. These should be linked to a network definition. A *network definition* is the distribution of the proposed system, both geographically and organizationally. Network definitions should include hardware already available to the client organization, like database servers, LAN equipment, and WAN equipment. The volumetrics should be broken down by network distribution, if applicable. They will be inputs to several decisions. The required size of database servers will be anticipated with the volumetrics. There's not much point getting a 2G server if the database is expected to grow to 200K over the next five years. Conversely, planning for a 500M server could be a mistake for a document management system that could produce 100M in versioned documents per month. Network requirements may be defined by volumetrics. If a regional office is required to pour over thousands of records of headquarters information directly from the headquarters database, upgrading from a 2400 baud modem is highly recommended. Volumetrics could also act as input to design and construction decisions. For example, if functions are distinctly split between headquarters functions and branch functions, perhaps two different executables, one for headquarters and one for branches, are in order. If a parts table is expected to have over 500,000 entries, but will only be accessed once or twice per day, caching this parts table in the workstation's memory may be overkill and even detrimental to the overall system performance.

Defining who is using the system is another part of the analysis stage. This would not be a compilation of names, but of job classifications, such as order entry clerk, shipping clerk, and management. This list would be used to create a security matrix. The matrix can compare users against data entities, business functions, or both. If comparing against data entities, the most common way to define permissions is to list which actions the user classification is allowed to perform on the data entity: create, read, update, and/or delete. If comparing against business functions, the most common way is simply to define whether the user classification can execute that function or not.

And what would any project be without time and cost projections! These should be constantly updated, so don't worry about incredible accuracy at the beginning. An overall timeline is necessary so that the client can ensure that the system is still valuable on the proposed schedule. For example, if a company doesn't even have a database server set up and needs something by next Tuesday, this might be a good time to suggest something other than client/server. Sometimes software development timelines can shock and panic a user. If pressure starts to reduce the time frame, remind the user that when development time is cut, cost, features, or quality must suffer. Political pressures may prevail. Just make sure your concerns are down in writing, so you are covered with an "I told you so." Presentation of a timeline might also be a good opportunity to remind the client that some of their staff may be required at various times for things like: requirements definition, requirements confirmation, testing, training, and application support. Costs are always a joy to discuss. However, better to warn them at this point than to discover that they've run out of money halfway through setting up the WAN and a third of the way through development. If the cost of setting up thirty T1 lines between headquarters and regional offices or the cost of six developers for six months causes them to claw the wallpaper off the walls, perhaps a change in scope is in order.

Infrastructure requirements before and during the analysis stage are primarily organizational. Responsibilities need to be defined at this stage, so that the appropriate people can be contacted in sufficient time.

Who is responsible for approval of life cycle documentation? Since the whole point of the documentation is confirmation of requirements, the success of the entire project rides on this person. If the project is being run by an outside IS organization, does the internal IS organization need to review documentation as well, since they will most likely be required to maintain the system after implementation?

Is data architecture a responsibility of the project team, or is there someone concerned with corporate data issue who must have input?

What about platform requirements? Does the equipment available to the client dictate parameters to the project team, or does the project team dictate what hardware the client must have to run the system?

Who defines what version of PowerBuilder should be used? Since new patches can solve some problems and introduce others (anyone who thinks this situation is unique to Powersoft should examine the history of word processors, or pretty much any other commercial product), a new patch that solves one system's problems might cause problems for another. Since having multiple versions of DLLs is always dangerous, someone may have to arbitrate which version and subrelease of PowerBuilder (and other related client/server software) should be chosen.

Who defines the application rollout strategy? Since this is probably done by the corporation on a regular basis, for both in-house products and off-the-shelf product upgrades, it might be more appropriate for someone in the organization to manage this instead of each project team reinventing the rollout wheel each time.

Who is responsible for planning the training strategy? Will it depend on on-line help, computer-based training, stand-up training, paper manuals, or a combination?

Although the end may seem far off, planning the responsibilities for post-implementation is also important in this stage. Is there going to be someone to call with application questions, and if so, who? Who is responsible for application maintenance? That might even be split up further into bug fixes and enhancements. And who is responsible for the day-to-day maintenance and upkeep of the database and LAN/WAN? To avoid finger pointing in the future, decide these things now. Once these steps are done, you have the necessary inputs for the design stage.

Design stage

Once the analysis stage has defined which business functions to automate, the design stage focuses on how to automate those functions. Much of the effort at this stage is effective communication with client representatives, in order to confirm or refine requirements. The primary output of this stage is a visual representation of what the application will look like at the end of the construction stage.

Physical data model

One of the first objectives of the design stage is the physical data model (i.e. a real database). This should take the logical data model as input. Any normalization should take place now and result in the planned tables and columns. Volumetrics should be used to define the storage requirements. The security matrix can be used to define database roles, if database roles are to be used as a line of security. The volumetrics by network distribution should be used to define data location and management, if data is to be distributed.

Defining the target platform is required in this stage. This platform definition should include: network software, database software, client workstation hardware (processor, memory, etc.), database server hardware. This may dictate some limits for your design. For example, if your target workstation is a 4M Windows machine, limiting the size of result sets returning from the database might become a high priority. If the target workstation is a slow processor, intensive processing should be moved to higher performance custom DLLs.

Prototype

The major product of the design stage is a prototype. This is the client's first glimpse of what is going to exist after all the work is done. The first step in producing the prototype is to group the business functions to be automated into windows. For example, if you've defined "Add Customer" and "View Customer" as different business functions, they could be combined into one window. After that, the windows should be grouped by executable, if the system is going to have multiple executables.

The next step is to produce the prototype itself. There are different kinds of prototypes you can generate, with varying degrees of effectiveness. The first kind is the paper prototype. These are prints of proposed windows. The windows are simply produced in the window painter, not necessarily using DataWindows where they are planned to be. Simply drawing a rectangle and putting text on top is sufficient to represent a DataWindow. The entire objective of the paper prototype is to produce an image. It is not likely that the windows developed for the paper prototype will be reused during construction.

The second type of prototype is the nonfunctional electronic prototype. This is an application that does little more than open and close windows via the same user interface to be employed in the final application (e.g. selecting a menu item will open the appropriate window or sheet). The windows for this type of prototype can be drawn by not using DataWindows where DataWindows are planned, or else by using external DataWindows. To show sample data without going to the database, external DataWindows can use the Initial Values option to fill in the values. Some elements of the prototype may be reused in the construction stage, but DataWindows should be reconstructed. However, if reuse is planned, class libraries have to be ready to be employed in the prototype too. Electronic prototypes have the advantage of allowing the user to experience firsthand how the GUI user interface will work. That could be particularly important if this is the user's first experience with GUI.

The third kind of prototype is the functional prototype. Its primary difference from the nonfunctional prototype is that its DataWindows are not external, but are connected to the database tables and columns. No code should be put in for DataWindows to SetTrans() or Retrieve() from the database; the Initial Values option should display data. This kind of prototype allows the greatest amount of reuse in construction. However it requires that the physical data model, as well as the class library, already be in place before the prototype's DataWindows are worked on. And as the user refines requirements through review of the prototype, and suggests changes, much of the work that went into the production of a functional prototype may be lost. For example, if an entire window is deemed unnecessary, the time spent on that window for a paper or nonfunctional electronic prototype would have been negligible. For a functional prototype, it might not have been.

Control/Action/Response chart

A Control/Action/Response chart should supplement the prototype. This is a high-level description of what your scripts will look like. For example, for a given control, such as an "Add" command button, and an action, such as "clicked," you would write in English (that the user will understand!) what will happen when the "Add" button is "clicked." Although from a PowerBuilder point of view, a DataWindow is one control, treat each of its fields as a separate control. This will simplify actions such as ItemChanged. Treating a DataWindow as one control in a C/A/R chart will only confuse the user, defeating the purpose of the prototype.

One thing to remember in the prototyping process is that it is supposed to be iterative. Developers who lose focus on this fact can become too identified with a prototype and take change suggestions as personal insults. There can be a fine line between suggestions that should be "discussed" and suggestions that should be taken as directives verbatim. If the suggestion does not contravene any GUI standards and is not contradictory to any analysis done to date, it should be considered your new marching orders. If it is contrary to GUI standards or previous analysis, it is something that should be discussed. While part of this process is to refine the requirements analysis, don't get caught in a game of Ping-Pong between two people who differ on how their business is run. Point out the contradictions and ask for clarification.

The infrastructure requirements for the design stage heavily overlap the infrastructure requirements for the construction stage. Application and GUI standards must be in place before design can start. For example, if the corporation wants all applications to use MDI frames, toolbars and microhelp, that needs to be defined now. Database standards are required before work on the physical data model can start. If a reusable electronic prototype is planned, the class library must be ready.

Once the prototype is done and approved, we're ready for the part we've all been waiting for.

Construction stage

So, what's left? We code (FINALLY!). We release the application. Right? Well, there's a little more to consider than that.

Avoid requirements creep

Item Number One: in case you've got a short memory, go back and read the part about requirements creep pull. Developers program to specifications. Nothing more. Nothing less.

Weekly discussion sessions can be particularly helpful in development. They can facilitate discussion between programmers to define common problems and share solutions. Does it make much sense to have one programmer frustrated about a problem that the next programmer solved last week? Having programmers give status reports can facilitate this kind of discussion. Short seminars can be useful to help people learn new aspects of PowerBuilder, or to refresh previously learned topics. Assigning the task of teaching to various people is useful, because each selected person is then forced to learn a topic well enough to teach it.

Quality control

Quality control is vital to software development, but often overlooked or neglected. Code walkthroughs can help catch problems before they get anywhere. A code walkthrough is simply the programmer explaining the window's code, line by line, to another programmer. The other person is looking for flaws, but more often than not, the original programmer spots the problems first.

Even this late in the software development life cycle, you need more infrastructure elements. One of the most important elements you'll need is an environment that is identical to the target environment. Often developers' workstations have more memory and power than the average user's workstation. Running your application on a workstation with 32M RAM isn't much of a test if your target workstation has only 4M. Get this environment and use it! Remember, the earlier a problem is diagnosed, the cheaper it is to fix. Information is what every programmer needs.

After spending thousands of dollars on workstations, don't skimp on the information resources. You've obviously already started with books. Don't forget magazines. An up-to-date version of Powersoft's Infobase is essential. And API issues always come up, so don't forget that documentation. For Windows, Microsoft issues the Microsoft Developer's Network CD: more information than anyone could possibly know, all full-text indexed for easy access. Check out what's available for the platforms you're working on. Don't forget that a couple hundred dollars is far cheaper than the labor costs involved in manual searches and workarounds.

Finally...

This outline is not complete, but it will give you a start on the software development life cycle. If you're still interested in learning more, go to a good computer bookstore and see what's available. If you're one of those people who reads the first and last paragraphs of each chapter, go back and read what's in between! Because until we all become perfect and communication is no longer a problem, a software development life cycle methodology might save your neck.

CHAPTER **14**

Designing a Strong Graphical User Interface in PowerBuilder

By Barry Gervin

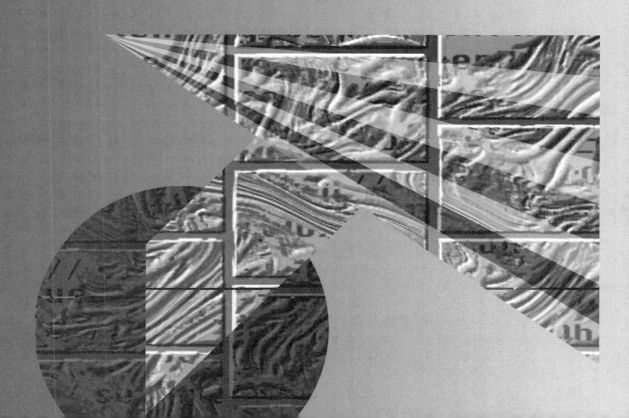

Designing a Strong Graphical User Interface in PowerBuilder

by **Barry Gervin**

Introduction

It is often said that a good user interface is one that is unnoticeable to the user. Your telephone and the faucets on a sink are two examples of a good user interface. While it may be difficult to prove that these examples are intuitive, for the most part, when you know how to use one telephone you know how to use them all. The goal of all software developers should be to design applications that are as easy to use as the telephone.

Part of what makes the telephone such an easy device to use is the standards that are in place for their development: all telephones have a handset and a keypad; phones with cords always have the mouthpiece closest to the cord. Users come to expect these features on all telephones, and these standards are what make them so easy to use, no matter who the manufacturer was.

Unlike most telephones, computer software has an infinite number of features. This makes the development of standards difficult, as well as an ongoing process. To date, published standards are rudimentary; however, the evolved standards that are being developed in today's commercial software have come a long way.

For Windows developers, the current standards are in *The Windows Interface: An Application Design Guide*, published by Microsoft. These standards form a good starting point for learning the rules, but knowing the rules does not necessarily make you a good hockey player. Knowing the rules and developing a strategy for implementing those rules are what differentiate the mundane from the elegant. This chapter will bring to light the important rules, and focus on the strategy that will make a Gretzky out of you.

Design Principles

The user's point of view

Perhaps the biggest hurdle for the mainframe developer to overcome in moving to a Windows client/server environment is the fact that the user is the center of all processing, not the application. This concept works hand in hand with event-driven programming. A good Graphical User Interface (GUI) will allow a user to control both how the application works and how it responds. In fact, when you program event-driven code, you are coding the individual responses for all possible actions, or events.

While you do not always have to coddle the user, there is also nothing wrong with a little bit of hand-holding every now and then either, especially with new users. Microsoft has realized that there are times when users must be guided through certain tasks, and has implemented the concept of a Wizard in their software. I will show you how to implement this concept in the chapter, "Building a Wizard in PowerBuilder."

I cannot stress enough how important it is to provide feedback to your users. This feedback may be as subtle as a warning beep or the pointer turning to an hourglass, but your users should sense that they are in control of the software.

Think of how a car handles. When users drive your application, they should feel as if they are driving a Porsche 911, which hugs every corner and responds to the driver's actions, rather than an old Lincoln Continental with bad shocks. When you are designing your application, think Porsche: there is no substitute.

Techniques for providing feedback

MicroHelp

MicroHelp is text that appears in the status bar at the bottom of an MDI frame. It is usually used to provide context-sensitive help. It can be used to show some extra information about a menu item or toolbar. Another effective use of MicroHelp is to provide a more descriptive label of the current edit control.

ToolBarTips

ToolBarTips are popup messages that appear when the mouse comes to rest over a toolbar button. In PowerBuilder 4.0, the message will be, by default, the toolbar text. However, you can specify something different by placing a comma after the toolbar text, and then entering a longer toolbar Tip (i.e. Exit, Shutdown the Application)

Audible cues

It is not a good idea to have the software "beep" at the user when they encounter an error or do something unexpected; this can be very annoying. It is acceptable, however, to use a well-placed beep from time to time when warning a user of some potentially destructive action. Audible feedback (such as a beep) can also be beneficial at the end of a long process.
When users must have feedback
Nothing makes a good application feel bad like poor performance. Unfortunately, it is often difficult to determine where performance is lacking in a client/server environment.

Inevitably, processes will not always be as fast as the user would like. In these cases, make sure to let the user know what is going on with the application.

> In cases where the wait will be short (0–10 seconds), display the hourglass pointer.

> When a process is going to take between 10 and 18 seconds, display MicroHelp to step the user through the process.

> For durations longer than 18 seconds, you will need to display a progress window.

> As mentioned, it is acceptable to issue an audible tone (i.e. beep(1)) at the end of long process. This will alert users if they have taken their eyes from their screen.

User customization

Wherever possible, allow your users to adjust the interface to your application. For a good example of customization, look at the Windows Control Panel, which lets users alter their desktop and Windows configurations. Make your application as customizable as possible for all levels of users.

Consistency

The most important aspect to remember when designing an interface is to be consistent within your application (or suite of applications), as well as being consistent with the Windows interface. Font, colors, 3D representations, spacing, and control dimensions all have to be consistent in look as well as functionality. Use common labels like "OK," "Close," and "Cancel," so that users do not have to guess at the functionality of a control.

While consistency is vitally important to a good user interface, it can also be taken to extremes. I recently saw a system in which each screen looked so much like the others in the application that users were becoming confused as to where they were in the software. Consistency should not interfere with the usability of the application. The give-and-take relationship between consistency and usability is often hard work, but like everything else, hard work usually pays off.

In making the components of your application consistent with each other, use the concept of the *object:action-* or *action:object*-based system. Most database applications can be said to have both "objects" and "actions" (for example, you *fire* an *employee*; you *approve* an *expense form*). You need to decide whether your user picks an object (noun) or an action (verb) first, and then try to keep that order consistent throughout the application.

There are two ways to determine which method to use:

Decide whether you have more objects or actions, and put the majority category first. This will flatten your menu structure and provide more visual indicators of what the users' options are. This rule generally only works when there are ten to twenty objects or actions at the top end. Determine how the users actually work. Do they work on expense forms, then have them approved? Or do they know in advance that they need to approve some expense forms?

Real world metaphors

Choosing the right metaphor is important; you should pick a metaphor that relates to real-world concepts. First-time GUI programmers tend to become enamored of particular metaphors, and may use them inappropriately. Sometimes interface metaphors can work their way into your class libraries, and there is a tendency to design the interface so that it becomes easy to program, not easy to use.
Choosing the right editing metaphor

Freeform

A *freeform* data entry window is useful when the user needs to maintain or view one record of information at a time. Figure 14-1 shows an example of a freeform data entry window. You will notice that every label has a colon, is left justified and left aligned. When designing freeform windows, try to keep in mind that unlike 8.5" x 11" paper, a computer screen has more horizontal than vertical space.

Figure 14-1: The freeform data entry window.

Tabular

The *tabular* window, by contrast, allows the user to maintain or view multiple rows of data at one time. Figure 14-2 shows an example of the tabular metaphor used as a selection dialog. The tabular metaphor can also be used for data entry, but this is usually only employed when the rows being edited are related to each other (i.e. the items of an order).

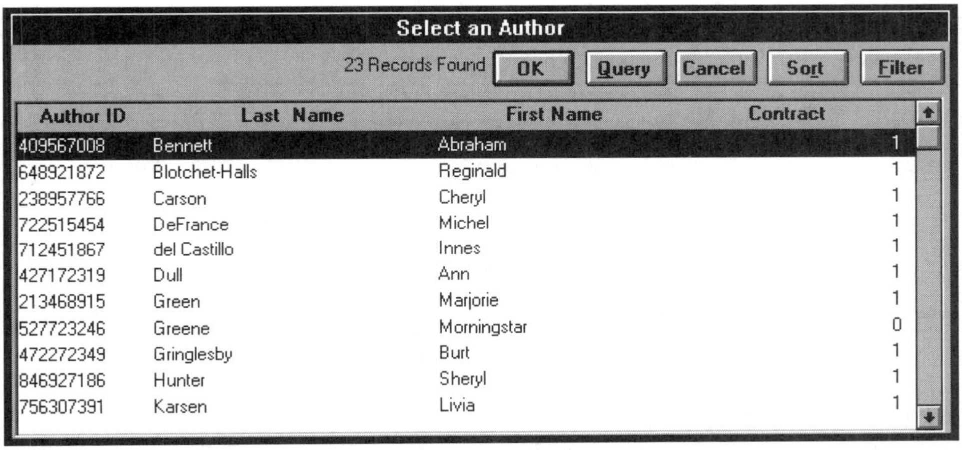

Select an Author						
23 Records Found	OK	Query	Cancel	Sort	Filter	

Author ID	Last Name	First Name	Contract	
409567008	Bennett	Abraham	1	
648921872	Blotchet-Halls	Reginald	1	
238957766	Carson	Cheryl	1	
722515454	DeFrance	Michel	1	
712451867	del Castillo	Innes	1	
427172319	Dull	Ann	1	
213468915	Green	Marjorie	1	
527723246	Greene	Morningstar	0	
472272349	Gringlesby	Burt	1	
846927186	Hunter	Sheryl	1	
756307391	Karsen	Livia	1	

Figure 14-2: The tabular window.

Master-detail

The *master-detail* window has gained a lot of acceptance in recent years. As you will see in Figure 14-3, the master-detail window is composed of two tabular portions (called the master and the detail). A master-detail window is used to graphically represent a defined business relationship between two sets of data. The example in Figure 14-3 displays a list of Authors (the master). When a particular author is selected, the bottom part shows the Titles that author as written (the detail). The top or master portion of Figure 14-3 could be freeform; however, this would imply that we are only interested in one master, and all of its detail.

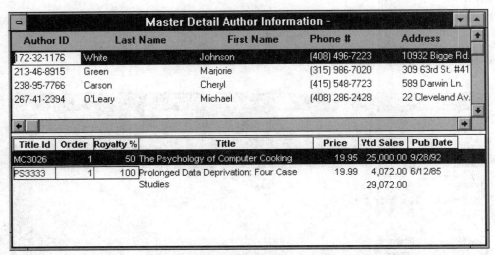

Figure 14-3: The master-detail window.

Tabbed dialog box

The *tabbed dialog* metaphor has very recently gained increasing popularity. In fact, the tabbed dialog will be a standard control in Microsoft's new version of Windows, Windows95.

The benefit of this metaphor is that it allows the developer to put a lot of information on the screen at one time without the resulting display looking crowded or intimidating. Figure 14-4 shows an example from Microsoft Word that takes advantage of tab folders. You will notice that the information on each panel is significantly different from each other panel. Also of importance is that the number of tabs is fixed. This differs from workbook tabs, as you will see in the next section.

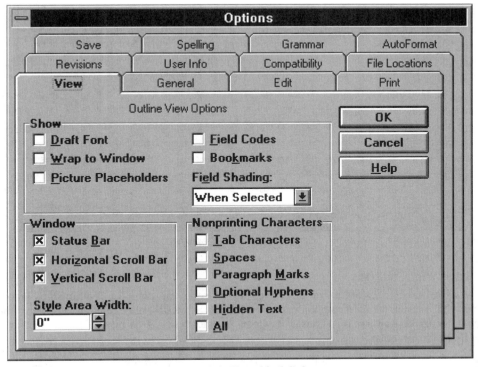

Figure 14-4: The tabbed dialog.

Workbook tabs

Workbook tabs are not as popular as the previous example of tabs. However, they can be effective in some situations.

Figure 14-5 shows how Microsoft Excel takes advantage of workbook tabs. The first thing you will notice is that they are at the bottom of the display rather than the top.

The type of data that is related to each workbook tab is said to be homogenous. Another way of stating this is that each tab is an instance of data. In Figure 14-5, each instance is a spreadsheet. The VCR buttons to the left of the tabs are a provision for scrolling through an indefinite number of tabs.

I do not expect that many of you will be writing spreadsheet programs in PowerBuilder. An effective use of workbook tabs in a PowerBuilder application might be to show a report by department, each department appearing on a separate tab.

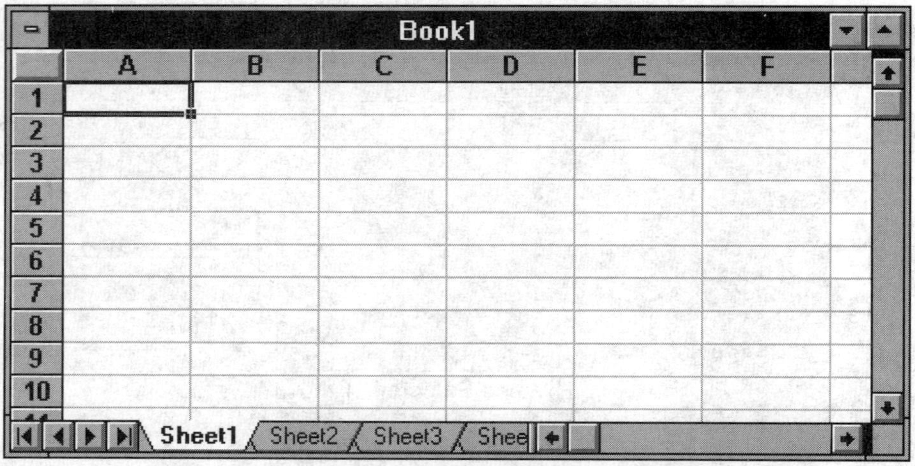

Figure 14-5: Workbook tabs.

Hierarchical list box

It is a challenge to create a graphical interface to represent complex relationships among data. The master-detail metaphor can only handle a one-to-many relationship. But what about recursive relationships–master to detail A and detail B and detail C., or master to detail, to further detail?

The *hierarchical list box,* as displayed in Figure 14-6, is a very elegant way of representing complex relationships. As is the case with tab folders, users find this metaphor easy to understand.

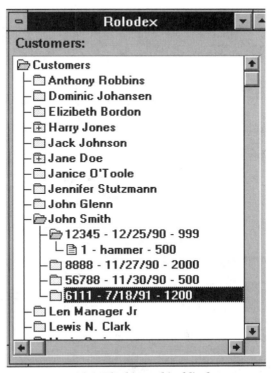

Figure 14-6: The hierarchical list box.

Wizard

So far, I have only discussed simple data entry or viewing of data. There are cases when a user must perform a series of actions in a specific linear order. Windows does not naturally have a mechanism for this type of behavior.

The concept of a Wizard (see Figure 14-7) is used in Microsoft Word to handle this situation. The concept provides for a series of dialog boxes with some simple navigation forward and backward in the process. For more information on creating a Wizard, see the chapter, "Creating a Wizard in PowerBuilder."

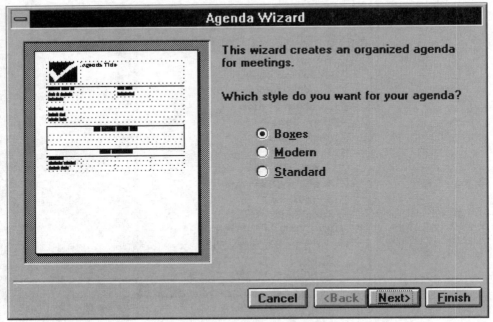

Figure 14-7: The Wizard.

Following operating system standards

Microsoft also hopes that one day the computer will be as easy to use as your telephone or sink faucets. As a developer, you can have an important impact on how successful this vision becomes, by making your applications look and feel the same as all other Windows applications. In following the rules of implementing a good user interface, you accomplish the following goals:

You make it easy for your users to *learn* how to use your application.
You also make it easy for users to *remember* how to use your application.
You propagate a standard for other developers to follow.

Most projects that I have been involved with have had a user base that I would classify as beginners. Quite often the application being built was the first Windows application these users were being exposed to. Following strict development rules might not make the application easier for these users (in fact, it might make it harder to use at first), but if you design your software to look like their existing system, either paper or mainframe, you are only propagating the old way of doing things at the cost of future flexibility.

You are not developing GUI applications simply because the technical team in your firm decided that Windows was a more stable operating environment than unix and COBOL. Experienced end users are demanding that applications developed for internal use be as easy to use as those they have at home. Investment in following the rules now will provide a big payoff later.

Remember, too, that the users you are currently developing for will not remain in your firm forever. Employees come and go in today's society. If you can base your application on standard rules, learning to use and develop that application will eventually prove easier for everyone.

PowerBuilder, like most Windows development tools, makes assumptions about how you will write your applications. These assumptions generally coincide with important concepts from the Microsoft *Design Guide*. Therefore, trying to work against the established rules means that you will, essentially, be working against PowerBuilder. If you do not follow established standards and rules when designing your application, you might as well try putting a square peg into a round hole; it will not work.

Other considerations

The problems encountered in trying to develop a good user interface are exaggerated by the fact that most of the people responsible for the development and design are programmers, usually with mainframe backgrounds. Remember that Windows became a popular corporate standard because *users* demanded that applications be developed on this platform.

As part of a regular training program, I strongly recommend that all PowerBuilder developers take the time to learn what comprises an effective GUI design before they begin a large project. I also recommend that any end users who will be involved in the design process do the same. The process of developing a good user interface often takes longer, and goes through more iterations, than programming tasks associated with the application's functionality. At the end of this chapter, I list other resources that you can use to develop your GUI design skills.

Making an application easy to use is not an easy task. The importance of making your application clear and straightforward is too often overlooked in favor of adding functionality. It is important to remember, however, that if the application is not easy to use, users will not be able to take advantage of the additional functionality.

Studies indicate that despite all of the functionality included in Microsoft Excel, most users take advantage of only three to five functions. My personal experience proves that these studies are true. My sister learned to use Lotus 1-2-3 about a year ago, and called me a week ago to ask how to add values on the spreadsheet. This example shows that users may use a product, but often do not know how to take advantage of the functionality included with that product.

Despite what programmers like to believe, to a user, the interface *is* the application. If an interface is too complicated to understand, the user thinks the system is too complicated and will opt for an easier-to-use product (that is, a product with a better interface). If the interface is easy to use, users will quickly adopt the system and become more productive.

Again, the most important consideration in designing a good interface is the user. Learn to develop applications from the user's point of view, and productivity for both programmers and users will be increased. Allow the user to be in control.

The First Steps to Good GUI Design

The user interview

The easiest way to understand the end users of your application is to do their job for a day, or at least an hour. I can guarantee that this will be a humbling experience.

Asking users how they do their jobs, and what would make their jobs easier to do, are the fundamentals of a user interview. User input is the first step in building a good interface, and should begin before any application development occurs. Determine what a user's most critical job functions are, and make those functions most prominent in the interface. Any information that may be secondary in nature (according to the user) should be placed in a secondary location in the application.

Make sure that you interview the right people. The people that you interview must be experienced in the tasks that they perform, and they must be respected by their peers. Ensure that the people you talk to are end users, and not managers who want to change the way their employees work. Get a wide range of input.

The best way to observe users at work is through the use of hidden cameras or network monitors. Personal interviews also work, but the information you receive may be skewed from the way the work is actually performed.

The following information will help you determine the requirements of the users:
List all activities within a given day. This may give you more information than you need, but it also might help the users think of things they would not have thought of otherwise.
Determine what problems users are encountering in performing their jobs.
Ask what they spend the most time doing during the day.

It is also important to understand the background of your users.

How many years of computer experience?
How many years using Windows, and with which applications?
How much employee turnover and orientation?

Other resources

Understanding the business problem and the nature of your end users' work only helps you solve half of the problem. With this understanding you will be able to detect a poorly designed interface. However, you will need to acquire skills that will help you translate that business understanding into practical designs.

There are many courses on the market that claim to teach the developer GUI design skills. These can be very helpful, but they require a lot of time and money. An easy way to start learning some of the necessary skills is to look at other applications–both good and bad. Try to remember how you felt the first time you tried using any piece of software. If you are unsure of how the standards should be implemented, a good place to start is the Microsoft Office suite of applications. Last but not least, you should read the actual standards. A short list appears at the end of the chapter.

Window Design

Choosing the right type of window

Windows are the main method of communicating to your user. It is very important that you pick a window type that is going to behave in the desired manor. Here is a summary of the various window types.

The primary window

The primary window is the initial or main window of your application. There are two types of primary windows you can choose from for your application.

For most applications that you will develop using PowerBuilder, the Multiple Document Interface (MDI) is the window you will use as the entry point to your application. This type of primary window will easily handle multiple instances of an object (for example, opening multiple orders). Each window that you open inside of an MDI frame is a sheet or MDI child window.

The primary window will present the user with a menu, a set of toolbar icons, and a status bar (also known as MicroHelp), as shown in Figure 14-8. Most complex applications on the market today use MDI windows as their primary windows.

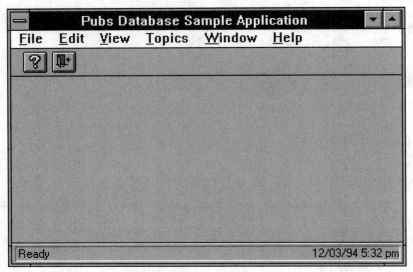

Figure 14-8: Multiple Document Interface (MDI).

For contrast purposes, Figure 14-9 demonstrates the other type of primary window, known as a main window. Main windows are useful for simple or single-purpose applications such as the Calculator applet that is included in Windows.

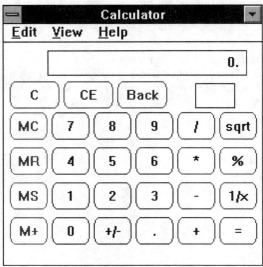

Figure 14-9: Main window.

The modal/response window

Response or modal windows require an immediate response from the user before any other action can be processed. They are useful for asking questions that must be answered before an action can proceed, as in Figure 14-10.

Characteristics of a response window:

> It is usually centered on the screen.

> It should contain at least one button to close the window. If the purpose of the window is to obtain user acknowledgment, the button should be labeled "OK." All other types of response windows should have at least two buttons, one to initiate or accept a process (the "OK" button), and a "Cancel" button.

> The "Cancel" button is associated with the <Esc> key, and abandons any changes made in the window.

> Use a "Close" button when there is no way for a user to undo the changes made in the response window.

> The "OK" button is usually the default button on the window, and can be activated from the keyboard by pressing <Enter>.

> Buttons are either stacked along the right border of the window, or aligned side by side on the bottom. The default button is usually the top or leftmost button, with the "Cancel" button placed immediately after the "OK" button.

> A "Help" button is optional on a response window, but is a good idea to include. The "Help" button should be placed at the bottom of the stack, or on the far right.

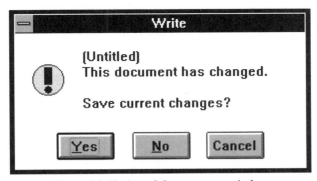

Figure 14-10: A modal or response window.

The popup window

Popup windows are not as frequently used as response windows, but they do have their purpose. PowerBuilder uses a popup window to display the status of a currently selected control (Figure 14-11). Popup windows can be useful for showing extra information or some sort of system status, because they always remain on top of the parent window.

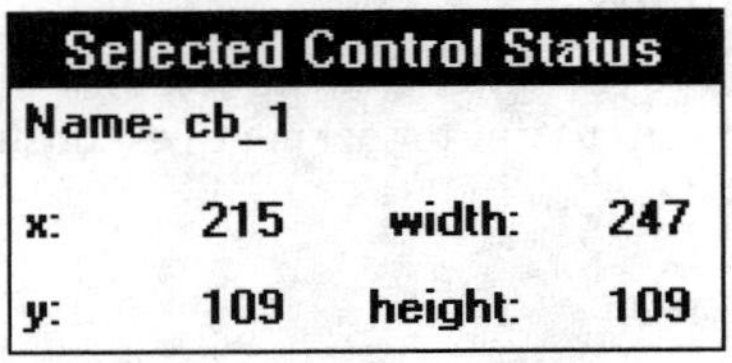

Selected Control Status			
Name: cb_1			
x:	215	width:	247
y:	109	height:	109

Figure 14-11: A popup window.

MDI applications

MDI menus

Should you choose to use the MDI window as your primary window, there are some standards in building the menu that should be adhered to. This will make your application look and feel like the other applications your end users may have installed.

Here is a breakdown of some of the more common MDI menu items.

File

Microsoft says that you should use this menu if your application deals with files. That is the original standard rule, and thus where the name of this menu originates from. However, this menu has become a standard component on any MDI application. Most of the commands that are associated with data files (New, Open, Save) can also be translated for database applications. This menu also provides a way of closing the current sheet (Close) and exiting the application (Exit).

Edit

The Edit menu provides the required clipboard functionality of all Windows applications (Cut, Copy, Clear, Paste). The Undo item can be used to reverse the last action that altered data.

For database applications, it is also customary to put record handling functions under the Edit Menu (Insert, Delete, Search).

View

The View menu can be very useful for database applications. The purpose of these items is to modify the user's view of the data.
Here are some things you could put in a View menu:

    Sort options
    Filter options
    Toolbar settings
    Status (popup) window

Window

The Window menu is crucial for MDI applications. It provides an important part of the sheet navigation facility. It usually contains the list of currently opened sheets, and allows for quickly jumping to any one of them. The Window menu also provides for sheet positioning preferences (Layer, Cascade, Tile, Arrange Icons). The Window menu should always be the second menu item from the right.

Help

The Help menu should be the last (far right) item on the menu bar. The Help menu usually contains items for accessing the application's on-line documentation (Contents/Index, Search). It is also customary to have an item for accessing the help hypertext engine's on-line help (How to Use Help).

Last, but not least, there should be a entry for displaying the "About" box. The "About" window should display the application name, version number or date, a copyright message if necessary, the application's icon, and optionally a serial number or user's name. Some applications go as far as displaying the available memory or system resources. An example of the Program Manager "About" box is shown in Figure 14-12.

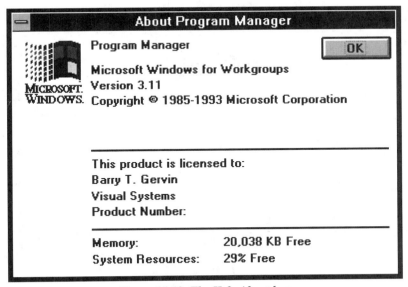

Figure 14-12: The Help About box.

Other considerations

Keep the number of menu options across the top of the MDI to eight or less. If you have more than eight menu options, make them optional.

The first menu item in a drop-down is not always the most obvious, even though it is highlighted.

Use an ellipsis ("...") to indicate that a response window will appear.

Avoid the use of nested cascading menus.

Do not group related menu items using separator bars.

Place the most frequently used functions on the toolbar.

Window navigation

Title bars on a window should indicate the object and/or action being performed in that window. An example is shown in Figure 14-13. If the window allows multiple instances of an object (for example, a sheet for each author), make sure that you indicate the specific instance of the window to which you are referring (for example, use the author's name in the title bar). This will be beneficial for identification purposes when the window is minimized, or in an MDI application, when the window name appears in the Window menu.

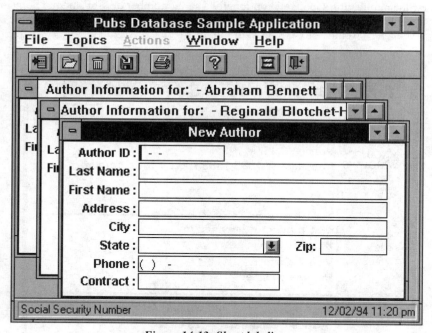

Figure 14-13: Sheet labeling.

Expanding windows

Most database application developers who begin developing under Windows soon discover that they run out of screen real estate very quickly. A helpful technique is the expanding window. An expanding window initially only shows the minimum amount of information that is required (See Figure 14-14). A button with two chevrons (>>) indicates to users that they can unfold this window to its full size if they need more information, or to change advanced settings. When the window is fully expanded (See Figure 14-15), the button with the chevrons is disabled. A preferred approach would be to change the label of the button to use the opposite chevrons (<<) to enable the user to collapse the expanding window.

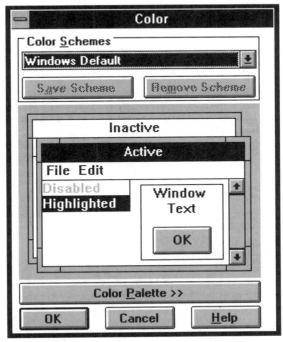

Figure 14-14: Initial state of an expanding window.

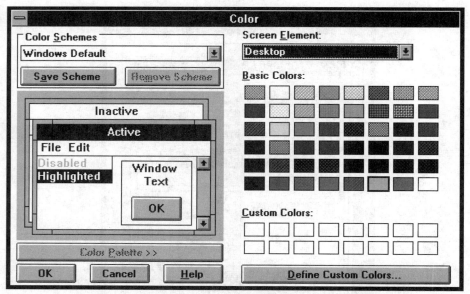

Figure 14-15: An open version of the expanding window.

Controls

All of the items you can place on a window are generally referred to as controls. Each type of control has a very specific purpose. In mainframe-style applications, the choice of controls was fairly limited (Label or Field). Microsoft didn't invent the various types of controls so that your screen would "look nice." Instead, controls have very specific definitions that communicate information about their nature to the user. For example, a command button tells users that when they click on it, some action will be performed. A single-line edit does not communicate the same message. When users see a single-line edit, they know that if they click on it, the cursor will be placed in that control and they can edit its contents.

It's very important to pick the right control for the job. You want to communicate all of the available functionality to your users in the least amount of time and screen real estate. Knowing how to properly place controls on a window is a real art. However, the more you do it, the better you will get at it. A user's eye will naturally peruse your window from the top left, and move to the bottom right. You can use this progression to your advantage when there is a natural business order to the information to be entered or read. The tab order of the fields on your window should also follow this flow; however, do not rely on that order being maintained by your users.

Command buttons

The command button is used primarily as a launching point for some processing. A command button should represent only one function. If that function is dependent on the mode of the window, make two buttons, disabling the inappropriate/unavailable button

Use an ellipsis on a command button to indicate that further information is required before processing an action (see the "Setup..." button in Figure 14-16). Use two chevrons on a command button to expand a folding window (see Figure 14-17).

Figure 14-16: The ellipsis on the "Setup..." button indicates that more information will be required.

*Figure 14-17: The two chevrons indicate that this button will unfold this window
(and reveal advanced options).*

According to Microsoft, command buttons should measure 14 "dialog units." On my machine, that relates to 93 PowerBuilder units, or a height value of 93–which is nowhere near the default value of 109 that PowerBuilder assigns to new command buttons.

To determine the proper width of a command button:

Put a lowercase "n" on each end of the button's label (for example, nClosen).
Change the width of the button (by holding the <Ctrl> key and using the left and right arrows) until the leftmost "n" touches the border of the button.

Delete the "n"s from the button label.

Following this procedure will ensure that your command button is the proper width (according to Microsoft).

When you place several buttons on a window, they should be aligned either vertically on the right side of the window, or horizontally along the bottom of the window. The exception to the rule occurs when the button is related to another control on the window; in this case, it is more appropriate to put the button close to the related control.

Multiple buttons on a window should be placed approximately 40 PowerBuilder units apart (27 units if the buttons are to be logically grouped together, and 60 units between groups).

Actions on a command button should be available both through mouse clicks and the keyboard. A "Cancel" button should be mapped to the <Esc> key, while the default button (usually the "OK" button) should be mapped to the <Enter> key. Having a responsive keyboard for each command button is easy; check the Cancel and Default attributes for the command button in the control style window.

Single-line edits, multiple-line edits, edit masks

Each of these controls is used to allow the user to type in some information from the keyboard. There is no processing associated with any of them; they are only used for capturing or displaying data from the user. An example of each of these controls is shown in Figure 14-18.

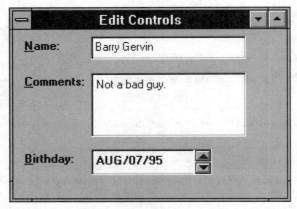

Figure 14-18: Single-line, multiple-line, and edit controls.

List boxes

List boxes typically allow users to make multiple selections from a list of choices. It is possible to make list boxes only accept a single selection from a list, but if this is the desired behavior, a DropDownListBox would be a more effective use of screen real estate. An example of a list box is shown in Figure 14-19.

Figure 14-19: A multi-selection list box.

DropDownListBoxes

A DropDownListBox looks like a single-line edit with an arrow to the right. The arrow allows the user to drop down a list box of available choices. The user can select only one choice from the list. An example is shown in Figure 14-20.

The list of available selections has no theoretical limit, but the practical limit for the user is about thirty or forty items. If the list gets much larger, you should not torture your users with a DropDownListBox, but institute some sort of search window.

If the list is rather small (less than five items) and you have the screen real estate available, you might want to consider using a set of radio buttons instead.

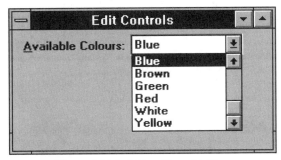

Figure 14-20: A DropDownListBox.

CheckBoxes

CheckBoxes, as seen in Figure 14-21, control individual choices that are logical– either On or Off. The user can change the state by clicking the CheckBox. There should be no other behavior associated with a CheckBox other than to capture the state of a field. Unlike Radio buttons, CheckBoxes have no explicit relationship to other CheckBoxes on the window. If you find you are placing a lot of related options together on a window with CheckBoxes (like Figure 14-20), you might want to consider a multi-selection list box instead.

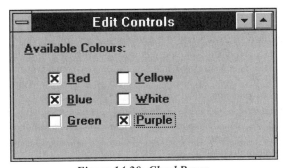

Figure 14-20: CheckBoxes.

Radio buttons

Radio buttons or option buttons are used for selecting one out of a limited set of mutually exclusive options. The available option list must be fixed. If you find the need to dynamically add a new option at runtime, consider using a DropDownListBox. You should also consider a DropDownListBox if you find the list getting beyond three to five.

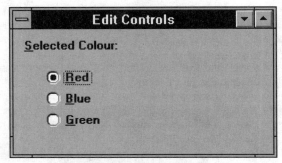

Figure 14-21: Radio buttons.

Keyboard Users

One of the most common oversights of new Windows developers is the simple fact that there are still quite a number of keyboard users. Although we may believe that their number is dwindling, that is not the case. With more and more laptop computers in the field, and more and more power users (who prefer keyboard shortcuts) in the office, keyboard use has become a more, not a less, important issue.

Accelerators

Most controls on a window can have associated accelerators. An accelerator is a special key that a user can select in combination with the <Alt> key to navigate or select a specific control or menu item. This is indicated in the label of a control by underlining the accelerator key.

Accelerators are indicated in PowerBuilder by placing an ampersand ("&") before the letter in the label to be underlined. Controls such as command buttons, radio buttons, and Check-Boxes are their own label (i.e. you don't need to place any extra static text next to these controls to identify them); therefore all you need to do is to put the ampersand in front of the appropriate character. In the case of single-line edits, DropDownListBoxes, and list boxes, you need to provide a static text label. Follow these steps for putting an accelerator key on these controls: Use the "&" on the static text label to indicate to the user what the accelerator key is. Double-click on the control to bring up the control style window, and specify the accelerator key on the actual control.

Be very careful with reserved accelerator keys and accelerator keys that are being used on the menu as well. Use consonants instead of vowels, and preferably the most meaningful character of a word (not necessarily the first character).

Shortcut keys

Shortcut keys are used only on menu items. They differ from accelerator keys in that they do not have to be visible to be activated. The shortcut key can be any combination of <Alt>,

<Ctrl>, or <Shift> and a letter or function key on the keyboard. These are helpful for power users. Make sure not to conflict with the reserved shortcut keys that can be found in Microsoft's *The Windows Interface: An Application Design Guide.*

Fonts

All developers seem to have their own personal preferences when it comes to colors and fonts in their applications. Most developers think that because you *can* change fonts and colors, you *should*. This is not so. There are some simple guidelines to follow that will make your application look professional and polished.

PowerBuilder defaults all fonts to Arial. Unfortunately, this is not necessarily the best font to use. The standard system font for Windows is either the Microsoft Sans Serif or Arial font, but keep in mind that they are not the same. The best bet for your screens is the Microsoft Sans Serif 8 point font. It is a bitmapped font, scaled properly for the installed resolution on your PC. Being a bitmap, and not a True Type font, means that it will be displayed faster. Not only are True Type fonts slower, they are usually poorly displayed on monitors.

Microsoft uses the MS Sans Serif font, and I suggest that you do too, with one exception. If you are creating a DataWindow that will be printed, use the Arial font; it will look better on your printout. If the DataWindow will be used both on the screen and for reports, use Arial. You will sacrifice a marginal performance gain and a slight visual impediment, but you will save having to create two windows.

Use bold text for labels, headings, and static text. Do not use bold for data fields. I strongly recommend against the use of italics, as it can be very harsh on the eye. Capitalize the first letter of all words used to label controls, except for short words such as "the," "of," "or," etc. All static text labels should have a following colon, and be left aligned.

Whatever font you decide to use, make it consistent throughout your application. The best way to make it consistent is to:

Set the defaults for your application object.
Set the defaults in your PowerBuilder extended table attributes for each table.

Color

Generally, you should design your windows with black text on a gray background (MDI windows usually have a white background), keeping in mind that ten percent of the population suffer from some sort of color blindness. Remember, too, that monochrome screens still exist, particularly in the laptop environment. Using different colors can render these screens a black, useless mess.

If you use color in your application, make sure that you use it for a reason, not just to differentiate a window or a field. Color should only be used as a real-world indicator or metaphor. Use the color consistently, within reason, and only when it is absolutely meaningful to your users.

On-line Help

On-line help (via the WinHelp engine) is not an optional component of a Windows application. Windows applications are targeted at a wide range of users, from the beginner to the advanced, and as such, require a detailed help system to guide users through processes and commands.

There are many third-party help authoring tools to aid in the process of designing a good help system. Doc-to-Help, RoboHelp, and HelpBreeze are all relatively easy to use, and are based on Microsoft Word for Windows. ForeHelp is an authoring tool that lets the writer create the help file without the use of an external word processor.

An important element of on-line help development is creating context-sensitive links to functions in the application. Using the ShowHelp() command in PowerBuilder, on-line help can be attached to any menu item, command button, or window. On critical response windows, do not rely on the user remembering to press <Shift>-<F>1 for context-sensitive help. Instead, put a help button on the window, and use the ShowHelp() command to link the appropriate information to the window.

For a complete description of the design, budgeting, scheduling, and manpower issues surrounding the development on on-line help, refer to *Developing On-line Help for Windows* by Scott Boggan, David Farkas, and Joe Welinske. For an introduction to on-line help development, see the corresponding chapter in this book.

Icons and Toolbars

Always try to use icons and toolbars that are easy for users to understand. In general, programmers do not make good graphic artists, so looking elsewhere for icons is advisable. There are several libraries of icons (available in shareware and commercial software), and we have included a small sample on the CD-ROM.

For toolbars, you can use the text attribute to display a very short, one-word description of the function, or you can use the ToolBarTips to display a more descriptive message when the user positions the pointer over a toolbar item and pauses.

Summary

This chapter has tried to equip you with some of the skills required to develop not only a functional application but a usable application. Personally, I have developed far too many applications that have been more than functional...yet somehow all that functionality the users demanded doesn't seem to get used. Is that their fault?

Remember that of the over four hundred functions available in Microsoft Excel, the average user only takes advantage of four or five. When you develop your next application, before you sign off on something as "working," ask yourself: Is it usable? If it's not, then there isn't much point in deploying it to your users.

Developing a functional and usable application means work. I have found that making an application usable often takes as much or more time as making it functional did. Interface is hard work, but it can pay big dividends for your end users' productivity–and that's what we are doing all this for in the first place.

And as a last thought, if you ever get frustrated with the hard work of interface design–try programming your neighbor's VCR!

Additional Reading:

The Windows Interface: An Application Design Guide. Microsoft Corporation. Microsoft Press, Redmond, WA (1987), ISBN 1-55615-439-9.

Object-Oriented Interface Design: IBM Common User Access Guidelines. QUE Corporation, 11711 N College Ave., Carmel, IN 46032, ISBN 1-56529-170-0.

Systems Application Architecture; Common User Access Advanced Interface Design Guide. IBM. International Business Machines Corporation, Purchase, NY (1989 & 1991).

The Design of Everyday Things. Donald A. Norman. Doubleday, New York, NY (1988), ISBN 0-385-26774-6.

CHAPTER 15

DataWindow Printing

By Derek Ball

DataWindow Printing

by **Derek Ball**

Once you have built your reports for your PowerBuilder applications, it is natural that you will want hard copies of some of them. To accommodate this, PowerBuilder 4.0 has a number of built-in functions for communicating with the printer of your choice. Given that your reports will probably be DataWindow objects, the most commonly printed object will be those DataWindows, but you can also print strings, bitmaps, graphic objects and even your entire screen!

Two Methods for Printing DataWindows

There are two easy methods that we can use for getting our DataWindows to the printer. We can send the DataWindow by itself, a simple and effective process, or we can choose to bundle a number of DataWindows (or combinations of other objects) together as a single print job.

Method 1: Sending the DataWindow on its own, without a specific print job

The easiest way of getting our report to the printer is to use the Print() function. To use the Print() function you simply specify the name of the DataWindow control that you want to print, i.e.:

```
dw_data.Print({cancel dialog})
```

The Print() function does not require any parameters, but there is one optional parameter which you can code to stop PowerBuilder from displaying the Print Cancel dialog window (otherwise it will appear automatically, as in Figure 15-1). The *cancel dialog* parameter is a boolean value which will default to True.

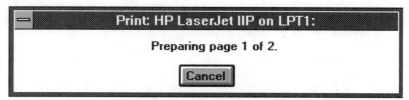

Figure 15-1: The Print Cancel dialog window appears by default
when printing unless you specify otherwise.

Other formats of the Print() function exist to allow printing of text strings, but they require the opening of a print job first. These formats will be explained after we have shown you how to open a print job.

Method 2: Bundling one or more DataWindows as a print job

You may decide you want to send a number of DataWindows to the printer as a single print order. To accomplish this you must open a print job (a single unit of work to be sent to a printer that may actually consist of many subtasks). A print job is uniquely identified in PowerBuilder by its job ID. We use the PrintOpen({job name}) function to obtain a print job number. PrintOpen() has a single optional parameter, and that is the *job name*. The job name is the name that will appear in the Windows 3.X Print Manager for this collection of reports.

When you use PrintOpen(), a new fresh page is created for you to print on. You will use other functions to call up new pages in the print job, such as PrintPage(), described later. You use the PrintOpen() function as follows:

```
INTEGER li_printjob

li_printjob = PrintOpen("Payables Report")
// Optional parameter of Payables Report identifies
// this particular job in the Windows Print Manager

// Check to ensure that print job opening was successful

IF li_printjob < 1 THEN
 MessageBox("Print Error","Unable to open a print job. Please call systems
support")
RETURN
END IF
```

Once you have the job number, you can proceed to print a variety of items within the scope of the job using the following functions.

Printing strings to the print job

Print(print_job_number, string)

This format of the Print() function can be used to print a string to the printer. The string will print in whatever font is currently defined for the chosen printer.

Print(print_job_number, string, tab)

This format of the Print() function can also be used to print a string to the printer, but once the string is printed it will tab to the distance specified in the *tab* parameter (measured in thousandths of an inch) without starting a new line. This allows you to print information in columns.

Print(print_job_number, tab, string)

This format of the Print() function is a variation of the above format except it will tab the specified distance from the edge of the print area, print the string in the current font, and then will start a new line.

Print(print_job_number, tab, string, tab)

This final format of the Print() function will tab the specified distance from the edge of the print area, print the string in the current font, and then tab over the specified distance in the second *tab* parameter and will not start a new line. Note that if the length of string places the cursor beyond the position specified in the second *tab* parameter, the cursor will stay at the end of the string.

All the above functions will provide an integer return value of 1 if they succeed and -1 if they fail. If you embed the string control characters ~n~r in your string, as is done in Power-Builder to create a new line, it will have the same effect when the string is printed. However the initial tab stop will be ignored on all lines past the first.

There is one function left that we use to print strings which is slightly different from the Print() function:

PrintText (print_job_number, string, x, y {, fontnumber})

This function will print a text string contained in the *string* parameter as though it were an object.

The string will begin at the coordinates specified by the X and Y parameters (in thousandths of an inch). The *fontnumber* parameter is an optional parameter. If it is not specified, the current font will be used. Otherwise the *fontnumber* is a value from 0 to 8, with 0 being the default font for the printer and 1-8 being fonts that you have defined using the PrintDefine-Font() function described later. This function, unlike other functions that specify coordinates, will change the position of the print cursor. The return value of this function is the new X coordinate of the print cursor.

Printing objects to the print job

The following functions will allow you to print a variety of different types of objects in your open print job. Any of these functions which specify an X and Y coordinate set will not change the position of the cursor for string printing.

objectname.Print(print_job_number, x, y {, width, height})

This function will print any object specified in *objectname* which is either a window or a descendant of DragObject (this covers all windows controls) to the print job specified in *print_job_number*.

The X and Y parameters designate the coordinates on the page where you want the left corner of the object to appear (this measurement is in thousandths of an inch). The *width* and *height* parameters are optional parameters that you can use to specify how wide and how high you want the object to print (again in thousandths of an inch). If you do not specify a *width* and a *height*, PowerBuilder will use the objects original dimensions.

The following example will print the picture button pb_exit at a position two inches to the right and one inch below the top left of the print area.

```
INTEGER li_printjob

li_printjob = PrintOpen( )
pb_exit.Print(li_printjob, 2000,1000)
PrintClose(li_printjob)
```

PrintBitmap(print_job_number, bitmap, x, y, width, height)

This function will print a bitmap image at a location in the print area specified by the X and Y parameters (in thousandths of an inch).

The *bitmap* parameter contains a string with the name of the file containing the bitmap image to print (i.e. brush.bmp). The *width* and *height* parameters will specify how wide and how high you want to the bitmap to appear. These are not optional parameters. Entering a 0 value will cause the bitmap to print in its original size. Example:

```
INTEGER li_printjob

// Define a new blank page.
li_printjob = PrintOpen( )

// Print the bitmap Greycol2.bmp in its original size at
// position 100,100
PrintBitmap(li_printjob, "greycol2.bmp", 100,100, 0,0)

// Close the print job (sends the page to the printer)
PrintClose(li_printjob)
```

PrintDataWindow(print_job_number, datawindowcontrol)

This function will print the formatted contents of a DataWindow control as part of the specified print job. Since PowerBuilder uses the fonts and formatting defined in the DataWindow object, functions like PrintDefineFont() and PrintSetFont() have no effect. Powersoft recommends that if you are going to use PrintDataWindow, it should be the only function that you use in the print job. It is a bit of a page hog and uses up the entire page. Every time you issue a PrintDataWindow, the next item you print will be on a new page.

PrintLine(print_job_number, x1, y1, x2, y2, thickness)

This function will print a line of a specified thickness. The line will begin at the coordinates specified in the X1 and Y1 parameters (in thousandths of an inch) and will end at the coordinates specified in the X2 and Y2 parameters (also in thousandths of an inch). The *thickness* parameter is an integer value specifying the thickness of the line in thousandths of an inch.

The following example will print a 1/4 inch thick line from the top left of the print area to a position five inches below.

```
INTEGER li_printjob

// Open a print job.
li_printjob = PrintOpen( )

// Print a line starting at the top left of the page (0,0)
// and ending five inches below that (0,5000).
// The line is 1/4 inch thick (250)
PrintLine(li_printjob, 0, 0,0, 5000, 250)
```

PrintOval(print_job_number, x, y, width, height, thickness)

This function will print an oval (or a circle if the width and height are the same) outlined with a line of a specified *thickness* (in thousandths of an inch). Every oval is surrounded by an imaginary box (the bounding box) which contains the entire oval within it. You must visualize this box when you want to physically place the oval, because the X and Y parameters specified are for the location (in thousandths of an inch) of the upper left corner of the bounding box.

PrintRect (print_job_number, x, y, width, height, thickness)

This function is exactly the same as the PrintOval() function, except it prints a rectangle.

PrintRoundRect (print_job_number, x, y, width, height, thickness)

This function is exactly the same as the PrintOval() function, except it prints a rounded rectangle (the corners are rounded instead of squared).

Print Control Functions

There are a suite of functions that you will use to control how things are going to print when you send them to the printer. The first one, PrintOpen(), we already introduced to you in the early part of this chapter. Now it is time to tell you about the rest.

PrintCancel(print_job_number)

This function will cancel the print job number specified without sending anything to the printer.

datawindowcontrol.PrintCancel()

This variation on the PrintCancel function will cancel the printing of a DataWindow control printed with the datawindowcontrol.Print() function.

PrintClose(print_job_number)

This function will close the print job specified and send it to the printer (or spooler). To avoid hung print jobs, all opened jobs should be either closed or canceled.

PrintDefineFont(print_job_number, fontnumber, facename, height, weight, fontpitch, fontfamily, italic, underline)

This function allows you to define one of the eight fonts that PowerBuilder supports for each print job. The print job number that this font is intended for is specified in the *print_job_number* parameter and the *fontnumber* parameter is which of the fonts for this print job (1-8) you are defining. The rest of the parameters describe how the font is to appear, including things like italics, bold, and underline.

The *facename* parameter is a string that contains the name of the font you are defining (i.e. Courier 10cpi). The *height* parameter is the height that you want for the font in thousandths of an inch (i.e. 250 would be an 18 point Courier 10cpi font). The *height* parameter could alternatively be used to specify the point size by using a negative value (i.e. -18 would be a point size of 18). The *weight* parameter holds the value you want for the stroke weight of the font (i.e. 400 in normal text, 700 is bold).

The *fontpitch* parameter is an enumerated datatype indicating the pitch of the font (Default!, Fixed!, or Variable!). The *fontfamily* parameter in another enumerated datatype indicating the family that the font belongs to (AnyFont!, Decorative!, Modern!, Roman!, Script!, or Swiss!). These two parameters are only used in the Windows-based operating system. In the Macintosh world, for example, the *fontfamily* and *fontpitch* are ignored, and only the *facename*, *height,* and *Weight* are used.

The *italic* parameter is a boolean value that sets the font to be italic (True) or non-italic (False), and the *underline* attribute is a boolean that functions in the same way.

The following example would define the font number 1 for the print job as Courier 10cpi with a pitch of 18, non-bold, italic, and underlined.

```
INTEGER li_printjob

li_printjob = PrintOpen( )
PrintDefineFont(li_printjob, 1, "Courier 10Cpi",-18, 400, Default!, &
Decorative!,TRUE, TRUE)
```

PrintOpen()
This function was described at the beginning of the chapter. It is used to obtain a print job number for grouping together items to be sent to the printer. The return value is the unique print job ID, with a negative value being returned should an error occur.

PrintPage(print_job_number)
This function will send the current page of the specified print job to the printer (or spooler) and sets up a new empty page for the print commands that follow it.

PrintSend(print_job_number, string {,zero_character})
This function is used to send a specific string to the printer for the print job specified. The string is usually a command string of escape characters used for printer setup or manipulation. These printer control codes are different for every printer, and you should refer to your printer manual for the appropriate codes.

The string will be a collection of ASCII characters that are required to communicate with the printer. One problem arises from this: the ASCII character 0 is used to terminate a string. If you need to send ASCII zeros to your printer, you can substitute a different character in your string for 0, then indicate that by giving the ASCII value of the substitute character in the optional parameter *zero_character*.

Typical uses for this function would include changing the paper orientation (landscape or portrait) or the paper tray to print from.

PrintSetFont(print_job_number, fontnumber)
This function will set the current printer font to be one of the eight that you defined using the PrintDefineFont() function.

PrintSetSpacing(print_job_number, spacing)
This function sets the spacing between lines of text to the value specified in the *spacing* parameter. This value is specified as a factor of the current font height. The default is 1.2.

PrintSetup()
This function calls the Windows Print Setup dialog box. The actual setup window that appears depends on the printer driver that you have installed.

PrintWidth(print_job_number, string)
This function will return the width of the string in the *string* parameter in thousandths of an

inch. This is based upon the currently selected font.

PrintX(print_job_number)

This function returns the X coordinate (horizontal) of the print cursor.

PrintY(print_job_number)

This function returns the Y coordinate (vertical) of the print cursor.

Unless otherwise specified, the above functions will return a value of 1 for success and a -1 if an error occurs.

The Print Attributes of the DataWindow Control

Using the Modify function, we can alter the specific attributes of a DataWindow's print characteristics in advance. Before we print our DataWindow we might call a window like the one in Figure 15-2 to get the parameters we want our users to set.

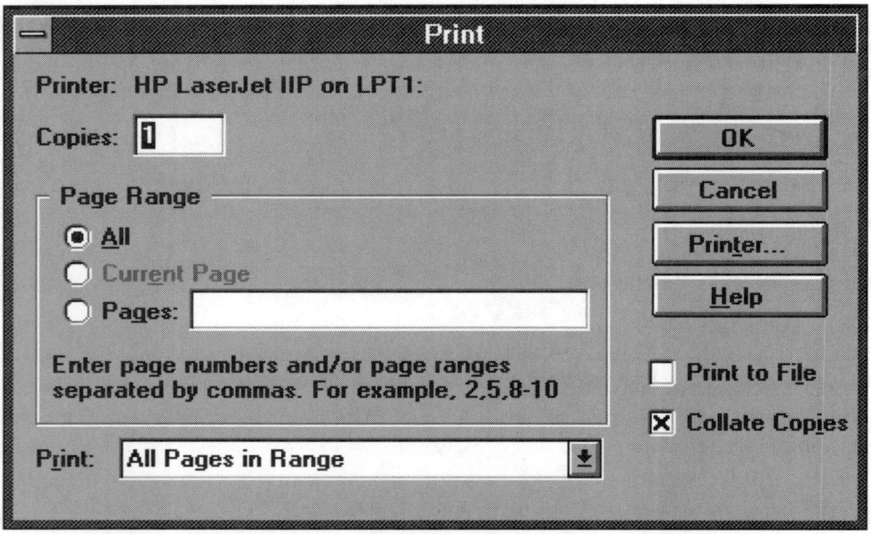

Figure 15-2: A print parameters window can be used to get the values to set into a DataWindow's print attributes.

As an example, we can change the number of copies that we want to print with the following statement:

```
dw_data..Modify("DataWindow.Print.Copies=3")
```

You can use the dwsyn40.exe DataWindow syntax application that comes with your Power-Builder Enterprise to help you build your Modify statements.

The following list of parameters that you can modify are all prefixed with DataWindow.Print, followed by the attribute.

Collate = Yes or No (Default is no, do not collate)

This attribute is used to indicate whether or not the printing will be collated. Collating is usually slower because the whole print cycle must be repeated in order to produce a collated result.

Color = 1 (Color) or 2 (Monochrome)

This attribute is used to indicate whether the output sent to the printer will be in color (if you have a color printer) or monochrome.

Columns = <an integer> (Default is 1)

This attribute is used to specify the number of newspaper-style columns the DataWindow will print on a page.

Columns.Width = <an integer>

This attribute is used to specify how wide the newspaper-style columns are (based upon the units of measure specified for the DataWindow).

Copies = <an integer>

This attribute is used to set the number of copies of the output you want generated.

DocumentName = <a string>

This attribute allows you to set the name for the document that appears in the print queue when the DataWindow is sent to the printer.

Duplex = 1 (Simplex) or 2 (Horizontal) or 3 (Vertical)

This attribute will set the orientation of printed output.

Filename = <filename string>

This attribute is only applicable if you are printing your DataWindow to a file. The attribute holds a string containing the name of the file that will be created.

Margin.Bottom = <an integer>

This attribute holds an integer specifying the width of the bottom margin on the page (in the units specified for the DataWindow).

Margin.Left = <an integer>

This is the same as **Margin.Bottom**, but is for the width of the left margin.

Margin.Right = <an integer>

This is the same as **Margin.Bottom**, but is for the width of the right margin.

Margin.Top = <an integer>

This is the same as **Margin.Bottom**, but is for the width of the top margin

Orientation = 0 (Default orientation for your printer) or 2 (Landscape) or 3(Portrait)

This attribute is used to indicate the desired print orientation. You can use the default printer settings, or if you want your DataWindow to always print in landscape or portrait mode you can override the default print settings.

Page.Range = <page range string>

This attribute contains a string that holds the numbers of the pages that you want to print. The numbers in the string should be separated by commas, or a range can be indicated using a dash between numbers. You can also combine these two techniques together, for example "1,2,3, 6-12". An empty string indicates that all pages should be printed.

Page.RangeInclude = 0 (Print All) or 1 (Print Even Numbered Pages) or 2 (Print Odd Numbered Pages)

This attribute is used to indicate what pages to print within the range indicated in **Page.Range**.

You can choose to print even numbered pages and then turn the pages over, reinsert them into the printer, and select odd numbered pages. This will effectively give you printing on two sides of a page, like a book.

Paper.Size = < an integer>

This attribute is used to indicate the size of the paper being printed on. The acceptable values are:

```
 0-Default paper size for the printer
 1-Letter 8 1/2 x 11 in
 2-LetterSmall 8 1/2 x 11 in
 3-Tabloid 17 x 11 inches
 4-Ledger 17 x 11 in
 5-Legal 8 1/2 x 14 in
 6-Statement 5 1/2 x 8 1/2 in
 7-Executive 7 1/4 x 10 1/2 in
 8-A3 297 x 420 mm
 9-A4 210 x 297 mm
10-A4 Small 210 x 297 mm
11-A5 148 x 210 mm
12-B4 250 x 354
13-B5 182 x 257 mm
14-Folio 8 1/2 x 13 in
15-Quarto 215 x 275 mm
```

```
16-10x14 in
17-11x17 in
18-Note 8 1/2 x 11 in
19-Envelope #9 3 7/8 x 8 7/8
20-Envelope #10 4 1/8 x 9 1/2
21-Envelope #11 4 1/2 x 10 3/8
22-Envelope #12 4 x 11 1/276
23-Envelope #14 5 x 11 1/2
24-C size sheet
25-D size sheet
26-E size sheet
27-Envelope DL 110 x 220 mm
28-Envelope C5 162 x 229 mm
29-Envelope C3 324 x 458 mm
30-Envelope C4 229 x 324 mm
31-Envelope C6 114 x 162 mm
32-Envelope C65 114 x 229 mm
33-Envelope B4 250 x 353 mm
34-Envelope B5 176 x 250 mm
35-Envelope B6 176 x 125 mm
36-Envelope 110 x 230 mm
37-Envelope Monarch 3.875 x 7.5 in
38-6 3/4 Envelope 3 5/8 x 6 1/2 in
39-US Std Fanfold 14 7/8 x 11 in
40-German Std Fanfold 8 1/2 x 12 in
41-German Legal Fanfold 8 1/2 x 13 in
```

Paper.Source = < an integer>

This attribute holds an integer value specifying the paper bin that will be used as the source. The acceptable values are:

```
 0-Default
 1-Upper
 2-Lower
 3-Middle
 4-Manual
 5-Envelope
 6-Envelope manual
 7-Auto
 8-Tractor
 9-Smallfmt
10-Largefmt
11-Large capacity
14-Cassette
```

Preview = Yes (Print Preview mode on) or No (Print Preview mode off–this is the default)
This attribute allows you to toggle the DataWindow in and out of Print Preview mode, which allows the user to see how it will appear on the printed page.

Preview.Rulers = Yes (Display rulers) or No (Don't display rulers–Default)

This attribute sets whether rulers will appear in the DataWindow object when it is in Print Preview mode.

Preview.Zoom = <an integer>

This attribute allows you to specify a zoom factor for previewing the DataWindow when it is in Print Preview mode. The default is 100% (Preview.Zoom = 100).

Prompt = Yes (Display prompt–default) or No (No prompt)

This attribute allows you to control whether PowerBuilder displays a prompt allowing the user to cancel the print job before the job prints.

Quality = 0 (Default) or 1 (High) or 2 (Medium) or 3 (Low) or 4 (Draft)

This attribute allows you to select the quality of the print output.

Scale = <an integer>

This attribute allows you to specify the scale of the printed output so that you can scale the output up or down.

Doing a Screen Dump: How to Print the Entire Screen

A new feature in PowerBuilder is the ability to take an image of the screen at any point and to dump the screen to the printer. We do this using one more print function called Print-Screen(). The syntax for PrintScreen() is:

```
PrintScreen(print_job_number, x, y {,width, height})
```

Executing this function will take the current screen and print it to a specified print job at the coordinates indicated by the X and Y parameters (measured in thousandths of an inch). The *width* and *height* parameters specify how wide and high you want the screen to print. These last two parameters are optional. If you don't specify them, the screen will print in its original width and height.

```
INTEGER li_printjob

// Open a print job to print the screen to
li_printjob = PrintOpen( )

// Print the screen one inch down and one inch from the left
PrintScreen(li_printjob, 1000,1000)
PrintClose(li_printjob)
```

Summary

With PowerBuilder 4.0 we now have a great deal of control over how we are going to generate hard copies of our reports. When we combine this with the composite DataWindow, we have the ability to generate and print almost any type of report that you can dream up. So get creative and have some fun, and in no time you will be amazing your family, friends, and co-workers with your outstanding reports!

CHAPTER **16**

Improving Your
Applications with Graphs!

By Derek Ball

Improving Your Applications with Graphs!

by **Derek Ball**

When it comes to conveying information in a quick, succinct, and intuitive manner, nothing beats the power of a good graph. Luckily for us, packaged into PowerBuilder 4.0 is a powerful graphing facility allowing us to present our data as charts, bars, pies and more! This feature was an exciting development for those of us who have been using PowerBuilder for awhile. In previous versions, if we wanted to display a graph we would have to do DDE to Excel or some other graphing utility.

We see graphs everywhere we look, and the users of the applications we build can easily understand data presented in the form of a graph whether they are technically oriented or not. Graphs are often underutilized in PowerBuilder applications today. Lists of data and summary values can be difficult to draw meanings from, but take that same data and present it as a graph and we have a new tool for analysis. Within our applications we need only specify the data that we wish to graph (usually from our relational database) and what we want the graph to look like (we can make bar graphs, pie charts, line graphs, scatter graphs, etc. and we can do them in 2D or 3D), and PowerBuilder takes care of most of the hard work for us.

The Three Ways of Using Graphs

There are three ways that you can integrate graphs into your application:

You can use the graph control in the Window Painter to paint a graph directly onto your window like any other control. This type of graph is not explicitly linked to any outside data source, which means that you must populate it manually using the PowerScript graph functions (i.e. grAddData, grAddSeries). This can be long and tedious if your graph has any degree of complexity at all, but can be useful for simple graphs, such as resource or memory graphs.

Graphs can be created as a DataWindow. There is a DataWindow presentation style called Graph which instead of displaying all the rows of data in the DataWindow control, will display a graph of the type that you specify, based on the data.

You can use a graph to supplement the information in a non-graph DataWindow. This allows you to have both the detail data that the graph is based on, and the summary information in the graph itself, available to the user. This gives you a great deal of flexibility. The graph can float in the foreground layer of the DataWindow, and thus not print out; or you may choose to include it in one of the band layers to provide summary information on all or a portion of a report; or you could place it in the background layer to serve as a backdrop image behind the detail data.

Basic Graph Elements

The graphs that you will build have a number of common elements that you will need to specify.

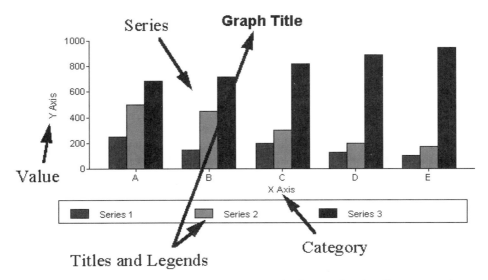

*Figure 16-1: All graphs contain a category and values, and optionally may contain
a series, titles, and legends.*

Category: The category, or X axis, represents the major grouping of your data or
the independent variable in your graph. For example, in a graph showing
employee salaries by department, department would be the category.

Value: The value, or Y axis, represents the plots of the dependent variable (or variables, if applicable) in your graph. In the above example, a graph showing
employee salaries by department, the sum of employee salaries for a given
department would be the value.

Series: The series, or Z axis, is not a required element in all graphs. It can be used
to further define your graph by adding a third axis on which to differentiate your data. In the example we have been using, we could further refine
the graph by adding a series which would show us the total salaries by
gender by department. The sum of salaries for a given gender in a given
department would be our series.

Titles and **Legends**: Titles and legends can optionally be added to the graph to
allow us to label the graph and its elements. Legends, if applicable, are
also available to allow us to label a category. Legends are often used with
pie graphs to label the segments of the pie.

2D Vs 3D—Presentation Styles and Data

The expressions "2D" and "3D" can be a little confusing when you deal with graphs in PowerBuilder, because the same terms are used to refer to both the presentation style (type) of the graph, and to the number of data components being tracked. In the latter case, a two-dimensional graph will track a value (Y-axis) and a category (X-axis)–for example, a two-dimensional graph for a company might track employee salaries by department. A three-dimensional graph has the value and category, but subdivides these into a third value the series (Z-axis)–for example, a count of the employees in each department subdivided by gender (Figure 16-2).

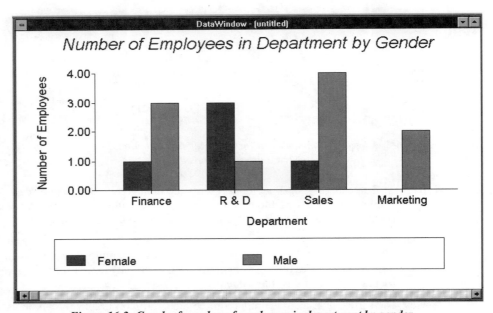

Figure 16-2: Graph of number of employees in department by gender.

When referring to a presentation style as being 2D or 3D, we are referring in particular to the graph type, and whether it is rendered visually in a two-dimensional or a three-dimensional manner. There are a variety of types that you can choose from, as shown in Figure 16-2. The graph type is just the first of the attributes that you will need to select.

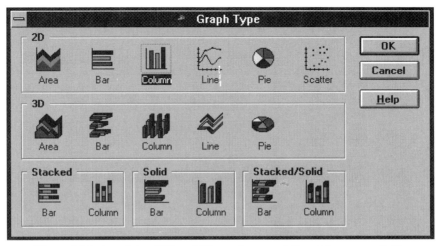

Figure 16-3: A variety of 2D and 3D graph presentation styles are available.

Building the Graph—Choosing a Category and a Value

We will focus our efforts on creating a DataWindow of a graph presentation style. The first step to create this graph is to create a new DataWindow. From the DataWindow Painter, select New. This will bring up the standard DataWindow options selection, where you choose a data source and a presentation style. Select a Graph presentation style and an appropriate data source. Once you have done this, you will get the Graph Data dialog box (Figure 16-4).

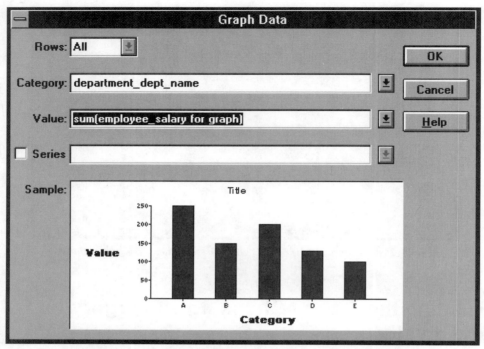

Figure 16-4: The Graph Data dialog box allows you to select the category, value, and series (X, Y and Z axes) for your graph.

There are four elements to the Graph Data dialog box:

> **Rows DropDownListBox**. Here you will select what rows you want to compose your graph. Initially there are two choices:
>
> > ALL–to show the data from all the rows in the result set
> > or
> > PAGE–to show the data in the graph for only those rows on the current physical page.
>
> If your graph is going to be of the Graph DataWindow presentation style, this box will be disabled and ALL will be selected by default: the assumption is that you will always show a summary of all the data in your result set. However, if you are adding a graph to an existing tabular DataWindow, there are a few different ways you may choose to show your data.
>
> If you want the graph in the footer of the DataWindow, you would probably want to graph only the data on that physical page, and so you would select PAGE. The data on each page would be different, and the graph on the bottom of the page would change accordingly.

You could also place the graph in the group header or trailer to show a summary graph for the rows of data in that group. If you add groups to the DataWindow, then the Rows DropDownListBox will allow you to select to graph by the rows in Group 1 (or any other group for that matter)

Category DropDownListBox. Here you will select what you would like to have for your X axis on the graph. The DropDownListBox will contain a list of all columns in your result set. Most of the time this will fulfill your requirements,. but there are times when you may want to use an expression instead of a straight column name as your independent axis–for instance, you might want to group all the sales in a particular month by using the Month() function. The Category DropDownListBox is an editable field and you can enter in any valid expression.

Value DropDownListBox. In this field you enter the expression for what you would like to show on the Y axis of your graph. This usually involves some kind of mathematical function. The available options in the drop-down list will provide you with all the standard counts, sums, and averages that PowerBuilder can deduce you might require, but these are only the simplest of calculations. You can select one of them, or enter your own expression into the field.

Series DropDownListBox. The final of the four fields is an optional argument that you can use to graph a third dimension in your graphs (the Z axis). If you wish to add this third dimension you must select the CheckBox beside the Series field to enable the DropDownListBox. You can then select a series from the list or enter a valid expression in the field. The series should provide a way to further subdivide the categories and values currently being graphed.

In our example, we will use the Powersoft Demo database in Watcom. I have selected a list of employees by department, including their salary and status. As indicated above, each of the three axis choices has a DropDownListBox associated with it. We can select Department Name for our category and Sum(employee_salary for graph) for our value. This will result in a graph like that in Figure 16-5.

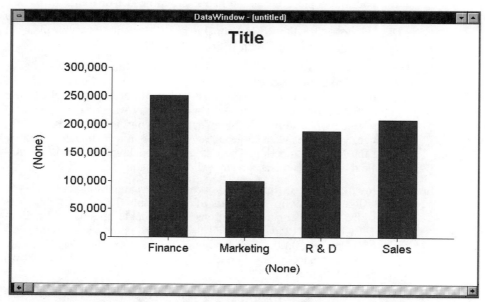

Figure 16-5: A 2D graph with the sum of employee salaries by department.

Keep in mind that the options presented in the list are not your only options. The list box is an editable field and you can enter any valid expression that you would like to graph by. We could enter Month(employee_birth_date) as the category and then Count(employee_last_name) as the value, and get a count of how many employees have birthdays in different months (see Figure 16-6).

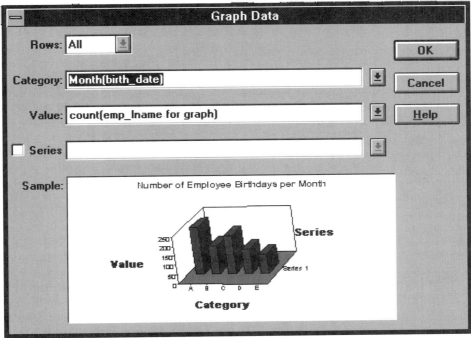

Figure 16-6: We can enter any valid expression as a category, value, or series in a graph.

We could get the month name to show up by using a LookUpDisplay() function in the expression to retrieve a lookup value from a code table.

Choosing a Graph Type

Now we have built a basic graph, but what if we want something other than the default column graph.? We can select any of the graph types from Figure 16-3 above. We can make area, bar, column, line, pie, and scatter graphs–and a number of those also come in a variety of sub-types.

To select a different type of graph, click with the right mouse button in the middle of the graph area (in the DataWindow designer). You will see a popup menu of graph attributes that you can alter. Select the Type... option.

We can now take our graph from Figure 16-5 above and change it into a 3D pie graph, as in Figure 16-7.

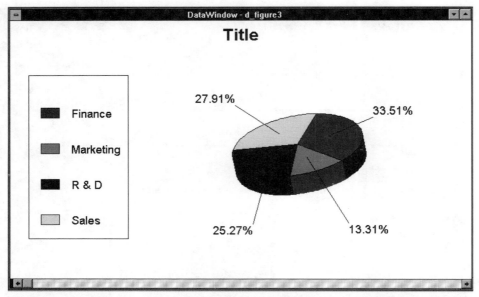

Figure 16-7: We can change the type of graph by clicking in the middle of the graph with the right mouse button.

The Different Graph Types

Line graphs are the traditional graph with discrete data points connected by a line. A separate line exists for each series in the graph.

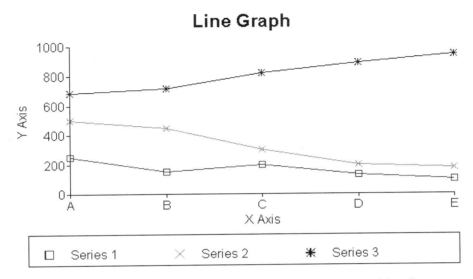

*Figure 16-8: A 2D line graph has discrete data points connected by a line.
A different line and data point symbol is used for each series.*

Bar graphs and column graphs allow you to present your data as a range covered by the bar or column on your graph area. Bar graphs extend from the left side of the graph to the right, and column graphs extend from the bottom upwards. Both display the same data, but a bar graph moves the X axis to the vertical axis and the Y axis to the horizontal.

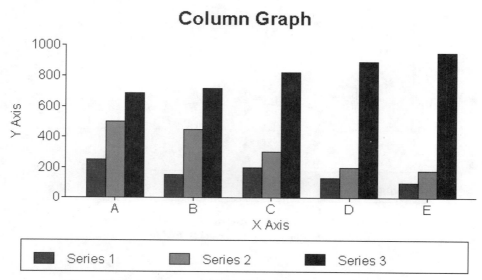

Figure 16-9a: A column graph extends from the bottom axis upwards.

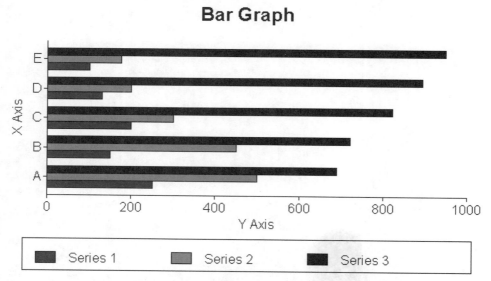

Figure 16-9b: A bar graph extends from the left axis towards the right.

Series are normally added as their own bars or columns extending from the appropriate axis. However, data from a series can be stacked together with the other series on the graph, as is the case in the stacked and stacked/solid bar and column graphs.

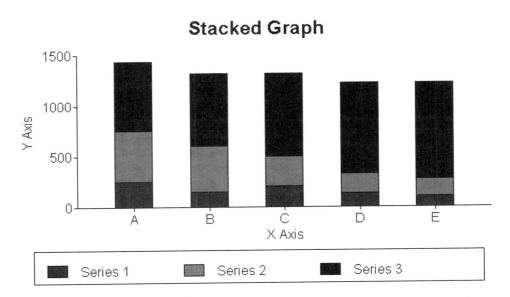

Figure 16-9c: Series can be represented as one bar by using a stacked or stacked/solid graph type.

The area graph is very similar to the line graph, but the area between the line and the X axis is shaded in. This graph type will not always yield the expected results when used with a series, as a given series will overwrite those portions of any previous series that has lower datapoints than the current series.

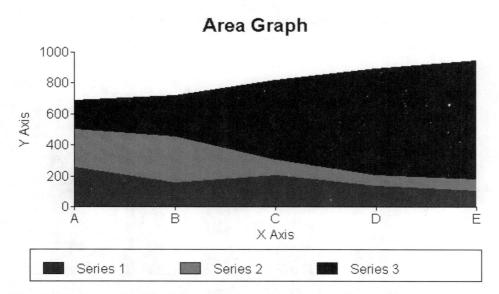

Figure 16-10: An area graph is similar to a line graph, but the area beneath the line is shaded in.

The scatter graph allows you to graph discrete data points against two axes. A typical use might be salaries by age of employee, which would allow you to determine trends to see if there is any correlation between the age of an employee and the salary earned.

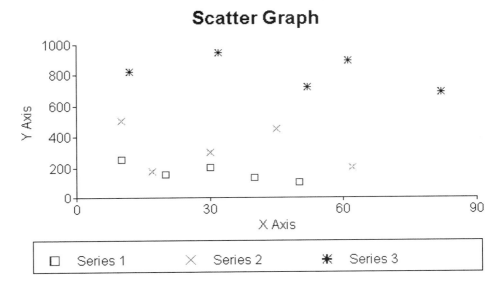

Figure 16-11–A scatter graph shows data points graphed against two value axes.

Pie graphs display data by taking the segments defined by the category and displaying them as pieces of a "pie." The size of the segment is the result of the data–for example, the sum of employee salaries by department.

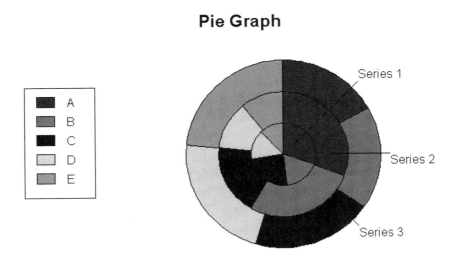

Figure 16-12–Pie graphs display data summaries as pieces of a pie.

Most of these graphs have both a 2D and a 3D version. The functionality is essentially the same, whether the graph is rendered in two or three dimensions.

Altering the Style of a Graph

To alter the specific attributes of the graph, double click in the graph area with the left mouse button. This will open the graph style window (Figure 16-13).

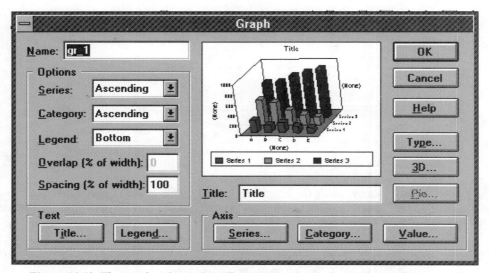

Figure 16-13–The graph style window allows you to change the attributes of your graph.

You can assign a name to the graph, and specify its title, in the style window. In the Options group box you can select some presentation options, such as how to sort the series and category (ascending, descending, or unsorted) and where to locate the legend (top, bottom, left, right, or none). The Overlap option allows you to designate if you want the width of the objects to overlap, and by what percentage (default is 0–no overlap). The Spacing option designates how much space you want between columns as a percentage of the width (default is 100%).

In the Text group box there are two command buttons, "Title..." and "Legend...", which are used to change the text details for the title and the legend areas. Pressing these buttons opens the text window (Figure 16-14).

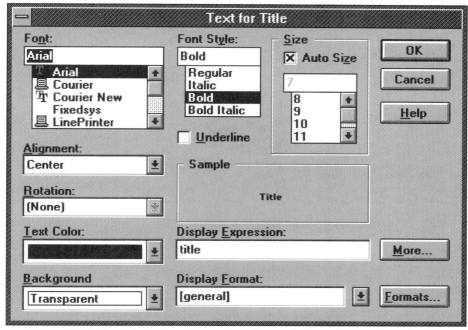

*Figure 16-14: The text window allows you to change the font characteristics for titles,
legends, and labels.*

This window allows you to select the font type, size, and style, as well as specify the alignment, of a given text field. The Rotation DropDownListBox allows you to rotate the text in your labels to a variety of angles. This only applies to labels, not to titles or legends. You can also select the color for the text and the background, and the display format that you would like to use. This display format is identical to the display format in the DataWindow Painter extended attributes, and if you select the "Formats..." command button it will take you into the formats definition window that the DataWindow Painter uses.

One new and powerful field in PowerBuilder 4.0 is the Display Expression field. We can alter a field to display not only text, but any valid expression. This means that our title can contain computed fields (such as the total salaries paid out across all departments), and that the labels on our pie graphs are no longer restricted to percentages. Now we can mix and match labels to show the total salary amount in that department *and* the percentage that represents by entering the following expression:

```
(string(sumforcategory,"$0,000.00") +" ("+string(per-
centofseries,"0.00%")+")")
```

This will result in a pie graph with labels as in Figure 16-15.

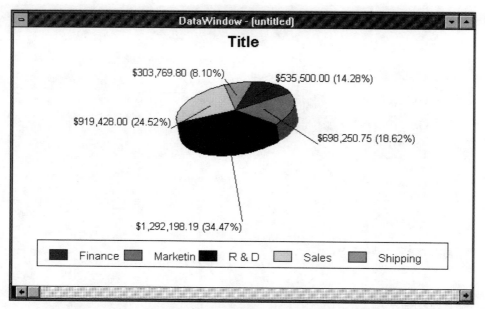

*Figure 16-15–The Display Expression field in the graph style window allows us
to display expressions as the labels for our graph.*

This expression is entered into the same text window, but the window is accessed by selecting the" Pie..." command button from the style window (only available if you are using a pie
graph type).

The Axis group box from the graph style window in Figure 16-13 contains command buttons that allow you to modify how each of the three axes is displayed. Selecting any of the
command buttons will open the axis window shown in Figure 16-16.

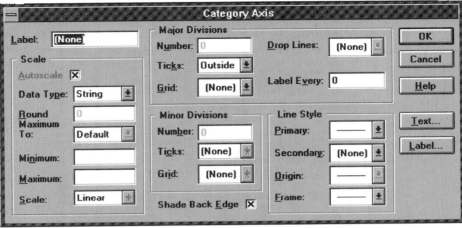

Figure 16-16: The axis window allows you to customize how each axis appears on the graph.

From this window you can assign a label to the axis. The scale box allows you to change how the values on this axis are presented. By default PowerBuilder will autoscale the graph, but if you choose to override this setting you can then select your own minimum and maximum values, rounding, and scaling. You can also set how you want the lines and tick marks to appear, and how often. Selecting the "Text..." or "Label..." command button lets you change the text for the axis and labels with the text style window from Figure 16-14.

The final command button from the graph style window in Figure 16-11 is the "3D..." button. This button allows you to alter the roll, pitch, and yaw of your 3D graph, and to select a width for the objects in the graph (Figure 16-17).

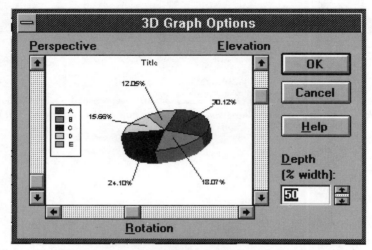

Figure 16-17: You can adjust the width, roll, pitch, and yaw of your 3D graph.

As you can see, there are a wide variety of ways that you can customize your graph to get it to appear exactly as you would like it to. Try experimenting with the different attributes; that is the best way to get a firm understanding of how they all work.

Adding a Series

Our graph is displaying the data as we wanted it, along with labels, titles and legends, but now we decide that we really need to have the data broken down into greater detail. We need to add a third axis, the series, to our graph. We decide to break down employee salaries by male and female. To do this we have to click on the right mouse button in the middle of the graph and choose Data... to get back to the Graph Data dialog. In this dialog we will click on the Series CheckBox to indicate that we want to add the third dimension. Then we will enter the employee gender description as the series value (Figure 16-18).

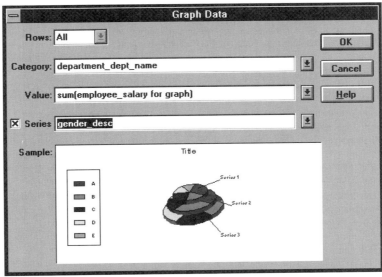

*Figure 16-18a and Figure 16-18b: We can add a series to our graph
to allow us to further define the data.*

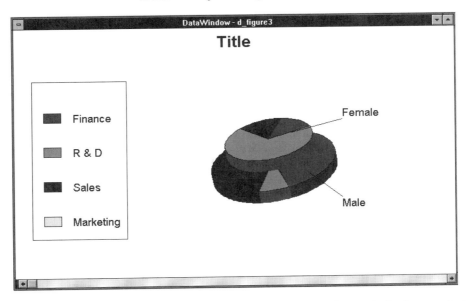

It would appear that now the data is not well represented by a pie graph. Perhaps a stacked
bar graph would be more appropriate (Figure 16-19).

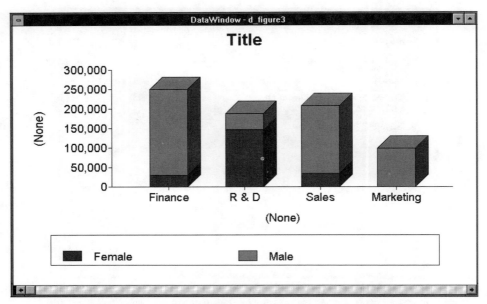

Figure 16-19: We can change the type now to the more appropriate stacked bar graph.

Enhancing the Graph

Having done a fine job of getting our data to display the way we want it, we now want to polish up our graph a little to enhance its presentation style. Just as with controls in the Window Painter, we can double click with the left mouse button to access the graphs style window (Figure 16-20).

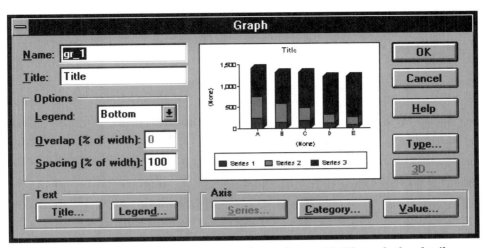

Figure 16-20: In the style window we can change the graph's titles and other details.

Aside from the name and title of the graph, we can now change other settings such as the location of the legend (if applicable), the graph type, the 3D settings (roll, pitch, and yaw are all user definable), and the fonts to be used. The separate command buttons for the various axes allow us to change the specific details for each axis (Figure 16-21).

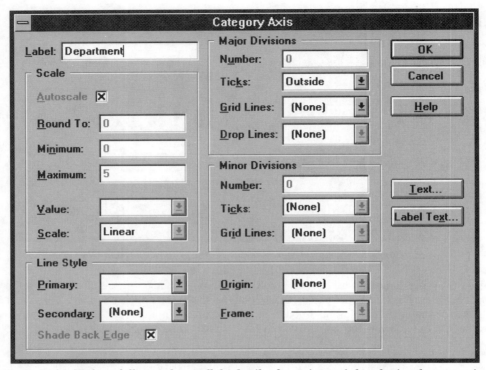

Figure 16-21: We have full control over all the details of any given axis by selecting the appropriate axis command button from the graph style window.

We now can alter details, such as having the axis automatically scale based upon the data or setting the scale ourselves. Other attributes that we can now control include scaling in a linear or non-linear (i.e. logarithmic) manner; the style of lines we want to use; and where we want to show tick and grid marks and how they are to appear. We can change the label text, and also the fonts used for the labels.

Other ways of altering the appearance of the graph include using the right mouse button to click on the graph and selecting the attribute to modify from the popup menu. From this menu you can choose attributes such as the system pointer that you want to see when the mouse is over the graph, or the colors you want the graph to use. (Note: Some colors are preset and can only be changed in your scripts.)

Individual items on the graph can be accessed by clicking on them with the right mouse button. This includes the graph title, axis labels, the individual axis, and the legend. You will get a popup menu that allows you to change the attributes of that particular area, or you can alter it by selecting items from the style bar.

Overlaying One Graph Over Another

In PowerBuilder it is possible to build two graphs and overlay them in the same physical space. We could take our graph of employee salaries by department from Figure 16-3 and overlay a graph showing the average salary in each department (Figure 16-22).

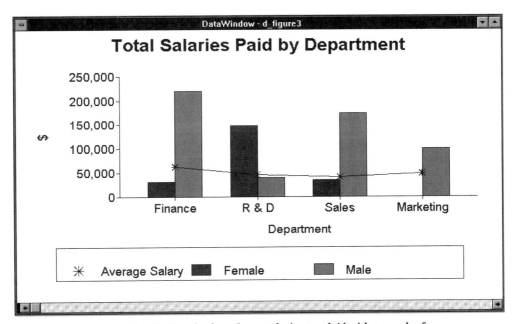

*Figure 16-22: Graph of employee salaries overlaid with a graph of
the average salary by department.*

To accomplish this we have to add the overlay into the Data... definition area of the graph. We separate the second graph from the first by entering the data for the second graph on the same line, but separating the two with a comma. In the series definition we set up the overlay section by placing a comma between the two segments, and in the series for the second graph we insert

```
@overlay~tAverage Salary
```

as in Figure 16-23.

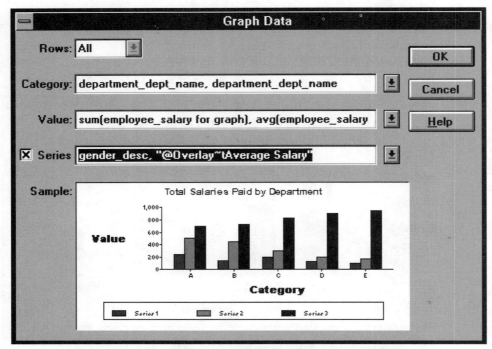

Figure 16-23: Two graphs can be overlaid in the same physical space using the @overlay function in the definition.

Using Modify to Change Your Graph at Runtime

You can use the ever-powerful Modify() function (this used to be dwModify in Power-Builder 3.0) to dynamically change all of your graph's attributes at runtime. To get the full list of all the attributes that you can modify, use the DWSyntax program that comes with your PowerBuilder Enterprise (dwsyn40.exe can be placed as a custom toolbar icon). Some examples of what you can do include:

1. Allow your users to change the type of graph they are looking at with:

```
<DW Control Name>.Modify(&
"<Graphname>.GraphType='<1-2DArea, 2-2DBar, 3-3DBar, 4-SolidBar, 5-Stacked-
Bar, 6-Stacked/Solid Bar, 7-2DColumn, 8-3DColumn, 9-SolidColumn, 10-Stacked-
Column, 11-Stacked/Solid Column, 12-2DLine, 13-2DPie, 14-2DScatter, 15-
3DArea, 16-3DLine, 17-3DPie>' ")
i.e.
dw_graph.Modify("gr_1.GraphType='17'")

changes graph type to 3D Pie.
```

2. Change the position of the legend.

```
<DW Control Name>.Modify(&
"<Graphname>.Legend='<0-None, 1-Left, 2-Right, 3-Top, 4-Bottom>'")
i.e.
dw_graph.Modify("gr_1.Legend='2'")
```

moves legend to the right side of graph.

Using Functions to Change Your Graph at Runtime

Another method for altering a graph at runtime is to use the PowerScript functions for working with graphs. There are many (around forty) different functions to affect things such as color, font style, labels, adding a series, adding a category, saving data to or importing from a clipboard, and much more. The full list of functions can be found in the on-line help section on graph functions.

Many of these functions serve useful purposes, but one function in particular stands out. It is difficult to change the foreground color of a series in a graph when painting it, but you can use the grSetSeriesStyle() function to make this change:

```
controlname.SetSeriesStyle ( { graphcontrol,} seriesname, colortype, color )
```

i.e.

```
dw_graph.SetSeriesStyle("gr_1", "Salary", ForeGround!, 255)
```

sets the series "Salary" to have a foreground color of Red. This is in the graph gr_1 in the DataWindow control dw_graph.

```
gr_salaries.SetSeriesStyle("Salary",ForeGround!, 255)
```

sets the series "Salary to have a foreground color of Red in the graph window's control gr_salaries.

This function can be used to change the foreground, background, line, and shading color for a series. On one project we needed to change the color of the bar graph so that its default color wasn't red, as red was not considered a good color to graph company financials in!

If you use this function to change the default color, create a user event for the dwGraphCreate event. This event will fire before the graph actually gets drawn on the window. By coding the grSetSeriesStyle function in this event, the color will be changed before the graph appears on the screen. This prevents having the graph drawn in the original color and then changed to the new color.

There are many other functions that are used in production applications. You may choose to use a graph that is not linked specifically to data to show things like system resources (a handy thing to keep your power users happy; then they know if they are about to overload the system). To show this kind of information we need to be able to manually add and delete data from the graph. The following functions may play a role:

1. Adding a new category to the graph (the user wants to show not only memory usage, but also CPU usage).

i.e.
```
controlname.AddCategory ( categoryname )

gr_resources.AddCategory("CPU Usage")
```

adds the category CPU Usage.

2. Adding some data to our new category.

```
controlname.AddData(seriesnumber, datavalue{,categorylabel})
```
i.e.

```
integer li_seriesnum

   li_seriesnum = dw_graph.FindSeries("CPU Usage")
   gr_resources.AddData( li_seriesnum, f_get_cpu_usage())
```

Another function that you may need will find out where on a graph the user has clicked the mouse. This may come into play if you want to build a drill down graph, or perhaps display detail or supporting information for the segment of the graph the user selected. To find out the series and datapoint that the user clicked on, we can use the function ObjectAtPointer(). This function will return to us an enumerated datatype indicating the type of object inside the graph that the user clicked on, and will place the series number or the datapoint number in a reference variable.

```
controlname.ObjectAtPointer( {graphcontrol,} seriesnumber, datavalue )
```

i.e.

```
// This script would appear in the clicked event of the Graph control
int li_seriesnum, li_datanum
double ldb_datavalue
grObjectType lgro_objecttype
string ls_series

lgro_objecttype = gr_annualsales.ObjectAtPointer(li_seriesnum, li_datanum)

CHOOSE CASE lgro_objecttype
   CASE TypeSeries!
     ls_series = gr_ annualsales.SeriesName(li_seriesnum)
// Build a choose case to show the details for the selected series
......
     CASE TypeData!
ldb_datavalue = gr_ annualsales.GetData(li_seriesnum, li_datanum)
// Show the details for the selected data value
......
END CHOOSE
```

There are many other PowerBuilder functions to support the usage of graphs in your applications. You will find the graphing very versatile and powerful.

New Functions for Version 4.0

If you have been doing graphing already in PowerBuilder 3.0 you will want to familiarize yourself with the new functions for working with graphs in version 4.0. These functions are:

controlname.SetDataPieExplode
({graphcontrol,} series, datapoint, percentage)

This function explodes a slice of the pie away from the main unit for a particular series and datapoint. How far out to explode the slice is indicated by percentage.

ControlName is the name of the control or the DataWindow control containing the graph that you want to explode.

GraphControl is used if the graph whose slice you want to explode is contained within a DataWindow control. This is the name if the graph in string form.

Series is the series number that identifies which series you are wanting to explode.

DataPoint is the number of the slice to explode.

Percentage is how far out you want to move the slice from the pie. This is measured as a percentage of the radius of the pie. A value from 0 to 100 is acceptable, and at 100% the tip of the slice is even with the edge of the pie.

The following example would explode a section of the pie chart that the user clicks on:

```
INTEGER li_series, li_datapoint, li_percent
grObjectType lgro_clickedtype

li_percent = 75 // Make sure graph is a pie graph

IF (THIS.GraphType = PieGraph! OR THIS.GraphType = Pie3D!) THEN
lgro_clickedtype = THIS.ObjectAtPointer(li_series, li_datapoint)

IF (li_series > 0 and li_datapoint > 0) THEN
// Explode pie slice out
THIS.SetDataPieExplode(li_series, li_datapoint, li_percent)
END IF
END IF
```

controlname.GetDataPieExplode({graphcontrol,} series, datapoint,
percentage)

This function will return to you the percentage of explosion of the specified pie slice (datapoint) for the specified series. The parameters are the same as for SetDataPieExplode(), except that percentage must now be an integer variable where the return value will be stored.

In an effort to be more polymorphic, powersoft has decided to remove the "gr" that used to prefix the graph functions. Any previous code that you have that used the "gr" functions will still function normally. This is similar to the removal of the "dw" prefix from the DataWindow functions that had it.

Where to Go from Here

This chapter has focused on one of the primary graphing methods (adding a graph to a DataWindow), but the techniques are relatively transferable through the three different methods. Try creating the different types of graphs and experiment with the different styles and functions that you have available to you. Get familiar with how to use the Modify function to change things about your graph. This can give your end users a great deal of flexibility in the way they can examine their data.

The best way to understand graphs is to begin including them in your applications. A picture truly does convey a thousand words, and the overall picture of your data that a graph provides can often tell you more in a moment than hours of analysis could reveal.

CHAPTER 17

Drag and Drop

By Robert Zenobia

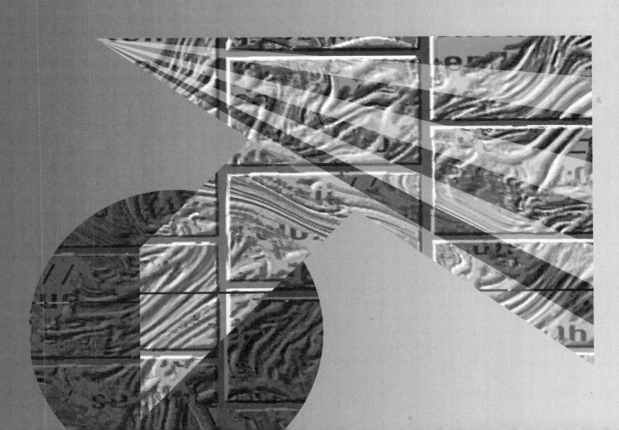

Drag and Drop

by **Robert Zenobia**

Overview

One way to make your PowerBuilder applications easier for users is to incorporate drag and drop functionality. Drag and drop allows users to interact with graphic controls on the screen in an intuitively familiar fashion. One way we deal with objects in real life is to pick them up, carry them someplace new, and put them down.

For instance, every day we pick up our mail from our mailboxes, examine it, and determine if it should be thrown away or saved. We could describe this process as a movement of mail from the mailbox to either a "trash object" or a "storage object." In drag and drop terminology, the mail is the drag object–the object we pick up and want to manipulate. The trash object and the storage object are drag targets. Each target encapsulates a certain functionality to be carried out when a mail object is dropped on it. The trash object's functionality is to destroy the mail, while the storage object's is to store the mail for later viewing.

This simple example illustrates the most traditional usage of drag and drop. There are other ways to use drag and drop and movement within our applications that can make our applications even more powerful.

To unleash the hidden power of drag and drop we need to look at another way in which we do things in real life. Think of the volume controls on a stereo receiver. Most are dials or slider bars that either turn or slide to manipulate the stereo's output level. Interaction with this type of object involves grabbing the object, turning or sliding it, and letting it go, usually in a new position. The movement here occurs within the object itself, and its functionality is subtly different from that of the previous example. As we move the dial or slider bar on the stereo, the volume automatically adjusts. The object's action is occurring *as the control is being manipulated*, not at the end of the movement, as with more conventional drag and drop applications.

To create PowerBuilder applications that incorporate different types of drag and drop controls, we first need to have a good understanding of what relevant tools are available to us in PowerBuilder. Immediately following is a breakdown of the PowerBuilder drag and drop tools.

PowerBuilder Drag and Drop Tools

DragObject datatype

All controls in PowerBuilder except drawing objects (lines, ovals and rectangles) can be dragged and are of the datatype DragObject. DragObject variables can be instantiated in scripts or as global or instance variables. References to objects of type DragObject can be stored in these variables, making the attributes of the referenced object directly accessible.

DragObject attributes

Autodrag

All objects of type DragObject have the autodrag attribute. Autodrag is a boolean attribute, which by definition is either true or false. If autodrag is set to False, the autodrag functionality is turned off and you will need to use the Drag function to drag the control. If autodrag is set to True, then the control will automatically be put into drag mode whenever it is clicked. In this case, the control's clicked event basically becomes This.Drag(Begin!). Any code written for the clicked event of a control set for autodrag will be ignored.

To simulate a clicked event for a control set for autodrag, place the script you want executed when a click occurs in the control's dragdrop event. Dragdrop will be triggered when the user drops the control on itself–which is now what happens when the control is clicked. Pushing the left mouse button down starts the dragging of the control, and letting the left mouse button up drops the control. If the control is over its original location it will trigger its own dragdrop event.

Dragicon

All objects of type DragObject also have a dragicon attribute. The dragicon attribute holds the name of either an enumerated icon or a custom-built .ico icon file. If this attribute is left blank it will default to a box the size of the dragged control.

Drag and drop events for DragObjects

Dragdrop

This event is triggered when a control being dragged is dropped (mouse button released) on a DragObject control. The dragged control has a drag-sensitive area, usually located near its center. DragObject controls respond to drag-sensitive areas. When a drag-sensitive area is over the perimeter of a DragObject control and the mouse button is released, the dragdrop event for the stationary control will be triggered. Controls can be dropped on themselves, and if this occurs quickly enough it can, as mentioned, be used to simulate a clicked event.

Dragenter

This event is triggered when the drag-sensitive area of a control being moved enters the perimeter of a stationary DragObject control. Controls dragged away from their original space can trigger their own dragenter event if dragged back to their original space.

Dragleave

This event is triggered when the drag-sensitive area of the dragged control is moved *away* from the perimeter of a stationary DragObject control. Controls dragged away from their original space can trigger their own dragleave event.

Dragwithin

This event is triggered when the drag-sensitive area of the control being moved is dragged within the perimeter of a DragObject control. This event is very powerful for making controls like dials and slider bars.

Drag and drop functions

Drag

This function is used to begin (begin!), end (end!) or cancel (cancel!) the dragging of a DragObject control that is not set for autodrag. "Begin" starts the drag mode. "End" stops the drag mode and automatically triggers a dragdrop for the object the dragged control is over . "Cancel" stops the drag mode and does not trigger a dragdrop event.

Draggedobject

This function is used to determine which control is being dragged. The return value is a pointer to the object being dragged (object of type DragObject). If no object is being dragged, an execution error message will be displayed. Storing the return value in a variable of type DragObject allows you to directly manipulate the attributes of the dragged object.

Sample applications: Sample One

Now that we have a good understanding of what PowerBuilder tools are available to us, let's look at some sample applications.

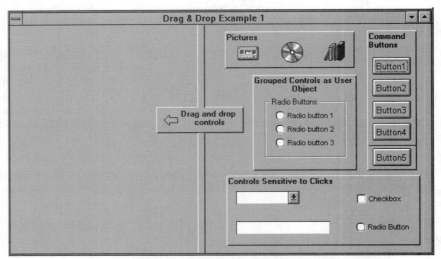

Figure 17-1: Drag and drop Sample Application One.

The first sample, shown in Figure 17-1, demonstrates how to use drag and drop with various types of PowerBuilder controls. The drag objects are the individual controls, and the intended drag target is the window. (We will see latter that there are other drag targets.) When this sample application is executed, the user will be able to drag controls from the right side of the screen and place them on the left. The control will be relocated, centered around the drop point on the window. Let's examine the different components of this application to see how they work.

The window: w_example1

W_example1 is a generic main window with one script. The script is for the dragdrop event and is given in Listing 1. It has four local variables: l_drag_obj of type DragObject; l_xpos and l_ypos of type Integer; and l_window of type Window.
The statement

```
l_window = This
```

gets a pointer to w_example1 and stores it in l_window.
The next statements,

```
l_xpos = l_window.pointerX()
```

and

```
l_ypos = l_window.pointerY()
```

set *l_xpos* and *l_ypos* to the x and y coordinates of where the mouse is in relation to w_example1 when the dragdrop event occurs. The next statement

```
l_drag_obj = DraggedObject()
```

stores a pointer to the object that was dragged in the variable *l_drag_obj*.

The next two statements change the x and y values of the object that was dragged, in reality moving the object to a new location. We use

```
l_drag_obj.x = l_xpos - (l_drag_obj.width/2)
```

to set the x value to the x value of where the mouse was minus half the width of the control. This centers the control horizontally around the dropped point. We use the same logic to determine the new y value for the control, except this time we want to center it vertically. The last statement

```
l_drag_obj.Drag(Cancel!)
```

stops the dragging of the control and does not trigger a dragdrop event. We use this statement for some controls that are not using autodrag; controls that are using autodrag will not be affected by it.

Listing 1: Dragdrop script for w_example.

```
/*
Object:   w_example
Event:    Dragdrop

Description: Move the dragged object to the location of where
the mouse pointer is when to object was dropped.
Note, we center the object around the mouse position
  "l_drag_obj.x = l_xpos - (l_drag_obj.width/2)" and
  "l_drag_obj.y = l_ypos - (l_drag_obj.height/2)".
*/

// Local Variables
// ----------------------------------
DragObject l_drag_obj
int l_xpos, l_ypos
window l_window

// Get a pointer to this window
// ----------------------------------
   l_window = This

// Get x & y position of mouse
// ----------------------------------
   l_xpos = l_window.pointerX();
   l_ypos = l_window.pointerY();

// Get the dragged Object
// ----------------------------------
   l_drag_obj = DraggedObject()

// Set the x & y of the dragged object to their new values
// ------------------------------------------------------
   l_drag_obj.x = l_xpos - (l_drag_obj.width/2)
```

```
    l_drag_obj.y = l_ypos - (l_drag_obj.height/2)

// IF the dragged object used the drag mode then cancel it
// ------------------------------------------------------
    l_drag_obj.Drag(Cancel!)
```

The pictures: p_1, p_2, and p_3

The three picture controls, p_1, p_2, and p_3–represented by bitmaps of a cassette, a compact disc, and a collection of books–have no scripts. These controls only use their autodrag and dragicon attributes. Autodrag is set to True for each picture control, and the dragicon attribute is set to the appropriate icon file. In traditional drag and drop utilizations, picture controls tend to work extremely well using autodrag. Try dragging these controls and see how they respond.

The command buttons: cb_1, cb_2, cb_3, cb_4 and cb_5

The command buttons cb_1 through cb_4 are all alike. They have autodrag set to True and one script for their dragdrop events. The dragicon is not set, causing it to default to a box the size of a command button. Their dragdrop scripts display a message box informing the user which button was pressed. This script is intended to show how the dragdrop event can be used to simulate a clicked event. Try clicking one of the command buttons cb_1 through cb_4; then try dragging the button to a new location. The message box should only display when the command button is clicked, and not when the command button is dragged to a new location.

Command button cb_5 is different from the others. It does not use autodrag and has a user event called left_button_down which has been mapped to pbm_lbuttondown. There are three scripts, one for each of the following events: left_button_down, clicked, and dragdrop. The script for left_button_down starts the drag mode. The script for the clicked event displays a message box indicating that command button 5 has been pressed, and the script for the dragdrop event stops the drag mode, in case the user just clicks the control.

The functional difference between cb_5 and the other command buttons is that every time cb_5 is dropped, its clicked event is automatically executed. When the control is clicked and not dragged, the control just executes its clicked event, as is normal. By coding cb_5's drag and drop in this fashion, we can see why PowerBuilder disables the clicked event when autodrag is on. If the clicked event was not disabled , it would be triggered every time the control was dropped. In typical drag and drop operations, this is not the desired outcome. Try clicking and dragging cb_5, and compare its operation to the other command buttons.

Grouped controls as user object: uo_1

The three radio buttons that are grouped together are intended to act as one functional unit. Only one radio button can be selected out of the three. When this group is dragged, all four controls (the three radio buttons and the group control) should drag together as one unit. To accomplish this, it seems logical that the group's autodrag attribute should be set to True. Then, if the group control is selected and dragged, the radio buttons should be included. However, this does not work. At runtime, group controls cannot be selected or dragged. The solution to this problem is to create a custom user object that has three radio buttons grouped together. The user object is placed on the window and *its* autodrag attribute is set to True.

The user object includes all four controls—the three radio buttons and the group control. As a result, only one radio button can be selected out of the three, as before, but now we can drag all four controls as a single object. In fact, all four controls *are* one object, a custom user object.

Try selecting the individual radio buttons within the group and see how they respond. Then try dragging the group of radio buttons to a new location. To select the user object and not one of radio buttons, make sure the cursor is over blank space within the group box and not over a radio button when beginning to drag. Remember, the controls will be centered around the drop point when dropped.

Controls sensitive to clicks: ddlb_1, sle_1, cbx_1 and rb_1

There are a handful of controls that are sensitive to mouse clicks and automatically perform operations when clicked. For example, when a single-line edit is clicked, the cursor is automatically placed inside the single-line edit in order to capture text entered. Examine the events for a single-line edit control. Notice that there is no clicked event listed. Single-line edits reserve the clicked event for their own use. Trying to drag this type of control becomes difficult. Autodrag cannot be used because it will negate the automatic operation that normally takes place for the control. The Drag function can be used, but it cannot be place the clicked event.

Let's examine these controls more closely to see how they handle drag and drop.

Check boxes & radio buttons

Check boxes and radio buttons have the option of being click-sensitive or not. Setting the control's automatic attribute to True makes the control click-sensitive. If the automatic attribute is set to True and autodrag is set to True, then the automatic toggling of the checked attribute will not occur when the control is clicked. To use autodrag with these controls, set automatic to False and in the control's dragdrop event, code the toggle of the checked attribute (see Listing 2). To emphasize the point that the automatic operation will not take place, the check box and radio button in our sample have their automatic attribute set to True and are also coded for dragdrop. Try clicking and dragging these controls. Then try commenting out the dragdrop script. Even though the control is set for automatic toggling of the checked attribute, without the dragdrop script the toggle will never take place while using autodrag.

Listing 2: Dragdrop script for cbx_1.

```
/*
 Object: cbx_1
 Event:Dragdrop

Description: Because we're using drag auto we need to mimic
the clicked event. When a check box is clicked
it automatically toggles its checked attribute.
The script below mimic the toggling of the checked
attribute.
*/

// Toggle checked attribute for this object
// --------------------------------------
```

```
IF This.checked = True THEN
    This.checked = False
ELSE
    This.checked = True
END IF
```

Single-line edits

Single-line edits are always click-sensitive and if set for autodrag, will never allow access to the text entry portion of the control. Test this by placing a single-line edit on a window and setting its autodrag attribute to True. Access into the text entry portion will never be granted.

To give single-line edits the ability to be dragged while remaining operational, use the Drag function. The single-line edit in our sample calls the Drag function from a user event entitled left_button_down. Left_button_down is mapped to pbm_lbuttondown and is activated when the left mouse button is pressed down. The script for this event is This.Drag(Begin!). The dragdrop event is used to stop the drag mode if the user just clicks on the control. The drag-drop script is This.Drag(Cancel!).

Try using the single-line edit in the sample. Put text in, drag it, click on it, and edit the text in it. Notice how it responds when clicked and dragged.

DropDownListBoxes

DropDownListBoxes are always click-sensitive. This is one of the few controls that tend to be difficult to use with drag and drop. When a DropDownListBox control is clicked, the drop-down list portion is displayed. If a DropDownListBox is set for autodrag, the drop-down list portion will never display. If pbm_lbuttondown is used, as in the single-line edit example, you will be able to drag the control and use it in typical drag drop utilizations. However, if we use pbm_lbuttondown in our sample application, the single-line edit portion of the control separates from the drop-down list portion when the control is relocated.

To solve this problem, the sample takes advantage of two user events: closeup, mapped to pbm_cbncloseup; and mouseup, mapped to pbm_lbuttonup. Closeup is triggered when the drop-down list portion of the control is closed. Mouseup is triggered when the left mouse button is released.

Try using the DropDownListBox in the sample. When the control is first clicked the drop-down list is shown, as is normal. After the list is closed, the control can be dragged. Once dropped, the next click will show the list again. What we have done is to *assume* that when the control is first clicked the user wants to see the list portion of the control, and that once the list has been closed, an immediate click on the control means an intention to drag it.

Other drag targets

We mentioned earlier that this sample includes other drag targets besides the window object. In fact, *all* the controls in this sample of type DragObject are drag targets. To emphasize this point, in the sample try dropping one of the picture controls on cb_1. Notice that cb_1's dragdrop event is triggered and its message box is displayed. If cb_1's dragdrop script was only intended to be used as a replacement for the clicked event, then the Draggedobject function would have to be used to determine which DragObject was dropped on cb_1.

Sample applications: Sample Two

Sample Two is a simple yet powerful example of a typical drag and drop application. It contains three picture controls and a custom user object. The pictures use autodrag to enable their dragging and have tag values set so that they can be identified. (The tag values here demonstrate one way to take advantage of tag attributes. Other means of identifying controls are outside the scope of this discussion.) Most of the functionality that occurs in this sample is coded in the trash can user object. This user object knows what needs to be done when objects are dragged to it, dragged away from it, or dropped on it. It also has the capability of performing different operations depending on which object is dropped on it.

Before examining the individual components of this application, run it and get a good feel of how it performs. Drag each picture object to the trash can. Notice how the trash can responds when the dragged object enters or leaves its space. Drop each one of the picture objects onto the trash can and notice that each produces a different response.
Now let's look at the components.

The window: w_example2

W_example2 is a generic main window with no scripts.

The pictures: p_1, p_2 and p_3

The three picture controls, p_1, p_2, and p_3, represented by the bitmaps of a cassette, a compact disc, and a collection of books, have no scripts. These controls use their autodrag and dragicon attributes. Autodrag is set to True for each picture and the dragicon attribute contains the appropriate icon file name. Each picture has an associated tag value. P_1 is assigned the tag value *Cassette*, p_2 is assigned the tag value *Compact Disc* and p_3 is assigned the value *Books*.

The inherited user object: uo_1

The inherited user object uo_1 looks like a closed trash can and contains only one script. This script is for a user event provided by its ancestor object. The user event is entitled info_delete and contains the script . Info_delete is mapped to pbm_custom01 in the ancestor object u_trash_can. All inherited instances of u_trash_can will have this user event. The script for info_delete contains two local variables, *l_drag_obj* of type DragObject, and *l_answer* of type Integer.

The first statement

```
l_drag_obj = DraggedObject()
```

stores a pointer to the dragged object in *l_drag_obj*.

The next group of statements checks the tag value of the dragged object to determine which one of the pictures was dropped.

```
IF l_drag_obj.Tag = "Cassette" THEN l_drag_obj.Visible = False
```

causes p_1, the cassette picture control, to vanish from the screen when it is dropped on the trash can.

```
ELSEIF l_drag_obj.Tag = "Compact Disc" THEN MessageBox("Delete
Denied","Sorry, you cannot delete any Compact Disc objects",Stopsign!)
```

displays a message box when p_2, the compact disc picture control, is dropped on the trash can.

```
ELSEIF l_drag_obj.Tag = "Books"
THEN l_answer = MessageBox("Confirm delete","Are you sure you want to delete
the book object?, Question!,YesNo!,2)
```

displays a message box asking users if they would like to delete the book object when a book picture control is dropped. If the user selects Yes from the message box, *l_answer* holds the value 1; otherwise *l_answer* holds the value 2.

```
IF l_answer = 1 THEN l_drag_obj.Visible = False
```

causes p_3, the book picture control, to vanish from the screen when the user responds to the message box with Yes.

The ancestor user object: u_trash_can

U_trash_can is a custom user object designed to be reusable. It includes one picture control, entitled p_trash, which is assigned the bitmap trash.bmp. Trash.bmp is a bitmap of a closed trash can. U_trash_can has scripts assigned to dragenter, dragdrop and dragleave.

The dragenter script contains only one statement:

```
p_trash.PictureName = "trash2.bmp
```

This statement dynamically changes p_trash's bitmap at run time. Trash2.bmp is a bitmap of an open trash can. We change the bitmap dynamically to keep the animation of the trash can smooth. If two picture controls were used instead and their visible attributes manipulated, a flash would be produced when the bitmaps redraw.

The dragdrop script contains two statements:

```
            p_trash.PictureName = "trash.bmp"
and
            Parent.TriggerEvent("info_delete")
```

The first statement closes the trash can by setting the bitmap back to trash.bmp. The second statement triggers the user event info_delete, which should contain the application-specific delete routine coded at the descendant level.

The dragleave script contains one statement:

```
            p_trash.PictureName = "trash.bmp"
```

This statement closes the trash can if the user does not drop the object but instead drags it away from the trash can.

Because bitmaps are being changed dynamically at runtime, each bitmap changed needs to be included in a .pbr, a PowerBuilder resource file. PowerBuilder resource files tell the compiler that there are other objects, beyond the ones detected, that need to be included in the executable file. Dynamically changed objects are not detected by the compiler when executables are created.

Sample applications: Sample Three

Sample Three is an advanced example that shows how to simulate movement within an object. In this example the movement occurs as a combination lock's dial is rotated. The dial object needs to be sophisticated, in the sense that it must update its own appearance as well as communicate to other objects what value is selected. Sample Three includes four instance variables, one picture object, one custom user object, two command buttons, and seven static text objects. All the dragging and dropping occurs within the user object.

Before examining the individual components of this application, run the sample and get a taste of how the combination lock works. Drag the dial's line indicator, first clockwise (right) to the value 15, then counterclockwise (left) to 35, and then clockwise (right) again to the value 10. Try to open the lock by pressing the "Try to Open Lock " command button. The lock should open, since this is the correct combination. Reset the lock by pressing the "Clear Combination" command button. Try another combination and see how the lock responds. Notice that the lock knows the direction you turn the dial. To emphasize this point, drag the dial's line indicator counterclockwise (left) instead of clockwise (right) for the first rotation. Notice the application forces the first right value to 0 and stores the selected value in the left text box.

Now let's examine the individual components of this application and see how they work.

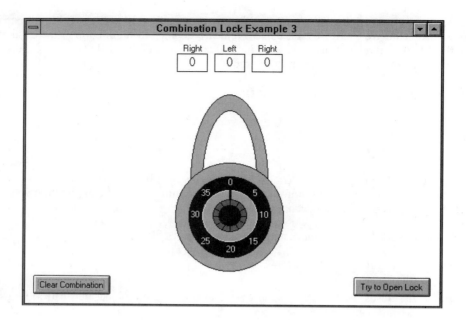

The window: w_example 3

W_example3 is a generic main window with one script, four instance variables, and one window function. The four instance variables are *start_value* of type Integer, *right1, left,* and *right2* of type Boolean.

The window's open script includes one line:

```
uo_knob.Initialize(st_right_1.Text, st_left.Text, st_right_2.Text)
```

Initialize is a function that belongs to the user object uo_knob's ancestor. Initialize sets all the text box indicators to zero and makes the dial's indicator point to zero. The window function wf_lookup_value() accepts an integer argument ,and depending on the argument's value, returns an integer that represents the value on the combination's dial to the left of the value passed. We'll see later on how the instance variables and window function are actually used._

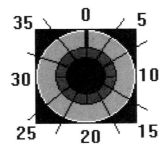

The picture: p_lock

The picture control p_lock is an instance of a generic picture control with its picture name attribute set to "locked.bmp". Locked.bmp is a bitmap of a locked combination lock.

The static text : st_1, st_2, st_3, st_right_1, st_left, st_right_2, and st_message

The static text objects are all generic static text objects. st_right_1, st_left, and st_right_2 have a box border, and st_message has red text and its visible attribute set to False.

The command buttons: cb_clear, cb_open_lock

Cb_clear has one script for its clicked event. This script is used to reinitialize the various controls and variables in order to reset the lock.

The first statement in the script

```
uo_knob.Initialize(st_right_1.Text,st_left.Text, st_right2.Text)
```

calls the user object's ancestor function to initialize the dial to zero and reset to text boxes. The next three statements

```
           right1 = True
           right 2 = False
```

and

```
           left = False
```

reset the instance variables used to determine which direction the dial is rotated. The next statement

```
           st_message.Visible = False
```

hides the static text message that indicates that the combination entered is incorrect. The last statement

```
           p_lock.Picturename = "locked.bmp"
```

reset the bitmap of the lock back to the locked bitmap.

Cb_open_lock has one script for its clicked event. The first statement

```
IF st_right_1.Text = "15" and st_left.Text = "35" and st_right_2.Text = "10"
THEN
```

checks the values in the static text objects to see if they match the combination. If the values match, then the statements

```
                Beep(1)
and
                p_lock.picturename = "unlocked.bmp"
```

are executed. The first statement sounds a tone. The second statement dynamically changes p_lock's bitmap to unlocked.bmp, which is a bitmap of a unlocked combination lock. However, if the values do not match, then the statements

```
                Beep(1)
and
                st_message.Visible = True
```

are executed. The first statement again sounds a tone. The second statement causes the st_message object to become visible. St_message has text informing the user that the combination entered is incorrect.

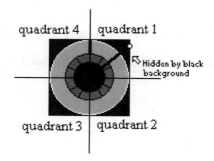

The new line's end point is forced to the edge of the user object to make the line appear to have a constant length. Notice how more of the line shows when the line is at either the three o'clock or 9 o'clock position. To make the lines length seem constant, the end point of the line is extended to the edge of the user object. Any portion of the line not required is masked by the black background of the dial.

The inherited user object: uo_knob.

Uo_knob is an inherited instance of the custom user object uo_dial. Uo_knob has scripts for the following events: left_button_down, dragleave, dragdrop, and dragwithin.

Left_button_down is a user event mapped to pbm_lbuttondown in uo_knob's ancestor object, uo_dial. The script for left_button_down, This.Drag(Begin!), starts the dragging of uo_knob. The script for dragleave, This.Drag(End!), stops the dragging of uo_knob and causes a dragdrop to be issued. The dragdrop and dragwithin scripts require a closer examination. Let's look at each of these scripts separately.

The script for dragdrop has four local variables: *quadrant*, *x_pos*, *y_pos,* and *value,* of type Integer; and *slope* of type Double. The first two statements

and

```
x_pos = This.PointerX()

y_pos = This.PointerY()
```

set *x_pos* and *y_pos* to the x and y coordinates of the cursor position, relative to uo_knob, when the dragdrop event is triggered.
The next statement

```
quadrant = this.locate_pts(x_pos,y_pos)
```

calls uo_knob's ancestor's function locate_pts, which sections the user object's area into quadrants and returns the quadrant number where the passed x and y values fall.

The next statement

```
slope = abs((y_pos - this.mid_y) /(x_pos - this.mid_x))
```

sets *slope* to the absolute value of the slope of the line which originates from the center of the user object and continues to the point where the cursor was when the dragdrop event occurred.

The next statement

```
value = This.find_value(quadrant,slope)
```

calls uo_knob's ancestor's function find_value, which determines the appropriate combination lock value using the quadrant and slope just calculated.

The last group of statements

```
IF right1 THEN
 st_right_1.Text = String(value)
ELSEIF left THEN
 st_left.Text = String(value)
ELSEIF right2 THEN
 st_right_2.Text = String(value)
END IF
```

uses the instance variables *right1*, *left,* and *right2* to determine the appropriate text box to store the value in.

Uo_knob's dragwithin script extends its ancestor's script (see uo_dial dragwithin). Uo_knob's dragwithin script has one local variable, *value,* of type Integer.

The first statement

```
value = This.find_value( This.quadrant, abs( This.slope ) )
```

calls uo_knob's ancestor's function find_value to get the combination lock value for the selected point. *This.quadrant* and *This.slope* are uo_knob's ancestor's instance variables already computed in the ancestor's dragwithin script.

The next group of nested statements

```
IF start_value <> value THEN
IF wf_lookup_value(start_value) = value THEN
IF right2 THEN
left = False
right1 = false
right2 =false
ELSE
left = true
right1 = False
right2 = False
END IF
 ELSE
IF NOT right1 THEN
left = false
right2 = TRUE
END IF
END IF
start_value = value
END IF
```

*s*ets the window's instance variables used to determine the direction of rotation. If the combination value just computed is different from the last value stored in the window instance variable *start_value*, then we call the window function wf_lookup_value to get the number to the left of *start_value* on the combination's dial. If the number to the left of *start_value* on the dial equals the new computed value, we know the user moved left. Otherwise, we know the user moved right. If the user moved left, we evaluate *right2* to determine if this is the first left rotation, and set the instance variable accordingly. IF the user moved right, we examine the value of *right1* to determine if this is the first or second right rotation, and set the instance variables accordingly. Finally we set the *start_value* to the new computed value so we can detect the next rotation that occurs._

The ancestor user object: uo_dial

Uo_dial is a custom user object used to create the combination lock's dial. Uo_dial contains nine instance variables: *mid_x, mid_y, min_x, min_y, max_x, max_y* and *quadrant* of type Integer; *slope* of type Double; and *ranges[]* of type Sections. Sections is a user object structure consisting of *section, lower,* and *upper* of type Integer; and *start_slope* and *end_slope* of type Double. Uo_dial has scripts for its constructor and dragwithin events and contains one user event, left_button_down, mapped to pbm_lbuttondown. Uo_dial also contains three user object functions: find_value, initialize, and locate_pts.

Let's examine uo_dial's scripts and functions to see how this object operates.

Uo_dial's constructor script is used to set up the dial user object. The first two statements

and

```
mid_y = This.height/2

mid_x = This.width/2
```

set the values of *mid_y* and *mid_x* to the center coordinates of the user object. The next two statements

and

```
min_x = 0

max_x = This.width
```

set the values of *min_x* and *max_x* to minimum and maximum values that the x coordinate can accommodate. The next two statements

and

```
min_y = 0

max_y = This.height
```

accomplish the same task for the y coordinate.

The remaining statements in this script are used to populate *ranges[]*, the array of section structures. *Ranges[]* holds the information required to divide the dial object into sections for the purpose of assigning values. We determine the sections of the dial by drawing lines from the center of the user object out to the edges. *Ranges[]* holds the slopes of the lines that define the different sections. We only store the information for sections 5, 15, 25, and 35, since these are all that is required to define the lines used to section the user object. All values can be determined from *ranges[]* by comparing the slope from a new line to the slopes in *ranges[]*. We'll see how this is done later in the find_value function.

The dragwithin script for uo_dial contains five local variables: *x_pos*, *y_pos* of type Integer; and *y_intercept, new_x,* and *new_y* of type Double. The first statement

```
This.SetRedraw(False)
```

turns off the redrawing of the user object. The next two statements

```
        x_pos = This.PointerX()
```
and
```
        y_pos= This.PointerY()
```

get the x and y coordinates of the cursor in relation to the user object when this event is triggered. The next statement

```
        quadrant = this.locate_pts(x_pos,y_pos)
```

calls the user object function locate_pts to determine the quadrant where *x_pos* and *y_pos* are located. The next two statements

```
        slope = (y_pos - this.mid_y) / (x_pos - this.mid_x)
```
and
```
        yintercept = y_pos - (slope * x_pos)
```

compute the slope and y intercept of the line originating in the center of the user object and extending to the coordinates of the cursor's position, referenced by *x_pos* and *y_pos*.

The next group of statements adjusts the endpoint of the new line to extend the line to the edge of the user object. Notice that each quadrant has two edges, one horizontal and the other vertical. The nested IF statements are used to determine which edge the new endpoint will be placed on. The statements inside the nested IF statements cause the dial's line indicator to move by reassigning the *endx* and *endy* values of the line. The final statement

```
        This.SetRedraw(True)
```

turns the redraw of the user object back on.

The user object function initialize accepts three string arguments passed by reference. These arguments are intended to be the static text controls that hold the combination values. The first two statements

```
        ln_dial.BeginX = mid_x
```
and
```
        ln_dial.BeginY = mid_y
```

set the indicator line's starting point to the center of the user object. The next two statements

```
        ln_dial.EndX = 170
```
and
```
        ln_dial.EndY = 1
```

set the indicator line's end point to 170,1. A line drawn from the center of the user object to 170,1 is a line pointing directly to the combination's zero value. The last three statements

```
        right_1 = "0"
```

and

```
left = "0"

right_2 = "0"
```

set the values of the static text controls to zero. Remember the arguments *right_1*, *left,* and *right_2* are passed by reference, allowing us to directly manipulate their attributes.

The user object function find_values has one local variable, *value,* of type Integer, and accepts two arguments, *quadrant* of type Integer and *slope* of type Double. The first argument is intended to be the quadrant where the indicator line lies. The second argument is intended to be the indicator line's slope. Find_values returns an integer that represents the combination lock's value for where the indicator line is pointing.

The first group of statements

```
IF Ranges[quadrant].start_slope < slope THEN
value = this.Ranges[quadrant].upper
```

compares the slope of the indicator line to the start_slope for the quadrant. If the *start_slope* is less then the slope of the indicator line then the indicator's slope falls in the upper value section of the quadrant. Otherwise,

```
ELSEIF this.Ranges[quadrant].end_slope > slope THEN
value = this.Ranges[quadrant].lower
```

compares the quadrant's *end_slope* to the indicator line's slope, and if the *end_slope* is greater then the indicator's slope then the indicator line falls in the lower value section of the quadrant. Otherwise,

```
ELSE value = this.Ranges[quadrant].section
END IF
```

determines that if the line is not in the upper or lower sections of the quadrant, then it must be in the middle section.

Let's look at an example of how the indicator's line value is determined. If the slope of the indicator line falls in Quadrant 2, which includes the sections 15, 10 (which is 15's lower) and 20 (which is 15's upper), we compare Section 15's *start_slope* and *end_slope* to the slope of the indicator. If the indicator's slope is greater then the *start_slope,* then the return value is section 15's upper value, or 20.

If the indicator's slope is less than the *start_slope*, then we compare it to the *end_slope*. If the indicator's slope is less than the *end_slope,* then the return value is Section 15's lower value, or 10. Otherwise, the slope of the indicator falls between the *start_slope* and *end_slope* and the return value is the value of the section itself, or 15.

The user object function locate_pts accepts two integer arguments, *x* and *y*. X and y are intended to be the coordinates that represent the cursor's location. Locate_pts returns an integer value that represents the quadrant where the values passed lie. The first statement

```
IF x >= mid_x THEN
```

compares the passed *x* value to the *mid_x* value of the user object. This determines if the passed *x* is on the right or left side of the user object. The next statement

```
IF y >= mid_y THEN
```

compares the passed *y* value to the *mid_y* to determine if the passed *y* is in the top or bottom half of the user object. Once we determine the left or right, top or bottom location of the points, we know the quadrant number. If the point lies in the top right, then the quadrant is 1. If the point lies in the bottom right, then the quadrant is 2. If the point lies in the bottom left, then the quadrant is 3. Finally, if the point lies in the top left, the quadrant is 4.

Sample applications: Sample Four

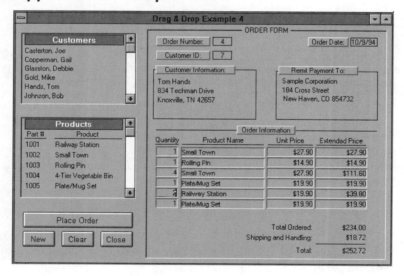

Sample Four shows how to create the illusion of dragging rows of information from one DataWindow object to another. In this example the user fills in an order form by dragging customer names from the customer DataWindow and product names from the product DataWindow to the order form. Products listed in the order form can be removed by dragging a line item back to the product DataWindow.

Sample Four includes one instance variable, *i_order_id,* and twelve controls. There are four command buttons (cb_clear, cb_close, cb_new and cb_order), six DataWindows (dw_customer, dw_products, dw_order_info, dw_order_detail, dw_order_disable and dw_detail_disable), and two static text objects (st_1, st_2).

Before examining each control in this application, run the sample and get a sense of how the controls interact. In order to run Sample Four, an entry for ORDERS must be added to your local odbc.ini file. odbc.ini is usually stored in the windows directory of your hard drive. Add the information to your odbc.ini file. Make sure the path statements pointing to wsqlodbc.dll (driver) and orders.db (database) are listed correctly for your system.

When the sample is run, notice that the order form initially comes up disabled (dragging and dropping do not work and text is grayed out). Pressing the "New" command button activates the order form and makes it ready to accept data. Once activated, drag a customer's name from the customer list to the order's customer information box. Notice all the information that fills in.

Try dragging different customer names, and pay attention to the number of lines in the address section. The number of address lines appears to dynamically adjust between three and four lines, as needed. Next, drag some products from the product list to the order's detail section. Notice that the price information automatically fills in and updates the totals.

Change a line item's default quantity value from 1 to 5 and notice the extended price and order totals are automatically adjusted. Add more products; then remove a product by dragging a line item by its quantity field from the order detail section back to the product list. To save the data to the database, press "Place Order"; to clear the order form and start over, press "Clear"; and to close the application, press "Close".

The application: Orders

The Orders application contains two scripts, one for the open event and the other for the close event. The open event's script sets up the transaction object and connects to the database. Notice that the transaction object's attributes sqlca.dbms and sqlca.dbparm are being populated from the file orders.ini. The close event's script simply issues a disconnect to detach the transaction object from the database.

The window: w_orders

W_orders is a generic main window with one instance variable and one script. The instance variable *i_order_id,* of type Integer, is used to hold the current order id number and keep the order information and order detail information synchronized. W_order's one script is for its open event. This script first sets the DataWindow transaction objects for dw_customers, dw_products, dw_orders_info, and dw_order_detail. It then inserts a row into dw_order_disable, making its columns visible. Finally, it retrieves the two DataWindows dw_customers and dw_products, which will be used to fill in the order form.

The Command buttons: cb_clear, cb_close, cb_new and cb_order

cb_clear

Command button cb_clear is used to reset orders that are not placed. Cb_clear contains one script for its clicked event. The first two lines in the script reset the DataWindows that make up the order form. The next three lines insert a new row into dw_order_info, and load the values for the order number and order date into the proper columns.

cb_close

Command button cb_close is used solely to close the orders window. It has one script for its clicked event, Close(Parent*)*. cb_new Command button cb_new is used to create new orders. It has one script for its clicked event. The first two statements

and
```
dw_order_disable.Visible = False

dw_detail_disable.Visible = False
```

are used to hide the disabled version of the order form. The next two statements

and
```
dw_order_info.Enabled = True

dw_order_detail.Enabled = True
```

make sure that the real order form is enabled and ready to accept data. We then fire off embedded SQL to get the last order number from the database. If we get an *SQLCA.SQL-CODE* other than zero, then we set the order number to 1. Otherwise we set the order number to the maximum number returned from the database, plus 1. The next three statement insert a row into dw_order_info and load the order number and order date into their proper columns. The last statement

```
i_order_id = l_order_id
```

sets the instance variable *i_order_id* to contain the current order number.

cb_order

Command button cb_order is used to update the database with the information stored in the current order form. Cb_order contains one script for its clicked event. The script starts by getting the number of rows contained in dw_order_detail. Then using a FOR loop, we step through the rows in dw_order_detail, getting the extended prices. We sum up the extended prices for the detail section and store that value in *l_total*.

The next two statements

and
```
dw_order_info.SetItem(1,4,l_total)

dw_order_info.SetItem(1,5,(l_total * 0.08))
```

are used to store the total price and total shipping and handling amounts into the correct columns for dw_order_info. This is done because dw_order_detail contains the totals as calculated columns for display only. It is dw_order_info which contains the columns for the order totals that will be updated to the database, and must be populated before the update function is called.

Next, the update function is called for both dw_order_info and dw_order_detail. We check the return value of each update to see if errors occurred. If either update fails, we display a message box and roll back the transaction; otherwise we commit the updates and return the order form to its disabled state.

The DataWindows: dw_customer, dw_products, dw_order_info, dw_order_detail, dw_order_disable and dw_detail_disable

dw_customer

The DataWindow dw_customer lists customer names, (last name, first name) sorted alphabetically. Dw_customer contains two scripts, one for its clicked event and the other for a custom user event entitled left_buttonup that is mapped to pbm_lbuttonup. The script for the clicked event causes the clicked row to become selected and then starts the drag mode. The script for the left_buttonup event causes the clicked row to become unselected. The net outcome created when these two scripts occur in sequence is that the clicked event highlights the clicked row when dragging begins, and the left_buttonup script unhighlights the row when the item is dropped. This is serves to let the user know which row is being dragged to the target.

dw_products

The DataWindow dw_products lists product part numbers and names, sorted by part number. Dw_products contains three scripts–one for its clicked event, one for its dragdrop event, and one for a custom user event entitled left_buttonup. The clicked and left_buttonup scripts function in the same way as the clicked and left_buttonup scripts for dw_customer. The dragdrop script is used to remove line items from dw_order_detail that are dropped on dw_products.

The script starts with the statement

```
l_drag_obj = DraggedObject(
```

This stores a pointer to the object which is being dragged into *l_drag_obj*. The next statement

```
IF TypeOf(l_drag_obj) = DataWindow! THEN
```

checks the type of the dragged object to see if it is a DataWindow. The statement

```
l_DataWindow = l_drag_obj
```

stores a reference to the actual DataWindow object, allowing us access to its attributes. The next statement

```
IF l_DataWindow.dataobject ="dw_order_detail" THEN
```

checks the dataobject attribute of *l_DataWindow* to see if it is the order detail DataWindow. If *l_DataWindow* is pointing to the order detail DataWindow then we get the current row from dw_order_detail, get the product ID from that row, and display a message box asking the user to confirm the removal of the line item. If the user responds Yes to the message box, we execute the statement

```
dw_order_detail.deleteRow(l_row)
```

which removes the row from the order detail data window.

dw_order_info

The DataWindow dw_order_info represents the order information section of the order form. Dw_order_info updates the Orders database table and has scripts for losefocus and dragdrop.

The losefocus script, This.AcceptText(), simply makes sure that all modifications to dw_order_info are accepted when focus is directed toward another object.

The script for the dragdrop event starts with the statement

```
l_drag_obj = DraggedObject()
```

This stores a pointer to the object which is being dragged in *l_drag_obj*. The statement

```
IF TypeOf(l_drag_obj) = DataWindow! THEN
```

checks the type of the dragged object to see if it is a DataWindow. The next statement

```
l_DataWindow = l_drag_obj
```

stores a reference to the actual DataWindow object, allowing us access to its attributes. The next statement

```
IF l_DataWindow.dataobject ="dw_customers" THEN
```

checks the dataobject attribute of *l_DataWindow* to see if it is the customer DataWindow. If *l_DataWindow* is pointing to the customer DataWindow, then we get the current row from dw_customer, get the customer ID from that row (which is there but not visible), and trigger off embedded SQL to retrieve the customer's name and address information. Finally, we populate dw_order_info with the required information (customer_id, first name, last name, address1, address2, city, state, and zip).

The DataWindow object for dw_order_info uses calculated columns to display the customer name and address information. The calculations set up for these columns make it appear that the address lines are being allocated dynamically. This is required, since sometimes the column for address2 will be blank and other times it will not. Examine these columns using the DataWindow Painter to see how the calculations accomplish this illusion.

dw_order_detail

The DataWindow dw_order_detail represents the line item section of the order form. Dw_order_detail updates the Order_detail database table and has scripts for the following events: losefocus, clicked, dragdrop, editchanged, and custom user event recalc_line, which is mapped to pbm_custom01.

The losefocus script, This.AcceptText(), simply makes sure that all modifications to dw_order_detail are accepted when focus is directed toward another object.

The script for the clicked event consists of one statement

```
This.Drag(Begin!)
```

This statement puts the DataWindow in the drag mode so the user can drag a line item back to the product list and remove it from the order form.

The dragdrop script for dw_order_detail starts with the statement

```
l_drag_obj = DraggedObject()
```

This stores a pointer to the object which is being dragged into *l_drag_obj*. The next statement

```
IF TypeOf(l_drag_obj) = DataWindow! THEN
```

checks the type of the dragged object to see if it is a DataWindow. The statement

```
l_DataWindow = l_drag_obj
```

stores a reference to the actual DataWindow object, allowing us access to its attributes. The next statement

```
IF l_DataWindow.dataobject ="dw_products" THEN
```

checks the dataobject attribute of *l_DataWindow* to see if it is the products DataWindow. If *l_DataWindow* is pointing to the products DataWindow, then we get the current row from dw_products, get the product ID from that row, and trigger off embedded SQL to retrieve the product name and sale_price. Next, we insert a row into dw_order_detail, get the row number of the row just inserted, and populate that row with the required information (product_id, default quantity, unit price, extended price, order id, and product name).

The editchanged script and the recalc_line script for dw_order_detail work together. The editchanged script's first statement

```
IF This.GetColumn() = 2 THEN
```

checks to see which column in dw_order_detail the user is on when this event occurs. If the column is 2, the quantity column, then the statement

```
PostEvent("recalc_line")
```

is executed. The recalc_line script calls the function AcceptText(), which makes sure that dw_order_detail contains any modified data. Then we get the current row number from dw_order_detail, which is used to get the values for quantity and price. The statement

```
l_new_value = l_quant * l_price
```

recalculates the extended price for the line. The last statement

```
This.SetItem(l_row,4,l_new_value)
```

updates the extended price column for the line item in dw_order_detail. Since the "Total Ordered," "Shipping and Handling," and "Total:" columns are calculated columns in the dw_order_detail object, they automatically adjust when line item values change.

dw_detail_disable and dw_order_disable

DataWindow dw_detail_disable and dw_order_disable are used solely for visual purposes. They never get assigned to a transaction object and are never used for data manipulation. They have no scripts, no active columns and all the text is set to dark gray. We initially show these DataWindows so that the user can see what the order form looks like before we allow access to the actual order form.

The static text objects: st_1 and st_2

Static text objects st_1 and st_2 are used solely for visual purposes. St_1 and st_2 make up the order form's frame and title, which are used visually to group the DataWindows dw_order_info and dw_order_detail. These object have no scripts and are not enabled.

Conclusion

The sample applications given here are intended to demonstrate ways in which drag and drop can be deployed within the PowerBuilder development environment. While you are developing PowerBuilder applications, keep these samples and the concepts they demonstrate in mind. As we have seen in this chapter, creating applications that incorporate drag and drop functionality is not that difficult. It is well worth the minor effort it takes to make your application much more enjoyable to use.

CHAPTER **18**

The Data Pipeline

By Michael MacDonald

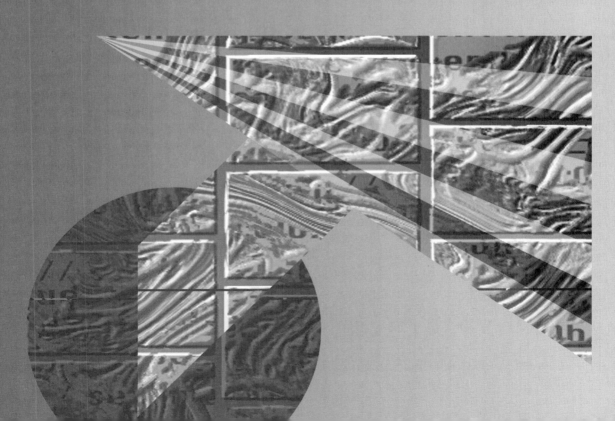

The Data Pipeline

by **Michael MacDonald**

One of the more exciting new features in PowerBuilder 4.0 is the data pipeline. Using this feature, you can move data from a table in one datasource to another table in either the same or a different datasource.

The data pipeline is a system object much like the transaction and mail objects. In this chapter we will explore the object itself, the painter used to create the object, and then the dynamic use of the pipeline object in your applications.

The data pipeline has just five attributes (shown in Table 18-1), five events (shown in Table 18-2), and seven functions (shown in Table 18-3).

Pipeline Attribute	Purpose
DataObject	The name of the pipeline previously created in the painter. For instance, in the first part of this chapter we will create a pipeline called c_funct_user which will be the data object when we create a pipeline object in our script.
RowsRead	The number of rows read in execution of the pipeline. See Figure 18-13.

RowsWritten	The number of rows written in execution of the pipeline. See Figure 18-13.
RowsInError	The number of rows that encountered an error in writing. There is a maximum limit set in the painter. If this limit is met, then the pipeline shuts down. See Figure 18-13.
Syntax	The description of the object, to include its source, destination, commit and error information, etc.

Table 18-1: Pipeline attributes.

Pipeline Event	Explanation
Constructor	The creation of the object via object_name = CREATE pipeline
Destructor	The destruction of the pipeline via DESTROY object_name
PipeStart	The start of the pipeline execution
PipeMeter	The completion of a block of reads and writes equal to the number of records specified by the commit parameter.
PipeEnd	The end of the pipeline execution.

Table 18-2: Pipeline events.

Pipeline Functions	Explanation
Cancel	A function that can be called after a pipeline Start or Repair to cancel further execution. All rows up to that point will be committed. Returns 1 for success and -1 for failure. pipeline_object.cancel ( )
ClassName	Returns the class name of the pipeline object as a string.
PostEvent	Adds an event to the end of the specified object's message queue. Returns TRUE for success or FALSE for failure. cb_ok.PostEvent (Clicked!)

Repair	This processes the data in the error DataWindow and can be triggered after the user has fixed it. Any rows that are still in error remain in the error DataWindow, and the Repair function can be executed as often as necessary. Returns 1 for success. See Table18-4 for failure reason codes. pipeline_object.Repair (dest_trans)
Start	This begins execution of the pipeline to apply rows from the query answer set of the source to the destination. Returns 1 for success. See Table 18-4 for failure codes. pipeline_object.Start (source_trans, dest_trans, error_dw {arg1, arg2, ... argx})
TriggerEvent	Trigger an event for the specified object and execute the specified script immediately (see also PostEvent). Returns 1 for success and -1 for failure. cb_ok.TriggerEvent (clicked!)
TypeOf	Returns the type of the user object as an enumerated datatype.

Table 18-3: Pipeline functions.

Return Code	Meaning	Start	Repair
-1	Pipe Open Failed	Yes	No
-2	Too Many Columns	Yes	No
-3	Table Already Exists	Yes	No
-4	Table Does Not Exist	Yes	No
-5	Missing Connection	Yes	Yes
-6	Wrong Arguments	Yes	No
-7	Column Mismatch	Yes	No
-8	Fatal SQL Error In Source	Yes	No
-9	Fatal SQL Error In Destination	Yes	Yes
-10	Maximum Number Of Errors Exceeded	Yes	Yes
-11	Invalid Window Handle	No	Yes

-12	Bad Table Syntax	No	Yes
-13	Key Required But Not Supplied	Yes	Yes
-15	Pipe Already in Progress	Yes	Yes
-16	Error in Source Data-base	Yes	No
-17	Error in Destination Database	Yes	Yes
-18	Destination Database is Read Only	Yes	Yes

Table 18-4 : Repair and start return codes.

In the following session, we will create a pipeline that will select data joining two tables from a source database and create a table with the results in the destination database. Note that the destination database can be the same as the source.

The Data Pipeline Painter is accessed via an icon. Figures 18-2 through 18-7 illustrate a typical session using the Data Pipeline Painter. First, Figure 18-2 illustrates the creating of a new pipeline. In Figure 18-3, we select the source of the data–the SampIn datasource. We next select the destination–the SampOut datasource. Both happen to be Watcom databases, though they could have been btrieve or Sybase or any other combination.

In Figure 18-4, we select one or more tables from which to draw the data that is to be transferred. In this case, we are selecting two tables: c_funct and s_uaccess. Figure 18-5 shows the familiar SQL Painter screen where we join the two tables, specify our WHERE and ORDER BY clauses, etc.

All of this leads to Figures 18-6 and 18-7, which are a graphical representation of the pipeline object itself. PowerBuilder suggests a number of defaults. Table 18-5 examines the screen item by item:

Data Pipeline Item	Explanation / Notes
Table	The name of the table to be created. PowerBuilder suggests as a default the name of the first table select as the source.
Key	The primary key of the destination table. You may want to change this if the Option is Create - Add Table or Replace - Drop / Add Table.
Options	Specific actions to be taken when the pipeline is executed. Options include: Create - Add Table; Replace - Drop / Add Table; Refresh - Delete and Insert Rows; Append - Insert Rows; Update - Update / Add Rows.
Max Errors	The maximum number of errors that will be tolerated before the pipeline operation is shut down. The default is 100.
Commit	The number of rows to process before committing data. The default is 100.
Extended Attributes	Whether or not to transfer extended column attributes information.
Source Name	The name of the column from which data is being selected.
Source Type	The column type of the source data.
Destination Name	The suggested name of the column being created/updated on the destination datasource.
Type	The column type of the destination data.
Key	Is the column a key column?
Width	The width of the destination column.
Dec	The scale of the destination column for numeric decimal values,
Nulls	Are nulls allowed for this column? Defaulted from the source.
Initial Value	The initial value to be assigned for the destination datasource. Normally spaces for characters, 0 for numbers, and null where nulls are allowed.

Table 18-5: The Data pipeline screen elements.

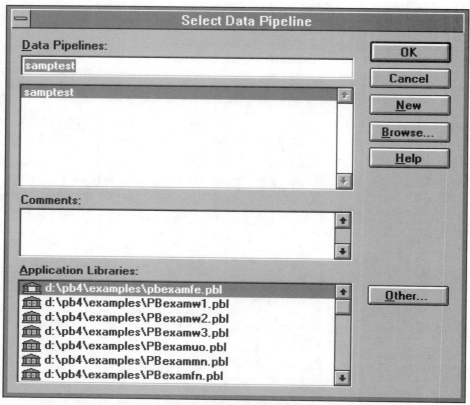

Figure 18-2: After opening the pipeline painter, a dialog is presented showing existing pipelines. In our example, we selected New.

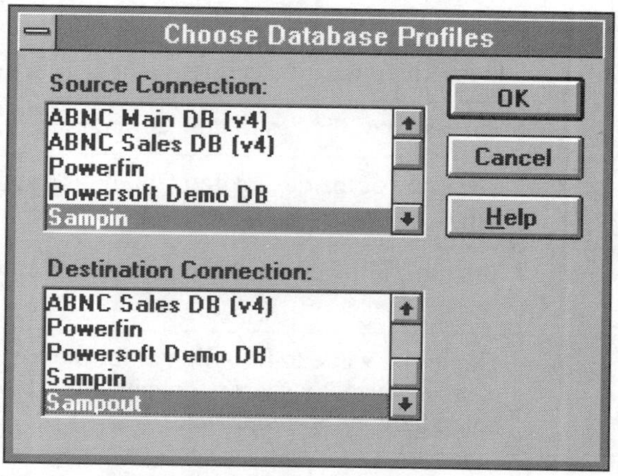

Figure 18-3: Specify the source datasource and the destination datasource.

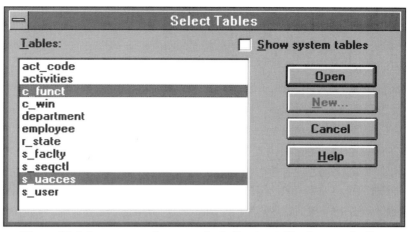

Figure 18-4: In our example, we are including two tables for our pipeline.

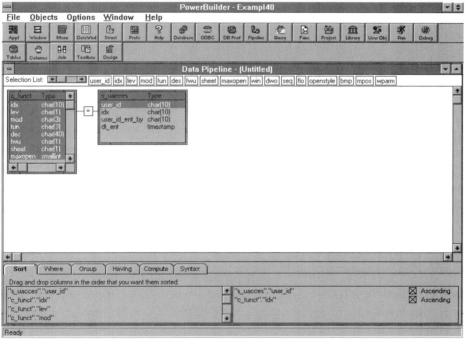

Figure 18-5: Paint a query as per normal.
The query result will be what is transferred to the destination datasource.

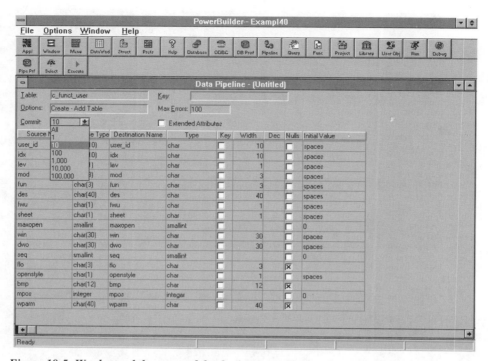

Figure 18-5: We changed the name of the destination table to c_funct_user to show that this is a table joining two other tables. Below the name of the table is a series of options for the destination datasource. We chose Create Table. In subsequent operations, we will change that to Drop/Add Table. Below that we are specifying to commit every ten rows. The default is 100.

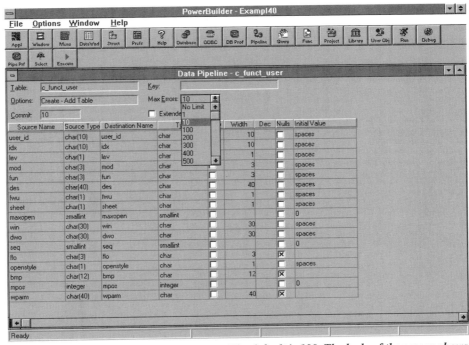

Figure 18-6: Permit no more than ten errors. The default is 100. The body of the screen shows all of the columns being selected and the proposed column names in the new table.

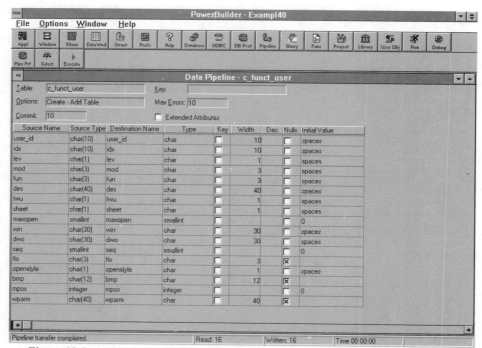

Figure 18-7: As can be seen on the bottom of the screen, the query has finished and the results have been transferred to the new table.

The pipeline can be run by pressing the Execute icon. This triggers the pipeline start event. The bottom of the screen shows the progress of the execution by updating the records read and the records written. This is refreshed every time a pipeline meter event is completed. Recall that the meter event is completed each time *x* rows are read and then written, where *x* is defined as the number of rows after which data is to be committed. Thus, because we have chosen to commit after each ten rows, the screen is refreshed every time ten rows are read and then written. A more practical interval would be 100 or even 1000 rows.

Once you have created and tested your data pipeline, you are ready to use it in your Power-Script in an application. We will spend the remainder of the chapter doing this by creating the window shown in Figure 18-13.

First, you need to create a user object of the type Pipeline System Object. To do so, open the User Object Painter and select the class Standard as shown in Figure 18-8. Select the Standard Class Type of pipeline (Figure 18-9).

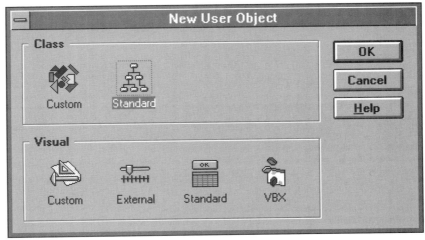

Figure 18-8: The pipeline system object is created by entering the User Object Painter and first selecting the standard class.

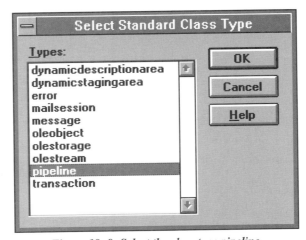

Figure 18- 9: Select the class type pipeline.

Powersoft recommends a nifty little trick for relaying the progress of your pipeline to your user which we will use. The next step then is to create three instance variables of type Statictext as shown in Figure 18-10. From the user object, select Declare and Instance Variables. Type in:

```
statictext i_st_status read, i_st_status_written,
i_st_status_error
```

Next, open the Script Painter for the pipemeter event and code the following, as shown in Figure 18-11.

```
i_st_status_read.text    = string (rowsread)
i_st_status_written.text = string (rowswritten)
i_st_status_error.text   = string (rowsinerror)
```

We will use these instance variables later in our script.

Now, save the user object as u_pipe_test.

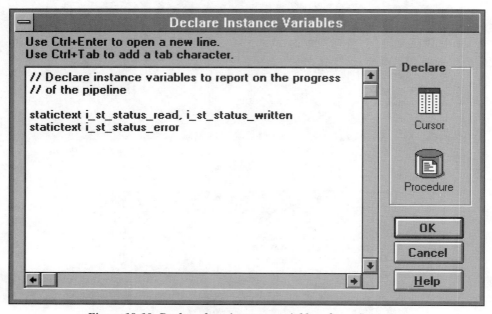

Figure 18-10: Declare three instance variables of type Statictext.

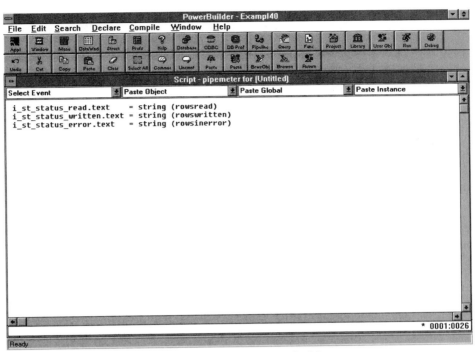

Figure 18-11: Code this script in your PipeMeter event.

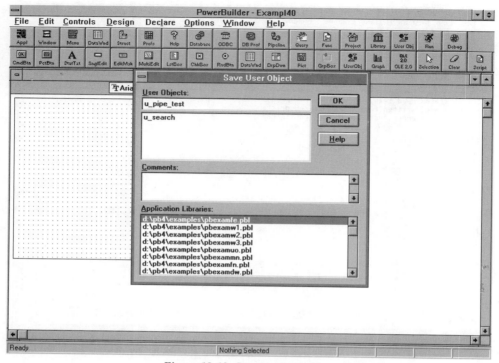

Figure 18-12: Save the user object.

Now, open the window painter and create a window similar to that shown in Figure 18-13. You will need seven static text objects, with the first four being titles ("Pipeline Example," "Read," etc.). The last three will be the counters shown. These should be called st_read, st_written, and st_error respectively. Add three command buttons as shown. Their names are not critical.

Next, add a DataWindow control to the window but do not assign a DataWindow to it. Size it similarly to that shown and let its name default to dw_1. Lastly, create a multi-line edit control and let its name default to mle_1. Size it as shown.

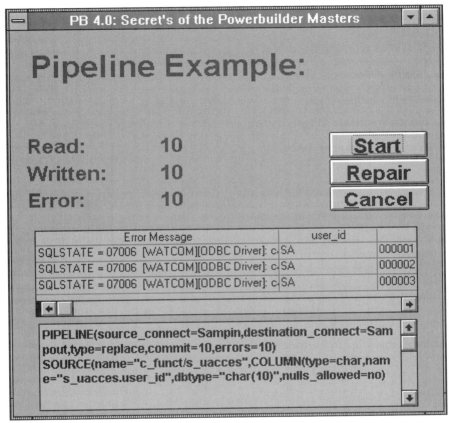

Figure 18-13: An example of the pipeline being used in the application.
Errors were deliberately introduced to show the error DataWindow being populated.
The bottom multi-line edit shows the pipeline syntax attribute.

Create two instance variables as shown in Figure 18-14:

```
transactionSQLCA1
u_pipe_testi_uo_pipe_test
```

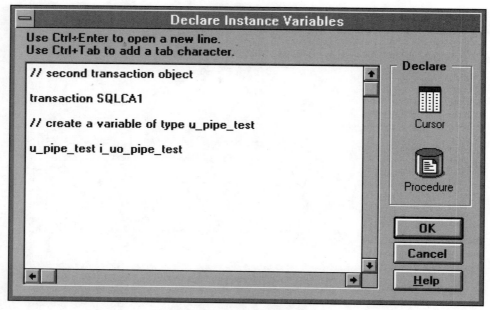

Figure 18- 14: Two instance variables.

Add the following script to the window's open event:

```
// fill in the values for the source datasource
SQLCA.DBMS = "ODBC"
SQLCA.DbParm = "Connectstring='DSN=sampin'"

// create the second transaction source

SQLCA1 = create transaction

SQLCA1.DBMS = "ODBC"
SQLCA1.DbParm = "Connectstring='DSN=sampout'"

// now connect

Connect using SQLCA ;

if sqlca.sqlcode < 0 then
messagebox ("Error","Connect Failed: "+ sqlca.sqlerrtext)
return
end if

Connect using SQLCA1 ;

if sqlca1.sqlcode < 0 then
messagebox ("Error","Connect Failed: "+ sqlca1.sqlerrtext)
disconnect using sqlca ;
return
end if
```

The above establishes the second transaction object and connects both to the database. Use your own connect parameters.

Code the following for the "Start" command button clicked event:

```
int i_result

// create pipeline user object

i_uo_pipe_test = create u_pipe_test
i_uo_pipe_test.dataobject = "c_funct_user"

// now, connect the static text counters
i_uo_pipe_test.i_st_status_read    = st_read
i_uo_pipe_test.i_st_status_written = st_written
i_uo_pipe_test.i_st_status_error   = st_error

// display the syntax
mle_1.text = i_uo_pipe_test.syntax

// execute the pipeline
i_result = i_uo_pipe_test.Start (SQLCA, SQLCA1, dw_1)

// evaluate the result
if i_result < 0 then
Messagebox ("Error","Return Code = " + string (i_result))
else
Messagebox ("Transfer Complete","Rows Transferred Successfully.")
end if
```

The above script is the meat of our applet. First, recall that we declared the instance variable i_uo_pipe_test. Now, we instantiate it as u_pipe_test via the CREATE statement. Next, we assign to the dataobject the pipeline c_funct_user. The next three statements connect the counters within the pipe user object's pipemeter event to our three static text variables, creating the ability for out pipe object to update the display each time a block of rows is read and written (where a block is equal to the number defined in our commit parameter). In the next line, we display the pipeline's syntax in our mle for illustration purposes.

In the line after, the pipe's Start function is fired, specifying SQLCA as the source, SQLCA1 as the destination, and dw_1 as the DataWindow for any errors. Notice that we did not have to actually create a DataWindow–the pipe takes care of that automatically.

Lastly, we evaluate and display the result.

The above is the recommended way of instantiating and initiating a pipe function. However, the pipeline can be invoked without going through a user object. The following script will work just as well (though less elegantly since we cannot display the counters to the user):

```
int i_result

// create pipeline user object
pipeline i_uo_pipe_test
i_uo_pipe_test = create pipeline
i_uo_pipe_test.dataobject = "c_funct_user"
```

```
// display the syntax
mle_1.text = i_uo_pipe_test.syntax

// execute the pipeline
i_result = i_uo_pipe_test.Start (SQLCA, SQLCA1, dw_1)

// evaluate the result
if i_result < 0 then
Messagebox ("Error","Return Code = " + string (i_result))
else
Messagebox ("Transfer Complete","Rows Transferred Successfully.")
end if

//Hang on, let's code the Repair function. Add the following script to the
Repair button's clicked

// apply repair of errors to pipeline

int i_rtn

i_rtn = i_uo_pipe_test.Repair (sqlca1)

if i_rtn = 1 then
Messagebox ("Cancel","Repairs Successfully Applied!")
else
Messagebox ("Error","Error " + string(i_rtn) + " Encountered")
end if
```

When errors are encountered, as shown in Figure 18-13, they are written to the DataWindow dw_1. The user is then able to change the individual rows and press the "Repair" button to again try to apply the changes/updates. This is accomplished via the control's Repair function.

The first thing to notice is that the destination datasource is no longer in play. In fact, after the Start function completes, you can safely disconnect the source database. All of the remaining rows are contained within the error DataWindow.

The above script, which fires the Repair function and evaluates the result, can be run repeatedly. As rows are successfully applied to the destination database, they are removed from the DataWindow. Notice that the error displayed in the message box is not necessarily the error that prevented the rows from being applied. For instance, to create the errors that you see in Figure 18-13, I deliberately changed a character column to numeric. As far as the Start and Repair functions were concerned, no errors were encountered. It was "only" the rows themselves that were in error!

Since the Repair function can be run repeatedly, the user can take as many tries as are necessary to correct the data.

Next, enter the following script for the "Cancel" button's clicked event:

```
// cancel execution of pipeline

int i_rtn

i_rtn = i_uo_pipe_test.Cancel ()
```

```
if i_rtn = 1 then
Messagebox ("Cancel","Pipeline Operation Cancelled")
else
Messagebox ("Error","Unable to Cancel Operation")
end if
```

This script triggers the pipe's Cancel function to cancel any processing that is taking place. For instance, as soon as the Start function is fired, control is returned to the user even through processing may well occur for the next few minutes (or hours!). Pressing the "Cancel" button will trigger the Cancel function, which will halt processing after the next block is read or written.

The last script for our application is critical and is placed in the window's closequery event:

```
// Window is closing so clean up

disconnect using sqlca ;
disconnect using sqlca1 ;

destroy i_uo_pipe_test
destroy sqlca1
```

After disconnecting from the database, we destroy our pipeline object to free the resources that it consumes. Failure to do so, especially if running the app several times, can leave Windows short on resources and unstable. As a rule of thumb, CREATE and DESTROY should be thought of as like left and right parentheses–there should an equal number of both.

In this chapter, we have explored the pipeline object and its various attributes, events, and functions, presenting tables for all. We have also examined error codes and their causes. We explored the Data Pipeline Painter and its use, and then using the Pipeline in your application via practical script examples. You should now be able to fully exploit the power of the data pipeline.

CHAPTER **19**

Using Drop-Down DataWindows

By Tom Flynn

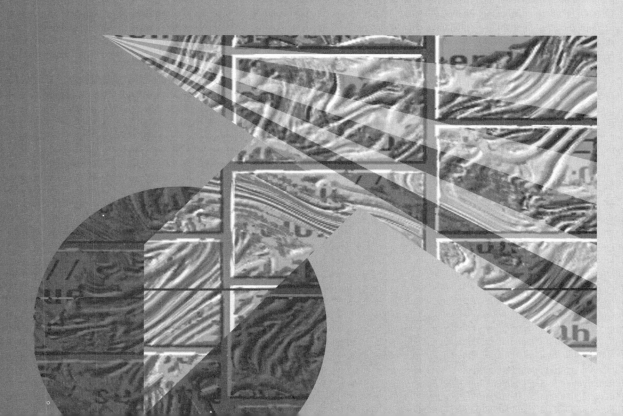

Using Drop-Down DataWindows

by **Tom Flynn**

All of us have been faced with the requirement more than once: a window used for data entry needs one or more drop-down listboxes on it. These listboxes contain data that must be retrieved from a database before the window can be displayed. To accomplish this, a script is written in the window open event which will open a cursor to retrieve the listbox data and use the SetValue function to add this data to the drop-down listbox edit style code table. An example of such a window open event script is shown in Listing 1. The problem with this is that scrolling through one or more cursors can be a slow process, not to mention the time required to call the SetValue function. When it comes to data retrieval, it's hard to beat the power of a DataWindow. What we really need is a way to harness that power within a drop-down listbox. The dropdownDataWindow–first added to PowerBuilder in Version 3.0–provides us with this capability, allowing us to implement the listbox as a DataWindow.

Listing 1: Window open event script to populate the code table for a drop-down listbox edit style.

```
integerli_cnt=1
stringls_stateid, ls_statename

// Declare cursor that will return
// state codes and names
DECLARE state_cr CURSOR FOR
SELECT states.state_id,
       states.state_name
```

```
FROM  states
USING SQLCA;

if SQLCA.sqlcode<0 then
 close(this)
 messagebox("Error","Declare Of Cursor Failed")
 return
end if

OPEN state_cr;

if SQLCA.sqlcode<0 then
 close(this)
 messagebox("Error","Open Of Cursor Failed")
 return
end if

do while SQLCA.sqlcode=0
 FETCH state_cr into :ls_stateid, :ls_statename;
 if SQLCA.sqlcode<0 then
 close(this)
 messagebox("Error","FETCH Of Cursor Failed")
 return
 elseif SQLCA.sqlcode=0 then
 dw_1.setvalue("state",li_cnt,ls_statename + "~t" + string(ls_stateid))
 end if
 li_cnt++
loop

close state_cr;
if SQLCA.sqlcode<0 then
 close(this)
 messagebox("Error","Close Of Cursor Failed")
 return
end if

//Add 1 blank row to DataWindow
dw_1.insertrow(0)
```

Let's start with a simple example. Figure 19-1 shows a New Customer DataWindow with a dropdownDataWindow on the State column. To create this listing of states we start by defining a tabular DataWindow. The SELECT statement for this DataWindow will retrieves the state code and state name columns. The state code column will be removed from the display, but it must still be retrieved, since this is the value that will be written to the database for each customer.

Often you will need to use the same list in several DataWindows. For example, there could be several places within an application where a list of states is needed. Consequently, it is a good idea to give the DataWindow which will act as the listbox portion a name that can be easily identified. For this reason, the DataWindow which retrieves the list of states will be called d_states_dddw.

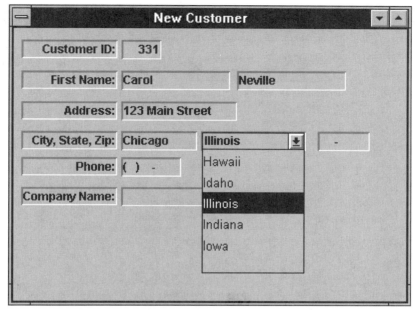

Figure 19-1: A dropdownDataWindow on the State column.

The next step involves defining the freeform DataWindow which will act as the New Customer data entry window. We will click the right mouse button on the State column and choose "dropdownDataWindow" as the edit style for the column. When this edit style is selected from the pop-up menu, we will see the window illustrated in Figure 19-2.

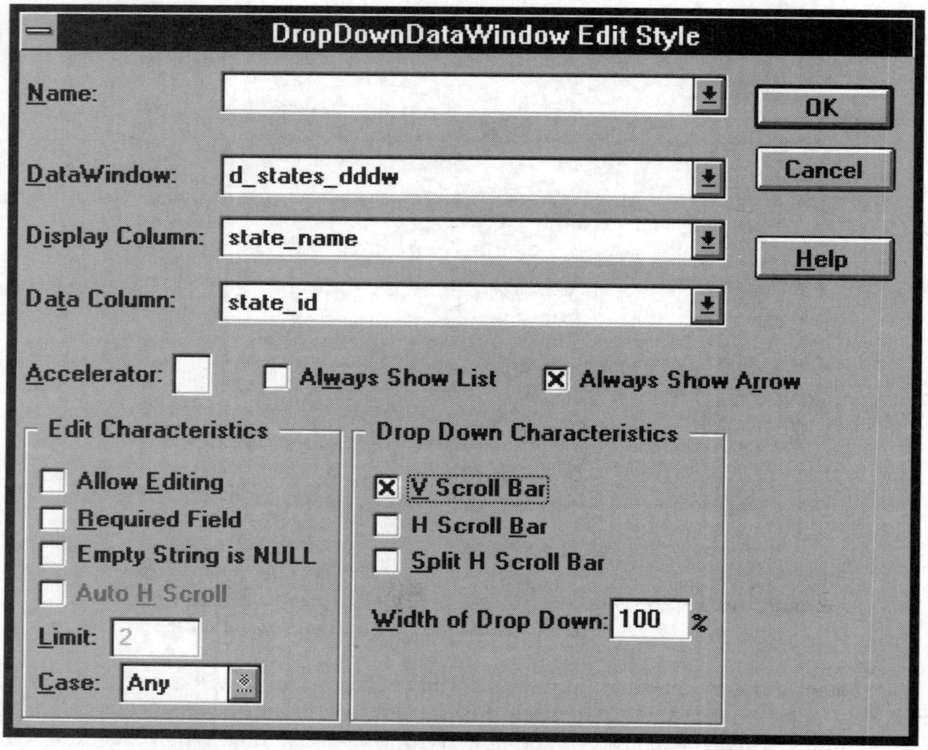

Figure 19-2: The dropdownDataWindow edit style definition window.

As you can see from Figure 19-2, the DataWindow edit field will contain the name of the DataWindow which will act as the listbox portion of our edit style. The display column will be **state_name**–the value from the dropdownDataWindow that will be seen in the edit box portion of the State column's edit style. **state_id** will be specified as the data value, since this is the value that will be written to the database for each customer. Several other attributes can be set for the edit style, including whether or not scroll bars should be included and how wide the dropdownDataWindow will be. The width is entered as a percentage of the width of the column: it defaults to 100%, or exactly as wide as the column.

Now the customer DataWindow object will be placed in a DataWindow control on the window. When the DataWindow functions InsertRow() or Retrieve() are called, PowerBuilder will check to see if there are currently any rows in the dropdownDataWindow. If the dropdownDataWindow is empty, then a retrieve will be executed on it which will retrieve all the states. This retrieval will execute in a fraction of the time it would take to open a cursor and populate a drop-down listbox edit style's code table.

DropdownDataWindow Retrieval Arguments

The technique we have just presented has many advantages. The dropdownDataWindow approach required no additional coding, and also performs better than an open event processing a cursor. Let's take this a step further and add a retrieval argument to our dropdown-DataWindow: now we only want a list of states for a particular region. The SELECT statement for this DataWindow will contain a retrieve argument called :arg_region:

```
SELECT "states"."state_id",
       "states"."state_name"
  FROM "states"
 WHERE "states"."state_region" = :arg_region
```

Once we have defined this DataWindow we will associate it with the customer window as a dropdownDataWindow, just as we did in the previous example. In our window open event we will issue a SetTransObject(SQLCA) followed by an InsertRow(0) to display a blank customer row in our window. However, when we open the window, instead of seeing our customers we see the window shown in Figure 19-3..

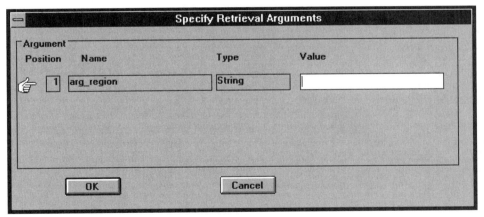

Figure 19-3: Window that shows when we try to use a dropdownDataWindow
requiring a retrieve argument.

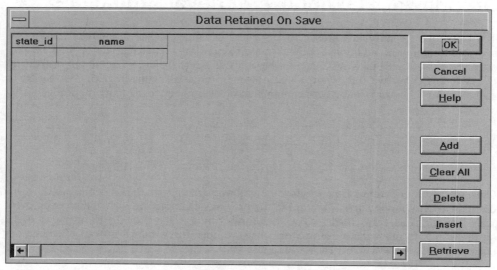

Figure 19-4: The window that is seen when Rows..Data is selected in the DataWindow Painter.

Now that we have stopped PowerBuilder from forwarding the request for our retrieve argument, how do we populate the dropdownDataWindow? We want to have the listbox contain all the states for a particular region. When we know what region we want to see, we will issue our own Retrieve(). The function dwGetChild can be called to provide us with a reference to the dropdownDataWindow. Once we have this reference, we can call the various PowerScript functions to manipulate the dropdownDataWindow just as though it were any other DataWindow in our application. In our example, we will use the reference to issue a SetTransObject on the dropdownDataWindow followed by a Retrieve(). In the call to the Retrieve() function we will pass a region as a retrieve argument. This region is being passed to the window by opening the window with the OpenWithParm function. The script shown in Listing 2 would run in the window open event.

Listing 2: The window open event script for a dropdownDataWindow with a retrieve argument.

```
string ls_region
DataWindowchild dwc_state
// Get the region which is passed
// To the window using OpenWithParm
ls_region=message.stringparm

// Obtain a region to the
// dropdownDataWindow
dw_1.dwGetChild("state",dwc_state)

// Retrieve the states for the
// Region that is passed
dwc_state.SetTransObject(SQLCA)
dwc_state.retrieve(ls_region)

// Add a blank customer
// To the window
dw_1.InsertRow(0)
```

Changing The SELECT Statement for DropdownDataWindows

The reference to the child DataWindow that we get by calling dwGetChild can be used in a number of different ways. For example, we can use dwModify to change the characteristics of the dropdownDataWindow. Let's assume that we need to change the WHERE criteria at runtime. Based on some circumstances, we will use dwModify to change the SELECT statement for the dropdownDataWindow. The script in Listing 3 shows a call to dwGetChild and then a call to dwModify to change the attribute DATAWINDOW.TABLE.SELECT.

Listing 3: Script to dynamically add a WHERE clause to a DDDW.

```
DataWindowchild dwc_state
string ls_sql,ls_syntax

// Obtain reference to DDDW
dw_1.dwGetChild("state",dwc_state)
// Get the current SELECT statement
// For the DDDW
ls_sql=dwc_state.dwDescribe("DataWindow.table.SELECT")
// Add a where clause to the SELECT statement
ls_sql=ls_sql + " WHERE country='CAN'"
// Build dwModify syntax
ls_syntax="DataWindow.table.SELECT=~"" + ls_sql + "~""
dwc_state.dwModify(ls_syntax)
// Retrieve existing customers
dw_1.retrieve()
```

Sharing DataWindow Result Sets

Even with the performance benefits of DataWindow retrievals, if the dropdownDataWindow's SELECT statement is complex or if it is returning a large result set we can experience performance problems. For example, let's assume that there are several windows in our application that require a drop-down list of customers. It seems a shame that we will have to retrieve the same list every time we want to show a list of states. A better approach would be to retrieve the list of states once, and use that list for any dropdownDataWindow that needs a list of states. This can be accomplished by using the DataWindow's ability to share result sets.

The first step will be to create a window containing a DataWindow that displays a list of states. The open event for this window will execute a retrieve on the included DataWindow. This window will be opened from the application open event; however, the window's Visible attribute will be set to FALSE so that the user will not see it.

Since this window is open–even though it is not visible–other DataWindows can share its result set using the function dwShareData. In the open event for any window that needs a list of states, a script similar to Listing 4 will be executed. The script obtains a reference to the State column's dropdownDataWindow, and then uses the dwShareData function to allow the column to use the hidden window's DataWindow result set.

Listing 4: Script to allow a DDDW to share another DataWindow's result set.

```
DataWindowchild dwc_state

// Obtairn reference to DDDW
dw_1.dwGetChild("state",dwc_state)

// Share the data in the hidden window
w_hidden_window.dw_1.dwShareData(dwc_state)
// Retrieve existing customers
dw_1.settransobject(SQLCA)
// Add a blank customer to begin data entry
dw_1.insertrow(0)
```

These examples do not begin to exhaust the possible uses for child DataWindows. By taking these techniques and applying them to your own applications you will discover lots of other things that can be done.

CHAPTER 20

Controlling DataWindow Actions with the SetActionCode Function

By Mike Pflieger

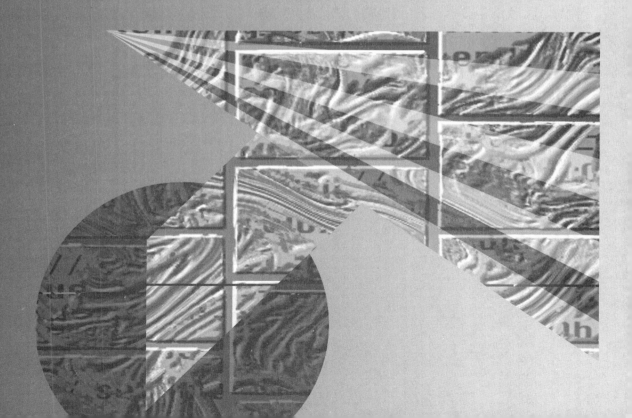

Controlling DataWindow Actions with the SetActionCode Function

by **Mike Pflieger**

Some DataWindow events have an action code which allows you to change the default action that follows the event. By using the PowerBuilder function SetActionCode, you can set the value to control processing that occurs in these events. The DataWindow events that utilize action codes are:

Clicked
DBError
ItemChanged
ItemError
PrintPage
RetrieveRow
RetrieveStart
UpdateStart

The valid action code values vary between events, as does the processing which is affected.

Clicked Event

The Clicked event fires whenever the user clicks inside a DataWindow control. If the user clicks on a valid row, the DataWindow will automatically make that row the current one. If you don't want to process the row change, use SetActionCode(1) to stop it.

```
0   Continue with row change and clicked event. (Default.)
1   Stop processing the clicked event.
```

The following code only allows users to click on rows with their own user id.

```
// Clicked Event
// We'll assume there is an instance variable with the current user's
// User ID: string is_user_id

long l_row
string s_user_id
l_row = GetClickedRow()

// No need to continue if the user didn't click on a valid row
if l_row < 1 then
 return
end if

s_user_id = GetItemString(l_row, "user_id")
// If the user_id is not the current user then disallow row change
if s_user_id <> is_user_id then
 beep(1)
 SetActionCode(1)
 return
end if
```

ItemChanged Event

The DataWindow ItemChanged event can achieve several useful goals. One such goal is to control whether or not a new value for a field is accepted, rejected with an error, or rejected but processing continues. The values are as follows:

```
0   Accept the new data value. (Default.)
1   Reject the new data value ( fire the ItemError event).
2   Reject the new data value but allow the focus to change.
```

One use of SetActionCode in the ItemChanged event is for cross-validations. For example, to validate that if field Account Status is changed to "Inactive" then the field Balance is checked for zero:

```
//ItemChanged Event

Decimal {2} d_balance // Customer Account Balance
Long    l_currow // Current Row Number
String  s_column_name // The name of the column that changed
```

```
String s_status // Customer Account Status
l_currow = this.GetRow()
s_column_name = this.GetColumnName()

CHOOSE CASE s_column_name
...
...
CASE "STATUS"
 s_status = this.GetText()
 // If STATUS is Inactive
 IF s_status = "I" THEN
 d_balance = this.GetItemDecimal(l_currow,"BALANCE")
 IF d_balance <> 0 THEN
 //SET AN ERROR
 this.SetActionCode(1)
 RETURN
 ELSE
 //ACCEPT THE VALUE
 this.SetActionCode(0)/* not required since 0 is default */
 RETURN
 END IF
 END IF
END CHOOSE
```

While SetActionCode does not have to be the last line in the script, other DataWindow functions may reset the action code. To avoid this problem, code a Return function after the SetActionCode to terminate the script.

Another use of the SetActionCode function in the ItemChanged event is to set a field to a value other than the one the user gave it. For example, the user changes a date to a Sunday, but we want to ensure that the field holds the first business day after the entered date, figured through a function. To set the field to the Monday's date might seem simple at first:

```
//ItemChanged Event

date  dt_process      // Process date
long  l_currow        // Current Row Number
string s_column_name  // The name of the column that changed

l_currow = this.GetRow()
s_column_name = this.GetColumnName

CHOOSE CASE s_column_name
...
...
CASE "process_date"

 dt_process =f_get_next_bus_date( date(this.GetText()))
 this.SetText(dt_process)
 this.AcceptText()

...
```

While this might look like it would work, you would end up in an infinite loop. The AcceptText would cause the ItemChanged event to fire. But the column changed would still be process_date, and it would try to change the date, and then AcceptText would cause the ItemChanged event to fire... I am sure you see the point. You should never code an AcceptText in the ItemChanged event. You can use SetActionCode to accomplish this:

```
CASE "process_date"
dt_process =f_get_next_bus_date( date(this.GetText()))
this.SetItemText(l_currow,"process_date",dt_process) // set value in buffer
this.SetActionCode(2) // reject edit control value RETURN
```

This would set the value of process_date to dt_process in the Primary! buffer. The SetAc-
tionCode(2) would reject the value in the edit control (the Sunday date that was entered) and
allow focus to change (meaning no error would occur).

ItemError Event

The ItemError event is fired whenever a DataWindow field fails validation, or when the
value is rejected from the ItemChanged event. As with the ItemChanged event, its action
codes can be set to accept or reject the newly entered value for a field. It also allows you to
suppress a display of the error message box when the value is to be rejected. The action
codes for the ItemError event are:

```
0  Reject the new data value and show an error message box. (Default.)
1  Reject the new data value and suppress the error message box .
2  Accept the new data value .
3  Reject the new data value but allow the focus to change.
```

If we want to display a custom error message on a certain field instead of the PowerBuilder-
generated error message box, we could use SetActionCode to suppress the standard message
box. For instance, in our previous example we tried to change the status to inactive when the
balance was not $0. For the same edit we could, in the ItemError event, display a message
stating the error:

```
//ItemError Event

Long  l_currow      /* Current Row Number*/
String s_column_name  /* The name of the column that changed*/

l_currow = this.GetRow()
s_column_name = this.GetColumnName

CHOOSE CASE s_column_name
 CASE "status"
 MessageBox("Error","Account cannot be changed to Inactive"+
     "Balance is not zero.")
 this.SetActionCode(1)
 RETURN
...
END CHOOSE
```

Using SetActionCode in the ItemError event also allow us to selectively override a validation entered in the DataWindow object column. For example, say we have the following validation rule on balance:

```
Real(GetText()) <= 10000
```

This rule means that customer balances cannot go over $10,000. If we wanted to allow customers who have "Corporate" accounts to go over $10,000, we could do the following:

```
//ItemError Event
CHOOSE CASE s_column_name
 CASE "balance"
 // Allow balance over $10,000 on Corporate accounts
 IF d_balance not <= 10000 AND s_type = "C"
 this.SetActionCode(2)
 RETURN
 END IF
...
```

We could also reset the value in the Primary! buffer and reject the new value, as we did in the ItemChanged, but the action code would then be set to 3.

DBError Event

The DBError event fires after a dw.Retrieve, dw.Update(), or imbedded SQL statement is issued and a database error is encountered (SQLCode equal to -1). Many PowerBuilder shops will develop standard database error message displays for these situations. In order to keep PowerBuilder from displaying the default database error message boxes ,we can use SetActionCode. The action code values for the DBError event are:

```
0  Display the error message box. (Default.)
1  Do not display the error message box.
```

An example would be:

```
//DBError event

MessageBox("DB Error:"," Number "&
+ string(this.DBErrorCode) + " "+ this.DBErrorMessage( ),StopSign!)
// Supress PB generated DB Error Message.
this.SetActionCode(1)
return
```

PrintPage

The PrintPage event fires after the dw.Print() function and before the data is sent to the printer. When printing a DataWindow you can set an action code to skip a page before printing the DataWindow. The action codes for the PrintPage event are:

```
0  Do not skip a page. (Default.)
1  Skip a page.
```

To skip a page before printing you would code the following in the PrintPage event:

```
//PrintPage event
this.SetActionCode(1)
```

RetrieveRow

The RetrieveRow event fires after each row is received from the server. In this event you can set an action code to stop the retrieval. The following are the valid action codes for the RetrieveRow event:

```
0 - Continue. (Default.)
1 - Stop the retrieval.
```

If a DataWindow could potentially bring back a large number of rows and you wish to stop the retrieval after a certain number are retrieved, you would use SetActionCode in the RetrieveRow event:

```
//RetrieveRow event
// Instance variable Long i_l_count
...
IF i_l_count++ > 100 THEN
      // Maximum rows retrieved, stop retrieval
      this.SetActionCode(1)
      RETURN

END IF
```

When the instance variable i_l_count, used to count the number of rows retrieved, is greater than 100, the retrieval will stop.

Note: If any code exists in the RetrieveRow event, then the event is fired after every row. This could slow down the retrieval.

RetrieveStart

The RetrieveStart event fires after the dw.Retrieve() function and before the generated SQL is sent to the server. In certain situations it might be desirable to stop a retrieval before it starts. The following are the action codes for the RetrieveStart event:

```
0  Continue. (Default.)
1  Do not retrieve
```

For example: If we have a window that allows the user to enter search criteria, we could determine in the RetrieveStart that an excessive number of rows would be returned, then stop the retrieval and force the user to narrow the criteria.

```
//Retrieve Start event
Int i_count  /* Expected Retrieve Count */
...
//Get Count of Rows to be retrieved
...
```

```
IF i_count > 1000 THEN
    MessageBox("Stop", "Please narrow your search",Stop!)
    This.SetActionCode(1)
    RETURN
END IF
...
```

UpdateStart

The UpdateStart event fires after the Update() function and before the generated update SQL is sent to the server. By setting the action code you can prevent the update from being sent to the server.

The valid action code values for the UpdateStart event are:

```
0   Continue. (Default.)
1   Do not Update.
```

If you need to prevent the update from being performed, you would code the following in the UpdateStart event:

```
//UpdateStart event
...
this.SetActionCode(1)
RETURN
...
```

Summary

There are several other situations where setting the action code is beneficial. These samples are intended to give an idea of some of those situations. As you gain experience using PowerBuilder and coding using PowerScript, you will find that SetActionCode is very useful.

CHAPTER **21**

Understanding
DataWindow Events

By Tom Flynn

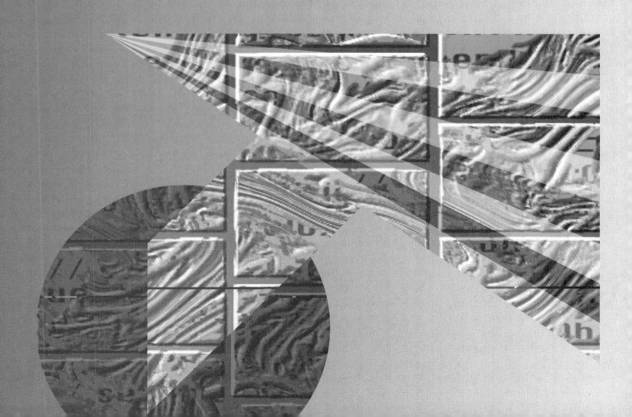

Understanding DataWindow Events

by **Tom Flynn**

Most of us get up in the morning, get ready for work, and commute to the office. These events, which make up our day-to-day lives, are a reliable and necessary sequence. Just as we can chronicle a day in the life of a PowerBuilder developer, we can examine the events that a DataWindow experiences. Let's analyze the events that occur as we perform such common DataWindow tasks as retrieving data, entering data, and performing updates.

Figure 21-1 shows a DataWindow with a list box that displays events as they occur. In the open event for the window we are issuing a retrieve, and its associated events are displayed in the list box. The first event we see is the Constructor event. When a window is created, each of its controls requires a constructor event. Think of the constructor event as being the open event for each control. We are all aware that the close of a window is signaled with the window close event. Just before a window close activates, the destructor event is triggered for each control on the window. Think of the destructor as the close for a control.

Continuing on with the events in Figure 21-1, the RetrieveStart event signifies the beginning of a retrieval: think of it as the DataWindow's way of warning us that a retrieval is about to begin. The retrieval can be canceled at this time with an action code of 1. By default, the DataWindow will reset the DataWindow buffers before retrieving new rows. If you want a retrieval to be appended to the end of any existing data, call SetActionCode(2), which will prevent the DataWindow buffers from being reset.

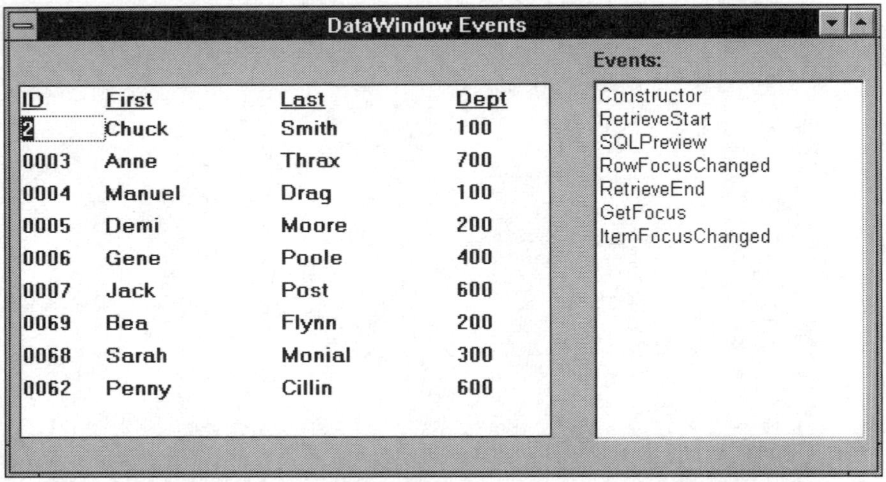

Figure 21-1: The events fired when retrieving data in the open event of a window.

The SQLPreview event follows the RetrieveStart event. SQLPreview provides us with the SQL statement(s) that are about to be sent to the server due to a Retrieve( ) or Update( ) function call. Calling the function dwGetSQLPreview( ) from the SQLPreview event will return to you the SQL statement about to be sent to the server. While there are not many instances where the SQLPreview event is used in live applications, it is useful when debugging a DataWindow. There are two action codes associated with this event. An action code of 1 in SQLPreview will cancel the retrieval. There is also an action code of 2 associated with this event, but we will look at that code a little later when we analyze the update process.

Once the SQLPreview event has been triggered, the retrieval process is ready to begin. Rows are fetched into the DataWindow one at a time. As each row is brought into the DataWindow, a RetrieveRow event can be triggered. In the example in Figure 21-1 only one RetrieveRow is being displayed, but the event will be trigger once for every row brought in. While at first the RetrieveRow event may seem handy, it has its drawbacks. Having any script (even a comment) in the RetrieveRow event will typically *double* the amount of time the retrieval takes. There are two reasons that RetrieveRow is such a performance stopper. First, if each time a row is fetched into the DataWindow a script is processed, the process is obviously going to be slower than if PowerBuilder was able retrieve all the rows without stopping to execute a script. Second, whenever there is anything in the RetrieveRow event, PowerBuilder will do an implicit yield. This means that after each row is retrieved, PowerBuilder hands control back to Windows. At that point any waiting messages will be processed.

The next event to be triggered is the RowFocusChanged event. We typically associate this event with moving from row to row within a DataWindow. It is also triggered when a DataWindow is receiving focus. In this example, the DataWindow is the first control in our tab order. Consequently it is the first control to receive focus when the window opens. Oddly enough, in our example the RowFocusChanged event seems to be occurring before the

RetrieveEnd event, which signifies the end of the retrieval process. I would have thought that the RetrieveEnd event would surely occur before RowFocusChanged. Obviously it is not a good idea to rely too heavily on the order of events within a windows application.

At this point the retrieval has completed. Since, as mentioned, the DataWindow control is the first control in the tab order, it now receives focus. Notice that after the GetFocus event activates, an ItemFocusChanged event is triggered in the DataWindow control. Like the RowFocusChanged event, ItemFocusChanged fires when focus is moved to a new item in the DataWindow–including the initial focus one the DataWindow itself.

Entering Data

Now that our DataWindow contains data, the user can scroll through making changes where appropriate. Figure 21-2 shows what will occur if the user tabs from the employee id column to the employee first name column, and then changes the first name. Notice the sequence of events associated with these moves.

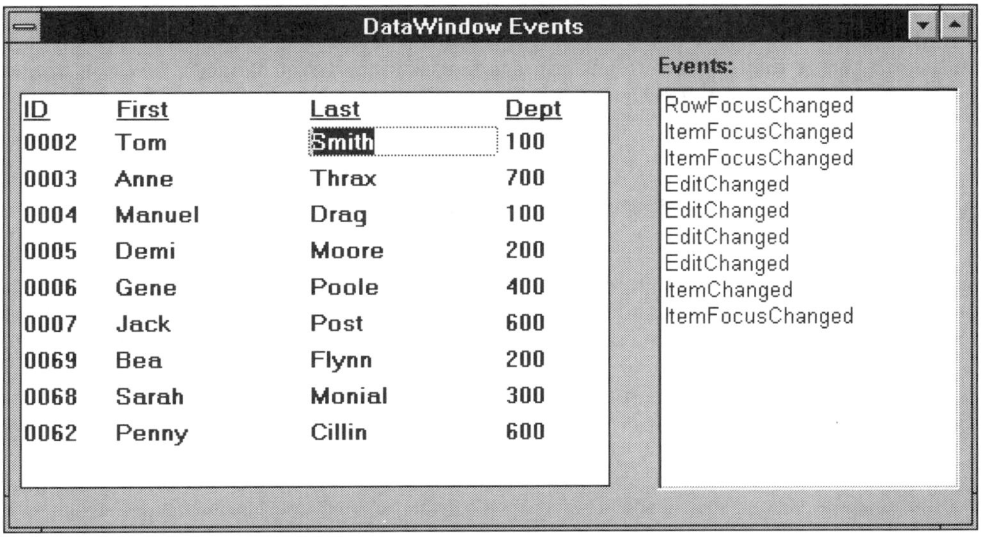

*Figure 21- 2: Events fired after tabbing from ID to First, changing
the first name, and tabbing to Last.*

As was mentioned in the retrieval example, when the DataWindow control receives focus the RowFocusChanged and ItemFocusChanged events trigger first. The third event in the list is another ItemFocusChanged. This is generated when we hit the Tab key to move to the first name column. When we get to that column, we type in the name "Tom". This results in three EditChanged events–one for each character that is entered. Remember that EditChanged simply signifies that another character has been entered into the edit control. Then when the user presses the Enter or Tab key, the ItemChanged event fires.

Validation Levels

When the Enter or Tab key is pressed, four levels of validation must be passed.

To start the validation process, the DataWindow checks to see if anything new has been entered into the edit control. If the value in the edit control is the same as the value in the DataWindow buffer, validation stops. An ItemChanged event is not triggered, but an Item-FocusChanged event is.

Assuming that something new has been entered into the edit control, the datatype of the newly entered value is checked. If the value entered is not of the correct datatype, an ItemError event is triggered in the DataWindow control. If the value entered is of the correct datatype, then validation continues. The third level activates any validation rules or code tables that are associated with the column. Once again, if a validation rule or code table validation is not met, an ItemError event fires. (There are a number of action codes associated with the ItemError event. The most useful is 1, which will suppress the standard Power-Builder error message.)

If all validation rules are passed, then the fourth and final level of validation executes in the ItemChanged event. ItemChanged is triggered just before the value is transferred from the edit control into the DataWindow buffer. It is our last warning that the value in the edit control is going to be moved. Setting an action code of 1 in the ItemChanged event will trigger an ItemError event, thus stopping this value from moving into the buffers.

Sending Changes to the Server

After the user has made all the necessary changes, he or she will want to save those changes back to the database by calling the Update( ) function. Figure 21-3 shows the sequence of events associated with the update process. The file menu in our example has an option called Save which is selected to start that process. The first SQLPreview event shown in the listbox in Figure 21-3 is associated with the initial call to the Retrieve( ) function in the window open event.

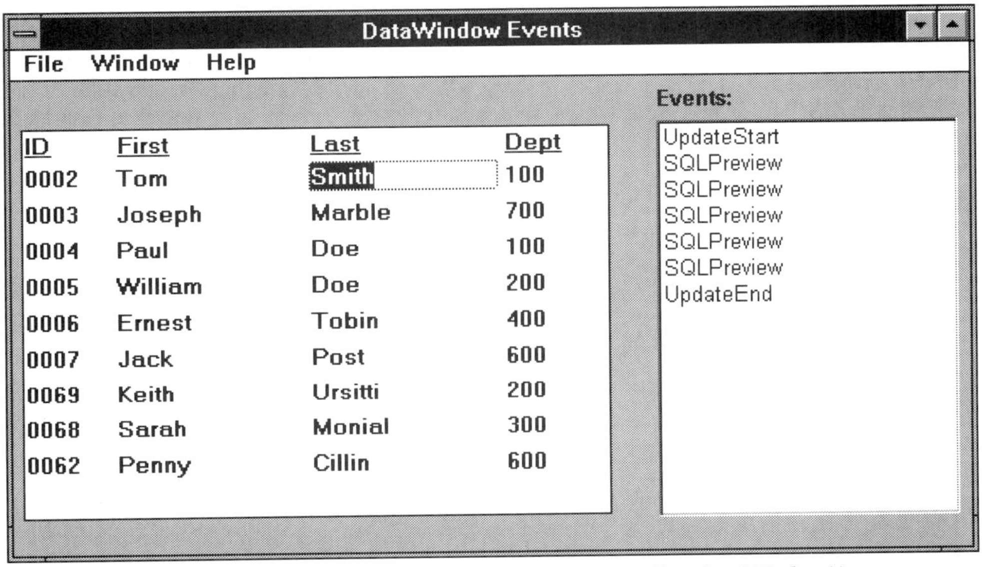

Figure 21-3: Sequence of events associated with a call to dw_1.Update( )

The first event associated with a call to the Update( ) function is UpdateStart. The event serves as a warning that PowerBuilder is about to begin sending SQL statements to the server. The update can be canceled at this time by setting the action code to 1. Otherwise, right after the UpdateStart event, SQL statements will begin going to the server. As each SQL statement is sent, an SQLPreview event executes. (This event was discussed earlier when we looked at retrieval, but we deferred discussion of the action code 2. Action code 2 prevents the current statement from being sent, but continues on with the rest of an update. This might be useful in a debugging environment where you want to see what SQL statements are being generated but you don't want the database to be changed.) The completion of the update process is signaled with the UpdateEnd event.

Printing the DataWindow

After calling the Print function to print a DataWindow, the PrintStart event is triggered to signal that printing is about to begin. As each page is sent to the printer, a PrintPage event fires. Calling a SetActionCode(1) from the PrintPage event will stop that page from being printed. When the printing has completed, the PrintEnd event executes. Just as the UpdateEnd and RetrieveEnd events signified the end of their respective functions, so PrintEnd signifies the end of the print process.

Custom Events

In addition to the standard events that are defined for all DataWindow controls, there are other events available for DataWindows that can be defined as custom user events. Figure 21-4 shows the list of DataWindow events available for the user event definition window. All the DataWindow event ids begin with pbm_dwn. Unfortunately, documentation on these events is sketchy at best. I was unable to find any!. Let's try to highlight a couple of these events that might be useful in your applications.

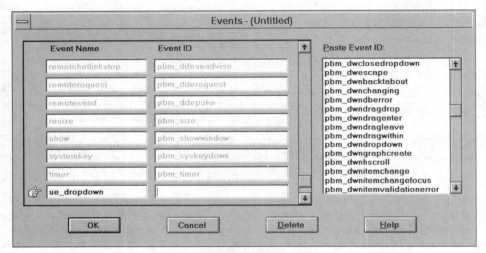

Figure 21-4: Defining custom events.

Conclusion

That concludes our look into the life of a DataWindow. As you have seen, even in a relatively simple DataWindow there is quite a bit of activity. Knowing how to use these events effectively is what separates the DataWindow guru from the novice.

CHAPTER 22

PowerBuilder (Windows) Events

By Michael MacDonald

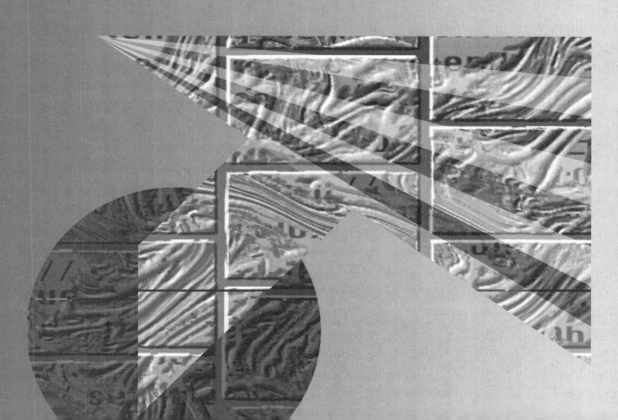

PowerBuilder (Windows) Events

by **Michael MacDonald**

Windows programming is much more complex than straight DOS, COBOL, or xBase programming ever was–and yet, in some ways, it is easier. Consider that the programmer is provided, free of charge, with many routines that were always difficult to do in a DOS program. Mouse movements and events, such as pressing the left button, are recorded by Windows and transmitted as Windows messages to whatever programs might care to intercept them. Previously complex multimedia routines are also available, including joystick, MIDI, and waveform services.

There are over two hundred such messages that Windows provides for the programmer, starting with Activate (a window has become active) and Create (a window has been created). PowerBuilder passes each and every one on to you, the programmer, as a PowerBuilder event, and provides you with pre-built script handlers for the most common ones.

For instance, click in the window area of a sheet and then select User Events from the Declare menu. The first event you'll see is activate. Go to the Script Painter, and activate is one of the events for which you can record script. In this way, PowerBuilder 4.0, as well as previous versions, shelters you from much of Windows' complexity. However, if you return to the User Events dialog, you will observe that PowerBuilder does allow you to access any Windows message directly. Look down the right side of the window and you will see events such as pbm_activate and pbm_bmgetcheck. Notice that the common activate and clicked events are actually mapped to the pbm_activate and pbm_lbuttonclk events.

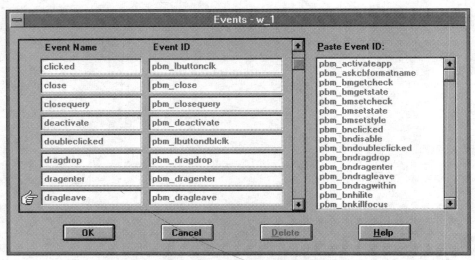

Figure 22-1: The Declare -> User Events dialog box.

Message types, windows, events, or messages actually begin with two or three characters denoting the source or object of the message. For instance, pbm_activate is actually WM_ACTIVATE, where WM stands for Window Message. Other message prefixes include:

```
BM   Button Message
BN   Button Notification
CB   Combo Box Message
CBN  Combo Box Notification
DM   Dialog Box Message
EM   Edit Control Message
EN   Edit Control Notification
LB   List Box Message
LBN  List Box Notification
MM   Multimedia Messages
SBN  Scroll Bar Notification
```

While DDE messages are technically window messages, they are broken out separately in the following tables and begin with DDE. PowerBuilder does not support the complete range of DDE message services.

Messages usually tell an object, such as a button, to perform some action. Notifications are usually sent by a control and inform the application that some event has taken place. *The Waite Group's Windows API Bible* details 200 messages that can be sent to controls using PowerBuilder's Send(handle, message_no, word, long) function.

All events that PowerBuilder automatically maps for you begin with the "pbm" prefix. In the case of window events, the "WM" is stripped off. For example, pbm_activate is really the wm_activate event. Other types of messages retain the prefix: for example, BM_GETCHECK becomes pbm_bmgetcheck.

By adding events through the Declare -> User Events dialog box, the programmer may intercept these messages as required. Enter a meaningful name in the left hand column. Then enter the corresponding pbm_ event name in the right hand column.

In Figure 22-2, we've added a new event called rbuttonup which is mapped to the windows message pbm_rbuttonup. You can either type in the event_id or double-click in the Paste Event ID list box.

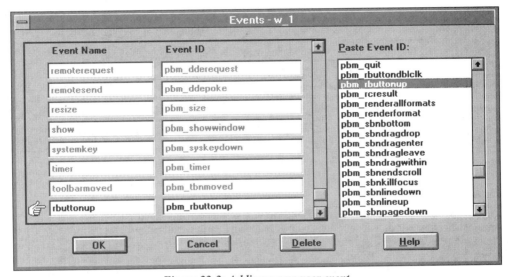

Figure 22-2: Adding a new user event.

There are times when you want to add an event of your own that won't map to any of the normal Windows events. These events might be for data validation, inserting or deleting rows, or performing functionality. I recommend adding the prefix "ue_" to your event name, so that any programmer looking at your code will know that the event doesn't map to any message which Windows might generate.

Custom Events (Figure 22-3) shows how to create an event called ue_validate. This event is mapped to the event called pbm_custom01. There are seventy-five custom events that will only be called when you, the programmer, trigger them. The way you'll get this event to fire is to use the function TriggerEvent("ue_validate").

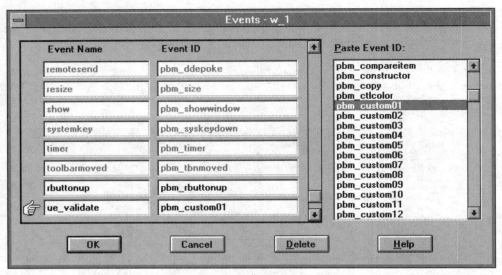

Figure 22-3: Adding a custom event for validation.

DataWindow events

PowerBuilder has another class of messages preceded by a "dw" or "dwn", such as pbm_dwnretrieveend. These are messages and notifications relating to DataWindows. While standard Windows messages are documented in a variety of third-party references, DataWindows are not standard Windows objects, and thus have their own events. You can review how some of the built-in DataWindow events are defined by selecting a DataWindow control on a window and opening the Declare -> User Events dialog.

In the remainder of this chapter, you'll find a list of the various events to which PowerBuilder has built-in mappings.

* * *

Button messages (prefix = pbm_bm)

```
getcheck  Is the radio button or check box checked?
getstate  Is the button highlighted?
setcheck  Change the radio button or check box from checked to unchecked
          or vice versa.
setstate  Highlight or unhighlight the button.
change    Change the style of the button; for example,
          to a radio button or a group box.
```

Button notifications (prefix = pbm_bn)

```
clicked         A button control was clicked.
disable         A button control was disabled.
double-clicked  A button control was double-clicked.
```

dragdrop	An object was dropped on the button control.
dragenter	An object was dragged onto the control.
dragleave	An object was dragged off of the button control.
dragover	An object is being dragged over the control.
hilite	A button control will be highlighted.
paint	A button control will be painted.
setfocus	A button control will have focus.
unhilite	A button control will be unhighlighted.

Combo box messages (prefix pbm_cb)

addstring	Adds a string to the combo box.
deletestring	Deletes a string from the combo box.
dir	Adds a directory listing to the combo box.
findstring	Finds a string beginning with a set of characters.
findstringexact	Finds a string exactly matching the set of characters provided.
getcount	Number of items in the list box.
getcursel	Number of items currently selected.
getdroppedcontrolrect	The screen x, y position of the list box.
geteditsel	Range of characters selected in the edit control.
getextendedui	Default or extended user interface.
getitemdata	4-byte item in redrawn list box.
getitemheight	Height of an item in list box.
getlbtext	Text from the list box control.
getlbtextlen	Length of text in the list box control.
insertstring	Add a new string or 4-byte item to the list box.
limittext	Limit the number of characters that can be typed into the list box.
resetcontent	Remove all elements from the list box.
selectstring	Find matching string and display it.
setcursel	Select and display an item in the list box.
seteditsel	Select a range of characters in the edit area of the list box.
setextendedui	Set either the default or the extended user interface.
setitemdata	Set the 4-byte (32-bit) item in the list box.
setitemheight	Set the height of an item in the list box.
showdropdown	Toggle (show or hide) the drop-down area of a list box.

Combo box notifications (prefix = pbm_cbn)

dblclk	The user has double-clicked an item in the list box.
dragdrop	An object was dropped on the combo box control.
dragenter	An object was dragged onto the control.
dragleave	An object was dragged off of the combo box control.
dragover	An object is being dragged over the control.
dropdown	Drop down portion of list box is about to be made visible.
editchange	Text in the edit control was changed.
editupdate	Windows is about to change the text in the edit control of the list box.
errspace	Windows has run out of room and cannot add another item to the list box.
killfocus	Combo box has lost focus.
selchange	Current selection in the list box has changed.
selendcancel	User pressed the "Cancel" button.

selendok	User pressed the "OK" button.
setfocus	Combo box control now has focus.

DataWindow messages (prefix = pbm_dw)

closedropdown	Close the DropDownDataWindow.
scrollend	Scroll to the last row in the DataWindow.
scrollhome	Scroll to the first row in the DataWindow.
scrolllineend	Scroll to the end of the current line.
scrolllinehome	Scroll to the beginning of the current line.

DataWindow notifications (prefix = pbm_dwn)

backtabou	About to leave the control via the <Shift>-<Tab> combination.
changing	Control is about to change.
dberror	There was a database error. ActionCode 0 = display the error; 1 = do not display.
dragdrop	An object was dropped on the DataWindow control.
dragenter	An object was dragged onto the DataWindow control.
dragleave	An object was dragged off of the DataWindow control.
dragover	An object is being dragged over the DataWindow control.
dropdown	Drop-down portion of list box is about to be made visible.
graphcreate	About to create a graph.
hscroll	About to scroll horizontally.
itemchange	Field in the DataWindow has been changed and loses focus. Also triggered when an item is selected in a column with a drop-down edit style. SetActionCode 0 (default) accepts the new data value. 1 rejects the change, while 2 rejects the change but allows the field to lose focus.
itemchangefocus	The current item in the DataWindow control focus changed.
itemvalidationerror	The change to the current item caused a validation error.
key	A key was pressed. Use KeyDown() to process the keystrokes.
killfocus	A DataWindow control has lost focus.
lbuttonclk	A left button clicked event has occurred. Use the GetClickedRow and GetClickedColumn functions to determine where this occurred.
lbuttondblclk	A left button double-clicked event has occurred.
lbuttondown	The left mouse button was depressed.
lbuttonup	The left mouse button, which was down, was released.

DataWindow notifications (prefix = pbm_dwn), continued

mbuttonclk	The middle button was clicked.
mbuttondblclk	The middle button was double-clicked.
mousemove	The mouse was moved.
printend	The current print job has ended.
printmarginchange	The print margin has changed.
printpage	A page on the current print job is about to be printed. Use Action Code = 1 to skip the page.

printstart	The current print job is about to start.
processenter	The <Enter> key was pressed.
rbuttonclk	The right button was clicked.
rbuttondblclk	The right button was double-clicked.
rbuttondown	The right mouse button was depressed.
rbuttonup	The right mouse button, which was down, was released.
resize	The DataWindow control was resized.
retrieveend	The current retrieve has completed.
retrieverow	A row has been retrieved from the database. SetActionCode = 1 means do not perform additional retrievals.
retrievestart	A retrieval from the database is about to start. An Action Code of 1 means do not do the retrieval. An Action Code of 2 means do not reset the DataWindow first.
rowchange	Focus has changed from one row to another in the DataWindow.
setfocus	The DataWindow control has received focus.
sql	The SQL Preview event occurs after a retrieve, update, or reselect row function call, and immediately before the event in the SQL script takes place. An Action Code of 2 means to stop processing, while an Action Code of 3 means to skip this request and go on to the next one.
tabdownout	The user has pressed the down arrow on the last DataWindow row.
tabout	The user has pressed the tab key on the last row/column of the DataWindow.
tabupout	The user has pressed the up arrow on the first DataWindow row.
updateend	All of the updates to the database have been completed.
updatestart	Occurs just before a database update starts. Use an Action Code of 1 to cancel the update.
vscroll	The DataWindow has been scrolled vertically.

Dynamic Data Exchange (DDE) messages (prefix = pbm_dde)

ddeack	A DDE message has been received.
ddeinitiate	A DDE conversation has been started.
ddeterminate	A DDE conversation has been ended.

Edit control messages (prefix = pbm_em)

canundo	Can an edit control undo the last change?
emptyundobuffer	Empty the undo buffer maintained by Windows.
fmtlines	Add or remove carriage returns and line feeds at the end of each line in a multi-line edit.
getfirstvisibleline	Return the line number of the first visible line in the edit control.
gethandle	Get the handle to the memory being used by the edit control.
getline	Copy a line from the edit control to a buffer in memory.
getlinecount	Return the number of lines in a multi-line edit control.
getmodify	Has the text been modified by the user?

getrect	Return the rectangle surrounding the control.
getsel	Return the start and end positions of the selected text.
limittext	Restrict the length of the text that may be keyed in by the user.
linefromchar	Return the line number of the selected text.
lineindex	Return the 'xth' position within the string in the edit control of the first character of the selected line.
linelength	Return the number of characters in the selected line of the edit control.
linescroll	Scroll the edit control horizontally or vertically.
replacesel	Replace the selected text with new text from the clipboard or from the keyboard.
sethandle	Set the handle of the edit control to a buffer area in memory.
setmodify	Set the modified flag for the edit control.
setpasswordchar	Set the character that will display whenever the user enters text. Used for password-type displays.
setrect	Set/reset the rectangle within which the edit control appears. Text is repainted.
setrectnp	Same as setrect, except that text is not automatically repainted.
setsel	Select the characters in a given range.
settabstops	Set the positions of tab stops in a multi-line edit.
setwordbreak	Set a new word break function.
setwordbreakproc	Set a new word break procedure.
undo	Undo the most recent change to the edit control.

Edit control notifications (prefix = pbm_en)

change	The text in the control has changed.
dragdrop	An object was dropped on the edit control.
dragenter	An object was dragged onto the edit control.
dragleave	An object was dragged off of the edit control.
dragover	An object is being dragged over the edit control.
errspace	The edit control has run out of memory buffer space.
hscroll	The user has clicked the horizontal scroll bar.
killfocus	The edit control has lost focus.
maxtext	The user has attempted to enter more text than the control can take.
setfocus	The edit control has obtained focus.
update	The edit control is about to display changes made by the user.
vscroll	The user has clicked the vertical scroll bar.

List box messages (prefix = pbm_lb)

addstring	Add a string or item to a list box control.
deletestring	Delete an item from a list box.
dir	Fill the list box with a directory listing.
findstring	Find the first item in a list box that partially matches the characters provided.
findstringexact	Find the first item in a list box exactly matching the characters provided.
getcaretindex	Find the item in the list box which has focus.
getcount	Determine the number of items in the list box.

getcursel	Determine the item number which is selected.
gethorizontalextent	Find the width of the list box, accounting for horizontal scrolling.
getitemheight	Determine the height of an item in the list box control.
getitemrect	Determine the dimensions of the list box control.
getsel	Get the currently selected item in the list box control.
getselcount	Get the number of selected items in a multi-select list box.
getselitems	Fills a provided array of integers with the numbers of the items in the list box that have been selected.
gettext	Get the text of the currently selected item in a list box.
gettextlen	Find the number of characters for the currently selected item in a list box.
gettopindex	Determine the item number of the topmost visible item in a list box.
insertstring	Add a new string to the list box.
resetcontent	Reset (clear) the contents of the list box.
selectstring	Find and highlight a string matching the provided characters.
selitemrange	Select / deselect a range of items in a list box.
setcaretindex	Set the focus on an item in the list box.
setcolumnwidth	Set the width of columns in the list box.
setcursel	Select and highlight an item in a list box. Scroll the list box if necessary.
sethorizontaltext	Sets the number of units that the list box can be scrolled horizontally.
setitemdata	Sets the 32-bit / 4-byte value associated with a list box.
setitemheight	Set the height of items in a list box.
setsel	Select a string in a list box.
settabstops	Set the position of tab stops in a list box control.
settopindex	Scroll the list box so that a specified item is the top visible in a list box.

List box notifications (prefix = pbm_en)

dblclk	The user has double-clicked an item in a list box control.
dragdrop	An object was dropped on the list box control.
dragenter	An object was dragged onto the list box control.
dragleave	An object was dragged off of the list box control.
dragover	An object is being dragged over the list box control.
errspace	The user has attempted to exceed the maximum number of characters for the list box.
killfocus	The list box has lost focus.
selcancel	The current selection has been canceled.
selchange	The user has selected or deselected an item in a list box control.
setfocus	The list box has gained focus.

Multimedia messages (prefix = pbm_mm)

```
joy1buttondown      One of the buttons on Joystick 1 has been pressed.
joy1buttonup        One of the buttons on Joystick 1 has been released.
joy1move            Joystick 1 has been moved to a new position.
joy1zmove           A three-axis Joystick Number 1 has been moved in
                    the Z dimension.
joy2buttondown      One of the buttons on Joystick 2 has been pressed.
joy2buttonup        One of the buttons on Joystick 2 has been released.
joy2move            Joystick 2 has been moved to a new position.
joy2zmove           A three-axis Joystick Number 2 has been moved in
                    the Z dimension.
mcinotify           A multi-media control interface (mci) process
                    has started.
mimclose            A MIDI input device has been closed.
mimdata             A MIDI message has been received.
mimerror            An invalid MIDI message has been received.
                    An error was encountered.
mimlongdata         A MIDI long message has been received.
mimlongerror        An invalid MIDI system exclusive message has
                    been received.
mimopen             A MIDI input device has been opened.
momclose            A MIDI output device has been closed.
momdone             A system exclusive message has been transmitted.
momopen             A MIDI output device has been opened.
wimclose            A waveform audio input device has been closed.
wimdata             A waveform audio input buffer is full.
wimopen             A waveform audio input device has been opened.
womclose            A waveform audio output device has been closed.
womdone             A waveform audio output device has completed playback.
womopen             A waveform audio output device has been opened.
```

Scroll bar notifications (prefix = pbm_sbn)

```
bottom              The user has scrolled to the bottom.
dragdrop            An object was dropped on the scroll bar control.
dragenter           An object was dragged onto the scroll bar control.
dragleave           An object was dragged off of the scroll bar control.
dragover            An object is being dragged over the scroll bar control.
endscroll           Scrolling action has ended.
killfocus           The scroll bar has lost focus.
linedown            The user has scrolled down a line.
lineup              The user has scrolled up a line.
pagedown            The user has scrolled down a page.
pageup              The user has scrolled up a page.
setfocus            The scroll bar has gained focus.
top                 The user has scrolled to the top.
```

User object notifications (prefix = pbm_uon)

```
dragdrop            An object was dropped on the user
                    object control.
dragenter           An object was dragged onto the user object
                    control.
dragleave           An object was dragged off of the user
                    object control.
dragover            An object is being dragged over the user
                    object control.
external01-external25  Used to process messages received externally.
```

Windows messages (prefix = pbm_)

activate	A window has become active or inactive.
activateapp	The window being activated belongs to another application.
askcbformatname	Asks that the contents of the clipboard be copied into a text buffer using a custom format.
cancelmode	The system has canceled a mode (i.e. modal) that it was in.
changecbchain	The window in the clipboard viewer chain of applications is being removed from the chain.
char	Transmits the character pressed on the keyboard.
chartoitem	Assists list boxes in locating items by converting the character from the keyboard.
childactivate	A child window has been moved or activated.
clear	The user is deleting the contents of the current edit control.
close	The window will be closed via the system menu or <Shift>-<F4> from the keyboard.
command	The user has selected a menu item, control, or has used an accelerator key.
compacting	The system is running low on memory. This message is generated when Windows is spending more than 1/8 of the CPU cycles compacting memory.
compareitem	Generated when a new item is added to a list box or combo box. Windows uses this to facilitate comparison of items.
constructor	A PB event indicating that a control is about to be created.
copy	Copies selected text to the clipboard.
create	A window is being created. Generated before the window is visible.
ctlcolor	A control is about to be drawn. Colors may be changed at this point.
cut	Selected text was cut to the clipboard.
deadchar	The user has selected a non-English accent or other special character that will change the next character about to be typed.
deleteitem	An item has been removed from a list or combo box.
destroy	A window is being destroyed after it was removed from the screen.
destroyclipboard	The clipboard contents have been cleared.
devmodechanged	The name of a device in the win.ini file has been changed.
drawclipboard	The contents of the clipboard have changed.
drawitem	One of the contents of a list box or combo box has changed.
dropfiles	This message is transmitted when the left mouse button is released over an application which is registered as a recipient of dropped files.
enable	A window has been enabled or disabled.
endsession	Windows is being shut down.
enteridle	A modal dialog has been activated but has no messages to process.
erasebkgnd	The client area of a window needs to be repainted.
fontchange	The number of fonts available to the application has changed.
getdlgcode	Notification of what type of keyboard is active.
getfont	Retrieves the currently active font.

getminmaxinfo	Windows is checking the size of the minimized or maximized window.
gettext	Copies text from a control, such as a button or edit control, to a memory buffer.
gettextlength	Used to determine the number of characters on a control.
hscroll	The user has adjusted a horizontal scroll bar.
hscrollclipboard	The clipboard's horizontal scroll bar has been used.
iconerasebkgnd	A minimized window needs to have its background repainted.
initdialog	A dialog box is about to be displayed.
initmenu	A menu is about to be displayed.
initmenupopup	A popup menu is about to be displayed.

Windows messages (prefix = pbm_), continued

keydown	A key on the keyboard was pressed.
keyup	A key on the keyboard was released.
killfocus	The window is about to lose focus.
lbuttondblclk	The user has double-clicked the left mouse button.
lbuttondown	The user has pressed the left mouse button.
lbuttonup	The user has released the left mouse button.
mbuttondblclk	The user has double-clicked the middle mouse button.
mbuttondown	The user has pressed the middle mouse button.
mbuttonup	The user has released the middle mouse button.
mdiactivate	A child MDI window (sheet) is being activated.
mdicascade	Arranges all of the sheets in a cascade form.
mdicreate	Creates an MDI child window (sheet).
mdidestroy	Removes a sheet from an MDI frame.
mdigetactive	Obtains the handle of the currently active MDI sheet.
mdiiconarrange	Arranges the icons of the minimized sheets on an MDI frame.
mdimaximize	Maximizes an MDI child sheet.
mdinext	Activates the next MDI sheet (the one immediately behind the active one).
mdirestore	Restores an MDI sheet to its previous size.
mdisetmenu	Links a menu to an MDI sheet.
mditile	Tiles all MDI sheets.
measureitem	This message is sent to the window owning a button or other control about to be created.
menuchar	A keyboard shortcut was used but did not match any shortcuts available.
menuselect	The user has selected a menu item.
mouseactivate	The user has clicked the mouse in an inactive window.
mousemove	The user has moved the mouse.
move	The window has been moved.
ncactivate	The non-client area of a window is about to be activated.
nccalcsize	The size of the window needs to be recalculated.
nccreate	The window is about to create the non-client area of the window.
ncdestroy	The non-client area of the window is being destroyed.
nchittest	Sent every time the mouse is moved in the non-client area.

nclbuttondblclk	The user has double-clicked the left mouse button in the non-client area.
nclbuttondown	The user has pressed the left mouse button in the non-client area.
nclbuttonup	The user has released the left mouse button in the non-client area.
ncmbuttondblclk	The user has double-clicked the middle mouse button in the non-client area.
ncmbuttondown	The user has pressed the middle mouse button in the non-client area.
ncmbuttonup	The user has released the middle mouse button in the non-client area.
ncmousemove	The mouse has been moved in the non-client area.
ncpaint	The non-client area needs to be painted.
ncrbuttondblclk	The user has double-clicked the right mouse button in the non-client area.
ncrbuttondown	The user has pressed the right mouse button in the non-client area.
ncrbuttonup	The user has released the right mouse button in the non-client area.
nextdlgctl	Moves the focus to another control within a dialog box.
paint	The client area of the window needs to be painted.
paintclipboard	The clipboard app transmits that the viewer needs to be repainted.
palettechanged	The system color palette has changed.
paletteischanging	The system color palette is about to be changed.
parentnotify	Notifies the parent window that a child window is being created.

Windows messages (prefix = pbm_), continued

paste	Copies text from the clipboard to an edit control.
querydragicon	The user is about to drag a minimized window.
queryendsession	Notification that Windows is about to be shut down.
querynewpalette	The application is about to receive input focus and should perform any necessary color changes.
queryopen	A minimized window is about to be restored.
quit	The final message processed by an application.
rbuttondblclk	The user has double-clicked the right mouse button.
rbuttondown	The user has pressed the right mouse button.
rbuttonup	The user has released the right mouse button.
renderallformats	Notification to the owner of a clipboard format that the application is losing all formats.
renderformat	Notification that data placed on the clipboard should be sent in a specific format.
setcursor	Notification that the mouse cursor is moving in a window.
setfocus	The window has gained focus.
setfont	Used to change the font in dialog box controls.
setredraw	Sent to a list or combo box prior to adding a new item.
settext	Used to change the title or text on a window.
sizeclipboard	The clipboard viewer application has changed size.
spoolerstatus	A print manager job has been added or subtracted.
syschar	The <Alt> key, plus another key, has been pressed.
syscolorchange	One or more of the system colors have changed.
syscommand	The user has selected a system menu command.
sysdeadchar	Notification of a system dead (non-English precedent) character.
syskeydown	The user has pressed a key plus the <Alt>key.
syskeyup	The user has released an <Alt>-key combination.

```
timechange              The system clock has been changed.
undo                    Copies text from the undo area onto the edit control.
vkeytoitem              The user has pressed a key while a list box
                        has focus.
vscroll                 The user has clicked on the vertical scroll bar.
vscrollclipboard        The clipboard viewer's vertical scroll bar has been
                        clicked.
windowposchanged        The window position has changed.
windowposchanging       The window position is about to change.
wininichange            The win.ini file has changed.
```

Custom messages (prefix = pbm_custom)

```
custom01-75             Seventy-five events that the programmer can
                        create and use.
```

Visual Basic messages (prefix = pbm_vbxevent)

```
vbxevent01-50           Fifty events that are mapped to specific
                        VBX events.
```

An Ad Hoc Query Tool

By Sean Rhody

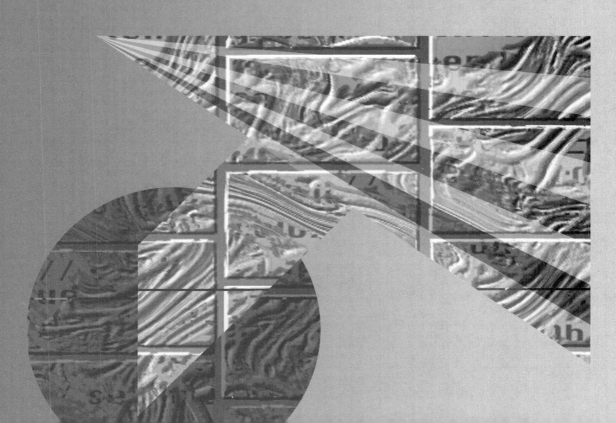

An Ad Hoc Query Tool

by **Sean Rhody**

Users frequently want an ad hoc query tool in their applications. There are several good general purpose tools on the market today that provide this functionality, but all require additional purchases. Rather than asking end users to buy and install these products themselves, I believe it is often better to supply a simple ad hoc tool that will meet most anticipated user needs. When users have a flexible method of saving query data–for instance, to an Excel spreadsheet or a simple text file–they can work with their existing software products to produce reports and charts.

One of the problems with creating a general purpose database-independent query tool is that each RDBMS uses a different method–different system tables–to store additional information such as table names, column names, and relationships. PowerBuilder relies on these tables to display relationship information in the various database-related painters. We're faced with a design choice right at the beginning. Do we try to cover all the bases and build a large system capable of recognizing *all* system tables, or do we go for a smaller, implementation-specific tool, which won't be very portable?

Well, we can do both. We can create PBDs that are specific to a single database from the PBLs that have specific database code. We can then make use of the fact that PBDs can be delivered separately from the executable to deliver the tool we need for whatever database system we decide to work with. We'll do Watcom to learn how to use the RDBMS-specific tables.

Two topics are vital to the approach taken in developing this application. The first of these is dynamic DataWindow creation. This is not an extremely difficult task. It merely involves generating valid SQL syntax to create a new DataWindow. There are several commands to do this, and we'll explore them when we look at the query results window. The main point is that we need to be able to dynamically submit the SQL, because the ad hoc tool has no way of knowing what the query will be before runtime. This technique allows us to do that easily.

The second topic is user objects. There are three user objects in this application, each with a different purpose. Some of these will be assigned to windows at compile time, while others will be created dynamically at runtime. User objects are important because they allow us to extend the functionality of standard objects within PowerBuilder. In this application, we'll take a DataWindow and make it into a table object.

The Application Design

We want the application to be robust, yet simple for user to understand.

We'll use an MDI frame with Microhelp as our main window. We'll treat this as an MDI application, with the query layout and results as the two types of windows supported. To simplify the design, only one layout window will be allowed at any time, although we will allow multiple result windows. In addition, we'll need a window for the where clause information. We'll make this a child of the layout window and let the layout window own it.

The general idea is to allow the user to pick a number of tables, which are then displayed in the layout window as table objects. The user can then select columns from these tables by double-clicking on the column name in the table object. The where clause window will allow the user to create where clause arguments. The next step is to build a query, which will display results in a grid DataWindow.

In order to systematically design and discuss the components of this application, I've broken it down into several PBL files. I'll discuss the application in depth on a PBL by PBL basis. A little background on these files purposes will probably be useful.

The adhoc.pbl file contains all of the application specific functionality. This includes the application open script, the MDI frame and the base menu for the system. This is one of the smaller PBLs in terms of number of objects and code associated with it as well.

The tables.pbl file contains all of the table specific objects and code. The table user object, as well as several support objects are stored in this file. There is a great deal of code associated with this user object.

The common.pbl file holds several common functions, including a string parser, and methods for highlighting single and multiple selection DataWindows.

The layout.pbl file contains the layout window and all associated objects. This is the main file in the application, along with the tables file. There are several windows and two user objects as well as many scripts in this library.

The results.pbl file contains the objects for the results windows. This includes the window and results menu. This is a fairly simple file.

The main thrust of the application lies in the tables and layout files, and in the interaction between the two objects. The layout window is a very complicated object, composed of many table objects as well as other objects, and it provides a great deal of functionality.

Let's take a look at what the finished application will look like.

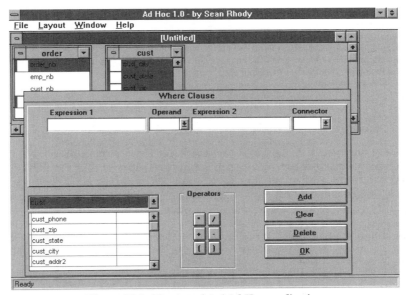

Figure 23-1: The completed Ad Hoc application.

The picture above shows the ad hoc tool with the query layout window open, and the where clause selection dialog box open. After selecting the correct where clause and column names, we'll select build query from the layout menu to generate a result window.

The library files

Let's get the simple libraries out of the way and then progress to tables and layout. We'll start with the adhoc.pbl library. This library contains only three entries–the application object, the main MDI frame, and the base menu.

The application object's sole script is for its open event. This script reads the adhoc.ini file and sets up the sqlca transaction object with the values obtained. It then attempts to connect to the database. If it is successful, the application opens. Otherwise, the application displays an error message and then closes. Here's the script:

```
// fill the transaction object

sqlca.DBMS = ProfileString("adhoc.ini","connection","DBMS","")
sqlca.Database = ProfileString("adhoc.ini","connection","Database","")
sqlca.UserId = ProfileString("adhoc.ini","connection","UserId","")
sqlca.DBPass  = ProfileString("adhoc.ini","connection","DBPass","")
sqlca.LogId   = ProfileString("adhoc.ini","connection","LogId","")
sqlca.LogPass = ProfileString("adhoc.ini","connection","LogPass","")
sqlca.ServerName = ProfileString("adhoc.ini","connection","ServerName","")
sqlca.DBParm  = ProfileString("adhoc.ini","connection","DBParm","")

Connect USING sqlca;

IF sqlca.sqlcode <> 0 THEN
MessageBox("Connection Failed","Could not connect to database.~n" + &
"Transaction information is:~n" + &
"DBMS="+sqlca.DBMS+"~n" + &
"Database="+sqlca.Database+"~n" + &
"DBParm="+sqlca.DBParm)
HALT
END IF

open(w_ad_hoc)
```

Watcom really only needs the DBParm parameter filled in order to connect, but this allows us to develop a database-independent open script. The script checks the SQL code of the transaction object sqlca after the connect is issued. A non-zero value indicates an error, which means we cannot connect to the database. Further processing makes no sense at this point, since the entire application depends on the database connection.

In addition to this application object there is an MDI frame, with a menu. This menu serves as the basis for all other menus in the application. The layout and results menus are both copied directly from here, and then modified.

The menu, m_adhoc_base, has four main choices: File, Actions, Window, and Help.

The Actions choice is not visible, as there are no actions for a base class menu. Instead, the two menus for layout and results add items to this menu.

The File menu offers typical functionality. It provides choices to create a new layout; open an existing layout; print and do print setup; and close and exit the application. Not all of these choices are visible. In particular, Print and Close are not visible.

Since we are going to allow only one layout window, the new layout script ensures that only one instance of the window is in fact open.

```
IF Handle(w_layout) <> 0 THEN
 MessageBox("Open Layout","Only one layout window is allowed!",StopSign!)
 RETURN
END IF
OpenSheetWithParm(w_layout,0,w_ad_hoc,4,Original!)
```

Note that the command to open the window is OpenSheetWithParm. MDI applications use this to help manage the child or "document" windows. Its parameters are the name of the window to be opened; the passed parameter; the MDI frame; the number of the top-level menu that will contain the open window list; and the arrangement type. The open window list is typically attached to the second-to-last menu choice. This is a Windows standard, and should be followed. The Original! enumerated value opens the window at its normal size, rather than attempting to size it to fit in the MDI frame.

The Open Layout choice is similar to the new layout. The difference is that we need to pass a one instead of a zero as the second parameter in the OpenSheetWithParm function. The layout window uses this parameter to determine whether to create a new layout or open an existing layout.

Printing is available for the results windows, but not for the layout windows. The print choice is not visible on the base menu, but is set to be visible on the results window menu, which does implement printing.

Print Setup is available on all menus, and is implemented by calling the function Print-Setup(). This function calls the Windows printer setup dialog box and allows users to change the settings to whatever printer is available.

Close is not visible, because there is nothing to close when the base menu is visible. On the layout and results menus Close is implemented to close their respective windows.

The Actions menu has no submenu, and is not visible on the base menu. It is another place-holder, with actual choices for actions implemented in the layout and results menus.

The Windows menu provides the standard MDI application choices for arranging documents within the MDI frame. These include tiling the windows, cascading the windows, and arranging the icons along the bottom of the MDI frame. It is on this menu that Windows places the open windows list. This list never actually appears on the base menu, because anytime there is a window open, either the results or the layout menu will be active.

Last we have the Help menu. This is another Windows standard. Typically, on-line help is available from this menu. I have not developed an on-line help file for this application, but if you wish to, this is where the file should be called.

In practice, all this menu really does is allow the user to open a layout window. But in reality, the entire application structure is defined here, and copied to all the other menus in the application. I say "copy" because I have opted to copy rather than inherit. This was a personal preference. Although inheritance is a wonderful feature, it still seems to have one or two bugs in it. The next library is the file common.pbl. This library contains some routines that I commonly use to do various tasks. In this case there are only three functions: f_get_token, which is a string parser; udf_dw_hilight, which does single item highlighting in a DataWindow; and udf_multi_hilighting, which does multiple item highlighting in a DataWindow. Let's look at the code.

First of all, f_get_token is a function that is used to parse strings. String parsing is nothing more than breaking one big string into several smaller strings, which are typically called tokens. This function will be used repeatedly in the code to break up lists into individual items. In order to parse a string, we need a string and a delimiter, sometimes called a separator. The delimiter that I use is the semi-colon (";").

Let's look at the function.

```
/*
function udf_get_token(ref string pzSource, string pzSep)

Purpose: Parse pzSource to obtain a token
Returns: String - the token
*/

int   liPos
string  lzRet

liPos = Pos(pzSource, pzSep)

if liPos = 0 then
 lzRet = pzSource
 pzSource = ""
else
 lzRet = Mid(pzSource, 1, liPos - 1)
 pzSource = Mid(pzSource, liPos + 1)
end if

return lzRet
```

The function first searches for the delimiter within the source. If there's no delimiter, it simply returns the whole string and sets the source to the empty string. If there is a delimiter, it gets the token in front of the delimiter by using the Mid()function, and then removes both the token and the delimiter from the source. Finally it returns the token.

The two other functions in common.pbl both have to do with highlighting rows in the DataWindow. Highlighting places a blue background on the row, indicating that it has been selected. Two different situations require this technique, each of which has its own function. In the first situation we want to allow only one row in a DataWindow to be selected: when the user clicks on a new row, the new row is selected and the old row is deselected. The second situation call for multiple selection: the new row is selected, but the old row is *not* deselected. We'll use both techniques when we deal with the layout window. Let's look at the code.

```
/*
function udf_dw_highlight(REFERENCE DataWindow p_dw)

 Purpose: Collects the highlighting code for a DataWindow into
 a function that can be called in all DataWindows

Parameters: p_dw - the DataWindow to be changed.
  passed by ref, so it can be changed.

 Called from: The clicked event of a DataWindow.
*/

// local variables
intl_int_clicked // the row clicked

l_int_clicked = p_dw.GetClickedRow()
if l_int_clicked = 0 THEN
 RETURN
ELSE
 p_dw.SelectRow(0,FALSE)
```

```
   p_dw.SelectRow(l_int_clicked,TRUE)
END IF
```

This function gets the clicked row and checks to make sure that it is valid. (The row could be invalid if the user clicked somewhere else in the client window than in a row.) Next it deselects all selected rows by passing the 0 argument and the FALSE argument to SelectRow(). This is the function that actually performs the highlighting. Last, it selects the new row. Let's look at the multi-selection version.

```
/*
 function udf_multi_highlight(REFERENCE DataWindow p_dw)

Purpose: Collects the highlighting code for a DataWindow
 into a function that can be called in all DataWindows
 Differs from udf_dw_hilight in that it allows multiple selection

Parameters: p_dw - the DataWindow to be changed.
 passed by ref, so it can be changed.

Called from: The clicked event of a DataWindow.
*/

// local variables
int l_int_clicked  // the row clicked
int l_int_selected // the first selected row after the clicked row -1

l_int_clicked = p_dw.GetClickedRow()
if l_int_clicked = 0 THEN
 RETURN

ELSE
 l_int_selected = p_dw.GetSelectedRow(l_int_clicked - 1)
 IF l_int_selected = l_int_clicked THEN
 p_dw.SelectRow(l_int_Clicked,FALSE)
 ELSE
 p_dw.SelectRow(l_int_clicked,TRUE)
 END IF
END IF
```

This one is a little trickier. It starts off the same, by determining if the clicked row is valid. Then it calls GetSelectedRow() with the clicked row minus one as a parameter. GetSelected-Row() returns the next selected row *after* the row passed. In this case, if this row is equal to the clicked row, then the row is already selected and must be deselected. This is done in the IF...THEN statement.

To talk about the results.pbl library before the layout and tables libraries seems like putting the cart before the horse. However the result library is fairly simple, and will give us an understanding of where we are headed when we design the table and layout library entries.

There are only two objects in the result library, the result window w_result and the corresponding menu m_adhoc_result. The w_result window is very simple–it has only a single DataWindow control. No DataWindow object is assigned to this control. Instead, we will dynamically create and assign a DataWindow object in the open event of the window. This is not as difficult as it sounds, since we intend to provide only a basic grid DataWindow for display purposes. There are two functions involved in this process, dwSyntaxFromSQL(), and dwCreate().

The dwSyntaxFromSQL() function generates a string containing the syntax needed by dwCreate() to create a new DataWindow. It requires a connected transaction object (sqlca); the SQL syntax; an optional string which contains additional information about how to build the DataWindow (which we provide); and a string in which to store error information.

In the event that an error occurs in the SQL syntax, a message is returned and the window is closed. Otherwise, the DataWindow is built and retrieved.

```
/*
 open event for w_result

 Purpose: Open the window and create a new DataWindow with results based
 on the passed query.
 Parameters: Message.StringParm contains the SQL statement to be used to
 build the DataWindow
 Called from: The clicked event of a DataWindow.
*/

string  lzSQL            // the SQL syntax
string  lzErr            // used to check for errors
string  lzSyntax         // the DataWindow syntax

lzSQL = Message.StringParm   // get the SQL string

// build the DataWindow syntax from the SQL
lzSyntax = dwSyntaxFromSQL(sqlca,lzSQL,"Style(type=grid)",lzErr)

// check for syntax errors
IF LEN(lzErr) > 0 THEN
 MessageBox("Syntax Error Occurred","Database Message was" + &
 ": "+lzErr+"~r~n~r~n" + &
 "Syntax was: "+lzSQL,StopSign!, Ok!)
 close(this)
ELSE

 // create the DataWindow
 dw_1.dwCreate(lzSyntax)
 // set the transaction object
 dw_1.SetTransObject(sqlca)
 // retrieve the results
 dw_1.Retrieve()
 // show the DataWindow
 dw_1.Show()
END IF
```

The m_adhoc_result menu adds only two functions to the basic menu. It implements the Print command and the Save command, which allows the user to save the results to a file for further manipulation. Both functions are short, with only one real line of functionality in each. There's one subtle point, though, that deserves a closer look.

We want to have the DataWindow print itself using the Print() function. We need a way to reference this from the menu, as this particular application offers no command buttons or other controls to activate these functions from the window. So we declare a variable of type w_result, called lwMyWin.

Ordinarily, just as in the structure painter we create a structure definition and not a structure variable, so in the window painter we create a window definition. Since that is so, how is it that we can open a window by using the definition name? It works because PowerBuilder automatically creates a variable of the same name when we use the definition in that way.

So why do we need to declare our own variable? Well, we can't just refer to the w_result window in the menu script by using the ParentWindow keyword. ParentWindow is a window type that does not contain our dw_1 DataWindow. Why not? Because PowerBuilder creates all window objects as descendants of a base window class, the window datatype. (And you thought we avoided inheritance!) The ParentWindow keyword refers to this base window type, which can be used to refer to any window object. The problem lies in the fact that this window is completely empty. Therefore it cannot reference any control on our actual w_result window. For example, trying to compile ParentWindow.dw_1.Print() will result in a compiler error indicating that dw_1 is not a control on ParentWindow.

In C/C++ programming, a technique known as casting converts one datatype into another. We can use a similar technique here to do the work we want. We declare a variable of the type w_result. We then assign ParentWindow to it. This has the effect of assigning the correct window to lwMyWin. Now, since lwMyWin is of type w_result, we can reference the DataWindow dw_1 on it as follows.

```
/*
 clicked event for m_print

Purpose: print the DataWindow.
*/

w_result  lwMyWin
lwMyWin = Parentwindow
lwMyWin.dw_1.Print()
```

Similarly we can do the same type of thing in the m_saveresult clicked script.

```
/*
 clicked event for m_saveresult

 Purpose: save the DataWindow.
*/

w_result  lwMyWin
lwMyWin = Parentwindow
lwMyWin.dw_1.SaveAs()
```

This event script allows the user to save the data in the DataWindow in any number of file formats.

The next library is tables.pbl, which contains all of the various PowerBuilder objects needed to represent a table for the layout window. The table object is built by creating a standard user object derived from a DataWindow. Next a specific DataWindow is associated with the object, which permits the required column information to be retrieved from the database. This DataWindow will need to change with each different database, as it will access the database system tables to obtain its information.

Several objects are needed to create the table object. The first is a structure for passing information into the table as it opens. The picture below illustrates the definition:

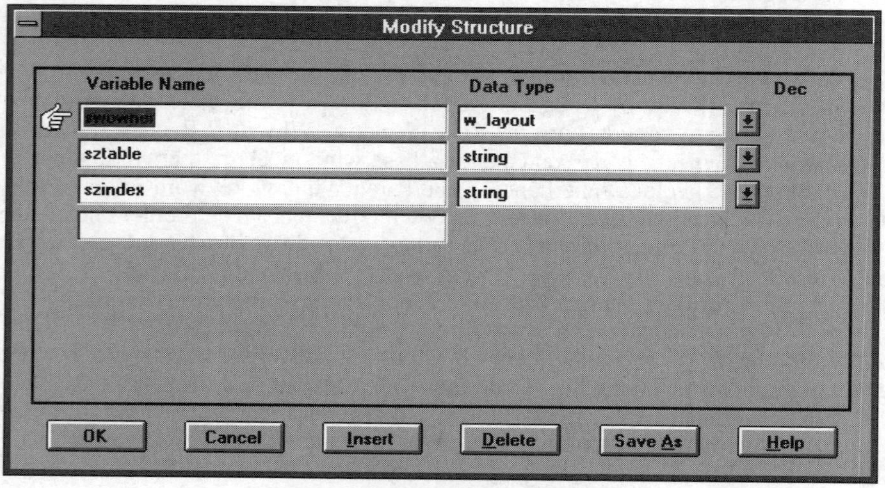

Figure 23-2: Structure s_uo_parm.

There are three parameters in this structure. The first, swowner, is of the type w_layout, which is the layout window datatype. This is used so that the table object can reference its owner. The second parameter is sztable, which tells the object the name of the table that it represents. The last parameter, szindex, tells the table what its array index is on the w_layout window. The array index, by reusing closed table objects, helps minimize the amount of memory space used for table objects. We will see this in detail when we discuss the layout.pbl file.

This structure is passed in as a parameter to the user object via a call to OpenUserObjectWithParm(). The w_layout window populates the structure with the appropriate parameters, and makes the call.

The second structure needed for the table object is a DataWindow. This DataWindow is called d_table2. It accesses Watcom's sys.sys_columns table.

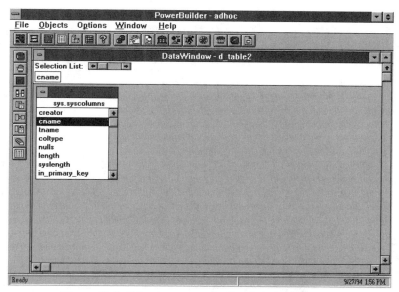

Figure 23-3: Select statement for DataWindow d_table2.

Only one column, the cname column, is selected from this table. The table name already passed in via the structure above is used in the where clause to define which table to select. For example, if this were the employee table, sztable in the structure would read "employee." When the retrieve is issued for the DataWindow, its argument would be "employee." In the where clause this is used as a retrieval argument, which effectively setting the SQL statement to the following:

```
SELECT   sys.sys_columns.cname
FROM     sys.sys_columns
WHERE    sys.sys_columns.tname = "employee";
```

Although only one column is selected from the table, there appear to be two columns in the DataWindow. In fact one of them is a bitmap, set to a bitmap called nk.bmp. The nk part stands for "No Key." This field is not currently used, but may be used to support a display of bitmaps indicating primary keys. All the tab orders on this DataWindow are set to 0. The user should not be able to modify any of this information.

The last piece of the table object puzzle is the most complex: the table object is implemented as a standard user object called uo_dw_table. This object implements all of the extended functionality added to the basic DataWindow to make it behave as a table. It looks like this.

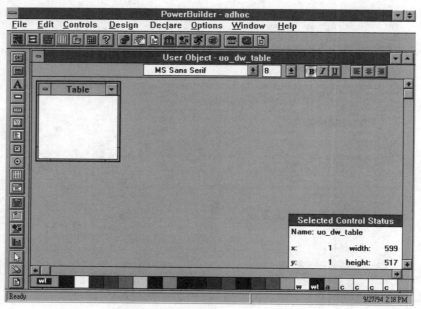

Figure 23-4: User Object uo_dw_table.

This is a very complex object containing user object functions, several instance variables, and several user-defined events. The best place to start in on it is with the instance variables. These are declared as follows:

```
string iz_uo_tablename // the tablename
string iz_uo_index     // the place in the user object array on w_layout
w_layout iw_uo_owner   // the layout window
boolean ib_active      // whether the table is active
```

Each of these variables stores some key piece of information that is needed at some point in processing. The iz_uo_tablename variable stores the name of the table. The iz_uo_index stores where the table object is in the user object array on the w_layout window. The iw_uo_owner variable stores a reference to the layout window, so that window functions can be called. The boolean ib_active variable indicates whether the table object is currently active or if it has been closed. One important point is that closing the table object, by double-clicking on the control menu, does not trigger or cause the destructor event. This only occurs when the user closes the entire program, or if somehow the event is triggered from a script.

In addition to the instance variables, there are several window functions. These functions are:

```
1. udf_get_selected()        Returns a list of selected columns
2. udf_get_x()               Returns the X coordinate
3. udf_get_y()               Returns the Y coordinate
4. udf_set_selection()       Toggles a columns selection
5. udf_uo_get_tablename()    Returns the table name of
                             the object ( iz_uo_tablename)
```

Let's examine these functions.

```
/*
 Function  udf_get_selected()
 Purpose: returns the selected columns, in a string containing
 the row, and the data. Used when opening a saved layout
*/

string lzColRows[]
string lzReturn
long llRow
long llCounter = 1
long llSize

// get the first selected row
llRow = This.GetSelectedRow(0)

// loop through the selected rows
DO WHILE llRow > 0
 lzColRows[llCounter] = String(llRow)  // add an entry
 llrow = This .GetSelectedRow(llRow )  // get the next selected row
LOOP

// build lzReturn, the return string
llSize = UpperBound(lzColRows)
FOR llCounter = 1 to llsize -1
 lzReturn = lzReturn + lzColRows[llCounter]+";"
NEXT

lzReturn = lzReturn + lzColRows[llSize]
return lzReturn
```

This function relies on the database to return the column names in the same order every time. It only saves the row number. This information gets stored in a layout file, and fed back in when an existing layout is opened.

The udf_get_X() and udf_get_Y() functions simply return the current x and y coordinates so that the table can be positioned in the same place when a saved layout is reopened. They simply return This.X and This.Y.

The udf_set_selected() function is used to select rows (which correspond to the columns of a table) when a saved layout is reopened.

```
/*
function udf_set_selected(string pzcols)

Purpose: restore the selected columns list from a saved layout
*/

string    lzToken
string    lzIn
string    lzTable
```

```
string    lzColumn
int       liRow
w_layout wLayoutWin

// get the layout window in order to update it's selections too.
wlayoutWin = iw_uo_owner

// the passed in list
lzIn = pzCols
lzToken = f_get_token(lzIn,";")

// loop and parse
DO WHILE lzToken <> ""
 liRow = Integer(lzToken)
 This.SelectRow(liRow,TRUE)

 // update the layout selections
 lzTable = iz_uo_tablename
 lzColumn = This.GetItemString(liRow,1)
 wLayoutWin.udf_wf_update_selection(lzTable,lzColumn,TRUE)
 lzToken = f_get_token(lzIn,";")
LOOP
```

The function gets a list of rows that are to be reselected. (The list was stored in the file that contains the saved query.) It parses the string of numbers to get the individual rows to be selected, and selects them. Then it updates the layout window selection list by calling its udf_wr_update_selection() function.

The next function is udf_uo_get_tablename().

```
/*
function  udf_uo_get_tablename()

Purpose: If the table is active ( i.e. visible ) return the name of the table
 otherwise ( table is closed, not visible ) return an empty string
*/

IF ib_active THEN
 return(iz_uo_tablename)
ELSE
 return("")
END IF
```

This function is used when the where clause window is updated. If the table is visible then it returns its name. If it's not visible, the function returns the empty string. Remember that closing the table does not destroy it–as long as it exists in the array on w_layout, it's still going to be referenced by w_layout. When w_layout opens its where clause window, it updates the list of tables by looping through its array of table objects. Because the closed tables still exist in the array, this function is called for them as well. To prevent their names from appearing in the list we return the empty string.

The next step is to discuss the events that a table will process. These events are constructor, clicked, doubleclicked, and two user defined events, ue_do_retrieve and ue_close. The ue_do_retrieve event retrieves the column names for the table, and is defined as pbm_custom01. The ue_close event intercepts the close of the window to perform processing, and is defined as pbm_showwindow. Note that pbm_showwindow occurs when the table opens as well as when it closes, so the script needs a way to distinguish between these two states. This accomplished by use of the ib_active instance variable.

The constructor event is used to set up the table object.

```
/*
constructor event for uo_dw_table

Purpose: Sets the Transaction object, and retrieves the
 passed table name
*/

// local variables
w_layout  MyOwner
string lzTable
s_uo_parm Parm

// get the passed parameter
Parm = Message.PowerObjectParm

// unload the passed parameter into the instance variables
iz_uo_tablename = Parm.szTable
iz_uo_index = Parm.szIndex
iw_uo_owner = Parm.swOwner

// setup a transaction object and retriev the column names
This.SetTransObject(sqlca)
This.Retrieve(iz_uo_tablename)

// set the table title
This.Title = iz_uo_tablename

// set to false so that ue_close can work correctly
ib_active = FALSE
```

The clicked and doubleclicked events are exactly the same. Their purpose is to highlight or dehighlight the clicked row. This is an important event, because selecting a row must add it to the selection list for w_layout, while deselecting a row must remove it from the list.

```
/*
 clicked or doubleclicked event for uo_dw_table

Purpose:  Control selection of column names
*/

long llRow
long    llNext
w_layout  wLayoutWin
string    lzTable
string lzColumn

// get the layout window
wLayoutWin = iw_uo_owner

// get the clicked row
llRow = this.GetClickedRow()

// check for errors
IF llRow = 0 THEN
```

```
RETURN
END IF

/*

Check to see if llrow is highlighted.

This is done by calling getselectedrow with llrow - 1 as the argument

This returns the number of the next selected row after llrow - 1.
If llrow is selected, then llNext will be equal to llRow
*/

llNext = this.GetSelectedRow(llRow - 1)
lzTable = iz_uo_tablename
lzColumn = this.GetItemString(llRow,"cname")

// change the selection DataWindow on w_layout by calling its
// udf_wf_update_selection function

IF llRow = llNext THEN        // llNext is already highlighted
  this.SelectRow(llRow,FALSE)
  wLayoutWin.udf_wf_update_selection(lzTable,lzColumn,FALSE)
ELSE
  this.SelectRow(llRow,TRUE)
  wLayoutWin.udf_wf_update_selection(lzTable,lzColumn,TRUE)
END IF
```

The ue_do_retrieve event script is a one liner that simply does a retrieve on the DataWindow. It's not currently used, but can be used to refresh the data in the table object, if needed.

The ue_close script is used to update the table object array on the w_layout window. The pbm_showwindow event ID corresponds to the event that occurs when the user double-clicks the control menu on the table object. It also happens to occur when the table is initially displayed.

```
/*
ue_close event for uo_dw_table

Purpose:  update the table array on w_layout
*/

// local variables
w_layout  wLayoutWin

// see if the window (table) is open
IF NOT ib_active THEN // this is what happens when the table opens
                      // initially
ib_active = TRUE
ELSE                  // this is what happens when the table is closed
wLayoutWin = iw_uo_owner

// update the free entry list, so that this array slot can be reused.
  wLayoutWin.udf_update_free_entry(iz_uo_index)
  ib_active = FALSE
END IF
```

Summary of table object

The table object receives its name and other information at creation via a structure that's passed to it as a parameter. Using this name it retrieves from the database system table a list of the relevant column names, and places them in rows in the DataWindow. Clicking on a row selects or deselects the row and updates the selected rows list for the w_layout window. The ue_close event works with the w_layout window to minimize the memory needed for the table objects by allowing the w_layout window to reuse an array member (which is a table) that has been closed. This limits the size of the array to the highest number of table objects open together at any one time.

The most complex part of the entire application is the layout window, w_layout, which is part of the layout.pbl file. It includes three windows, three DataWindows, two user objects, and one menu. The best way to explore this is to look at the windows in turn. The simplest window is the w_sql_syntax window.

The w_sql_syntax window is used to show the current SQL syntax based on the tables selected, the columns selected, and the data in the w_where_clause window. This window has only two controls–a multiline edit control which is used to display the SQL, and a command button which is used to close the window.

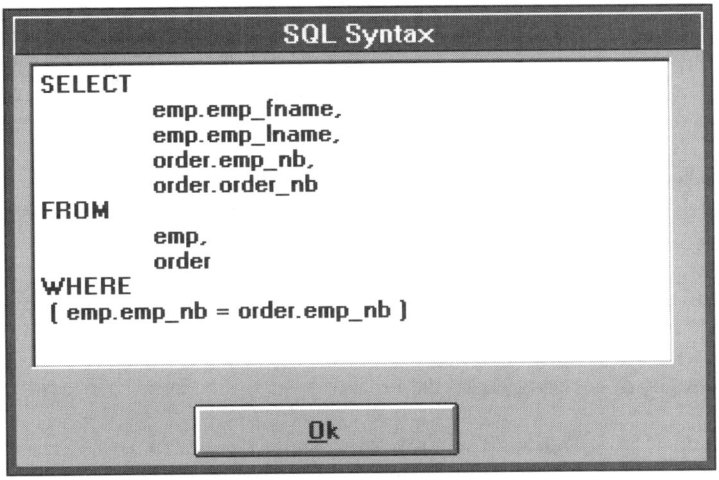

Figure 23-5: The w_sql_syntax window at work.

The open script is only three lines of code, used to assign the passed-n string to the text of the multiline edit.

```
/*
 open event for w_sql_syntax

 Purpose: Assign text to the mutliline edit control
*/

String lzParm
lzParm = Message.StringParm
mle_1.Text = lzParm
```

The w_where_clause window is used to build the where clause for the SQL statement. It provides an interface similar to that of PowerBuilder for selecting the parts of the where clause, although it is slightly simplified. The window is composed of two DataWindows, a drop-down list box, a user object for arithmetic controls, and four command buttons. The Add button adds a new line in the where clause. The Clear button clears the entire where clause. The Delete button removes the current line from the where clause, and the OK button simply hides the where clause.

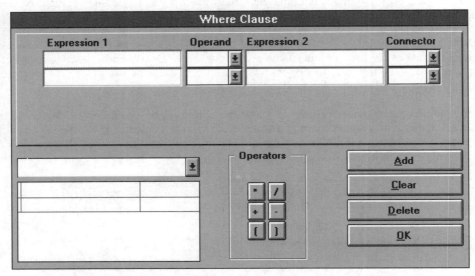

Figure 23-6: The w_where_clause window.

This is a fairly complex window. In addition to allowing the user to select the statements for the where clause, it is responsible for supplying two forms of the statement: one, with line feeds embedded, is for use with the w_sql_syntax window, and the other is for use in building the result window. It must be updated every time a table is opened or closed so that it can update the table list of the drop-down list box.

It will be easier to understand the window as a whole if we look at several of the window controls separately. The first of these is the DataWindow d_where_clause. This is an external DataWindow with a tabular presentation style.

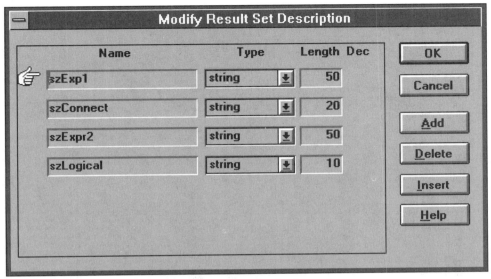

Figure 23-7: Result set for d_where_clause.

There are four fields in this DataWindow. They are szExp1, the first expression; szConnect, a connector; szExp2, the second expression; and szLogical, a logical connector between statements. szConnect and szLogical are drop-down list boxes with code tables assigned. The szConnect contains the most common connectors, such as =, <>, >, <, >=, <=, NOT, LIKE, IN, BETWEEN. The szLogical contains only two logical connectors, AND and OR.

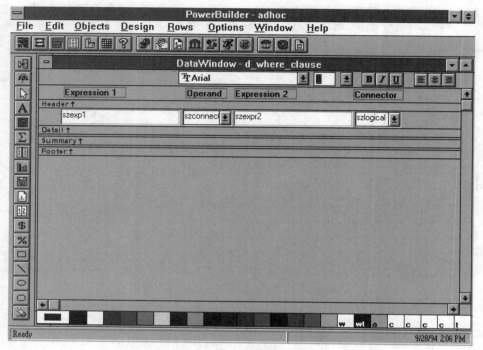

Figure 23-8: The d_where_clause DataWindow.

The d_where DataWindow is composed of only two fields, the table name and column name for a table. The data source for this DataWindow is also external, with a grid presentation style. On the DataWindow itself the size of the table name column has been reduced almost to nothing so as to hide it from the user. The table name will be used to set up a filter expression so that only columns from the table selected (via the drop-down list box) are displayed.

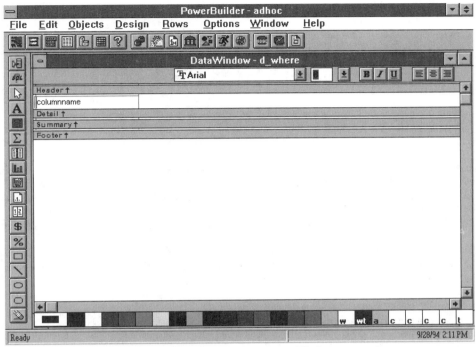

Figure 23-9: The d_where DataWindow.

The operator controls are a single user object, uo_where_controls. These controls simply add the appropriate operator to the active edit. For example, the "*" control triggers a user event, ue_multiply, on the user object control. The script for this is formally identical to all the other scripts for this control. Only the text differs.

```
/*
 ue_multiply event for uo_1

Purpose: Add a multiplication element into the active edit
*/

string lzSelected
string lzText

// il_row and il_col contain the last active row and
// column numbers in the dw_where_clause dw
IF ((il_row = 0) OR (il_col = 0)) THEN

 MessageBox("Invalid Row","Please add a row to the where clause first!")
 RETURN
END IF

// set the focus back to the where clause and select the appropriate row and
column
dw_where_clause.SetFocus()
dw_where_clause.SetColumn(il_col)
dw_where_clause.SetRow(il_row)
```

```
// get the current text
lzText = dw_where_clause.GetItemString(il_row, il_col)

// prevent nulls from causing an error
IF IsNull(lzText) THEN
 lzText = ""
END IF

// add the multiply
lzText = lzText+"*"

// set the new text back to the DataWindow
dw_where_clause.SetItem(il_row,il_col,lzText)
```

This script illustrates an important point. In order to provide its functionality, the window (by using dw_where_clause) needs to keep track of which row and column last had focus. Focus should always be on a row and column in this DataWindow. Whenever a user makes the focus leave the DataWindow by clicking on one of the other controls, the window must store the current row and column positions so that focus can later return to the proper place.

What happens when a table name is selected from the drop-down list box? The DataWindow dw_where has its filter set to the name of the table. This effectively filters out all the data in the DataWindow which is unrelated to the table in question.

```
/*
 selection_changed event for ddlb_1, the table listbox

Purpose: Set the dw_where filter to show only the columns from
 the selected table.
*/

string   lzFilter
string   lzTable
int      liRetCode

// get the new table name
lzTable = This.Text

IF IsNull(lzTable) or lzTable = "" THEN
 RETURN
END IF

// set the filter condition
lzFilter = "table = '"+lzTable+"'"

// set the filter - SetFilter does not actual do the filter, just sets it up!
liRetCode = dw_where.SetFilter(lzFilter)

// To actually make the filter happen Filter is required.
dw_where.Filter()
```

Now that we've examined some of the controls on the window, let's try to understand the window itself. The window has two instance variables, both of type long, which store the row and column information that was mentioned above. These two variables are il_row and il_col.

There are four window functions.

1.udf_add_columns	Adds columns to the DataWindow dw_where based on table
2.udf_wf_build_clause	Builds a where clause for the w_sql_syntax window
3.udf_wf_str_clause	Builds a where clause for the results window generation
4.udf_wf_update	Updates the window.

Let's take a look.

```
/*
udf_add_columns(string pztablename, DataWindow pdwcols)

Purpose: selects the column names from the database
         and adds them to the DataWindow
*/

string    lzColName
long      llRow

// use a cursor, because dw_where_clause is an external data source
// cursor gets the column names from the database

 DECLARE c_col_names CURSOR FOR
   SELECT "sys"."syscolumns"."cname"
     FROM "sys"."syscolumns"
    WHERE "sys"."syscolumns"."tname" = :pzTableName   ;

OPEN c_col_names;

FETCH c_col_names
INTO  :lzColName ;

// loop through the cursor until out of data
DO WHILE sqlca.sqlcode = 0
 // update dw_where
 llRow = pdwcols.InsertRow(0)
 pdwcols.SetRow(0)
 pdwcols.SetItem(llRow,"columnname",lzColName)
 pdwcols.SetItem(llRow,"table",pzTableName)

 FETCH c_col_names
 INTO  :lzColName ;
LOOP

// always close the cursor!!!
CLOSE c_col_names ;
```

This function adds the table and column names to the dw_where DataWindow.

```
/*
 udf_wf_build_clause()

Purpose:  build the where clause and return it differs from
 udf_wf_str_clause in that it inserts carriage returns
 for screen display.
*/
```

```
string    lzExpr1
string    lzExpr2
string    lzOp
string    lzConn
String    lzClause
long      lRowCount
long      lCounter

// loop through the rows in dw_where_clause
llRowCount = dw_where_clause.RowCount()

IF llRowCount = 0 THEN
return ""
END IF


FOR llCounter = 1 to llRowCount
// set the row to the current count
dw_where_Clause.SetRow(llCounter)

// get the variables
 lzExpr1 = dw_where_clause.GetItemString(llCounter,1)
 lzOp    = dw_where_clause.GetItemString(llCounter,2)
 lzExpr2 = dw_where_clause.GetItemString(llCounter,3)
 lzConn  = dw_where_clause.GetItemString(llCounter,4)

// prevent null values
IF IsNull(lzExpr1) THEN
lzExpr1 = ""
END IF
IF IsNull(lzExpr2) THEN
lzExpr2 = ""
END IF
IF IsNull(lzOp) THEN
lzOp = ""
END IF
IF IsNull(lzConn) THEN
lzConn = ""
END IF

 // add a line feed
 IF llCounter > 1 THEN
 lzClause = lzClause +"~r~n"
 END IF
 lzClause = lzClause +" ( " + lzExpr1 + " "+lzOp+" "+lzExpr2+" )"+lzConn
NEXT

// return the completed where clause
Return lzClause
```

The function loops through the rows in the dw_where clause and builds the clause in the lzClause variable. It adds line feeds to automate formatting of the w_sql_syntax window. The udf_wf_str_clause is almost identical, but leaves out the line feeds.

The udf_wf_update() function updates the drop-down list box and the dw_where DataWindow.

```
/*
 udf_wf_update(string pzTables)
```

```
Purpose: This function updates the ddlb and DataWindow. It takes a
 list of tables and repopulates these objects
*/

string   lzTables
string   lzToken
int      liPos

lzTables = pzTables
// reset the ddlb and DataWindow
ddlb_1.Reset()
dw_where.Reset()

IF IsNull(lzTables) or lzTables = "" THEN
 RETURN
END IF

// parse the string
liPos = Pos(lzTables,";")

IF liPos = 0 THEN
 lzToken = lzTables
 lzTables = ""
ELSE
 lzToken = Mid(lzTables,1,liPos - 1)
 lzTables = Mid(lzTables,liPos+1)
END IF

// loop through the table list, updating the ddlb and DataWindow
DO WHILE ( (NOT IsNull(lzToken)) AND (lzToken <> ""))
 ddlb_1.AddItem(lzToken)
 // now build the DataWindow part
 udf_add_columns(lzToken,dw_where)

 // more parsing
 liPos = Pos(lzTables,";")

 IF liPos = 0 THEN
 lzToken = lzTables
 lzTables = ""
 ELSE
 lzToken = Mid(lzTables,1,liPos - 1)
 lzTables = Mid(lzTables,liPos+1)
 END IF
LOOP
```

This function takes a list of table names and populates the drop-down list box and dw_where DataWindows with the appropriate data, using udf_add_columns to fill the DataWindow. It gets called whenever the w_layout window shows the where clause window.

Before we cover the layout window, let's take a look at the other user object in layout.pbl. This object is uo_dw_selection, and is a standard user object derived from a DataWindow. This DataWindow keeps track of all the selected columns for the layout.

This user object uses the d_selection DataWindow as its base. It adds two functions for adding and removing columns. The DataWindow is an external source DataWindow with a grid presentation style, and it has two string columns: table and column name.

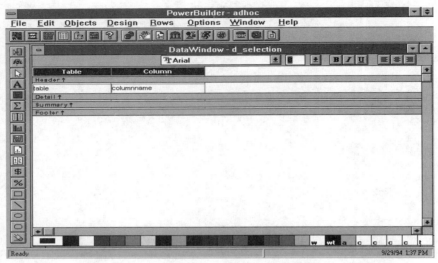

Figure 23-10: The d_selection DataWindow.

The user object looks like this.

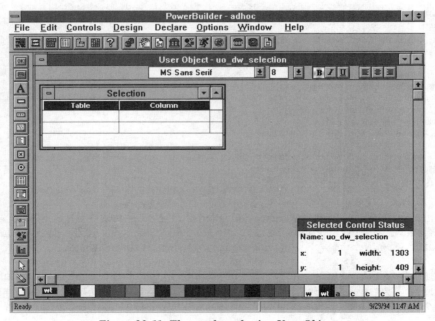

Figure 23-11: The uo_dw_selection User Object.

The two user object functions are called udf_uo_add_col() and udf_uo_delete_col(). They are used to add and remove columns from the selection list. The udf_uo_add_col() function is easier, it simply needs to insert a row and fill the values.

```
/*
 udf_uo_add_col(string pzTable, string pzColumn)

 Purpose: add a table/column to the DataWindow
*/

long llRow

// insert a new row
llRow =this.InsertRow(0)
// set the values
This.SetItem(llRow,"Table",pzTable)
This.SetItem(llRow,"Columnname",pzColumn)
```

The udf_uo_delete_col() is a little more complicated, because it needs to find the correct row and then delete it.

```
/*
 udf_uo_delete_col(string pzTable, string pzColumn)

Purpose: Delete a specific table/column
*/

string lzTable
string lzColumn
int liCount
int liRowCount

// find out how many rows
liRowCount = This.RowCount()

// loop through the rows
FOR liCount=1 TO liRowCount

// get the table name for this row
 lzTable = This.GetItemString(liCount,"table")
 IF lzTable = pzTable THEN

 // table name matches, see if this is the right column too
 lzColumn = This.GetItemString(liCount,"columnname")
 IF lzColumn = pzColumn THEN
 This.DeleteRow(liCount)
 liCount = liRowCount+1
 END IF
 END IF
NEXT
```

The m_adhoc_layout menu is the next logical step in discussion the layout window. It is based on the m_adhoc_base menu, but it implements functions on the actions menu. Let's take a look.

The file menu now supports two additional choices, Save Layout and Close Layout. The Save Layout choice triggers the ue_savelayout event on the w_layout window. The Close Layout choice simply closes the layout window. The services menu is disabled. This menu was part of the original design, but is not used in the actual implementation, so it's hidden. The action menu has changed titles to read Layout. The layout menu allows the user to add tables to the layout, build a query, show the selection window, use the where clause window, and show the SQL syntax for the layout. Almost all of these selections simply trigger an event on the w_layout window. Let's go down the list.

```
/*
 clicked event for m_addtables
*/
TriggerEvent(myWin,"ue_addtables")
 The Build Query choice works a little differently, because it needs to open
a window.
/*
 clicked event for m_buildquery
*/

w_layout myWin
String lzSQL

myWin = ParentWindow

// get the SQL
lzSQL = MyWin.udf_get_sql_syntax()

// open the results window
OpenSheetWithParm(w_result,lzSQL,w_ad_hoc,4,Original!)
```

The Where Clause selection is used to display the where clause window. This window is not actually opened by this selection although that is how it appears to the user. Instead the window is hidden so that it can retain the values between uses.

The ue_togglewhere event is used to show and hide this window.

```
/*
 clicked event for m_whereclause
*/

TriggerEvent(ParentWindow,"ue_togglewhere")
```

There's a little more code to the Show/Hide Selections menu choice, simply because it manipulates the text of the menu choice, changing it from Show to Hide and back again in response to user actions. It uses the ib_show variable to determine which state it is in and toggles that value each time.

```
/*
clicked event for m_showselection
*/

w_layout wOwner
wOwner = ParentWindow

IF ib_show THEN
 ib_show = FALSE
 wOwner.dw_1.Hide()
 This.Text = "Show S&election"
ELSE
 ib_show= TRUE
 wOwner.dw_1.Show()
 This.Text = "Hide S&election"
END IF
```

The layout window

At last we can discuss the layout window itself. Most of the functionality of the entire application is here. This window has to manage all of the table objects, the where clause, and the selection DataWindow. It implements all of the functionality to save a layout, load a layout, add tables, and open a result window.

Again the best place to start is with the instance variables. These are declared as follows:

```
uo_dw_table          iu_dw_table_array[]
string               iz_free_entry
integer              ii_xspace, ii_yspace
integer              ii_level, ii_count
w_where_clause       iw_where
boolean              ib_where
```

The iu_dw_table_array is an array of uo_dw_table objects. This is how the window manages all of the table objects and coordinates the various other activities that deal with table objects. The iz_free_entry string is a list of entries in the iu_dw_table_array that have been marked as available. When a table object is closed, its array entry is marked as available. The next time a table object is opened, rather than expand the array, the next free entry is used.

The ii_xspace and ii_yspace variables are used to keep track of the default spacing between table objects in the layout window. These values are read from the adhoc.ini file, so the user is free to modify these as desired.

The ii_level and ii_count variables are also used to determine placement of the table objects in the layout window. The ii_level is used to control the y coordinate and the ii_count is used to control the x coordinate. These values ensure that the layout window opens no more than four table objects across, and also help to ensure that a new table is not opened on top of an existing one.

The iw_where variable is the where clause window for the layout. This is used in several scripts. The ib_where variable is used to determine if the where clause window is open (visible).

In addition to the instance variables, there are several window functions. These functions are:

```
1. udf_get_free_entry()        Returns the first free enty in the table array
2. udf_get_sql_syntax()        Returns the current SQL Syntax
3. udf_update_free_entry()     Updates the free entry list
4. udf_wf_build_table_list()   Builds a list of tables for SQL
5. udf_wf_update_selection()   Updates the selection DataWindow
```

Let's examine each function.

```
/*
udf_get_free_entry()

Purpose: This function returns the first free
array entry on the list. This prevents
the array from growing out of control as
```

```
the user opens and closes tables.
 If the list is empty it returns zero, otherwise
 it grabs the first array entry off of the list
*/

int liRet

IF IsNull(iz_free_entry) or iz_free_entry = "" THEN
 RETURN(0)
ELSE
 liRet = Integer(f_get_token(iz_free_entry,";"))
END IF

return(liRet)
```

This function is actually fairly simple. If the list is empty, it simply returns a zero to indicate that the layout must increase the iu_dw_table_array size by one. Otherwise it peels off the first entry in the iz_free_entry string and returns it as an integer. Storing the list as a string simplifies many functions, although it does add the need to convert back and forth from integers to strings.

```
/*
 udf_get_SQL_syntax

 Purpose: Return the current SQL statement
 based on the selection window and the
 Where clause window. No validation
 checking is performed.
*/

// build sql statement

string     lzTableList
string     lzSelection
String     lzTable
String     lzColumnname
string     lzWhereClause
string     lzSQL
long       llRowCount, llCounter

// build the select statement
lzSQL = "SELECT "

llRowCount = dw_1.RowCount()
FOR llCounter = 1 to llRowCount
 dw_1.SetRow(llRowCount)
 lzTable = dw_1.GetItemString(llCounter,"table")
 lzColumnname = dw_1.GetItemString(llCounter,"columnname")
 lzSelection = lzTable+"."+lzColumnname
 lzSQL = lzSQL +lzSelection
 IF llCounter < llRowCount THEN
 lzSQL = lzSQL + ","
 END IF
NEXT

// build the from list
lzTableList = udf_wf_build_table_list()

IF IsNull(lzTableList) OR lzTableList = "" THEN
```

```
return ""
END IF

lzTable = f_get_token(lzTableList,";")
lzSQL = lzSQL + " FROM "
DO WHILE lzTable <> ""
 lzSQL = lzSQL +lzTable
 IF lzTableList = "" THEN
 lzTable = ""
 ELSE
 lzSQL = lzSQL + ","
 lzTable = f_get_token(lzTableList,";")
 END IF
LOOP

// get the where clause
lzWhereClause = iw_where.udf_wf_str_clause()

IF lzWhereClause <> "" THEN
 lzSQL = lzSQL +" WHERE"
 lzSQL = LzSQL + lzWhereClause
END IF

return lzSQL
```

This function has three distinct phases. The first phase loops through the rows in the selection DataWindow to obtain the column names for the select portion of the statement. It the calls the udf_wf_build_table_list() function to obtain the tables needed for the from portion of the statement, and then calls the udf_wf_str_clause() function of the where clause window to obtain the expressions for the where portion of the statement.

```
/*
 udf_update_free_entry( String pznext)

 Purpose: This function updates the free entry list
 for the layout window. This list contains
 a string with semicolon seperated integer
 values, that denote array entries that are
 available for reuse. This minimizes the
 amount of memory allocated for the table array.
*/

IF iz_free_entry = "" or IsNull(iz_free_entry) THEN
 iz_free_entry = pzNext
ELSE
 iz_free_entry = iz_free_entry+";"+pzNext
END IF
```

This function's sole purpose is to manage the free entry list for the layout window. It adds the entry to the list either by appending it to the existing list or by assigning it to the currently empty list.

```
/*
 udf_wf_build_table_list()

 Purpose: this function builds a list of table names by calling
 the udf_uo_get_tablename function for each table object
 in the iu_dw_table_array array. It relies on the
 fact that the udf_uo_get_tablename function returns
 an empty string "" if the table has been closed.
```

```
*/

string lzRet, lzTable
int   liBound
int   liCount

liBound = UpperBound(iu_dw_table_array)
lzRet = ""
FOR liCount = 1 to liBound - 1
 lzTable = iu_dw_table_array[liCount].udf_uo_get_tablename()
 IF lzTable <> "" THEN
 lzRet = lzRet + lzTable
 lzRet = lzRet + ";"
 END IF
NEXT

lzTable = iu_dw_table_array[liBound].udf_uo_get_tablename()
IF lzTable <> "" THEN
 lzRet = lzRet + lzTable
END IF
Return ( lzRet)
```

This function builds a table list from the iu_dw_table_array variable. It uses the fact that a closed table returns an empty string from its udf_uo_get_tablename() function to ignore closed tables in the array. These are the tables that are on the free entry list.

```
/*
 udf_wf_update_selection(string pztable,,string pzcolumn, boolean pbtoggle )

Purpose: This function updates the selection window
  ( actually a DataWindow ), by either inserting
 or deleting an entry, based on the value of
 pbtoggle.
 dw_1 is the selection window.
*/

IF pbtoggle THEN
 dw_1.udf_uo_add_col(pztable, pzcolumn)
ELSE
 dw_1.udf_uo_delete_col(pztable, pzcolumn)
END IF
```

This function simply adds or removes a column form the selection DataWindow.

The w_layout window also defines several user events. These events are:

```
1. ue_addtables     Used to add tables to the layout
2. ue_save_layout   Used to save the layout to a file
3. ue_togglewhere   Used to show and hide the where clause window
4. ue_showsql       Used to display the current SQL Syntax
5. ue_opensaved     Used to open a saved query layout
```

In addition to these user events, the layout window process the following standard events:

```
1. Open    Used to setup layout
2. Close   Used to close a layout
```

Let's look at the functionality in each.

```
/*
 open event for w_layout

 Purpose: Initialize the spacing, open and hide the where clause
 window, initialize the location value for each table
 and open the table selection window by triggering the
 ue_addtables event.
*/

int liSwitch

// the parameter for determining open new, or exisiting
// 0 = new, 1 = existing

liSwitch = message.DoubleParm

// initialize the spacing
ii_xspace=Integer(ProfileString("adhoc.ini","adhoc","xspace","10"))
ii_yspace=Integer(ProfileString("adhoc.ini","adhoc","yspace","10"))

// open the where clause
open(iw_where)
iw_where.hide()
ib_where = FALSE

// initialize the levels for table placement
ii_count=0
ii_level=0

// open the table selection window
IF liSwitch = 0 THEN
 TriggerEvent(this,"ue_addtables")
ELSEIF liSwitch = 1 THEN
 TriggerEvent(this,"ue_opensaved")
END IF
```

This script performs several actions. First it decodes the passed-in parameter to determine whether it is opening a new layout or an existing layout. It initializes the spacing and placement parameters from the initialization file using the ProfileString() functions. It then opens the where clause window and hides it. Finally, depending on the value of the passed parameter, it triggers either the ue_addtables event to add tables to a new layout, or the ue_opensaved event to open a saved query.

The closed event simply closes the where clause window first. It's a one-liner.

The user events are very interesting. The first event is the ue_addtables event. Let's take a look at it.

```
/*
 ue_addtables for w_layout

 Purpose: This script opens the table selection window and
 then opens all of the selected tables
*/

string lzTables, lzToken, LzTableName
int liFree, liPos, liX, liY
s_uo_parm sParm
```

```
// open the window
open(w_select_tables)

// capture the table list
lzTables = message.StringParm

// parse the table list
liPos  = Pos(lzTables,";")
IF liPos = 0 THEN
 IF IsNull(lzTables) or lzTables = "" THEN
 return
 ELSE
 lzToken = lzTables
 lzTables = ""
 END IF
ELSE
 lzToken = Mid(lzTables,1,liPos - 1)
 lzTables = Mid(lzTables,liPos+1)
END IF
DO WHILE lzToken <> ""

 // open a new table object, but check the free entry list first
 liFree = udf_get_free_entry()
 IF liFree = 0 THEN
 liFree = UpperBound(iu_dw_table_array)+1
 END IF

 // build the input parameter for a table
 sParm.szTable = lzToken         // table name
 sParm.szIndex = String(liFree)  // index entry
 sParm.swOwner = This            // parent window

 // determine the spacing
 liX = 10 + (ii_count * ii_xspace)
 liY = 10 + (ii_level * ii_yspace)

 // open the table
 OpenUserObjectWithParm(iu_dw_table_array[liFree], sParm , liX, liY)

 liPos  = Pos(lzTables,";")
 IF liPos = 0 THEN
 IF lzTables = "" THEN
 lzToken = ""
 ELSE
 lzToken = lzTables
 lzTables = ""
 END IF
 ELSE
 lzToken = Mid(lzTables,1,liPos - 1)
 lzTables = Mid(lzTables,liPos+1)
 END IF

 // deal with table positioning
 ii_count++
 IF ii_count >= 4 THEN
 ii_count = 0
 ii_level++
 END IF
LOOP
```

There's a lot going on here. First, it opens w_select_tables to obtain the desired tables to open. It then parses the list to obtain individual table names. It loops through these names, establishing spacing and location for each table. It fills the structure sParm with the parameters needed to open the table object and then calls OpenUserObjectWithParm() to open the object. Lastly, it updates the ii_count and ii_level variables to ensure proper placement of the next table.

```
/*
 ue_savelayout for w_layout

 Purpose: Save the layout information to a file
*/

int    liRet             // return from the file save dialog
string lzFileName        // the file name
string lzPathName        // the full path
string lzTable           // a table name
int    liX,liY           // the table position
string lzRows            // the selected rows
int    liTableCnt        // the number of tables
int    liBound           // the number of array entries
int    liCounter         // a counter
string lzSection         // the section name
int    liFile            // the file handle

// get the file name
liRet = GetFileSaveName("Save Layout",lzPathName,lzFileName,"QRY","Query Lay-
outs" + & "*.QRY),*.QRY")

IF liRet <> 1 THEN
 RETURN
END IF

// deal with the fact that setprofile won't create a file
liFile = FileOpen(lzPathName,LineMode!,Write!,Shared!,Replace!)
IF liFile = -1 THEN
 MessageBox("File Error","Cannot create layout file!",StopSign!)
 RETURN
END IF

// write a line
FileWrite(liFile,"[summary]")
FileClose(liFile)

// initialize some variables
liTableCnt = 0
liBound = UpperBound(iu_dw_table_array)

FOR liCounter = 1 to liBound
 IF iu_dw_table_array[liCounter].ib_active THEN
 liTableCnt++
 lzTable = iu_dw_table_array[liCounter].udf_uo_get_tablename()
 liX = iu_dw_table_array[liCounter].udf_get_X()
 liY = iu_dw_table_array[liCounter].udf_get_Y()
 lzRows = iu_dw_table_array[liCounter].udf_get_Selected()
 lzSection = "table"+String(liTableCnt)
 SetProfileString(lzPathName,lzSection,"tablename",lzTable)
 SetProfileString(lzPathName,lzSection,"X",String(liX))
   SetProfileString(lzPathName,lzSection,"Y",String(liY))
```

```
    SetProfileString(lzPathName,lzSection,"selections",lzRows)
    END IF
NEXT

    SetProfileString(lzPathName,"summary","tablecount",String(liTableCnt))
    This.Title = lzFileName
```

This is the script that performs the save of the layout. It makes extensive use of the SetProfileString function to save the data. The actual query layout file is identical in format to any INI file, with sections and keys.

The function first calls GetFileSaveName() to obtain a valid file name. It then opens the file, writes one line, and closes it. This may seem confusing, but it really is necessary. Although the SetProfileString function will create a section and key entry in a file if none exists, it will not go so far as to create the actual file as well. The file functions that are used here create the file for further use.

Next the script loops through the table array and obtains all of the necessary information needed to save each table. It then writes this information. Note that it includes the information needed to save the selection list.

Finally it writes a table count to the summary section. Let's take a look at an actual file produced by this script.

This is a .QRY file–test3.qry.

```
[summary]
tablecount=2

[table1]
tablename=order
X=10
Y=10
selections=1;2

[table2]
tablename=cust
X=710
Y=10
selections=1;2

// end of file
```

The next script is for the ue_togglewhere event and is used to show and hide the WHERE clause window.

```
/*
ue_togglewhere event for w_layout

Purpose: Shows or hides the where clause.
*/

string lzTables

IF ib_where THEN
 ib_where = FALSE
```

```
 iw_where.Hide()
ELSE
 ib_where = TRUE
 lzTables = This.udf_wf_build_table_list()
 iw_where.udf_wf_update(lzTables)
 iw_where.Show()
END IF
```

This is a simple enough function. If the where clause window is already showing, it hides it. If the where clause window is hidden, it gets a list of tables from the layout window, then refreshes the table list on the where clause using the udf_wf_update() function.

The next event, ue_showsql, is used to display a window with the current SQL syntax.

```
/*
ue_showsql event for w_layout

Purpose: Build and display the current sql statement.
*/
string     lzTableList
string     lzSelection
String     lzTable
String     lzColumnname
string     lzWhereClause
string     lzSQL
long       llRowCount, llCounter

// build the select statement
lzSQL = "SELECT"+"~r~n"

llRowCount = dw_1.RowCount()
FOR llCounter = 1 to llRowCount
 dw_1.SetRow(llRowCount)
 lzTable = dw_1.GetItemString(llCounter,"table")
 lzColumnname = dw_1.GetItemString(llCounter,"columnname")
 lzSelection = lzTable+"."+lzColumnname
 lzSQL = lzSQL +"~t"+lzSelection
 IF llCounter < llRowCount THEN
 lzSQL = lzSQL + ","
 END IF
 lzSQL = lzSQL + "~r~n"
NEXT

// build the from list
lzTableList = udf_wf_build_table_list()

IF IsNull(lzTableList) OR lzTableList = "" THEN
return
END IF

lzTable = f_get_token(lzTableList,";")
lzSQL = lzSQL + "FROM"+"~r~n"
DO WHILE lzTable <> ""
 lzSQL = lzSQL + "~t"+lzTable
 IF lzTableList = "" THEN
 lzTable = ""
 lzSQL = lzSQL + "~r~n"
 ELSE
 lzSQL = lzSQL + "," +"~r~n"
```

```
   lzTable = f_get_token(lzTableList,";")
  END IF
LOOP

// build the where clause
lzWhereClause = iw_where.udf_wf_build_clause()

IF lzWhereClause <> "" THEN
  lzSQL = lzSQL +"WHERE"+"~r~n"
  lzSQL = LzSQL + lzWhereClause
END IF

// show the syntax in a window
OpenWithParm(w_sql_syntax,lzSQL)
```

This script builds the SQL syntax and then displays it by opening the w_sql_syntax window.
Note that the functions used to build the SQL are almost identical, except for the where
clause. In addition the SQL is formatted with line feeds using the "~r~n" characters. These
are not needed in actually building the SQL in order to create a new DataWindow.

The next script performs the exact opposite of the ue_savelayout script. The script for
ue_opensaved opens a saved layout.

```
/*
ue_opensaved event for w_layout

Purpose:Open a saved layout
*/

int       liTableCnt       // the number of tables
string    lzTable          // the table name
int       liX, liY         // X and Y coordinates for the table
string    lzRows           // selected rows for the table
string    lzFileName       // the saved file
string    lzPathName       // the full path name
int       liRet            // the file open return value
int       liCounter        // a counter variable
string    lzSection        // the section name for each table
int       liFree           // next table array entry
s_uo_parm sParm            // the structure used to open a table

// get the query file name
liRet = GetFileOpenName("Open Layout",lzPathName,lzFileName,&
 "QRY","Query Layouts (*.QRY),*.QRY")

IF liRet = 1 THEN

 // find out how many tables to open
 liTableCnt = ProfileInt(lzPathName,"summary","tablecount",0)

 // loop to open tables
 FOR liCounter = 1 to liTableCnt

 // get the section name
 lzSection = "table"+string(liCounter)

 // get the table name
 lzTable = ProfileString(lzPathName,lzSection,"tablename","")
```

```
// don't get trapped by errors
IF lzTable = "" THEN
continue
END IF

// get a free entry - actually should not be needed.
liFree = udf_get_free_entry()
IF liFree = 0 THEN
liFree = UpperBound(iu_dw_table_array)+1
END IF

// fill the open parameter for the table
sParm.szTable = lzTable
sParm.szIndex = String(liFree)
sParm.swOwner = This

// get the position of the table in the window
liX = ProfileInt(lzPathName,lzSection,"X",10)
liY = ProfileInt(lzPathName,lzSection,"Y",10)

// open the table
OpenUserObjectWithParm(iu_dw_table_array[liFree],&
sParm, liX,liY)

// now update the tables selections
lzRows = ProfileString(lzPathName,lzSection,"selections","")
IF lzRows <> "" THEN

// update the selections
iu_dw_table_array[liFree].udf_set_selected(lzRows)
END IF
NEXT
this.Title = lzFileName

ELSE            // user cancelled the open file dialog box
 return
END IF
```

First this function calls the GetOpenFileName() function to obtain the file name of the query to open. Then it finds out how many tables are stored in the file. It then loops through each table, reading the information needed to restore it on the layout, and opens it with the OpenUserObjectWithParm() function.

Summary and Future Directions

With all that it does, there is still plenty of room for improvement in Adhoc. I would have liked to display relationship information graphically, with lines between the tables to indicate relationships–but this can't be done directly in PowerBuilder, and I didn't want to bring external functions into Adhoc at this time. I also would have liked to have created the DataWindow objects needed for access to many other databases, such as Oracle, Sybase, etc. Error handling in this application is only rudimentary: Adhoc does not address the problem that occurs when a table is deleted from the database, but still stored in a query layout file. And the layout window builds the SQL from portion based on the open tables, rather than on the tables that have columns in the selection DataWindow. I'd also like to have included a window that would allow the user to type in SQL directly and generate a result window.

Adhoc provides the ability to work with the database in a manner that is fairly intuitive to the user. It represents tables as objects on the screen and allows users to graphically build queries and obtain results. It can save the layout for later use, and can print the results and save them to any supported file format. And it introduces the MDI frame paradigm in a simple, straightforward manner. Overall, I think Adhoc does a good job of addressing simple needs without having to resort to separate products. It was a great deal of work, and a learning experience. I hope that you get as much out of it as I did.

CHAPTER **24**

Data Driven Architecture

By John Olson

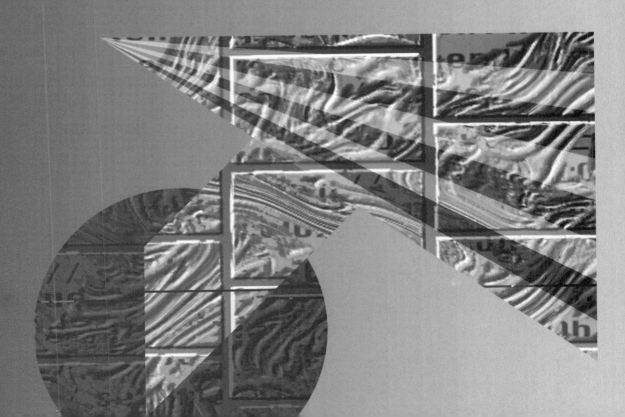

Data Driven Architecture

by **John Olson**

If Gallup pollsters were to survey PowerBuilder developers asking them what they like to do least, the following tasks would probably be among the most common responses: "testing," "painting thousands of DataWindows," and "recoding the same thing over and over." Each of these answers indicates a general dislike of repetition.

Testing is tedious and repetitive in nature, but if you use an automated testing mechanism, the amount of work required in successive repetitions declines dramatically. The repetition of painting DataWindows for each table in your database can be eliminated by creating DataWindows dynamically. By setting up functionality which allows you to dynamically create DataWindows you may never have to paint one again: the next time your boss tells you to build a DataWindow for every table in the database you can surprise him by coming back after a long lunch and saying "Done!" (It won't hurt your career if he thinks you are a PowerBuilder magician). Likewise, if you don't want to code the same functionality over and over you can design for reuse.

This chapter will demonstrate the power of data-driven architecture to create applications which have dynamic behaviors that can be modified without changing code. In order to illustrate this, we will walk through the process of building a small application. By the end of the chapter you will have learned how to apply basic concepts of data-driven architecture to menus/navigation, development of generic objects, and application security, enabling you to reduce coding repetition while increasing the functionality of your applications.

A large aspect of designing for reuse is to make objects generic. Instead of hard-coding your object names in scripts, use the pronouns provided: this, super, parent, etc. For script in your

DataWindow controls, instead of specifying DataWindow, table, and column names, contain their values in string variables. In fact, you could pass those values as parameters to the window which has the DataWindow control on it.

Although you can develop very generic objects using these coding techniques, there is a certain point where you can't get any more generic; you'll need information specific to the data or objects with which you are working. Let's suppose you have a window, w_dw_entry, which provides standard DataWindow functionality such as insert, update, and delete. You could pass the DataWindow object name as a parameter to w_dw_entry, but that would mean that the script which called w_dw_entry would have to know the name of the DataWindow object. Perhaps you want your calling script to be generic and not contain a DataWindow object name. You may have several data-specific calls to a generic object with each variation having to be coded separately. Sooner or later you will reach a point where you can go no farther: your objects and the calls to those objects are as generic as they can get. You have used pronouns in all cases, variables for all references, and all data-specific information is passed as parameters. You think you're about to reach the peak of maximum genericness, only to find a higher peak coming in to view.

The next step is to store the specific information you need in a database table or a file so that it doesn't have to be hard-coded into the application. Instead it can be retrieved at runtime. This isn't much different than using ini files. While ini files are used to store personal preferences and application settings, data-driven architecture takes that concept one step further. It allows you to tap into vast quantities of data from complex databases. Once you do begin using tables to store application information, a whole new world of generic coding will open up to you. Your applications will no longer have finite functionality. You will be able to change your application by simply changing data in the underlying tables. (Keep in mind though, there are limitations to what you can do. Your application will still need to contain your processing logic and possibly some very complex generic objects.) Undoubtedly, your mind is racing now, thinking of all the areas to which you can apply this concept. While the uses for this technique are seemingly endless, there are a few areas in which it is used most: menus/navigation, application security, and generic data entry objects. As mentioned, we will examine all three of these here.

The application we will build will be a simple purchase order tracking system. Since many of the class libraries on the market today use DOS-type menus to provide navigation between major application functions, we also will use this menu paradigm. (This menu structure is particularly useful when there are more menu options than can be displayed on a standard menu.) The application will have a generic window which will be used to perform data entry on a DataWindow. The name of the DataWindow on which data entry will be performed will be passed as a parameter to the generic window. The DataWindows used will have dropdownDataWindows (dddws) which will display a list of values based on an entry in another column. The window will check table values to determine which values to display in the DDDW. Finally, we will add security features to the application. The application will read user access information from a table and display only those menu options to which the current user has rights. We'll use a Watcom database to store both the application and the architectural data. Throughout this chapter I'll refer to the architectural tables as the Application Administration database.

Menus/Navigation

In MS-Windows applications, menus are used to trigger processes and to provide a means of navigation through applications. I have combined menus and navigation together in this section because they are virtually inseparable.

According to the Microsoft's *The Windows Interface, An Application Design Guide*, a menu should have no more than three levels of hierarchy. The first level contains the menu options which are always visible. This level typically contains File, Window, and Help, but may also contain Edit, View, and other items specific to the functionality of the attached window. The second level is the pull-down menu. These menus appear when you select a top-level menu item. The third level is the cascading menu which is associated with a pull-down menu item. While not specifically forbidden, it is considered poor design if a menu contains more than these three levels of hierarchy. The reason is that it becomes very difficult for the user to find a desired menu item in a menu that has four or more levels.

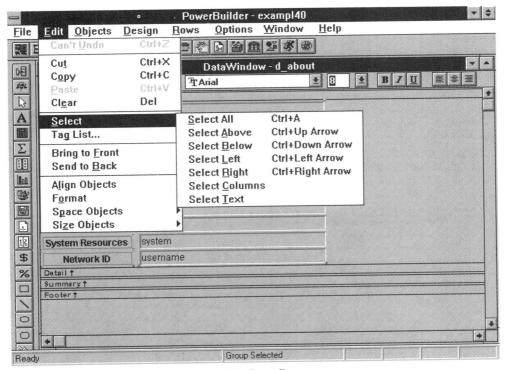

Figure 24-1: Cascading menu.

Data-driven architecture can provide flexibility in developing menus and reduce complexity in several problem areas. First, there are some cases where menu options may change frequently. This may occur if a production application is undergoing frequent modifications and features are being added regularly. Second, the navigational options on a sheet menu may need to change substantially based on information specific to the current sheet. Imagine an application which allowed the user to open data entry windows for database tables which have key relationships foreign to the table currently being accessed. In this case the navigational menu options may be completely different for each data entry window. Third, there may be so many menu options that the menu would extend off the screen when opened. This scenario may require using a different menu structure. Regardless of the problem, using data driven menus provides a means for changing an application's menus without modifying code, rebuilding the deployment files (exe and pbds), and redeploying the application. The application administrator needs only to modify the data in the Application Administration database.

Building Menus

The PowerBuilder 3.0 demonstration database application is a good example of using data-driven architecture to control menus and navigation. Although the demonstration database doesn't store the data in database tables, it does store first level menu items in a listbox object and import second level menu items from a file. The application menu is very generic in nature and doesn't contain any window-specific navigational script. It simply uses the stored information to show the user a list of options and opens the appropriate windows based on that stored information.

To create our own menu system we will build a window, w_main_menu, which will provide two levels of menu hierarchy. When the user selects an item from the Level 1 list, a list of items will be displayed in the Level 2 selection box. Initially, we will retrieve all values for the Level 2 menu, but we will filter the records so that only the appropriate ones are displayed based on the Level 1 selection. When the user highlights a Level 2 menu item a description of the menu item will be displayed in a multiline edit, 'mle_Description'. Instead of using a listbox as in the PowerBuilder demonstration, we will use DataWindow controls to display both menu lists.

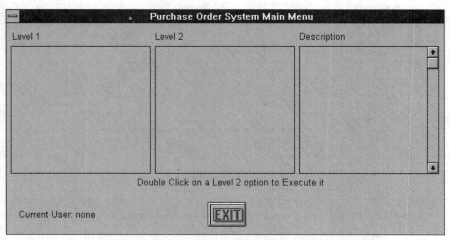

Figure 24-2: Empty w_main_menu from PowerBuilder samples.

First we will need to design and create database tables to contain our menu hierarchy information. These tables will be added to our Application Administration database. For simplicity we'll assume that each Level 2 menu item can be related to only one Level 1 menu item. Items at both menu levels should have ID and display values. Level 2 items will also have a description, a window to open if they are selected, and a DataWindow name to pass as a parameter to the window. Once we have created the Watcom tables, we will paint a DataWindow for each of the tables. The DataWindow for Level 1, dw_Level1, should include both the display column and the menu ID. Although the user will only see the display column, we need to be able to access the values from the ID column for the relationship to Level 2. The Level 2 DataWindow also should include all columns. Again, the user will only be able to see the display value, but we need the ability to access the other columns so that we can show the menu description in a multiline edit, mle_Description–and also because we need to know which window to open and the parameter to pass it.

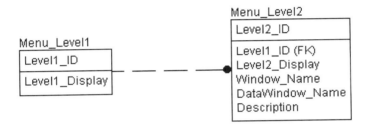

Figure 24-3: Entity-Relationship diagram of menu Level 1 to Level 2

In keeping with good programming style let's create a we_init event for w_main_menu, and post that event from the w_main_menu Open event. For the sake of brevity I will not include error checking code in these scripts; however, there is error checking in the sample application which accompanies this book.

```
// Open event of w_Main_Menu
this.PostEvent(  'we_init' )
```

In we_init of w_main_menu we need to set the transaction objects for dw_Level1 and dw_Level2, then retrieve all records for the DataWindows.

```
// we_Init event of w_Main_Menu
dw_Level1.SetTransObject( SQLCA )
dw_Level2.SetTransObject( SQLCA )
fw_Retrieve_dw( dw_Level1, 'Level1' )
fw_Retrieve_dw( dw_Level2, 'Level2' )
```

The we_Init event uses function fw_Retrieve_dw to perform the retrieve, so as to avoid duplicating error checking code. (Again, error checking code does not appear in this chapter's text, but is included in the sample application.) Also, when we add security features later in this chapter, we need only change script in one location. For now the function performs a simple retrieve of the DataWindow.

```
/*
fw_Retrieve_dw()
Retrieves dw menu items which are accessible to the current user

Arguments:
adw  DataWindow  DataWindow to retrieve from
--------------------------------------------------------------- */

adw.Retrieve()
```

When w_main_menu opens, we want the first menu item (row) in dw_Level1 to be selected. Based on that selection we'll apply a filter to dw_Level2 so that only those menu items which are associated with the selected Level 1 menu item will be displayed. We'll put script in we_Init to select the first row in each list. Since we'll want the filtering to occur every time the user selects a different Level 1 item, we'll put the filtering script in the RowFocus-Changed! event of dw_Level1. Our we_init will trigger the RowFocusChanged! event of dw_Level1 to force the first filter to be applied.

```
//we_init continued...

// select the first item in the Level1 list
dw_Level1.SetRow ( 1 )

// trigger RowFocusChanged! so that Level2 is filtered
dw_Level1.TriggerEvent( RowFocusChanged! )
```

So the entire script for we_Init looks like this:

```
// we_Init for w_Main_Menu
// set trans objects, retrieve menu values, set filter on Level2

SetPointer( HourGlass! )
dw_Level1.SetTransObject( SQLCA )
dw_Level2.SetTransObject( SQLCA )
fw_Retrieve_dw( dw_Level1, 'Level1' )
fw_Retrieve_dw( dw_Level2, 'Level2' )

// select the first item in the Level1 list
dw_Level1.SetRow ( 1 )

// trigger RowFocusChanged! so that dw_Level2 is filtered
dw_Level1.TriggerEvent( RowFocusChanged! )
```

Previously, I mentioned that a new filter should be applied to dw_Level2 every time the user selects a different dw_Level1 row. There are three additional things we must also do when the user selects a different Level 1 menu item before we can apply the filter.

```
1. Get the current row.
2. Unhighlight the previous row.
3. Highlight the current row.
```

Now we're ready to apply the filter to dw_Level2 based on the selected dw_Level1 row. We need to program all these behaviors in the RowFocusChanged! event of dw_Level1.

```
// RowFocusChanged event for dw_Level1 of w_Main_Menu
// Get selected row, change Level2 list based on Level1 selected
```

```
long ll_rownum

// get selected row
ll_rownum = this.GetRow ()

// unhighlight all rows
this.SelectRow ( 0, FALSE )

// highlight current row
this.SelectRow( ll_rownum, TRUE )

// call a function to set the filter for Level2
fw_Set_Level2( ll_rownum )
```

Notice that I called a function to handle the dw_Level2 filtering. That function should filter
out all dw_Level2 rows except for the ones which have the same Level1_ID as the selected
dw_Level1 row.

```
/*
fw_Set_Level2()

Filters dw_Level2 based on dw_Level1 selection

Arguments:
al_rownum   long   dw_Level 1 row number to base filter on
-------------------------------------------------------- */
// turn off Redraw so that the dddw doesn't flicker
dw_Level2.SetRedraw (FALSE)

// create the filter string then apply it
dw_Level2.SetFilter ("Level1_ID=~"" + &
dw_Level1.GetItemString(al_rownum, 'Level1_ID') + "~"")
dw_Level2.Filter ()

// unhighlight all rows
dw_Level2.SelectRow (0, FALSE)

// turn Redraw back on
dw_Level2.SetRedraw (TRUE)

/*
if all menu rows have been filtered out then indicate that there are no Level2
menu options

// otherwise display the description for the selected menu item (the default
// selection is item 1)
if dw_Level2.RowCount () > 0 then
 dw_Level2.SelectRow (1, TRUE)
 mle_Description.text = dw_Level2.GetItemString ( 1, 'description' )
else
 mle_Description.text = "(No Level 2 menu options available for this Level 1
option.)"
end if
```

We're almost done with scripting for the menu selections. Now we need to add script to handle a Level 2 selection change as well as a double click on a level 2 option. As with Level 1,
if the user selects a different Level 2 menu item we want to unhighlight the previously
selected row and highlight the newly selected row. We also want to change the description

display so that it shows the description for the newly selected row.

```
// RowFocusChanged Script for dw_Level2 of w_Main_Menu

long ll_rownum

// get selected row
ll_rownum = GetRow ( this )

// unhighlight all rows
this.SelectRow ( 0, FALSE )

// highlight the selected row
this.SelectRow ( ll_rownum, TRUE)

// display the description text for the selected row in mle_Description
mle_Description.text = dw_Level2.GetItemString ( ll_rownum, 'description')
```

w_Main_Menu instructs the user to double-click on a Level 2 option to execute that option. We designed our application so that we only need to get the window and DataWindow names for the selected option and pass the DataWindow name as a parameter when the window is opened.

```
// DoubleClicked event for dw_Level2 of w_Main_Menu
// Get the name of the window for the selected row, open it,
// and pass the DataWindow name as a parameter

window lw_new_window
string ls_window_name, ls_dw_name
long ll_rownum

SetPointer (HourGlass!)

// get the current row
ll_rownum = this.GetRow ()

// get the window class name
ls_window_name = this.GetItemString( ll_rownum, 'window_name' )

// get the DataWindow name to pass as a parameter
ls_dw_name = this.GetItemString( ll_rownum, 'DataWindow_name' )

// Use OpenWithParm() Format 2
OpenWithParm( lw_new_window, ls_dw_name, ls_window_name)
```

Although we don't know the type of the window we will be opening, we do have a string which contains the name of the window class. In order to open an instance of a window for which we don't know the class name at compile time we have to use format #2 of Open() or OpenWithParm(). In our case we use OpenWithParm() because we want to pass the DataWindow name as a parameter.

We are now done coding w_Main_Menu. However, we need to populate the Watcom tables Menu_Level1 and Menu_Level2 so that the menus aren't empty. In the next section we will develop the data-driven portions of a generic data entry window.

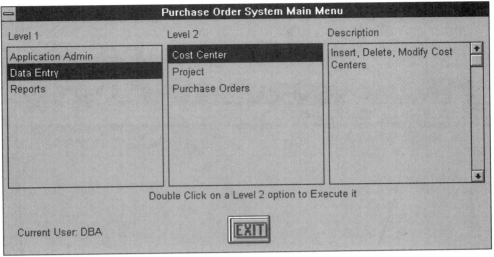

Figure 24-4: w_main_menu with values.

Generic Objects

Developing generic objects allows us to use objects to exhibit varied behaviors based on data values. A simple example of this is a generic message window. The window contains a static text object and a button. When the window is opened, two parameter values are passed: message text and button text. In some cases we may want the message to say "Retrieving Records. Please Wait" and the button to say "Cancel Retrieval;" in another case they might be "Login Name or Password Is Incorrect" and "OK." This example shows that we can get the display variance we need by simply passing two parameters. For more complex objects there may be functional differences based on several sets of parameters which are passed. In addition to having a large amount of parameter data, the parameter data may change frequently enough that we don't want to code the data values into our application. If we store the data in tables and pass an identifier as a parameter then all the data stored in the those tables can be retrieved using that parameter as a key.

PowerBuilder itself incorporates data-driven architecture. An example of this is the database painter. If you select a table and choose a data manipulation option from the menu, Power-Builder will create a DataWindow for the selected table. If you haven't specified formats, edit styles, or validations for columns on that table, the DataWindow will be very simple in nature. However, if you have entered specifications for that table the DataWindow could be quite complex. It could have edit masks, dropdownDataWindows, checkboxes and other column styles, and have special display formats and validation expressions for the columns. PowerBuilder determines how to build the DataWindow based on information in the PowerBuilder system tables. It retrieves font information for the DataWindow from pbcattbl, and for the individual columns it retrieves data from pbcatcol to determine label text, column height and width, edit styles, formats, validation expressions and more.

Coding For Generic DDDW Dependencies

For our application I have provided a window, w_dw_entry, which already has all the basic data entry functionality for a single DataWindow. w_dw_entry accepts a DataWindow object name as a parameter when it is opened and allows the user to perform data entry on that DataWindow object.

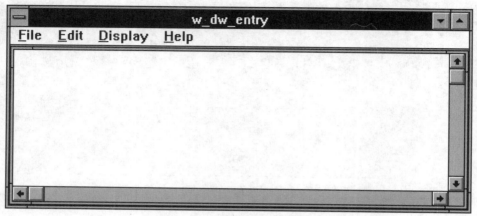

Figure 24-5: The w_dw_entry window.

Options on the attached menu are Retrieve, Update, Insert, Delete, First, Prior, Next, Last, Exit, and About.... We will now add a feature to the DataWindow control which will allow the values displayed in a dropdownDataWindow to be dependent on the value entered into another column. Specifically, our purchase order DataWindow will have a Cost_Center_ID column and a Project_ID column. When the user selects a cost center, only those projects which are valid for the selected cost center will be displayed in the Project_ID DDDW. Also, instead of passing the column information as parameters to the window, we will only pass the DataWindow name: w_dw_entry will retrieve the other information it needs from Application Administration database tables by using the DataWindow name as a key.

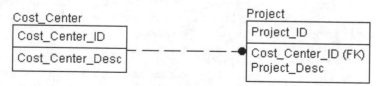

Figure 24-6: E-R Diagram of project and cost center relationship.

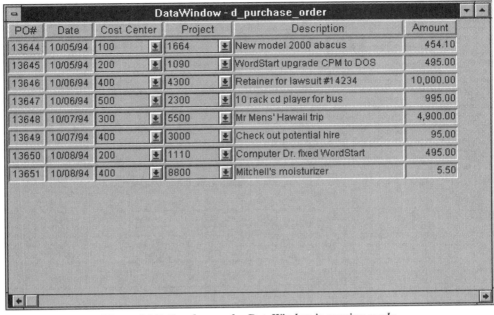

Figure 24-7: Purchase order DataWindow in preview mode.

For our example we will populate the Cost_Center table and the Project table with the following values.

Cost Center ID	Cost Center Description
100	Administrative Support
200	Data Processing
300	Sales
400	Tattoo Parlor
500	Child Care
600	Grounds Maintenance

Project ID	Project Description	Cost Center ID
1090	LAN Administration	200

1110	On-Site Software Support	200
1320	Help Desk	200
1664	Financial Accounting	100
1665	Budget Planning	100
2300	Bus Service	500
3000	Background Investigations	500
4208	Tattoo Removal	400
4300	Legal Defense	400
5500	Marketing Travel	300
5660	Telemarketing	300
8800	Steel Wool Scrubbers	400

To be able to create script which will filter a DDDW based on the value entered into another column, we need to know the names of the columns and how they are related. Instead of hard-coding this information into the application, the information will be stored in Application Administration database tables. Only one table, Dependent_dddw, must be created to contain the information we need: the name of the DataWindow object, the name of the DDDW column, and the name of the column on which the filter will be based. I will call these dwObject, Target_dddw, and Trigger_Column respectively.

```
Dependent_dddw
┌──────────────┐
│ dwObject     │
│ Target_dddw  │
├──────────────┤
│ Trigger_Column│
└──────────────┘
```

Figure 24-8: E-R diagram of Dependent_dddw.

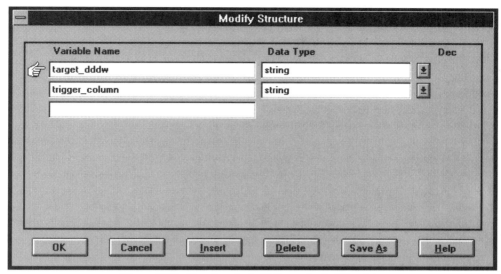

Figure 24-9: Structure to hold Dependent_dddw data.

Once the table is created we need to insert a record for d_purchase_order:

```
dwObject        = 'd_purchase_order'
Target_dddw     = 'Project_ID'
Trigger_Column  = 'Cost_Center_ID'
```

Next we need to create script to handle the filtering. For our example we'll create a window descendent of w_dw_entry, w_dw_entry_dddw. To this window we will add script that will read data from the table Dependent_dddw and filter the Target_dddw based on the value in Trigger_Column. A filter should be applied to Target_dddw whenever the value in Trigger_Column changes. Therefore, we will code a filter in the ItemChanged! event of the DataWindow control (dw_generic). Also, since the filter should change whenever the users selects a different row, we will code a filter in the RowFocusChanged! event.

First, we need to add script that will read into a structure all records in Dependent_dddw which apply to the current dwObject. The reason we want to read it into a structure is that we only want to select from the database once, after which we can check the structure whenever ItemChanged! or RowFocusChanged! is triggered. This is a much faster method than executing a SQL Select every time one of those events is triggered.

The structure which will store the table data (s_related_dddw), must have elements for Target_dddw and Trigger_Column. To allow a DataWindow object to have more than one column dependency we must declare an instance array of these structures for w_dw_entry_dddw.

```
s_related_dddw istr_dddw_info[]
```

We will also declare an instance variable which will track the number of DDDW dependencies for the DataWindow object (the number of records read from Dependent_dddw).

```
int ii_dddw_count
```

The Open event of w_dw_entry takes the DataWindow name, which is passed as a parameter, and puts it in a window instance variable, is_dwobject. In w_dw_entry there is also an event called ue_prepare_dw which is called when the window opens. This event sets the dataobject attribute and the transaction object for dw_generic. In ue_prepare_dw of w_dw_entry_dddw, we will call a function, fw_populate_dddw_str, which will retrieve Dependent_dddw data from the database and store it in istr_dddw_info.

```
// ue_Prepare_dw for dw_generic of w_dw_entry_dddw, ancestor
// script is executed first
// Read Dependent_dddw records

fw_populate_dddw_str()
```

The function fw_populate_dddw_str uses a dynamic cursor to fetch records from Dependent_dddw into the structure array istr_dddw_info[].

```
/*
fw_Populate_dddw_str

Populates the structure istr_dddw_info with all records in Dependent_dddw
which apply to this dwObject.

Arguments:    None
Return value  Boolean  Indicates success or failure
----------------------------------------------------------------------*/

string add_string, select_string

// Set up select statement using passed parameters, only retrieve the
// records for the current dw object

select_string = "SELECT Target_dddw, Trigger_Column FROM dependent_dddw " + &
"where dwObject = '" + is_dwobject + "'"

PREPARE sqlsa FROM :select_string;

DECLARE dyn_cursor DYNAMIC CURSOR FOR sqlsa;

OPEN DYNAMIC dyn_cursor;

DO WHILE SQLCA.sqlcode = 0
 ii_dddw_count++
 Fetch dyn_cursor into :istr_dddw_info[ii_dddw_count].target_dddw, &
 :istr_dddw_info[ii_dddw_count].trigger_column;
LOOP

CLOSE dyn_cursor;

Return TRUE

//Remember to add code the check SQLCA.sqlcode after every SQL statement
```

In the ItemChanged! event of w_dw_entry_dddw we need to determine if the column which has been modified is a trigger column. If it is, then we use GetText() to get the newly entered value and apply that value in a filter to the target DDDW. The filter is:

```
<target dddw DataWindowchild>.SetFilter ( <trigger column name> + "=~"" +
this.GetText() + "~"" )
```

This line sets a filter for the target such that the column in the target DDDW, which has the same name as the trigger column, must have the same value as was entered into the trigger column. So if the trigger column is named Cost_Center_ID, the target DDDW is named Project_ID, and "100" is entered into Cost_Center_ID, the filter would be:

```
<target dddw DataWindowchild>.SetFilter ("Cost_Center_ID=100" )
```

The ItemChanged event script contains a loop which checks the currently modified column against all records read into istr_dddw_info.

```
// ItemChanged! event for dw_generic of w_dw_entry_dddw
// Determine if the current column is a trigger, if it is then apply a Filter
// to Target_dddw based on Trigger_Column value, set Target_dddw value to null

string ls_colname, ls_filter_string, ls_colval
int li_trigger_index
DataWindowchild ldwc_target

ls_colname = this.GetColumnName()

for li_trigger_index = 1 to ii_dddw_count
 if ls_colname = istr_dddw_info[li_trigger_index].trigger_column then
 // processing for trigger

 // get handle to Target_dddw dwchild
 this.dwGetChild( istr_dddw_info[li_trigger_index].target_dddw, ldwc_target )

 // set Target_dddw filter
 ldwc_target.SetFilter ( ls_colname + "=~"" + this.GetText() + "~"" )

 // apply Target_dddw filter
 ldwc_target.Filter()

 // set Target_dddw value to blank
this.SetItem( this.GetRow(), istr_dddw_info[li_trigger_index].target_dddw, ''
)

 // even if a match was found continue loop because a column could
 // be a trigger for more than 1 dddw
 end if
next
```

Next, the RowFocusChanged! event must apply a filter to Target_dddw based on the Trigger_Column value for the selected row. This step is necessary because a filter applies to all rows in a DataWindow. If the user changes rows but the filter is not changed to reflect the values in the newly selected row, the Target_dddw may not display the appropriate values.

```
// RowFocusChanged! event for dw_generic of w_dw_entry_dddw
// Filters all Target_dddws based on Trigger_Column values
```

```
string ls_trigger_col_val
int li_target_index
DataWindowchild ldwc_target

// loop through Target_dddws and set filters on them

for li_target_index = 1 to ii_dddw_count
 this.dwGetChild( istr_dddw_info[li_target_index].target_dddw, ldwc_target )

 // get value in trigger column for the current row
 ls_trigger_col_val = this.GetItemString( this.GetRow(), &
 istr_dddw_info[li_target_index].trigger_column)

 // if trigger column value is null then don't apply filter,
 // the target_dddw will be protected
 if NOT ls_trigger_col_val = "" then

 // set target dddw filter
 ldwc_target.SetFilter ( istr_dddw_info[li_target_index].trigger_column + &
 "=~"" + ls_trigger_col_val + "~"" )
 // apply filter
 ldwc_target.Filter()
 end if
next
```

Finally, when the records are retrieved into dw_generic, a filter must be applied so that only the appropriate values are displayed in the Trigger_dddw's. w_dw_entry has a custom event, ue_retrieve, which contains script to retrieve records into the DataWindow. Immediately after the retrieve we want to apply a filter to the row selected by default (row 1). The desired behavior for this circumstance is exactly the same behavior as when RowFocusChanged! is triggered. Therefore, triggering the RowFocusChanged! event immediately after record retrieval will provide the desired functionality.

```
// ue_Retrieve event for dw_generic of w_dw_entry_dddw, continuation of ancestor script
// Immediately after retrieve, trigger RowFocusChanged! event

this.TriggerEvent( RowFocusChanged! )
```

We are now done coding this feature. If we run the application and select Purchase Orders from the menu, the w_dw_entry_dddw window will pop up, and upon opening will retrieve all purchase orders. If we select a Cost Center value, then click on the dropdown button for Project, only those projects which are valid for the selected cost center will be displayed.

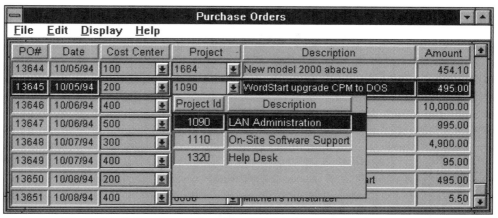

Figure 24-10: Purchase order with a DDDW showing limited selection list.

There is one last issue which we must address. When the user inserts a new row into d_purchase_order, the initial value for the Cost_Center_ID column will be null. Since the Cost_Center_ID value is null, the Project_ID DDDW will be empty if the user opens the dropdown. Rather than showing the user an empty DDDW we can use the new DataWindow column 'Protect' attribute. When a column is protected the user can't set focus or modify the value in that column. PowerBuilder 4.0 allows a column to be 'Protected' based on an evaluated expression. If the expression evaluates to 0 (False) the column will not be protected. If the expression evaluates to 1 (True) the column will be protected. For the d_purchase_order, we only want the Project_ID column to be protected if the Cost_Center_ID for the same row is null. The following expression will provide the result we want:

```
If ( isnull ( Cost_Center_ID ), 1, 0 )
```

To set the Protect attribute:

```
1. Open the DataWindow painter and load d_purchase_order.
2. Put the mouse pointer over the Project_ID column, press
   the right mouse button and select Attributes...
3. Click the down arrow on the vertical scrollbar until the
   Protect attribute is visible.
4. Enter the expression for the Protect attribute.
5. Click OK and save the DataWindow.
```

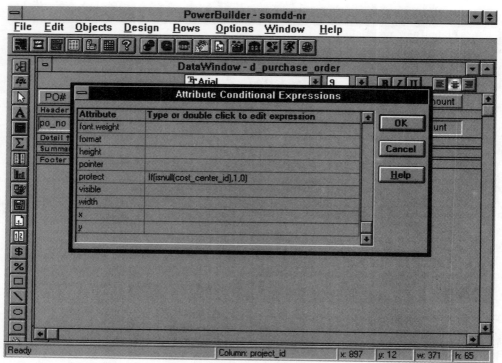

Figure 24-11: Setting the 'Protect' attribute for the Project_ID column of d_purchase_order.

Security

In addition to database table rights, there are two basic levels at which security can be applied to an application. The first is navigational security: the application can allow or disallow a user access to a screen based on the user's security level. The second level is functional security: once a user has accessed a screen, the application can control which menu options may be selected, which buttons may be pushed, and which data columns may be viewed or modified. These two areas do overlap, since menus are used to provide navigation and also to trigger processes. However, I have divided them into the two security levels which are common to most applications.

Navigational

Navigational security and dynamic menus go hand in hand. If your application uses data-driven architecture to meet your changing menu needs, consider adding a security check to determine whether any given menu option should be available to the current user.

Functional

Functional security goes one step further than navigational security. In addition to disabling menu options for a window you may also want to disable some window controls (CommandButton, SingleLineEdit, CheckBox, ListBox etc.) and make some DataWindow columns "display only" or even invisible. The data needed to track this information is more specific than that needed for navigational security. In addition to tracking user access to windows, you would also need to track each window control for which you want to limit access. This may include all controls on a window and all columns on a DataWindow.

How security should be applied to an application and how it is applied in actuality are often not the same. Typically, there are three ways in which developers handle application security: Allow all who log in to the application to have full access to everything.

This method is only good for an application which has no security considerations, i.e. if the user is able to log in to the database, then that user should be able to perform every function the application offers. However, using this method would be a nightmare for a user with a low security level in a multiple security level application. Imagine a user with few database table rights but full access. Every time this user attempts to perform a function he gets an endless stream of database errors.

Restrict access based on user names which are embedded in the application scripts.

This second method provides a means of restricting access based on the login name and would be acceptable if the list of users was static. However, as soon as you need to add or delete a user, or change the access level of a user, the maintenance team would need to modify code and redeploy the application. Few off-the-shelf software applications use this method. Although it does provide multiple access levels, those levels must be preprogrammed and are not modifiable.

Restrict access based on user names and rights which are read at runtime.

If this method is used, the application administrator could simply update the security table for that application on an as-needed basis. No code changes, no pbd or exe generation, and no redeployment would be necessary. Most importantly, the change can be made by the application administrator instead of calling in very expensive developers to do the work.

Obviously, if we want our applications to be user-friendly and provide multiple security levels, Option One can be eliminated. Although the second option may be reasonable in some cases, for the most part it won't meet real-world needs. The third option requires the lowest level of maintenance while providing the most user-friendly security levels. This option uses data-driven architecture to meet the security needs of the application owners.

Adding Security To Your Menus

To add security to our menus we need only do four things:

Design and build new security tables

Insert application specific security data

Add user arguments to dw_level1 and dw_level2

Add a security script to w_main_menu

1. Design and build Application Administration database tables to hold the security data.

What data do we need to store in the Application Administration database which will allow us to apply security to our menus by individual user? First, we need a table of users. For our application we will only store the user's name and an ID. Also, for each of the two menu levels we need to be able to track which users have access to which menu items.

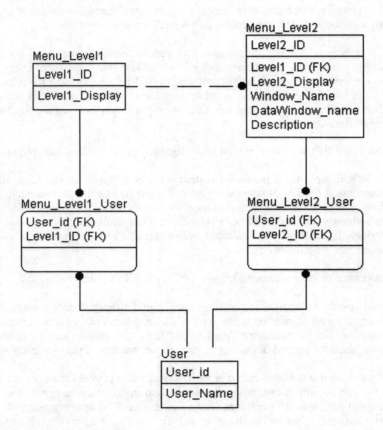

Figure 24-12: E-R diagram for security enhancements.

Figure 24-12 shows the tables which we have added to the Entity-Relationship diagram for our menus.

2. Insert records for the specific application into the database tables we created.

The menu items we will display to the user are only those menu items for which they have rights. If a user should have rights to a Level 1 menu, then a record must be entered into Menu_Level1_User for that user and the desired menu. So to assign rights for a menu with Menu_Level1_ID=5 to a user with User_ID=DBA, enter a record into Menu_Level1_User with Menu_Level1_ID=5 and User_ID=DBA.

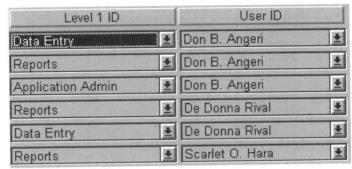

Figure 24-13: Security settings.

3. Add arguments to dw_Level1 and dw_Level2.

Originally, dw_Level1 and dw_Level2 performed very simple SQL Selects from a single table. Now, instead of retrieving all menu items, we want the DataWindows to retrieve only those records which have been assigned for the current user. Instead of retrieving records from only Menu_Level1 or Menu_Level2, the DataWindows should accept the current user's ID as an argument, and select only those records in Menu_Level1_User and Menu_Level2_User for that User_ID. The SQL Select for dw_Level1 changes from

```
SELECT
 Menu_Level1.Level1_ID ,
 Menu_Level1.Level1_Display
FROM
 Menu_Level1,
ORDER BY Menu_Level1.Level1_Display  ASC
```

to the following, where as_User_ID is the new dw_Level1 argument.

```
SELECT
 Menu_Level1.Level1_ID ,
 Menu_Level1.Level1_Display
FROM
 Menu_Level1,
 Menu_Level1_User
WHERE
 ( Menu_Level1.Level1_ID = Menu_Level1_User.Level1_ID ) and
 ( Menu_Level1_User.User_ID = :as_User_ID )
ORDER BY Menu_Level1.Level1_Display  ASC
```

The SQL Select for dw_Level2 would change in the same way. From

```
SELECT
 Menu_Level2.Level2_ID ,
 Menu_Level2.Level2_Display
FROM
```

```
  Menu_Level2,
ORDER BY Menu_Level2.Level2_Display  ASC
```

to the following, where as_User_ID is the new dw_Level2 argument:

```
SELECT
 Menu_Level2.Level2_ID ,
 Menu_Level2.Level2_Display
FROM
 Menu_Level2,
 Menu_Level2_User
WHERE
 ( Menu_Level2.Level2_ID = Menu_Level2_User.Level2_ID ) and
 ( Menu_Level2_User.User_ID = :as_User_ID )
ORDER BY Menu_Level2.Level2_Display  ASC
```

4. Add security script to w_main_menu.

Once the tables are designed, created, and the User_ID arguments have been added to the DataWindows, we are ready to add script to w_main_menu to apply the security to the menus. You should recall that when we scripted w_main_menu we used a function, fw_Retrieve_dw, to retrieve dw_Level1 and dw_Level2. Now by making a simple change to that function we can apply the menu security. When the Retrieve function is called, the Login ID of the current user must be passed as an argument to the DataWindow. For our example we can get the User_ID from the LogID attribute of the default transaction object, SQLCA. To run against a different RDBMS, or if connection to the database was made using a different transaction object, you may have to change the User_ID reference.

```
/*
fw_Retrieve_dw()

Retrieves dw menu items which are accessible to the current user

Arguments:
adw DataWindowretrieve records for this DataWindow
------------------------------------------------------------ */

// retrieve only those records for the current user ID
adw.Retrieve( SQLCA.LogID )
```

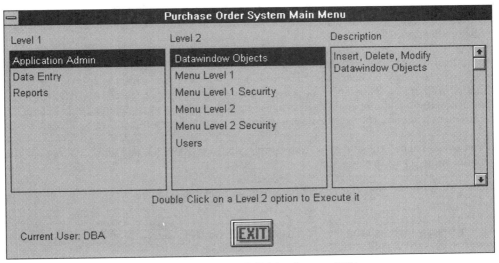

Figure 24-14: Menu definition for user DBA.

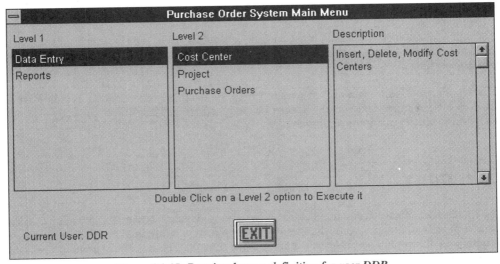

Figure 24-15: Restricted menu definition for user DDR.

Deployment Issues

A negative effect to using data-driven architecture is that the complexity of deploying your applications increases. Not only will your install routine become more complex, but you will have to provide your client with a way to modify the Application Administration database. The latter usually entails developing an application for the Application Administration database and deploying it with the applications which use the data-driven architecture. Not only will you have the normal headaches associated with deployment, but you will also be forced to develop a strategy for handling the Application Administration database and its accompanying application.

When determining where you will put your Application Administration tables you will generally have only two choices. You can either deploy an RDBMS with the application which contains your architecture tables, or you can create those tables on the client's RDBMS. You may encounter difficulties with both of these options, but you must determine a strategy for deployment and code your application and setup program accordingly.

If you choose to deploy an Application Administration database along with your application here are some issues to remember:

The Application Administration database files will have to be included in the install routine for the application.

All machines which will run the application must have the correct drivers and settings necessary to access the Application Administration database.
If the deployed application allows for multi-user access then the deployed database must also allow for multi-user access. This eliminates many desktop databases as options.
Alternatively, here are some issues if you choose to build the Application Administration tables on the client's RDBMS:

The application install routine must include executing SQL DDL against the client's RDBMS. The DDL must create the Application Administration tables and assign the appropriate user rights.

The Application Administration application must be database-independent; avoiding database-specific features and syntax. It must be designed so that it will run correctly with all RDBMS's which your application may use.

Summary

As you can see, data-driven architecture allows you to develop dynamic applications which can be modified, with no code changes, by the application administrator. The maintenance required for the application is lessened at the same time that the amount of coding repetition during the application's development is reduced. Although the main areas to which these concepts are applied are menus/navigation, generic objects, and application security, you could apply them to almost all areas of application design.

As with any concept, there are limitations and considerations. However, data-driven architecture provides a means to address various problems and issues, to offer flexibility and enhanced functionality–and all without modifying code. In essence, data-driven architecture enables you to create seemingly simple solutions for users' complex needs. It makes you appear to be a PowerBuilder wizard. What are you going to do with all the time you might save using this new-found power? I'm going to Disneyland!

CHAPTER 25

OLE 2.0 Container Support in PowerBuilder 4.0

By Barry Gervin

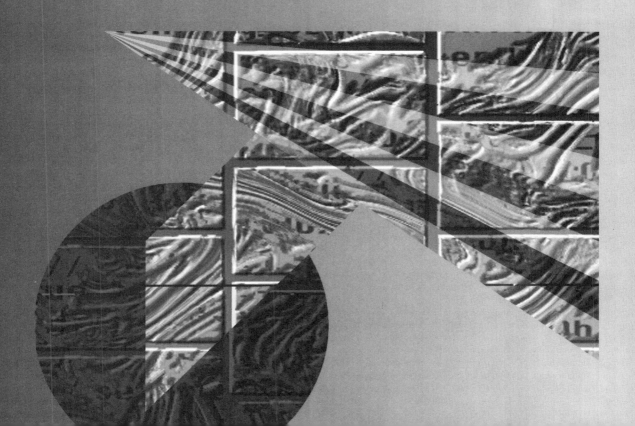

OLE 2.0 Container Support in PowerBuilder 4.0

by **Barry Gervin**

Introduction

Object Linking and Embedding (OLE) is an exciting technology that allows applications to communicate between themselves, not only transferring data, but sharing the processing as well.

PowerBuilder 3.0 allowed developers to create an OLE 1.0 client application. A client application is one that can store or contain data (an OLE object) that is generated by an OLE 1.0 server application. This support was provided through the DataWindow object (see Figure 25-1). For example, in your Employee Detail DataWindow, you could have a binary column represented as an OLE Picture via MS Paintbrush.

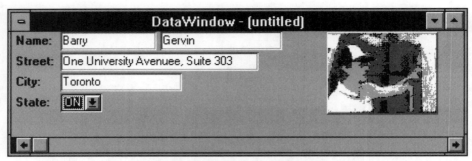

Figure 25-1: PB 3.0/4.0 OLE 1.0 DataWindow support.

Shortly before PB 3.0 was delivered to the market, a new specification for OLE was released by Microsoft–OLE 2.0. This new version brings many more features to the OLE technology. Microsoft defines the differences as follows:

While OLE 1.0 was solely a document technology, OLE 2.0 is built on the underlying OLE Component Object Model, making OLE 2.0 a foundation for object services that extend well beyond document technologies. As such, OLE provides a single, integrated architecture that addresses the needs of corporate developers building business solutions.[1]

Powersoft has not altered its DataWindow OLE 1.0 support; however, it has added OLE 2.0 Container support and OLE Server Automation Support in PowerBuilder 4.0.

The new OLE 2.0 Container support has been added via a new window control. This control will allow you to place an OLE 2.0 server object on the surface of a window. Powersoft's OLE server support is provided through new datatypes and functions.

The OLE Server Automation can be used in conjunction with an OLE Container Control within your PowerBuilder application, or against an external session of the OLE server. For example, with OLE Automation, you could instruct Word to print its current document, or instruct Excel to perform a calculation. This chapter will not address OLE Server Automation Support, but rather focus on the Container Control.

What is OLE?

OLE is a technological implementation of the Common Object Model (COM). COM allows software developers to build components that work in conjunction with other objects or components. This plug-and-play environment can benefit end users by allowing application developers to focus on the nuances unique to a particular business application instead of the techniques involved in building lower level technical blocks.

---

1. OLE Documents: Technical Backgrounder Part No. 098-56453 Microsoft Corporation

This approach is not unique to the software business. The hardware industry has been doing it for years with the IBM-compatible, ISA, or AT bus architecture. Using defined standard interfaces, hardware engineers can design components that will plug into a PC's bus. PC builders only need to focus on the business requirements of their customers (i.e. how much disk space, as opposed to how to build a hard drive).

OLE 2.0 technology is also being made available by Microsoft within the Apple Macintosh environment, and has even been licensed by some unix vendors. (Powersoft's support for OLE in these other ports remains to be seen.) Microsoft is pushing OLE very hard. In fact, starting with Windows95, all applications that use data must be OLE-enabled in one fashion or another to be able to use the "Windows Compatible" logo.

What Components Can I Use with PowerBuilder?

PowerBuilder is an OLE client application. That means that a PowerBuilder developer can embed or link OLE server applications inside of a PowerBuilder application. In Power-Builder 3.0, OLE 1.0 servers were supported through the DataWindow object. PowerBuilder 4.0's new support for OLE 2.0 servers is provided through a new class of window control, an OLE Container.

You cannot take advantage of either version of OLE server unless it is installed on your machine and registered properly. This registration normally occurs when the application is installed through its setup utility. To see a list of installed and registered applications, you can run the Registration Editor. Its filename is regedit.exe and it is installed as part of MS Windows. The easy way to run this is from the Run menu item, under File, in Program Manager.

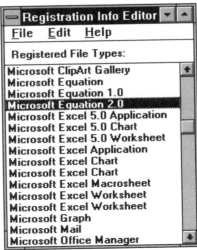

Figure 25-2: Registration Editor.

The Registry displays all of the installed or registered applications; however, not all of these will be OLE 2.0 server applications. To ascertain an application's status, you can run the Registration Editor with the Verbose option (*Run, regedit /v*). In Figure 25-3, take note of the *Protocol/StdFileEditing* notation. It indicates that this application is an OLE server.

If the application you wish to use is not listed, but you know it's an OLE 2.0 server, you may need to manually register it. You can use the File, Merge Registration File to manually register an OLE server application. However, this should be done automatically as part of the program's installation.

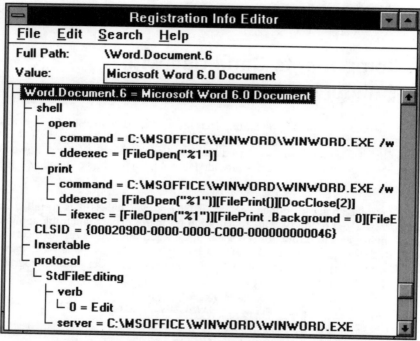

Figure 25-3: Verbose Registration Editor (run regedit /v).

An easier way to look at the OLE server list exists right within PowerBuilder. While in the Script painter, you can select Browse OLE Classes from the Edit menu. An example of the dialog is shown in Figure 25-4.

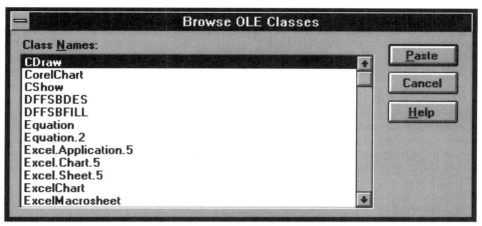

Figure 25-4: PowerBuilder's Browse OLE Classes.

A complete OLE applications catalog is available from Microsoft by calling the Microsoft Developer Solutions Team at (800) 227-4679.

Using the Window OLE Container Control

You can place an OLE object directly in a window using the OLE 2.0 control. The control has attributes that specify the control's appearance and how the user can interact with the object it contains. When you place an OLE control in a window, you can link or embed an object into it at development time, or leave it empty and insert an object during execution. You can write scripts that allow the application or the user to choose an object for the control.

To use the OLE Container Control from the Window Painter, select the OLE 2.0 item from the control menu and place it on your window. The first thing you will be asked is what class of OLE server this control will represent (Figure 25-5).

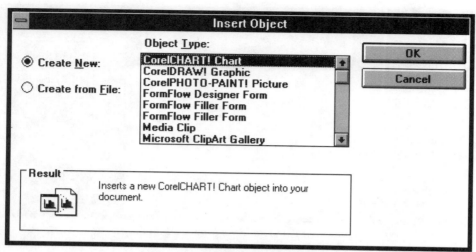

Figure 25-5: Insert Object dialog.

You can either specify a new object–in which case you can select the Object Type–or you can specify a filename. A third, subtle, option is also available: you can decline to specify an Object Type at all by hitting cancel. This would be the choice if you are going to give your user the option of selecting the OLE class at runtime. This could be done with the InsertObject Function.

The next thing you need is to edit the attributes of the OLE Control. This can be done by double-clicking on the control and bringing up the Control Style dialog (Figure 25-6).

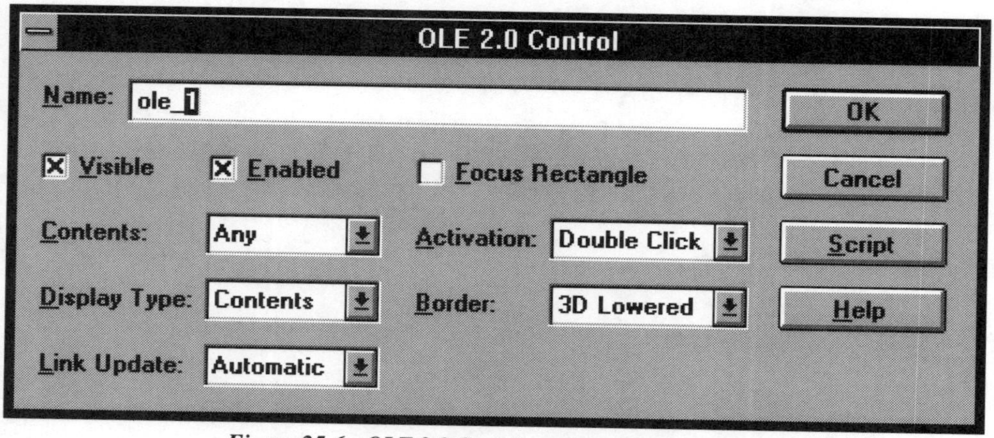

Figure 25-6: OLE 2.0 Container Control style dialog.

Contents

The Contents attribute indicates how the data being displayed in the control is stored. When Contents is Embedded, the data will be stored in your application. This means that the data will actually be stored in the window, saved in your .pbl, and compiled into your executable. Any changes to embedded data must be stored somewhere else; therefore, embedded Contents are generally only used for static data.

When Contents is Linked, it means that only a reference to the data will be stored in your application, not the data itself. The actual data is stored in a file. This is useful if you have many applications sharing the same data. If other applications sharing the data change it, the changed data will also be reflected in the control. If the file is moved, renamed, or the link is otherwise broken, the Link Update attribute will determine how this is handled.

When Contents is Any (the default), either method is allowed. This is probably what you are going to use most of the time. That is because in most cases you will be saving your information in a different file every time, or you will be storing it a database blob column. In either case, you will be manually moving data in and out of the control.

Display Type

This attribute specifies what PowerBuilder will show in the control. Some applications can never show the contents of the OLE object (i.e. a sound recording) and will always show the icon of the server application.

Link Update

If the Contents of an OLE Control are Linked (vs. Embedded) and the link is broken (i.e. file deleted, renamed, moved, etc.), PowerBuilder will need to know how to reconnect to that file. This attribute controls how PB will find the file. If the Link Update is Automatic, PowerBuilder will try to find the file. If PowerBuilder cannot find the file, it will display a dialog box to users at runtime, asking them to point to the file (see Figures 25-7 and 25-8).

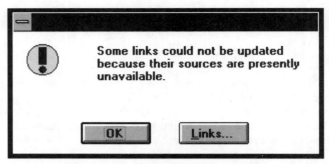

Figure 25-7: Broken OLE link warning.

Links:	Type	Update
d:\pb4\capb.bmp	Paintbrush Pictur	Unavail

Cancel

Update Now

Open Source

Change Source...

Break Link

Source:
Type:
Update: ○ Automatic   ○ Manual

Figure 25-8: Broken link editor.

Activation

The Activation attribute determines how the OLE server will be activated. Activation is invoked to play or edit the data that is in an OLE Container. This process launches the OLE server application so that it may take control of the data.

On today's machines, OLE activation may take some time, particularly with large applications such as Word or Excel. For this reason, the GetFocus event is a highly overrated activation method, since it makes it very likely that a user will accidentally activate the OLE server. If this takes thirty seconds, your users will be annoyed.

There are two ways that PowerBuilder may respond to the request for activation: In Place and Off Site. In Place activation is the default that PowerBuilder uses whenever the OLE server supports it. In all other cases, Off Site activation will be used–with one exception. If the data is Linked, as opposed to Embedded, Off Site activation will *always* be invoked. If you are activating manually, you will have to use the Activate function to perform the activation.

Off Site activation is what was previously supported in OLE 1.0. When the OLE server is launched, it is physically displayed in its own separate window. In Place activation allows the user to edit the data right within the OLE Control. The OLE server's menus are merged with the PowerBuilder application's menus.

Menus for In-Place Activation

When In Place activation is invoked, the OLE server application menus are merged with the menus of your PowerBuilder application. The Menu Painter allows you to control the settings of how the menus will be merged. (Important Note: The menu attributes for In Place activation only apply to the top level menuitems. They have no effect for any of the drop-down items.)

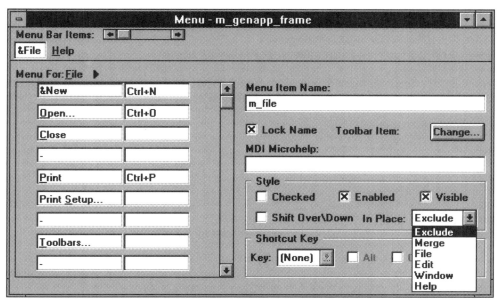

Figure 25-9: In Place settings in the Menu Painter.

Here are some tips for quickly setting up your menu items:

Mark your application's File menu with the In Place setting of File.

Mark your application's Edit menu with the In Place setting of Edit.

Mark your application's Window menu with the In Place setting of Window.

Mark your application's Help menu with the In Place setting of Help.

All other menu pull-downs should be marked as Exclude, unless you explicitly want them available during activation. Merging them may only make the menu too confusing.

Storing the Data

Unlike the DataWindow OLE 1.0 support, PowerBuilder's OLE 2.0 support will not automatically save information for you. Typically, you will want to store your data in a Long Binary/Raw column in your database. You can effectively do this by storing the contents of OLE objects in variables and saving them in files, or using the UPDATEBLOB SQL statement to write this information to the database. An example of this is in Figure 25-10.

```
blob lblb_blob
lblb_blob = ole_1.get_objectdata ( )

INSERT INTO "attachment" ("attachment_number")
 VALUES ( :ii_index_number) ;

UPDATEBLOB "attachment"
SET "attachment"."attachment_data"  = :lblb_blob
  WHERE "attachment"."attachment_number" = 1  ;
COMMIT;
```

Figure 25-10: Storing the blob information from an OLE 2.0 control.

Retrieving the data is very similar; however, instead of using a get_objectdata, a set_objectdata function call will place binary data into the control (Figure 25-11).

```
blob lblb_blob

SELECTBLOB "attachment"."attachment_data"
  INTO :lblb_blob
  FROM "attachment"
  WHERE "attachment"."attachment_number" = :ii_index_num  ;

ole_1.set_objectdata ( lblb_blob )
```

Figure 25-11: Retrieving the blob information for an OLE 2.0 control.

Vendors Providing OLE Support

ACCESS Communications
Access Softek
ADM Control Informatica
Adobe Systems, Inc.
Advanced Logic Research, Inc.

Alcom Corp.
Aldus Corp.
Allen-Bradley
Alliance Data Systems, Inc.
Alliance Infonet
Alliance Research Corporation
Alpha Pacific
Altamira Software Corp.
America OnLine Inc.
Applied Business Technology
Arabesque Software, Inc.
Arrowhead Systems Consulting
Asymetrix Corp.
Ataman Software, L.C.
Attachmate Corp.
AudioFile, Inc.
Aurum Software
Autodesk, Inc.
Automated Solutions
Avalan Technology
Banner Blue Software
BateTech Software
Berkley Speech Technologies, Inc.
Biodesic
Bits & Pixels
Blue Sky Software Corp.
Borland International
Brandon Fridley
Brevard FundRaising
Brio Technology, Inc.
Cadkey, Inc.
Calera Recognition Systems Inc.
California Software, Inc.
Catalytic Software
Chips and Technologies, Inc.
Chrisalan Designs, Inc.
Claris Corp.
CMD Technology, Inc.
Cognitive Technology Corporation
Cognos Corp.
Collabra Software, Inc.
Commerce Clearing House, Inc.
Compu-Color, Inc.
CompuServe, Inc.
Computer Associates International Inc.
Computer Concepts Corporation
Computer Mail Services, Inc.
Concentric Data Systems, Inc.
Consensys
Corel Corp.

Corporate Image Software, Inc.
Creative Interaction, Inc.
Crowe, Chizek & Company
Crystal Services
Cypress Software, Inc.
D.I.P., Inc.
Daniel W. Phifer Computer Systems Consulting
Datacap, Inc.
Datech Network Systems, Inc.
DB Software Consulting
DB Technologies
DCA
Deneba Software
Design Depot , Inc.
Design Science, Inc.
DevelopMentor
Diamond Head Software Inc.
Digital Communications Associates, Inc.
Digital Equipment Corp.
Digitalk Inc.
DMB Electronics, Inc.
Eden Systems Corporation
EM power Corporation
Emerald System Corporation
EPISYS, Inc.
Equinox Corporation
ESG, Inc.
Expert Choice, Inc.
EZX Publishing & Distributing
Falco Data Products, Inc.
FANUC ROBOTICS
FarPoint Technologies, Inc.
Finally Incorporated
Finnegan, O'Malley & Company, Inc.
First Floor, Inc.
Future Labs, Inc.
Geodesk
GlobalStream Corp.
Gold Disk, Inc.
Golden Software, Inc.
Graphics Development International
GST Software plc
Gupta Corp.
Howard Zuckerman & Assoc.
Hummingbird Software
Hydraulic Systems Software
I-Kinetics, Inc.
ICOT Corp.
IdentiTech, Inc.
Impact Technologies

Infinity Squared Corporation
Information Builders
Information Resources, Inc.
Informix Software, Inc.
Infotivity Technologies, Inc.
Innovative Ideas, Inc.
Instant Replay Corporation
Institute of Fundamental Physics (unregistered)
Intel Corp.
Intellution, Inc.
International Digital
Intersolv Q+E
IRI Software
Island Graphics Corp.
Kamel Software, Inc.
Kidasa Software, Inc.
Knowledge Garden, Inc.
Kofax Image Products, Inc.
LA Solution Logicielle
LABWERKS Development
LAPCAD Engineering
LBMS, Inc.
Lead Technologies, Inc.
Lenel Systems International, Inc.
Logis Technology
Loral Test and Information Systems
Lotus Development Corporation
Macromedia, Inc.
Mark V Systems, Ltd.
MathSoft Inc.
MBA Systems LTD.
MC3, Inc.
Merak Projects Inc.
Meridian Software Systems, Inc.
Metaphor, Inc.
MetaWare, Inc.
Micro Business Software
Micrografx, Inc.
MicroHelp, Inc.
Microseconds International Inc.
Microsoft Corp.
Microtest Inc.
Minolta Corporation
ModaCAD
Molecular Machines
Motion Works USA
NDECS
Netlogic, Inc.
Netsoft
Nielsen Marketing Research

No Hands Software
Object Design, Inc.
Object Management Lab
Objectsoft
Odyssey Computing, Inc.
OHB Software, Inc.
ONYX GRAPHICS, CORP.
Open Data Corp.
Optical Technology Group, Inc. (OTG)
Oracle Corp.
Orange Software
Outrider Systems
Pacific Telematics, Inc.
Panasonic
Paradigm Development Corporation
ParcPlace Systems, Inc.
PC DOCS, Inc.
Persoft, Inc.
Pictronics Corp
Pinnacle Publishing
POET Software Corporation
Portland Software
Powersoft Corp.
Practitioners Publishing Company
Premier Automation, Inc.
Primavera Systems, Inc.
Prodata
Prodea Software Corporation
Prodigy
Product Development Automation, Inc.
Professional Software Solutions
ProtoView Development Corp.
PTEX Systems
Q/Media Software Corporation
Quantitative Technology Corporation
Quick Quote
Real Software Solutions, Inc.
Resource Concepts Incorporated
Ring Zero Systems, Inc.
RWT Corporation
Sales Kit Software Corporation
Sales Productivity Systems, Inc.
SAS Institute, Inc.
SBL, Inc.
SBS - International
Scientific Programming Enterprises
Scientific Software Tools, Inc.
Scitor Corp.
SDRC
Serengeti Systems, Inc.

Shapeware
SIERRA ATLANTIC GROUP
Sigma Designs, Inc.
Simplify Development Corp.
SL Corporation
Softbridge, Inc.
Softklone UK
SoftNet Systems
SoftSolutions
Software AG
Software Frameworks Association
Software FX, Inc.
Software Publishing Corp.
Software Research, Inc.
SOMAR Software
SPSS, Inc.
StatSoft, Inc.
StereoCAD, Inc.
Sterling Technologies, Inc.
Stone Age Software
Summit Software Company
Sybase
Symantec Corp.
Symbiotics, Inc.
Symmetry Computing, Inc.
Synergy Engineering Technologies (SET)
Systems & Software, Inc.
Systemware, Inc.
TeamWrite Corporation
Telemagic, Inc.
Terrace Mountain Systems
The Midnight Software Co.
The Software Development Group (TSDG)
Thunderstone Software
TMS, Inc.
Tools & Techniques, Inc.
Traffic Software
Trax Softworks, Inc.
TriMetrix, Inc.
U.S. Computer Works, Inc.
Unisys OLTP
Vanguard Software Corporation
Visual Data Interface
W.D. Roberts Co., Inc
Wang Labs
WATCOM International Corp.
Watermark Software
Wierenga Software
Wilson WindowWare, Inc.
WordPerfect Corporation

WorldWare
XVT Software, Inc.

Conclusion

OLE 2.0 has some very promising new functionality. Version 4.0 contains Powersoft's first attempt at providing support for this specification. As is the case with other ground-breaking technologies, Powersoft's support for OLE 2.0 will likely improve in future versions, based on the experiences of developers with the current PB 4.0 support. I can only speculate, but future support may include OLE Control support (OCX replacements for VBXes) and OLE server support (i.e. letting you create an OLE server application in PowerBuilder).

While there are not many OLE 2.0 server applications available today, Microsoft has made support for this technology mandatory for the Windows 95 platform. If developers wish to use the Windows 95 logo on their product, and their application deals with data, they *must* support OLE 2.0. This is good news for PowerBuilder developers, as the market for OLE servers should continue to grow for years to come.

CHAPTER **26**

A Log File Manager
User Object

By Sean Rhody

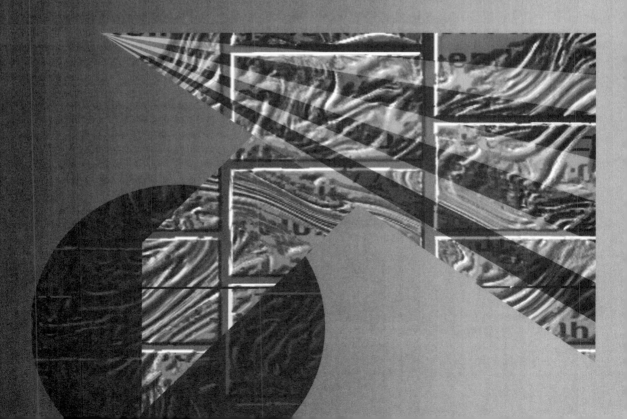

A Log File Manager User Object

by **Sean Rhody**

One of the most frustrating experiences in developing applications is tracking down problems and errors. It's an agonizing process–both for users, who do not understand what is going wrong, and for developers, who often have to rely on users for all their information. One way to ease this burden is to provide each application with a log file that can save information. And a good way to do this routinely in PowerBuilder is to create a non-visual user object to manage the log file.

A non-visual user object is a way of creating abstract classes in PowerBuilder. It is not tied to any user interface element, but rather provides encapsulation of data and methods. The non-visual user object we will design is called uo_lgmgr. The uo_logmgr object will encapsulate all the data and methods needed to implement a log file mechanism.

One reason that a user object is needed is to keep track of the file handle for the log file between writes to the log. The file handle is an integer value returned from the FileOpen() function. Conceivably, you could track this file handle using a global or instance variable and a number of user-defined functions, but that would prevent extensions to the functionality by inheritance. Additionally, it would allow other functions to write to the log file, which should not be allowed.

The user object has one instance variable, an integer called iiLogFileDesc. This is the file descriptor for the log file. All actions performed on the log file are done through the user object. There is no direct access to the log file within the program itself.

There are six different functions for uo_logmgr. They are the following:

```
uf_close()      Closes the file descriptor. This is a private function.
uf_init()       Opens the log file and initializes the logmgr.
uf_db_error()   Logs a database error.
uf_error()      Logs a non-database error.
uf_warning()    Logs a warning.
uf_message()    Logs a message.
```

Because this is a non-visual user object it cannot be placed on a window. Instead, it must be created and assigned to a variable. For example, in an MDI application, an instance variable for the frame might be declared as follows:

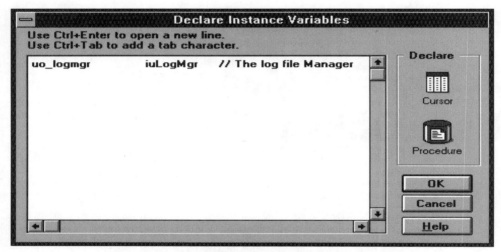

Figure 26-1: Instance variables for uo_logmgr.

This is just the declaration. The object still needs to be created and assigned to this variable. Thus in the open event for this MDI frame window, there might be several lines such as:

```
iuLogMgr = CREATE uo_logmgr
iuLogMgr.uf_log_init("c:\MyLog.log",1)
```

The first line creates a new logmgr object and assigns it to the instance variable iuLogMgr. The second line initializes the log manager as shown below.

```
/*
integer uf_log_init(string p_logfilename int p_mode)

Purpose:    Initialize the log file manager
  p_mode=0 overwrites, p_mode = 1 appends
Returns: 1 for success -1 for failure
/*

string lzInit  // the init string
```

```
date   ldDate    // today's date
time   ltTime    // today's time

IF p_mode = 0 THEN        // overwrite
 iilogfiledesc = FileOpen(p_logfilename, LineMode!, Write!, &
 LockReadWrite!, Replace!)
ELSE
 iilogfiledesc = FileOpen(p_logfilename, LineMode!, Write!, &
 LockReadWrite!, Append!)
END IF

IF iilogfiledesc = -1 THEN
 Return -1
ELSE
 ldDate = Today()
 ltTime = Now()
 lzInit = "Log file initialized: "+String(ldDate)+" at "+ String(ltTime)
 FileWrite(iilogfiledesc,lzInit)
 Return 1
END IF
```

The uf_log_init() function opens the log file in one of two modes, append or overwrite. It uses the FileOpen() function either to open an existing file and append to it, or to truncate a file and start over. The other parameters tell it that the file is opened in write mode, and is locked to prevent other users from modifying it.

If the function can open the file, it writes a new initialization entry to the file and then returns a 1 to indicate success. Otherwise, it returns -1, indicating failure. Note that the file descriptor is kept in the instance variable of the object, and is not accessible elsewhere, as it would be in a global variable.

There are two different types of messages that the object processes, database and non-database messages. Database messages are handled by the uf_db_error() function, while non-database messages can go to uf_error(), uf_warning() or uf_message().

The database message handler uf_db_error() is used to log a database error.

```
/*
integer uf_db_error(transaction p_trans, string p_mess)

Purpose: Writes transaction info and the message to the
 log file.

Returns: 1 for success -1 for failure
*/

Date    ldDate    // the current date
Time    ltTime    // the current time
integer liError  // checks for log write errors

ldDate = Today()
ltTime = Now()
liError = FileWrite(iilogfiledesc,"Database Error: "+String(ldDate)+&
" at "+String(ltTime))

// We won't check for file write errors from here on because we'll assume
// if the first one worked, they all will. In real production code you
// would want to check the return code for each one
```

```
FileWrite(iilogfiledesc,"~tTransaction Values")
FileWrite(iilogfiledesc,"~t~tDBMS="+p_trans.DBMS)
FileWrite(iilogfiledesc,"~t~tDatabase="+p_trans.Database)
FileWrite(iilogfiledesc,"~t~tUserID="+p_trans.UserID)
FileWrite(iilogfiledesc,"~t~tDBParm="+p_trans.DBparm)
FileWrite(iilogfiledesc,"~t~tLogID="+p_trans.LogID)
FileWrite(iilogfiledesc,"~t~tServerName="+p_trans.ServerName)
FileWrite(iilogfiledesc,"~t~tsqlcode="+String(p_trans.sqlcode))
FileWrite(iilogfiledesc,"~t~tsqldbcode="+String(p_trans.sqldbcode))
FileWrite(iilogfiledesc,"~t~tsqlerrtext="+p_trans.sqlerrtext)
FileWrite(iilogfiledesc,"~tMessage: "+p_mess)
FileWrite(iilogfiledesc,"*** End Database Error Entry ***")

return 1
```

The uf_db_error() function calls the Today() and Now() functions to obtain the current date and time for the log file. It writes a header indicating that this is a database error, and then writes the transaction information out, using the passed transaction object p_trans to provide the information. Finally, it writes the user defined message p_mess, and then the database error trailer. The function uses the tab character "~t" to embed tabs in the log file to make it easier to read.

One important point is that some of the transaction information is left out by design. The DBPass and LogPass attributes are not written, as these contain password information. It's a difficult decision to include the DBParm attribute, because this can include passwords, but since this is most often a source of database errors with ODBC, it was included.

The uf_error(), uf_warning(), and uf_message() functions are almost identical, so much so that only one is included here for illustration. The other two can be created simply by changing several of the text fields that are written to the log. The reason that these functions are separate is to provide the capability to extend them if a new user object is inherited from uo_logmgr.

```
/*
integer uf_error(string p_mess)

Purpose: Logs a warning condition to the log file

Returns: 1 for success -1 for error
*/

Date   ldDate     // today's date
Time   ltTime     // current time
int    liError    // errors

ldDate = Today()
ltTime = Now()

liError = FileWrite(iilogfiledesc,"Error Condition: "+&
String(ldDate)+" at "+String(ltTime))

IF liError < 0 THEN
MessageBox("Log Error","Could not write Error to log file")
return -1
END IF
```

```
liError = FileWrite(iilogfiledesc,"~tMessage: "+p_mess)
IF liError < 0 THEN
 MessageBox("Log Error","Could not write Error to log file")
 return -1
END IF

liError = FileWrite(iilogfiledesc,"*** End of Error ***")
IF liError < 0 THEN
 MessageBox("Log Error","Could not write Warning to log file")
 return -1
END IF

return 1
```

The function writes a header with the date and time, the error message, and a trailer.

The last function is uf_close(). This is a private function called in the destructor of the object that simply closes the file descriptor. The line of code is:

```
                return FileClose(iilogfiledesc)
```

It merely returns the close status. This status is not used in the destructor. The destructor simply calls the uf_close() function.

One possible use for uo_logmgr would be to create an instance variable in an MDI frame, as discussed above. All messages and errors could then be written to the log simply by calling one of the functions. The log should be initialized in the open event of the frame, so that it is available as soon as possible. If the frame was called w_my_frame, then a call to the uf_db_error() function would look something like this:

```
w_my_frame.iu_logmgr.uf_db_error(sqlca, "My Error Message")
```

As with all non-visual objects, it's important to destroy them before closing up shop. This would be done in the close event for the w_my_frame window as follows.

```
w_my_frame.iu_logmgr.uf_message("Application Terminating.")
DESTROY iu_logmgr
```

Remember that the destructor event for uo_logmgr automatically closes the file descriptor, so there's no need to try to close it.

What does a log file look like? Here's an example.

```
Log file initialized: 10/11/94 at 11:36:00
Message Condition: 10/11/94 at 11:36:00
Message: Kennel 1.0 Initializing...
*** End of Message ***

Log file initialized: 10/11/94 at 11:37:11
Message Condition: 10/11/94 at 11:37:11
Message: Kennel 1.0 Initializing...
*** End of Message ***

Log file initialized: 10/11/94 at 11:37:16
```

```
Message Condition: 10/11/94 at 11:37:16
Message: Kennel 1.0 Initializing...
*** End of Message ***

Log file initialized: 10/11/94 at 15:07:37
Message Condition: 10/11/94 at 15:07:37
Message: Kennel 1.0 Initializing...
*** End of Message ***

Database Error: 10/11/94 at 15:07:50
   Transaction Values
   DBMS=ODBC
   Database=KENNEL2
   UserID=dba
   DBParm=ConnectString='DSN=KENNEL3;UID=dba;PWD=sql'
   LogID=
   ServerName=
   sqlcode=-1
   sqldbcode=-84
   sqlerrtext=SQLSTATE = 08001
[WATCOM][ODBC Driver][WATCOM SQL]Unable to connect to database server: speci-
fied database is invalid
Message: Connection Failed. Terminating.
*** End Database Error Entry ***
```

This can be a pretty useful tool to have as part of an application. It is even possible to put in a switch that would turn off the log file, simply by adding another function to the object, or writing the code outside of the object using IF THEN statements.

CHAPTER 27

PowerBuilder
Naming Conventions

By Michael MacDonald

PowerBuilder Naming Conventions

by **Michael MacDonald**

There is no subject more boring, yet more vital, than naming conventions in your Power-Builder programming efforts. Anybody looking at your script should be able to tell instantly where a variable is defined (its scope), its type, and its purpose. Likewise, functions and other objects should also be clearly scoped and labeled. Failure to follow these simple rules results in anarchy, and inevitably leads to hard-to-find bugs in your programs.

In the following pages, I will review the naming conventions that I use in PowerBuilder programming. These conventions are based on those published and donated to the public domain by PowerCerv™ Corp. of Tampa, Florida.

First, let's review variable names. PowerBuilder allows you to use up to ninety-nine characters for names, including special characters such as underlines. Avoid names such as temp1 and tempstring. These make it tough for other programmers following you (and indeed for yourself six months later) to determine the variable's purpose. Don't be afraid to create descriptive names such as payable_amount and cursor_index. Recognizable abbreviations, such as idx and ctr for index and counter, are okay.

The one exception I make is to the index variable on FOR ... NEXT loops, where I tend to code FOR i_i = 1 to 10 ... NEXT. Even that can become hairy when you have multiple nested FOR ... NEXT loops.

528 PowerBuilder 4.0: Secrets Of The PowerBuilder Masters

It is customary in PowerBuilder programs to use lower case for variables, and to use the underscore character as a separator. Use the separator for easy readability.

Variables may be scoped to four, or arguably five, levels: global; shared; instance; and local. One could argue that a fifth level is valid, that level being function arguments. The scope of any variable should be the first character, so that i_i_counter is recognizable as an instance variable and g_s_user_id is discernible as a global variable. Omit the scope for local variables:

Scope	Abbreviation
function argument	a
global	g
instance	i
shared	s

Variable type abbreviations are as follows:

Type	Abbreviation
Boolean	b
Blob	blb
Date	date
Datetime	dt
Decimal	dec
Double	d
Graphic Object	gr
Integer	i
Long	l
Real	r
String	s
Time	t
Unsigned Integer	ui
Unsigned Long	ul

Examples of proper variables names would include i_i_customers_found and dec_ar_balance, recalling that variables declared locally have their scope omitted. Some programmers like to omit the underscore between the scope and the type, resulting in ii_customers_found. This is perfectly acceptable, so long as it is applied consistently.

Windows

Windows should adhere to the convention:

```
w_<ancestor>_<number of datawindows>_<db op><cardinality>
```

or

```
w_<name>
```

for an ordinary window.

The ancestor component of the name appears only if this window is an ancestor object not meant to be directly instantiated. Use w_a for windows and MDI sheets. Use w_fa for an MDI frame ancestor. The number of DataWindows is self-explanatory and can be omitted if there is only one. The database operation and cardinality should always be present, and may be strung together (i.e. no separator character in between). Use the following tables:

Data Base Operation	Abbreviation
Update	u
Insert	i
Delete	d
Query	q
Cardinality	c
Single Row Update	s
Multiple Rows Update	m

Thus, a valid name for an ancestor window meant to provide update, delete, and insert capabilities on single rows would be w_a_udis. Note that the _a_ denotes a window not meant to be directly instantiated and that the window would have one DataWindow control. A customer update window inherited from w_a_udis, would be simply w_customer.

User Objects

User-defined DataWindow objects are denoted similarly to windows:

```
u_dwa_{<number of datawindows>}<db op><cardinality>
```

Thus, a typical ancestor DataWindow user object would be named u_dwa_udis. Leave out the number of DataWindows if there is only one, and denote a DataWindow object providing update, delete, and insert capabilities on single rows.

Other user objects have the syntax of:

```
u_<object>{a}_name
```

where the optional a_ denotes the object is not meant to be instantiated directly.

Use the following table to denote the type of object:

Object Type	Abbreviation
Application	app
Command Button	cb
Check Box	cbx
Edit Mask	em
DropDownListBox	ddlb
Group Box	gb
Horizontal Scroll Bat	hsb
List Box	lb
Line	ln
Multi-Line Edit	mle
Non-Visual Object	nvo
Oval	oval
Picture	p
Picture Button	pb
Rectangle	r
Round Rectangle	rr
Radio Button	rb
Single-Line Edit	sle
Static Text	st
Structure	str
Vertical Scroll Bar	vsb

Thus, an "OK" command button would be ucb_ok.

Functions

Like variables, functions also have scope. Functions may be global or declared at the window, menu, etc. level. Function names take on the form:

```
<scope>_name
```

Function Scope	Abbreviation
Global	f
Menu	fm
Non-Visual	fnv
User Object	fu
Window	fw

A global function to verify passwords would be f_password_verify, while a function belonging to a security non–visual object might be fnv_access_verify.

Custom User Events

Custom user events have the format:

```
<event type>_<name>
```

The event type will be either a **ue_** for a user event or **we_** for a standard Windows event. For user events, the name should be descriptive, such as **ue_validate** or **ue_ok**. These events should be mapped to one of the PB custom events, **pbm_custom01** through **pbm_custom75**. For Windows events, the name should be the Windows event, thus **rbuttondblclk** would map to **pbm_rbuttondblclk**.

Event Type	Abbreviation
User Event	ue
Windows Event	we

CHAPTER 28

Creating On-Line Help

By Bruce Armstrong

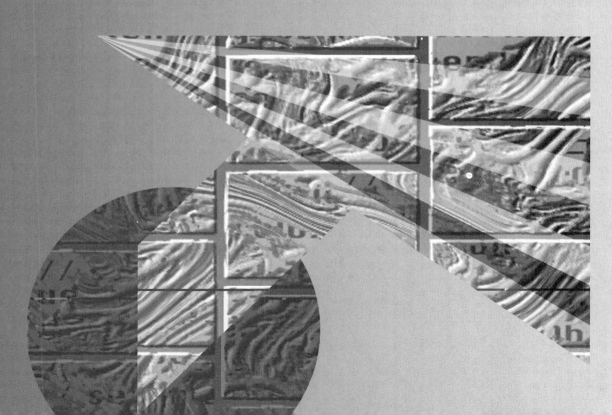

Creating On-Line Help:
How to Get Your Users to Actually Read the Manual

by **Bruce Armstrong**

Introduction

Why do on-line help?

Unfortunately, writing documentation for an application is a task that is often disregarded until the final phases of development. The results often suffer from being incomplete and poorly designed. Effective on-line help involves additional effort beyond that required to develop paper-based manuals. Therefore it is sometimes abandoned entirely–or when developed, is done even less well than the paper documentation.

One of the difficulties in developing on-line help has been that the Windows help compiler only accepts input in the form of RTF (Rich Text Format) files. In addition, the nomenclature used to distinguish various help file features, such as "popup links" and "jump links," is rather cryptic.

However, there are a number of utilities available to the developer now that will prepare the RTF files that the Windows help compiler requires, without requiring the developer to understand or use the arcane nomenclature.(A few of those tools will be discussed below, and information on where to obtain information about them is contained in the end of the chapter.) So these complications need no longer be stumbling-blocks.

There are significant advantages to on-line help that should not be overlooked. It is certainly much less expensive to distribute: you simply include it on the same disk(s) that you use to distribute the application. It is more difficult for on-line help to be misplaced or "borrowed"; as a result, it is always available to the end user. On-line help provides the ability to hot link and browse, and to search through the documentation much more easily than can be done with conventional documentation. Proper on-line help can increase the chances that your end users will actually read the instructions!

This chapter is intended to help explain some of the procedures for implementing on-line help. My hope is that, with a fuller understanding of how to design it, application developers will be encouraged to use on-line help more extensively, and also to consider developing it concurrently with the application itself.

Some features of on-line help files

Hot link

A hot link is a defined relationship between a word, phrase, image, or section of an image in one topic of the help file and another topic in the help file. If the user clicks on the word, phrase, image, or section of an image, the related topic is displayed. If the hot link is defined as a jump, that topic becomes the current topic. If the hot link is defined as a popup, that topic simply displays is a small window on top of the current topic, and will disappear when the user clicks the mouse button again.

Browse

When the help file is developed, you may indicate that some topics are related as peers rather than through hot links. From within the help file, the user will then be able to use a set of prior/next buttons to browse through those topics in order.

Search

As the help file is being developed, you may also specify one or more keywords for each topic. When users run the help file, they will then be able to perform searches on those keywords as a quick means for finding the information they want.

Some Resources You Will Need

Text editor, word processor, and/or RTF file generator

Text editor

It is fully possible to develop adequate on-line help using nothing more than a simple DOS text editor and the help compiler. For example, qdhelp is a utility that will read a standard DOS text file and convert it to a Windows help compiler-compatible RTF file for you. qdhelp uses its own syntax to implement the various help file functions; however, its syntax is much more comprehensible than the directives one would need to use in the RTF file.

Word processor

Several word processors are also capable of saving their documents in RTF format, most notably–and hardly unexpectedly–Microsoft Word for Windows. However, developers still have to know what formattings they need in order to produce the codes in the RTF file that will result in the desired functions in the help file. Fortunately there are a number of utilities to make this easier. They range from simple document templates through sophisticated commercial products such as Doc-To-Help. (The Windows help compiler requires a project file (HPJ), but all of the utilities discussed below generate that file for you as well.)

RTF file generator

The previous approaches work well when the person developing the on-line help is comfortable with writing, particularly if the paper manual and the on-line help will be developed from a common source document (Doc-To-Help is particularly good for the latter). However, if the help file is being generated by developers who are more comfortable with point/ shoot/code procedures, they will probably find other tools easier to use. There are a number of standalone programs that are designed specifically for use in developing on-line help, including Visual Help, Robo-Help and Help Magician.

Screen capture utility

Though you can certainly develop text-only on-line help, it is usually more useful for your end users if you include some graphics. In particular, it is often very helpful to include screen shots from the application you are documenting. These can be incorporated into your on-line help in a number of ways.

Some utilities you already have

Perhaps the simplest approach is to use some of the features and utilities provided within, or along with, Windows itself. If you press <Print Scrn> within Windows, it will copy an image of the entire screen to its own clipboard. From there, you can paste that image (or at least a portion of it) into the PaintBrush program that is provided with Windows, or directly into your document if you are using a compatible word processor or RTF file generator. If you press <Alt>-<PrintScrn>, Windows will copy the active window, rather than the entire screen. If you are not using a compatible word processor or RTF file generator, you should save the image to disk as a .bmp file and then reference that image from your document.

Some better utilities

While the above approach works, it doesn't give you much control over the image you capture. And it will not work if you want to capture images of your drop-down menus, since they will no longer be dropped down when you attempt the screen shot. To gain more power over the images you want to include in your on-line help, you can use a screen capture utility. Some graphics utilities, for example the Watcom Image Editor, provide this capability (though the Watcom Image Editor still cannot capture drop-down menus). There are also a number of utilities that are designed specifically for capturing screen shots with a high degree of control, such as the ability to capture drop-down menus. One such tool is Snag-It.

Image Editor

While screen shots are useful, you may want to incorporate additional graphics in your on-line help simply to make it more pleasant to use. You could, of course, take advantage of stock images, which are available from a number of sources. But you might also want to develop some of your own images–for instance, you might want to include a graphic of your corporate logo at appropriate locations within the help file. An image editor is also useful for cleaning up some of your screen shots.

There are a great number of image editing utilities on the market, either available commercially or as shareware. CorelDraw is one of the most popular commercial products, and comes with a large selection of clip art. PaintShop Pro is a well-known shareware product. Finally, many of you may already have another useful tool, the Watcom Image Editor.

Segmented Hypergraphics Editor

One of the more sophisticated features of on-line help is the ability to assign "hot spots" to your screen shots, so that users can "drill down" graphically in your help file to find the information they need. The image file used to provide this capability originates as a bitmap file (BMP), but in the process of assigning the hot spots is converted to a format called segmented hypergraphic (SHG). The utility used to convert BMP files to SHG files is the Segmented Hypergraphics Editor (shed.exe).

One interesting feature of SHG files is that although they provide the same resolution as BMP files and contain additional information, they are actually smaller. In fact, depending on the image, a SHG file may be only one-fourth the size of the original BMP file. This is largely because the BMP format is an uncompressed format. It means, however, that regardless of whether or not you wish to implement graphic hot spots in your on-line help, you might consider using SHG files rather than BMP files in order to keep down the size of your file.

Help compiler

Once you've developed your source for the RTF file, added whatever graphics you want to include, and generated the RTF file, you'll need to compile it all into the on-line help file format (HLP). The program that accomplishes this is the Windows help compiler. Unlike its sister utility shed.exe, the Windows help compiler is a DOS executable. It comes in three versions:

> hc.exe–The Windows 3.0 help compiler. This version is not recommended..

> hc31.exe–The Windows 3.1 help compiler. This version is primarily designed for generating help files from the DOS command line.

> hcp.exe–The protected memory version of the Windows 3.1 help compiler. This version is primarily designed for generating help files from a DOS shell

invoked from within Windows.

An Example

Introduction

For our example, we're going to develop some on-line help for the sample application that comes with PowerBuilder 4.0. I'll be using Windows Help Magician to create the RTF file: a demo copy of that program is included on the CD-ROM that comes with this book, so that you can create the same on-line help following the same steps. If the segmented hypergraphics editor and the help compiler are not included on the CD-ROM, they can be obtained from the WINSDK forum on CompuServe. A shareware version of Snag-It is also provided on the CD-ROM to help capture the screen images. You will need to register that utility with the developer if you intend to use it beyond a short trial period.

Grabbing a screen shot

The first thing we want to do is grab a bitmap of the main window for the sample application. If the window is maximized, tools like Windows PaintBrush and the Watcom Image Editor can't handle the size of the bitmap that would result from a <Print Scrn> capture to the clipboard. Instead, let's use Snag-It to copy the entire screen directly to a file. Creating a SHG file

Selecting a hot spot

Next we read the bitmap into shed.exe in order to convert it into a segmented hypergraphic. Once it's loaded, we create our hot spots by doing a click and drag from one corner of the rectangular area we need to define to the opposite corner. The following figure shows what the image looks like after we have selected the DataWindow that displays the topics as a hot spot.

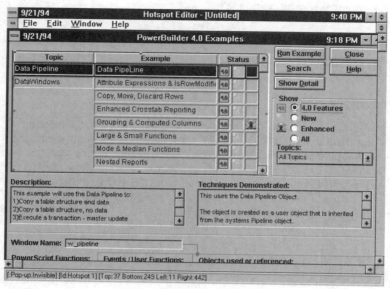

Figure 28-2

Assigning attributes to the hot spot

Double-clicking on the newly defined hot spot brings up a dialog box for defining its characteristics. Here we detail the context string, type, attribute, ID, and bounding box for the hot spot. Each of these is explained in more detail below.

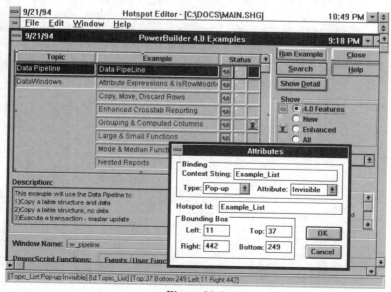

Figure 28-3

Context string

Unique context strings are used to identify the different windows in the on-line help file. Clicking on this hot spot will perform an internal link (based on the type, defined below) using this context string as the value to link to. Therefore the context string is usually the title of the window that you will later use to display help for that area.

Type

The type of the hot link can be popup (a small window is displayed on top of the current topic) or jump (the window associated with the context string becomes the new topic). The type could also be defined as macro or searchable, but we won't be covering those types.

Attribute

"Attribute" determines whether the user will be able to see the border of the hot spot in the graphic shown in the on-line help file. It is usually set to Invisible.

ID

"ID" can provide a more convenient name for the hot spot within the file. It is optional, and we will not use it within the on-line help file.

Bounding box

This may be used to fine tune the size or location of the borders of the hot spot.

Finishing the SHG File

We then repeat this process for the other object on the image that we want to have hot spot hypertext links. Once done, we save out the file in a SHG format.

If I have trouble remembering the context string we defined in the SHG file, I can simply select Edit, Select from within shed.exe when viewing the SHG file. It will provide me with a list of the defined hot spots:

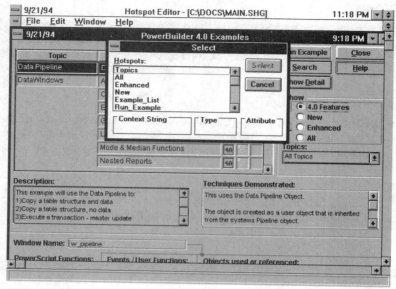

Figure 28-4

Referencing the SHG file

Once the file is defined, we specify its filename in the help file source that we are preparing with Help Magician and mark it as a bitmap using the "Bitmap" command button at the bottom of the Help Magician frame.

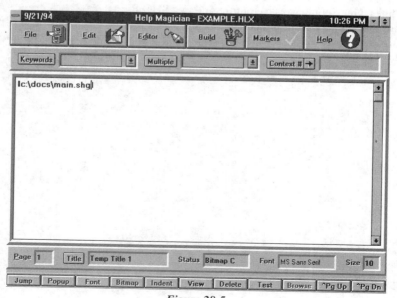

Figure 28-5

Defining hot link topics for the SHG file

We then define windows for the context strings that we want to call from our segmented hypergraphic. For simplicity, we define the title, the context string, and the keyword identically. (Each of those terms is explained below:)

The following is an example of one of the topic screens—in this case the one that will be displayed when the user clicks on the portion of the segmented hypergraphic to which I have assigned the keyword "Topics."

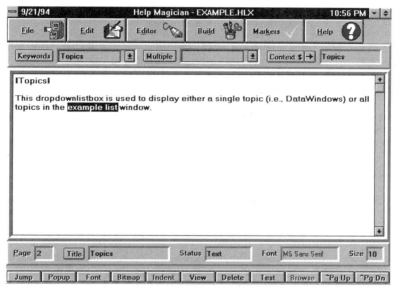

Figure 28-6

Context string

The context string is used within the on-line help system to uniquely identify each window and to provide the links between windows.

Title

The title is used within Help Magician as a more convenient way to reference an individual window.

Keywords

Keywords are used by the on-line system to allow the user to search for help on any subject. You may define a significant number of keywords for a single window in the help system, but at a minimum I would recommend including the title of the window.

Defining additional hot links

Notice in the last figure that the words "example list" have been highlighted. That's because I've already defined another help topic with that title, and we are going to define a jump link between the selected text and that window. To do that, after selecting the text, simply press the "Jump" command button on the bottom of the window and a list of available topics is displayed (see below).

Since we used the "Jump" command button to define this hot link, when the topics window is shown the phrase "example list" will appear in color (the default is green), and will have a solid underline. If the user clicks on that phrase, the Example List topic will become the current topic.

If we had used the "Popup" command button instead of the "Jump" button to define this link, the phrase would have appeared with a broken underline, and a popup window with the Example List topic would have appeared when the user clicked on the phrase. The topic currently in the window would have remained there.

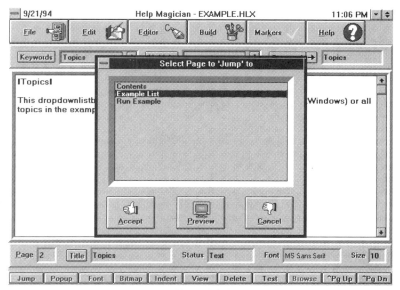

Figure 28-7

Allowing browsing

We want to allow end users to browse through the help for related topics–for example, the help for all of the command buttons. To do this, we create a browse group definition by clicking on the ""Browse" command button:

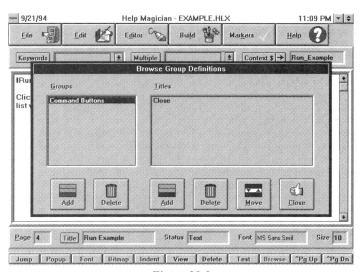

Figure 28-8

In this case, I've already created the group definition and added one of the command button topics to the group. To add the other command button topics, I simply press the "Add" button. I am presented with another dialog box from which I can choose another topic:

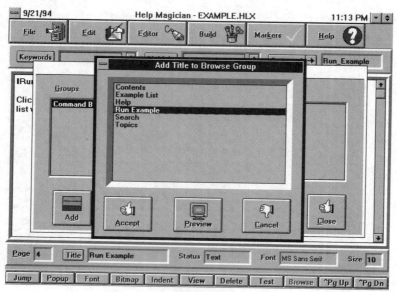

Figure 28-9

Since a topic can only belong to one browse group, this dialog box only shows those topics that have not already been assigned to a browse group.

When the help file is run, two command buttons ("Prior" and "Next") will appear on the frame. When a topic that is part of a browse group becomes the current topic, the command buttons will enable, and the user may then use them to step back and forth between the related topics.

Allowing searching

To allow the user to search for information in the help file, simply define one or more keywords for the important topics. When the help file is run, users may request a search dialog box that will list the keywords in alphabetical order. When they select one of the keywords, a list of topics that reference that keyword will be shown.

Compiling the help

The demo version of Windows Help Magician provided on the CD-ROM only allows a maximum of seven topics (the non-demo version has no such limit). Once you have defined seven topics (or as many short of that as you want), you can compile the help file by selecting the "Build" command button on the top of the Help Magician frame.

If any errors occur during the compile of the on-line help, you will be provided with a list of them (see below). You can then choose to ignore them or to correct them, and recompile the help file.

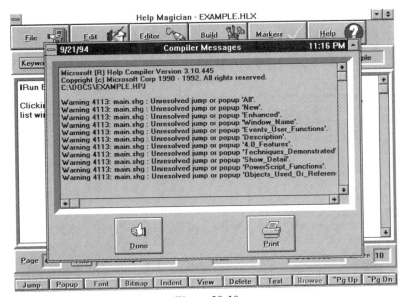

Figure 28-10

Running the help file

If there were no major problems with the compile, you can call the winhelp engine from a menu option under the "Build" command button, and it will run your newly created help file.

Popup

Here is an example of a popup link from the segmented hypergraphic I defined in the example help file we generated. It is invoked by clicking on the large DataWindow in the bitmap. Note that the window that the help appears in is sized for the amount of text that needs to be shown. That window will also only remain visible until the user clicks the mouse button again.

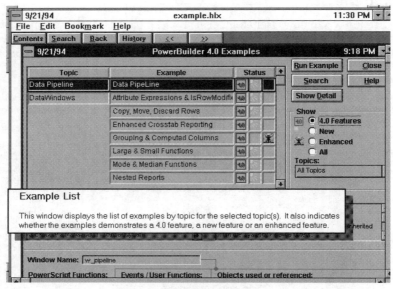

Figure 28-11

Jump

Here is what a jump link would look like. (I didn't include any in the example.) Note that the topic window fills the entire frame, regardless of how much text there is. Also note that the topic window is the current topic.

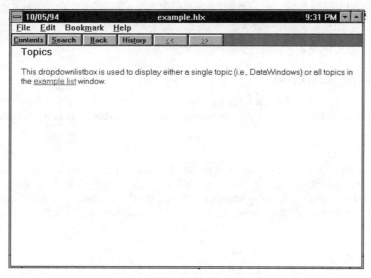

Figure 28-12

Searching

This is an example of the search dialog box that appears if the user attempts to search the on-line help.

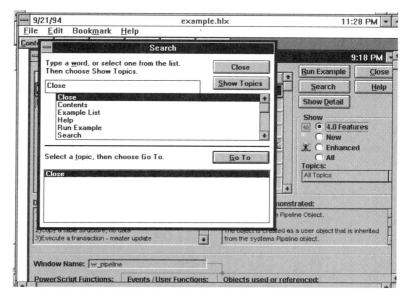

Figure 28-13

Browsing

Note in the following window that the last two buttons on the help file toolbar are enabled. That is because the "Run Example" command button is a member of a browse group. If users click on one of those two command buttons, they will be able to step through the related topics (in this case, the topics cover the other command buttons on the example window).

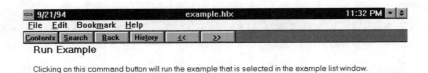

Figure 28-14

Additional Information

CorelDraw
Corel Corp.
1600 Carling Ave.
The Corel Bldg
Ottawa, ON, CD K1Z 8R7

Doc-To-Help
WexTech Systems, Inc.
310 Madison Avenue, Suite 905
New York, NY 10017
(212) 949-9595

Document Templates

A number of these are available in the MSWORD and WINSDK forums on CompuServe.

Help Magician

Software Interphase Inc.
82 Cucumber Hill Road, Suite 104D
Foster, RI 02825-1212
Phone: (800) 542-2742
Fax: (401) 397-6814.

PaintShop Pro

JASC, Inc.
10901 Red Circle Drive, Suite 340
Minnetonka, MN 55343
Phone: (612) 930-9171
Fax: (612) 930-9172

QDHELP

QDHELP is available as shareware from the WINSDK forum on CompuServe.

Robo-Help

Blue Sky Software
7486 LaJolla Blvd, Suite 3
LoJolla, CA 920037
(619) 459-6365
(800) 677-4946

SHED.EXE

Microsoft Corporation
One Redmond Way
Redmond, WA 98052-6399
Phone: (800) 227-4679

Snag-It

Snag-It is available as shareware from the WINSDK forum on CompuServe.

Visual Help

Visual Help is available as shareware from the Powersoft forum on CompuServe.

Watcom Image Editor

A beta version of this product was provided with the Enterprise edition of PowerBuilder 3.x.

CHAPTER 29

Debugging Tips and Tricks: How to Get Your Users to Actually Read the Manual

By Peter Horwood

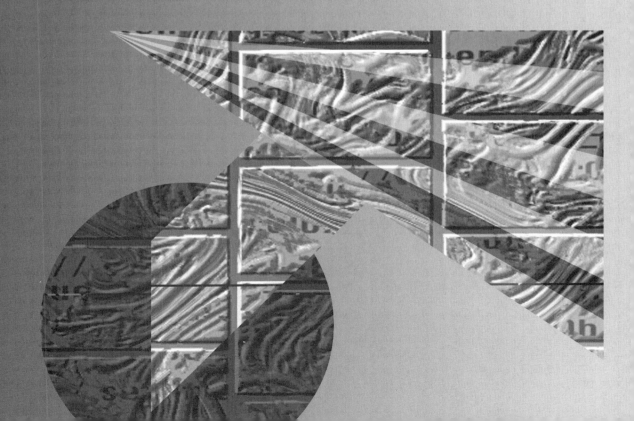

Debugging Tips and Tricks

by **Peter Horwood**

Why Are There Bugs?

In the beginning, computers were toys for electronic engineers and mathematicians. Very few other people had direct experience with them at the time. It was during this era that people started thinking of computers as magical devices and of the people who worked them as magicians.

Over the years, the domain of computers grew, and claims for their abilities began to outpace the ability of developers and hardware to deliver. Despite this, there was a low-level fear that computers would bring an end to human civilization and rule the world. To managers; however, the computer was described as a panacea that would solve all their administrative and information needs.

In the Seventies, the promises started coming more into line with reality, and the extremely high cost of computers made managers think about their cost benefits. The mainframe programmers of the time had to get more and more sophisticated in their development, testing, and debugging methods to meet the new efficiency demands.

In the Eighties, a new style of computer was brought out–one for which IBM initially estimated the total market as only thousands. The PC, or personal computer, over the next few years brought computer power down to a cost that many individuals and most companies could afford.

Like the bigger companies before them, the new-style computer purchasers were taught that PCs would be a blanket solution to all their ills. As the Eighties drew to a close and recession hit much of the world, the average person started to find out that computers were not a cure-all. In the Nineties, as micro-computers become more powerful than the mainframes of a decade ago, companies are starting to require that micro-computers too prove their value.

While the personal computer was growing up, many people started using standard programming languages on the PC. In the database arena, the most outstanding successes have of course been the xBase languages. Of those, we found that dbase (the original flavor) lost a lot of its favor due to its slow speed and number of bugs. Wayne Ratliff was once quoted as saying the product was considered stable when only two *new* bugs were reported per week. As the need for multiple people to access the same data became greater, tools like Power-Builder came along to propel us to the next level.

However, the vast majority of developers who use PC software, not being well-trained, get sloppy. One area that has been found wanting is program correctness. In the Nineties, micro-computer programmers are going to have to improve the overall reliability of their programs. To make matters worse, the sophistication, user friendliness, and portability now expected of programs are at least two orders of magnitude greater than they were a decade ago.

The lessons learned on the larger computers are going to have to be re-learned by the new developers, and learned better and faster. As Coleman Sisson from Powersoft has repeatedly said to those who come from mainframes, "Don't forget what you already know." Just because client/server software lets you do more in a shorter time period, doesn't mean you should start creating LOTS of poor quality programs.

In our company, I was giving a "pep" speech, and one of my phrases quickly became a motto of our developers. "We want to develop a little bit of excellence, not a whole lot of crap." Tools like PowerBuilder will help you do either. Too many choose a whole lot of poorly written, designed, debugged, and tested applications.

If you, like my staff and me, want to produce as much as you can–so long as it is quality...then this book, and this chapter, will attempt to help you reach this goal quickly and wisely.

Who's at Fault?

What types of problems are we going to face? Whenever bugs are encountered, it is almost always claimed to be someone else's fault. Users blame developers; developers blame analysts or the software they use; analysts blame users' inability to know what they want; and compiler writers blame Microsoft.

Regardless of whose fault it is, developers and analysts find out very quickly that the user does not *care* who is to blame–and the user pays the bills. If the current set of developers and analysts cannot solve the problem, users will look around until they find others who can. If you blame someone else, the user will simply assume you made a bad decision in trusting that someone else.

PCs are no longer "personal" computers. Networks of PCs, or PCs with operating systems like unix, can now run hundreds of terminals. As PCs move more and more into traditional mainframe areas, the demands on developers and analysts are going to do nothing but increase. If developers and analysts want to have jobs, they will have to find the solutions.

So where *do* the bugs come from? To get a handle on the issue I have spent some time, in the companies I own and manage, tracking bugs to their final source. Over about five years, working first with Fox Software and then Powersoft, I have estimated the following approximate ratios:

```
Hardware               1%
Operating systems      3%
Powersoft's software   5%
Third-party utilities  2%
In-house errors       90%
```

I think the value for the third-party utilities is so low because we avoid using too many of them. This is due to having been stung too many times waiting for third-party libraries to be released on the newest platform our main tool is on.

Admittedly, I find it appalling that ninety percent of the errors were caused by me and my employees–and like most, I find the Powersoft bugs the most frustrating. It is an area that we (and fortunately Powersoft) are constantly striving to improve. In practice, our productivity has almost doubled for each of the last seven years, while the frequency of bugs per hour of development has only increased slightly. This is encouraging, but almost everyone in the industry needs continual improvement in this area.

Our experience with PowerBuilder gives a further insight into where the time spent finding bugs actually goes. I found that when my staff and I started working with PowerBuilder, the bulk of the errors we tracked down turned out to be syntax and/or concept bugs on our part. As we became intermediate users, we started finding that a lot of our bug hunting time was spent finding PowerBuilder bugs. Eventually, as we learned to avoid the bugs, we got to the point that the majority of debugging time was spent searching for logic and design problems. This is the same pattern I have seen with previous languages I've worked with.

What about the costs of testing and correcting programs? It has been estimated by many sources that fifty percent or more of the average commercial developer's productive time is spent on debugging and fixing bugs. The cost of a developer's time is staggering, but the cost of live systems re-runs, bad data correction, and the time wasted by top personnel who must assist in finding the problem, dwarfs the cost of the developer's time.

The hidden cost is the frustration factor. On the users' side, the feeling of helplessness–people's inability to accomplish their objectives with those "useless computers"–can often bring a high level of hostility in the relationship between user and developer. Indeed, users have often been called unwilling victims of developers.

On the other side, no developer likes to have users clamoring about problems, and very few developers enjoy the time spent resolving bugs. This is especially true when it was the customers who found the bugs and are complaining! Many developers hope that they have done their job when the program is coded, and will do almost anything to leave a project and start the next one. One would think that developers would jump at the opportunity to reduce post-coding problems. Unfortunately most developers are either unwilling, unable, or both. This chapter, of course, is aimed at the willing but unable, as well as those who are able, but want to improve.

If a program is used in mission-critical areas–medical and military equipment controls, vehicles or space shuttles–problems can mean loss of life, all due to one "little" mistake by a developer or analyst. Consider the Patriot missile that did not even try to shoot down a Scud missile in the Gulf War of 1990. The result was twenty-eight deaths. All because of one "small" computer bug.

In programs used in accounting or management software, single bugs have been known to cause problems in the hundreds of thousands of dollars.

On a more personal level, many companies have gone bankrupt because they were unable to control the quality of their systems. This has not happened to me, and I hope it hasn't happened to you. Gut a bug in a system could cause it to occur.

It has been said that no program is better than the false conclusions derived from it. The phrase GIGO (Garbage In, Garbage Out),is generally taken as a computer phenomenon. However if a manager is handed false values, then the decisions made from those reports will often be just as bad. So GIGO applies to anyone who uses the computer's output.

Types of Errors

In the previous section I discussed the percentages of failures we see. In the coming section we are going to take a brief look at what each of those types of failures is.

Hardware errors

In the hardware section, most people include the actual computer circuitry and the BIOS, the low-level program that comes built into the computer. It is fortunate that for the last few years errors in this area have been very small. Most people have BIOSes written by companies with a reputation for high quality, such as AMI.

One interesting problem comes from the general reliability of the hardware. Since the hardware is very seldom at fault, people very rarely consider it–even when it *is* at fault. The seeming randomness of such errors, and the conditioning to trust hardware, often makes hardware failures very difficult to detect. They may exist for a long time before anyone even looks at the problem. As a result, when they occur, hardware errors are frequently the most costly and time-wasting, despite their low frequency. Of course, if you fiddle with your hardware frequently, this may not be a problem, because you are used to having a lot of hardware errors!

When I get a sudden rash of unresolved and non-reproducible bugs on my system alone, I will often remove and reset all the cards in my system, to see if that is the problem. I carry my computer to and from work every day, and this "fix" works about once a month.

Operating system errors

Sticking my neck out, I include under operating systems the so called "true" operating systems such as PC-DOS and unix, along with Windows or XMotif, networking software–and of course, the accursed screen drivers.

Like hardware problems, operating system errors can be very difficult to find or even suspect. As operating systems have been getting more complicated, the problems attributed to them have definitely been increasing, while hardware problems have been declining.

Powersoft's software

Powersoft takes a lot of flak for bugs, much of it undeserved. Many of these bugs are our fault, or the fault of one of the myriad of components or software we have connected (e.g. DBMS back ends). Many of us, who came from simpler operating systems like unix, DOS and mainframes, got used to the bulletproof character-based applications of these environments. When we switched to Windows, we learned very quickly with the first Windows language we worked with that Windows programs tend to have a lot more bugs. This is because 1) they are newer and have not, like old cheese, matured yet; and 2) they try to do ten times more than their character-based counterparts.

We developers also want PowerBuilder to catch every bug we create, and we want it done while creating programs that are as fast as C. There is nothing wrong with wanting this, but we need to realize that there are tradeoffs. Personally, I feel PowerBuilder has done a reasonable job of giving us enough latitude and freedom to hang ourselves, while constraining us in areas that do not cause unreasonable restrictions for database-based applications.

Recently one of my employees was bemoaning the fact that it took him two hours to write a particular program and work around a PowerBuilder bug. The he realized that when he had written the same program a few years ago in FoxPro, it had taken him *three months*!

I am not going to try to defend Powersoft as being "bug-free." PowerBuilder *has* bugs, and I hope Powersoft continues to improve it and reduce the bug count. But in the meantime, I am convinced that I can produce more and better programs with it than I can with the other alternatives currently available. I will do my part to help Powersoft find and define their own bugs, so that they can remove them.

Third-party software

Linking in third-party software can save a lot of programming time by not reinventing the wheel. One of the big advantages of using third-party software (if you are not one of the first to buy it) is that it has been tested by many other people.

However, this can lead to finger-pointing. One product I work with recently gave up trying to use PowerBuilder 3.0a– in large part because when it copies more than 32k to the clipboard, PowerBuilder corrupts memory. It took us a few days to find out where the problem was, and even then, until the third-party vendor or Powersoft fixes the problem, the library is useless.

Also, many third-party libraries have been tested with C++ or VB. When you tell their developers you are using these libraries with PowerBuilder, their first instinct is to blame any bugs on PowerBuilder. On closer examination, I have found that most such bugs are due to my interface (calling the library functions wrongly or in the wrong order) or are due to the fact that the third-party library has more holes than Swiss cheese. Other libraries have proven to be rock solid and relatively bug-free.

In-house errors

These are the most voluminous, and the ones you and I have the most control over. Often they are the most complicated–partly because we suspect that "maybe the hardware is malfunctioning" or because we start out by saying "here's a bug in PowerBuilder." In our office, almost all such cases have turned out to be entirely or primarily our own fault.

I like to break in-house errors into the following categories:

1. **Design errors**: the system was not designed to handle some situations that arise. Sometimes what has been missed is a "minor" situation that only occurs once in a very long time. Other times it is a very frequent situation that was simply overlooked. Working with users, we have found that there are three normal reasons why they might not have discussed a requirement with the designer.

> The user (after seeing the final product) says, "It was obvious, you should have realized."

> Users were not aware of the case themselves. The special situation was handled without ever being consciously considered.

> "It only happens once in a while; you don't need to worry about it." Users don't realize that special cases are just as important as the normal case in design.

> Design errors are often the most expensive to fix, as they frequently require rewriting major portions of the system.

2. **Specification interpretation errors** occur when a developer doesn't remember what a note meant, or doesn't understand what the designer meant on a specification. These errors can also occur when a developer only looks over the design quickly, without fully appreciating it. And that can happen even when the developer was the designer.

3.**Logic design errors** result when a developer fails to clearly understand the problem in its fullness, and as a result doesn't deal with the problem at a detailed enough level.

4.**Logic slips** occur when a developer states < 0 when <= 0 is meant, or says > 7 when < 7 is meant. It is sometimes difficult in retrospect to tell logic design errors from logical slips. In the final analysis it may not matter to the user, but logic slips are often easier to detect and fix. Logic design errors can take a lot longer to find because the attempt to fix them may make the same error of not dealing with the whole problem.

5.**Structural errors** are comprised of such mistakes as forgetting to put a space between END and IF. PowerBuilder catches many of these. The ones that are the hardest are those passed to commands like dwModify (now called Modify in Version 4!). This is because the syntax of these commands cannot be compiled until runtime, since the contents of the string are not always known until then.

6.**Transcription errors** will mostly be detected by the compiler, but others can remain hidden for long periods of time. For instance, if you have two variables I_1 and I_I, you might use I_I when you meant to use I_1. Proportional fonts can make this even more difficult. Recently one of our developers accidentally inserted a space in a filename. When it was reported as a bad filename or disk full error, he had other developers look at it. Not one person saw the space until we took the file into Word and sorted it. The item was no longer in the proper order. Suddenly we saw there might be a space. Using the arrow keys we were able to determine that there *was* a space in the middle of the name.

7.**Detail errors** are similar to structural errors and transcription errors and indeed, are often structural or transcriptional. These occur through simple carelessness or by working back and forth between two languages. They are often errors of omission (omitting a comma, a bracket) or insertions of a similarly insidious statement. If you never forget the space between the END and IF, you probably still have problems sometimes with the " vs ~" vs ~~~" details.

Why Is So Little Written on This Topic?

One would think that, with over fifty percent of programming time and cost being spent on debugging or testing programs and systems, there would be a large number of books written on the topic. Unfortunately, it is a lot easier to write a book on syntax and coding techniques, and an awful lot more fun to write a book or article showcasing your algorithms.

Similarly, book authors want to *read* books on "how-to's" and other fun things, not on boring topics like testing and debugging. A couple of years ago I was querying publishers about writing a book on testing and debugging with FoxPro (a language I used to be fairly proficient at). One publisher said quite bluntly that "no one wants to read books about that–they want to know about the latest tricks and features. How about you write a book on...." And I have to admit, I'm really looking forward to reading and studying the work by the other authors in this book!

One would also think that there would be a large bank of transmitted knowledge on how to test, given all the experience that every developer acquires. It seems; however, that most developers and systems managers do not expand and polish these techniques. They simply wish over and over again that they had a better way of doing it, and then rush out and start out wrong all over again.

So What Do I Hope to Accomplish in This Chapter?

I will be dealing with work habits, tools, and techniques that are designed to minimize time spent in the total development cycle–the total development cycle meaning the time it takes until the product is out, working, and "complete." It is specifically *not* going to help you get the first draft of the code done in the shortest possible time. It *will* help you to get the working product done in the shortest realistic time.

The emphasis will be on avoiding, finding, and removing bugs, in that order of priority. More than one developer has been heard to say, "just don't put the bugs in, in the first place!" Having avoided many of the bugs, we will then work on finding those that remain.

For managers, this chapter and the next will help you set out policies and procedures that will minimize the number and extent of programming errors. We will look at the cost/benefit trade-offs as well as discussing specifically what you, as a manager, can do to help your developers and designers achieve your goals. In the latter portion of this chapter, we will deal with some of the touchy-feely issues that can really help.

Developers can use this book to evaluate their programming methods and styles to become, in many cases, drastically more productive.

Students can use this book to avoid making the mistakes of the current and past generation of developers (e.g. me).

Finally, this discussion is intended and designed to be extremely practical. About half the topics are not specific to PowerBuilder. Yet where we get down to the specifics, I am not discussing "all languages in general": in a PowerBuilder book I have deliberately chosen, wherever possible, to base the tricks on PowerBuilder. This way you can directly, immediately, and exactly apply the techniques and tools discussed.

When you are finished going through this section, even if you only apply a few of the techniques, the programming achieved by you or your developers will be improved. If most of the techniques are new for you and you apply most of them, then the improvement should be nothing short of phenomenal.

Don't Put the Bugs In, In the First Place

Why do I talk about bug avoidance first? One day while talking with a customer, I received the response, "Well, why do you put the bugs in, in the first place?" Around the shops of many offices, it is stated, "Just don't put them in." I realize that this is nothing new to developers. One of many similar statements has been around for years: an ounce of prevention is worth a pound of cure (or here in Canada, a gram of prevention is worth a kilogram of cure).

It takes a lot less time and a lot less money to keep the majority of bugs out in the first place than to look for them after the fact. There is a balance, of course–but the industry is way off balance. Far too much time and money is spent finding bugs that should not have been put there in the first place.

Walkthroughs

Don't run your code: walk through it first. Remember the old adage (adapted for my own purposes), "You have to walk through before you can run." It is absolutely amazing how much you can learn about your code by going through it carefully in a walkthrough (or desk check if you prefer) before ever running it. When I fix a bug, too, I always try to walk through it before running the fix. When I find a series of bugs in an object or section of code, I try to do a walkthrough with at least one other developer before running it again.

There is a tendency to "run first, debug later" with tools like PowerBuilder, but this is unfortunate. Remember that the goal is usually not just to get something to show quickly. The goal is to get the program working and to a level of quality as soon as possible. That level will depend on the purpose of the program. Doing walkthroughs before you run your code will help you get to that level much quicker.

Naming standards

There are a few different (but similar) naming standards used in the PowerBuilder world. Another chapter in this book discusses one of these in detail. Whatever standard you choose, there are three tricks to help keep bugs out:

Stick to your naming standards. Make sure all developers in the company follow the same standards, and don't allow "personal" standards that they or you use instead.

Don't use temporary variable names saying or thinking, "it's okay, I'm just using it for this test, then I'll delete it." It is amazing how many "quick temporary variables" can end up as necessary and permanent variables in the production system and get in your way when you are trying to debug. The variable names temp, lb_temp, and ls_temp are very hard to debug–

especially if they exist as different types and/or purposes as you step through various scripts and functions.

Use self-documenting names. You have lots of characters in PowerBuilder: don't be afraid to use them. Code where the variables are descriptive is much easier to read than code with comments explaining what the variables mean. And don't ever use the default names cb_1, cb_2, sle_1, dw_1, etc. Always give variables proper names like cb_OK, cb_cancel, sle_filename, or dw_results. This will make your script much easier to read and simplify your debugging tremendously.

If the meaning of the variable, function, or event changes such that it doesn't match its name, change it! Yes, if it is widely used or accessed, it may take a few minutes to an hour to find it everywhere. But it will make it easier to understand your code. And since the meaning changed, you SHOULD be checking every use of it to see whether the change in meaning will break something else. This will mean fewer bugs, and the bugs that you do put in will be easier to find.

Comments

Avoid using /* and */ for comments. If you use these to comment out code, it can be VERY hard to notice when debugging, unless you are using the debugger to step though that point. Fortunately, PowerBuilder uses nested /* */, so that /*...*/...*/ will produce an error (unlike some languages we all know).

As a consequence, we do permit–in very rare cases–use of the /* */ for in-line comments.

```
IF lk_someval=3 /* 3 means exit */ or lb_quit THEN
uf_quit()
END IF
```

Of course, we prefer to use values and variable names that make sense, but you may be accessing sources written for some other purpose or controlled by someone else, and may not have that option. If you decided not to permit /* */ at all, I think that would also be a safe and reasonable standard. However, I strongly suggest that you not go the other way and permit unlimited use of /* */ until PowerBuilder gives us an editor that has a different color for comments than for actual code. This is because it's hard to tell whether a section is a comment or actual code–especially when the comment line is off the top or bottom of the screen, or when the commented out section is large. If you assume it is actual code, you could easily be sent on a wild goose chase.

```
/* the following is commented out
lk_someval = 2
IF lk_someval = 2 THEN
uf_initialize ()
END IF
*/
```

When PowerBuilder gives us a color editor, I expect I'll change my attitude because the commented-out code will be a different color; therefore, easy to spot.

Find the Bugs

Finding bugs is best done by trying these steps first:

```
Propose a hypothesis.
Design a test.
Define results and their meaning.
Do the test.
Compare the results.
Reach a conclusion, and if necessary go back to Step One.
```

Skipping Step Three will often prolong your debugging time and cause incorrect conclusions. Despite the adage, when it comes to debugging, hindsight is nowhere near 20/20.

There are times these steps don't help. In such cases, you may just want to shoot blind, look at variables in the debugger as you go along, and try random changes based on intuition. But this should be *after* you've tried the methodical way. Most bugs can be found more quickly by following careful procedure than by wild random guesses.

Inconsistent bugs don't really exist (very often). Almost every bug that I have encountered that was not PowerBuilder-related eventually could be demonstrated in a non-inconsistent way. Although it may take a long time, if you start with this attitude you are much more likely to be able to find the problem. And if you talk to Powersoft support, Team Powersoft, or other helping hands on CompuServe, the Internet or in your own office, having this attitude and some methodical tests will usually get you a problem resolution more quickly.

All this leads us to the most powerful of debugging tools, the human brain.

The debugger— the human

Debugging is an art, just as programming and development is an art. Unfortunately, the skills of programmer/developer and debugger do not necessarily exist in the same individual. Most developers can do debugging, but not all developers make great debuggers.

There are certain things you can do to become a better debugger. Like most things in life, practice is required. There is a story of a wealthy old man and a young boy. When the young boy asked the old man how he became wealthy, he replied, "I made good decisions." "How did you make good decisions?" the boy pursued. "I became experienced." "And how did you become experienced?" "I made bad decisions," the old man said. So it is with becoming a top notch debugger.

To become a really good debugger, it is important to really understand what is happening behind the scenes, both in your code and in Powersoft's. Some of the topics you can study to assist in this include assembly, compiler design, and operating system design. If you desire to be a top notch debugger, studying these topics in your spare time will be invaluable in the long term.

I have noticed that recent graduates tend to act as if they have a greater mystical belief in computers than did graduates of ten years ago. It is not that they think computers are magic, it is just that, not having had to work at low levels, they do not really understand what is going on behind the scenes. Besides knowing how to use the high level tools that do a lot of behind-the-scenes work for you, you should also have an understanding of *how* Power-Builder et al are doing all that work. You might get this familiarity through dabbling with lower level languages like Assembly and C/C++. (Note I'm not advocating "real" development in these languages!)

One of the important items that you will probably have to really understand before doing major debugging is the picky syntax details of ~" ~~~", and other related items in dwDescribe and dwModify. To help you learn, you can use the debugger to show you what the variable looks like before you call dwDescribe or dwModify. You can store the string into a variable, then simply say:

```
dwDescribe (ls_dwdescribe)
```

By doing this, the debugger can let you see the contents of ls_dwdescribe before it is interpreted by dwDescribe or dwModify.

If you have more than one developer, make sure you have at least one developer who is very conversant in dwDescribe and dwModify so he or she can help the others get these details right the first time. About ten to twenty percent of the time I am wrong the first time, so I still have some work in this regard myself.

Another of the important items to understand is the matter of pointers vs. variables. Power-Builder tries to hide the difference from you, but the difference is still there. Understanding it can make your debugging easier. A pointer is a variable which, when passed, passes a "pointer" or an "address" for the real object. If you've worked with other languages with pointers, basically PowerObject variables are all pointers, while all other variables are standard. When you say:

```
transaction my_trans
sqlca.DBMS = 'ODBC'
my_trans = SQLCA
my_trans.DBMS = 'trace ODBC'
```

the variable my_trans is pointing at the same information that the SQLCA variable is pointing to. Anything you do to my_trans will be the done to SQLCA, since both variables point at exactly the same area of memory. For example, when I changed the DBMS value to be "trace ODBC" above, I changed it for my_trans and SQLCA, since they are both the same transaction. When debugging, you can see this by changing one of the attributes of SQLCA, then looking at the my_trans attributes. You will find that it was changed there too. If you then were to write:

```
my_trans = my_other_trans
```

my_trans no longer is the same as SQLCA because SQLCA has been left alone. Now any changes to my_trans will also be done to my_other_trans. Compare this to:

```
transaction my_trans
sqlca.DBMS = 'ODBC'
my_trans = create transaction
my_trans.DBMS = 'trace ODBC'
```

This creates a whole new object of type Transaction, and my_trans points at it. Now the only transaction object that says 'trace ODBC' is my_trans, the other transaction object, SQLCA, still says 'ODBC.' Also compare the first example to:

```
integer i,j
I = 3
j = I
j = 4
```

The line j = 4 does NOT change I because I is not a pointer. I still has the value 3. My_trans was a pointer. I and J are not.

Similarly, when you pass a variable that is any PowerObject (transaction, window, menu, etc.) to a function, you are not passing the whole PowerObject. You are only passing a pointer to it. In practical terms, passing by reference or by value has, in most cases, no effect, UNLESS you do something like a create object or my_trans = my_other_trans on the passed variable. There, if you passed the parameter by value, only the variable in the function will point at the new object. However, if you passed by reference, the variable in the calling script will also point at the new object.

If you pass a PowerObject by reference or by value, and just change one of the attributes, you will change it for both the variable inside the function AND the variable in the calling script. This is because the item you passed by reference or value was not the PowerObject itself. Rather, when passed by reference, the variable points at the PowerObject. When passed by value, it points to the *address* of the PowerObject.

When passing an integer or other non-PowerObject variable by reference or value, you are not passing a pointer, but rather the variable itself. If you pass by reference, you are passing the address of the memory that contains the integer, by value you are passing the VALUE of the integer.

	Pass by value	Pass by reference
PowerObjects (windows, menus etc.)	If you create, destroy or assign a new object to it, the calling routine will not see that change or any other changes you make after that point. Otherwise, all changes will be seen.	If you create or assign a new object to it, the calling routine will also get the new object. All other changes will also be seen.
All other variables (Integers, Booleans, etc.)	Any changes are hidden from the calling routine.	Any changes directly affect the calling routine's variable.

As a side point of interest, for those that want to create linked lists in PowerBuilder: now that you know PowerObjects are really pointers, you should have no trouble at all creating any linked list you want.

Starting to attack the problem

How many developers are there? Take that number and multiply by ten and that is the approximate number of different ways to hunt for bugs. There are some general guidelines; however, that can save you a lot of time.

Start at the big picture and work down

When a program is brand new, it is safe to assume that the problem is more likely with the program than with the end user or tester. However, when the program has been working for a few years, it is safer to assume the problem is more likely with the end user. This should affect the questions you ask and generally how you go about identifying the problem.

The first attack, then, will be to find out whether the problem is with a setup configuration—something the user did that *should* have caused the results seen—or whether the problem is deeper than that. At this level, you will be interviewing the person who found the bug. If you are the one who found it, try interviewing yourself. Ask yourself what you just did, what you saw, what you expected to happen, and how the results differed from what you expected. If it "has been working all along," then what is different from "all along?"

If this is not a program that you are constantly working on, the next step is to do a review of the design and code. Find out what the requirements were–that is, what it was supposed to do. Then find out what the design was–how was it supposed to achieve these requirements. You can then move on to a static review of the code. Look at the code itself, not running it, to get a feel for how it is written and how it tries to match the design.

Having this good overview to start with will usually make it a lot easier to zoom in on the actual bug. It will also help when it comes time to fix the bug. Having a good overview of the program will make it a lot less likely that the fix you implement will cause more problems.

Once you have the overview, your attack may depend on the type of problem.

Easily reproducible problems

If the problem is easily reproducible, count yourself lucky–especially if it is a GPF problem. You should run some tests to try to narrow down where the problem is. Then go and look at the code in that area to see if the problem is obvious or not.

Intermittent problems

These are much, much harder. Begin by finding out whether the problem happens on only one machine, but not another. If it is only on one machine, consider starting to work on the assumption that hardware is at fault. One really big trick for this is to remove each of the components one at a time to a similar machine and see if the problem moves with the component. Don't forget the operator as one of the components. I have seen situations where the problem was "only at one station," so we switched operators and the problem moved! In these cases, we have had good luck in trying to find out what that operator was doing differently from the other operators.

Once you have ruled out hardware, and you have come to believe that the problem is your interaction, move on to the next step. With intermittent, non-hardware problems, I find I have better luck starting with a detailed inspection of the code to see if there is anything that might be causing the problem. In many cases, going through the code, I can find a way that might make the bug consistent. Possibly I see that "it looks like variable x is not being initialized when I start the function from the OK button."

When you have exhausted the easy tests mentioned above, you are now ready for more invasive steps to find the bug. Imagine yourself as a detective trying to solve a crime. You have a bug, it was caused by something, you *know* it is not magical. When you start out you have hundreds of suspects. You need to eliminate all of the suspects until you find the culprit. In the spirit of Sherlock Holmes, when you have eliminated all other possible causes of the bug, the one remaining, no matter how improbable, must be the true cause.

We want to find that cause, no matter how improbable. But don't forget, just as in real life, bugs may have accomplices. A bug is often caused by a combination of factors and is not as simple as a single error.

We can remove suspects in code, by changing the code. For example, you may want to skip a loop and hard code a value the loop was supposed to generate. Likewise, to chop out a chunk of code, you can surround it with:

```
IF FALSE THEN
.... Code that you want to quarantine
END IF
```

Don't forget to put the code back when you are done! I put in a comment:

```
//B This code commented out for debugging purposes
only.
```

In our documentation standards, //B means "known bug." Before I ship the product to the testing group, I can then use the browser to search for any occurrences of //B. If I find them, I check or fix them before forwarding the code to the testers.

The next step is to use tools, like a debugger. I go through the code, stopping at various points and changing the values of variables, if necessary. It is frequently handy to combine changes to the code with use of the debugger. This will be discussed more fully in other portions of this chapter.

Break the problem down

If you do not find the problem quickly, one really good trick is to break the possible location down into smaller chunks. A common method is called binary division.

Let's assume you have a long LAN BNC cable with dozens of segments, and one seems to be broken. (If you are not familiar with these cables, if one segment is bad, *none* of the segments works.) You could start at the first segment, put a terminator on the line, and see if the first two computers can now talk to each other. If they cannot, you have probably found the bad cable. If, after fixing the cable, they still cannot talk, the problem probably was not related to cabling to start with. If they *can* talk to each other, then that cable is good and you have virtually proven that the cable was at fault. You then connect the second cable and put the terminator on the end of the third computer. If they can talk, the second cable is good. If they can't, the second is bad. You continue to do this, segment by segment, until you find the bad cable.

If you have less than ten segments, this might be practical. But when you have dozens, it isn't.

With larger LANs you start in the middle. (Oh all right, for larger LANs you'd have to be nuts to use BNC, but lets assume you don't have a choice—dumb management decision and all that.) Terminate the cable on both ends, and test a couple of computers on both ends to see if they can talk to any other computers on their half of the LAN. Whichever end doesn't work is the end that has the problem. (If both fail, the cable is probably not the cause of the problem.) You then take the bad side, split it in two, and perform the same tests until you have narrowed it down to the bad segment.

You can apply the same methodology to debugging. Break the program at the halfway point. You might do this with a stop point on a debugger, and see if the problem happens before or after that point. Keep breaking the problem down into smaller and smaller chunks until you have isolated it. Unlike the LAN example, a program could have hundreds of thousands of steps, and you could spend hours trying to get to the point where the bug exhibits itself, if you start at the beginning and go one step at a time.

Unlike LAN cabling; however, bugs often don't call for a strict binary division. I tend to randomly break the problem into four to six sections, then break the bad section down into four to six sections and so on, until I find the exact problem spot. The technical details of how you might want to tell when you've gotten to the end of one of those sections is discussed more fully below. You would use techniques like multiple stop points in the debugger and/or set microhelps, beeps, or other methods.

When I say "randomly break the problem into four to six sections," I sometimes mean that literally. Just plop down four to six points at a run. However, usually I will use some intuition or judgment to put these points at somewhat logical locations. As you become more and more experienced, both as a debugger and with a specific language, (PowerBuilder in our case), your "intuition" will get luckier and luckier.

If you still can't find the problem, the final step is to call for help. If you have a debugger guru or a coworker who knows how to debug—now is the time to call that person in, explain the problem, and let them try. If *you* are the debugger guru, it is usually better not to let the developer tell you too much of what has been tried already until you have tried things yourself. Otherwise, you will often be biased in a way that makes you miss the bug for the same reason that the other developer missed it.

Your mental attitude

Roles

When you are working with a bug that is not trivial, you will find yourself having to control many emotions and attitudes. At times you will get bogged down in details and have to pull yourself back out to take a look at the overall picture.

This can require a lot of personal management. Personally, if it is taking more than an hour to find a bug, I try to get myself to sit back each hour and look at the forest for a few minutes before getting back into the trees. I try to evaluate, in the big picture, what I have found out so far, review what it is I'm trying to work on, and see if there is not something in the overall picture that I am missing.

Presumptions

I try to look at my presumptions, first by looking at my conscious presumptions, the presumptions I know I'm making. I find it helpful to speak them out loud or write them down to see if maybe I should stop making some assumption. You may, for example, have assumed that "three rows of data is normal," entered three rows of data, and done the testing. Maybe the bug only shows up with four rows of data or 100 rows of data.

Then I try to look for my unconscious presumptions. Am I assuming that the data has not become corrupted? Maybe you are reading in a text file that has been corrupted since the initial tests. Maybe you assumed that a variable was initialized when you entered a function, but it isn't in some circumstances–particularly the circumstances that exhibit the bug.

Clarity of thought

When you first start looking for a bug, you probably can memorize a lot of the details and just go hunting for it. But once you have passed the easy-find stage, you need to start writing down the details as clearly as possible. You should write down the values of variables at various points, note the exact address of every GPF (if this is the type you are tracking), and document what you did step by step–exact keystrokes and mouse clicks. You need to be careful how you think about a bug. I have made reference to "the circumstances that exhibit the bug." This is distinctly different from saying, "the circumstances that CAUSED the bug." This second statement implies that you have already found the location and cause of the bug. If you mentally take the attitude of your words, this can lead you into a wild goose chase. It would be easy to get into lots and lots of details, spending hours in one section of code and painstakingly recording values of variables, only to find out that the code was simply where the evidence of the bug showed up, not where the bug actually resides.

You may think that this wording is a petty issue, but I have found through the years that the words I and others use are usually much closer to how we are thinking, believing, and acting than we would like to accept. I have seen many cases, probably weekly, where I have challenged the wording of a problem, or others have challenged my wording, someone has said something like, "Yeah, that's what I meant," and then, suddenly, "Ohhhhh! Of course!" At which point it became possible to go on to find the real problem. Forcing yourself to use correct wording on a consistent basis, and not slipping into incorrect phrases, will help you to do this check without requiring a second person nearly as often.

Everyone in my shop has learned to self-critique. This self-critiquing is most important when we are in the midst of a deep dark debugging cycle. Remember to step back and critique your problem definition and interim conclusions, and get someone else to critique them periodically. Remember, if you haven't found the bug, then by definition your conclusions are not correct. They may be completely off base, or they may simply be not definitive enough.

Finally, though debugging is in large part an art, don't think of it as a "black art." Yes, it can be difficult, but it is seldom impossible. Often intuition–or if you prefer, "lucky guessing"– is what finds the problem. People with lots of experience may seem to be a lot luckier, but that may simply be because they *have* more experience, and can make better guesses because of that experience.

This does not mean that *you* cannot find the bug. If you are inexperienced at finding bugs, it is not unreasonable that, on average, it will take you a lot longer to find them than someone who *is* experienced. If you look at debugging as an evil task that is to be avoided at any cost, or have the attitude that it is not part of your work ("I want to get rid of this bug so I can get back to my real job"), then you are going to have a lot of problems. If you think this way, you are not as likely to spend the necessary time understanding the forest. You will be look-ing for shortcuts to solve the problem without fully understanding it. Once you find "the bug," you will be more likely to do a quick fix that introduces a new bug,–and if you do not understand what really was going wrong, you will have learned nothing that will help you out next time...other than thinking that maybe it is time to become a burger flipper at a fast food outlet!

I try to feel (and often succeed in feeling) that each new debugging session is a journey, a challenge to be savored, and a victory to be enjoyed. I am frequently the one who is called in when others can't find the bug, so I don't get many of the easy bugs these days. Indeed, hav-ing spent years tracking them down, I don't get a thrill out of the easy ones anymore–but boy, do I get a kick out of the brain teasers.

Also, remember that your whole purpose in developing is...to make gobs and gobs of money. No! Your whole purpose in developing, including debugging, is to get your end users the best possible code, that will give them the maximum benefit for the money spent. Yes, some developers make gobs of money (Mr. Bill for example). But most of us will make signifi-cantly less than a doctor would (though many of the top-notch developers are smarter than a lot of doctors I have met). If you are not doing this because you want to serve and bring sur-prise (the good type!), enjoyment, and productivity to your end users, then you are going to have a lot of problems in the debugging cycles.

So try to manage yourself; think with clarity; be careful and meticulous; remember for whom and why you are doing this work; and try to learn from each and every debugging ses-sion. And I have no qualms in saying that the people I have known who hated debugging have *never* become good debuggers. On the other hand, most of those who had a positive attitude towards it have become, at worst, "good" debuggers. Many of them have become "great" debuggers.

Testing tools and suites

I hope that you will have already developed a series of tests that you perform against your code. You may also have a tool like SQA TeamTest for PowerBuilder. When you are notified of a bug in your program, you should strongly consider applying your suite of tests against the program to see if something has gotten broken since the last time you checked. If the test suite runs fine, then once you define the bug, you should add it to the suite, so that it can't happen again.

When you look at your tests, whatever they are, you should examine them in the same way that you examine your programs. Every time your test suite does not catch a bug, it means the test suite itself is buggy and needs to be debugged and repaired. The better your test suite, and the easier it is to run, the fewer bugs you will send out to your end users.

When reading the rest of this chapter, consider many of the issues as applying both to your test suite and to your programs. For example, if you find a bug in some part of a program, I recommend you spend more time in the same area seeing what else you can find. The same is true for your test routines. When you find that you are not testing for some condition, have a look at what other conditions you should be checking for that you might not be. This is especially valuable just after a debugging session, because you will have a much better idea of some of the problems you might run into right away, or when you make future changes to the system.

The debugger–the program

Depending on what your past experiences are, your opinions of the PowerBuilder debugger will vary. If you have never had a debugger, you will think it is the greatest thing since sliced bread. If you have used other PC-based debuggers like VB's, Watcom C++'s, or many other Windows-based debuggers, then you will be disappointed with PowerBuilder's. Given the scope of this book, I am not going to parrot the PowerBuilder manuals, which give you the "how-to" of the debugger in sufficient depth. If you are not familiar with the features of the debugger, you should read "Debugging and Running Applications" in the User's Guide, and/or check out the debugging sections in one of the beginners' books on PowerBuilder.

Don't think that debugger=debugging. The debugger is simply one of many tools in your debugging toolbox. Although it is powerful, it is minor in comparison to your most important tool–your imagination and logic skills.

If you didn't use "real" names for the objects when you built your windows, a few hours of debugging should convince you of the need for them. Notice the easy-to-read "Control or Object" names in the following screen shot:

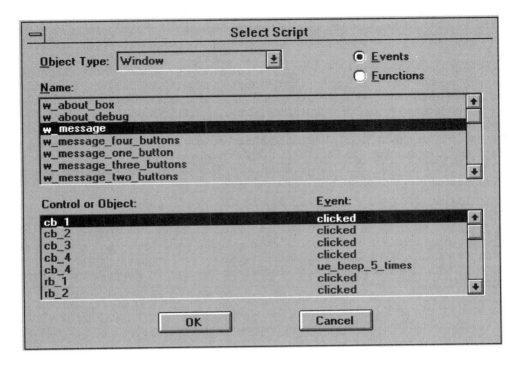

Cb_1, cb_2, rb_1, etc., just does not cut it in debugging. Personally, I refuse to help anyone in my office debug if they show me a screen like this. It's even worse if they use cb_1.function()–I figure that has *got* to be a capital offense! Real names like cb_OK, cb_close, or cb_redraw_picture are much better to work with. Remember you are allowed to have dozens of characters in the file and variable names–use them!

When you first start debugging, make sure that you can see the bug from the debugger. Nothing is more frustrating than spending an hour on a problem, only to find out that "it works when I run the debugger." At a minimum, run through the debugger with only a few stop points and see if the bug is ever going to show up. That way, if it turns out the bug *isn't* going to show up, you can modify your strategy.

This does not mean that you cannot use the debugger to help solve the problem. It will become a secondary item used after you have narrowed the problem down. You might turn to it to check values at certain points, then run the program normally, after adding some code that acts based on the information you found.

When using the debugger, watch out for the Posted, Activate and GetFocus events.
Debugging is obtrusive. In an event-driven model, the very act of debugging can cause your program to run drastically differently from how it will run when you are not debugging. At a minimum (obviously, I hope), most timing tests are out of the question.

Then we have to deal with Activates and GetFocuses. If you have a debug stop in an Activate or GetFocus, the debugger takes over, causing a LoseFocus event. Then, when you come back into the debugger, you have the pending Activate or GetFocus waiting where you were stopped *and* you just caused a brand new Activate and GetFocus to occur.

The same thing can happen when you get a message box or response window to come up this way, possibly through a function called by the GetFocus or Activate event. If you understand that PowerBuilder, when it comes back from the debugger, will let the application run script until it comes to a STOP, you will see there is a partial solution to this problem. Normally, when not in a GetFocus event, the debugger returns, and since there is no code that is launched by that activity, it STOPs at the next line. The trick then is to get your code *back* to that line of code as quickly and as unobtrusively as possible. To do so I create a variable of type Boolean. Let's call it ib_in_the_getfocus_event. This variable is declared in the instance variables section of the object:

```
Boolean ib_in_the_getfocus_event
```

Then, if we are already in the GetFocus event. we want to make sure we *get out* right away. What we are doing is checking for unwanted recursion, and if we find it, terminating it. At the very start of the GetFocus event we put code in that says, "if we are in the GetFocus event, GET OUT."

```
IF ib_in_the_getfocus_event THEN
RETURN // we are recursive
END IF
```

If we get this far, we set our variable to True, indicating that we are in at least one level deep.

```
ib_in_the_getfocus_event = TRUE
```

Now, this is *very* important. NEVER, EVER put a debug stop before the line of code that says ib_in_the_getfocus_event = True. Then before each and every RETURN, except the first one (the one that says Return // we are recursive), we set the ib_in_the_getfocus_event variable back to False.

```
ib_in_the_getfocus_event = FALSE
RETURN
```

Here is a representative sample of the code we put in, with comments:

```
// Never put ANY code before this comment!
IF ib_in_the_getfocus_event THEN // do NOT put a debug
STOP on this line
RETURN // we are recursive, // do NOT put a debug STOP
on this line

END IF // do NOT put a debug STOP on this line

ib_in_the_getfocus_event = TRUE // do NOT put a debug
```

```
STOP on this line
// you can put a debug STOP on any lines after this com-
ment.
.....Code
IF somecondition THEN
ib_in_the_getfocus_event = FALSE
RETURN
END IF
.... Some more code
ib_in_the_getfocus_event = FALSE
RETURN
//end of getfocus event
```

Now, this solution is not without its failures. The first problem is that if you debug through a GetFocus event on an object that occurs before the Window Open event is completed, the object will probably not be visible on the window. If it will not mess up what you are debugging for, this problem can be solved with another variable. Let's call it ib_first_time_in. Start it out as False, then put this code in the first part of the script:

```
IF ib_first_time_in THEN // do NOT put a debug STOP on
this line
ib_first_time_in = False
RETURN // do NOT put a debug STOP on this line
END IF
```

If you have descendants, you must also put similar code in them. Otherwise you will pile up a bunch of descendant GetFocus events that will get executed after the ancestor GetFocus event. And there may be other flaws that I have not encountered yet.

Despite the flaws, there are times when I really, really want to debug through a GetFocus. This trick usually lets me do that.

Post events

Now, what happens if you post an event? If you have worked with PostEvent, you know that a PostEvent basically waits until there are no other triggered events pending. Then, while the system is waiting for the user to do something, the posted event occurs.

But the debugger causes a drastic change: it throws the event stack away–that is, all pending PostEvents. This means that if you Postevent('ue_I_was_posted') and then get to a debug stop before the ue_I_was_posted event happens, the ue_I_was_posted *won't* happen. It gets removed from the stack.

Unfortunately, I have not yet found a way around this one. The best I can suggest is to be really aware of it and take it into account when debugging. Where possible, stop *before* the event is posted, then choose "Continue," so that the posted event will execute.

There are other tricks you can use outside of the debugger. The following examples tend to be less obtrusive than the debugger, but depending on your application, any one of them may be a problem for you.

Code a beep(n). On some systems beep(5) and beep(1) sound the same; on others the differences can be easily counted. If your system will let you count beeps, you can use different numbers of beeps for different values or situations.

```
w_thiswindow.title = 'The value of I is '+string(i)
w_main.setmicrohelp( "The first variable is
'+ls_first+', the second is '+string(second) )
```

Similarly, you can set microhelp with '>>>>>>>>>>>>>>>>>>>>>>>>>>>>>>>'.

When initializing our system, we display "more" and "more greater than" signs so that we can tell where in the startup it "hung" without having to display technical descriptions to the end user. You may prefer to have more descriptive status notes. The point is, you can use setmicrohelp to display the values of variables, notes about what point you've gotten to in a script or object, or any other information that could help debug your program.

Be aware that the setmicrohelp can have some problems if you use the tag value to display microhelp throughout your program. If you do, you may have trouble seeing the messages as they go by.

If you have a turbo switch, turning it off can help debug "timing" issues, when you want to figure out what is happening before what. If you don't have a turbo switch or it is too slow, create another program that chews up CPU cycles for lunch. When you get to the point you want to debug slowly, start that program. If you have the Windows SDK, there is a program Microsoft wrote that can do this for you.

Finding a variable in the debugger

One of the first things you will find is that locating a specific variable in a specific window can be a daunting job. This can be further complicated when there is more than one way to access an object. Some are impossible or darn near impossible to get to–for example, windows that are opened using a script-local variable. That sort of object cannot be found in the debugger after the script ends, yet it is still a valid variable.

If you want to know the value of a particular variable–for example, in a user object on a specific window–you *can* go through the debugger and try to find the variable. Alternatively, in a moderate or large system, you might want to declare a local variable of the same type, and assign the variable in question to it. This way you can find it as a local variable.

Sometimes you learn by trial and error. This can be especially true with dwModifys. In the anti-bugging section, I suggested that you become very familiar with the dwModify syntax. Don't just get it working; try to understand *how* you got it working. To get to that level, you can use the debugger to help.

PowerBuilder does not have an "immediate execution" option in its debugger. However; when you are playing, or trying to find a dwModify that will work, try the following code to *simulate* immediate execution.

```
string ls_dwModify
string ls_error
Boolean lb_debug_loop = True
ls_dwModify = // whatever your best guess is
DO WHILE lb_debug_loop = False
ls_error = dwModify ( ls_dwModify)
LOOP
```

Now you can try the dwModify function over and over again until it works. After each attempt, double-click on ls_dwModify and make the change you want to try next time. You can (should?) also check the ls_error after each line to see if it caused any PowerBuilder errors. When you are done, you set lb_debug_loop = False by double-clicking on it and changing it to True. This will cause the loop to terminate. WARNING: If you tell the debugger to continue, you will have created an infinite loop that won't result in a stack fault error. Depending on the code in the loop, you may be able to double-click on the PowerBuilder icon. If it pompts, "An application is running - terminate it?", click on Yes.

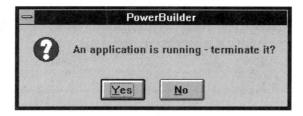

Unfortunately, this trick does not always work. If you are in a tight loop with no interaction to Windows calls, you may have to use Windows <Ctrl>-<Alt>-<Del> to terminate the application. This will also terminate the current instance of PowerBuilder. One alternative to the code above then would be:

```
string ls_dwModify
string ls_error
integer lk_i
ls_dwModify = // whatever your best guess is
FOR lk_i = 1 to 100
ls_error = dwModify ( ls_dwModify)
NEXT
```

This is similar, but it lets you try up to exactly 100 times (unless you modify lk_i on the fly). When you are done, before the 100th time you can set lk_i = 100 in the debugger, just as you would have with lb_debug_loop. Now you will not get an infinite loop if you accidentally "continue." The loop will execute a maximum of 100 times.

Faster debug stepping

If you use the mouse on the step button several times in a row, you may be better off press-

ing <Ctrl>-<S>. Try it ten times with the mouse and then ten times with <Ctrl>-<S>. You will find the keyboard method is significantly faster. The extra delay time is due to Windows having to interpret which object the mouse was over when it was clicked. With the keyboard, Windows can pass it through quickly, without nearly the overhead.

If you are stepping through a script and you are about to go to a function or trigger event, put a stop on the next line. That way, if you get tired of stepping through the function and just want to get out, you can hit Continue and it will proceed until it gets to your stop point.

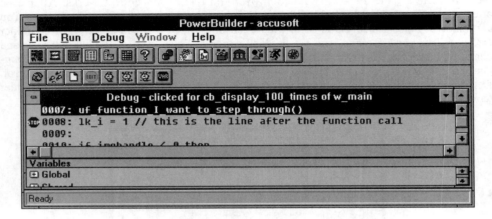

When working with the debugger, you will probably find that watching the local variables is the most common set for you. However, when going down through your windows, the local variables can get pretty far away. Did you know you can move the local group to the watch window just like any individual variable?

Now, in version 4.0, we can store watch variables between runs. When you assign variables to the watch window, PowerBuilder will now remember not only your stops and the size of each of the three sections of your debug window, but also your watch variables for the next iteration of testing.

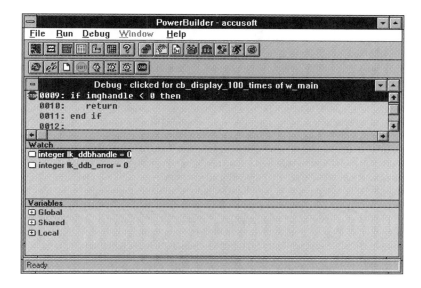

You can also, theoretically, edit the variables in the Preferences Painter, as below. But you should simply leave them alone here, and instead, add and remove them through the Debug Painter.

Don't double-click on the debugger control menu icon (the little minus sign at the upper left corner of the debugger window), unless you really have to. PowerBuilder has a number of situations where the debugger will crash PowerBuilder, or your whole Windows system, if you do. Version 4.0 has a dialog box display which asks if you want to risk crashing. Only use this option when the risk of possibly crashing Windows is better than continuing on with the program. If you are going to answer Yes, make sure all data in all other applications is saved first. Terminating the debugger while stopped may violate *more* than just Power-Builder integrity. It may violate Windows integrity–or under NT, the Win16 subsystem, causing all applications other than Win32 applications to crash. So, answer No unless you have no other choice.

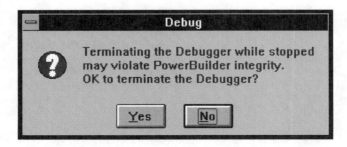

Develop a Debug Window for DataWindows.

I estimate that about ninety percent of PowerBuilder developers use DataWindows for about ninety percent of their design, yet the PowerBuilder debugger does not give us access to the majority of attributes of a DataWindow (yet!). The information has to be gathered using dwDescribe. The problem is that, at runtime, you can't *reach* the information through the debugger. You have to think it through beforehand and execute the dwDescribe function in question into a local variable, which you can then look at from the debugger. But there is a significantly better way.

Create a series of windows that display the information as appropriate. To make this as easy as possible, make this object aware of your base class DataWindow object. In our case, we keep track of the master and child windows, and if you press <Ctrl>-<Shift>-<Alt> while clicking on the secondary (right) mouse button, the standard DataWindow object will launch this window, passing the window a handle to itself.

By double-clicking on the master or a child, we let the developer walk up and down the tree to see the values. You may want to show other values that are in your generic DataWindow object so the developer does not have to go to the debugger for the information. You can also tie these windows back to the calling DataWindow object, so as changes occur in it, you can have these windows updated. Alternatively, you could put the code to update these screens in the timer event. Finally, you could provide the developer with a "Refresh" button.

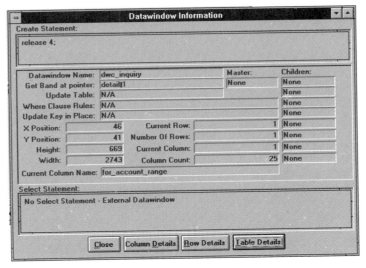

You will notice that the Create Statement and Select Statement windows are resizable. We do not use this interface design style on "end user tools," but for developers we found it to be quick and convenient, especially for long select statements.

When the window itself is resized, the Select Statement DataWindow shrinks or expands along the bottom and the right border. The Create Statement DataWindow expands only on the right border. If you press the "Column Details" button, you display a screen similar to the following. (The exact details and display vary depending on the column type.)

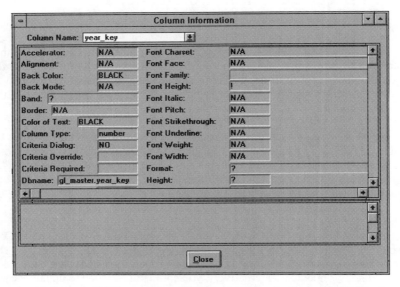

If you press the "Row Details" button, you display a screen similar to the following. In this specific window there is only one row, and its type is New. The bottom half displays the contents of the highlighted row.

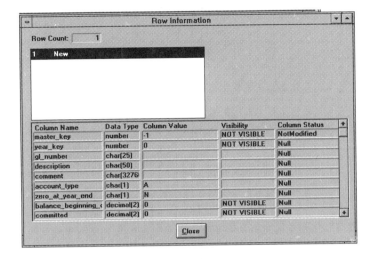

Finally, if you press "Table Details," you get the following screen:

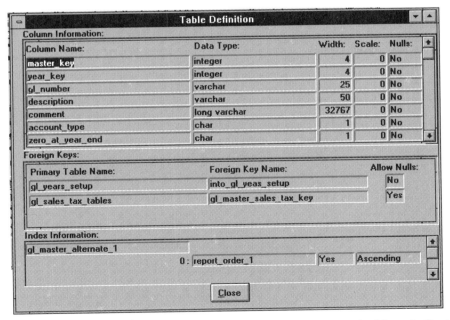

These screens would make an excellent candidate for turning into a tab object similar to the Word 6.0 options box. Our tabs would say something like "dw," "columns," "rows," and "tables."

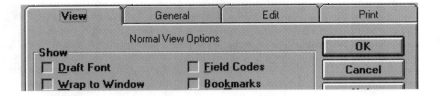

Use your screen effectively

Use as large a resolution screen as you can afford and your eyes can handle. I use a 1280x1024 on a 14 inch screen, but everyone thinks I'm nuts. If I could find and afford a 16000x12000, 48" screen–I'd buy it. The bigger the screen and higher the resolution, the easier it is to debug.

If your screen has high enough resolution, place the running program on the left hand side of the screen and the debugger on the right hand side. This will let you see both the running program and the code at the same time. I place the debugger on the right side so that I can move it partially off the screen and still see the first few characters of the script, yet move it back easily when I want to see the whole line.

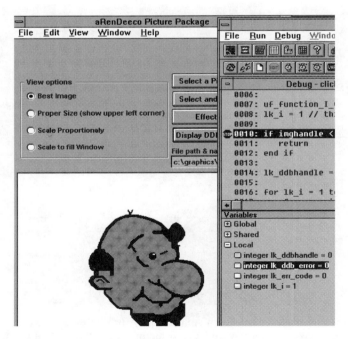

Remember you can resize the three sections of the debugger. Sometimes I want the script section to show me lots of code. Other times, I want to see all the variables. Usually I keep the watch window one or two variables high, but occasionally I want the watch window larger. With version 4.0 remembering watch variables from one run to the next, I am more likely to expand the watch window and keep more variables close at hand than I was under 3.0 or 3.0a.

Use ISQL. If you have purchased the "full" version of Watcom SQL, you received a text-based interface to Watcom. When debugging SQL-related problems, I will sometimes run ISQL in one window and the application in another. This lets me step through my program, possibly with the help of PowerBuilder's debugger, and then see the results at Watcom's end by using ISQL to show the results.

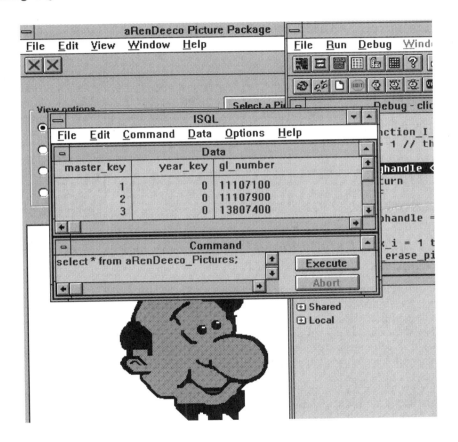

Include special code to be run only when you are debugging

Use code like:

```
IF gb_debug THEN
    // code that will give more useful info.
END IF
```

You set a global variable. (Personally, I keep this variable on a special user object, not as a global variable.) Having set this variable, you can then bring into play any diagnostic routines you want to write.

If you want to get really fancy, you can implement your own compile time code. Put something like //X in front of all lines of debugging code. Then you can run a program which exports the object, moves all the //Xs to the end of the line, and imports the object. When you are done debugging, you have a companion program move all the //X's back to the beginning of the line and re-import. This allows you to put in a lot of error checking on the test machines, while having none of the time-consuming error checking on the production system.

You can extend this concept as far as you want to make it much more complicated, but this is far enough for now. To do more we will wait until version 5.0 of PowerBuilder, which I hope will introduce proper conditional compilation. (No I don't have ANY information on version 5.0–this is a hope only.)

Finally, if you haven't already, make sure you check out *all* the options on the debugger toolbar. There are only eight choices on the bar. Almost everyone learns very quickly about Continue and Step. Most learn about Show/Add/Remove, but I have seen a number of developers who never Select or Edit Stop from here. They go back to the development environment, add their stops, and then re-run the application. Don't you be one of them! Make sure you have used *each* of the choices on the bar at least two times and know what it is for.

Display hidden DataWindows and/or show extra columns in DataWindows

When going back and forth on particularly difficult bugs, I will make visible my normally invisible DataWindows. The risk here is that I will forget to remove them when the program goes to the end user. Because of this, we color ours using the bright, or lime, green color. That way, when our testing group runs the program, if they see anything lime green they know that it is debugging stuff, and will immediately inform the developer to get rid of it. We add extra fields and color their background green for this same purpose.

If you are switching back and forth between wanting to see this extra information and not wanting to see it, consider putting it on the DataWindow at the bottom of the band. When you do not want to see it, just pull the band up to hide it.

/pbdebug

The /pbdebug is an option you can put on the run line of any .exe you create from Power-Builder. This will create a debug file with the name of the .exe and the extension .dbg. In this example, it will create the file myapp.dbg. Below is an edited-for-brevity sample of the file it would produce for myapp.exe.

```
Executing event script CREATE for class MYAPP, lib entry MYAPP
End event script CREATE for class MYAPP, lib entry MYAPP
```

```
Executing event script OPEN for class MYAPP, lib entry MYAPP
   Executing system function OPEN
   Executing event script CREATE for class W_MAIN, lib entry W_MAIN
      Executing event script CREATE for class M_MYMENU, lib entry M_MYMENU
         Executing event script CREATE for class M_DW_FEATURES, lib entry
M_MYMENU
           Executing event script CREATE for class M_EDITCHANGEDEVENTORDERING,
lib entry M_MYMENU
(many more CREATES)
         End event script CREATE for class M_MYMENU, lib entry M_MYMENU
      End event script CREATE for class W_MAIN, lib entry W_MAIN
End event script OPEN for class MYAPP, lib entry MYAPP

Executing event script CLICKED for class M_CTRLTAB-WRONGFIELD, lib entry
M_MYMENU
   Executing system function OPENSHEET
   Executing event script CREATE for class W_MYTEST_2, lib entry W_MYTEST_2
   End event script CREATE for class W_MYTEST_2, lib entry W_MYTEST_2
   Executing system function OPENSHEET
   Executing event script CREATE for class W_MYTEST, lib entry W_MYTEST
   End event script CREATE for class W_MYTEST, lib entry W_MYTEST
End event script CLICKED for class M_CTRLTAB-WRONGFIELD, lib entry M_MYMENU

Executing event script DESTROY for class W_MYTEST, lib entry W_MYTEST
End event script DESTROY for class W_MYTEST, lib entry W_MYTEST

Executing event script DESTROY for class W_MYTEST_2, lib entry W_MYTEST_2
End event script DESTROY for class W_MYTEST_2, lib entry W_MYTEST_2

Executing event script DESTROY for class W_MAIN, lib entry W_MAIN
   Executing system function ISVALID
   Executing event script DESTROY for class M_MYMENU, lib entry M_MYMENU
      Executing event script DESTROY for class M_DW_FEATURES, lib entry M_MYMENU
(many more DESTROYS)
      End event script DESTROY for class M_CONNECT, lib entry M_MYMENU
   End event script DESTROY for class M_MYMENU, lib entry M_MYMENU
End event script DESTROY for class W_MAIN, lib entry W_MAIN

Executing event script DESTROY for class MYAPP, lib entry MYAPP
End event script DESTROY for class MYAPP, lib entry MYAPP
```

As you can see, this records calls to events and functions in the order they occur. Through indentation, you can see whether they were nested. For example, in the open for class MYAPP create, the create of W_MAIN is called. create for class W_MAIN in turn calls others, which call others. Eventually it winds its way back to the open for class MYAPP. So don't ignore the indentation–it is very significant. /pbdebug also specifically notes where an event ends ("End event" vs "Executing").

There are lots of interesting things to see in exe_name.dbg; however, it is an all-or-nothing choice. Either it records every single call, or it doesn't record any. It can easily and quickly end up creating a multi-megabyte file for you to parse through. If you have an editor, like MS Word, you can read the whole huge file in. You can also do tricks to let you find where you want to start. For example, if you wanted to see what happens when you load a particular window, you might code in two menu choices:

```
parent.triggerevent('Start here') // this of course
assumes you have created an event with the name
Start_here that doesn't do anything.
```

and

```
parent.triggerevent('End_here')
```

You would then hit the menu choice for the "Start here," open the window, and select the menu choice for "End here." Then when you edit the pbtrace.log file, you can cut out all the text before and after these two lines.

The most unfortunate part of this feature is that it only works with .exes you create. It does not work in development mode. And don't bother trying c:\pb3\pb040.exe /pbdebug. I tried it for you. PowerBuilder ignores the /pbdebug option in development mode. So if you have a large application and want to do many tests to see event orders as you change the code, you are better off with one of the other techniques in this chapter. The create .exe time is usually just too long. But if your application is failing at a customer site, this is one level of debugging reporting that the client can do for you. Similarly, if you have already created the .exe, this is one extra tool in your bag of tricks. Certainly, if you are trying to learn in what order events occur, there is no easier way. You have to append the /pbdebug option to the end of the command used to launch the application, and then have them send the myapp.dbg file to you for inspection.

DBMS = TRACE NAME_OF_DBMS

There is a feature I call TRACE that most people who know about it feel is very similar to /pbdebug. It has two significant differences from the /pbdebug command:

> TRACE records all the commands and response codes from/to the DBMS; (the data from the DBMS is not recorded), whereas /pbdebug records which events of which objects ran.

> TRACE works at development time *and* when you press the blue "runner" (File, Run or <Ctrl>-<R>) and execute the application without creating an .exe. At runtime, only /pbdebug works.

You can also put this in your application where you assign the value to the DBMS parameter of the transaction object. This must be done prior to connecting. At development time or when running your application, you will get the file pbtrace.log in your Windows directory.

If the above message comes up over and over again for every SQL statement and response, shut down Windows and try again. It will only show up once for the connection.

The following is a pbtrace.log, edited to show a representative sample of what you would find in this file.

```
LOGIN
CONNECT TO trace ODBC:
USERID=dba
DATA=Madman Local
DBPARM=Connectstring='DSN=Madman Local;UID=dba;PWD=sql'
 CURRENT_OF_CURSOR
 PARSE_ONLY
 SPECIAL_CURSOR
```

```
    START_TRAN
RUNTIME_EXECUTE:
Set temporary option Blocking = 'OFF'
 CANCEL
RUNTIME_EXECUTE:
Select "aaa_Support_Info"."Name" ,"aaa_Support_Info"."Address"
,"aaa_Support_Info"."City" ,"aaa_Support_Info"."Province"
,"aaa_Support_Info"."Postal_Code" ,"aaa_Support_Info"."Phone"
,"aaa_Support_Info"."Fax" ,"aaa_Support_Info"."Modem" from "aaa_Support_Info"
 RTFETCHNEXT
 RTFETCHNEXT
 Error 3 (rc 100)
 CANCEL
RUNTIME_EXECUTE:
Select "aaa_municipal_constants"."municipality"
,"aaa_municipal_constants"."addr1" ,"aaa_municipal_constants"."addr2"
,"aaa_municipal_constants"."serial_number" FROM "aaa_municipal_constants"
 RTFETCHNEXT
 RTFETCHNEXT
 Error 3 (rc 100)
 CANCEL
RUNTIME_EXECUTE:
SELECT "gl_setup"."gl_display_mask" ,"gl_setup"."gl_edit_mask"
,"gl_setup"."number_of_sales_taxes" ,"gl_setup"."gl_maximum_length" FROM
"gl_setup"
 RTFETCHNEXT
 RTFETCHNEXT
 Error 3 (rc 100)
 CANCEL
 CURSOR_CONNECT
 SPECIAL_CURSOR
 CURSOR_LOGIN
CONNECT TO trace ODBC:
USERID=dba
DATA=Madman Local
DBPARM=Connectstring='DSN=Madman Local;UID=dba;PWD=sql'
 CURSOR_CONNECTION
RUNTIME_EXECUTE:
SELECT "aaa_packages"."description" ,"aaa_packages"."owned"
,"aaa_packages"."passkey" FROM "aaa_packages" WHERE "aaa_packages"."owned"
='Y'
 FETCH_FIRST
 RTFETCHNEXT
 RTFETCHNEXT
 Error 3 (rc 100)
 CANCEL
 DISCONNECT
 SHUTDOWN_INTERFACE
RUNTIME_EXECUTE:
SELECT ( Today ( * ) ) FROM Dummy
 RTFETCHNEXT
 RTFETCHNEXT
 Error 3 (rc 100)
 CANCEL
 CURSOR_CONNECT
 SPECIAL_CURSOR
 CURSOR_LOGIN
CONNECT TO trace ODBC:
USERID=dba
DATA=Madman Local
DBPARM=Connectstring='DSN=Madman Local;UID=dba;PWD=sql'
```

```
 CURSOR_CONNECTION
RUNTIME_EXECUTE:
select today(*) from sys.dummy WHERE EXISTS(SELECT * FROM aaa_user_id)
 RTFETCHNEXT
 CANCEL
 DISCONNECT
 SHUTDOWN_INTERFACE
RUNTIME_EXECUTE:
SELECT "aaa_user_id"."user_key" ,"aaa_user_id"."user_id"
,"aaa_user_id"."full_user_name" ,"aaa_user_id"."password" FROM "aaa_user_id"
WHERE "aaa_user_id"."user_id" ='Madman'
 RTFETCHNEXT
 RTFETCHNEXT
 Error 3 (rc 100)
 CANCEL
PREPARE:
 SELECT "aaa_user_id"."user_id" ,          "aaa_user_id"."full_user_name"
FROM "aaa_user_id"
 DESCRIBE
 DW_EXECUTE
 FETCHNEXT
 FETCHNEXT
 Error 1 (rc 100)
RUNTIME_EXECUTE:
SELECT "aaa_user_id"."user_key" ,"aaa_user_id"."user_id"
,"aaa_user_id"."full_user_name"  FROM "aaa_user_id" WHERE
"aaa_user_id"."user_id" ='Madman'
 Error -143 (rc -1) : SQLSTATE = S0022
[WATCOM][ODBC Driver][WATCOM SQL]: column 'rowfocus_indicator_colour' not
found
RUNTIME_EXECUTE:
SELECT "gl_years_setup"."year_key" FROM "gl_years_setup" WHERE
"gl_years_setup"."year" =1994
 RTFETCHNEXT
 RTFETCHNEXT
 Error 3 (rc 100) : SQLSTATE = S0022
[WATCOM][ODBC Driver][WATCOM SQL]: column 'rowfocus_indicator_colour' not
found
 CANCEL
RUNTIME_EXECUTE:
update "aaa_user_id" SET "default_gl_year" =1994 WHERE user_key =18
 COMMIT
 DISCONNECT
 SHUTDOWN_INTERFACE
```

There are lots of interesting things to see in the pbtrace.log, though it can become very large, very quickly. This TRACE log file, like the exe_name.dbg of /pbdebug, is an all-or-nothing approach. And, like the exe_name.dbg, you can do tricks to let you find where you want to start. For example, if you wanted to see what happens when you load a particular window, you might code in two menu choices:

```
string ls_trace // a throwaway variable
SELECT "Start here" into :ls_trace from "sys"."dummy"
RETURN
and
string ls_trace // a throwaway variable
SELECT "End here" into :ls_trace from "sys"."dummy"
RETURN
```

You would then hit the menu choice for "Start here," open the window and then hit the menu choice for "End here." These statements will create the following:

```
EXECUTE:
select 'Start here' from "sys"."dummy"   (50 MilliSeconds)
 GET AFFECTED ROWS: (0 MilliSeconds)
 ^  1 Rows Affected
 GET NUMBER OF COLUMNS SELECTED: (0 MilliSeconds)
 ^  1 Columns
 DESCRIBE SELECT: (0 MilliSeconds)
 BIND SELECT OUTPUT BUFFER (PowerScript): (0 MilliSeconds)
1 Bind Columns
 CHAR Length 40
 FETCH NEXT: (11 MilliSeconds)
COLUMN=1

 GET AFFECTED ROWS: (0 MilliSeconds)
 ^  1 Rows Affected
 FETCH NEXT: (20 MilliSeconds)
 Error 3 (rc 100)
 CANCEL: (10 MilliSeconds)
```

Then, when you edit the pbtrace.log file, you can do a search on "Start here" and cut out all the portions of the TRACE file that are irrelevant to you. If you want more than just a plain start and end, try:

```
// initial code
string ls_trace // a throwaway variable
SELECT "1" into :ls_trace from "sys"."dummy"
... // some code
SELECT "2" into :ls_trace from "sys"."dummy"
... // more code
SELECT "3" into :ls_trace from "sys"."dummy"
... // the rest of the code
```

Obviously, there are many other variations on the theme, and where possible, you should use more descriptive strings than "1," "2," and "3". You should have the basic idea now.

Some DBMSes, like Oracle, have their own built-in trace features. Watcom does not. You should check your DBMS to see what its support is and compare it to the pbtrace.log file. You should decide if and/or when you would want to use your DBMS trace feature, and if and/or when you would want to use the PowerBuilder TRACE. You should do this before you "need" it, of course, so you know how to get it!

Create an "event" window

We have a special window we call the "event" window. To understand its use, think about the English word "event," not the PowerBuilder or SQL term. An event has been defined as an "occurrence," or more to our purpose, as "a noteworthy happening." Every time something happens that we want to keep track of, we send a message to that window telling it to record the event. We send this message by invoking a function on the window or in a user object that controls the window. I may send a string that reads, "going through the loop for the "+string(lk_i)+"th time," or it may be "entering RowFocusChanged event". Frequently, as in the first example, we will record the value of variables at that point. This allows us keep a trace of just those events or SQL statements that we want, making it much easier.

SQLPreview

For every database select, delete, insert or update PowerBuilder is going to make to the DBMS, you get a chance to look at it before it executes.

Put code similar to the following in the SQLPreview event to see the statement before it is sent. Uf_message is our replacement for the message box. It formats long messages, such as the SQLPreview, better than message box does. If you do not have a similar function, use the message box to display the SQL code. I have stripped out other "fluff" code from the actual code that I use.

```
if uo_debug.ib_display_sqlpreview then
 uf_message('The SQL about to be executed is:~n~r' &
 +this.dwGetSQLPreview(),'')
 end if
end if
return
```

If you program .dlls for PowerBuilder in C++, then you should be using the most recent Watcom C++ compiler with PowerBuilder. It allows you to step through the PowerBuilder code debugger, and when you get to the .dll, it steps through it using the Watcom debugger. This alone may be reason to switch to the Watcom compiler. The only downside to this is once you get to play with the Watcom debugger, you'll never be happy with the PowerBuilder debugger!

You may also prefer to send the this.dwGetSQLPreview() to your "event" window, discussed in the section just prior to this one, rather than sending it to the screen in a message box. This way you can do a postmortem and not have to hit the <Enter> key until it wears out.

Stack fault errors

If you get a stack fault error, you can be pretty sure it is your fault and not PowerBuilder's. A stack fault is caused when your program goes into uncontrolled recursion. Doing an accept-text in the ItemError event is a favorite way of mine to create a stack fault error. Changing the size of a Window in the Resize event is another convenient way to cause a stack fault.

There are times when you want controlled recursion, but recursion can be a little tricky to manage if you don't use it regularly. If you are a competent developer, you will find that though there are situations where recursion is really useful, there are others where recursion is the simple, but wrong, answer.

Re-entrance is similar to recursion. This can happen when you have a function to display a message: if an error occurs, you call the same function to display the error about the original message. (Indeed, this may represent recursion in the true sense of the word.)

Your biggest problems with recursion or re-entrance are going to come from system or application globals, or from object shared variables. Some examples to give you an idea of what to watch out for:

System global:
A file at the operating system level
An .ini file
The printer port

Application global:
SQLCA
Window variables if opened using format 1

One of the biggest mistakes in debugging recursion is losing track of what level you are actually at. In most cases you can create an instance variable initialized to 0, and then use it in the recursive event or function to keep track of how deep you are. For example:

```
long ig_recursion_depth = 0

event ue_recursion_test
ig_recursion_depth ++
// Bunch of code that can cause recursions
ig_recursion_depth --
```

You can also extend this trick to catch illegal recursion or re-entrance.

GPFs

If you have used any Windows application for a few months, you have probably run into a General Protection Fault (GPF). Some programs, including some competitors of Powersoft, capture and rename these errors so that the user doesn't realize what happened. A rose by any other name....

Whatever the application calls it, a GPF occurs when an instruction in an .exe or .dll tries to write to a location in memory for which it has not received write permission from Windows. In most cases there is little you can do other than to try to find the cause of the problem and fix it. In some cases the fault is not yours, but Powersoft's. Then it becomes necessary to write a workaround until Powersoft fixes it. If you can create a small reproducible test and send it to them, Powersoft is much more likely to be able to fix it.

Even more so than with most bugs, if you can duplicate the GPF in the smallest possible application, it will make it easier for you, TeamPS, and/or Powersoft support to find the cause of the problem.

One cause of GPFs is bad video drivers. Some programs, like PowerBuilder, seem to be affected by bad video drivers more than others are. I was able to get rid of a lot of GPFs by updating my ATI video card software.

Be careful about the difference between the *cause* of the GPF and the *symptom*. The GPF does not always happen at the point of corruption. For example, if you copy more than 32K to the clipboard using the SaveAs(",Clipboard!,...) function, under 3.0a and the beta 4.0 that I am using while working on this chapter, Powersoft will corrupt memory. The result of that corruption is sometimes immediate, but the first time I saw this, and a few times thereafter, I stepped through a hundred or more lines of code with the debugger before it GPFed. Fortunately, most GPFs happen at the line of code that caused the GPF–but don't discount the possibility of it being somewhere else. If you change some code and the GPF "moves," give serious consideration to the possibility that it is happening because of some other section of code.

Working on bugs like this is not easy for anyone. It is done with a combination of intuition and careful, painstaking research. Many times you will find that your code was at fault. But if you get a solid problem definition, please make sure Powersoft has been told. Experience shows they will try very hard to get it fixed once they know about it.

The exact cause of specific GPFs, especially those caused by Powersoft, is a moving target. This book is being written while version 4.0 is in beta. To mention specific GPFs would not make sense, as they will probably be outdated and mostly fixed by the time you read this. Therefore, if you have the InfoBase CD, see if it has a problem listed that is similar to yours. You can even try to search for the exact GPF address. You probably won't get a hit very often if you are running with patches released after your InfoBase. This is because the specific segment:offset is usually only applicable for a specific .dll. When Powersoft modifies it, even if the same bug is occurring, there is a good chance it will now be at a different address.

I would also humbly suggest you download my pb_gpf.zip file on CompuServe. It will also be on the Powersoft Internet FTP site when that is operational–by the time you read this, I hope. I upload an updated version of this document every couple of months. It discusses all the reproducible GPFs and similar problems that I know about.

If these don't reveal the problem, call Powersoft support or put a message out on CompuServe.

When trying to track down a GPF (or the equivalent, in products that have re-worded it so they can say that they don't have GPFs), one of the most frustrating aspects is the reboot factor. Once you have had a GPF, any other GPFs you get in that session–whether in the product that caused the GPF in the first place or in a different product–may be side effects directly caused by the first GPF. Once memory is corrupted, GPFs can happen frequently. If PowerBuilder or your PowerBuilder code is the cause of the GPF, shutting down PowerBuilder will often not let you do other things, because you will get GPFs in the strangest places.

This, of course, assumes that you can continue. Many times when you get a GPF, your system will be locked up tighter than a drum, the mouse won't move, the screen may go black, and no matter what you do, you can't get to your other programs to save their data.

If you are trying to track down this type of bug, here are a few steps that will make the process a little less painful.

There are certain programs that let you unload .dlls from memory. These programs will show you everything that Windows has loaded. After a GPF, you can go in, select all the Power-Builder .dlls, then tell the program to remove them from memory.

Personally I find that I am not fast enough with the mouse to make this method practical; however, one of my developers moves the mouse around faster than the rest of us can see, and he uses one of these programs to great effect. Although you still have to reboot some-times with tools like this, it can drastically reduce the number of times you have to reboot. When it removes the .dlls from memory, it usually seems to remove the corruption at the same time.

If you have data in other programs that you want to save but your system is locked up, try the three finger salute: <Ctrl>-<Alt>-<Del>. This will sometimes have Windows come back and tell you that the application is not responding and ask if you want to terminate it. If you get this screen, that is good. Tell it to terminate your program, then save your data in the other programs and reboot.

Get NT 3.1 or 3.5 so that, in most cases, it will only lock up your PowerBuilder session. All other sessions, be they Win16 or Win32 sessions, will usually stay up. In the few months I've worked with NT, I have only twice lost work in other applications under it–this despite working with earlier betas in which I measured the GPF rate in number of times per hour.

Of the two, get NT 3.5, if for no other reason than it is far faster than 3.1. If you are running with 3.1, trust me, you really want to switch to NT 3.5. One reason is that the hot keys work in NT 3.5, but they don't in NT 3.1. Ask me for details on CompuServe, if you wish, because I'm sure my list of reasons will be longer.

Now that you are running in 3.5, you will quickly find that NT can be frustrating to reboot, because it makes you type <Ctrl>-<Alt>-<Del> to log on. It then asks for your password, and if you have connected to any Windows for Workgroups machines, it asks you for the passwords of each and every one of those machines.

But as you may have guessed, I have some ideas here too. The first one is, if you don't need the W4WG connections, get rid of them, and only connect when you need to. If you can, have those you connect to switch to NT, so that you have compatible password schemes. Now the big one. You can set up your NT machine so it will *not* ask you to hit <Ctrl>-<Alt>-<Del>, or for your password, to log on. Rather, if you log off, it will automatically re-enter NT with your user id and password. This is obviously NOT a good idea for a "secure" sys-tem and it violates almost all the security built into NT, but it saves lots and lots of time when debugging GPFs.

To set your system up to reboot automatically, you need to have a password. If your pass-word is the empty string–that is, you just hit the <Enter> key when NT asks you for your password–you need to change your password to be a real string. The trick I'm about to show you will only work once, and then you will have to set it up again and again and again–every time (before) you reboot.

Type <Ctrl>-<Alt>-<Del> to get a window that will let you change your password.

Next you need to launch the program regedt32.exe. If you want to be able to turn this feature on and off, set up a program item group as in the following screen shot.

```
┌─────────────────────────────────────────────────────────────┐
│ ─              Program Item Properties                        │
├─────────────────────────────────────────────────────────────┤
│                                                               │
│  Description:     │Regedt32              │   ┌──────────────┐  │
│                                             │      OK       │  │
│  Command Line:    │C:\NT\SYSTEM32\REGEDT32.E│ └──────────────┘  │
│                                             ┌──────────────┐   │
│  Working Directory: │C:\NT\SYSTEM32       │  │    Cancel     │  │
│                                             └──────────────┘   │
│  Shortcut Key:    │None                  │                     │
│                                             ┌──────────────┐   │
│                                             │   Browse...   │  │
│         ┌────┐     ☐ Run Minimized          └──────────────┘   │
│         │    │     ☒ Run in Separate Memory Space              │
│         └────┘                              ┌──────────────┐   │
│                                             │ Change Icon...│  │
│                                             └──────────────┘   │
│                                             ┌──────────────┐   │
│                                             │     Help      │  │
│                                             └──────────────┘   │
└─────────────────────────────────────────────────────────────┘
```

Now, launch regedit32 and select the sheet titled "HKEY_LOCAL_MACHINE on Local Machine." From there, expand the HKEY_LOCAL_MACHINE subdirectory, then expand SOFTWARE, MICROSOFT, WINDOWS NT, CURRENTVERSION, and select WINLOGON. This will leave your screen looking roughly like the next screen shot.

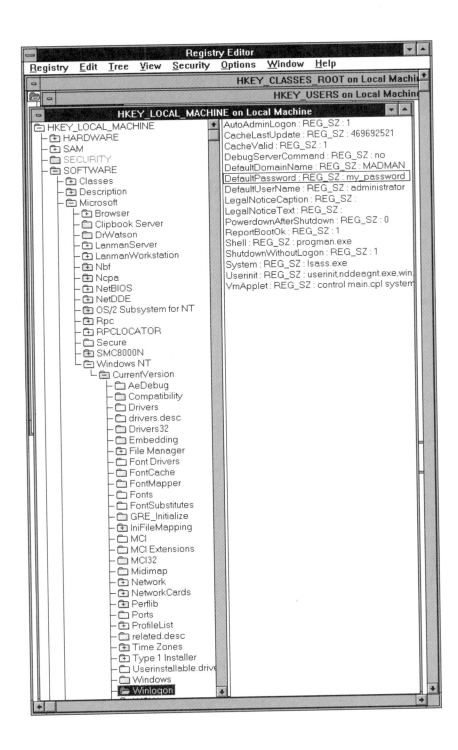

You are going to change the value of AutoAdminLogon to 1. (Personally, I love this choice since one of my companies is "Auto-Administrator," and I like to think of it is being Number 1). Setting AutoAdminLogon to 1 means "Yes." Windows NT will immediately log you in when you turn the computer on and when you log off. (Remember that in Windows NT, Shutdown is the way to turn it off for real.) If you set it to "No," it will not automatically log on.

Second, you are going to make sure the DefaultDomainName is set to you. As above, you will see that I am "MADMAN." Finally you will put your password in the DefaultPassword. Then, to change an item, double-click on the value (the right-hand side) and edit it as desired.

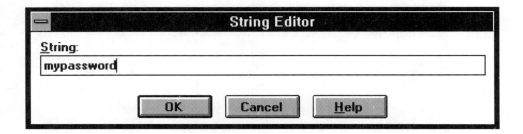

Notice that your password is in clear text. For this reason, make sure you use a different password here than you use when logging in to CompuServe, the Internet or other computers, just in case someone sees your password. If you find that this trick does not work for you, look at the big screen shot of regedit32 and see if there are any other settings you have changed from those on my machine.

Although this trick takes a couple minutes to set up, if you are frequently rebooting as part of your debugging process, this can free up hours of time. This gives you time to get a coffee, study your code or do other things, rather than baby-sitting Windows while it shuts down and reloads.

5.Take everything other than PowerBuilder out of your startup. Normally I like to run with all sorts of software including Word 6.0, MS-Scheduler, MS-Mail, File Manager, Power-Builder and a handful of others. This is really handy under normal circumstances, but when I am frequently rebooting, it is a big pain waiting for all these applications to load. To solve the problem I created a "Temp. Startup" group. The result is that the reboot cycle is much shorter. Then, when I get involved in a whole bunch of reboots, I drag all the icons from my "Startup" group into my "Temp. Startup" group. When I have licked the problem, I drag them all back. Another trick is to hold down the shift key while Windows is loading, which causes the applications in the Startup group not to load.

Object oriented-caused problems

As most people know, PowerBuilder is fairly object-oriented (OO). This means there is a *lot* more dependency between objects than there was with procedural code. On the whole this is good, very good. But there are times....

One of the biggest problems appears when you change an ancestor object. When you save an object, PowerBuilder "compiles" a copy of it into the same .pbl where the source code is stored. That "compiled" copy knows lots of information about its ancestors. For example, it knows when to call their events. (Someday, export an object and look through its code to see all the references to the ancestor.)

Any given object may be used by multiple programmers on multiple projects. The ancestor has *no way* of knowing what all its descendants are. Yet when you change an ancestor, it is important to regenerate all its descendants in all projects. (If all you do is edit some script, you do not need to regenerate the descendants.) Regeneration is especially necessary if you add or delete an event, function or variable, or if you change the definition of a variable that is public or protected.

If you don't regenerate, the compiled descendants are going to reference their ancestor and find that part of their ancestor is not there, or not where they expected it to be. If you execute this, you can expect REALLY strange results. GPFs, wrong event scripts being executed, and other such problems should be expected and are not a sign of a defect in PowerBuilder.

Some people blame PowerBuilder for this. Please read the whole paragraph before throwing the book down– I hope they *don't* fix it. Why? Because I'm a crazy Madman? No, because I believe the performance or development penalty would be too great. I fear that the only ways PowerBuilder could fix this would be:

> Drastically slowing the run time down by doing all the linking and checking at runtime.

> Maintaining static links to all descendant objects in all projects, and regenerating all of them every time the ancestor is changed. This would mean we would not be permitted to work on an application unless *all* its descendants (in *all* programs) are available to be updated.

I prefer the current alternative–put the developer in charge of doing regenerations. This way, I may decide to leave some projects un-regenerated for weeks, and only regen them the next time I work on them.

Now, PowerBuilder may come up with a better way in the future, and I'm sure there are other options that I haven't considered, so let me revise my statement. I hope they *do* fix it– but I hope they only fix it when they find a way that will not cause a huge slowdown at runtime or in the development environment.

In the meantime, PowerBuilder gives us the regenerate options to assist us. We have adopted Three Complete Bug-Free Regens as a rule of thumb before creating any .exes or (as in the following) doing a migration.

The first regen is done in the Browse Class Hierarchy on the Utilities menu of the Library

Painter. The other two are done by opening all the .pbls and selecting the first object in the first .pbl. Then, using the mouse and holding down the shift key, select the last object in the last .pbl. Choose Regenerate from the menu or click on the Regenerate icon on the toolbar.

The Browse Class Hierarchy choice is a nice way to ensure your application is regenerated in the correct order. When you select this choice you get the following response window:

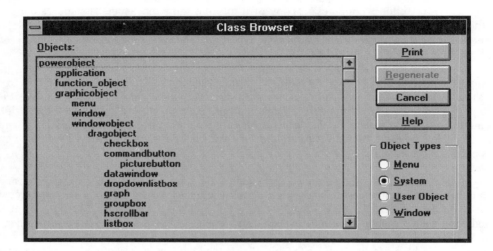

We start by regenning the menus, then the user objects, and finally the windows. Notice that I have highlighted the xw_parent_of_all_windows choice. When I select Regenerate, it will regenerate the tree in object inheritance order. This means all the ancestors will be regenerated, then their descendants, then their descendants, and so on.

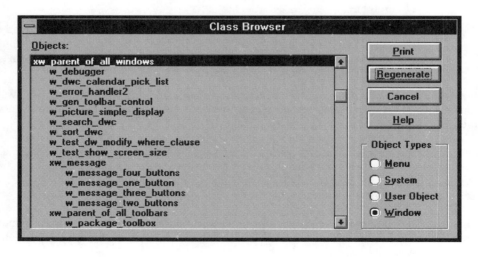

This removes the problem of regenning by selecting a bunch of objects in the Object Painter, as in the following screen shot:

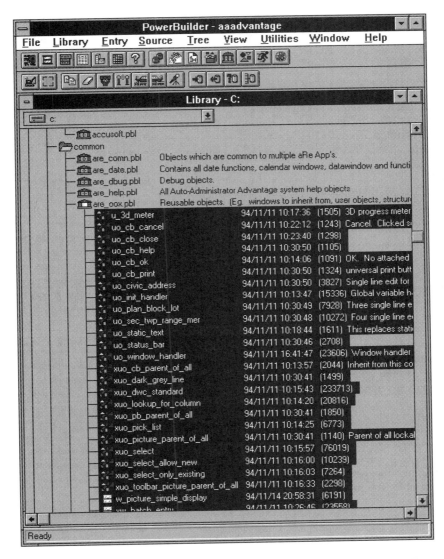

When you regenerate using this method, there is nothing stopping PowerBuilder from regenerating some of the descendant objects before the ancestors. This means the descendants may require regenerating again.

Migration

As you read this chapter, many of you are going to be migrating your Version 3.x apps to version 4.0. In fact, some of you will have purchased this book because you were migrating.

If you have a moderate- or large-sized application, you are bound to run into some migration issues. You may run into problems with small applications. While I was writing this chapter, I was also in the process of migrating a moderate-sized application (thirty .pbls, about eighteen megabytes total size). I was working with a beta version of 4.0–that is, a version where I *expected* to see bugs. My job was to help find them. I was surprised to find a number of bugs that should have caused problems in 3.0! For the life of me, I couldn't understand why they had not.

For example, I found a call to an external .dll where I was specifying a 32bit Long, but it was expecting a 16bit Integer. Under version 4.0 it caused a GPF in pbshr040.dll (the memory resource handler). Under 3.0, it seemed to work fine! As far as I can determine, I was causing a memory leak in Version 3.0 that did not show up at the problem point.

To date, half of the errors we found in converting to Version 4.0 were errors of ours that "slipped by" in Version 3.0.

Some of the other errors were caused by using PowerBuilder in undocumented ways and having this fail in Version 4.0. For example, we were triggering an event on an object that did not exist "yet." Under Version 3.0, we never found the bug. Under Version 4.0 we got a friendly "Null object reference on line 3 of ..." error message. We fixed the object in both 4.0 and 3.0 (we check if IsValid() and not IsNull() before triggering it now) and–surprise, one of the intermittent GPFs we had had in 3.0 seems to have disappeared. While it might be argued that this was a bug in Version 3.0 of PowerBuilder, I also accept equal responsibility. I'm just glad that the migration caught this long-standing bug in our code.

The rest of the bugs we encountered were caused by the beta. Some have been fixed already, and I expect most or all will be fixed by the time Version 4.0 ships. I also suspect that the ordering of some events may have changed. I have not completed my tests in this regard (I have found no changes yet), but many people, myself included, rely on the order of events. If there *are* changes in Version 4.0, we will all have to make minor adjustments to accommodate them.

When you convert, you may find still other problems. Don't immediately assume the fault is with PowerBuilder. Give equal or greater consideration to the possibility that Version 4.0 has caught an old bug, and by giving you an error or crashing "consistently," is now giving you an easier job of finding it.

Old wives' tales

Be wary of these. When you have a bug, there is a great tendency to jump at the first solution you find. Sometimes this is reasonable–such as when you find a value being set to 2 when it is supposed to be 1, and you know the line of code where it is happening. But other times, in the process of debugging, you may make a small change and find that the problem went away. If the change you made has little bearing on the problem, then you are likely to assume it was a generic problem and carry on with that assumption, probably blaming Power-Builder. If you were wrong, you have just created an "old wives' tale."

Once we have created an old wives' tale and taken it as true, we have needlessly restricted and complicated our lives. Also, we obviously make debugging just that much more difficult, as we add fancy workarounds for problems that never existed.

As a result, I have a habit of checking my fixes. Once I have found a bug and coded a fix, I put the bug back and cause it to happen again. Then I take it out once more, to make it go away. This proves that I know the exact reason for the bug. I will often go on and perform other tests in other programs, on other machines, and in other projects, to prove or disprove my hypothesis. This can be time-consuming and frustrating, especially when it proves I *don't* really know the cause. But it the long term, this attitude will stop you from creating mental "no-nos" that are actually perfectly fine. It also means you are more likely to have *really* found the bug, not just moved it somewhere else.

As an example, we once had a window that would not accept a menu at runtime (under 3.0a patch level 12). We changed one of its attributes–and then it would accept a menu. I was tempted to claim that it was the value of the attribute that caused the problem. However, I was challenged to follow our standard and reintroduce the bug. I couldn't. In retrospect, had I regenned the object, the bug would probably have gone away without any other changes.

Also, be aware that for every bug you fix, there is a fifty percent chance that you have introduced a new bug. Be very careful when repairing after debugging. Debugging finds the cause of the immediate problem, it does not necessarily provide the solution. Carefully consider the possibility that the obvious solution may be creating a new bug elsewhere.

Fix the bugs

Okay, now you've spent all this time finding a bug. Maybe it was easy to find this time; a variable was not initialized. You are tired, it is after midnight, and the product is shipping tomorrow morning. So what do you do?

There is a tendency at this point to think, "Finally, I'm almost done." But this is not the case. As mentioned, every time you fix a bug you are running the risk of adding one or more bugs elsewhere. Also, the fix you do may be thought by another programmer to be a bug itself! You may have painstakingly found a bug and fixed it, only to have someone come along and put it back the way it was before.

When you fix a bug, DOCUMENT the fix, and do it well. For example, if you have worked with True/False/Null logic for any amount of time, you are no doubt aware that the following two code segments are drastically different:

```
IF ib_somevar = TRUE THEN
  do it one way
```

```
         END IF
```
and
```
         IF ib_somevar  = FALSE THEN
           do something
         END IF
```

In both cases, if ib_somevar has the value Null, the ELSE clause will be used, so it will never be done. This is because Null is not True and it is not False. We had a bug a while ago where someone (me) "optimized" the code. It read:

```
         IF NOT ib_somevar = TRUE THEN
           do something
         END IF
```

I unwisely decided to improve performance and make it easier to read (so I thought) by changing it to:

```
         IF ib_somevar = FALSE THEN
           do something
         END IF
```

This, of course, made the program fail on the Null case. When I went back and fixed the bug, I changed it to read:

```
         //IF ib_somevar = FALSE THEN <- NO!!! You are not
         allowed in here if ib_somevar is NULL
         IF NOT ib_somevar = TRUE THEN // WARNING remember to NOT
         do this if the value is NULL
           do something
         END IF
```

I now document every trinary logic condition so I won't make a mistake like this again.

The lessons to be learned from this and similar mistakes are:

Always document a change. Since it wasn't done correctly the first time, neither the original nor the fix is "obvious." It NEEDS to be documented with WHY and WHAT (explained below).

Always be careful when making a change. Don't apply a bandage. Apply a solution.

A similar rule I have that has come from experience with these types of debugging sessions and resolutions is:

> When debugging or reading code, if I do not understand WHY a piece of code is doing what it is doing, or if I do not understand WHAT a piece of code is doing, once I figure these out, I go back and document them. This will

help me and others understand the next time through.

Earlier I said that when you find a bug, make sure you really understand why the bug was fixed by what you did. Try to fully understand the problem and don't just jump at the first solution that comes to mind. This can be especially true with a fix involving PostEvents vs. TriggerEvents. How many times have developers realized, "Oh, this event needs to be posted to work," only to find out later that under some conditions, a response window pops up and all the posted events immediately start to execute while waiting for the end user to respond to the response window?

Before applying a fix, ask yourself a few questions:

Why did the original programmer put this bug in, in the first place? The event may have been triggered because of the response windows. Or a variable may be uninitialized because some other portion of the program is specifically checking to see if it has been initialized or not. Often bugs are not put in a program without reason. When resolving a bug, you have to try to make sure you understand both the original reason for the bug being put in the code *and* the reason why the solution is expected to remove the bug.

Is the bug local? Will its variables and functions have no effect outside themselves, or does it employ a variable that is widely used? If it is widely used, you have to be ten times more careful that your fix is not going to blow up one of those other users.

What type of bug is it? Is it syntactical, lexical, a problem understanding the specifications, or some other type of bug? If it is syntactical, on the first run of the program, you are much safer taking only a cursory look for side effects. However, if the problem is logical and the program has been in use for some time, you have to be VERY careful.

As a general rule, whenever I fix a bug in an area, I spend a few more minutes, hours, or days looking at the code, to see if I can find "the other bugs" that may be hiding there. Experience has shown that where one bug lies, the probabilities are very high that there are more. More important, I have found that approximately twenty percent of the code contains eighty percent of the bugs. So I know that when I find a bug, I have probably found one of the areas that contain most of the bugs. It has proven to be a very good investment to continue looking in the same area for other bugs, known or unknown.

The second benefit is that this gives me a further check to see whether my fix is going to break anything else. If the bug was intermittent it is a lot harder to feel comfortable that it has actually been caught. If the problem occurred twice daily and to four or five customers out of hundreds, it will take weeks, and program use by hundreds of different customers, before I will feel comfortable that the bug has been irradiated. I have seen bugs that happen, on average, two or three times daily and then do not show up for weeks.

One particular example was a bug that seemed to turn up only occasionally. We wouldn't hear about it for months, and then it would happen again everywhere. We sent out "the latest patches" and the problem "went away"–for a couple of months. It turned out the bug only appeared when the day of the month was greater than 30.

We had a similar bug that only happened on Feb. 29th. This was also hard to find. But in both cases, once we isolated the real problem and turned it into a reproducible failure, we had a very high degree of confidence that we had found and fixed the problem.

The point is, a fix for a bug that you cannot reliably reproduce is less likely to be a real fix. It is more likely to simply cover the problem up or move it around–possibly making it easier, but more often making it harder, to find.

With any intermittent problem, you will have to do much more extensive tests in order to make it fail with some statistical certainty. And you will have to test it like crazy after you "fix" it. With most intermittent bugs, you can only be sure if your fix has worked or not if, after it has been applied, it still fails! A "null failure" does not imply that the bug has been found and eradicated.

When you have found and repaired a bug, you may have an opportunity to help double check your solution, as well as to help other developers learn about solving the problem. If you have learned a particular lesson from a specific debugging session, consider letting other developers try to find the same problem while you watch. If they get stuck, help them out. This can help them become better debuggers, but they might also point out other flaws in the program and/or your solution.

This suggestion works best in an atmosphere where there is little hostility and competition is friendly. This has the least benefit in a union shop, or where individual improvement is rated higher than group achievement. If you work in an office where you feel this sort of sugges-tion would not be well received, I would suggest you should plan on looking for a better environment.

Closing Thoughts

Debugging is part science, part art. Although some people are "naturally" better at it, most decent developers will be able to become reasonably competent at debugging. The more you try debugging, the better you will get. Very few people are excellent debuggers from day one. The vast majority of excellent debuggers got that way by constant practice on harder and harder debugging cases.

As tools, like PowerBuilder, become more and more powerful, the number of jobs they do for you "per bug" becomes higher and higher. But the bugs that you create often become harder to find. Although, like most, I get frustrated when I have a bug I can't find, I fre-quently look back and realize that if I were using my two-year-old tools, I would have had ten to a hundred times as many bugs per feature.

I have discussed a large number of tools ranging from the hard to the very wishy-washy. Most of them will do a better job for you if you practice with them before you have a serious bug to find. Using a tool for the first time while trying to track down a difficult bug is not the best way. Having said that, you will never "really" learn the more powerful tools until you have used them under real bugs.

Recommended Reading:

*Debugging: Creative Techniques and Tools for Software Repai*r by Martin Stitt, published by Wiley. ISBN 0-471-55831-1.

CHAPTER 30

Debugging, Part II: Environment, Staffing, and Management

By Peter Horwood

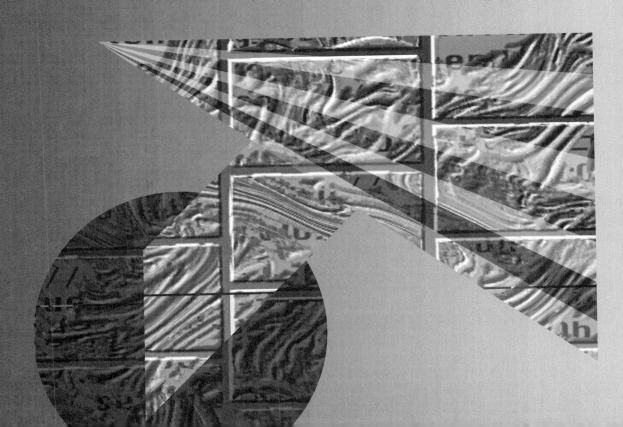

Debugging, Part II:
Environment, Staffing, and Management

by **Peter Horwood**

Environment

Lighting

You can now buy what are called "full spectrum fluorescent lights." These produce a more pleasant blue light than normal fluorescent bulbs, which is less stressful on the eyes (and some claim healthier in other ways). They are currently about three times the price of normal bulbs, but produce ninety percent of new light after ten years. Even considering interest, they are cheaper in the long run than normal bulbs. We found the incidence of headaches among people who worked on computers (secretaries, managers, and developers) were cut in half when we first installed them about six years ago.

Refreshments

Remember that developers often (usually, in our office) work hours that most white-collar workers consider "odd." It is necessary to insure that developers can get food and drink at 3:00pm and 3:00am. You may have a kitchen or you may have a vending machine. If you do, make sure you stock items that the developers want! A fridge and microwave are also very worthwhile investments.

Noise levels

Programming is usually a concentration-intensive task. Most developers do not do well in noise other than music of their own choosing. If they want music (and it is permitted), it must be controlled in a way that does not bother others, since very seldom will everyone like the same music. Most radio stations are a significantly less desirable source of music, as the speaking breaks concentration too easily and too often.

We have found that three to four people in an open room is about the limit before you need partitions to block the noise. Try to put people who usually work on the same project together in the same area, so they do not have to take long walks to discuss design problems.

You will find some developers who have to be in a separate room, either because they are an interruption to others or because they cannot tolerate any noise. Give them their request! We accommodate this request with movable partitions and self-standing bookcases so we can easily rearrange as needs and projects change, or just because we are bored and want a change. This way we can still keep teams in close proximity for necessary discussions. We don't want the different noise needs to interfere with the communication bandwidth more than necessary.

Don't make the room dozens of little cubbyholes, unless the developers really want it that way. We have found that developers need to bounce ideas off their peers to keep the creative juices flowing.

Interruptions

This is why developers who work from home seldom are as successful as those who work in an office. Unless they are single, it is difficult to avoid breaking concentration. If work is done both at home and at the office, you should plan to do the non-logical or non-mental jobs from home. I have four kids aged two to five, and work at home an average of four to five hours per night. I have found that in order to concentrate I either have to work after everyone else has gone to bed, and/or get up before they do. Fortunately, I have been blessed with a very low requirement for sleep. If you haven't, try to avoid working at home, or find suitable solutions that work for you.

Colors

The color of the office can make a big difference. Programming can be stressful, and we want to lower the stress to reduce the bugs. You want neither excessively sterile nor gloomy environments. I have found that pastels in well-lit rooms work well. Oak offices or hospital-white rooms just don't seem to work for developers. Our main work area in Calgary is done in dusty rose–a very relaxing color.

Couch

In our board room, seldom used in the traditional way, we have a couch. Any employee who needs to rest, needs to lie down and think, has a headache, or is simply feeling over-stressed, can go and lie down as long as he or she wants. We do our utmost to never disturb people when they are on the couch. It would be nice to think that the environment is so perfect that developers would never feel the need or desire to lie down, but that is not realistic. That $300 couch has bought far more than $300 worth of value many times over.

Screens

Staring at computer screens for hours can cause a high level of tension through sore eyes. Bad screens are one of the worst causes of tension, discomfort, and malaise among developers. There are a number of issues to consider with screens.

For now, stick with "standard" screens, except with portables. The various options on portables are still too hard to work with for long hours. When members of my staff need a portable, I provide a "real" screen at the office.

Refresh rate is a personal issue. I need a non-interlaced screen that has a refresh rate of 70 Hz or higher. Any slower, and I constantly see a flicker and get a headache. My father, on the other hand, uses an interlaced screen that has a refresh rate of only 60 Hz and he cannot see the flicker. We figure that his eyes, being older, don't react as quickly; therefore, don't register the flicker. Mine do register it, and constantly try to adjust for it.

Size is more of a budget question. Bigger is better! However, when we last evaluated monitors, within the budget I was willing to allocate, the 14" monitors we found were crisper than the 17". We chose clarity over size. Burn-in is simple to deal with. If you can see images on the screen when there is nothing there, replace the screen.

You want the highest resolution you can work with on your screen without getting tired.

So what do I use? I use 1280x1024 on a 14" monitor. (Remember I'm Madman– as in crazy.) I admit this is a very high resolution for such a small screen, but I find the more I can cram on it, the faster the bugs get squeezed out; so I put up with it. Just as soon as I get paid big bucks for writing this chapter, I'm going to move up to a monster 21" monitor—who knows what resolution I can get then? Most of my staff uses 1024x768 on the same 14" monitor.

Don't forget desk space. Current monitors, 14" and larger, use up an awful lot of the desk depth. With 17" and larger monitors, we find we have to move the desk away from the wall.

When positioning the monitor, give consideration to the new "in the desk" method. The screen is imbedded in the desk at an angle that lets the head look down on it.

Finally, don't have a screen positioned where the user is facing out a window, or with a dark background. There will be a lot of sore eyes trying to adjust looking back and forth.

Whiteboards

Computers are wonderful tools, but sometimes manual methods are easier. One non-computerized tool we have found to be invaluable is a whiteboard. We have a few small ones (4'x3') and a few large ones (4'x12'). The small ones are mounted in each work area. The large ones are on wheels and are used in our development rooms, classrooms and boardrooms.

We use whiteboards to keep track of the major elements of each developer's to-do list and immediate to-do list. This usually consists of the next three "major" tasks, along with the detailed list for the next couple of weeks. This is also excellent for management, who can just look at the whiteboard to see where someone is, without having to ask (and break people's concentration). Yes, we have computerized to-do lists, which the developers and managers can access when they need detail, but usually managers only need the overall view. Wiping an item off the whiteboard gives a certain feeling of accomplishment!

Their other functions are more important than to-do lists. We use whiteboards to do basic design– drawing our data-flow diagrams, writing field requirements pseudocode, tracing how and what happened, and documenting our hypothesis. They are especially excellent when more than one person is involved with the design.

For testing and debugging, we sometimes hang the scripts up by magnets and do our dry runs with pens on the whiteboards. We trace the variables and other states by erasing and changing the values as we go along.

Unlike paper and pen, it is easy to move things around on them. Our next modification will be to build a calculator in!

Computerized whiteboards

You have started to see these showing up at conferences. If you do development across telephone lines with the same people all the time, they are definitely worth looking into. Basically, everything you draw on the whiteboard gets transmitted, so people at both ends can see the whiteboard. Also, you can hook them up to a computer and save your design onto a computer screen.

"Developers' dummy"

As a general rule, we find it is best if developers have one or two of their peers they can talk to and bounce ideas off of. Although sometimes the other developer can help, we usually find that the very fact of telling someone about a problem helps to give it structure and substance, and ultimately leads to its solution. We have a saying in our office: "I need a developers' dummy!" This results in someone coming along who just says "uh huh" and "hmmmm" from time to time. Depending on the problem, dummy developers have been known to read a book or debug their own unrelated objects while "listening" until the other developer has solved the problem.

We have played around with a chair that has a painted face and "uh huh" written on it. We found that, once you got over feeling funny about speaking aloud to a chair, talking to it would often get the problems solved! It is said that you learn more by teaching than you do by being a student. If you feel foolish talking out loud to a chair, try going into a separate room where you can't be heard, and explain the problem to a picture, or a mirror, or something. If this fails, ask someone to be your developers' dummy. (Make sure people read this section before you call them that, though!)

Keyboards

All developers and analysts should either be touch typists or be taking a course in touch typing. Keyboard layout is important, most people preferring the 101 keyboard layout that IBM created. Keyboards are the one major weakness of most laptop and portable computers.

Dvorak Layout

You may want to consider the Dvorak layout. The layout we are familiar with is called the QWERTY layout (for the six keys in the upper left area of the alpha keys). It was designed to *slow typists down,* because the original typists were too fast for the mechanical devices. The Dvorak layout is designed to let you type some ninety percent of English words on the home row. It is less tiring to type on and can double your typing speed. (Another benefit that I personally got from switching to Dvorak layout was that my hands were not so tired each night.) Along with increasing your speed by up to a hundred percent, the Dvorak keyboard will reduce the number of "typos"–as long as you are not switching back and forth between layouts.

The only disadvantage, and one that must be weighed seriously, is that it takes at least a week to go back and forth between QWERTY and Dvorak layouts. That is the time it takes to retrain yourself. So if you work at customer sites, you will have to carry your keyboard with you. But if you always work at your own office, Dvorak is a reasonable consideration.

Just don't expect a quick training time. It took me a couple months to regain my QWERTY speed with Dvorak.

Ergonomic Keyboards

The other keyboard layout to consider is the new Microsoft split keyboard. This is a less radical choice than the Dvorak layout. We are considering changing all our existing keyboards over to this one. The idea has existed for many years, but Microsoft seems to be the first to offer it at price close to normal keyboards.

Chairs

Chairs should be adjustable, supportive and comfortable. The most important adjustments for most people are height and back angle. Beware of cheap chairs which shift or slip on their adjustment. Spend a little bit more to get good chairs so you won't have to throw them away and buy the good ones later.

Desks

Desks should be comfortable and big enough for working on, with either a dropped keyboard section or a pull-out keyboard. Secretarial desks are not practical, because you cannot put the screen back far enough from the keyboard for comfort without putting the screen at such an angle as to cause neck strain. Consider the desks with the screen sunk in them at an angle. This appears to be a more natural and less stressful position than the traditional "eye-level."

Step stool

If you have developers who are shorter than average, you should provide a step stool to rest feet on. All of these environmental factors are designed to reduce stress and make the developer's job more enjoyable, and will almost always result in fewer errors.

Management: Self and Others

Time management

If you have not taken a time management course, NOW is the time to take one!
I have given such a course, and virtually all those who have taken it–from me or anyone else–have found that they can get more done in the same period of time and feel better about themselves. They don't have that feeling that they never accomplish anything, because they are accomplishing what they set out to do. So am I perfect at this? No, I still take on more than I can handle and try to do too much in too little time. But...I more than doubled my useful productivity within a couple of months of taking that first time management course.

To go into detail or to train new employees, I spend about four hours "lecturing," followed by about eight weeks of follow-up verification and evaluation. Rather than go into that much detail here, I will give some basics. Keep a "to-do" file. I call mine simply "todo.doc". Very original, I thought! In that file there are four sections that I would recommend everyone should keep.

```
Section 1. List of to-dos
Section 2. List of to-talk-tos
Section 3. Long term ideas
Section 4. Completed
```

You should go through Section 1 daily, and make sure that the MOST IMPORTANT items are at the top of the file. Then start at the top and go as far as you can down the list during the day. Don't worry if you don't do everything; go home secure in the thought that you did the most important things. If you also work at home, you can go to bed satisfied that you kept your priorities.

The other sections are far less important
.
In the to-talk-to section I have a lot of items I want to ask or tell other people about, whether

in or out of the company. If those items are urgent, I put a note in Section 1 to e-mail or call the person. Other items wait until the next conversation. Every time people call me or I am about to call them, I immediately check under their names in the list. By doing this, I save my time and theirs.

If you are a manager of developers and you follow this method, you will find that in most cases you will interrupt your developers less, and therefore not break their concentration. There is nothing a developer hates more than unnecessary interruptions, and managers should be of the same mind. Unnecessary interruptions cause bugs. Try to keep non-urgent interruptions down to once or twice a day, or less if you can. I refer to Section 3 list at least once a month, to allow my subconscious to continue to work on the long-term projects. In Section 4 I keep a list of all the people I talk to that I may want to remember. I record the time, date, and topic of the conversation, along with any resolutions. I can then find them when needed. Once a year I go through and purge this section.

Exercise

This topic may seem out of place to those who do not exercise regularly–but t all hose who do, understand why exercise is one of the most powerful tools available to the developer. I won't go into details here, other than to say that I have found (and most authors on exercise seem to concur) that exercise that gets your breathing and heart rates up is the most effective. My personal preference used to be to swim hard forty-five to sixty minutes three times weekly. Now that my kids are older, I play with them instead. The swimming was more effective.

My crude estimates are that developers who exercise sufficiently at least three times weekly make about twenty percent fewer mistakes in every category. Why is this? Exercise seems to increase the blood and oxygen flow to your brain, and has significant residual effects for a couple of days. All the tools, tricks, and techniques in this book are designed to multiply the effectiveness of the developer's or designer's powers of thought. If people are not thinking properly, tools only give a slight improvement. If they are thinking properly, tools give a great improvement.

Often, designers–and even more often, developers–spend long hours working on problems, frequently with "overnighters." My personal record is four and a half days without sleep. I do not advocate going for a hundred hours without sleep, The point is, that despite the best design and testing there are occasions when time pressures require long hours with high levels of logical thinking. This is easiest when you are physically fit.

Developers should not feel that they are the only ones who have to be mentally productive for long hours. I recently heard an interview on TV with a world-renowned chess master, who said he exercised four hours per day in preparation for chess tournaments. He said he needed the fitness to maintain his brilliance for the long hours it took to play against other masters. He claims he didn't become a master until he started rigorous exercise. Similarly, when the top team of chefs from Canada was preparing for a world championship competition, they included regular exercise as part of their practice, since they would work upwards of thirty-six hours at a time preparing the best meals that the world can offer. In almost every case, it seems to me that the majority of top performers in any field requiring intensive thought are the ones who, besides being brilliant and hardworking, exercise as a regular part of their training program.

My experience is that people who don't exercise, and don't try it for a few weeks, do not believe the results. Indeed, when they try exercising, they find that they are more tired, sleep longer, and do not increase productivity at all. This is true for most people when they first start. Their metabolism is still running at the old speed. But if you keep it up for a few weeks, your metabolism cranks up, and keeps going at the new speed. The great part, of course, is that it keeps going all day long, the next day, and to a lesser degree the third day. And there are lots of ways to get exercise. I get most of mine from playing rough with my kids each night. The rest I get where I can–taking stairs rather than elevators; running through the office rather than walking; and just trying to be "bouncy" rather than sedated. I am not the "go to the gym and be bored" type. Some of my other top staff are. If you can, don't stop once you start. When I fall back, I find it harder to get started again than it was to keep up. If you are already an "expert" and don't exercise–just think how good you could be if you also exercised! Since there are a lot of good books written on this topic, I refer you to your closest bookstore or library for further information.

Food

I am going to be careful on this one. Over the long term, I believe in eating "healthy"–but once you get sufficient nutrition, and if you are exercising regularly, I believe there are few rules for the rest of the calories. When working past fifteen hours in a stretch, sugar (i.e. candy) works great. According to more than one doctor I have talked with, this is because sugar is easy to digest and the body does not have to divert as much blood from the brain to digest it. Next time you're in a hospital, take at look at the food in the IV–it's often pure sugar and water!

I would like to reemphasize that you can fill up on the so called "empty calories" only if you are getting sufficient nutrition. If you don't exercise regularly, there is a good chance you will get too many calories before you get sufficient nutrition. The normal recommendation to talk to your doctor before radically altering your diet is wise. If you have had a high sugar diet, it is possible (and not all that uncommon) to make yourself sick by changing too quickly to a "healthy" diet! I believe it from experience.

It is very hard to think logically after a large meal. The reason? Your body has shunted blood from your brain and other portions of your body to your stomach, in order to digest the food. Thus you will make fewer mistakes after a small meal than after a large meal. Again, tools simply amplify your effectiveness. Eating a large meal before an intensive mental task lowers your effectiveness, and therefore the effectiveness of the tools–resulting in poorer debugging, testing, and development.

Again, those who know me might argue that I'm not one to speak. I'm definitely never accused of being thin, and a lot of top-notch developers eat too much. But the evidence seems to suggest that being healthier will help you to think and reason better.

On a similar front, if you want alcohol, you're best to leave it until after your mental work is done. And, of course, drinking large quantities at one time can permanently lower your peak ability, so it is not advised. Some (all?) ex-smokers I know also claim they could think more clearly once they kicked the habit. I suspect it comes from extra oxygen to the brain.

Staff

Staff considerations

All too often managers and developers evaluate performance by how fast it takes to get the first release of the software completed. It is true that speed should be one of the most important considerations in evaluating performance, but it is speed in producing a completed, working program that should be counted, not time it takes to first draft.

Obviously the competency of individuals, like the analyst and the developer, make a large difference in the quality of the produced product, but other factors come into play as well. We will be looking at the structure of the department and other "human factors."

Hiring of staff

When recruiting, do not slough off the job of interviewing as a punishment for someone or because it is "their turn." Have the person with the best judgment of skills deal with the hiring. It can easily take six months to a year to train an analyst or developer to the culture and standards of a company. That is a lot of money to spend, and sloughing off the interviewing job will cost a great deal of money in the long run.

I have had very good luck working with local colleges, taking students on work practicums. Have them work with the team to see if they measure up and can fit in.

If you are planning to hire people or move them from a different department, what do you look for? Do you hire the child prodigy who can write thirteen programs in thirteen minutes (not "quite" following standards), or do you hire the slower, steadier developer who ensures that all the standards are met?

Those of you who have read my standards document on CompuServe, or talked to me, know how emphatic and sold I am on the idea of having and following standards. Even if not, you may have expected me to say, "the slower, steadier developer, of course"–but life is not that simple. In anti-bugging and debugging, we are dealing with trade-offs to find the best balance. In most larger shops, there is room for one whiz-bang developer who can take on the emergency programs, and write the "one-up" programs that will be used in-house for a short period of time, then discarded. Sometimes the cost of bugs is so low and the existence of bugs will be so obvious, that you are better off writing the program quick and dirty. The problem is, once you have developers trained in "doing the job right," it is very hard to have them switch gears to quick and dirty. And if you succeed in getting a developer to write a Q&D program or suite of programs, there is a good chance that it will take weeks or even years to retrain for "normal" programming! For this reason, if there is enough work to keep a developer doing just those programs, it is often better than risking the corruption of your other developers.

Be aware of the potential that the whiz-bang developer *may* corrupt your other developers. Or your other developers may become jealous over issues of freedom and "special privileges." This may remove the benefits of the separate position.

Indoctrinating new staff

You should make sure developers know, before being hired, roughly what will be expected of them. After that point, you should plan on working with new developers, to ensure that they get the standards and methods ingrained.

You will have developed a standards manual with many more standards than this book lists, and you will want to ensure that all new developers study it (not just read it once). You will also want to go over each stage of their work with them, to find areas where it does not conform to your standards.

If you need help drafting your standards, see other sections of this book, PowerBuilder magazines, are_st.zip in the PowerBuilder forum, and various commercial products.

Department structure

In any company other than a one-man shop there will have to be a structure of some sort. In many companies, the programming department is made up of analysts, developers, testers, and technical writer(s). The analysts design the program from the user's point of view and the developers design it from the computer's point of view. If this is your structure, your analysts should have a very good feel for what PowerBuilder, your base class, and other libraries can and cannot do, and what the normal "look and feel" is. They should also know what the skill sets of the development team are. If they do not know, they are likely to design a system that is outside the team's ability. This will mean more mistakes and more bugs to have to find and debug. This obviously goes against my anti-bugging philosophy.

Information passing between the analyst and the developer should be in written form. If the developer feels there are changes necessary, then the written document should be changed to reflect this, usually after the approval of the analyst. If your company works with "Developer/Analysts," where each person does both jobs, the specifications should still be written down, and no actual changes should be made until the specifications are changed.

This will help immensely in the testing and debugging stage. It can also drastically cut down the time it takes to write a manual. If there are special considerations, exceptions or side-effects, these should all be included in the design document.

CHAPTER 31

Writing C DLLs for PowerBuilder: A Primer

By Sean Rhody

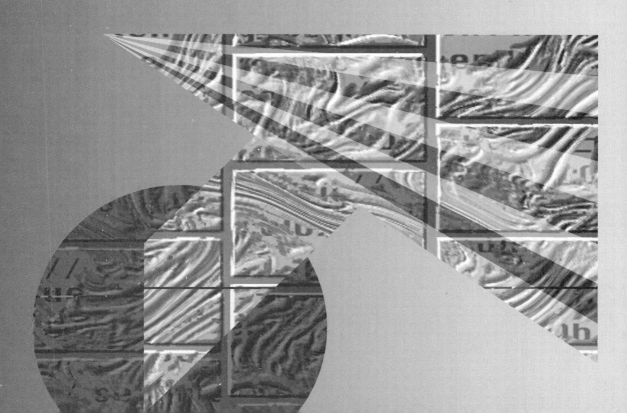

Writing C DLLs for PowerBuilder: A Primer

by **Sean Rhody**

Introduction

PowerBuilder offers over four hundred functions for use in developing applications. With so many provided functions available, it's easy to think that there is no need to use external functions (which are functions that exist in Dynamic Link Libraries, or DLLs for short). Yet the Windows Application Programming Interface, or API, includes over a thousand functions. It's important to realize that PowerBuilder is not intended to be a general purpose programming tool, although we can use it as such. PowerBuilder's strength lies in its ability to provide an easy mechanism for developing interfaces for database management systems.

Nevertheless, we often want to provide our users with functionality that is not available within PowerBuilder itself. For example, Windows maintains a list of current tasks. Power-Builder has no built-in functions for accessing this task information–but as we will see, there are API functions for accessing and manipulating this data. Another area that PowerBuilder provides no functionality for is in accessing the list of fonts available on a Windows system. Again, there are functions within Windows that can provide this information. By the end of this discussion we will have developed a DLL that will provide functionality in both of these areas.

We will also examine in detail the mechanism that PowerBuilder offers for calling external functions, so that we can understand what happens when PowerBuilder data meets C.

A little review of PowerBuilder and Windows C datatypes is probably in order. Let's start with the side that's most familiar to PowerBuilder programmers, namely how do Power-Builder datatypes translate into C datatypes under Windows. The following chart will explain the conversions, and we'll discuss a couple to further round out the details. Several of the PowerBuilder datatypes have no native representation in C. For example, C has no native datatype representing a Date or a DateTime. Similarly, there is no datatype or representation for Blobs.

PowerBuilder Datatype	Windows C Datatype
Blob	No Native Datatype
Boolean	BOOL or Integer
Char	char far
Date	No Native Datatype
DateTime	No Native Datatype
Decimal	Similar to float
Double	double
Integer	int
Long	long
Real	Similar to float
String	char far *
Time	No Native Datatype
UnsignedInteger (UInt)	unsigned int
UnsignedLong (ULong)	unsigned long

Figure 31-1: Comparison of PowerBuilder and C datatypes.

The PowerBuilder datatypes that C does support map almost completely to C datatypes. The ranges for Decimal and Real are not identical to the ranges for float in the Microsoft C/C++ compiler. Based upon the documentation, they differ in the size of the smallest number (i.e. the most negative number) allowed. C does not typically represent decimal numbers; they are handled by float.

The other side to this coin is how the Windows C datatypes are related back to Power-Builder. Windows has some datatypes in use that are not really C datatypes, but have been defined as such through the C precompiler directive 1'TYPEDEF, which allows us to define our own datatypes. Since these appear often in Windows programming, the following chart shows what they currently map to in C and in PowerBuilder. These datatypes are abstractions designed to aid portability in the event that the architecture of Windows changes.

Windows Datatype	C Datatype	PowerBuilder Datatype
HANDLE	int	Integer
HWND	int	Integer
HINST	int	Integer
WORD	int	Integer
DWORD	long	Long
LPSTR	char far *	String

Figure 31-2: Equivalent Windows, C, and PowerBuilder datatypes.

There are many other less common Windows datatypes, but these are the ones that we will encounter most frequently. A HANDLE is a 16-bit integer which provides a reference to an object, such as a window . Windows uses handles to provide a layer of indirection above pointers, so that it can implement memory management. Most Windows API functions require some kind of handle. In PowerBuilder the Handle() function can provide the Windows handle of a window so that we can use it in an external function call. This will be the most common use of the Handle() function. The HWND and HINST datatypes are object-specific handles, to a window or an application instance respectively. In Windows, each window has its own handle, and each application has its own application instance handle, so that windows can distinguish between multiple copies of the same application which are executing at the same time. WORD and DWORD are used by many Windows functions. The LPSTR datatype stands for Long Pointer to a STRing. An LPSTR is used to define a reference to a null ("\0") terminated character string. C has no native datatype called string. Instead, it represents strings as arrays of characters, terminated by the null character.

If C uses arrays for characters, then why don't we see any array declarations? Is a pointer the same as an array declaration? Yes and no. C represents arrays as a name and a specific amount of space in memory. The name becomes a sort of variable that tells C where to start looking for the string. In C, there are many functions that allow the programmer to manipulate arrays. One of the most common ways to manipulate arrays in C is to treat the name of the array as a pointer. Remember that the name of the array is used to hold the address of the starting point of the data. Since a pointer is basically an address of data, just like the name of an array, C allows pointer operations and representations of strings. There's one important difference that should be noted. An array typically declares an amount of space that will be used. Unlike PowerBuilder, C arrays are not dynamic and must be declared at compile time. A pointer, on the other hand, does not allocate any space for data at compile time. It just holds the address of some data. So to create a new string in C we need to allocate space for that string at runtime. We'll see how we do this in just a moment.

OK, that should be pretty clear, but what might seem less clear to those familiar with C under other operating systems is what the keyword *far* means. One of the most difficult problems in developing applications under Windows is the segmented architecture of the memory on a PC. Due to the design of the original IBM PC, memory is divided into segments, which can be no larger than 64K. To refer to data in these segments, two 16-bit values are used. These values are the segment and the offset of the data within the segment. Now when all of the data is within a segment, our program can use just the offset, which is called a near pointer, because it contains only an offset, with the segment value assumed to be the same as the current data segment. When the data that we are referring to is not in the same data segment, then the segment address is needed as well, resulting in a 32-bit far pointer. We won't go into further detail about the memory scheme in Windows except when we describe how a DLL interacts with other programs. Basically, in all of our DLL programs pointers will be far pointers. [For a thorough discussion of Windows memory management and general DLL creation, see *Programming Windows 3.1*, Third Edition, by Charles Petzold. Published by Microsoft Press.]

So now we ask ourselves, why do we need to use far pointers? Can't we just keep all our data in one segment? After all, typically we are only creating a small amount of data; why can't it all be in one segment? The answers to these questions are based upon the nature of a DLL. A DLL is designed to allow multiple programs to share a single code resource. Let's think about this. Prior to Windows, all PC programs had to load all of their code at once, and could not share it with any other program. Windows allows non-preemptive multitasking. This allows several programs to execute at the same time. But one of the problems with this is that if each program instance has to be completely loaded into memory, we quickly run out of memory. Another problem is that we are completely duplicating all of the code and resources in each program each time we load another copy. And finally, we can't share our work with anyone without releasing source code to them.

The DLL changes all of that. It allows code to be loaded as needed, rather than all at once. It also allows several instances of a program to share one copy of code, reducing memory usage. And most importantly, it allows different programs to share the same code. In fact, Windows itself is mostly made up of DLLs, although they have different extensions.

That still doesn't answer the question of why we need far pointers, but let's look at one other concept first: then we can tie it all together and start working on some development. The concept I'm referring to is a data structure called a stack. A stack is basically similar to the lunch tray pile in a cafeteria. The first item on it is the last item off it. And you can only take things off from the top of the stack. What's this got to do with programming? Well, it happens that all parameters passed to a program, as well as all local variables in a function, are placed in a data structure called the stack in the data segment (there's that word again) of a program. What's significant about this is that each program has its own stack where it places variables. It also has its own area called a heap where it places data that is created in the program. Normally the stack segment is the same as the data segment, so there are no problems with near pointers. But not in the case of DLLs.

DLLs do not have their own stack, but instead use the stack of the calling program. A DLL can have its own (single) data segment and create storage on its local heap. Variables are placed on the calling program's stack, which is in a different data segment. This means that all variables that we create on the stack that reference data in the DLL's data segment must be declared far. Otherwise they would look in the stack data segment of the calling program for the data, which would be wrong. It also means that when the DLL function finishes execution, all of the variables are popped back off the stack and dereferenced so that they cannot be used by another function to access data from a different program.

It's also important not to store these pointers in global variables within programs. We can't do this in PowerBuilder anyway, but it's vital that we don't do it in C–the data is moveable and the segment address of the data may change, making the pointer we stored in the global variable invalid. Instead we should simply create functions in the DLL that let us access the data whenever we need it.

Wow. We strayed pretty far from the topic of DLLs with PowerBuilder, but that's just a glimpse of the background information that's needed to create DLLs. If you got lost along the way, don't worry. You can use the examples that we'll develop as a starting point to get your feet wet.

Writing and compiling C under Windows is a little trickier than on some other operating systems, but not horribly so. What's important to understand is what kind of files are needed to create a Windows program, in this case a DLL.

All Windows programs require source files, typically .c and .h files. A definition file, with a .def extension, is also required. The current generation of compiler environments automatically generates a project or make file, so make files are normally generated by the compiler in the background, with no intervention from the programmer. In Windows executables several resource files, with an .rc extension, are typically required to define things like menus and bitmaps for the compiler. No resources are used in the following examples, so an .rc file is not needed.

The definition file contains the following information.

```
LIBRARY   C2PBDLL
EXETYPE   WINDOWS
CODE PRELOAD MOVEABLE DISCARDABLE
DATA    PRELOAD MOVEABLE SINGLE
HEAPSIZE 1024
EXPORTS
WEP PRIVATE
```

This tells the compiler several things. First, the LIBRARY entry tells the compiler that this is a DLL named C2PBDLL. The EXETYPE tells the compiler that this is a Windows executable (my compiler will create DOS executables as well, and some other compilers will create NT and OS/2 executables). The CODE and DATA sections contain information pertaining to how the code and data segments will be loaded in memory. The MOVEABLE declaration allows Windows to move the segments around in memory, to allow Windows to compact memory. The SINGLE declaration in the DATA segment description is used to tell the compiler that the DATA segment will have only a single segment, which is the way a DLL operates. The HEAPSIZE tells the compiler how much memory to allocate in the DATA segment for the heap.

The last declaration is not strictly needed. It's used to declare what functions are exported by the DLL. This has already been done in the source code itself, so there's no need to add the entries here. If the _export keyword had not been used, then this is where the exported functions would be declared.

Let's begin by looking at a bare-bones C DLL, which will have only one exported function. An exported function is a function in a DLL that is visible (and therefore callable) from another program. For example we may have several intermediate functions that we do not wish to make available to the user, preferring to make available the final result. One possible reason we would do this is to prevent the user from misusing the functions and causing errors or data corruption (or plague, famine, war, etc.). That's enough description. Let's take a look at the code.

```
/***************** sample.c *************/
#include <windows.h>
/* Function prototype */
int FAR PASCAL _export  Square(int x);
/* LibMain takes the place of WinMain in a DLL */

int FAR PASCAL LibMain(HANDLE hInstance, WORD wDataSeg, WORD wHeapSize,
 LPSTR lpszcmdline)
{
 hInst = hInstance;     /* we need this info later */
 if (wHeapSize > 0)     /* unlock local data segment */
 UnlockData(0);
 return(1);
}
int CALLBACK WEP(int nParameter) /* DLL terminator function */
{
/* cleanup activity goes here */
return(1);
}
long FAR PASCAL _export  Square(int x)
{
return ((long)x)*((long)x);
}
```

Let's look at this line by line (not counting the comments). The first line is an include statement, which tells the compiler to use the windows.h file to include various definitions that are placed there. This file is almost always included.

The next line is a function prototype for the one function that we are providing. There is no real need for this declaration, as no other functions call Square(), but it's good programming practice. Later we will see some examples that require prototypes, or require us to change how we order the functions in our source code. I prefer to place prototypes at the top, make the main loop the first function, and proceed to define the rest in a logical order. If you can anticipate all of the functions needed and define the functions that depend on other functions later, then you can avoid prototypes.

The next line is the beginning of the LibMain function. In a DLL, LibMain takes the place of the WinMain function. If you have written Windows programs in C, you can see that this function is much simpler than any WinMain function you have ever written. This is because a DLL cannot process messages. That means that no Windows message ever goes to a DLL. Therefore, the LibMain function does not need to define switch statements to handle all of the various messages, such as WM_CREATE, which a normal program must manage.

LibMain is declared as int FAR PASCAL. That's a pretty weird definition, so let's break it down to simpler terms. The int part should be familiar, it's just the return type for the function. FAR and far are interchangeable on my compiler. This tells the compiler that this is a function that will be called from a different code segment. When we think about this, it makes sense, because this function will be called by Windows to initialize the library when it's loaded into memory. Windows itself is a program, with a different code segment than our DLL, and it expects this. If Windows did not know that this function was going to be in a different code segment, it would cause an error by looking in its own code segment for this function. The PASCAL part of the declaration tells the compiler to use the PASCAL method of function processing rather than the C method. These two conventions differ in how they manage the stack, with the PASCAL convention being slightly more efficient. You will frequently see functions defined as FAR PASCAL in our work.

What about the parameters to LibMain? Well, we will use one or two of them, and ignore the rest. The *hInstance* parameter is an instance handle. In regular Windows programming, the main function also gets a handle to a previous instance of itself, if one exists. In DLL programming, only one instance can ever exist, so the previous instance handle is not needed. The *wDataSeg* parameter specifies the data segment register value (DS) that is used for this DLL. This will not be used in our work. The *wHeapSize* specifies the amount of memory allocated for the heap for this DLL. The *lpszcmdline* parameter is a command line string, something that is almost never used with DLLs. We won't use this either.

So what does LibMain do? In our applications, it won't do much of anything. First it saves the instance handle to a global variable so that we can use it at will. We won't bother to make use of it in this simple example, but we will use it later. Next it determines if there is a local heap. If so, it unlocks it so that windows can move it around in memory. Then it returns a status. If this were a more complicated function, perhaps one that depended on other DLLs for functions, it might check to see whether they were available. If not, it would return a failure code of 0, which would indicate to Windows that the DLL could not load. As a courtesy, in that case, we should probably display a message box indicating the cause of the problem. In our examples there is no chance for failure, so the return value is hard coded.
The next function is the CALLBACK function WEP. This function is the Windows Exit Procedure and is called by Windows when the DLL is unloaded. It is used to perform any processing prior to the unloading of the library. In this case, no processing is needed, so the function simply returns a value.

A callback function is a function that is passed to another function as a parameter for use within that function. Later on we will see an example of a callback function when we develop the routines we need to get the font list from Windows.

Finally, there is the Square() function. This function takes an integer and squares it. It's declared FAR PASCAL as usual, but there's an additional line that says _export. This keyword is used to indicate that this function is exported and can be called by other programs.

This can also be done in the DLL .def file, which is used to define various options in creating the DLL. We won't really look at this option; instead we will rely on the _export declaration to do the work.

Square() is really a very simple function. It just multiplies the parameter by itself and returns the result. The only subtle points are the return type, and what's known as a cast. The return type isn't integer, it's long. This makes sense, because it's very easy with an integer close to the maximum integer value to generate a value that exceeds the maximum by squaring it. The long return type takes care of that problem. The other problem is making sure that the multiplication does not cause an overflow. This is done by casting the values to long. A cast simply converts one type of data to another, with limits. You can't cast a string to an integer, for example.

The Square() function is not a very useful illustration–it's a little too simple, and could easily have been implemented in PowerScript. It's time to look at our first concrete example, obtaining information on current tasks.

Windows maintains information on all running tasks in taskentry structures. In order to compile a program that uses a taskentry structure, the toolhelp.h header file must be included. In addition, the linker must be told to link the toolhelp library with the program, or the linker will report undefined symbols for TASKFIRST and TASKNEXT, the two task functions that are used. The method of doing this varies by compiler. In Visual C++ the method is to go to the Options menu and choose Projects... . This brings up the following dialog box.

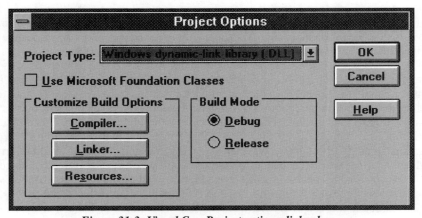

Figure 31-3: Visual C++ Project options dialog box.

The Dialog Box in Figure 31-3 is used to select the various options available in Visual C++. To have the linker include the proper libraries, click on the "Linker..." button. This brings up the linker dialog box.

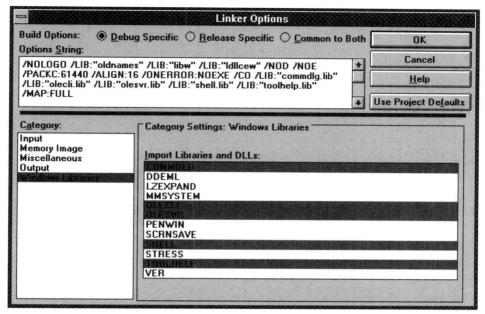

Figure 31-4: Visual C++ linker options dialog box.

Select Windows Libraries from the Categories list. Click on TOOLHELP to add it to the list. When this is done, the entry /LIB "toolhelp.lib" is added to the list of options as shown above.

The taskentry structure declaration is shown below.

```
#include <toolhelp.h>
typedef struct tagTASKENTRY { /* te */
  DWORD    dwSize;
  HTASK    hTask;
  HTASK    hTaskParent;
  HINSTANCE hInst;
  HMODULE  hModule;
  WORD    wSS;
  WORD    wSP;
  WORD    wStackTop;
  WORD    wStackMinimum;
  WORD    wStackBottom;
  WORD    wcEvents;
  HGLOBAL  hQueue;
  char    szModule[MAX_MODULE_NAME + 1];
  WORD    wPSPOffset;
  HANDLE   hNext;
} TASKENTRY;
```

The TASKENTRY structure contains information about one task. We won't use most of this information; we're simply interested in listing the current tasks. The name of the task is contained in the character array szModule.

Armed with this information, we can now write the function that we need to return the names of the current tasks. The first thing we'll do is declare several global variables and constants.

```
/* Global Variables and definitions */
/* define the maximum number of tasks that will be returned */
#define LF_TOTTASKS 64
/* global variables */
/* a list of tasks */
char far lpszTaskArray[LF_TOTTASKS][MAX_MODULE_NAME+1];
```

We will store the names of the tasks in the lpszTaskArray array. Unlike PowerBuilder, C cannot easily dynamically resize its arrays. Rather than overcomplicate the code for a rather small return, we will pick a fairly large number as the size of the array. In this case, sixty-four tasks seems fairly generous. MAX_MODULE_NAME is defined in toolhelp.h, as the maximum size of a module name.

Windows provides two functions for obtaining the task entries. The TaskFirst() function is used to get the first task on the task list. To obtain subsequent tasks the TaskNext() function is called repeatedly, until it returns a status that indicates that there are no more tasks. We obtain the specific task entry by passing the functions the address of a taskentry variable. The functions then fill the taskentry variable with the appropriate information. It then becomes a simple matter to loop until all the tasks are obtained.

The ListTask() function that we are writing will return a comma-separated list of the task entries. In order to build this string, we need to allocate space for the string, and then loop through the array to obtain the values.

The complete function looks like this.

```
char FAR * PASCAL _export ListTasks(void)
{
int nRetSize;              /* total space for the return string */
HANDLE hString;            /* a handle for localalloc */
char far * lpszString;     /* The returned string */
 TASKENTRY TaskEntry;      /* task entry structure */
BOOL Status; /* determines when we are finished with task list */
WORD i,n = 0;              /* loop counter */
 char far *lpszNull = "";
/* set the size of the taskentry */
TaskEntry.dwSize=sizeof(TASKENTRY);
/* load TaskEntry with the information on the first task in list */
Status=TaskFirst(&TaskEntry);
/* walk through task list */
while (Status!=FALSE)
{
  lstrcpy(lpszTaskArray[n],TaskEntry.szModule);
Status=TaskNext(&TaskEntry);
n++;
}

/* if n > 0 then there are task entries in the array */
if ( n > 0 )
{
```

```
/* calculate the maximum size needed for the return string.
Size is n ( the number of entries ) * the maximum name
size plus the number of entries -1 to add the commas
*/
nRetSize = ( n * (MAX_MODULE_NAME+1)) +( n-1) );

  /* allocate the needed space */
if ( NULL == (hString = LocalAlloc(LHND,nRetSize)))
return (lpszNull);

/* Get a pointer from the handle */
lpszString = LocalLock(hString);
/* concatenate the entry with the string */
for (i = n; i >= 0; i--)
{
lstrcat(lpszString,lpszTaskArray[i]);
/* Add the comma separator */
lstrcat(lpszString,",");
}
/* add the last face name, without a comma separator */
lstrcat(lpszString,lpszFontArray[nFontNumber-1]);

/* free the handle */
LocalUnlock(hString);

/* return the string */
return(lpszString);
}
else
return(lpszNull);
}
```

One further topic for discussion is how the memory for the return string is allocated. Remember that lpszString is simply a pointer to a character it has no storage space. In order to use it to build and return the string, we first need to allocate memory for it.

We can calculate the amount of memory needed as follows: there are n task entries, so n times the maximum size of a task entry will provide space for all the task names. Then we want to add n - 1 commas to separate each entry, so we need space for n - 1 of them.

Next we need to allocate the space for this on the local heap. C coders from other operating environments will be looking for a call to malloc or calloc at this point. Unfortunately, this is Windows, and memory management is part of the Windows domain. Instead of these familiar calls we need to use the somewhat more exotic LocalAlloc() function. The call we make asks for the number of bytes and asks that all the bytes be moveable and set to zero. We make the bytes moveable because we have defined our data segment as moveable.

One of the consequences of making the bytes moveable is that in order to use the memory, we need to lock it. This is done with the LocalLock() function.

This works, but after viewing this information in PowerBuilder it's inevitable that we come to the conclusion that it's not really what we want. What actually shows up in the szModule attribute is a simple module name, with no additional information. So, for example, if we had several PowerBuilder programs running, the module names would all be PBSTUB, which is not at all helpful in determining which programs are there.

What we really need is the actual file name that is executed. In order to get that information we need to call another function within our DLL, the GetModuleFileName() function. This function places the path name of the executable in a buffer for our use. The code is shown below.

```
char FAR * PASCAL _export ListTasks2(void)
{
int nRetSize;              /* total space for the return string */
HANDLE hString;            /* a handle for localalloc */
char far *  lpzString;     /* The returned string */
 TASKENTRY  TaskEntry;     /* task entry structure */
BOOL Status; /* determines when we are finished with task list */
WORD i,n = 0; /* loop counter */
  char far * lpNull = "";
  char buf[64]; /* debugging */
 int ret;

TaskEntry.dwSize=sizeof(TASKENTRY);
/* load TaskEntry with the information on the first task in list */
Status=TaskFirst(&TaskEntry);
/* walk through task list */
while (Status!=FALSE)
{
/* MessageBox(NULL,TaskEntry.szModule,"Debug", MB_OK); */
  ret = GetModuleFileName(TaskEntry.hInst,buf,64);
  lstrcpy(lpzTsk2Array[n++],buf);
Status=TaskNext(&TaskEntry);
}

if ( n > 0 )
{
nRetSize = ( n * (64+1)) + ((n-1));

  /* allocate the needed space */
 if ( NULL == (hString = LocalAlloc(LHND,nRetSize)))
 {
 MessageBox(NULL,"Could not allocate space","error",MB_OK);
return (lpNull);
}

/* Get a pointer from the handle */
lpzString = LocalLock(hString);

/* concatenate the entry with the string */
for (i = 0; i < n - 1 ; i++)
{
lstrcat(lpzString,lpzTsk2Array[i]);
/* Add the comma separator */
lstrcat(lpzString,",");
}
/* add the last name, without a comma separator */
lstrcat(lpzString,lpzTsk2Array[n-1]);
/* free the handle */
LocalUnlock(hString);

/* return the string */
return(lpzString);
}
else
return(lpNull);
```

```
}
```

This does little more than replace the szModule entry for the actual filename, but it does provide a way to differentiate between programs. For example, if I ran two PowerBuilder programs, pba.exe and pbb.exe, I could now distinguish between the two.

Sometimes we may want additional information about the task, such as its instance handle or its module handle. Rather than convert this to a string, it's a pretty useful illustration of PowerBuilder concepts to pass in an array of structures. The next function, ListTasks3(), uses an array to return this information. It also uses a c structure defined below to map the PowerBuilder structure.

```
struct ModInfo
{
 HTASK hTask;
 HINSTANCE hInst;
 HMODULE hModule;
 char szPath[260];
};
```

This corresponds to the following PowerBuilder structure declaration.

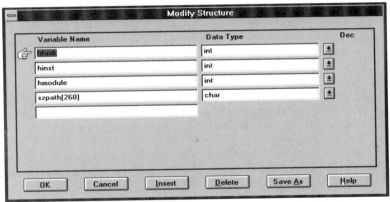

Figure 31-5: PowerBuilder structure equivalent to ModInfo.

Notice that the handles map to integers, while the character array maps to a character array. We use an array of characters rather than a string because it simplifies the programming in the DLL. With a character array the storage is already allocated.

The function has been simplified to take an array with storage for up to sixteen tasks. This was done arbitrarily, and could easily be converted to deal with any number of tasks. ListTasks3() is listed below.

```
int FAR PASCAL _export ListTasks3(struct ModInfo ModArray[16])
{
// Return value is the actual number of tasks returned

 TASKENTRY  TaskEntry; /* task entry structure */
BOOL Status; /* determines when we are finished with task list */
int n = 0;/* loop counter */
```

```
      char buf[260];/* full path*/
      int ret;

   TaskEntry.dwSize=sizeof(TASKENTRY);
   /* load TaskEntry with the information on the first task in list */
   Status=TaskFirst(&TaskEntry);
   /* walk through task list */
   while (Status!=FALSE)
   {
   /* MessageBox(NULL,TaskEntry.szModule,"Debug", MB_OK); */
      ret = GetModuleFileName(TaskEntry.hInst,buf,260);
      lstrcpy(ModArray[n].szPath,buf);
   ModArray[n].hInst = TaskEntry.hInst;
   ModArray[n].hModule = TaskEntry.hModule;
   ModArray[n].hTask = TaskEntry.hTask;
   n++;
   Status=TaskNext(&TaskEntry);
   }

   return(n);
   }
```

Up to this point we have been dealing with functions that, although complex, could have been coded completely in PowerBuilder using external functions. But there is a whole class of Windows API functions that cannot be coded in PowerBuilder. These are functions that require a callback function. Remember that a callback function is used to implement custom processing in many situations. A perfect example of this is the task of obtaining available font information. The API functions that provide this type of information require a callback function. PowerBuilder currently does not support callbacks, so this function must be encapsulated in a C DLL in order to be used.

The function that we need to use is EnumFontFamilies() function. This function takes four parameters: a device context, a font family name which we will set to NULL in order to get all the information, a callback function, and an additional parameter which we will not use.

The device context is obtained from the window handle that is passed into the function. When this function is called from PowerBuilder it must be passed a valid handle. We also need to make the callback function into what is known as a PROCINSTANCE. This obtains a valid address for the function that we want EnumFontFamilies() to use for each font. We use this function to load the font array (which is why it is declared as a global variable) with the font name information.

Let's look at the code. First some definitions.

```
#define LF_TOTFONTS 256 /* the maximum number of fonts this will return*/
/* global variables */
char far lpzFontArray[LF_TOTFONTS][LF_FACESIZE];/* array of font names */
int nFontNumber = 0;   /* counts the number of fonts */
HANDLE hInst;          /* the instance handle */
```

Because I've written the callback function after the actual function in the code, I need to declare a function prototype.

```
/* Function Prototypes */
int CALLBACK FAR PASCAL _export EnumProc(LOGFONT FAR *lpnlf, TEXTMETRIC FAR *
lpntm,
```

```
int FontType, LPARAM lParam);
And now the functions.
char FAR * PASCAL _export ListFonts(HWND hWnd)
{
/*
HWND hWnd is the handle of a window. Use the PB Handle()
  Function to obtain this handle.
*/

FONTENUMPROC  lpEnumFamCallBack; /* The ProcInstance for EnumProc */
HDC hdc;                         /* a device context */
intnRetSize;                     /* space for the return string */
HANDLE hString;                  /* a handle for localalloc */
char far * lpzString;            /* The returned string */
int i;                           /* a counter */

hdc = GetDC(hWnd);               /* Need the device context */

/* build a procinstance */
lpEnumFamCallBack = (FONTENUMPROC) MakeProcInstance(
(FARPROC)EnumProc,hInst);

/*Enumerate the fonts*/
EnumFontFamilies(hdc, NULL, lpEnumFamCallBack,0);

/* get rid of ProcInst.*/
FreeProcInstance((FARPROC) lpEnumFamCallBack);

/* free up the DC */
ReleaseDC(hWnd,hdc); /* VERY IMPORTANT !!!!!!!!!!! */

/*
  calculate the total size needed for the return string.
  Note that the space may be larger than the actual string
  because, we are assuming that each face name is the maximum
  size. Not always true, but it simplifies the task without
  causing undo problems.
*/
nRetSize = ( nFontNumber * LF_FACESIZE ) + ( nFontNumber -1);

  /* allocate the needed space */
if ( NULL == (hString = LocalAlloc(LHND,nRetSize)))
return ("");

/* Get a pointer from the handle */
lpzString = LocalLock(hString);

/*
  nFontNumber is the number of fonts, But C uses 0 based arrays
  SO, all array references using the nFontNumber must subtract 1.
  Also, we don't want to place a trailing comma, so we do the
  last face name separately.
*/

for ( i=0; i< nFontNumber - 2; i++)
{
/* concatenate the entry with the string */
lstrcat(lpzString,lpzFontArray[i]);
/* Add the comma separator */
lstrcat(lpzString,",");
}
```

```
/* add the last face name, without a comma separator */
lstrcat(lpzString,lpzFontArray[nFontNumber-1]);
/* free the handle */
LocalUnlock(hString);
/* return the string */
return(lpzString);
}
/* EnumProc:The EnumProc function is a callback function that is
used by EnumFontFamilies to step through the fonts.
*/
int CALLBACK FAR PASCAL _export EnumProc(LOGFONT FAR *lpnlf, TEXTMETRIC FAR *
lpntm,
int FontType, LPARAM lParam)

{
/*
lpnlf is a newlogfont structure, which holds the information we need
We can basically ignore the other parameters in this particular
case.
*/
/* check if the EnumFontFamiles has run out of fonts */
if ( lpnlf->lfFaceName == NULL )
return(0);
else
{
/* make sure we don't go past the array boundary */
if (nFontNumber < LF_TOTFONTS - 1)
{
/* copy the font face name */
lstrcpy(lpzFontArray[nFontNumber++], lpnlf->lfFaceName);
/* 1 = continue */
return(1);
}
else
return(0);
}
}
```

And that's all there is to it. What we did was call EnumFontFamilies(). It in turn calls Enum-
Proc() for every font that's available for the device. EnumProc() in turn places the name in
the array, for up to 256 different fonts. After the last font is done, EnumFontFamilies()
returns. We then build a string in a similar fashion to what is done in the various ListTasks()
functions.

Now that we have all these functions we use them in PowerBuilder by declaring external
functions, either at a global or object level. For example, the following picture shows all the
functions discussed above declared as global external functions.

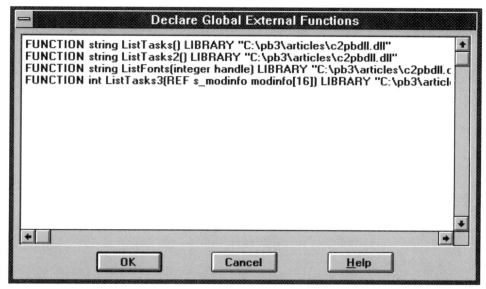

Figure 31-6: Declaring global external functions.

The syntax for declaring functions in PowerBuilder is fairly straightforward. They begin with one of two keywords: FUNCTION, for routines returning values, or SUBROUTINE for routines that do not return values. For functions, the returned datatype is listed next. Either method is then followed by the function name, and in parenthesis the datatypes and names of the parameters. The optional keyword REF in front of a datatype declaration, such as the declaration for ListTasks3(), specifies that the function can modify the data. Lastly, the keyword LIBRARY is followed by the name of the DLL, either the relative name if it is in the path, or the absolute name if it is not. In this case the DLL is called c2pbdll.dll, and since it is not in the path, the fully qualified path name of c:\pb3\articles\c2pbdll.dll is used.

A sample PowerBuilder application, DLLTEST, is included on the disk. It basically tests each of these functions. It consists of one main window, a multiline edit, a DataWindow, and four command buttons.

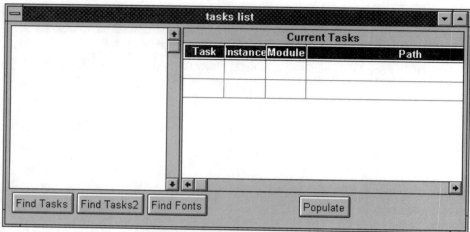

Figure 31-7: Task list window.

The "Find Tasks" and "Find Tasks2" buttons call the ListTasks() and ListTasks2() functions; the "Find Font" button calls the ListFonts() function, and the "Populate" button calls the ListTasks3() function.

Here are the scripts.

```
cb_findtask:
string lzTasks
lzTasks = ListTasks()
mle_tasks.Text = lzTasks
cb_findtask2:
string lzTasks
lzTasks = ListTasks2()
mle_tasks.Text = lzTasks
cb_findfont:
string lzTasks
integer liHandle
liHandle = Handle(w_main)
lzTasks =ListFonts(liHandle)
mle_tasks.Text = lzTasks
cb_populate:
s_modinfo Modinfo[16]
int i,count
long lrow
string  lzName
count = ListTasks3(modinfo)
dw_tasks.reset()
dw_tasks.SetTransObject(sqlca)
IF count < 1 THEN
```

```
MessageBox("Error","no tasks")
ELSE
FOR i = 1 to count
lrow = dw_tasks.InsertRow(0)
dw_tasks.SetItem(lrow,"task",ModInfo[i].hTask)
dw_tasks.SetItem(lrow,"instance",ModInfo[i].hInst)
dw_tasks.SetItem(lrow,"module",ModInfo[i].hModule)
lzName = f_convert_to_string(ModInfo[i].szPath)
dw_tasks.SetItem(lrow,"path",lzName)
NEXT
END IF
dw_tasks.SetRow(1)
```

There is one PowerBuilder function, called f_convert_to_string(), which takes a character array and returns a string, It is used in the cb_populate button script to convert the file name from a character array to a string.

Conclusions

DLLs can provide a wealth of additional functionality to the PowerBuilder programmer by providing access to functions in the Windows SDK. Although some of these functions can be called directly as external functions, many others require callback functions, such as the one we used in ListFonts(); these must be encapsulated in a DLL in order for PowerBuilder to use them.

There are several practical uses for these functions. ListTasks3() can provide sufficient information to allow PowerBuilder to work with many other SDK functions, including functions to perform task switching. The ListFonts() function can be used to provide a drop-down list box in a custom toolbar user object that can change fonts based on the selection. Good luck.

CHAPTER **32**

Class Libraries

By Rey Bango

Class Libraries

by **Rey Bango**

One of the greatest benefits provided by PowerBuilder is inheritance. A suite of tested objects can contain enough logic to process many of the common operations of an application. Because of this wonderful feature, a whole new breed of PowerBuilder-related products has started to blossom: the class library.

Geared toward providing project teams with the foundations for mission-critical applications, class libraries allow developers to base their work upon a tested methodology that provides standardization and subsequently increases maintainability.

Class libraries have been crucial to the success of many PowerBuilder projects because of the speed they give to the development cycle. A class library can generally provide a forty to sixty percent reduction in application development time. Furthermore, project managers can better estimate the development effort when the applications foundation has already been laid. And since a common methodology and consistent development architecture is being used, the learning curve for new PowerBuilder developer with access to class libraries is usually far less than for a developer starting from scratch.

One of the biggest pitfalls in application development is a lack of consistency in several key areas, specifically naming conventions and code placement. Inattention here serves up a plateful of nightmares for any developer who has to maintain such an application. Most class libraries provide proper naming conventions and proven coding practices which afford a developer the peace of mind of knowing where various pieces of code will be handled.

A New Market

The benefits of class libraries are universally recognized and have opened a new market for PowerBuilder add-on products. A growing number of development firms are producing and/ or actively marketing class libraries that not only provide the traditional application framework but also expand into such areas as code generation, tab folders, navigation control, security, three-tier support, and specialized services (i.e.: DDE, printing, etc.). There are many advantages to using a commercial class library:

Product support: support policies are usually available from the vendor. Upgrades: commercial libraries are usually upgraded on a regular basis to increase product functionality or to add compatibility with new releases of PowerBuilder. Purchase cost vs. in-house development: chances are that the cost of developing a class library in-house will be far greater than the cost of purchasing a commercial library. Proven methodology: most of the well-known class libraries have been available for several years and have been thoroughly tested

The biggest drawback of commercial class libraries is price. Most of the top products available run into thousands of dollars. In response to this, some vendors have begun to offer "desktop" editions of their tool in an effort to attract PowerBuilder Desktop users. They are also making evaluation copies more readily available. Generally, usage licenses for these libraries vary, ranging from single-user versions to full enterprise-wide licenses.

There are a number of choices to select from, but making an effective buying decision is becoming increasingly difficult. Most vendors provide a standard set of objects that provide the basic functionality of an application. These include:

Window objects: sheets, response windows, single-row updates, multi-row updates, master/ detail, MDI frames, query windows, pick lists, login screen. Menu objects: base menus for frames and sheets. User objects: objects with underlying code and error checking, application control, and value storage. Functions: Security checks, database connectivity, .ini file manipulation.

Many vendors have expanded upon the traditional offerings by providing specialized business objects to handle common business requirements. "Componentware" is also booming as vendors begin to dismantle their traditional libraries in order to generate further revenue. In the near future, expect to see some of the following products available as extensions to the traditional application frameworks:

Security libraries that specialize in object-level security and can work interchangeably in any PowerBuilder application. Specialized business objects, including calendars, schedulers, word processors, etc. Focused business software components–reusable components for such systems as order entry, POS, manufacturing, inventory control, and accounting.

These features will certainly increase the end user's productivity as well as the ease with which applications can be upgraded and enhanced.

Choosing an Approach

In-house development

Developing an in-house application framework is far from being a menial task. Most frameworks take several man-years to develop to a fully mature and stable level. The effort requires not only a clear understanding of the business logic, but also expert knowledge of programming methodologies such as object-oriented programming, event processing, and relational database handling. Here are some considerations that must be looked at before undertaking this type of development:

Does the project team have several months to properly develop an in-house application framework? The estimate must include analysis, design, proper object modeling, process model development, and unit and system testing. Is there sufficient budget allocated? (Expect to spend well into the hundreds of thousands of dollars to develop an extensive framework.) How good are the resource people currently available? Do they have a firm understanding of object-oriented programming? Do they have a firm understanding of the business requirements? Will outside consultants be needed? If they are needed, the budget demands must be increased accordingly. Are the business needs unusual enough to require a home-grown design? Can the cost of developing a framework be justified in comparison to the cost of purchasing and adapting a commercial product? What will be the ongoing maintenance and upgrade costs for an in-house framework?

Although in-house developing is always an attractive option, the above list spells out some very valid concerns. Does the desire for vendor-independence significantly outweigh unsatisfactory answers to the previous questions? In most cases, probably not. The whole philosophy of application development is to spend the least amount of time and to commit the fewest resources. Reinventing the wheel (i.e.: developing an in-house framework) detracts from accomplishing the ultimate goal of a project: to solve a business problem.

Going the commercial route

Purchasing a commercial class library is no easy task either. More and more offerings are hitting the market on a daily basis. Here are a set of features that should be included in the class library you choose: An **inheritance methodology** that significantly reduces the amount of application-specific code that must be written. This helps to reduce development time, maintenance overhead, and code defects.

A development architecture and methodology that **enforces GUI and coding standards** so that a consistent interface is provided not only to the developers, but to the application users as well.

A **comprehensive collection of PowerBuilder objects** that can be immediately used for application development. This should include predefined windows (frame, main, and response styles), menus, functions, and user objects that can communicate with each other but are encapsulated for independent functionality. **Support for MDI** and SDI-style applications. Extensive use of **user-defined events** to allow object-level processing as opposed to menu-level processing. This is also a benefit for inter-object communication. The library should also provide user-defined events for data initialization, validation, updating. Support for **multiple RDBMSes**. This should be seamless. Also, with the support that three-tier architecture is generating, will the product be able to properly support legacy data access (e.g.: RPC support)? A built-in, customizable **error-handling** routine.

Security. Security should exist at all levels, including applications, windows, controls, and even DataWindow columns for individual users or groups or users.

Complete documentation. This should fully detail the development methodology, including standards and coding conventions. Each object's function and specific attributes (such as instance variables, structure usage, etc.) should be clearly given. An ancestor tree description is also extremely helpful. Documentation is one of the most important components of a class library. ServerLogic, the makers of PowerClass, has a fine example of complete and concise documentation. Every object is fully detailed and the implementation clearly explained.

Price. Prices range from less than two hundred dollars to a couple of thousand dollars. The phrase "'You get what you pay for" definitely applies here, because not all class libraries are in the same league. Be sure to get a technical overview of the library's functionality. There may be features that differentiate one library from another which would justify paying a bit more.

Technical support. This is a key item. A product is only as good as the company that supports it. Insure that the vendor has a dedicated staff of technical support representatives to offer assistance in case of a problem. Most vendors offer this as an additional purchase.

Training. As these products become more and more specialized, the need for user training will increase exponentially. Most class library vendors offer on-site training courses to properly explain the methodology behind their products.

Source code. This is one of the most important considerations when purchasing a class library. Insure that the vendor provides source code for the product. If the vendor will not provide the source, either look at another product or convince the vendor to place the source in escrow. One of the biggest fears for a prospective class library purchaser is vendor dependence. Having source code eliminates the need to have a vendor maintain the product. The source code can be invaluable not only for future support, but also as a learning tool for new developers.

Vendor commitment to future upgrades as well as support for future revisions of Power-Builder.

A proper evaluation should be done before any purchase is made. This will insure that the product meets certain standards and will meet the demands of application development efforts.

The following is a list of recognized class libraries:

PowerTOOL by PowerCerv
Tampa, Florida
(813) 226-2378

PowerClass by ServerLogic

Bellevue, Washington

PowerFrame by MetaSolv
Dallas, Texas

ObjectStart by Greenbrier & Russel
Chicago, Illinois
(800) 453-0347

These libraries are best of breed. Their respective companies have made a commitment to continually improving and supporting each product.

Powersoft's offering

Powersoft bundled an application development library with PowerBuilder 3.0. Although it does provide some of the functionality that is necessary for an application foundation, it is far from being a complete package. It doesn't touch upon some of the advanced features of the commercial products, such as master/detail window processing with maintenance capabilities; advanced security capabilities; multi-row updating; intersheet communication; and specialized objects such as tab metaphors and outline objects. The Powersoft Application Library is best suited for prototyping or small, non-critical applications. It can certainly serve as a learning tool for new developers.

Class Library Implementation

The key to proper usage of a class library is to inherit, not modify, the base class library objects. This insures that a proper application foundation is maintained and decreases the possibility of errors. Generally, a class library will consist of a set of .pbl files containing the objects and process models that will be inherited. These should not be modified unless absolutely necessary. A better approach is to create a separate .pbl file to house the application-specific objects that extend the functionality of the base class library. Figure 1 shows a graphical representation of this thinking.

This helps in maintaining the generic functionality of the base class library, especially when developing multiple applications. A base class library system administrator should be designated to handle any modification to the base objects. This process is extremely important when deciding to go with a commercial class library. By maintaining extensions to the base classes in a separate .pbl file, you insure that future revisions of the class library will upgrade smoothly.

Summary

The bottom line is that a class library, whether developed in-house or purchased, can dramatically affect the development of an application. The derived benefits of reduced development times and maintainability more than justify the cost of implementing an application framework. The above-listed criteria and a proper analysis of the business needs will help you to make an educated choice.

CHAPTER

33

Using ERwin/ERX for PowerBuilder

By Barry Gervin

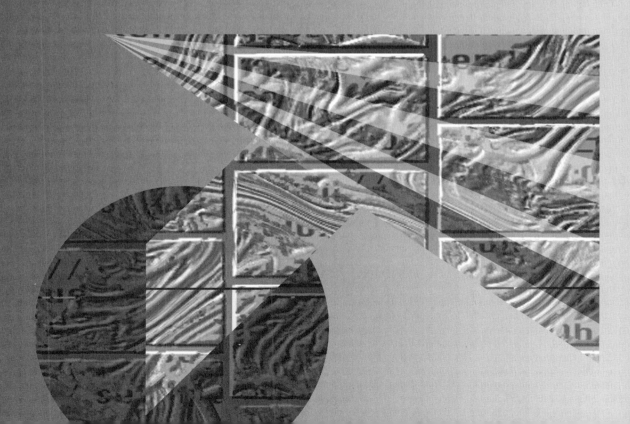

Using ERwin/ERX for PowerBuilder

by **Barry Gervin**

Introduction

I know you must be wondering, "Why is there a chapter on ERwin in a PowerBuilder Book?" Let me try to answer that question. Regardless of the front end development tool, I would always choose ERwin to design and create the data model for any project I was involved in. I know most of my associates and co-authors would say the same. Specifically, however, ERwin/ERX for PowerBuilder has some compelling benefits for PowerBuilder Developers–namely, better control over the PowerBuilder Repository of Extended Attributes.

I cannot assume that my readers will know much if anything about ERwin–after all, this is a PowerBuilder book. Therefore I will start by giving a brief introduction to ERwin data modeling. I will also show you some of the reverse engineering capabilities of ERwin. Lastly (and most importantly), I will show you how ERwin can make using the PowerBuilder Repository easy. This collection of extended attributes is perhaps one of the most underutilized, yet very powerful, features of PowerBuilder.

ERwin isn't a CASE tool

ERwin is generally considered to be the choice of the PowerBuilder masters when it comes to CASE tools. But I have to admit that when I started my first client/server project in PowerBuilder and decided to use such a tool, ERwin didn't even make it to my short list for evaluation. Of course not–it doesn't formally qualify. ERwin's stated focus is on quickly creating high quality robust physical databases. But though I didn't recognize it at the time, that's really what I wanted a CASE tool for. And that's why ERwin has been winning Reader's Choice awards for CASE tools for years in the DB magazines. The creators of ERwin, LogicWorks, while flattered, have also been surprised, because they do not even advertise ERwin as a CASE tool! ERwin is sold as a database design tool.

LogicWorks has basically pulled the carpet from underneath the upper CASE tools by focusing their product's attention on the physical side of data modeling. That's not to say there are no logical modeling components in ERwin. However, it is to say that ERwin does not create processing modeling diagrams, just Entity Relationship diagrams (known as ER diagrams–thus the name ERwin).

ERwin's specialization on the physical side means that it beats its CASE big brothers hands down. The big flaw with upper CASE tools is that, after spending a couple of years designing something, you still don't know that much more about good relational database design....and that is critical for client/server success. ERwin takes a lot of the mystery out of data modeling by exposing the physical results to the designer from the start, not hiding it like upper CASE tools do. As Bill Murray said, "if you want to catch a chipmunk, you have to think like a chipmunk." The same goes for client/server development. To build a good database model, you have to think like a relational database. ERwin keeps you in that mindset.

Benefits

So what's so great about ERwin? We can break the benefits into two categories. The first one you will notice is increased productivity. This is true for those projects that already have an existing database, and also for those us lucky enough to work on new projects with a blank slate for a data model.

The second benefit you will see after you create your database. The quality and robustness of the physically generated SQL DDL (Data Definition Language) is unsurpassed by even the largest and most expensive CASE tools on the market. LogicWorks has been continually improving this and has made great leaps in Version 2.0.

An interesting point to note is the lifespan of ERwin's usefulness on a project. I have found that when ERwin is the tool of choice it is used throughout the entire project, without exception. Where upper CASE tools are used (LBMS, IEF, etc.), the tool is usually abandoned somewhere during the initial development phase. I've never seen a project that adopted an upper CASE tool in the middle of development. However, on many occasions, I've seen projects that weren't using any form of CASE tool easily pick up ERwin in midstream and keep with it to the end.

Data Modeling In ERwin

Data modeling is actually fun in ERwin. ERwin uses a traditional methodology called IDEF1X, but don't let that scare you. Not unlike other tools, with ERwin you start creating an ER diagram by placing entities (tables) on your diagram and adding relationships between them. Figure 33-1 shows the ERwin toolbox, which allows you to do this.

Figure 33-1: The ERwin toolbox.

Entity modeling

There are two types of entities, independent and dependent, as seen in Figure 33-2.

Independent entities are those that can be uniquely identified without determining their relationships to another entities. Conversely, dependent entities cannot be identified uniquely without determining their relationship to other entities. Both types are available from the ERwin toolbox seen in Figure 33-1.

Figure 33-2: Independent and dependent entities.

TIP: If you always use the Independent entity type, ERwin will automatically convert it to Dependent when necessary (i.e. when you add an identifying relationship to the entity).

To add an entity to your diagram, select the appropriate icon from the toolbox and click anywhere on your diagram. ERwin will give your entity a default name. To change the name, you will need to use the right mouse button and click on the entity to bring up the list of available editors for that entity. Invoke the Entity-Attribute Editor (see Figure 33-3).

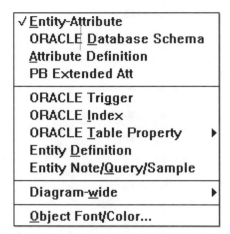

Figure 33-3: The popup menu for an entity.

The Entity Attribute Editor as seen in Figure 33-4 allows you to enter not only the entity name, but the attributes (fields, columns) for the entity. When you enter attributes, you need to decide whether an attribute forms part of the primary key or not, and enter it into the appropriate window. Keep in mind that what we are entering so far are only logical names for attributes and entity. These names can have spaces in them. The logical names will be used to generate default physical names. It might be wise to limit your logical names according to the specifications of your particular database. That way, you may never need to adjust your physical names.

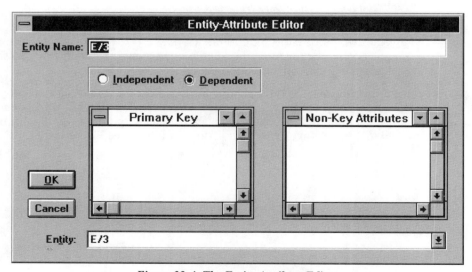

Figure 33-4: The Entity-Attribute Editor.

Relationship modeling

One of the nicest features of ERwin is its foreign key migration capability. It's a feature you really need to understand before you start adding relationships between entities. In the IDEF1X terminology, there are two types of relationships between entities, identifying and non-identifying. Identifying relationships are used when a child entity is identified through its association with the parent entity. In other words, The foreign key column of the child table is also part of the primary key. Non-identifying relationships indicate that the child entity is not identified by its relationship to the parent entity. Identifying relationships and non-identifying relationships are represented by solid and dashed lines respectively.

Relationships in ERwin are generally referred to as foreign keys on the physical level. In fact, the way foreign keys are graphically displayed in the PowerBuilder Database Painter is often mistaken for an ER diagram. Normally, when you create foreign keys you first define the parent table (with a primary key) and the child table (with some columns in common). Afterwards you add a foreign key on the child table's related columns, and make that point to the primary key of the parent table. You'll always get an error if the number of columns in the foreign key is not the same number of columns in the primary key of the parent table (or if the datatypes don't match). This is where the foreign key migration comes into place.

To create a relationship in ERwin, select the appropriate icon ("Identifying"/"Non-Identifying") from the ERwin toolbox, click on the parent table and then on the child table. ERwin will automatically migrate the primary key attributes of the parent table into the child table. PowerBuilder will also migrate the physical name and datatypes of those columns as well. If you draw an identifying relationship (solid line), the primary key attributes of the parent table will migrate into the primary key section of the child entity. Conversely, non-identifying relationships will migrate the primary key columns of the parent table into the non-key area of the child entity.

Figure 33-5: Before adding a relationship.

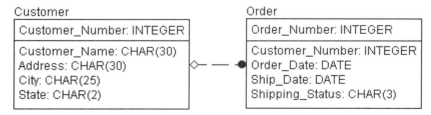

Figure 33-6: After adding a non-identifying relationship.

Take a look at Figures 33-5 and 33-6–a before-and-after look at adding a non-identifying relationship. You'll notice that ERwin automatically added the customer number field in the Order table. The relationship was a non-identifying one, so the customer number was automatically inserted in the non-primary key are of the Order table.

The best part about this foreign key migration is that it is dynamic. If you change the datatype of a primary key column in a parent table, the change is reflected in all child tables. If you add columns to the primary key of a parent table, they are migrated down to the child tables.

> **TIP:** When adding attributes to an entity, avoid manually adding those attributes that caneventually be migrated from a parent table. That way you save typing the name of the attribute (and its datatype) twice.

Referential integrity

After a relationship has been added between tables, ERwin lets you control the referential integrity between them. To access this feature, you need to right click on the relationship line to bring up the relationship's menu, and select "Referential Integrity". (See Figure 33-7).

```
√ Relationship
  Referential Integrity
  Relationship Definition
  Relationship Template
  ─────────────────────
  Object Font/Color...
```

Figure 33-7: The relationship menu.

Once in the Referential Integrity Editor, ERwin will display the parent and child table names, as well as the name of the relationship. The first thing you can do is change the verb phrase and physical name of the relationship. This will be used for the name of the foreign key.

ERwin allows you to control the behavior for an insert, delete, or update on either the parent or the child. Your options for any given action are Restrict, Cascade, Set Null, Set Default, and None.

The *Restrict* option will cause the database to return an error if the action will violate referential integrity. For example, on a Parent Delete–Restrict setting, if an attempt is made to delete a customer that has orders, the deletion will fail.

The *Cascade* option will cause the database to trickle any changes between the related entities. A Parent Delete–Cascade setting would cause the attempt to delete a customer with orders to also delete the associated orders. A Parent Update–Cascade setting would result in any attempt to change a customer number (the primary key of the Customer table) also changing the customer number for all orders that belong to this customer.

The *Set Null* option will cause the database to null out the foreign key columns in the child table during a deletion or an update. For example, a Parent Delete–Set Null option would result in Order records having a null customer number for any orders that once belonged to a deleted customer.

The *Set Default* is very similar, but instead of setting the foreign key columns to null, it resets them to their original default values.

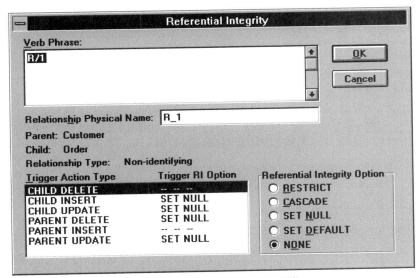

Figure 33-8: The Referential Integrity Editor.

Not all of the options are available for each action. For example, a Child Update–Set Null setting doesn't make much sense if you think about it for a minute. Also, not all of the options are available for foreign key declaration syntax in your particular DBMS. In fact, most of the options are not supported by the popular DBMSes. However, ERwin provides physical support for all of its options through the use of triggers. If your DBMS supports triggers, you can take advantage of most, if not all, of the options.

ERwin accomplishes this through a set of trigger templates. These templates are created with a large and feature-filled set of macros. You can customize and even create your own triggers–however, the macro language is poorly documented. This same macro language has now been extended in Version 2.0 to support stored procedures and ad hoc scripts. You can create your own stored procedure templates and apply them to tables or to the schema as a whole. This can be powerful for creating standard select, insert, update, and delete stored procedures to use in your DataWindows.

Supported Databases

One of ERwin's big strengths is its wide support for various databases. Figure 33-9 shows the Target Server dialog with all of the supported databases. ERwin doesn't make a big deal out of it, but you can change databases on the fly. ERwin maintains a datatype map between databases, so the process of porting from one database to another is only a few clicks away.

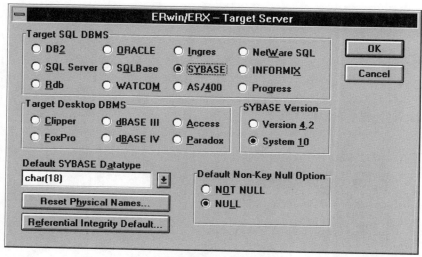

Figure 33-9: Supported databases.

It may also be noteworthy to mention that ERwin/ERX 2.0 supports physical storage parameters for Oracle and SQL Server (both MS and Sybase). This information can be reverse engineered; however, forward engineering is only supported with Oracle.

Reverse Engineering

Most of us are not fortunate enough to begin working on a project that has no legacy data or existing data model. LogicWorks has included the capability to reverse-engineer from any of the supported databases. Reverse engineering is the process of examining the previously existing table structure and getting your ERwin data model up-to-date with what's going on in the real database.

In previous versions of ERwin, reverse engineering required you to have the original SQL DDL that was used to create your tables. However, quite often you can find yourself with a DDL that is out of date–or in the worst case, you have no DDL. ERwin 2.0 solves this problem by providing "Server FRE" to the rescue. You can still use the traditional approach in the latest version. Here are the steps.

1. Start ERwin.

2. From the File menu, select Open.

3. Change the File type to SQL, and specify the SQL file that you wish to reverse engineer from.

4. Specify the DBMS type that the SQL syntax is written for.

In the Reverse Engineer Window (Figure 33-10), you now have several options. You can specify which components of SQL you want to capture. You must reverse-engineer tables for obvious reasons, but you can capture foreign keys and indexes as well. You also have the ability to set case conversion options. Lastly, for the inquisitive, you can display the parse of the SQL as it is happening.

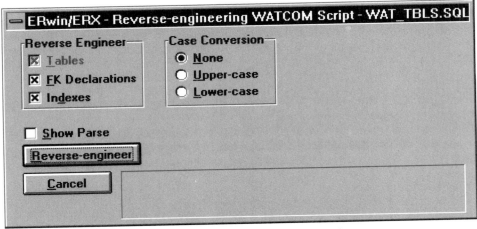

Figure 33-10: DDL reverse engineering options.

When all options are set, press the "Reverse-engineer" button. Now would be a good time to calculate how much time you are saving by letting ERwin do the reverse engineering as opposed to doing it yourself! Unfortunately, you may not even have time to do that–it's pretty fast. It even runs in the background, so you can press <ALT>-<Tab> and go do something else.

ERwin has a much better method of reverse engineering in ERwin 2.0. In fact, it's an insult to call it forward and reverse engineering. LogicWorks thinks so too, and they have coined a new term, Server FRE (Forward/Reverse Engineering). With this new capability, ERwin will actually connect to your DBMS and read directly from the system catalogs. This is not a one-time process, but an ongoing synchronization. If a developer makes a change directly on the database, it is very easy to pick that up the next time you synchronize. This capability can only strengthen the product's project longevity.

PowerBuilder Extended Attributes

PowerBuilder extended attributes have to be the most underutilized feature of the program. In fact, most people don't even know what they are, so let me start with a brief refresher. Every column in your database has some attributes associated with it–the name, the datatype, the length, a column constraint, a default value, a comment, etc. These attributes are maintained by your DBMS and are usually stored in the DBMS's system catalogs. PowerBuilder also has system catalog tables. These are created in your DBMS the first time you connect to it with PowerBuilder. This repository maintains extra attributes about your tables and columns that can be useful when you use these columns in a DataWindow. Some of these attributes are the label, the heading, the edit style (checkbox, radio button, DropDown-ListBox, etc.), the validation rule, and the display format.

The advantage to using this repository can be seen when a developer creates a DataWindow. All of the default styles, validation rules, etc. will be taken from the repository when a column is placed on a DataWindow. This means that the chief architect of a project can decide how certain columns will behave, and this decision is not left up to the developer. There is also a large productivity benefit to be gained. You only need to define the attributes once in the repository, not for every single DataWindow.

ERwin allows you to maintain these attributes through the Schema or Physical Attribute Editor. Figure 33-11 shows two displays that are available to you. All of this information can also be reverse-engineered from an existing database. The same forward and reverse engineering synchronization that is available with entities and attributes is also available for the PowerBuilder extended attributes. A change can be made either in ERwin or directly in PowerBuilder's Database Painter. In either case, ERwin will perform a synchronization for you.

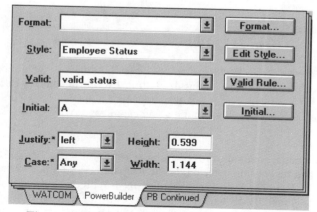

Figure 33-11: PowerBuilder extended attributes.

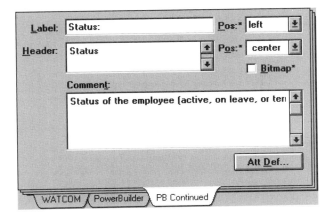

The Future of ERwin

LogicWorks positioned ERwin as a tactical database design tool, but it became the wannabe CASE tool of PC developers. PC developers have traditionally shied away from upper CASE tools that made their Clipper projects take longer than necessary. That's why ERwin won the *Databased Advisor* CASE Tool of the Year award: *DB Advisor* used to be read only by Clipper heads, and that's what Clipper heads thought a CASE tool was. Wrong.

Upper CASE tools have traditionally been focused on mainframe programmers...but now there is this new crossbreed of development, client/server. The winner in the client/server CASE tool arena remains to be decided. Like the technology itself, the people involved in client/server come from two schools, the COBOL folk and the Clipper folk. (That's a large generalization. Perhaps PC People and Mainframers is a better characterization.) And up until now, upper CASE vendors have been saying bigger is better, while ERwin has been saying faster is better.

In my opinion, ERwin has been winning in the trenches of the client/server CASE battle. However, Companies such as LBMS, Popkin, and Bachman have their sights clearly aimed at ERwin. LogicWorks have been keeping up the battle, and Version 2.0 shows a significant leap ahead of the competition. How long this will keep up is anybody's guess, for now. ERwin helps me get the job done.

CHAPTER 34

Object-Orientation in PowerBuilder

By Steve Benfield

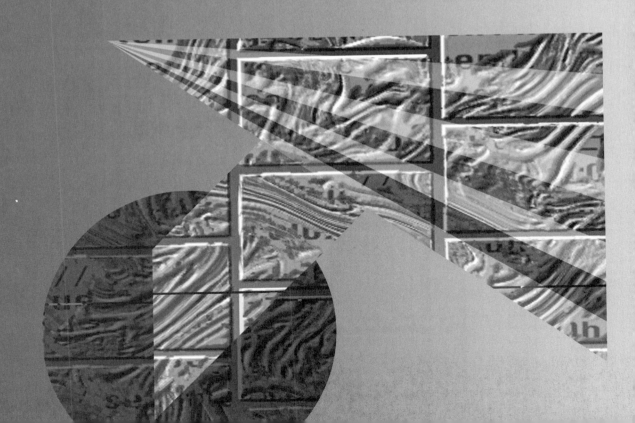

Object-Orientation in PowerBuilder

by **Steve Benfield**

Introduction

Object-Oriented Programming (OOP) in PowerBuilder isn't a requirement. If you are writing applications that are query and report front-ends for pre-existing data, you may not need to learn about objects and how they work.

However, if you want to move past the initial programming efforts you might have made and begin to craft larger, more complicated applications, you'll want to take advantage of Power-Builder's object-orientation.

The good thing about PowerBuilder is that it doesn't force you into using OO. You don't have to know OO to take advantage of some of its features. Many of those features, Power-Builder gives you "under-the-hood". However, without learning about OO and applying what you've learned in your programming, you won't reap the full benefits of reusability, maintainability, and increased productivity that you've been led to believe PowerBuilder gives you. It's not that PowerBuilder doesn't allow you to have these benefits, but you've got to do things correctly to fully harness the program's power.

Several months ago I wrote about spaghetti objects. Spaghetti objects are what you get when you don't do OO correctly. You get a jumbled mess that, on the surface, appears to be good reusable code. However, once changes come down the pike and your systems jump in complexity, you find that you've got to reengineer, improvise, and generally scrap what you've already done. Based on my personal experience, spaghetti objects are about a magnitude worse than traditional spaghetti code. Not only is your code out of whack but you then have to figure out where your code is! Which object? Which event? Which sequence of events?

It is with the problems of spaghetti objects in mind that I'm writing this chapter on Object-Oriented Programming in PowerBuilder. In it, I hope to convey my understanding of OO in PowerBuilder as it relates to real-world programming practices. In addition, I hope to pass on sample code and techniques that I've developed, borrowed, or otherwise acquired over the years! In the process, I hope you learn something and can then contribute to the greater knowledge of how to do this PowerBuilder thing correctly. I don't know all the answers. I just know what works for me and others that I talk to. Hopefully I'll hear from you and find out what works for you: the Professional PowerBuilder Developer.

Objects

One layman's definition of an object is a person, place, or thing. That's close enough in my book. An object is some independent entity that needs to keep data and functionality in your system or enterprise. Objects can be people, customers, orders, line items, purchase orders, windows, and command buttons. Mitchell Kertzman was joking last year at the Power-Builder User's Conference (which you should not miss in 1995) and made some passing reference about David Litwack mimicking Barney singing, "I'm an object, you're an object, wouldn't like to be an object too." Well Mitchell, well said! (I hope they still let me in this year after I've printed this!) Each object is unique. Each is independent of other objects.

Now, what makes these objects unique? Let's look at the characteristics all PowerBuilder objects have: Attributes, Events, and Functions (AEF).

These three characteristics: attributes, events, and functions, have the following rough meanings:

- Attributes: What do I know about?
- Events: What can happen to me?
- Functions: What things can I do?

Data: Attributes

Every object contains data about itself. For example, a person may have eye color, hair color, hair content, height, weight, etc. These are attributes. They are what help distinguish one object from another.

In PowerBuilder, we have two types of attributes: PowerBuilder Defined and User Defined. When you look in the PowerBuilder manuals and see the word "attributes", they are referring to the ones PowerBuilder defines for you. For example, a window has many, many attributes including width, height, x, y, title, visible, enabled, etc. These are created for you when you define a window using the window painter.

User defined attributes are the instance variables and shared variables that you declare for an object. They are accessed the same way PowerBuilder defined attributes are. The only thing we can do with our instance variables is that we can "hide" them from other objects. We'll cover that concept in encapsulation.

Some examples of attributes are:

window.title
window.height
window.control[]
customer.name
customer.balance
customer.dw_1

Events

Not only does PowerBuilder have functions, but it also has events. Events in PowerBuilder are mapped to Windows events. Events are executed (commonly referred to as "fired") when some action happens, triggering that event. For example, the command button has an event called clicked. The clicked event gets fired when the user clicks on the command button. Windows detects the mouse click and sends the "clicked" message to the command button. The PowerBuilder runtime engine intercepts the event and then executes the proper Power-Script code. Most of the events used in PowerBuilder are those directly mapped to Windows events that the user can invoke.

Another type of event is a User Event. These are events which you, the programmer, can declare and call when you wish. PowerBuilder gives us seventy-five custom events which are guaranteed never to be triggered unless we do so programatically in our code.
Some examples of events are:

window::open
window::ue_insert   <-- User event
commandbutton::clicked
datawindow::clicked
datawindow::itemchanged
datawindow::ue_dwdeleterow <-- User Event

Functions

Each object needs to know how to do work. In OO terminology, we call the things an object knows how to do, methods. One way PowerBuilder implements methods is by using object-level functions. So when you declare a window function, you are, in reality, declaring a method for that window object. In addition, PowerBuilder provides many object functions for you automatically, such as Hide() or Show().

The methods of an object are important because they essentially let other objects know what the current object can do. In pure OO, we don't allow other objects to directly modify attributes. Instead, we declare methods or functions to allow manipulation of those attributes. Why do we do this? To protect our data from being changed incorrectly. This method of protecting our data is called encapsulation, which we'll cover fully later.
Some examples of functions are:

```
window.hide()
window.show()
window.f_calculate_balance()
menu.show()
dw_1.reset()
```

Telling Objects What to Do

If you've looked at any OO systems or done even a little PowerBuilder programming, you've seen the following notation:

> object.attribute, or
> object.function(), and also
> object::event.

When you want an object to either give you information or do something, you first have to address the object. (This reminds me of a honeymooner's episode about addressing the ball. Hello, ball. But I digress.) So, we will, in fact, do something akin to saying, "Hello, Object". After addressing the object, we then have to tell the object what we want. Think of it as telling someone who works for you what to do:
Hey! Ditchdigger. Dig me a ditch.
What I've done is asked the object (The Ditchdigger) to do something (dig a ditch). In effect, I've done the following:

```
Ditchdigger.f_dig_ditch()
```

Likewise, when we want to set an attribute or get an attribute value we say, "Object, what is your attribute?" So, don't ever be intimidated by the object.attribute or object.function() notation. It is simply telling an object something that you want.

Classes

A class is an abstraction of an object. *It is a definition of objects of similar type.* For example, take you, me, and David Litwack. We are all objects, correct? And we're objects of the same type: we're people. We are all part of the class person'. So, if person is our definition and that definition includes eye color, hair color, etc., then all individuals of that class will have those characteristics. If a house is an object, then the plans and blueprint for the house is the object's class. By taking those plans, I now know how to build other houses.
Let's take this example to a more abstract level. Look at the windows you create in Power-Builder. Aren't they all fundamentally the same thing? They're windows. They are all objects of the window class. In fact, when you create a new window in PowerBuilder, the window inherits from the built-in window class of PowerBuilder. So even when you build your first PowerBuilder window, you are using inheritance! You're inheriting from the window class!

So, after all that, the simple definition of a class is: A Class is a definition of a similar set of objects.

Instantiation

Let's say I have a class called **w_cust**. That is, a window I've defined in PowerBuilder called **w_cust**. Now I've saved **w_cust**. Have I saved an object? No, I haven't. An object never exists until runtime. Why is this? Well, one reason is that I can't have data in my attributes until runtime. Until then, it's just lines of code! What exists during compile time is my class definition.

So, I've got this class definition of **w_cust** sitting around. Now, once I open **w_cust**, I've got an object in memory. Where does this object get its characteristics? It gets them from the **w_cust** class. Now let's say I open another customer window. Now I have two on the screen. I now have two objects instantiated based on the **w_cust** class. Oh, there's that word: Instantiate. Instantiate is just a three-dollar word that means to create an object based on the class. So, to sound really cool at your next PowerBuilder User's Group, just say, "I instantiated the **w_cust** window three times." Then when they ask you what you said you can look at them and say with a dry tone, "Open. I opened three customer windows."

Now, during runtime, although each object of the same type shares the same attributes of the others, the actual values of the attributes are different. My hair color is different from yours and is definitely different from David Litwack's. This goes for objects also. Each window instance can have separate attribute values. The title for each open window is different as is the x and y location, and a whole host of other attributes.

Let's take a look at how instantiation works during runtime. I created a window called **w_cust** in the Window Painter. Then during runtime, I've opened three different customers on the screen using the variables *w_cust1*, *w_cust2*, and *w_cust3*. Here's what my memory will look like after I have opened (a.k.a. instantiated) each window and retrieved the appropriate data:

Class: w_cust integer cust_id string name	w_cust1 (class w_cust) cust_id = 20 name = Payne

Methods: CalculateBalance() GetNextCustomerID()	w_cust2 (class w_cust) cust_id = 53 name= Helmuth

	w_cust3 (class w_cust) cust_id = 93 name =Roberts'

Table 34-1: Example of Window instantiated three times

Notice that the definition, **w_cust**, is only in memory once. That's because there's no reason to duplicate attribute definitions and programming code. The only thing duplicated is the individual values for each customer. Therefore, opening the first copy of the object, **w_cust1,** may take slightly longer than opening **w_cust2** and **w_cust3** because the object has to be fully initialized into memory.

Review

So let's do a quick review. If you can't fully understand the following paragraph, please reread the previous section.

Objects are things that I'm going to put in my system. These objects are essentially independent of each other. Objects have attributes, functions, and events. An object gets its definition from something called a class. Also, an object doesn't exist until runtime and until it is instantiated. When an object is instantiated, its definition is only in memory once, while each instance has its own memory area. Finally, each instance of a window has its own attribute values.

The "Big Three" of Object-Orientation

For a language to be object-oriented, it must have three things: inheritance, polymorphism, and encapsulation. If it lacks one of these three things, then you've got an object-based system, not an object-oriented one. PowerBuilder does have all three so we are in good hands! Let's find out what these three things really mean.

Inheritance

A good simple definition of inheritance means that one class gets its definition from another classÑjust like children get their "definition" from their parents. Inheritance is the most visible and easily understood concept of object-orientation. The fact that a descendant window can get its definition from a parent window is a pretty powerful concept. It means the end to the copy-paste method of code reuse. In a nutshell, an inherited object derives its base definition from another object. Think of it as a "real-time" template; when the parent object changes, so does the descendant.

The most visible way of showing inheritance is to use window objects as an example. We can show inheritance in less than five minutes. Here are the steps:

1. Create a new window.

2. Put a button on it. Label the text one'.

3. Save the window. Call it **wa_1.**

4. Now create another window through inheritance. Go to the Window painter and

click on "Inherit".

5. Select **wa_1** from the list of windows.

6. Voila! Your new window should now have the button labeled one' on it.

7. Add another new button and label it two'.

8. Save this window and call it **wa_2**.

9. Now create another window through inheritance. Go to the Window painter and click on "Inherit".

10. Select **wa_2** from the list of windows.

11. Voila! Your new window should now have the button labeled one' on it as well as one called two'.

12. Save this window and call it **wa_3**.

There you go! Done.

As you saw in the demonstration, **wa_2** contained the button that **wa_1** originally had. This is inheritance at work! **Wa_2** got its definition from **wa_1**. We then added something to **wa_2** and extended **wa_1**.

In PowerBuilder, there are three types of objects you can inherit from: Windows, Menus, and User Objects. You can't inherit DataWindow Objects, Structures, Pipelines, or anything else. When you inherit from these objects, here's what you actually inherit:

attributes
instance variables
shared variables
controls
user-defined events
object-level functions
event scripts

As you can see, when you inherit, you get a lot! One caveat, you can't delete anything you've inherited. There are several things you can do to inherited attributes, functions, and events of an object. We'll cover that in a few more paragraphs.

Benefits of Inheritance

There are many benefits of using inheritance. These include:

Ability to reuse pre-existing, tested objects.
Reduction in learning curve for new PowerBuilder developers.
Increased application consistency.
More accurate estimation of delivery dates and rates.

Polymorphism

Polymorphism is one of the least understood features of Object-Oriented Programming. The reason is that you really don't wind up understanding how to do polymorphism until you've tried to write some OO systems! Polymorphism is easy to explain but takes a mental leap to really understand. I can tell you that the specific objects we are calling don't need to be known at runtime and that we can call the same function on these unknown objects and get different results, but that won't help.

Let's take our real-world example again. Now, I'm going to address an object: YOU. And I'm going to tell you to do something: Relax. So, You.Relax() is what I'm saying. Do I know exactly who YOU are? No, I don't; we've got over 10,000 readers and I'm bad with names to begin with. But YOU know how to relax (except for type A personalities). Do I know how you'll relax? No, I don't. Do I care? Should I? Not really. All I'm doing is telling you to relax. You, the object, know how to relax. I'm just telling you to perform a function that you know how to do. That is polymorphism.

Let's try to apply this to PowerBuilder. In PowerBuilder, you can get the name of an object by using the function called Print(). So, issuing w_cust.Print() would print a window. During runtime, I may pass to a function of a control or window object (if you didn't realize it, you can pass objects as arguments in a function call). My function can then simply issue the Print() function against the passed object and the object prints itself. Do I know how a window goes about printing itself? No, I don't care. I should not care. I just tell whatever you pass to me to print and I'm done. Did I know that I'd be passed a window when I wrote the function? No, I didn't. Can I anticipate exactly how programmers will use my function in the future? No, I can't. So I'll try to write it in a way that I can take advantage of polymorphism. (Editorial Note: The Print function in PowerBuilder is actually implemented in a way that trying to make it truly polymorphic isn't as straightforward as I've led. Sorry! But maybe if you read on, I can tell you how to make it work.)

Encapsulation

Encapsulation: Data Hiding. Data Protection. What does this really mean?

The goal of encapsulation is to separate the implementation of an object from how other objects interact with that object. (OK, sorry for the bad definition again.) Let's figure out what this really means. Let's say you have implemented something in an object by using an array. This object and array look like the following:

```
object: w_companies
integer    company_id [ 20 ]
string     company_name[ 20 ]
string     contact_id[ 20 ]
```

Now, in all your code throughout your program, you refer to things such as w_companies.contact_id[i] and w_companies.company_name[10] and direct references like that. Well, this works fine until the day comes when you decide you need to keep track of multiple contacts for each company on the **w_companies** window. So, your maintenance staff goes in and changes the declaration of contact_id to contact_id[20, 10] (up to ten contacts per company). Well the **w_companies** object may be changed and updated but all your other objects that try to do w_companies.contact_id[i] will now break. This is clearly not acceptable. The goal of encapsulation is to provide an interface for other objects to interact with your object. So, instead of allowing other objects to directly manipulate your object's attributes, provide events and functions that other's must go through first. This way, when the way you actually implement the object changes, you won't have to go rewrite lots and lots of code in all your other objects. So, when you define your objects and work with them, if you ever find yourself doing things like w_companies.contact_id[i], stop and look at your system. Are there functions you could write to return the information you need such as f_GetCurrentCompanyID() or f_GetPrimaryContactID()? Sure it takes a little time to write these types of things correctly, but if you do take the time, you'll reap the increased performance benefits from then on. And, you'll have a system that is much more resilient to change.

So, how do you actually protect your attributes from being modified by others? You do so by using access modifiers. In OO systems there are three of them: public, protected, and private. (By the way, you can hide functions from other objects alsoÑnot just instance variables.) By default, instance variables and object functions you declare are public. Public means that any other object can access your data. Clearly something we want to avoid. So, to protect our data, let's use one of the other choices: protected and private. Private means that only the current object can access the instance variable or function. Protected means that only the current object and any of its descendants can have access. By far, the most common use is protected.

So let's look at our previous example of asking you to relax. You have the way you relax encapsulated. I don't know how you relax. And knowing some of the PowerBuilder people I do knowÑI don't *want* to know how people relax! Now, if you change how you relax, will that break my programming of telling you to relax? No, it won't. Heck, you could ignore my request to relax. I'm still OK. All I'm doing is telling you something. You are the object that has to decide what to do with that message. I'm just the messenger.

Objects Should Be Loners

I have a saying when I teach: Objects should be loners. They shouldn't know much about other objects. All that happens is that some other objects tell them what to do. When asked, the object responds and performs whatever it was asked to do and returns to the calling object what was advertised. So in the case of something like *decimal {2} customer.GetBalance()*, the customer object calculates the balance and then returns the balance. So, it is a loner, but has a well defined interface that lets other objects know what can be done and retrieved from the object. Outside of that interface, other objects don't know anything. And that is exactly how we like it.

PowerBuilder OO Implementation

We've discussed the features of object-oriented systems. Now let's look a little closer at how PowerBuilder actually implements our three features: inheritance, polymorphism, and encapsulation.

What can you inherit in PowerBuilder?

In PowerBuilder we can inherit from things:
>Windows,
>Menus, and
>User Objects.
>So you can create reusable Windows, Menus, and User Objects. The term User Objects covers many things such as:

Custom Class Object Formerly known as a non-visual user object
Standard Class Objects New in 4.0. You can inherit from other non-visuals such as transaction, message, error, etc.
C++ Class Object New 4.0 Class Builder lets you create C++ DLLs
Custom Visual Objects Composites of other visual elements used as a set
Standard Visual Objects Inheritable windows controls. Especially the DataWindow!
External Visual Objects External DLL with visual interfaces
VBX Visual Controls Visual Basic 1.0 VBXs

What gets inherited

Once an object is inherited in PowerBuilder, what happens? What are the elements that are inherited. Well, they are:

A E F

Attributes: What do I know about?

Events: What can happen to me?

Functions: What do I know how to do?

So after inheritance, your new object will be able to use the attributes of the parent object. In addition, the parent's events will show up in the event list of the descendants. Finally, the functions of the parent are brought down and are available to the descendant.

How Does Inheritance Work?

Inheritance works in different ways. The inheritance mechanism works differently for attributes and controls than it does for events or functions.

Attributes and Controls

Overriding Attributes and Controls
All the attributes and controls of an ancestor are inherited into the descendant. You can't remove them from the descendant. You can; however, override the values of the ancestor's attributes or controls. If you set the value of an attribute to 10 in the ancestor, you could override that value and set it to 20 in the descendant. There is no way; however, to not inherit the fact that the attribute exists.

Likewise, you cannot pick and choose which controls are inherited from the ancestor. If the ancestor window has command button **cb_1**, then the descendant will also have **cb_1**. You can't rename **cb_1** in the descendant but you can change the attribute values such as x, y, height, width, and most importantly, visible. Because you can override the attribute values of **cb_1**, you can make the command button invisible. To the user, the button doesn't exist any-moreÑit's invisible. However, it is still there and still taking up Windows resources.

Extending Attributes
There is no concept of "extending" an attribute. You can't "add" things to an attribute. You can; however, declare your own attributes on the descendant object. You can also add new controls to a descendant window. So adding to an ancestor is fairly easyÑjust declare new attributes or place new controls on it.

Events

When events are inherited, the scripts for those events are extended by default. You can choose to extend or override the script. These behaviors are detailed below.

Extending Scripts
By default, scripts are extended. This means that the code in any ancestors is executed first, then the code for the descendants is executed. Assume that you have the lines of code A, B, and C in your ancestor window **w_1**, ue_test event, lines D, E, and F in your second level ancestor **w_2**, and Z in your descendant, **w_3**. If you don't tell PowerBuilder otherwise, your code will execute in the following sequence: ABCDEFZ. This is extending a script and it is how PowerBuilder defaults script execution.

Overriding Scripts

There are times in your descendant objects when you won't want to execute the functionality of the ancestor. Perhaps, for this one special case, you need some other functionality to execute. When you need to do this, you'll override the ancestor script. To do so, choose Override Ancestor Script from the Compile menu. Following the example above, if you override the ue_test event in the window **w_3**, the only line of code that will execute is Z. Likewise, if you override script in **w_2**, then lines DEFZ will execute. So, in simple terms, overriding a script really means "ignore the ancestor."

If you override a script, there will be times when you want to execute the descendant and then execute the ancestor. You can do this by specifically calling the ancestor script using the CALL function. Assume we've overridden our ancestor in **w_3**. Then only line Z will execute. However, if we put the following line of code into our **w_3**, ue_test event:

```
CALL w_2::ue_test
```

 then the order of execution will be ZABCDEF. Why? Because originally, the code for **w_1** and **w_2** was overridden. However, by explicitly calling **w_2**, then **w_1** and **w_2** are executed because **w_2** was inherited from **w_1**.

Functions

Functions work differently than events or attributes. You can override functions, but its harder to override them than it is for events or attributes. Nevertheless, functions can be overridden and overloaded. Despite the similar name, the behavior of these functions is completely different.

Overriding

If you don't need the functionality that a function provides, you can override that function with your own code. However, its not as easy as checking an override box. To override a function, you must redeclare the function. This redeclaration must be exactly like the original; it must have the same return type, same function name, and same argument list. Once declared, PowerBuilder will execute the descendant version of the function during runtime. It has now been overridden.

During runtime, PowerBuilder begins to look at the functions in the lowest level descendant and then works its way up the ancestor chain until it finds a function with the same argument list as the one called.

Overloading

Overloading is unique to functions. An overloaded function is one with the same function name as another but with different arguments or parameters. During runtime, PowerBuilder looks for the function declaration that matches the one that you are calling. This allows you to have the same function call with different parameter lists. This simple technique is called overloading. It seems very simple but it gives object-oriented systems lots of power. I'm often asked, "when would I use such a thing?" The answer is that you use it all the time in PowerBuilder. Think of some PowerScript you've coded. One of the most common functions in PowerBuilder has been overloadedÑMessageBox.

Think of MessageBox. You can call it several ways:

MessageBox(string title, string text)
MessageBox(string title, boolean text)
MessageBox(string title, numeric text)
MessageBox(string title, string text, icontype icon)
MessageBox(string title, string text, icontype icon, buttontype button)
MessageBox(string title, string text, icontype icon, buttontype button, integer default)

Also, there are another six forms, three for boolean text and three for numeric text.

Because of function overloading, we can declare a function that has default operations as well as special, more specific functionality.

There is one caveat, however. You can only implement function overloading through Power-Builder's inheritance mechanism. You can't define the same function twice in the same level of inheritance. Try it. You can't do it. The only way you can have function overloading is to redeclare the overloaded function in a descendant object. Because of this limitation, many people aren't aware of PowerBuilder's overloading capability. Until Powersoft gives us the ability to overload in an easier way, it will be a little used feature of PowerBuilder.

In addition, PowerBuilder 3.0 didn't even allow you to see function declarations that existed in an ancestor. The only way to determine which functions existed in an ancestor was to either actually open the ancestor and look around or use the object browser and open every ancestor of your current object. Unless you had good documentation of your objects, you'd never have known that a function existed without stumbling across it in an ancestor. Power-Builder 4.0 has helped this situation a bit with its object level browser. You can now see the functions defined and available for an object by using the "Browse Object..." menu item under the Edit menu in the Script painter. Don't confuse this with "Browse Objects..." One is plural, one isn't. The plural version is the same object browser you had in PowerBuilder 3.0. The singular version shows the attributes and functions available to the current object.

Figure 1: Object Browser in PowerBuilder 4.0

PowerBuilder Class Hierarchy

Everything in PowerBuilder (except for your data types such as string, integer, datetime, etc.) are objects inherited from the mother of all objects: The PowerObject. From PowerObject, objects are generally divided into graphic objects and nonvisual objects. Within the graphic objects there are menus, windows, and controls (a.k.a. windowobjects), and drawing objects. The Nonvisual objects include the cplusplus object (used with the C++ Class Builder), the error, message, and transaction objects. In PowerBuilder 3.0 you couldn't inherit from these functional nonvisual objects. In PowerBuilder 4.0 you can.

Let's take a look at how the internal PowerBuilder objects are inherited:

Object	Added Functions	Added Atributes
PowerObject	ClassName, TypeOf, TriggerEvent, PostEvent	None
GraphicObject	Hide, Show	visible, tag
Menu	Check, Disable, Enable, Uncheck	Checked, ShortCut, Microhelp
Window	WorkSpaceX, GetActiveSheet, SetRedraw, Print	Border, WindowType, Vscroll, Control[]
WindowObject	Move, Resize	None
DragObject	Drag, PointerX, SetRedraw, Print	DragAuto, BringToTop
CommandButton	Print	Default, Cancel
PictureButton	SetPicture	OriginalSize, PictureName
DataWindow	AcceptText, Retrieve, Update	DataObject, HSplitScroll
DropDownListBox,..	AddItem, DirList, FindItem	AllowEdit, ShowList, Sorted
DrawObject	None	LineThickness, LineColor
Line	None	None
Rectangle	None	None
Nonvisual Object	None	None

cplusplus	None	None
error	None	None
message	None	None
transaction	None	None

Table 34-2: Object inheritance

Polymorphism

Polymorphism can be implemented in PowerBuilder in several ways. Event polymorphism is implemented more loosely than function or attribute polymorphism. Let's take a look at how these are implemented in real PowerBuilder systems.

Events

We've seen that every object in PowerBuilder is inherited from PowerObject. PowerObject includes the TriggerEvent and PostEvent functions. Since triggering events is simply a call to the Trigger or PostEvent function, then we can call events on any object, and those events don't have to exist at compile time. This is because we aren't referencing the event directly, we're referencing the TriggerEvent function. If the event doesn't have any code in it, then the TriggerEvent function will return a -1; if the event exists and has code, you'll get a return code 0 from TriggerEvent. What you won't get if the event doesn't exist is a runtime errorÑyour program will still run. Because of this flexibility, most people use events in PowerBuilder to implement polymorphism.

To use events polymorphically, you simply declare a user event on your window and trigger it. For example, you might want to create an event called ue_insert. You can then use the following code in your menu to fire off the ue_insert event of your window:
ParentWindow.TriggerEvent("ue_insert")

This code will always runÑeven if the ue_insert event doesn't exist on your window. Now let's contrast the use of events with the use of functions in PowerBuilder.

Functions

PowerBuilder is much stricter with functions that it is with events. A function must exist on an object before the compiler will allow your script to compile. If PowerBuilder detects that the function doesn't exist, you'll get an unknown function compiler error. Let's assume that you have a window, **w_cust**. On this window is a command button named **cb_insert** and a function named f_insert. This window is attached to a menu called **m_menu**. Can you compile the following lines in your **m_menu** menu?

```
ParentWindow.f_insert(), or
```

```
ParentWindow.cb_insert.TriggerEvent(clicked!)
```

No, you cannot. Why? Because the object type of ParentWindow is built in the Power-Builder window object. If you declare a new window in PowerBuilder, do you see an f_insert function? Likewise, do you see a button named **cb_insert**? No, you don't. And neither does PowerBuilder. The reason these statements won't compile is that the object type window does not have the function or the command button on it. Therefore the compiler doesn't see them on the ParentWindow and your code won't compile. So what do you do? The approach you have to use is to cast the ParentWindow variable into a window type that does have the function f_insert. Here's how you do that:

```
w_cust lw
lw = ParentWindow
lw.f_insert()
```

This code compiles fine. What you've done is created a variable, *lw* of the **w_cust** object type. In the variable *lw*, we can hold a reference to a **w_cust** window. Assuming the ParentWindow of our menu is, indeed, a customer window, then this code will work at runtime. Why? Because the actual type of the window held in ParentWindow will be a customer window during runtime. The assignment lw = ParentWindow works because you're assigning a customer window to *lw*.

Now, what happens when the new menu is attached to window, **w_emp**? (Remember, a menu can be associated with multiple windows.) OK, we're in runtime and we have an employee window open. What happens when the insert menu item is clicked? Well, what happens is you get a runtime error.

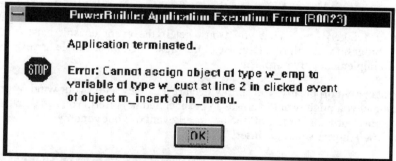

Figure 34-2: Runtime Error from Conflicting Window Type Assignment

So, the problem with the second form is that although it compiles correctly, you run the risk of getting a runtime error. This is why events are the safest call possible in PowerBuild-erN events never give runtime errors. The drawback of events is that they are always publicly available. You can't "hide" events like you can functions. Any object can call an event on your window at any time.

Functions vs. Events?

So what should you do regarding functions and events? I recommend that you call events on a window to perform functionality. Now, what that event does on your window is up to you. If you are more comfortable with events, use events. If you prefer functions, use functions. I prefer calling functions from my window events. Functions allow me to pass well-defined parameters easily. Also, functions return a value. To me, they are just plain more object-oriented than events are. However, events always work and they aren't as rigorous as functions. Also, I can look at ancestor events during programming time and choose to override or extend as needed. It's not as easy to see what is going on in an ancestor function.

Encapsulation

Encapsulation is more a technique than an actual feature. You can develop an object-oriented system that isn't too encapsulated. However, you won't gain all the benefits from OO unless you learn and enforce encapsulation. Let's take a look at some of the ways PowerBuilder helps us hide code and data.

Access Modifiers

Alright, let's look at a PowerBuilder example. Examine the following objects and their declarations:

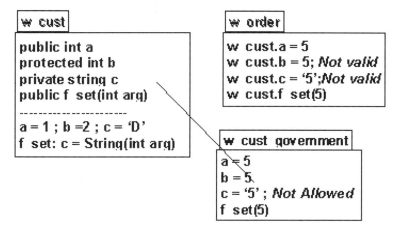

Figure 34-3: Object declarations

The window, **w_cust,** has three instance variables declared: *A*, *B*, and *C*. *A* is public, *B* is protected, and *C* is private. There's also a public function. Now, a completely unrelated window, **w_order**, can access the variable *A* of **w_cust,** but cannot access *B* or *C*; the compiler won't allow it. **W_order** *can* call the function f_setc() and indirectly set the private variable *C*. And look, **w_order** doesn't know how *C* is stored, it doesn't even know that *C* exists! **W_cust** does know and takes care of it. *C* is encapsulated.

Now, look at **w_cust_government**. It is inherited from **w_cust**. Since it is inherited, *w_cust_government* *can* see the instance variable *B*. It still can't see *C* and doesn't know that *C* exists. It can still call f_set to manipulate *C* but **w_cust_government** doesn't *know* about the instance variable *C*.

Now, when someone makes a decision that *C* should be a long instead of a string, what happens? Well, go to **w_cust** and change the declaration of *C* to a long and change the function w_set to the following:

```
f_set ( long value)
c = value
```

After these changes, both the **w_order** and **w_cust_government** windows still work: **Nothing Breaks**. This is our goal with encapsulation: systems that don't break.

Loosely Coupled Systems

Have you ever worked on a relational database design? Are you familiar with a normalized database? A fully normalized database means that if one fact changes outside of your database, you only have to change data in one place in your database. If you have to make more than one update, your database isn't normalized. (RememberÑthe database *should* handle foreign keys for you.) Just as the goal of normalization is to reduce update, insert, and delete anomalies in your database, the goal of a well-designed object-oriented system is to reduce the code and functionality that you have to change when your business requirements change. So, what we're after is a system that is resilient to change; where changes to one object don't break other objects. A system where objects don't assume or know how other objects work is called loosely coupled. We want loosely coupled objects. Loosely coupled objects can be reused easily because you don't have nearly as much "setup" to perform. And the object isn't making assumptions about what is calling it. Think of the following scenario. Let's say you have a customer window, **w_cust,** and an order window, **w_order**. Assume **w_order** gets its current customer from an instance variable on **w_cust**. So for **w_order** to work, it will have some sort of code that reads as follows:

```
stringis_cust
is_cust = w_cust.is_cust_id
```

Well, this seems innocuous enough. It will work fine until one of three things happens. First, when you decide to allow more than one customer open at a time, you'll then have more than one instance of **w_cust** open. Which one do you now reference instead of **w_cust**? You don't know at compile time. So your code breaks. The second thing that could happen is you decide to change how you store the customer id in your **w_cust** window. If you change the name of the variable, *is_cust_id*, then the code in **w_order** breaks. Finally, if you decide to use your **w_order** window, you've got to have a customer window open. What if you want to allow a different way of viewing orders? You'll have to change your code.

So how do you overcome these problems? The simplest solution, and the most sound, is to pass **w_order** the information it will need when it is opened. You can do this through the message object and OpenSheetWithParm. Remember, by passing data to the object that needs it, you've uncoupled the two objects. In this case **w_order** won't need to know which window is calling it. All **w_order** really needs to know is which customer to work with. Don't tell **w_order** more than it needs to know. If it really needed a customer window, then let it know about the customer window. However, in this case, there isn't any need for that. Also remember you can use the access modifiers to help enforce this type of programming. Just declare the variable *is_cust_id* in **w_cust** as protected or private. Then **w_order** would never be able to access that specific variable and you'd be forced to think of a different way of getting the customer number. By using access modifiers, you've helped the **w_cust** window protect itself.

A Real-World Perspective

Let's put all of this into a real-world perspective. How much of this OO stuff are people really doing? And how much is it costing them to do it?

The PowerBuilder OO Continuum

Each IS shop is different. Each has different skills, different backgrounds, different budgets, and different goals. Each shop needs to determine where along the object-oriented spectrum they currently are and where they want to wind up. The following chart shows what I call the OO continuum. As you move from left to right on the continuum, you get more object-oriented. Unfortunately, you also get much more expensive in up-front training and "learning" costs. As an IS organization moves to each successive level in the continuum, they'll have to spend money *and* time. Time is needed for the programmers, analysts, and management to fully absorb and learn the techniques needed at each successive level. I do not believe an organization can move from the left to the right easily. It takes time. Mistakes will be madeÑthey have to be made. The statement that you'll throw the first one away is true; you will throw your first efforts in each of these areas away. Well, if not completely away, you'll only reuse part of what you had at each level. Developing good object-oriented systems is hard work. It really is a new way of thinking, and working. And it gets very expensive to really do OO right. However, what this continuum doesn't show is that maintenance costs will decline over time. Productivity will increase. The payoff, in the end, will be worth it.

Besides training and mentoring, the use of a well-designed class library can help companies move along the OO continuum. The library allows a less experienced team to gain the benefits of OO while not knowing all the techniques and theories of OO. By leveraging work done by others, you and your team can not only get to OO faster but you can also learn by studying the class library you purchase.

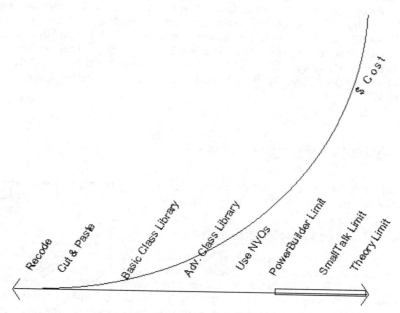

Figure 34-4: Object-orientation continuum

Easing into OO

Most companies I talk to use inheritance when it comes to windows. However, at least half of them aren't using an inheritable DataWindow control. My suggestion to you is to make sure you've got the minimum architecture needed to allow for a fuller use of OO in the future. To do this you need to make sure all your windows are inherited from a common window such as **wa_main**. In addition, instead of using PowerBuilder's built-in DataWindow on your windows, create a DataWindow user object. To do so, create a new DataWindow user object in the User Object painter and save it as **dwa_main**. Now, instead of placing the built-in PowerBuilder DataWindow control, use your new DataWindow user object. Notice that I haven't told you to put any code in your ancestors yetÑyou don't need to. By using, at a minimum, these two reusable objects, you've set yourself up to reap many benefits from inheritance in the future.

As you learn more about OO, you can make changes to **wa_main** and **dwa_main.** These changes will filter down to each of your windows and DataWindows. In the future, if you wanted to add security to all your windows, you'd have to change dozens, maybe hundreds, of windows if you created new windows each time. In addition, if you find new functionality for DataWindows, such as a Quicken-like scroll bar, then you'd have to add that code to each DataWindow control in your system. By using inheritance, you'd only have to add these changes to one place. Clearly a better alternative. For more information on easing into OO and changing ancestor objects after the fact, see the September 1994 issue of the *Power-*

Builder Developer's Journal for my article titled, "Reengineering Early PowerBuilder Projects" and the November 1994 issue for my article, "Changing Your Ancestry".

Conclusions

The first object-oriented feature people learn is inheritance. However, there's more to meet the eye in an well designed system than inheritance. Polymorphism and encapsulation are the additional two features of object-oriented systems that allow for reuse. PowerBuilder has a fairly complete implementation of object-oriented features, but using the event approach is easier to implement.

Object-oriented systems can't be rushed into; they can't be learned and implemented immediately. They require a team who knows OO. However, moving a team from the cut-and-paste method of reuse to full OO is a long, time-laden process. I recommend that your team either develop a class library or purchase one. Either way, you are going to pay to get further along the OO continuum. In the end it will be worth it as you reap the benefits of reusable objects, loosely coupled systems, and proven development methods.

CHAPTER **35**

Managing Resources

By William Green

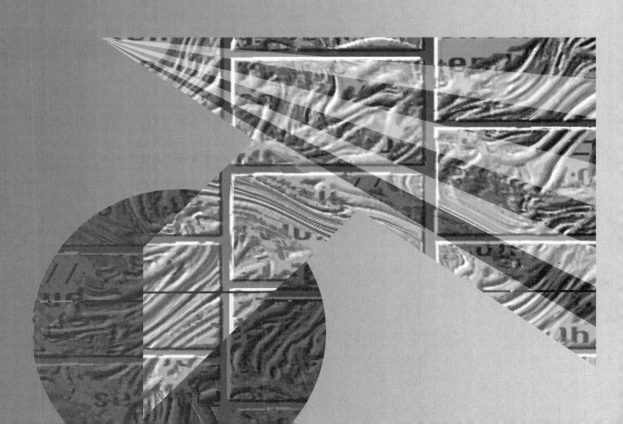

Managing Resources

by **William Green**

In this chapter we will discuss some techniques to improve the performance of your Power-Builder application, and how to manage resources from within your application to provide improved stability.

Managing resources with PowerBuilder is still a closely kept secret. Developers who have experimented with different techniques have discovered some that work, *but they aren't telling!* We're going to set the record straight. It's no secret that PowerBuilder requires significant resources to run well. It's also no secret that most of the tools available today require significant resources to run comparably. The real secret lies in discovering how to make your application run faster with the resources available.

We will discuss some of the methods available today which allow PowerBuilder applications to require significantly less footprint (the amount of memory/space required to run an application); methods for improving the performance of your application, even if the performance improvement is only visual; and method for managing resources dynamically (i.e.at runtime.)

Using the PowerBuilder .PBD

The first technique is well-known among developers: using PowerBuilder Dynamic Link Libraries. The concept is simple. A PowerBuilder Dynamic Link Library (or .pbd), is the binary representation of your source code in libraries that match your source code. Objects (including functions), are loaded from the .pbd into memory on an as-needed basis. This means that your executable size will be smaller (by far), and execution will be more efficient–not necessarily faster, but more efficient. Because only the required objects are loaded at any point in time, memory swapping is far less likely, and that *would* make your application faster.

Although this immediately seems like the best way to implement a PowerBuilder application, it has some pitfalls of its own. You are now required to perform version control on the runtime version of each .pbd. Every .pbd can be swapped out by another version of that .pbd without recompiling the application. This can make things simpler and, at the same time, much more difficult. If objects are inherited, then the objects' descendants must also be regenned, and the libraries they reside in, rebuilt. .pbds remain more efficient, however, as long as the basic rules are followed.

One factor *forces* the use of .pbds: use of the Open.... functions with a string variable to identify the object. If a developer employing these function does not utilize .pbds, the object requested *will not be included in the runtime*. (Pre-loading, discussed later, alleviates this problem.)

When using .pbds, follow these simple steps to ensure success.

Always regen and recreate .pbd s based on your class hierarchy.

Make sure you regenerate all descendants of an object.

Make sure you replace all of the .pbd s that have been rebuilt.

Provide a means of runtime versioning for your applications that can check each .pbd as necessary.

There are two immediate drawbacks to this technique. The first is the danger of replacing a .pbd at any time. If linked objects (inherited or descendant), are in different .pbds, the developer must ensure that all of the required .pbds are replaced. The second drawback is in software distribution. Instead of distributing your .exe file whenever changes are made and tested, you now have to distribute multiple files, increasing the risk of error. Some automated software distribution programs can alleviate the problem, but the danger remains.

There are also less predictable drawbacks, which lie in the sometimes incorrect techniques used in generating the executable. Techniques range from attempting to place the .pbds in specific sequences to facilitate quicker location of source code, to dynamically modifying the search sequence with special code. These techniques, while they may be successful in some cases, are not reliable and expose the application to dangers not conveyed by the User Guide.

Why is this better than compiling everything into a standalone .exe?

A huge executable file needs to load itself, generally across a network, whenever your application is run. Also, when memory resources are low, a large executable will either not load at all, or will swap in and out of virtual memory more often. It is therefore a recommended practice to use .pbds, despite the possible drawbacks. The key to success is in organization.

Organizing Your Objects

It is true that the correct sequencing of .pbds will provide an improvement in performance. If ancestor objects are located faster, objects will load faster. The difference in speed, however, is noticeable only to the CPU, unless your load sequence is in reverse (that is, your most often used and/or highest level ancestors are in the last of more than four .pbls). The average user will not notice the nanoseconds ticking by while the object ancestry is located. It is far more important to place objects in a sequence that makes sense to the object scanner that searches for your objects, and to pre-load objects that provide the basis of your object hierarchy. While from the interpreter's point of view it may be logical to place objects of common ancestry or style in the same .pbl (or .pbd), it is more practical to be able to locate objects in an ordered fashion.

If you have used inheritance in PowerBuilder, you will know that the deeper you go down a hierarchy, the slower your objects seem to perform. This occurs because whenever a descendant object is required, the interpreter must first locate the object's ancestor and load it. Remember that an object's inheritance never tells the interpreter any more than the object's immediate ancestor, and this ancestor may be a descendant itself. In this way the circle repeats itself until the highest level ancestor is located and loaded. Only then can the object begin to perform its processing.

Since, ideally, the highest level of ancestry should be highest in the search path, the second level next; and the other descendants afterward, it would seem to make sense to place the highest level of ancestors in a single .pbl located first in your search path. While this is true, it is not always workable. Search paths are used much more in the development environment than in the production environment. The gains are minimal and the effort could be substantial.

> **TIP:** If you choose to adopt this method, save your search path into a .txt file that can be imported and copied into each developer's library, so that everyone uses the same path. There is nothing worse than building an application paying attention to your search path, only to find that another developer, with a different search path, has regenned and rebuilt it with a very different search path sequence.

One solution to all these difficulties would be to pre-load certain objects into memory ahead of time. This would substantially reduce the load time of individual objects. But alas! No such feature is provided with the development tool. However, there is a way.

Pre-Loading Objects

Pre-loading objects definitely improves performance. This technique will give the user the impression that *everything* loads faster. All you are doing, however, is altering the point in time when the initial load of the object takes place. Instead of loading it when the user requests it (by opening a window for example), you will load it when the user is not expecting performance from the application. The most recognizable place to do this is in your application open event, when a simple nonvisual object can become your best friend.

> **TIP:** Remember that some objects, such as nonvisuals, load completely into memory when called, while other objects, such as functions, load pieces as needed. Therefore a nonvisual object might be faster than a global function (depending on size and functionality).

How to win time and influence objects

You do not have to pre-load every object in your application. The key is to pre-load those objects which are most commonly used as ancestor objects in your application. This is especially true if you are using a base class library of any kind. The way it works is to assign objects to variables within the nonvisual object. The nonvisual object remains open until your application terminates. This can have a marked impact in your application.

> **TIP:** If you cast a pointer to this object, you can utilize it as a global repository for such functionality as application constants, external functions, and many other useful application-wide features.

Step 1: Create the pre-loader.

Create a user object of type Non_Visual_Object. Save this object under the name of your choice. For this example, I will use NVO_Object_Pre-loader.

Within the object, create a dynamic array of Powerobjects called IPO_Pre-loaded_Objects[ ]. Why Powerobjects, you might ask? Powerobjects are the highest level of object in the PowerBuilder object hierarchy and will therefore cast to any PowerBuilder standard or custom object.

Now create a variable of type Integer for the index to the array. We'll call this ii_Idx, and assign an initial value of 0. Your instance variables should now look like this.

```
PRIVATE: /* We want to limit access of this data to this object only */

/* We will assume a maximum of 10 objects although this limit can be set by
the developer to however many objects are required. */

PowerObject ipo_Pre-loaded_Objects[10]
Integer     ii_Idx=0
```

TIP: Pre-size the array if possible. This will reserve memory ahead of time and your pre-load will run faster itself.

Step 2: Create the pre-load function.

Now create a user object function called NVOF_Pre-load_Object. This function takes a single argument, APO_Object, of type Powerobject. The function itself is simple.

```
/*
FUNCTION:  NVOF_Pre-load_Object
PURPOSE:   To pre-load often used ancestor objects
ARGUMENTS: PowerObject apo_Object
RETURNS:   integer
1 - Success, -1 Failed
*/

// Increase the index count by 1
ii_Idx++

/* assign the object to the array */
IPO_Pre-loaded_Objects[ii_Idx] = APO_Object

/* Check of the object assign worked */
If isvalid(IPO_Pre-loaded_Objects[ii_Idx]) then
 Return 1    // Return a successful return code value
else
 Return -1  // Return a failure code
end if
```

Now save the function and return to the nonvisual object.

Step 3: Create a user event where calls to the user object can be placed.

We now want to create, on this object, a method for the developer to place calls to pre-load objects. I employ a user event called a declarations event, which is posted from the object's Constructor event.

Name the user event on the object NVO_UE_Declarations, and place the following code into the object's Constructor event.

```
This.PostEvent("nvo_ue_declarations")
```

In the NVO_UE_Declarations event you can now place calls to pre-load objects.

Step 4: Pre-load objects.

We will assume a class library with several often-used ancestor objects. We will call these objects w_WindowBase, udw_DataWindowBase, uo_UserObjectBase, and m_MenuBase. These objects represent the ancestor objects for our window classes, user object DataWindow classes, user object classes, and menu classes. Your application may need more or fewer objects pre-loaded.

In the NVO_UE_Declarations event we code the following:

```
/* declare some local variables which will be the assignment point for objects
*/
Window       lWindow
UserObject   lUO
DataWindow   lDW
Menu         lMenu

/* For each object requiring pre-loading, create an instance of the object
using the Create function and call the pre-load function to store them in
instance memory */

/** Create an instance of the Base window class **/
lWindow = Create w_WindowBase
NVOF_Pre-load_Object(lWindow)

/** Create an instance of the UDW class */
lDW = Create udw_DataWindowBase
NVOF_Pre-load_Object(lDW)

/** Create an instance of the User Object base class */
lUO = uo_UserObjectBase
NVOF_Pre-load_Object(lUO)

/** Create an instance of the Menu Class */
lMenu = Create m_MenuBase
NVOF_Pre-load_Object(lMenu)
```

These objects will pre-load into memory and speed up our object loads substantially. The same variables can be used for multiple objects. Once the pre-load function has executed, the object variable is free to be used again. All of the variables are freed at when script execution ends.

> **TIP:** Objects called dynamically, such as those called using string variables, are not ordinarily included in an .exe. For example, if you open a window using Open(mywin, "My_Window"), the window My_Window is *not* automatically included in your .exe. If compiled as a .pbd, it is. However, if you pre-load the object using this method, it will be included under both the .pbd and .exe compilation techniques.

Step 5: Instantiate the pre-loader.

To get the objects into memory, one final step remains. We must load the pre-loader object into memory itself. You can choose to do this anywhere before the heavily used portions of your application begin to come into play. I most often use the application open event. The code required is:

Application instance variable:
NonVisualObject anvo_object_pre-loader

Application Open event:
anvo_object_pre-loader = Create NVO_Object_Pre-loader.

This will create the nonvisual object, which will in turn fire the Declarations event on the object, which will then pre-load the objects.

Memory leaks

IMPORTANT: Remember to code a DESTROY anvo_object_pre-loader in your application close event.

Of great concern to developers and users alike is the memory leak. A memory leak occurs when an object is loaded (and memory is allocated), and the memory is not freed up when the object is closed. While we are not responsible to monitor memory leaks created by the development tools we use, we *are* responsible for the memory leaks we create with our code.

The biggest culprit for memory leaks is the CREATE of an object without a corresponding DESTROY. Any time you create an object using the CREATE function, you are responsible for destroying the memory allocated to that object once completed.

Example: I create my own transaction object:

```
Transaction  MyTransaction
MyTransaction = CREATE Transaction
```

When I have finished using this object, I should destroy the object.

```
DESTROY MyTransaction
```

(NOTE: SQLCA is created by your application automatically and is also closed automatically.)

The nonvisual user object is often involved in memory leaks. This object can only be instantiated by a CREATE, and is therefore very susceptible to the omission of the corresponding DESTROY. Another common culprit is the dynamic user object, which is created using OpenUserObject... OpenUserObjectWithParm. Such objects require a corresponding CloseUserObject when you have finished with them.

Why doesn't PowerBuilder destroy these objects automatically, as it does with regular objects placed on a window? Because PowerBuilder can only destroy those objects which are in its control list, and only objects present on an object's surface are listed in the control list. (This includes invisible objects.) Dynamic user objects and nonvisual objects, as well as instances of PowerBuilder global objects (transactions, messages, errors, etc.), are added to the object *after* its control list is created. Closing the parent object will *not* automatically mean the parent object knows to destroy these dynamically added objects. If you leave them open, such objects remain in memory until you can recover memory through a utility, or until you close down Windows itself. Using a memory resource monitor, such as that provided by the Windows 3.1 Resource Kit, will allow you to check during test cycles to ensure that resources are freed as expected.

Getting More Speed from Your Application

There are ways to get more real speed from your application...but you should pay more attention to good coding methods than to the global techniques listed here!

> **Tip:** Methods like not using a function to determine loop or DO WHILE limits will improve code execution speed. For example: FOR 1 TO upperbound(arrayname), or DO WHILE Rownumber < RowCount() will force re-execution of the upperbound or RowCount() functions for each iteration of the loop. Simply setting a variable for your loop limit before executing the loop can have a significant impact on code execution speed.

```
DON'T:
int ii
For ii = 1 to upperbound(arrayname)
...
Next
DO:
int ii, iupper
iupper = upperbound(arranyname)

For ii = 1 to iupper
...
Next
```

This and many other tips are available in the PBTIPS.HLP file distributed with Power-Builder. The global techniques I have used successfully are described below.

Compiling resources into the application

PowerBuilder supports the use of a file known as a .pbr. This is simply a line indicating a path that identifies a resource file (such as a bitmap, icon, cursors, dynamic DataWindow/window, etc.). Remember that this path name must exactly match the path name you originally supplied for the object. .pbrs allow a copy of the bitmap or icon or cursor to be attached to the executable and loaded into memory when called upon. This is much faster than searching paths for objects that may not be there, and if they are, opening them and loading the resource into the object. When the object's memory is freed, so is the memory of the location of the resource file. Next time, the circle repeats.

Should I run my application on the client or the server machine?

Tests we have run have indicated, in some cases, a performance improvement of *fifty percent* when the software is run on the client machine. This may entail additional software distribution problems, but if your application is performance-dependent, you may be well served to run your application locally.

Why do I get "out of memory" messages no matter how I compile, and usually, no matter what is running on my user's machine?

The "out of memory" message in Windows is a misleading one, and usually is accompanied by irritable grunts of disbelief and yells of "I have 32 MB of RAM on this machine. How can I run out of memory with only two applications running?" Annoyed users experienced in Windows programs will immediately begin shutting down other applications until they find one that frees up enough room for their PowerBuilder application to run. Almost without fail, the developer will blame PowerBuilder, and the user will blame the developer. In most cases, neither one is to blame. Windows is.

Keep in mind that Windows is not an operating system. It is a DOS program. It still requires program address space that is fixed. This space is located below the 1MB memory line, in upper memory. If you use the DOS MEM program with the /C option, you will see something like the display below:

Modules using memory below 1 MB:

Name	Total =		Conventional		+ Upper Memory	
MSDOS	17,533	(17K)	17,533	(17K)	0	(0K)
HIMEM	1,120	(1K)	1,120	(1K)	0	(0K)
EMM386	4,144	(4K)	4,144	(4K)	0	(0K)
POWER	80	(0K)	80	(0K)	0	(0K)
COMMAND	3,888	(4K)	3,888	(4K)	0	(0K)
win386	44,816	(44K)	2,384	(2K)	42,432	(41K)
NAVTSR	7,984	(8K)	7,984	(8K)	0	(0K)
MOUSE	25,328	(25K)	272	(0K)	25,056	(24K)
SHARE	26,368	(26K)	26,368	(26K)	0	(0K)
DOSKEY	4,144	(4K)	4,144	(4K)	0	(0K)
WIN	1,760	(2K)	1,760	(2K)	0	(0K)
COMMAND	4,048	(4K)	4,048	(4K)	0	(0K)
POWER	4,672	(5K)	0	(0K)	4,672	(5K)
SMARTDRV	29,024	(28K)	0	(0K)	29,024	(28K)
Free	581,312	(568K)	581,312	(568K)	0	(0K)

Memory Summary:

Type of Memory	Total =	Used	+ Free
Conventional	655,360	74,048	581,312
Upper	101,184	101,184	0
Reserved	393,216	393,216	0
Extended (XMS)	19,821,760	18,773,184	1,048,576
Total memory	20,971,520	19,341,632	1,629,888
Total under 1 MB	756,544	175,232	581,312

Largest executable program size 581,296 (568K)
Largest free upper memory block 0 (0K)
MS-DOS is resident in the high memory area.

Figure 35-1: Available memory display.

Notice that although there is 360K (approx. 384,000 bytes) of memory available between the 640K DOS limit and the 1MB upper memory block, the display shows a total of almost 500K available between "upper" memory and "reserved" memory. Most of this is "reserved." This is memory not available to the developer. This "reserved" space is usually for network software and other drivers. The memory available is the remaining 42K shown in the "win386" line. This is the memory used by applications that require fixed address space. Some programs use more of this memory, in small pieces, than others. When Windows creates a new task, the Windows loader module creates a task database (TDB) for it. The task database must be loaded below the 1MB line and will be a minimum of 200 bytes in length. The reason is that the second portion of the task database entry is a program segment prefix (PSP), an artifact from Windows 1.0, 2.0 and 3.0 real mode. The only reason this is still used is to make things easier for the built-in MS-DOS extender, as it is not actually required for protected mode Windows. Why is this still implemented in Windows 3.1 protected mode? Only Microsoft engineers have the answer.

Regardless of the reason, your program still has to compete for this available space, and there is no way to extend it further. Even systems with 32MB RAM are bound by this restriction. (This, along with the 64K GDI and USER heaps mentioned below, is among the most restrictive pieces of code in Windows today). Windows programs all require some of this "below the line" memory in order to function, and all will allocate some fixed memory. Sometimes programs will allocate storage in this area although the memory required is not fixed. These are "misbehaving" programs, and will chew up this space quickly. Fortunately, PowerBuilder prevents us from being able to grab this scarce resource for ourselves. Unfortunately, this also means we have no control over what does or doesn't.

C programmers will be familiar with the GMEM_FIXED memory allocation, and possibly GlobalDosAlloc. Both of these functions will try to allocate memory below the 1MB line. A program such as heapwalk.exe (with the Windows SDK or C++ compilers), will allow you to view the allocated memory blocks below the 1MB line to determine more accurately which applications are eating up your most valuable resource. Also, experiment with the LoadHigh features of MS-DOS. Loading high frees up conventional memory, but r at the same time educes the amount of upper memory available. Balance is the key. (See the program MemScan, included for you on the CD.)

Other Windows resources

There are two other resources used in Windows that often cause applications some grief. These are the USER and GDI resources. These resources, like the task database area described above, are limited by Windows and not by your machine's capabilities. They have a 64K limit. This means that the amount of memory you have on your machine usually will *not* play a part in out-of-memory situations.

GDI resources are probably more well-known than the USER resources. GDI resources are handles to resources and device contexts used in your application. Every bitmap, icon, cursor, DataWindow, user object, and window will require these resources. Large custom toolbars are the biggest culprits of GDI mania, but are by far the least of your problems. Every window, DataWindow, and button will use up GDI resources—and these will, almost without fail, be the first resource that dwindles down below twenty percent free. At that point you are at the mercy of the system, and may or may not get your next object opened.

USER resources are also required by each object. If a user object comprises a collection of objects, each of these objects needs USER resources (handles, task management, etc.)–so the call for dynamically opened and closed objects might prove beneficial. To make use of a DataWindow as a collection of objects is also a good way to place less of a burden on these resources, since a DataWindow is truly a single object.

It should be quite clear now that you have far less memory available for applications than you might at first think. Windows95 apparently will alleviate this problem...but that remains to be seen.

Monitoring resources dynamically

Finally, I would like to share some routines with you that will help keep track of your system resources at runtime. A few simple SDK function calls, and your application will be in much more control of its fate. We are again going to use a nonvisual object as the SDK interface object, but you can declare the SDK functions as global external functions, and write global functions to access them, if you prefer. I like encapsulation and prefer to work within the scope of a redistributable object. This object will be declared either as needed, or within your application object as an instance variable.

Step 1:

Create the API access object NVO_API_ACCESS.

Create a user event for declarations, NVO_UE_Declarations, and trigger this event from the constructor event.

Create a user event for setup–NVO_UE_Setup–and post this event from the Constructor. (Yes, posting events in nonvisual objects is a feature of PB 4.0.)

Step 2:

Declare the following local external function:

```
//*****************************************************************
//** Windows API Functions for Resource monitoring
//*****************************************************************
FUNCTION uint GetFreeSystemResources(uint SysResource) LIBRARY 'user.dll'
```

Step 3:

Declare the following instance variables:

```
Private:
/* Resource minimum limits */
Long    il_usermem_limit
Long    il_gdimem_limit
Long    il_memory_limit
Long    il_standard_threshhold

/* Constants for resource access */
Integer sdkUser=0, sdkGDI=1, sdkResources=2
```

Step 4:

Create the following user object functions:

```
//*****************************************************************
// FUNCTION:   NVOF_Check_Resources
// PURPOSE:    To check system resources
// ARGUMENTS: (None)
// RETURNS:   integer
// 1 - Success, < 0 - Failed. Value * -1 indicates the resource that failed.
//
//*****************************************************************

/* Function checks all vital system resource for violations */

if GetFreeSystemResources(sdkUser) < il_usermem_limit THEN
 return (sdkUser * -1)
end if

if GetFreeSystemResources(sdkGDI) < il_gdimem_limit THEN
 return (sdkgdi * -1)
end if

if GetFreeSystemResources(sdkResources) < il_memory_limit THEN
 return (sdkMemory * -1)
end if

Return 1
```

Step 5:

We need to create a function to establish our limits.

Create function NVOF_Set_Resource_Limit. Input argument is an integer called ai_ResourceType containing one of the available resource constants and a threshold limit for that resource type.

```
//*****************************************************************
// FUNCTION:   NVOF_Set_Resource_Limit
// PURPOSE:    Sets resource threshhold limits
// ARGUMENTS: integer  ai_resourcetype
// (constant value indicating resource type)
//       integer ai_threshhold
// (value indicating threshhold limit)
// RETURNS:   integer
// 1 - Success, -1 - failed.
//
//*****************************************************************
```

```
/* Set the resources limit */
Choose Case ai_ResourceType
 Case sdkGDI
 il_gdimem_limit    =    ai_Threshhold
 Case sdkUser
 il_usermem_limit   =    ai_Threshhold
 Case sdkSystem
 il_Memory_Limit    =    ai_Threshhold
End Choose

Return 1
```

Step 6:

In the Declarations event, set the il_default_threshold to a number you feel comfortable with. Thirty percent is about the lowest you want resources to go to without warning the user, so we will use this as our default value.

Declarations Event:
il_Default_Threshold = 30

In the Setup event, build default functions to set the threshold limits. (The functions allow you to reset these limits at runtime as well. Set limits higher during development to ensure that resources will be okay when in production mode.)

```
NVOF_Set_Resource_Limit(sdkUser, il_Default_Threshold)
NVOF_Set_Resource_Limit(sdkGDI, il_Default_Threshold)
NVOF_Set_Resource_Limit(sdkMemory, il_Default_Threshold)
```

Summary

Instantiate the object. By calling the object's NVOF_Check_Resources() function before opening a window or dynamically opening a user object, or when creating an object, you can determine whether or not you have sufficient resources to allow your application to continue to open normally. These functions can also be called from anywhere within your application (as long as the object is instantiated) to reset limits or to check resources.

I hope that these techniques will help you to develop faster and safer applications. Happy PowerBuilding!

CHAPTER 36

Introducing Client/Server Technology to Your Organization

By Randy Hompesch

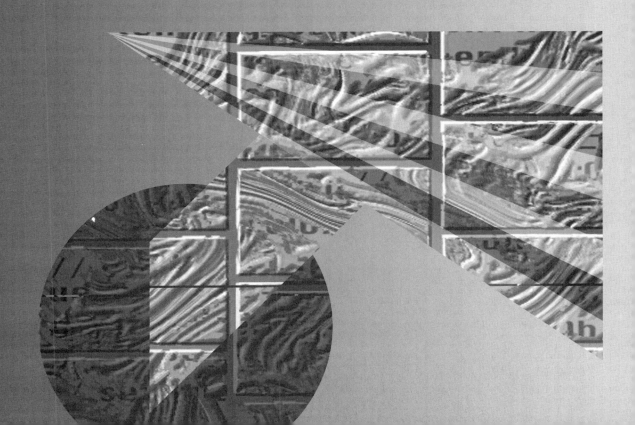

Introducing Client/Server Technology to Your Organization

by **Randy Hompesch**

I. Client/Server is the Answer....

Now, what was the question? Client/server (C/S) technology is the current, most favored buzzword in the computer industry. Every application development tool vendor is targeting this market, and many traditionally mainframe- and midrange-based application software firms are migrating their products to this hot new environment. Every applications programmer who is interested in staying abreast of technology is attempting to get management to fund course work from the C/S development tool vendors. But before we get too carried away, consider yourself in the position of this corporate IS Project Leader as he or she gets a visit from a high level IS manager.

Manager: We have decided that it's time our firm caught up with the industry trends and got on the client/server bandwagon. So we'd like you to develop this new mission-critical Flowerpot Tracking application using the best client/server technology you can find.

PL: Sounds good, I'd really like the opportunity. Who will the users be, where are they located geographically, and how much of their time can I have for the requirements specification phase?

Manager: The users are scattered throughout our branch offices, so they really can't be practically consulted. The project sponsor has agreed to give you fifteen percent of Sally's time for the next few weeks to help you out. She used to do this job and can tell you all about what the users need. Use prototyping and that RAD/JAD stuff–all you need to do is bang out a prototype while the user is watching and the requirements should be just about complete. Sally is available next Monday. How long do you think you'll need?

PL: I really won't know until I've had some time to talk to Sally and get some idea of the scope of the project. We really should make an effort to talk to the remote users too–after all, they're the ones who are going to be running this software once it's developed. How much money have you budgeted for travel?

Manager: We sold the VP of Flowerpots on this project by showing him how much time his people will save because of the ease of use of the software. We estimate each of his people will save five hours a week using this new system instead of their text-based mainframe/midrange application. We also heard that there's as much as a tenfold increase in productivity by using client/server tools, so we budgeted $100,000 for the whole project.

PL: How did you come up with that figure?

Manager: Well, we estimated it would cost about $1,000,000 if we were doing it with our existing mainframe/midrange platform using procedural languages, so we just divided this by ten.

PL: Okay, but I don't really know much about the details of this technology. I've read a lot but I'm a mainframe/midrange COBOL/RPG programmer. How much time can I have to research this area and pick some tools? I'd also like help from some of the other IS groups, and we need to talk to the database administration group about our requirements for a database server.

Manager: From everything we've read, this technology is so easy to use and offers such productivity gains that we've committed to a very short development cycle, so you'll have to get moving on the tools. You've got a lot of years in this business; we know you'll pick the best toolset. Don't worry about the database server. Joe's group is using one and they're having no problems.

PL: But how about support? Joe is only using this as the engine for a single-user system, and that user is local. I think we'll probably also need some help from Telecommunications and PC Support. I don't even know what kind of equipment our remote users have.

Manager: That shouldn't be a big deal. I think they all have PCs, and we've been buying some pretty powerful ones lately. And the network is just fine–everyone already has terminal emulation to our mainframe/midrange.

PL: What about my team? I'd like to have some say in picking whom to work with. John and Mary have both expressed interest in client/server tools and I know Bill has done some research on his own on development tools. I know George has some pretty good SQL skills, which we'll probably need and....

Manager: Look, we're working this in with our existing workload. Moe, Larry, and Curley are just coming off of the Underwater Accounting system–they're good COBOL/RPG programmers so we're going to assign them to your team full time. This system has very high visibility and we're really counting on your team to lead our organization into this technology. We've built some real expectations in the user community and they're anxious to start. When can you meet with Sally to get this thing on the road?

What should the Project Leader in this hypothetical but not too far-fetched scenario do? The correct answer of course is to run, not walk, to the nearest Human Resources rep or headhunting firm. That tinkling sound you hear in the future is not the users showering the hapless Project Leader with praise, but rather his career going down the drain!

It might seem that this is completely unreasonable, but many high level individuals, both users and IS, have been completely taken in by all of the trade press regarding C/S technology. The software tool vendors haven't done us developers any favors either. It's hard to come up with a convincing argument as to why your project should take longer and cost more than anyone thinks when they've all seen that slick presentation where the sales rep builds a working application right in front of their eyes during an hour-long product demonstration.

In this chapter I'd like to impart some information that may be helpful to you if you are in a position to migrate your organization to a C/S environment, or have been asked to provide input on such an effort. It is by no means exhaustive, and the conclusions and recommendations are my own. As they say on TV, the opinions expressed do not necessarily reflect those of this station, the software tool vendors, or anyone else at all! I'll try to explore some of the more common mistakes and oversights, some of which I've learned by hard experience, some from seminars and conferences, and the rest from other embattled developers who are expected to turn this technological panacea into working applications.

Since technical and environmental issues differ so drastically between organizations, it tends to be easier to concentrate on mistakes to avoid than to offer specific suggestions applicable to the reader's own environment. But I will try and focus on some of the good practices, and give some tips that I hope will increase your chances of success. You might be surprised to find that most of these things you already know. But first let's start slowly with some basics– after all, there may be some managers reading this!

II. What is Client/Server Technology?

This is an obligatory section of every article, book or presentation concerning C/S, so I guess I can't ignore it. My answer to "What is C/S?" is "What do you want it to be?" Almost any system in which more than one machine participates will be considered a C/S implementation by someone. If you said that a DOS Paradox application on one PC, with its data files on a file server, was a C/S implementation–I wouldn't argue. However I *would* argue that a system where data is downloaded from a host machine to a PC file, then manually imported into a PC database, is not a C/S application. Hmm...maybe both machines should be involved in the process at the same time. I'll have to think about that.

It's easier to say what C/S is not. Client/server technology is *NOT*

simple or easy

inexpensive

rapid (at least not at first)

a reason to abandon sound MIS principles.

If you read no further, but remember these four points, you have probably gotten eighty percent of the value I had hoped from this chapter!

Client/server has probably as many different definitions as there are industry "experts" trying to make a living by lecturing on the subject. In the simplest sense, this technology involves one process that performs services for another process. In most cases, these processes run on different machines, but this is not, strictly speaking, a requirement. When using Dynamic Data Exchange (DDE), for example, the processes both run on the same Windows-based PC. In this case the only real difference between the client and server processes is that the client is the one that initiates the conversations. Other than that, they can both request and supply information, terminate the conversation, and are essentially peers in the relationship.

But let's get practical and just look at the more common implementation. In most cases the client is a PC, usually running Windows, although OS/2 and Macintosh operating systems are also supported by many C/S products. When people think of the server they usually picture a dedicated machine running a database engine (with Oracle and Sybase being the current front runners in this arena). The application software actually runs on the Windows PC, requesting data from the server via some dialect of SQL (Structured Query Language). The server processes the request and returns the information, or performs the function and also supplies information to the client indicating the success or failure of the requested operation. When the application ends, the conversation between the client and server machines terminates.

There are a great many other types of servers, though, and they are becoming far more popular. Communications servers have been around for quite a while. You could even consider a Novell file server to be a provider of services (shared file storage and printing)! More recent entries into this arena include specialized data handling engines optimized for decision support applications. These are called On-Line Analytical Processing (OLAP) servers and are supplied by an increasing number of vendors. Similarly, Lotus Notes is becoming extremely popular and useful in corporations desiring workflow automation and groupware solutions, and is another specialized type of server.

In fact, the only real difference between these specialized servers and the venerable database engine is the method by which requests are made. With database servers, the conversation is conducted in some dialect of SQL. With the others, the conversation is usually conducted via a set of proprietary APIs called by the host language.

Although C/S technology is usually associated with "down-" or "right-" sizing, it is not necessarily integral to either of these processes. Many firms have downsized mainframe applications to midrange platforms without any C/S component at all. Nor is C/S technology necessarily going to be either smaller, cheaper, or faster for application development than traditional mainframe or midrange implementations. The promise is there, and now that the C/S toolsets are becoming more robust, it is largely being realized–but is far from guaranteed. You can miss delivery dates, overrun budgeted estimates, and disappoint end users just as well with a C/S application as you can with COBOL and IMS DB/DC on a mainframe. In fact you can prove you don't know what you're doing far faster with this technology than with traditional main/midrange-centric development!

III. The Architecture of a Client/Server Implementation

There is no one correct system architecture for C/S computing.

The simplest architecture is two-tiered. You merely hook PCs up to your existing midrange or mainframe platform and use the database engine which is currently running on the host as your database server. This approach has one major drawback.: all of the data access from the C/S applications will be occurring on the host machine, which is currently being utilized to run all of your production applications too. Unless you have a great deal of spare capacity on these boxes, you will soon be looking at upgrading some comparatively expensive platforms.

The most common model is the three-tiered architecture. It involves mainframe machines at the top level, and then an intermediate level of midrange or "superserver" machines running a Relational Database Management System (RDBMS). The third level is composed of PC clients who are interacting with the RDBMS. Client/server functionality provides the linkage between the PC clients and the RDBMS. The mainframes normally run legacy systems, either custom developed in third (e.g. COBOL, PL/1, RPG...) or fourth (FOCUS, NOMAD, RAMIS...) generation languages.

Many organizations find themselves with a need for a fourth level. The middle RDBMS level of the architecture is split in half to a single enterprise-wide RDBMS server and a set of distributed RDMS engines, usually of lesser power but running the same RDBMS as the enterprise server. This addition to the model allows PC client interaction via C/S technology with both the enterprise and/or the local RDBMS servers, depending on the end users' need for information access and aggregation. This configuration has the advantage of distributing the computing power closer to the end users, and is especially popular with companies that have a large number of remote sites.

For this architecture, the transmission of data from the enterprise to and from the local remote site RDBMS engines becomes a critical component. Most of the large RDBMS vendors offer some capability to allow automated transfer of all, a subset, or individual transactions between RDBMSes on different machines based on a predefined selection set and scheduling parameters.

To help you visualize the various scenarios, consider the example of a Sales Reporting application implemented in C/S technology for a multi-divisional company. The Order Processing application resides on a mainframe, and customer service reps take orders all day long. At night a batch program runs that cuts invoices for all orders shipped that day and also prepares an extract file of the sales activity. This extract file is transferred to a unix machine running an RDBMS, where it is loaded into the database. The preparation, transfer, and loading of the extract file are normally done by custom-developed programs and scripts. The following day the end users running Windows look at the data, report on it, and perform "what if" and modeling etc. using a variety of custom-developed C/S applications and packaged PC software applications.

At night, updated forecasts may also be extracted from the RDBMS and transferred into the mainframe system. Data may also be replicated between the central unix machine and remote PC or unix servers on scheduled intervals during the day or night. The central RDBMS may hold data for all divisions, but in the early morning, after the sales extract file from the mainframe has been loaded, replication scripts developed using the RDBMS vendor's proprietary scripting language take the subset of data belonging to the Widget division, extract it into a file, transfer it over the network, and then load it into a similar RDBMS engine running in the Widget division's offices.

As you can see from this example, there are a lot more components involved in the C/S environment than in traditional mainframe or midrange development efforts. These traditional platforms involve a single development language, a single file system on the same machine, and some limited interaction with that machine's operating system. There is virtually no dependence on the telecommunications network past terminal emulation, and there are normally Operations or Data Center personnel dedicated to the running of the host platform operating system and file system. It's a nice single, well supported and centralized environment, when contrasted with the complexities of our C/S architecture!

C/S complexity engenders a need for multiple support personnel, multi-faceted applications developers, middleware and/or gateway products and robust networking tools–and is the main reason why C/S technology is no longer considered to be the utopia originally propounded by the vendors.

IV. The Benefits of Client/Server Technology

With all of the inherent complexity, why would we even want to bother considering using this technology? Where are the benefits that will outweigh the costs associated with C/S computing? After all, text-based screens and green bar paper reports have been good enough for twenty years.

The single most significant answer to this question is that the users want it. Text screens and hard copy reports are no longer adequate for them to do their jobs. They have experienced the ease of use and productivity gains promised by the GUI-based PC application software packages (Word, Lotus, Excel, Harvard Graphics...) and this is the environment to which they've become accustomed. The more advanced ones are even using multiple programs at once, a capability formerly only available on mainframe and midrange operating systems.

Every desktop machine now has this ability, and users are happily cutting and pasting, importing and exporting ,and formatting data to their hearts' content. When they can set up their own databases and run mail merges on the data, it's hard to explain to them why the professionally developed mainframe and midrange systems for which they pay so much money don't have the same ease of use, capability and flexibility. The user community is increasingly demanding GUI interfaces and increased access to their own information.

Some additional benefits of C/S technology are examined below.

Scalability and rightsizing

The RDBMS can be run on a platform that is appropriate for the workload to be performed. Many RDBMSes run on a variety of different platforms. For example, Sybase runs on PCs using IBM's OS/2, Microsoft's NT, and even Novell's Netware. It also runs on a variety of unix systems including those from Hewlett-Packard, IBM, Sun, and many others. Both the Intel-based PCs and unix machines are very scalable and can be incrementally upgraded for a relatively small cost.

Faster applications development

The C/S tools offer the promise of greatly accelerated applications development. The migration from procedural languages to the event-driven paradigm can not only make the applications development life cycle shorter, but also make the resultant applications more intuitive and user-friendly.

Code reuse

Many of the current generation of C/S tools offer some level of object orientation. The ability to create complex logic or model generic business entities and encapsulate them into modules easily reused by many different applications certainly saves the cost of reinventing the wheel. Besides the time savings realized from not having to build from the ground up for each application, consistent reuse of code will also reduce the ongoing maintenance expenses and increase the accuracy of all applications using these modules. Even tools that are not intrinsically object oriented (such as Microsoft's Visual Basic) can benefit from this concept, since advanced interprocess communications protocols (DDE and OLE 2.0) allow the developer to interact with special purpose software packages already resident on the desktop. If you need complex spreadsheet-like capability, say to do a mortgage amortization calculation, just pass the parameters to a spreadsheet on the same desktop and let *it* perform the calculations. These shrink-wrapped PC applications become modules whose functionality you can incorporate into your own custom-developed programs with very little effort.

Incorporation of business rules into the RDBMS

In older technology, referential integrity constraints and business rules had to be enforced by each application program written to work against the data. For example, if customers could be deleted from screens controlled by five (or fifty!) different COBOL programs, each of those COBOL programs had to perform the logic to assure that the customer did not have an outstanding balance, had no open orders, etc. Obviously this approach is maintenance-intensive, and furthermore can never guarantee the accuracy and integrity of the corporate data resource. Moving these rules into the RDMS via triggers and stored procedures eliminates the recoding and enhances the quality of the data.

Support for open system standards

The industry is increasingly migrating away from the single-vendor-controlled "glass house" and into an environment where multiple vendors' products reside in and communicate across a communications network. Open system standards allow the business to eliminate its reliance on a single vendor, and force vendors to competitively bid against each other. They set the stage for seamless incorporation of new products and technologies as they become available, and reduce the amount of expertise necessary to keep track of multiple proprietary interfaces.

Data access is probably the most significant example of the benefits of standards. Before SQL, each database or file management system had its own proprietary access method, and programmers needed to understand the complexities of each before they could use any data stored in that format. If an MVS shop used both IMS and VSAM, programmers would have to be versed in both access methods. Once a few more systems were added, the nightmare of incompatible and inaccessible data stores became a reality. Now almost all products either offer a SQL front end (which allows SQL statements to be translated into their own proprietary access mechanisms) or are built from the ground up with SQL as the only data manipulation language.

Portability of application code

Most of the C/S tool vendors are enhancing their offerings to allow the developed applications to be run on a variety of client operating systems. PowerBuilder joins this group with this release, through deployment options for MS Windows, Macintosh, HP UX and other flavors of unix. Similarly, the emergence of database connectivity products (e.g. Q+E) and standards (ODBC, IDAPI) allow the code to access multiple different back end databases. An application, for example, that runs off of a Novell file server accessing data from an Oracle RDBMS on a unix machine in a C/S mode can also be run on a standalone laptop using MS Access as the database engine. As long as the database tables are structured and named the same, the only things the application has to worry about is changing the connect and disconnect logic for each engine and minor syntactic differences in the generated SQL.

Imagine your field sales force running the same application on their standalone laptops, with just their subset of the information, as the national sales manager runs in a C/S mode at headquarters. We may soon see the day where both the RDBMS and the client operating system are merely commodities to be chosen by each user on the basis of his or her own personal requirements.

(This is the promise, and it is real– to a limited extent. See the later section on middleware for the other side of the story!)

Effective use of all CPU cycles

The price/performance curve for desktop processors is perhaps the single most significant driving force behind C/S technology. The old Intel 286 processors (remember those?) of only a few years ago cannot run the new generation of GUI-based applications and operating systems. Never before in the industry has technology been made obsolete so quickly. As desktop processors have become more powerful and so much cheaper, it makes sense to port the presentation logic component of the application to this platform. Why have a multi-million dollar mainframe spend its expensive CPU cycles formatting a user's screen display when the same function can be performed so much more inexpensively on the user's own desktop? This can lengthen the productive life of existing mainframe and midrange investments while still delivering new application functionality. Similarly, the cost of PC- and unix-based servers is so much less than that of propriety mainframe and midrange hardware that new systems development efforts are increasingly migrating to them.

V. How to Fail at Client/Server

In this section we'll examine some of the more common mistakes made by people trying to get their first client/server project into production. This list is by no means complete (with every new project I find more things to worry about!) but it does cover the areas where I've seen most projects fail. Call it a blueprint for disaster...

Make the first project mission-critical.

Let's first discuss mission criticality. I consider a mission-critical application one where an application failure will result in lost lives or lost revenue, or which will incur significant economic penalties. I would not want to fly on an airline that used C/S technology in the cockpit. Can you imagine a Windows-based application that controls the plane hooked up to a database on a PC in the galley that has all of the flight schedule and airport layout information? The pilot uses the plane control application to put the plane into a dive, then accesses the database to get a layout of the airport that he or she is approaching. Windows locks up—and by the time the pilot reboots the system, the dive has terminated about six feet below ground level. *That's* a mission-critical application!

As C/S tools have reached the second generation (or so the industry says!) they have become more stable and reliable. Similarly, the client operating systems have increased in isolation and fault tolerance (Windows 3.1 crashes a lot less the version 3.0, and NT is even better). But why should your first effort at a completely new technology be put under this type of pressure? Don't decide to migrate to C/S for your next order processing application. The users will be far more tolerant of an occasional failure if it is not causing them a major loss.

This is a rule I'd apply to any new technology: Start slow with a pilot project that is relatively small and self-contained, but that does provide significant business benefits and has most of the components that you expect to use in future applications developed using the same technology.

Reporting and decision support applications are the ones that I've found to be prime candidates for a first foray into the world of C/S. If you can offer users a new capability that they've never had before, in a GUI environment with which they're already familiar, and which allows them to make better business decisions–they'll forgive a lot of mistakes. Due to the "read only" nature of this class of application the need to worry about transaction commit and rollback, concurrent access by multiple users, backwards and roll forward recovery schemes, and off-site storage is eliminated. This additional complexity can be ignored until later development efforts, when you have more experience with the basics of this environment and the toolset which you have chosen.

This class of application is extremely well suited for another reason: no matter how many reports are provided, most users will want to massage the data using their own tools. I've rarely met a business or financial analyst who didn't want to have the data in his or her own PC-based spreadsheet or database program for further manipulation. In many organizations this interface is currently accomplished by taking hard copy reports and retyping the numbers manually into the PC package. Show them an application where their data is displayed in their native environment (i.e. Windows) and that has seamless export (via DDE links and OLE) functionality into their spreadsheets and database packages, and they will quickly divorce themselves from the old paper-based reports altogether. This integration with the existing desktop applications will highlight some of the productivity improvements that are one of the primary benefits of C/S technology solutions.

Underestimate the first project.

Assume that everything you read in the trade journals is true and that you really can get into this new technology with no more effort than having your developers learn another programming language. Then estimate the project schedule as you would a corresponding system on the mainframe or midrange. Next divide this estimate by four to reflect the great productivity gains you're sure will result. Sell the project to management on the basis of this schedule, minimal training, and the cheapest C/S toolset that you can find advertised.

In this era of decreasing IS budgets and staffing levels and increased demand for rapid development, the risk of underestimation is quite real. Most IS development efforts need to be cost justified, and a foray into the world of C/S may seem to require selling the first project as a standalone effort, perhaps even bidding against proposals in which the system would be developed in your company's traditional toolset and host environment. This puts an unreasonable and inaccurate burden on that single application.

Most of the initial investment which you make in C/S technology will be in the areas of obtaining server hardware and software, purchasing development toolsets, providing training for your staff, evaluating and selecting your middleware or gateway product, and upgrading user and developer machines to a level where they can serve as clients. These up front expenditures are applicable to all C/S applications which you develop in the future and should not all be attributed this first project. Unfortunately, in many organizations this is exactly how the expenditure is viewed, and IS management is forced to understate many of these costs and to cut corners as often as possible in order to make this one application palatable from a cost-benefit perspective. Then even if the project succeeds (against all odds if the underestimation is severe), it is likely to overrun budget and will still taint the technology in the mind of the organization.

The correct method is to look at IS as you would any standalone business. Any business has a certain level of infrastructure and administrative overhead that must be borne merely as a cost of doing business. While no one believes that they get any competitive advantage from having a tax department, try eliminating that function and see how long Uncle Sam lets you continue to operate! In a true business these overhead costs include bookkeeping, office supplies, office space, telephone services, human resource functions, and a host of others too numerous to itemize. For IS departments the costs of network support tools, PCs, application development tools, training, and a research and development function are all part of the infrastructure costs.

Although this can be argued many ways, my feelings are that the only costs that should be attributed to a single C/S project are the incremental ones. For example if developing the first project in a C/S environment requires upgrading the telecommunications network, the upgrade costs should be attributed to the project. The same logic should be applied to the other components. I will argue that a database server is a necessary cost of doing business for any IS shop (even if just to keep abreast of the technology). So these hardware and software acquisition costs should not be counted; merely any additional money that might need to be spent to upgrade them to a production level. Similarly for the client machine upgrades: the developer upgrades are merely a cost of doing business, but end user upgrades should indeed be attributed, at least in part, to the first application developed. The research and development effort involved in toolset, middleware, and RDBMS selection should certainly not be charged against any one project.

Don't allow enough time and money for preliminary research and development. Before you can write your first line of code, you will spend many man-months involved in just researching the current hardware, software, and middleware components that make up the total solution. Skimping on the amount of time spent in this phase of the migration is sure to come back and haunt later, say about when the first project is due.

This might sound unrealistic, especially if you are in an organization which does not even have a research and development function (though if you are, you might want to start seeking new employment opportunities before you become obsolete), but time spent here in hands-on evaluations will more than pay for the costs incurred.

Research and development departments are also great places to charge for the type of upfront research and acquisition efforts required for a move into C/S technology. Since these costs are not directly allocated to any one project, the burden is fairly accounted for as a cost of doing business. If such a function is not permanently staffed in your company, you might try and sell the concept of putting together a working group to do specific research into this rapidly emerging technology on a one-time (rather than ongoingly staffed) basis. This way at least these costs are out of your hair when it comes time to use the information generated to prepare cost estimates.

The more enlightened shops don't have this problem to such a degree. They are more attuned to the need to stay competitive by keeping up with changes in technology, and tend to spend a great deal of time evaluating new toys to see if they might have a use for the corporation. Thus much of the groundwork for a C/S migration is already laid when the first project is conceived. But without IS management support for the long term benefits of C/S technology, it will be very difficult for the first project to be successful. If you're in a situation where IS manages project by project without a view to the longer term implications of technology on competitive advantage, then you have two strikes against you before you start.

Use only the first available internal resource on the team.

This mistake actually manifests itself in three ways. First, the next available people may not be the best individuals for the job. Second, failing to use external resources that already have experience with this technology means that you incur the entire cost of the learning curve for your own organization. Third, the composition of a C/S development team must differ dramatically from that of a traditional host-based development team.

With luck your management has made a long-term commitment to this technology and everyone on the development staff will eventually be exposed to it. However, for your first project you should be extra careful to select those individuals who are most likely to make a rapid adjustment to this new method of programming. The learning curve in migrating from a procedural coding environment to the event-driven (and often object-oriented) paradigm can be daunting to many individuals. Some will never be able or willing to make this transition.

For the first project, try to identify individuals who have shown an enthusiasm for new technology. If they've done some research on their own time, so much the better. I've found it is far easier to identify individuals who *want* to make transitions than to spot those who *can*— and it seems that those who want to, usually can. If a potential team member seems to be demonstrating an "Everything is fine right now, why are we bothering with this stuff" attitude, avoid him like the plague. You'll have enough to worry about without trying to keep the team together and motivated.

Once the team has been selected, be sure to provide them sufficient training opportunities. This is best done over time, giving them perhaps some small projects to work on between classes. Running a COBOL programmer with no knowledge of SQL and a brand-new PC through the entire PowerBuilder developer's series of courses in a month is not an activity conducive to maximum learning!

But training alone will not be sufficient. Consider hiring contract employees who have been through this process before. If you choose good ones and listen to their advice, their expertise will save you a great deal of time and money in the long run. Let them interact with the permanent team members, and be sure they realize that part of the service expected is the transfer of skills.

For these types of individuals you're probably better off using a smaller dedicated consulting firm than one of the Big Six. They are likely to have more hands-on experience, which is what you're really after. As a rule of thumb, I figure if potential consultants wants to spend their interview time talking about process models, business reengineering and data warehousing concepts, they are not the individuals for this job. (Question: What do you call a hundred management consultants chained together at the bottom of the ocean? Answer: A good start to any project.)

Lastly, be flexible about changing the roles of team members from the traditional Programmer, Senior Programmer, Programmer/Analyst, Sr. Programmer/Analyst... model. A client/server development team will require many more diverse skills than a traditional one and different individuals may migrate naturally to different functions. One consultant has suggested that the ideal team consists of the following functions:

Project Manager
Business Analyst
Chief User Liaison
System Architect
GUI Designer
Features Programmer
Back End Programmer
Database Analyst
Help Documentation Specialist
Usability Tester
Quality Assurance Tester.

Fortunately the Infrastructure Coordinator, Development Coordinator, System Integrator, and TQM Engineer roles are optional. I understand the spirit of the functions, but I've worked for shops that don't have that many people in the entire staff!

The points made are valid, though. C/S technology will take a lot more expertise in a lot more areas than traditional development efforts. Be open to individual team members leaning towards these functions. They all need to be done by someone, and if a person has aptitude and desire, why temper that enthusiasm by insisting on adherence to rigorous IS titles and job descriptions? Your people are your greatest asset, and this environment gives lots of opportunity to match project needs with employee desires.

This is kind of a backhand admission that you will either need more of them, or they will wear more than one hat. I told you this wouldn't be cheap!

Assume the client machines and telecommunications network are already in place.

The client machines are really not too much of a problem. Spend a little time with the prospective users and see what type of PC equipment they have installed. If you see a lot of dumb terminals around, you might want to address that issue before you start estimating the equipment costs. It is notoriously hard to do a GUI front end with a text-based terminal.

The hardware side can always be solved by money; it's the software configuration that is likely to bite you. Some shops have very good PC standards, and you'll find the same tools and setups on each machine. This makes your job relatively easy. But if every machine you touch has a different memory manager, private TSRs, and obnoxious extensions, you may need to cover yourself by including a supported platform specification in your requirements document. That way, when end users complain your system doesn't work right on their machine, at least you can point to one properly configured, show them the application working, and make reference to your document. This helps, but not much. Most PC users seem to think that everything should work together and you should know enough to make it happen.

If you're not doing the first C/S project in your organization, you should find the person who did (try looking in the nearest sanitarium if they're no longer in the office) and thank them for working out the telecommunications issues. I'll be the first to plead ignorance of the seven-layer OSI model and disavow responsibility for anything that happens after the SQL leaves my program. I personally believe that making any two machines communicate requires black magic. Intermittent communications failures are caused by people getting too close to the equipment with silver, with garlic on their breath, or with any other charm designed to protect one from the unnatural. So don't be surprised if I give very little concrete information in this section.

You need to carefully review the telecommunications setup at each site in which you expect to have users of your applications. Again it is going to come down to standards and corporate recognition of the value of similar configurations and interconnected offices. If some of your remote sites are not connected in a Wide Area Network and don't have access to the LAN on which your server is running, then you will not be able to set them up as clients. You'll have to budget for the costs involved in the WAN connectivity. If they have no local LAN at all, you will have to allow the time and money necessary to install one. Even if they do have access to the RDBMS server LAN, you will still need to test at each site to determine what else may be required.

I would recommend configuring a few remote machines before you finish your project estimates. This will allow you to test the installations, and also to verify that performance is acceptable. If it's not, you may have to dip into the project budget again and add the incremental cost of supplying more bandwidth to "underconnected" sites.

Use RAD/JAD as an excuse to ignore standards.

Rapid and Joint Applications Development methodologies and practices have become very popular lately. The emphasis in each is getting the user involved in the development process as early as possible, and for as long as possible. These techniques are basically an admission that waterfall-style system development methodologies don't suit all projects. They are actually almost identical to the prototyping methods which emerged during the mid- to late Eighties and were used extensively with fourth generation language tools (FOCUS, NOMAD, RAMIS).

As with prototyping, end users are there to provide instantaneous feedback as programmers make changes to a "look and feel" mock up of an application. For example, rather than supplying a paper document describing how a certain screen or report will look, the programmers develop it as part of the prototype and let the users interact with the working application. This gives them the ability to see how the panel itself looks and how it interacts with other components of the application. When the user is happy with the prototype, IS goes away and either refines it into the final application (by adding security, error trapping, performance enhancements, and other such elements ignored during the requirements prototyping) or uses it as a living requirements document from which the final application is developed, possibly even in a different language.

The current generation of C/S development tools lend themselves well to this type of approach. In fact I've found that it's easier to develop a panel in PowerBuilder and take a picture of it, than to produce a sample of the panel using a drawing tool. Plus the former method has the advantage that it can be immediately incorporated into the overall prototype, which is rather hard to do with a piece of paper! The danger for developers in this type of "gee whiz, look how fast he did that!" interaction is that, like the sales rep's working application in a product demo, it builds up unreasonable expectations in the minds of users. When these methods are employed, managing users' expectations becomes a major challenge and provides a real incentive to shortcut existing standards and practices in order to rush the application through to production.

Although IS has done quite a lot wrong over the last twenty years, we have at least made some attempt at quality control for development efforts. Most organizations have in place policies on how to assure consistent quality for custom development efforts, and if these are not already present or are not directly applicable to your C/S toolset, you had better take the time to develop them yourself before beginning to program.

There are several types of controls which I would recommend as a minimum for every shop:

User Signoff Points: providing documentation that the features to be included into the application are the ones that the users require. These assure that the specifications don't continually change while the application is under construction.

Naming Conventions: defining a framework for naming each component of an application (tables, windows, functions, variables etc.). This will reduce maintenance over the long term

GUI Standards: giving the application developer a set of rules to which the visual component of the application must conform. This provides consistent look and feel to all applications developed by the organization and decreases training and support requirements.

Peer Reviews: allowing each programmer's and database analyst's work to be reviewed by other project participants. This allows for the early identification of bugs and areas for improved efficiency or functionality. It also increases the overall knowledge level of the project by all participants, provides assurance that standards are being followed, and is a great way to pass along tips and techniques to less experienced developers.

Make sure you allow enough time in your project schedule for these activities. They may seem difficult to justify when the end user is breathing down your neck for you to deliver the application he or she believes they just saw working in your prototype, but they will be well worth it from a product longevity standpoint. The C/S projects that succeed share one major point in common with traditionally developed ones–the ones that succeed are the ones that are properly managed. These types of controls help to assure that the management is done properly and that the resulting system will meet the users' needs and be maintainable over the long term. Every effort should be made to resist pressure to implement any project where taking shortcuts will bypass proven and valuable control points.

Pick the wrong toolset for your organization.

I am going to assume here that the client workstations and telecommunications network are already in place within your organizations. The most common client platform is MS Windows, and the most common network operating system is Novell's Netware, so all that leaves you to choose are the database engine, the host platform for the database engine, the applications development tools, and the middleware component(s) necessary to hook up the development tools to the database engine. If the client operating system or network operating system are not already standards, get ready to choose them as well.

Remember also to at least give consideration to additional development tools outside of the pure programming one. For example, don't forget about version control software. If this is the first project your organization is doing in C/S technology it will probably fall on your shoulders to select a tool for this purpose as well. Additionally, most toolsets have a host of add-on products that should be considered in order to give yourself a jump start on your own programming efforts. With PowerBuilder you can purchase a number of third party class library add-ons. These will save you a lot of time in developing ancestor objects for your applications. These sorts of control and development productivity enhancement products should be part of your evaluation efforts.

All of these components are necessary to the success of your products and no one set is right for all organizations. This is where the research and development time comes in. Although any or all of these components may be new to you, the principles for choosing them are no different from those you need to choose any other programming tool or piece of application software.

The best way I've found is to do a high level feature comparison of from three to five of the leading projects in each of these areas. I like to stick with products that already have a significant market share. I've been burned by a company that promised a great deal in the way of capabilities in future releases, so I'm very concerned with anything that has a "1." in its version number (beware of brochure-ware, beta-ware etc.). Choosing a product with a significant installed user base should provide some hedge against risk–after all, if a lot of companies are already using the product, it should work to some degree.

After the selection of each of these components has been narrowed down to three or four, try a feature comparison to eliminate one or two more. Don't worry, each vendor will supply you a list of the features that are absolutely critical for any product in his/her market. Strangely enough, no two vendors' lists will be the same and each list will exactly match the feature set of the product being peddled (hmm....).

Preliminary evaluation can begin on each component separately, but try to defer any final purchase agreements until you have tested all selected components *together*. This is where the real difficulties lie. There are so many components involved that there is almost guaranteed to be a compatibility issue somewhere. If there's not, there will be a performance problem. And if you think performance tuning was tough on the mainframe, wait until you get to try it on a C/S architecture! There is no common model that you can use as a benchmark, and hence, few tuning tools. If performance is a critical component of your application solution, spend extra time here.

Remember that defining the toolset that is right for your organization will depend on a lot of factors besides the technical ones. Personally, I prefer a purely object-oriented toolset like Smalltalk, but would not recommend it for general use in Corporate America due to the high learning curve and dearth of truly skilled professionals. (This is one reason why I like PowerBuilder, by the way: it offers most of the practical benefits of object-oriented technology, with a gentler learning curve.) If enterprise-wide computing is important to your firm, look for C/S tools that are integrated with high end CASE tools. One of the largely legitimate knocks on C/S applications is that they tend to rely more on talented individuals than on exhaustive analysis (more art than engineering!).

If you think all of the above was a little vague and not very earth-shattering–you're right! Choosing these tools is really is no different from selecting any other software component. Test, test, and retest the products together on your site, with your application and your hardware, telecommunications and software environment. Other than that, the only real insights I can give you are encapsulated in the following.

Randy's Rules of Product Compatibility

> If the vendor claims his product works with another, it won't.
>
> If you see the two products working together during a demo, it was probably a slide show.
>
> If they work together in your environment, get a second opinion.
>
> If they still work together, wait until the next release of either. They won't.

VI. What Is This Middleware Stuff?

After all, database access is seamless and any front end tool can now talk to any RDBMS, right? If you still believe that after reading this far, how would you like to hire a virtual consultant?

Although SQL is the industry standard data manipulation language and is now employed in practically every modern database management engine, there are major differences in dialects and implementations. The SQL standard is the result of the SQL Access Subgroup of the American National Standards Institute (ANSI). This subgroup is composed of representatives from various vendors and the business community and is designed to set the technical specifications for SQL. SQL thus suffers from all of the problems that plague anything else developed by a committee. Consensus is difficult to achieve when multiple competing products have different capabilities, and the compromise is usually a standard that identifies the least common denominator rather than one which optimizes the technology for business usage.

As mentioned, virtually all RDBMSes which you may wish to use as database engines are SQL-compatible. Then why is "middleware" required? Middleware consists of the products that let the SQL generated by the front end application (whether a custom-developed Power-Builder application or MS Excel) communicate with the database engine. Each RDBMS implements its own dialect of SQL, and each of these possesses certain features that are not found in the SQL language as specified by the ANSI subgroup. Additionally, each RDBMS must implement SQL against its own proprietary data storage structures and algorithms. The result is that the SQL, in whatever dialect, that is sent to the RDBMS server must be parsed into a set of lower level instructions particular to the data access methods utilized behind the scenes by the RDBMS.

There are two types of middleware products. The first are the native APIs supplied by the RDBMS vendor. Sybase's product, for instance, is called Open Client, and this software is an additional component that must be purchased for and installed on each client machine. These APIs have the benefit of allowing you to use the specific SQL extensions offered by that vendor in its superset of ANSI SQL. Extensions include the ability to do outer joins (the ANSI standard is limited to the inner equijoin), remote procedure calls, top and top percentage SELECT statements, etc. The SQL which you prepare from your program code is passed to the API on the client machine and from thence sent to the RDBMS, which processes the statement and returns the result set (if any) and the vendor's return codes.

This type of middleware product is supplied by the RDBMS vendor, not by a third party. The problem is that it binds you to that particular RDBMS. If you use Oracle or Sybase as your engine and implement the native API of that vendor as your middleware, you have access to all of the features of their SQL dialect, but these are not going to be the same ones offered by another vendor. Although the native APIs are the fastest and most reliable middleware products, they don't allow you to view the RDBMS engine as a commodity. Any functionality that you use past the ANSI standard can most likely not be ported to another engine without modification. This tends to be less of a problem for corporations than for software vendors. You will most likely use a single RDBMS for the C/S applications custom-developed by your organization, while the vendors of front end tools and products are selling into a market in which they may be called upon to support a variety of back end database engines.

The second type of middleware addresses this cross-platform requirement. It sits between the RDBMS engine and the application program to translate the SQL prepared by the program into the dialect of *any* supported RDBMS. The most popular of these products support Microsoft's Open Database Connectivity standard (ODBC), which has emerged as the de facto standard in the industry. Competing, though less widely used, specifications include IDAPI (Borland/Lotus) and DRDA (IBM). All such specifications define the datatype conversions, the specific SQL dialects, and the return code indicators that must be adhered to. Most also allow a pass-through capability that sends on the SQL with no conversion and merely remaps the vendor-specific return codes to those specified by the standard. These middleware products can either live on each individual client or on a separate machine that acts as a gateway.

Although ODBC is a prevalent industry standard and middleware products can be found to link virtually any RDBMS with any front end product, the concept does have its drawbacks. As illustrated, it requires an additional layer of software on each database call–and this, of course, adversely impacts response time for the application. Additionally, these products are usually supplied by a third party vendor, and you now have to deal with compatibility issues between three vendors' products instead of just two. This will greatly increase your aggravation and testing time.

I would recommend that you use the vendors' API whenever possible. You will find it faster and more reliable than resorting to a third party ODBC middleware product. If you still feel the need to be able to change RDBMS engines over time, try to structure your application's SQL calls to use as few vendor-specific extensions as possible. Where you must, see if another RDBMS to which you might want to connect supports the same extension. If this is the case you can still probably get away without a third party middleware layer. I think you'll find that the compatibility issues you encounter over time and the performance degradation you'll suffer will be worse than if you tried to stick with the vendor's own APIs, but as usual this will depend to a large degree on your organization's standards and your application's requirements, so you'll have to make your own decisions after testing several options.

VII. So Where Do We Go From Here?

If reading about all the potential mistakes, pitfalls, and issues to be dealt with have made you feel like the transition to client/server computing is going to be a lot like herding spiders, Good! I've successfully eliminated some of the wide-eyed enthusiasm that one of the larger contributors to failure. But take heart: many firms have indeed made the transition and are reaping the benefits, and there is no reason why yours can't do so as well. As long as you meet a few preconditions.

CHAPTER **37**

Proper Placement
of Script

By Scott Virtue

Proper Placement of Script

by **Scott Virtue**

In object-oriented programming, a key ingredient for project development is the proper placement of the code or, in PowerBuilder, script. Where script is placed can make a substantial difference in application performance and maintenance. PowerBuilder provides the developer many ways to execute the same action. This flexibility can lead to a randomized method of script placement, which can lead to future pitfalls. In the following chapter I will discuss the proper placement of code. I will try to answer questions that at times may be overlooked. When should code be placed in events as opposed to functions? Should we place script in a control event or in an object event? In general, what placement of code will allow us to develop and maintain an application most efficiently?

A common method of coding that does not always utilize object-oriented programming to the fullest is the coding of controls. At the purest level, all script should be at the object level. Objects, such as windows and user objects, should be self-contained, to keep the logic centralized in one location. Keeping all of the logic together makes the code easier to debug and maintain. Another benefit is that when changes occur—and we know changes *always* occur—the object will be less prone to unwanted side effects.

Now let's discuss how we achieve this. Lets take, for example, the case where a user depresses a command button on a window. Instead of writing the associated action in the clicked event of the command button, we should post to a window user-defined event. (This is similar to the way that we code menus: menus initiate actions; they do not perform the actions themselves.) By placing this code at the <u>window level</u> we can initiate the action in our user-defined event easily from a command button and, in the case of sheets, from a menu item. By creating this user-defined event, our code now has more accessibility from other areas of the application.

A benefit of window level user-defined events is that similar logic obtains between windows and will always be kept in the same event. This is especially useful when all or most windows in an application are inherited from a main or ancestor window. In this case any button or menu item can call the event that has the associated logic. This allows all windows in an application to have a uniform layout, which makes it extremely easy for maintenance work to be done by a developer who may be looking at the window for the very first time. In the illustration shown here we see some user-defined events for a window that may be used as an ancestor for other windows.

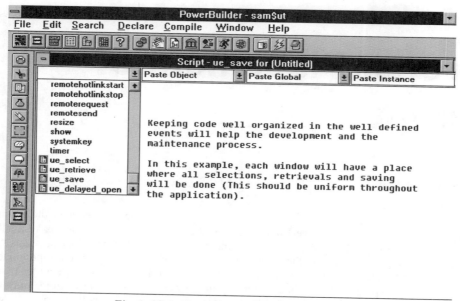

Figure 37-1: Common user-defined window events.

You can see that simply by laying out the user-defined events in an organized and logical manner, maintenance is greatly improved. Each window of the application will handle similar logic in the same event. As per our example, the initial retrieve for each window will be handled in the event ue_retrieve.

We can now see the advantage that can be gained by using events appropriately. When do we use functions? Also, what type of function–object level or global–is appropriate in each situation?

Functions are a powerful and useful tool provided to us in PowerBuilder. This tool, though, should not be overused. Functions should be employed only when their logic will be accessed from more than one place in an application. The overhead required to call a function that is used in only one place cancels any benefits that the function might offer. If a piece of code is used in a variety of places, then a function becomes very beneficial. What scope do we then give our function? Function scope should be kept to a minimum, dependent on the required use of the function. We should try to keep functions at an object level, such as window or user object functions. Only in the case where a function will be used globally throughout an application should global functions be used.

There are a few other points that should be passed along. The open event in a window should have a minimal amount of script. The reason for this is that a window does not begin to be "drawn" until the open event has been run. This leaves the user waiting for the window to appear, and possibly getting the impression that your application is running slowly. Though not coding the open event will not speed up the opening of the window, the user will get the impression that it is faster. Instead of placing a large amount of code in the open event, you should post to a user-defined event that will run once the window is drawn.

The placement of code is sometimes discarded as a secondary issue in development. With the proper placement of scripts, a developer can reuse code to its fullest. That will shorten development time and improve organization and effectiveness which will, in turn, promote maintainability and performance.

CHAPTER **38**

Using the Windows API The Other 500+ PowerBuilder Functions

By Bruce Armstrong

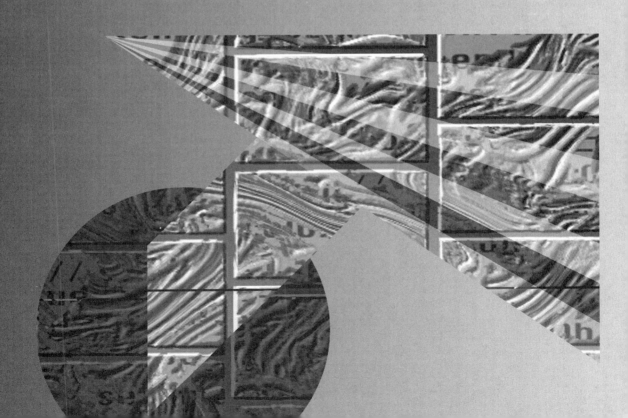

Using the Windows API The Other 500+ PowerBuilder Functions

by **Bruce Armstrong**

Working with Windows

Automatic scroll bars

By default, MDI sheets are resizable. Of course, this gives the user the ability to make the window smaller than you originally specified it. Unless you provide scroll bars, the user would then be unable to access some of the controls on the window. On the other hand, there's no need to provide the scroll bars unless the window is actually too small to show all the controls.

Many MDI applications address this by only turning the scroll bars on when the window is too small to show all of the controls and turning them back off when it is properly sized. Unfortunately, PowerBuilder doesn't supply a feature to handle this automatically for us, but it's easy enough to add ourselves.

We could do that without bothering with the Windows API calls. However, if the user has scrolled the window when the scroll bars were on and then resizes it large enough that the scroll bars are turned off, we need to move the window back to its original before we remove them. We can still do that without a Windows API call, all we need to do is send a message to the window. However, in this example we want to check to see if the user scrolled the window and only send the message if they did. To do that, we need to determine (a) the range for the scroll bar and (b) the current position of the thumb on the scroll bar. To do this, we need to use two Windows API calls: GetScrollPos and GetScrollRange.

Putting it together

To implement them, the first thing we need to do is declare them as local external functions in the window where we want to use them. In the local external function dialog box, add the following:

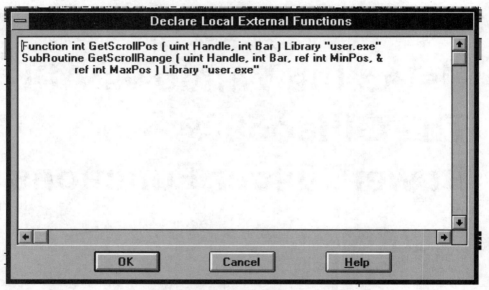

Figure 38-1: Local external functions for scroll bars.

Also declare the following as instance variables in that window:

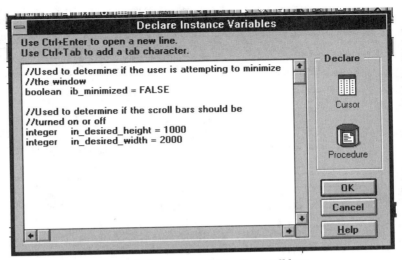

Figure 38-2: Instance variables for scroll bars

As indicated, the two integer variables are used to determine what size triggers the addition or removal of the scroll bars on the window. Of course, this would require you to set those two variables in each window. To make this window even more generic, we could define a window-level function that could parse the control[ ] attribute of the window during the open event to determine what those variables should be set at. We won't be covering that in this example, though.

The Boolean instance variable is used to determine if the user is attempting to minimize the window. If so, we need to deal with the scroll bars somewhat differently. We'll discuss that a little later.

In the open event, add the following script:

```
//Set the number of page down/ups needed
// to scroll entire window
//Not required, but convenient

this.LinesPerPage = 10
this.ColumnsPerPage = 10
this.UnitsPerLine = this.in_desired_height * .009
this.UnitsPerColumn = this.in_desired_width * .009
```

What we want to do is monitor the resize event and, depending how the user resizes the window, vary the scroll bar status. The problem is that removing or providing the scroll bars causes another resize event. Therefore, attempting to directly manipulate the scroll bar status within the resize event will cause recursive calls to that event, something we would like to avoid.

To prevent that, we're going to define a series of custom user events that will remove or provide the scroll bars for us. In the user event dialog box, enter the following:

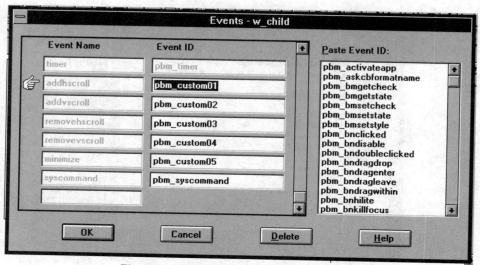

Figure 38-3: Custom user events for scroll bars.

There is an additional user event declared above that we will discuss later. For now, add the following to the first four custom user event scripts:

AddHScroll user event

```
//Turn on the scroll bar
this.hscrollbar = TRUE
```

AddVScroll user event

```
//Turn on the scroll bar
this.vscrollbar = TRUE
```

RemoveHScroll user event

```
//Declare local variable
uint WinHandle
integer ScrollPos, MinPos, MaxPos

//Get the window handle
WinHandle = Handle ( this )

//Determine the position of the scroll button
ScrollPos = GetScrollPos ( WinHandle, 0 )

//Determine the range for the scroll bar
GetScrollRange ( WinHandle, 0, MinPos, MaxPos )

//Scroll the window
IF ScrollPos > MinPos THEN Send ( WinHandle, 276, 5, 0 )
ScrollPos = GetScrollPos ( WinHandle, 0 )
```

```
//Turn off scroll bar
this.hscrollbar = FALSE
```

RemoveVScroll user event

```
//Declare local variable
uint     WinHandle
integer  ScrollPos, MinPos, MaxPos

//Get the window handle
WinHandle = Handle ( this )

//Determine the position of the scroll button
ScrollPos = GetScrollPos ( WinHandle, 1 )

//Determine the range for the scroll bar
GetScrollRange ( WinHandle, 1, MinPos, MaxPos )

//Scroll the window
IF ScrollPos > MinPos THENSend ( WinHandle, 277, 6, 0 )

//Turn off the scroll bar
this.vscrollbar = FALSE
```

We need to add some code to the resize event to determine when these custom events should be called.

Resize event

```
//If we're trying to minimize the window, don't process this
IF ib_minimized THEN
  Return
ELSE

//Otherwise, see if the scroll bars are needed
  IF this.width < in_desired_width AND NOT this.hscrollbar
THEN PostEvent ( this, "AddHScroll" )

  IF this.height < in_desired_height AND NOT this.vscrollbar
THEN PostEvent ( this, "AddVScroll" )

  IF this.width > in_desired_width AND this.hscrollbar
THEN PostEvent ( this, "RemoveHScroll" )

  IF this.height > in_desired_height AND this.vscrollbar
THEN PostEvent ( this, "RemoveVScroll" )
END IF
```

We need to add one more piece of code before we're done, and then we'll explain how it all works. Add the following to the syscommand user event:

Syscommand event

```
//If the user is trying to minimize the window,
//dump the scroll bars right away
IF message.wordparm = 61472 THEN

//Tell the resize event not to process its script
ib_minimized = TRUE
```

```
//Remove the scroll bars
 this.vscrollbar = FALSE
 this.hscrollbar = FALSE
ELSE
 ib_minimized = FALSE
END IF
```

How it works

The code in the Open event simply adjusts the scroll rate for the scroll bar and the code in the AddHScroll and AddVScroll simply add the horizontal and vertical scroll bars respectively. The RemoveHScroll and RemoveVScroll do the same thing in reverse, but they do a little extra something. That's where the Windows API calls come in.

The GetScrollPos function tells us what position the thumb on the scroll bar is at for our window. What we need to tell the function, though, is what window we want the information for, and for which scroll bar. The way we "point" to windows within the Windows operating system is by referencing their "handles." PowerBuilder provides us with its own function that will tell us the handle for a window within our own application, called the Handle function. Since these custom user events are declared within the window itself, we only need to pass "this" as the argument to the Handle function. Passing 0 as the second parameter tells the function that we want the value for the horizontal scroll bar; passing 1 calls for the or vertical scroll bar.

Comparing the current scroll position to the minimum position will then tell us if the user has scrolled the window. If so, we send the window a message to tell it to scroll the window back. The message numbers associated with the WM_VSCROLL and WM_HSCROLL messages are 227 and 226, respectively. For WV_VSCROLL we send the value of SB_TOP(6), which scrolls the window to the top. For WM_HSCROLL the Windows API documentation indicates we should send the same value. However, in this case the documentation is incorrect. The value we need to send to scroll the window to the far left is 5.

All this works fine until the user tries to minimize or maximize the window. Then it displays some unusual behavior. One thing we need to keep in mind is that the WM_SIZE event, the one that the PowerBuilder Resize event traps, is set after a window is resized. However, when the user is attempting to minimize a window, we need to turn the scroll bars off before the miminization occurs. Therefore, the code we have in our Resize event won't work for us in that case.

That's why we have the extra instance variable and the code in the event mapped to the WM_SYSCOMMAND message. The value 61472 is the value that is sent with that message when the user is trying to minimize the window. Therefore, if that's what the user is trying to do, we simply remove the scroll bars in that event. One problem, though, is that this will fire a resize event. That's where the instance variable comes in. We set that instance variable in the syscommand event and then check for it in the resize event. The variable tells the resize event that the user is minimizing the window, and the resize event then knows not to process its own script. If the user takes the window out of its minimized state, the syscommand event will be fired again, but the value passed to the message won't be 61472. Therefore the only portion of the script that will get processed is the section that turns the instance variable flag off (so the resize event will begin processing itself again).

Customizing your MDI sheets

You've probably already noticed that if you open your windows as MDI sheets using Open-Sheet or OpenSheetWithParm, the windows will not always have the same characteristics that you designed them with. In particular, the following attributes of a window are overridden when it is used as an MDI sheet: window type, visible, enabled, control menu, minimize box, maximize box, resizable, and title bar. In fact, unless you specify Original as the last argument in the OpenSheet or OpenSheetWithParm call, even the size and position of the window will be overridden. About the only things that aren't overridden when you open a window as an MDI sheet using OpenSheet or OpenSheetWithParm are the color and scroll bar attributes!

There may be cases, however, when you want to keep some of the attributes of the window style the way you defined them, even if they don't comply with the standard for MDI sheets. Some of those attributes (i.e. size and position) you can readily modify using standard PowerScript. However, others are not directly accessible to you from there. Fortunately, those style settings are accessible through a couple of Windows API functions, GetWindowLong and SetWindowLong.

Putting it together

The first thing we need to do is declare those two functions as local external functions within our window, preferably in the ancestor window for all of our MDI sheets.

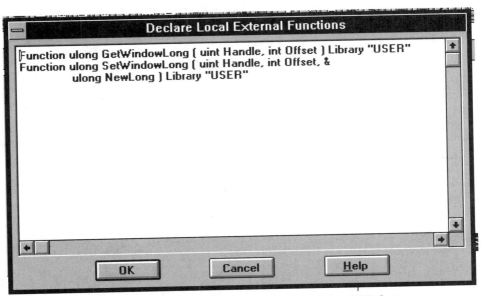

Figure 38-4: Local external functions for customizing MDI sheets.

Like the GetScrollPos and GetScrollRange functions discussed above, the GetWindowLong and SetWindowLong functions accept a handle to a window as an argument. (They will also accept handles to other window objects, but we won't be getting into that here). Both also take another argument, the offset. There are three possible values for the offset when working with a window object: GWL_WNDPROC (-4), GWL_EXSTYLE (-20) and GWL_STYLE (-16). All of the window style settings that we need to worry about are obtained by referencing GWL_STYLE, so we won't be concerning ourselves with the other two possible settings for this value. Both functions also return the value that the style setting for the window had when the function was called as a Long datatype. The primary difference is that the SetWindowLong function also passes a new value for that style setting.

You'll note that we only get one value back, yet that value somehow represents all of the style settings for the window. The key is that each of the possible style settings has a numeric value. Because of the way that the numeric values are assigned, it is possible to determine which of those style settings have been enabled. The following table will be helpful in trying to explain the method used to determine this:

Style	Hexadecimal	Decimal
WS_MAXIMIZEBOX	00010000	65,536
WS_MINIMIZEBOX	00020000	131,072
WS_THICKFRAME	00040000	262,144
WS_SYSMENU	00080000	524,288
WS_HSCROLL	00100000	1,048,576
WS_VSCROLL	00200000	2,097,152
WS_DLGFRAME	00400000	4,194,304
WS_BORDER	00800000	8,388,608
WS_MAXIMIZE	01000000	16,777,216
WS_CLIPCHILDREN	02000000	33,554,432
WS_CLIPSIBLINGS	04000000	67,108,864
WS_DISABLED	08000000	134,217,728
WS_VISIBLE	10000000	268,435,456
WS_MINIMIZE	20000000	536,870,912
WS_CHILD	40000000	1,073,741,824
WS_POPUP	80000000	2,147,483,648

One thing to notice about this table is that the values are a series of numbers that are a multiple of 2 greater than the previous number. This means, then, that it is not possible to add any combination of these number together and have them equal the value of one of the other numbers. This technique is used frequently within Windows, and is often called bitwise operations. Notice also that there are also some nonsensical combinations. You wouldn't actually define a window as being both WS_CHILD *and* WS_POPUP, or both WS_MINIMIZE *and* WS_MAXIMIZE.

Unfortunately, PowerBuilder doesn't have a set of built-in bitwise operators. There are some third-party products (i.e. FUNCky for PowerBuilder) that provide such functions. We may also simply develop some script that can perform the operations for us, albeit crudely. The following is one example:

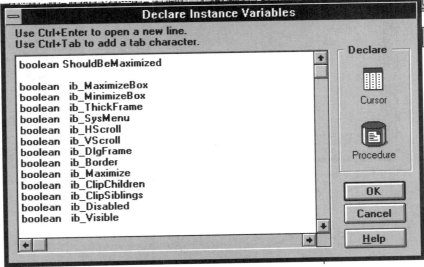

Figure 38-5: Instance variables for bitwise operations scripting.

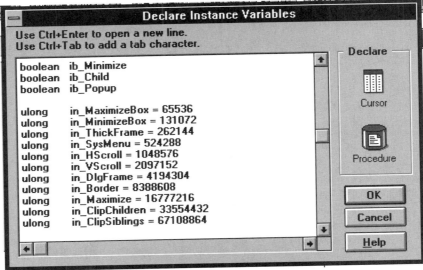

Figure 38-6: Instance variables for bitwise operations scripting, continued.

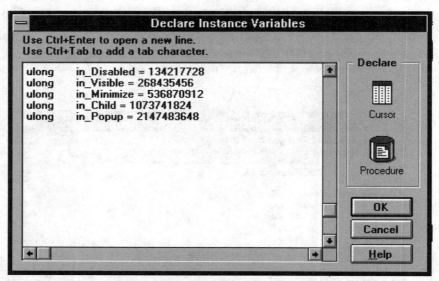

Figure 38-7: Instance variables for bitwise operations scripting, continued.

fw_check_style

```
//Returns:  boolean
//Arguments:
// an_window_style  ulong   reference
// an_style_value   ulong
//See if the window is the referenced style

IF an_window_style >= an_style_value THEN
  an_window_style = an_window_style - an_style_value
  Return TRUE
ELSE
  Return FALSE
END IF
```

fw_read_window_style

```
//Returns:    boolean
//Arguments:  none
//Declare local variables

ulong ln_window_style
  ln_window_style = GetWindowLong ( Handle ( this ) , -16 )
  ib_popup = fw_check_style ( ln_window_style, in_popup )
  ib_child = fw_check_style ( ln_window_style, in_child )
  ib_minimize = fw_check_style ( ln_window_style, in_minimize )
  ib_visible = fw_check_style ( ln_window_style, in_visible )
  ib_disabled = fw_check_style ( ln_window_style, in_disabled )
  ib_clipsiblings = fw_check_style ( ln_window_style, in_clipsiblings )
  ib_clipchildren = fw_check_style ( ln_window_style, in_clipchildren )
```

```
      ib_maximize = fw_check_style ( ln_window_style, in_maximize )
      ib_border = fw_check_style ( ln_window_style, in_border )
      ib_dlgframe = fw_check_style ( ln_window_style, in_dlgframe )
      ib_vscroll = fw_check_style ( ln_window_style, in_vscroll )
      ib_hscroll = fw_check_style ( ln_window_style, in_hscroll )
      ib_sysmenu = fw_check_style ( ln_window_style, in_sysmenu )
      ib_thickframe = fw_check_style ( ln_window_style, in_thickframe )
      ib_minimizebox = fw_check_style ( ln_window_style, in_minimizebox )
      ib_maximizebox = fw_check_style ( ln_window_style, in_maximizebox )
Return TRUE
```

fw_set_window_style

```
//Returns:    boolean
//Arguments   none
//Declare local variables

ulong ln_window_style
 IF ib_popup THEN ln_window_style = ln_window_style + in_popup
 IF ib_child THEN ln_window_style = ln_window_style + in_child
 IF ib_minimize THEN ln_window_style = ln_window_style + in_minimize
 IF ib_visible THEN ln_window_style = ln_window_style + in_visible
 IF ib_disabled THEN ln_window_style = ln_window_style + in_disabled
 IF ib_clipsiblings THEN ln_window_style = ln_window_style + in_clipsiblings
 IF ib_clipchildren THEN ln_window_style = ln_window_style + in_clipchildren
 IF ib_maximize THEN ln_window_style = ln_window_style + in_maximize
 IF ib_border THEN ln_window_style = ln_window_style + in_border
 IF ib_dlgframe THEN ln_window_style = ln_window_style + in_dlgframe
 IF ib_vscroll THEN ln_window_style = ln_window_style + in_vscroll
 IF ib_hscroll THEN ln_window_style = ln_window_style + in_hscroll
 IF ib_sysmenu THEN ln_window_style = ln_window_style + in_sysmenu
 IF ib_thickframe THEN ln_window_style = ln_window_style + in_thickframe
 IF ib_minimizebox THEN ln_window_style = ln_window_style + in_minimizebox
 IF ib_maximizebox THEN ln_window_style = ln_window_style + in_maximizebox

ln_window_style = SetWindowLong ( Handle ( this ), -16, ln_window_style )

Return TRUE
```

> **NOTE:** Although the Windows API documentation indicates that the Set-WindowLong and GetWindowLong functions return (and in the case of SetWindowLong, accept) Longs, the values are actually Unsigned Longs.

How it works

Note that we have included the values of the style attributes we are comparing against as instance variables. This is done largely for simplicity in this example. Ideally, these values should be declared as instance variables in a non-visual user object that we would then create as needed in local scripts. This is because window variables, even if private, could be inadvertently modified. As a result, they don't serve well to maintain what are actually constants. Using instance variables of local created instances of non-visual user objects ensures that the values could only be inadvertently changed within that local script and would not affect their values in any other location.

*--+

The fw_read_window_style could be called from the open event of the window itself to capture the initial style of the window. It should be noted, though, that the visible attribute of the window style won't be captured, because even if the window should be visible, the WM_SHOWWINDOW message hasn't been sent to the window yet, so the window won't be visible yet. One way to ensure that we capture the actual visible status is to declare a custom user event (i.e. ue_finishopen) that we do as a PostEvent to in our Open event, and then call the fw_read_window_style function from there. Since the PostEvent function puts the call to our custom user event in the message queue, it gets processed after the WM_SHOWWINDOW message, and we get the actual visible status of our window.

The fw_read_window_style function simply calls the GetWindowLong function to get the style of the window. That value is then decoded by a series of calls to our own fw_check_style function. We start with the window style attribute that has the greatest value, and then work backwards to the one with the lowest value. This allows us to subtract the value of any attributes we find set, and to continue to use the "greater than" operator to see if the next style attribute is set. Eventually, the fw_read_window_style function will set the values of all of the instance variables used to track the window style, and the value returned from the GetWindowLong function will have been reduced to zero.

When we want to modify one of the attributes of the window style, we simply modify the corresponding instance variable(s), and then call the fw_set_window_style function. That function then calculates the value that we need to pass to the SetWindowLong function to implement the new style. If we want to implement that style as the default style for the window, we could simply call it from the same event that we used to originally read the style of the window.

Working with Menus

Adding menu options to the system menu

Figure 38-8: Example of a menu item added to a system menu.

You may find occasions when you would like to add options not to your MDI frame menu, but to the system menu (the menu that appears when you click on the control on the upper left portion of the MDI frame, see above). I find it particularly useful when I'm developing an application or utility that does not require user input. One example is a scheduler that runs on the database server and simply processes tasks. In this case, the application always runs minimized, but I might want to include a couple of menu options for controlling the application. If so, I would probably want to do this in the system menu, because that can be used without needing to allow the user to take the application out of minimized mode. This is only an example. The technique I will show you will work whenever you want to add menu options to the system menu, regardless of what state you run the application in.

Powersoft doesn't provide us with functions that can be used to manipulate the system menu. There are a number of functions in the Windows API for working with any type of function, and a couple specifically for working with the system menu. The functions we'll be looking at are: AppendMenu, DrawMenuBar, GetMenu, GetMenuItemCount, GetMenu-ItemID, GetMenuString, GetSubMenu, and GetSystemMenu.

Putting it together

Once again, the first thing we need to do is declare these functions as local external functions within whichever window we want to alter the system menu (i.e., our ancestor MDI frame and/or ancestor MDI sheet).

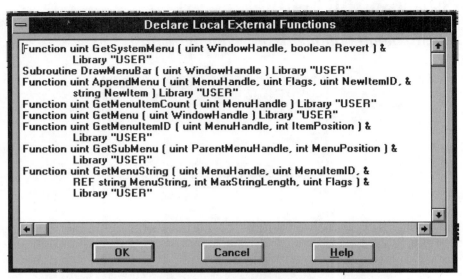

Figure 38-9: Local external functions for adding menu options to the system menu.

We also need to declare a custom user event to trap the WM_SYSCOMMAND Windows message, which is mapped to the pbm_syscommand event. This is the event that will be triggered when the user selects one of the options on the system menu, including our new option.

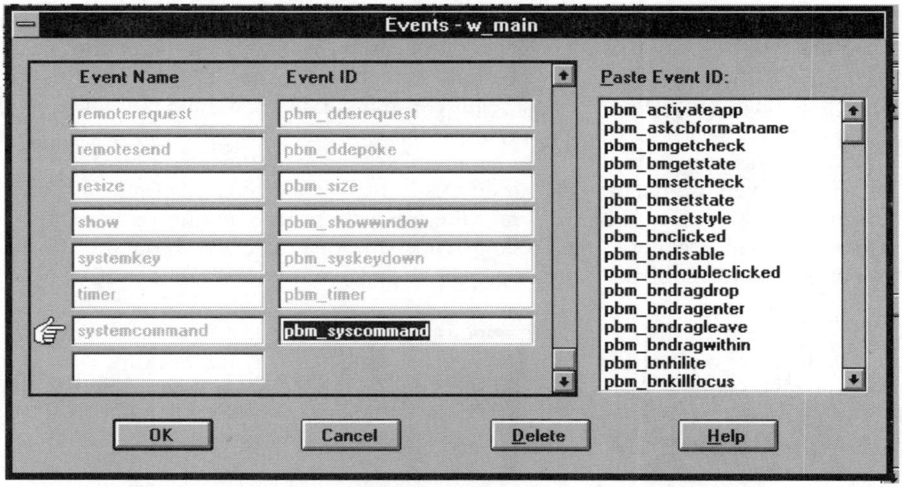

Figure 38-10: Custom user events for adding menu options to the systemmenu.

We also need to declare an instance variable in the window to track the id that we want to assign to the menu option we are adding: I've assigned an arbitrary number.

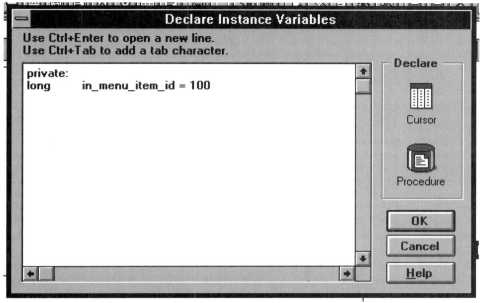

Figure 38-11: Instance variables for adding menu options to the system menu.

We then need to add the following to the open event of that window:

Open Event

```
//Declare local variables

integer ln_result, ln_mdi_items, ln_popup_items, &
ln_menu_item_text_length = 100
uint ln_system_menu_handle, ln_mdi_menu_handle
uint ln_popup_menu_handle, ln_popup_menu_item_id
string lt_menu_item_text = Fill ( " " , ln_menu_item_text_length )

//Get the handle for the menu for the mdi frame
ln_mdi_menu_handle = GetMenu ( Handle ( this ) )

//Find the last item on the main menu bar
ln_mdi_items = GetMenuItemCount ( ln_mdi_menu_handle )

//Get the handle for the popup menu for the last item
ln_popup_menu_handle = GetSubMenu ( ln_mdi_menu_handle, ln_mdi_items - 1 )

//Find the last item on the popup menu
ln_popup_items = GetMenuItemCount ( ln_popup_menu_handle )

//Get the menu item id for the last item on the menu
ln_popup_menu_item_id = GetMenuItemID ( ln_popup_menu_handle, &
ln_popup_items - 1 )

//Get the text off that menu item
ln_menu_item_text_length = GetMenuString ( ln_popup_menu_handle,
```

```
ln_popup_menu_item_id, lt_menu_item_text, ln_menu_item_text_length, 0 )

//Find the system menu
ln_system_menu_handle = GetSystemMenu ( Handle (this), FALSE )

//Add a horizontal line
ln_result = AppendMenu ( ln_system_menu_handle, 2048, 0, "" )

//Add our new item
ln_result = AppendMenu ( ln_system_menu_handle, 0, in_menu_item_id,&
lt_menu_item_text )

//Redraw the system menu with the new items
DrawMenuBar ( Handle ( this ) )
```

In this example, I want to add a menu option to the system menu that is mapped to one of the standard MDI menu options. What I will end up doing is capturing the selection of my custom system menu and triggering the MDI menu option that performs the same operation. Directly triggering that menu option would violate good object-oriented methodologies, because particular menu options within a menu aren't something that a window should directly reference. Instead, a window should call a menu-level function which would trigger the event. Maintaining the encapsulation of the menu object this way requires more code during development, but over the long haul there is less effort involved because maintenance is reduced. I can modify the menu itself significantly without having to change any windows that reference it because the windows uses the function call, which probably won't change.

Therefore, I add the following as a menu-level function:

mf_show_about

```
Returns:    boolean
Arguments: none
Return PostEvent ( this.m_help.m_about, Clicked! )
```

Finally, we add the following to the SysCommand event to check to see if the user selected our option, and if so, trigger the operation we want performed.

SysCommand Event

```
CHOOSE CASE message.wordparm
  CASE in_menu_item_id
  m_main.mf_show_about ( )
END CHOOSE
```

How it works

The majority of the work is done in the open event of the window. GetMenu, like many other Windows API commands, references a window by referring to its handle. It returns the handle to the MDI menu–which I then pass to the GetMenuItemCount function. That function reports back the number of top-level menu items on the menu. I pass this information to the GetSubMenu function, which gives me the handle to the popup menu that appears under the last option on the MDI frame.

Note that I subtract 1 from the number returned to me from the GetMenuItemCount function. That is because the GetSubMenu option is "zero-based": it counts the menu options starting with 0 rather than 1, so we need to subtract 1 to get the correct menu option.

The call to GetMenuItemID returns the identifier for the menu option we've passed, which we then use as input to the GetMenuString function. Finally, that function returns the text of the menu option.

The intent of all this is to return the text for the last menu option under the last menu item for the MDI frame (where Help/About normally appears), because I want to include that same text in the new system menu option. One good reason for doing that is that many programs include the name of the application after the word "About," so we don't know within this code what text that menu option might have.

(The obvious question is: "Why do all that?" We could have simply declared a menu-level function, like mf_show_about, that would have provided us with the same information. This is true, and might be a better way to implement that function. However, using this approach allowed me to demonstrate a number of the other menu functions in the Windows API that you might find useful in the future.)

Then comes the part of the code that we do need. The GetSystemMenu command, like the GetMenu command, accepts the handle to the window as an argument. It takes an additional argument as well. If this option is set to True, the system menu is reset to the Windows default state, and the return value has no meaning. We pass a False here because we want a reference to the system menu that we can alter, which is then what is returned to us.

We then use the AppendMenu function to create two new items on our system menu. The first is just a separator we use to distinguish our new option from the Windows default options. The second is the new menu option itself.

The first argument to the AppendMenu function is simply the handle to the menu. The second is a flag indicating the state (e.g., enabled, checked, etc.) that we want the option to appear in. In the first call, 2084 indicates the menu separator; and in the second case, 0 indicates that our new menu option should be enabled. The third parameter is the identifier for our new menu option. In the first call, it is 0, since menu separators don't have identifiers. In the second call, we pass the instance variable we declared for that purpose. The final argument is the text for the new menu option. Since menu separators don't have text, we pass a null string in the first call. In the second call we pass the text that we obtained from the MDI menu.

The last thing we do in the open event is use the DrawMenu function to force the menu to redraw itself with our changes. If the user selects any option on the system menu, the SysCommand event is fired. We then check the wordparm attribute of the message object to see which menu option was selected. If the value is equal to the id we reserved for our new menu option, we then process whatever code we want to associate with it (in this case, a call to our menu-level function in the MDI frame).

Working with Other Applications

Determining if another application is running

Putting it together

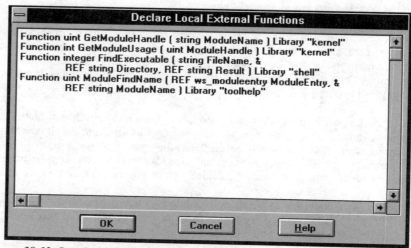

Figure 38-12: Local external functions for determining if another application is running.

fw_check_app_status

```
//Returns:        boolean
//Arguments:
//  at_filename    string
//  at_directory   string
//Declare local variables

integer  ln_size = 144, ln_result
string   lt_executable = Space ( ln_size )
integer  ln_module_usage
uint     ln_module_handle

ln_result = FindExecutable ( at_filename, at_directory, lt_executable )
IF ln_result < 32 THEN Return FALSE

//Get the module handle for the executable if loaded
ln_module_handle = GetModuleHandle ( lt_executable )

IF ln_module_handle < 1 THEN
 //It's not loaded, we're out of here
 Return FALSE
ELSE
```

```
//Find out how many instances are loaded
ln_module_usage = GetModuleUsage ( ln_module_handle )
Return TRUE
END IF
```

How it works

We've included the local external function declaration for another function that could be used to find the module for an application, ModuleFindName. However, we haven't taken the time to demonstrate its use here. The primary issue with that function is that the structure passed as the first argument requires as its first element a parameter which indicates its size. Until such time as PowerBuilder provides a SizeOf function for structures within Power-Script, use of such functions will be problematic.

We want to use the GetModuleHandle function of the Windows API to determine if another application is running. In order to do so, we need to know the fully qualified name of the file (drive and directory). We might include this in the .ini file for our own application, or (though I wouldn't recommend it) we might imbed it directly in our own executable by hard-coding it in the script. We want to be a bit more flexible than that, however. Therefore, in the window-level function shown, we first look for the win.ini file in the user's personal Windows directory.

This is because–at least for the application that we want to query on–a file association is made in the win.ini file between the application and certain document extensions. The first thing we do, then, is to look for that association in the win.ini file, so we can see where the application we are looking for was loaded from. We could either search the win.ini file ourselves, or we could use the FindExecutable function of the Windows API to find it for us. We've used the latter method here. We simply pass the file name and directory for a file that is associated with the executable we want to find, and Windows tells us the full path name to that executable. This is particularly useful when we need to run that executable if we don't find it already running.

Once we have that information, we pass it to the GetModuleHandle function. The return value from that function is a handle to the application, if it is loaded. (If it is 0, that application is not running, and in this particular function, at least, we simply exit.) If the application is running, we take the handle we just received and feed it back into the GetModuleUsage function. The return from that function will tell us how many different instances of the application are running. In our particular example we are querying against Microsoft Word, which doesn't allow multiple instances of itself to be running–but such information might be useful when working with other programs.

Making another application active

Putting it together

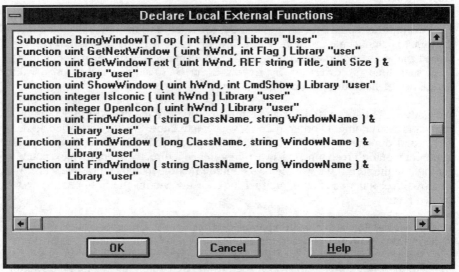

Figure 38-13: Local external functions for making another application active.

fw_make_app_active

```
//Declare local variables

boolean    lb_cont = TRUE
integer    ln_result, ln_size
string     lt_title
uint       ln_handle
ln_handle = Handle ( this )

ln_size = Len ( at_title ) + 1

//ln_handle = FindWindow ( 0, "Control Panel" )

DO WHILE lb_cont
  ln_handle = GetNextWindow ( ln_handle, 2 )
  If ln_handle = Handle ( this ) THEN Return FALSE
  ln_result = GetWindowText ( ln_handle, lt_title, ln_size )
  IF lt_title = at_title THEN lb_cont = FALSE
LOOP

//ShowWindow ( ln_handle, 3 )

IF IsIconic ( ln_handle ) > 0 THEN
  OpenIcon ( ln_handle )
ELSE
```

```
  BringWindowToTop ( ln_handle )
END IF

Return TRUE
```

How it works

Probably the simplest way to get a reference to another application's top-level window is simply to use the FindWindow function to search for it. FindWindow takes two arguments, the name of the window class for the window you are looking for and the title of the window. Note, however, that I've declared it three different ways in the local external functions. This is because you can pass a null to either of the arguments as a "wildcard." To pass a null, you declare the window argument type as long and then pass a 0 for that argument. Since we could pass a null for either argument, we need to declare the function in as many forms as it could possibly be used. When we actually use the function, PowerBuilder resolves which of the declarations we want to use and implements the correct one.

In the window-level function fw_make_app_active I've shown a sample of using the Find-Window function to search for the Control Panel window this way. It is then fairly simple to take the window handle returned by the FindWindow function and pass it to the BringWin-dowToTop function. That function would then make the Control Panel the active application.

All this works well–except for two things.

First, you don't always know the complete name of the top-level window for an application. For instance, when you are using Microsoft Word, the name of the document you are working on is included in the window title. Therefore, in that case, finding the top-level window requires another approach.

Second, the BringWindowToTop function doesn't work well if the window you're trying to make active is minimized. So we need to deal with that as well.

Actually, the second of these issues is easier to deal with. We add the IsIconic function to determine whether or not the window we want to make active is minimized. If it is not minimized, we use the BringWindowToTop function. If it is minimized, we use the OpenIcon function to make it active. That assumes, however, that we just want to show the other application in its most recent size and location. We can also use the ShowWindow function to exert more control over how the other application is shown. In the example, we pass a value that makes the window active in its maximized state. If you want to make it active in a different state, simply use one of the other values from the following table:

Value	Result
0	Hides the window (included for completeness)
1	Shows the window to its original size and position (if minimized or maximized) and makes it active (same as passing a 9)

2	Shows the window minimized and makes it active
3	Shows the window maximized and makes it active
4	Shows the window in its most recent size and shape without making it active
5	Shows the window in current size and position and makes it active
6	Minimizes the window and activates the top-level window in the system list
7	Minimizes the window without making it active (leaves the current window active)
8	Shows the window in its current state without making it active (leaves the current window active)
9	Restores the window to its original size and position (if minimized or maximized) and makes it active

To deal with the second issue, we declare a couple more functions, GetNextWindow and GetWindowText. (There is also a GetPriorWindow, but we don't need to use it.) If we pass the handle of a child window to GetNextWindow, it will cycle through all of the child windows that belong to a parent. If we pass the handle to a top-level window, however, then the function cycles through the top-level windows. It's the latter behavior we want, so the first thing we do is get the handle for the top-level window for our own application.

There are two reasons for this. The first is because we need a reference to a top-level window to start things off. The second is that we are using the GetNextWindow in a loop, and we need some indicator for when we've cycled through all of the top-level windows (in case the application we're looking for isn't there).

As we cycle through the top-level windows, we use the GetWindowText function to return their titles. The function takes three arguments: the handle of the window we want the text for, a string that we want the result returned in, and the maximum length of the field we want returned. We're going to use that last option to our benefit, because we don't want to match the entire window title, just that amount that ensures we've found the window we're looking for. For example, if we pass "Microsoft Word" to this window-level function, it determines the length of that text and adds 1. It then loops through the top-level windows looking for any that begin with that text. (Since we pass the size of the string we are going to compare against to the GetWindowText function.) If we find a match, we set the flag that takes us out of the loop and then continue. If we don't find a match, we'll eventually end up back at our own window. In that case, we simply exit this function.

Working with the Environment

There are a number of occasions during which we might need information about the environment our application is operating in. For instance, a "well-behaved" Windows application is supposed to monitor available system resources (i.e., memory) and, if it is becoming scarce, disallow certain resource-intensive operations until those resources are made available again.

For another example, we might consider what happens when our application is deployed against a number of machines that might be using video drivers with different resolutions. Since Windows has no built-in functions for automatically dealing with changing video resolutions, we might need to account for this ourselves within our application. In particular, we might want to vary the position and/or size of the windows in the application for different screen resolutions.

Finally, we might need information about what type of hardware we are operating on (e.g. the processor in use; whether or not a coprocessor is installed), or we might want to obtain or even change some of the operating characteristics of Windows itself.

All of these operations can be performed with a small number of functions that are built into the Windows API. The following is an example of some of them. Information is provided in the end of this section that explains some of the other uses of these functions.

Retrieving information from the environment

Putting it together

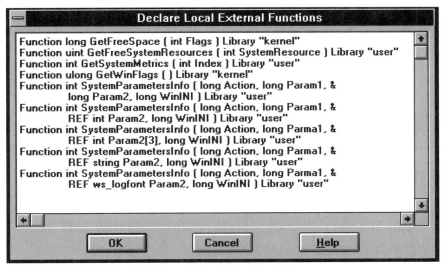

Figure 38-14: Local external functions for working with the environment: ws_logfont.

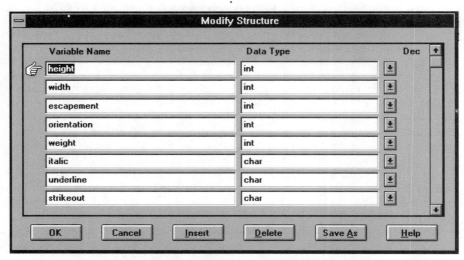

Figure 38-15: Window-level structures for working with the environment, continued.

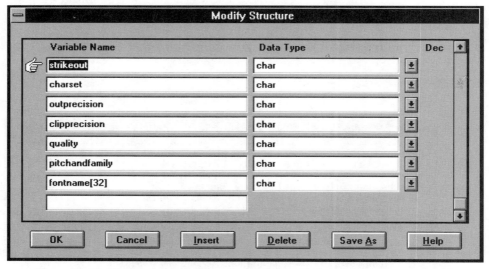

Figure 38-16: Window-level structures for working with the environment, continued.

fw_get_system_info

```
//Declare local variables

integer   ln_screenwidth, ln_screenheight
integer   ln_screensaveractive, ln_screensavertimeout
long      ln_freespace
uint      ln_system, ln_gdi, ln_user
```

```
ulong     ln_winflag
ln_freespace = GetFreeSpace ( 0 )
MessageBox ( "Free Space", string ( ln_freespace, "#,##0" ) )

ln_system = GetFreeSystemResources ( 0 )
MessageBox ( "Free System Resources", string ( ln_system/100, "##%" ) )

ln_gdi = GetFreeSystemResources ( 1 )
MessageBox ( "Free GDI Resources", string ( ln_gdi/100, "##%" ) )

ln_user = GetFreeSystemResources ( 2 )
MessageBox ( "Free User Resources", string ( ln_user/100, "##%" ) )

ln_screenwidth = GetSystemMetrics ( 0 )
MessageBox ( "Screen Width", string ( ln_screenwidth ) )

ln_screenheight = GetSystemMetrics ( 1 )
MessageBox ( "Screen Height", string ( ln_screenheight ) )

ln_winflag = GetWinFlags ( )
IF ln_winflag >= 2048 THEN
 ln_winflag = ln_winflag - 2048
END IF

IF ln_winflag >= 1024 THEN
 MessageBox ( "CoProcessor", "Is Present" )
 ln_winflag = ln_winflag - 1024
ELSE
 MessageBox ( "CoProcessor", "Is Not Present" )
END IF

IF ln_winflag >=512 THEN ln_winflag = ln_winflag - 512
IF ln_winflag >=256 THEN ln_winflag = ln_winflag - 256
IF ln_winflag >=128 THEN ln_winflag = ln_winflag - 128
IF ln_winflag >= 64 THEN ln_winflag = ln_winflag - 64

IF ln_winflag >= 32 THEN
  MessageBox ( "Mode", "Is Enhanced" )
  ln_winflag = ln_winflag - 32
  ln_winflag = ln_winflag - 1
END IF

IF ln_winflag >=16 THEN
  MessageBox ( "Mode", "Is Standard" )
  ln_winflag = ln_winflag - 16
  ln_winflag = ln_winflag - 1
END IF

CHOOSE CASE ln_winflag
  CASE 8
  MessageBox ( "Processor", "486" )
  CASE 4
  MessageBox ( "Processor", "386" )
  CASE 2
  MessageBox ( "Processor", "286" )
END CHOOSE

SystemParametersInfo ( 16, 0, ln_screensaveractive, 0 )
IF ln_screensaveractive = 1 THEN
  MessageBox ( "Screen Saver", "Active" )
ELSE
  MessageBox ( "Screen Saver", "Inactive" )
```

```
END IF

SystemParametersInfo ( 14, 0, ln_screensavertimeout, 0 )
MessageBox ( "Screen Saver Timeout", string ( ln_screensavertimeout ) )

Return TRUE
```

How it works

The first function we call in our window-level function is GetFreeSpace. This function takes one argument, which is actually ignored in Windows 3.1. (In Windows 3.0 it was used to qualify the type of memory we were asking about.) The function returns the total amount of memory available to our application, including a swap file if we are using one.

The value returned actually reflects the amount of "global heap" available, which is a majority, but not all, of the memory available to Windows. A discussion of the different types of memory within the Windows operating system, however, is beyond the scope of this chapter.

In Windows' protected mode (the default mode for Windows) this figure is an estimate. On the other hand, when applications are having problems because of a lack of resources, they usually don't run out of this memory. Instead, they usually are running low on one or more of a couple of other smaller memory pools (the GDI or USER).

The GetFreeSystemResources function is used to determine how much memory is remaining in those pools. However, as opposed to the GetFreeSpace function, which returns the information in bytes, the GetFreeSystemResources function returns a value that represents the percentage of the original pool that remains available.

The GetFreeSystemResources function takes one argument. The value of that argument determines which memory pool the function is reporting on, as follows:

Argument Value	Returned Value
0	Percentage of total system resources available
1	Percentage of GDI resources available
2	Percentage of USER resources available

The GetSystemMetrics function reports on a number of the system parameters, including the height and width of the video monitor in use (as expressed in pixels based on the resolution of the current driver). For example, when the "plain-vanilla" VGA driver that is supplied with Windows is indicated, the function reports back that the video monitor size is 640 by 480. If, however, a higher resolution video driver is in use, it might report back something like 1024 by 768.

The GetSystemMetrics function takes one argument, which determines what information it reports. As shown in our example, a 0 returns the screen width and a 1 returns the screen height. The valid arguments and the results for this function are:

Argument Value	Return Value
0	Width of screen
1	Height of screen
2	Width of the arrow button on a vertical scroll bar
3	Height of the arrow button on a horizontal scroll bar
4	Height of window title
5	Width of window frame that cannot be resized
6	Height of window frame that cannot be resized
7	The width of a dialog window frame
8	The height of a dialog window frame
9	Height of the 'thumb' (the movable button) on a vertical scroll bar
10	Width of the 'thumb' (the movable button) on a horizontal scroll bar
11	Width of an icon
12	Height of an icon
13	Width of cursor
14	Height of cursor
15	Height of single line menu
16	Width of client area for full size window
17	Height of client area for full size window
18	Height of Kanji window
19	If non-zero, indicates that a mouse is present
20	Height of the arrow button on a vertical scroll bar
21	Width of the arrow button on a horizontal scroll bar

22	If non-zero, indicates that the debugging version of the Windows shell is in use
23	If non-zero, indicates that the mouse buttons have been switched
24	Reserved
25	Reserved
26	Reserved
27	Reserved
28	Minimum width of window
29	Minimum height of window
30	Width of the bitmaps on the title bar
31	Height of the bitmaps on the title bar
32	The width of the window frame that can be sized
33	The height of the window frame that can be sized
34	Minimum tracking width of window
35	Minimum tracking height of window
36	The width of the rectangular area around the cursor within which the second click of the mouse button must occur to be considered a double-click
37	The height of the rectangular area around the cursor within which the second click of the mouse button must occur to be considered a double-click
38	Width between icons on the desktop
39	Height between icons on the desktop
40	If non-zero, indicates that the drop-down menu items are aligned along the right (rather than the left) edge
41	If non-zero, indicates that Pen-Windows is in use
42	If non-zero, indicates that double byte characters are in use
43	????

The GetWinFlags function is used to return information about the processors in use and the mode that Windows is operating in. It takes no arguments, and the value that is returned contains information about the system in a bit-masked mode. That is, the "bit" in a binary representation of the number returned indicates the status of particular feature of the system. Translated into decimal, it equates to this:

Return Value	Meaning
1	Protected mode in use
2	286 in use
4	386 in use
8	486 in use
16	Standard mode in use
32	Enhanced mode in use
64	8086 in use (time for a new machine)
128	80186 in use (time for a new machine)
256	LargeFrame?
512	SmallFrame?
1024	A coprocessor is installed
2048	The system has paging memory

The part that makes this interesting to use–at least when using a programming script language that doesn't have bit operators– is that the value returned is the sum of all applicable features. Therefore, unless we use some third-party or self-developed bit operator functions, we need to parse the information out to make it useful. (I've shown one "brute-force" method for doing this, by simply comparing for the highest bit value we might expect and then clearing that value by subtracting that value from the result, then continuing down to the last bit values.)

Finally, the SystemParametersInfo function is used to return information about some of the configurable attributes of the Windows environment. One major difference with this function is that we can also use it to *set* those attributes. Also unlike the other functions we've discussed in this section, the argument list for this function is a bit more complicated.

If you will look at the external function declarations for this function, you will note that I declared it five different ways. In each case, the function takes four arguments, and in each case the datatype of the third of those arguments changes. That is because, depending on the value of the first argument, the datatype that has to be passed to provide information to or receive information from this function varies. What happens within PowerBuilder is that the compiler checks to make sure that our use of the function matches one of those declarations. At runtime, the function uses the declaration that matches the datatypes current when it is called.

In our example, we only use one of those five different declarations. The others are shown for your reference.

When 16 is passed as the first argument, the function will report whether the screen saver is active. With this particular value for the first argument, the second argument is not used, so we provide a 0. We need to supply a variable of the appropriate datatype for the third variable, which will return the Boolean (i.e., 0=False, 1=True) to indicate the status of the screen saver. Since we aren't trying to modify the screen saver status, we pass a 0 for the fourth parameter.

Similarly, if we pass 14 for the first argument, the function returns the screen saver timeout value in the third argument. As above, the second and fourth arguments do not have meaning in this usage, so we simply pass a 0 for both.

Certain values for the first argument indicate that we want to modify the attribute of the Windows environment. In those cases, the fourth argument then has meaning as follows:

Value for fourth argument	Meaning
1	Update the WIN.INI file, but do not notify currently active applications
3	Update the WIN.INI file, and notify currently active applications

The Windows operating system notifies other applications of a change to the win.ini file by sending a WM_WININICHANGE message to all top-level windows. The valid values for the arguments of this function follow.

First	Second	Third	Meaning
1	0	integer variable	queries the warning beep status
2	new status (integer)	0	sets the warning beep status
3	0	integer array variable	queries the mouse speed and threshold values
4	0	new speed and threshold values (integer array variable)	sets the mouse speed and threshold values
5	0	integer variable	queries the multiplying factor for window border
6	new factor (integer)	0	sets the multiplying factor for window borders
10	0	long variable	queries the keyboard repeat speed
11	new speed (long)	0	sets the keyboard repeat speed
12	0	new driver (string)	sets the language driver
13	new horizontal spacing (integer)	0	sets the icon horizontal spacing
14	0	integer variable	queries the screen saver timeout value
15	new timeout value (integer)	0	sets the timeout value for the screen saver
16	0	integer variable	queries the screen saver active status
17	new status (integer)	0	sets the state of the screen saver
18	0	integer variable	queries the granularity of the desktop sizing grid

19	new grid granularity (integer)	0	sets the grid granularity for the desktop
20	0	new wallpaper (string)	sets the wallpaper for the desktop
21	0	new pattern (string)	sets the pattern for the desktop
22	0	integer variable	queries the keyboard repeat delay
23	new delay (integer)	0	sets the keyboard repeat delay
24	new vertical spacing (integer)	0	sets the icon vertical spacing
25	0	integer variable	queries the icon title text wrapping status
26	new status (integer)	0	sets the icon title text wrap status
27	0	integer variable	queries the pop up menu alignment status
28	new alignment status (integer)	0	sets the pop-up menu alignment
29	new width (integer)	0	sets the width of the area in which a second mouse click must be within for it to count as a double click
30	new height (integer)	0	sets the height of the area in which a second mouse click must be within for it to count as a double click
31	size of the structure used to retrieve the font information	ws_logfont structure	queries the font used for icon titles
32	new time (integer)	0	sets the time within which a second mouse click must be made to count as a double click
33	new status (integer)	0	sets the mouse button swap status

34	size of the structure containing the new font	ws_logfont structure	sets the font for icon titles
35	0	integer variable	queries the fast task switching status
36	new status (integer)	0	sets the fast task switch status

Working with Files, Part 1

A simple file copy routine

The Windows operating system is rather slim on low-level functions (i.e., file handling). To conduct many low-level operations, developers must obtain additional libraries (e.g., the FUNCky Library for PowerBuilder) or develop their own libraries in a language like C. We will actually look at this approach in a later section. However, we do want to illustrate one simple and fairly commonly required low-level function that can be performed using Windows API functions: a file copy.

The primary advantage of using this approach, rather than using an additional library, is that if this is the only low-level function you need, you do not need to distribute additional libraries with your application. However, if you are using an additional library to provide other services, and a file copy routine is included in that library's function set, you would probably want to simply use that function rather than take this approach.

Putting it together

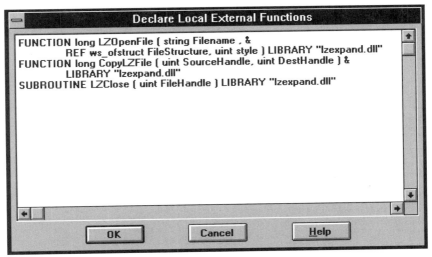

Figure 38-17: *Local external functions for a simple file copy.*

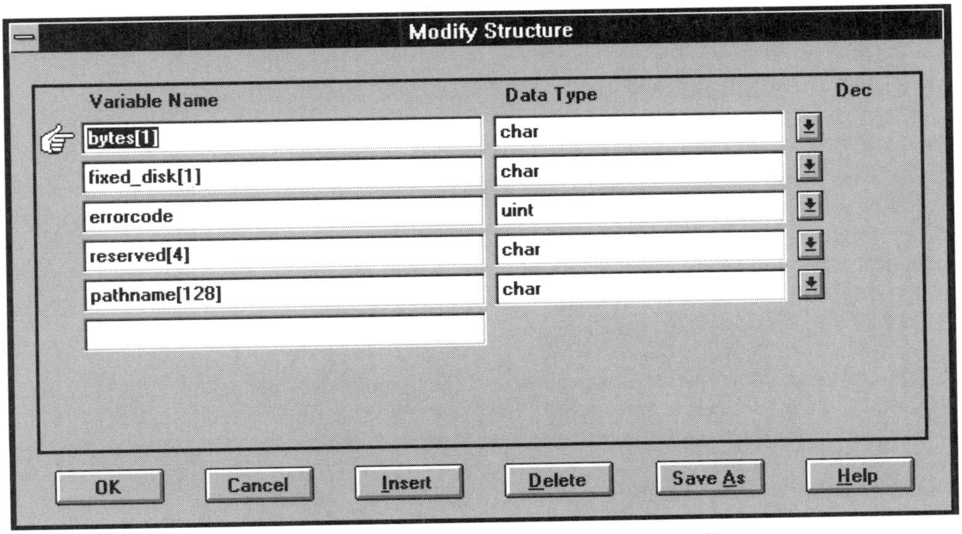

Figure 38-18: *Window-level structures for a simple file copy.*

fw_copy

```
//Returns:boolean
//Arguments:
    string   at_source
    string   at_dest
//Declare local variables
```

```
long ln_SourceFileHandle, ln_DestFileHandle, ln_result
ws_ofstruct s_SourceFileStructure, s_DestFileStructure

//Open the source file
ln_SourceFileHandle = LZOpenFile ( at_source, s_SourceFileStructure, 0 )
IF ln_SourceFileHandle = -1 THEN
  MessageBox ( "Program Error", "Could not open file: " + at_source )
  Return FALSE
END IF

//Create the destination file
ln_DestFileHandle = LZOpenFile ( at_dest, s_DestFileStructure, 4096 )
IF ln_DestFileHandle = -1 THEN
  MessageBox ( "Program Error", "Could not create file: " + at_dest )
  LZClose ( ln_SourceFileHandle )
  Return FALSE
END IF

//Perform the copy
ln_result = CopyLZFile ( ln_SourceFileHandle, ln_DestFileHandle )
IF ln_result < 0 THEN
  MessageBox ("Program Error","Could not copy file: " + at_source &
  + " to file: " + at_dest )
  LZClose ( ln_SourceFileHandle )
  LZClose ( ln_DestFileHandle )
  Return FALSE
END IF

//Close the files
LZClose ( ln_SourceFileHandle )
LZClose ( ln_DestFileHandle )

Return TRUE
```

How it works

Windows has built into it a number of functions for working with files that were compressed using the Lempel-Ziv algorithm (i.e., using the compress.exe file that comes with Windows). The LZCopy function is one of those functions and was intended as a decompression utility. However, the documentation for the LZCopy function notes that, "If the source file is not compressed, this function duplicates the original file." This makes it useful as a quick-and-dirty file copying function.

The LZCopy command takes two arguments, the handles for the source and destination files. Unfortunately, the file handle returned by the PowerBuilder FileOpen command is not the handle that this function requires. Therefore, when we use the LZCopy function of the Windows API, we need to use the LZOpenFile and LZClose functions of the Windows API as well, to make sure we have a file handle we can actually use.

The LZFileOpen command takes three arguments. The first is simply the name of the file to open. The second is a structure that will be filled with information about the file by the function. The LZFileOpen command, like the FileOpen command in PowerBuilder, is capable of creating files as well as opening them. The third argument indicates whether the function is being used to open the file for reading only (0) or creating it for writing (4096).

Once we have opened the source file for reading and created the destination file for writing, we simply pass the two file handles that were returned to us to the LZCopy function. We then use the LZClose command to close the files before we exit the function.

Working With Files, Part 2

Background

The Windows operating system doesn't have low-level operating system calls (particularly DOS function calls). In a previous section, we demonstrated how some Windows API functions could be used to obtain the same result as some low-level DOS function calls. However, for many low-level DOS functions, we need to find another approach.

One approach is to use a third-party DLL or develop our own that provides these low-level calls. For example, powersoft now markets one such third-party DLL, the previously-mentioned FUNCky Library for PowerBuilder, which contains over 500 low-level function calls.

To demonstrate how such libraries are used, we're going to implement a couple of other smaller third-party DLLs. The first, DRVPLUS, is a third-party shareware DLL that is available from CompuServe. This particular DLL provides a number of useful low-level functions, primarily file operations. The second, DIREC, is a DLL that was developed by a powersoft trainer for use in one of the training classes. DIREC is available from the powersoft BBS or from the powersoft forum on CompuServe.

DRVPLUS

Putting it together

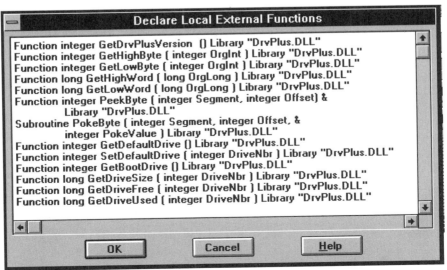

Figure 38-19: Local external functions for DRVPLUS low-level calls.

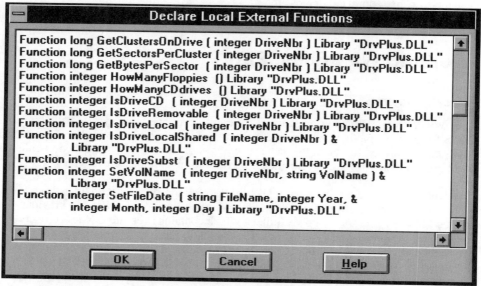

Figure 38-20: Local external functions for DRVPLUS low-level calls, continued.

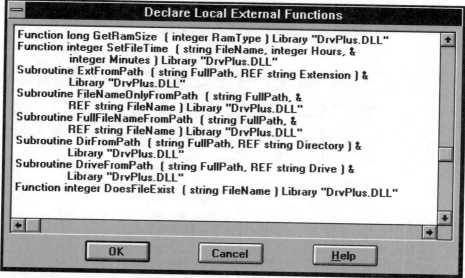

Figure 38-21: Local external functions for DRVPLUS low-level calls, continued.

GetRamSize

```
long ln_ramsize
ln_ramsize = GetRamSize ( 1 )

MessageBox ( "Ram Size", string ( ln_ramsize ) )

  DoesFileExist
  integer  ln_result
string lt_result

ln_result = DoesFileExist ( "c:\windows\win.ini" )

CHOOSE CASE ln_result
  CASE -1
lt_result = "Yes"
  CASE 0
lt_result = "No"
  CASE ELSE
  lt_result = "Error"
END CHOOSE

MessageBox ( "Does File Exist", lt_result )
```

DriveFromPath

```
string  lt_fullpath = "c:\windows\win.ini"
string  lt_drive = Space ( 255 )
DriveFromPath ( lt_FullPath, lt_Drive )

MessageBox ( "Drive From Path", lt_drive )
```

DirFromPath

```
string  lt_fullpath = "c:\windows\win.ini"
string  lt_directory = Space ( 255 )
DirFromPath ( lt_FullPath, lt_Directory )

MessageBox ( "Directory From Path", lt_directory )
```

FullFileNameFromPath

```
string  lt_fullpath = "c:\windows\win.ini"
string  lt_filename = Space ( 255 )
FullFileNameFromPath ( lt_FullPath, lt_FileName )

MessageBox ( "Full Filename From Path", lt_filename )
```

FileNameOnlyFromPath

```
string  lt_fullpath = "c:\windows\win.ini"
string  lt_filename = Space ( 255 )
FileNameOnlyFromPath ( lt_FullPath, lt_FileName )

MessageBox ( "Filename Only From Path", lt_filename )
```

ExtFromPath

```
string  lt_fullpath = "c:\windows\win.ini"
string  lt_extension = Space ( 255 )
ExtFromPath ( lt_FullPath, lt_Extension )

MessageBox ( "Ext From Path", lt_extension )
```

SetFileTime

```
integer  ln_hour, ln_minute, ln_result
string   lt_result
ln_hour = Hour ( Now ( ) )
ln_minute = Hour ( Now ( ) )

ln_result = SetFileTime ( "c:\windows\win.ini", ln_Hour, ln_Minute )

CHOOSE CASE ln_result
  CASE -1
  lt_result = "Successful"
  CASE ELSE
  lt_result = "Unsuccessful"
END CHOOSE

MessageBox ( "Set File Time", lt_result )
```

SetFileDate

```
integer  ln_year, ln_month, ln_day, ln_result
string   lt_result
ln_year = Year ( Today ( ) )
ln_month = Month ( Today ( ) )
ln_day = Day ( Today ( ) )

ln_result = SetFileDate ( "c:\windows\win.ini", ln_Year, ln_Month, ln_Day )

CHOOSE CASE ln_result
  CASE -1
  lt_result = "Successful"
  CASE ELSE
  lt_result = "Unsuccessful"
END CHOOSE

MessageBox ( "Set File Date", lt_result )
```

SetVolName

```
integer  ln_result
string   lt_result
ln_result = MessageBox ( "Warning", "Using this function will delete the &
  volume label on the disk in drive A. Are you sure you want to do this?", &
  Exclamation!, YesNo!, 2 )

IF ln_result = 2 THEN Return

ln_result = SetVolName ( 1, "" )

CHOOSE CASE ln_result
  CASE -1
```

```
      lt_result = "Successful"
    CASE ELSE
      lt_result = "Unsuccessful"
END CHOOSE

MessageBox ( "Set Volume Name", lt_result )
```

IsDriveSubst

```
integer ln_drive, ln_result
string  lt_result
ln_drive = GetBootDrive ( )

ln_result = IsDriveSubst ( ln_drive )

CHOOSE CASE ln_result
  CASE -1
    lt_result = "Yes"
  CASE 0
    lt_result = "No"
  CASE ELSE
    lt_result = "Error"
END CHOOSE

MessageBox ( "Is Drive "+ Char ( ln_drive + 64 ) + " a CD Drive?", lt_result )

  IsDriveLocalShared
  integer ln_drive, ln_result
stringlt_result

ln_drive = GetBootDrive ( )

ln_result = IsDriveLocalShared ( ln_drive )

CHOOSE CASE ln_result
  CASE -1
    lt_result = "Yes"
  CASE 0
    lt_result = "No"
  CASE ELSE
    lt_result = "Error"
END CHOOSE

MessageBox ( "Is Drive "+ Char ( ln_drive + 64 ) + " a shared &
local drive?", lt_result )
```

IsDriveLocal

```
integer ln_drive, ln_result
string  lt_result
ln_drive = GetBootDrive ( )

ln_result = IsDriveLocal ( ln_drive )

CHOOSE CASE ln_result
  CASE -1
    lt_result = "Yes"
  CASE 0
    lt_result = "No"
  CASE ELSE
    lt_result = "Error"
```

```
END CHOOSE

MessageBox ( "Is Drive "+ Char ( ln_drive + 64 ) + " local?", lt_result )
```

IsDriveRemovable

```
integer ln_drive, ln_result
stringlt_result
ln_drive = GetBootDrive ( )

ln_result = IsDriveRemovable ( ln_drive )

CHOOSE CASE ln_result
  CASE -1
  lt_result = "Yes"
  CASE 0
  lt_result = "No"
  CASE ELSE
  lt_result = "Error"
END CHOOSE

MessageBox ( "Is Drive "+ Char ( ln_drive + 64 ) + " Removable?", lt_result )
```

IsDriveCD

```
integer ln_drive, ln_result
string  lt_result
ln_drive = GetBootDrive ( )

ln_result = IsDriveCD ( ln_drive )

CHOOSE CASE ln_result
  CASE -1
  lt_result = "Yes"
  CASE 0
  lt_result = "No"
  CASE ELSE
  lt_result = "Error"
END CHOOSE

MessageBox ( "Is Drive "+ Char ( ln_drive + 64 ) + " a CD Drive?", lt_result )
```

HowManyCDDrives

```
integer ln_cddrives
ln_cddrives = HowManyCDdrives ( )

MessageBox ( "Number of CD Drives", string ( ln_cddrives ) )
```

HowManyFloppies

```
integer ln_drives
ln_drives = HowManyFloppies ()

MessageBox ( "Number of Floppies", string ( ln_drives ) )
```

GetBytesPerSector

```
integer  ln_drive
long     ln_bytes
ln_drive = GetBootDrive ( )
ln_bytes = GetBytesPerSector ( ln_drive )

MessageBox ( "Bytes Per Sectors", string ( ln_bytes ) )
```

GetSectorsPerCluster

```
integer  ln_drive
long     ln_sectors
ln_drive = GetBootDrive ( )
ln_sectors = GetSectorsPerCluster ( ln_drive )

MessageBox ( "Sectors Per Cluster", string ( ln_sectors ) )
```

GetClustersOnDrive

```
integer  ln_drive
long     ln_clusters
ln_drive = GetBootDrive ( )
ln_clusters = GetClustersOnDrive ( ln_drive )

MessageBox ( "Clusters on Drive", string ( ln_clusters ) )
```

GetDriveUsed

```
integer  ln_drive
long     ln_driveused
ln_drive = GetBootDrive ( )
ln_driveused = GetDriveUsed ( ln_drive )

MessageBox ( "Drive Used", string ( ln_driveused ) )
```

GetDriveFree

```
integer  ln_drive
long     ln_drivefree
ln_drive = GetBootDrive ( )
ln_drivefree = GetDriveFree ( ln_drive )

MessageBox ( "Drive Free", string ( ln_drivefree ) )
```

GetDriveSize

```
integer  ln_drive
long     ln_drivesize
ln_drive = GetBootDrive ( )
ln_drivesize = GetDriveSize ( ln_drive )
```

```
MessageBox ( "Drive Size", string ( ln_drivesize ) )
```

GetBootDrive

```
integer ln_drive
ln_drive = GetBootDrive ( )

MessageBox ( "Boot Drive", Char ( ln_drive + 64 ) )
```

SetDefaultDrive

```
integer ln_drive
ln_drive = GetDefaultDrive ( )

SetDefaultDrive ( ln_drive )

MessageBox ( "Default Drive", Char ( ln_drive + 64 ) )
```

GetDefaultDrive

```
integer ln_drive
ln_drive = GetDefaultDrive ( )

MessageBox ( "Default Drive", Char ( ln_drive + 64 ) )
```

PokeByte

```
integer ln_result
ln_result = PeekByte ( 64, 23 )

//Reverse the caps lock setting
CHOOSE CASE ln_result
  CASE 32
  ln_result = 64
  CASE 64
  ln_result = 32
END CHOOSE

PokeByte ( 64, 23, ln_result )

MessageBox ( "Poke Byte", string ( ln_result ) )
```

PeekByte

```
integer ln_result
ln_result = PeekByte ( 64, 23 )

MessageBox ( "Peek Byte", string ( ln_result ) )
```

GetLowWord

```
long ln_lowword
ln_lowword = GetLowWord ( 12345678 )

MessageBox ( "Low Word", string ( ln_lowword ) )
```

GetHighWord

```
long ln_highword
ln_highword = GetHighWord ( 12345678 )

MessageBox ( "High Word", string ( ln_highword ) )
```

GetLowByte

```
integer ln_lowbyte
ln_lowbyte = GetLowByte ( 256 )

MessageBox ( "Low Byte", string ( ln_lowbyte ) )
```

GetHighByte

```
integer  ln_highbyte
ln_highbyte = GetHighByte ( 256 )

MessageBox ( "High Byte", string ( ln_highbyte ) )
```

GetDrvPlusVersion

```
integer  ln_version
ln_version = GetDrvPlusVersion ( )

MessageBox ( "Drive Plus Version", string ( ln_version/100 ) )
```

How it works

Actually, the functions provided with DRVPLUS are fairly simple, and the examples I've provided should show fairly well how they are used. Of course, some of these functions are already provided in PowerBuilder, or can be implemented relatively easily using standard Windows API calls. For example, I've already discussed functions that can be used to determine system memory , as GetRamSize does here, and PowerBuilder has a FileExist function that accomplishes the same thing as DoesFileExist. All the same, there are some very useful functions included in DRVPLUS, and it's good to find them packaged together into one DLL (which means you only have to distribute the one file with your application). A few of the most useful functions contained within DRVPLUS are SetFileDate, SetFileTime, and GetDriveFree. If you aren't ready to invest in something like FUNCky for PowerBuilder yet, and you're not capable or willing to write your own DLLs, shareware DLLs like DRVPLUS are worth considering.

DIREC

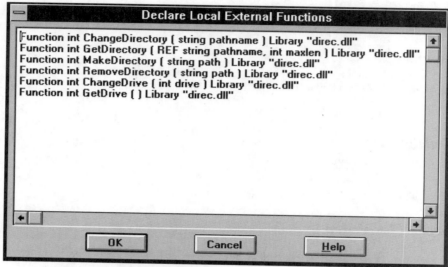

Figure 38-22: Local external functions for DIREC low-level calls.

fw_cd

```
//Returns: boolean
//Arguments
//  string  at_dir
integer ln_result

ln_result = ChangeDirectory ( at_dir )

CHOOSE CASE ln_result
 CASE 0
 Return TRUE
 CASE ELSE
 Return FALSE
END CHOOSE

fw_gd
//Returns     boolean
//Argumetns
// string  at_dir  reference

ln_result = GetDirectory ( at_dir, Len (at_dir) )

CHOOSE CASE ln_result
 CASE 0
 Return TRUE
 CASE ELSE
 Return FALSE
END CHOOSE
fw_md
```

```
 //Returns   boolean
//Arguments
// string    at_dir

integer   ln_result
ln_result = MakeDirectory ( at_dir )

CHOOSE CASE ln_result
 CASE 0
 Return TRUE
 CASE ELSE
 Return FALSE
END CHOOSE
fw_rd

//Returns    boolean
//Arguments
// string   at_dir

integer ln_result

ln_result = RemoveDirectory ( at_dir )

CHOOSE CASE ln_result
 CASE 0
 Return TRUE
 CASE ELSE
 Return FALSE
END CHOOSE
fw_cdr (string at_dir)
//Returns   boolean
//Arguments
// string    at_dir

;integer   ln_result, ln_drive

ln_drive = Asc ( Left ( at_dir, 1 ) ) - 64

ln_result = ChangeDrive ( ln_drive )

CHOOSE CASE ln_result
 CASE 0
 Return TRUE
 CASE ELSE
 Return FALSE
END CHOOSE
fw_gdr

//Returns boolean
//Arguments
string at_dir reference

integer ln_result

ln_result = GetDrive ( )

CHOOSE CASE ln_result
 CASE IS >0
 at_dir = Char ( ln_result + 64 )
 Return TRUE
 CASE ELSE
 Return FALSE
```

```
END CHOOSE
```

How it works

As good as DRVPLUS is, it is missing some things, particularly a change directory function. Fortunately, direc.dll provides a number of the standard DOS directory function commands that can be called from Windows applications. As with DRVPLUS, the functions are fairly simple and the examples I've provided clearly indicate their use.

Working with the Serial Port

Reading incoming serial data

One of the advantages of the Windows environment is that it gives the developer higher-level access to hardware control. This is particularly true for the printer ports, where the developer can code to device-independent functions and rely on Windows and the device driver for that printer to implement the request correctly. To some degree, it is true for the serial port as well. Rather than working at the device level, the developer can use a set of higher-level functions provided in the Windows API to control the port. While this does reduce some of the complexity of the problem, it still doesn't make it simple.

As an example, we're going to look at an application that reads data coming in from the serial port.

Putting it together

First we need to declare a number of local external functions for our window. In fact, we need to declare ten in all, nine that are specifically related to controlling the serial port and one (GetWindowsDirectory) that we will be using to allow the end user to configure the serial communications.

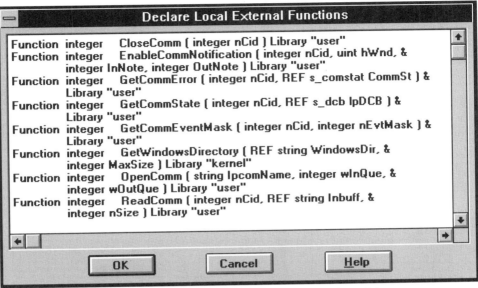

Figure 38-23: Local external functions for reading the serial port.

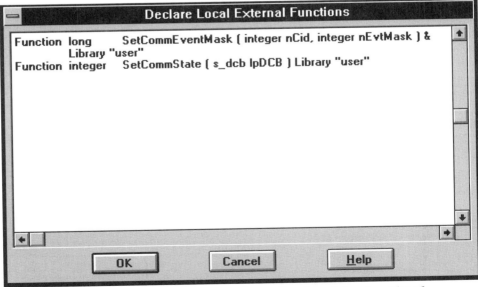

Figure 38-24: Local external functions for reading the serial port, continued.

This particular window was originally designed to serve as an ancestor object that would be inherited to provide the base functionality for a number of different serial communications requirements. Normally, we would use nonvisual user objects to encapsulate base class behavior. However, certain Windows features (e.g., DDE) require encapsulation in an object that can receive standard Windows messages (i.e., a window). In this particular case, we are going to declare a custom user event to trap the WM_CommNotify message, called the pbm_commnotify event in PowerBuilder. Once we have configured the communications port, this is the message (event) that Windows will use to tell us that there is data coming in at the serial port that we need to process.

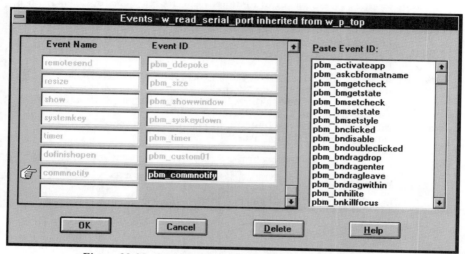

Figure 38-25: Custom user events for reading the serial port.

In order to provide for good object-oriented functioning, we want to include the majority of our code in a combination of object-level events and functions. In this particular case, we are going to use primarily object-level functions. Specifically, we define four window-level functions to do the bulk of the work in this window.

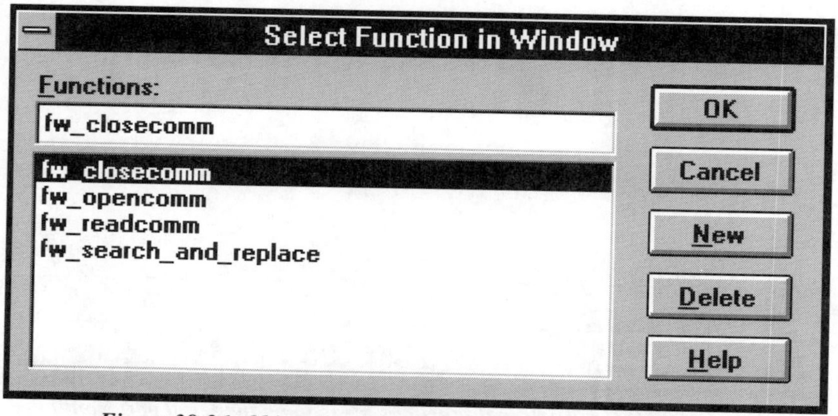

Figure 38-26: Object-level functions for reading the serial port.

The fw_closecomm event is used to shut down the communications link between this window and the serial port when the window is closed.

fw_closecomm

```
//Returns:    Boolean
//Arguments:  none
//Declare local variable
u_win_api      lu_win_api

lu_win_api = Create u_win_api

lu_win_api.CloseComm ( in_CommID )

Destroy lu_win_api

Return TRUE
```

The fw_opencomm function is used to configure the serial port and link it to this window. It is called from the open event of the window.

fw_opencomm

```
//Returns:   boolean
//Arguments
  an_trigsize  integer
//Declare local variables
character  lc_flow_control, lc_parity, lc_data_bits
integer    ln_result, ln_EventMask, ln_count = 144
integer    ln_baud_rate, ln_data_bits
string     lt_WindowsDir = Fill ( " ", ln_count ), lt_INIFileName
string     lt_com_port, lt_flow_control, lt_parity, lt_inifile_section
ws_dcb     ls_dcb

//Find the windows directory
ln_result = GetWindowsDirectory ( lt_WindowsDir, ln_count )
IF ln_result = 0 THEN Return FALSE

//Find the application .INI file
lt_INIFileName = lt_WindowsDir + "\" + i_application.appname + ".INI"

lt_inifile_section = it_inifile_section

//Read the com port from the .INI file
lt_com_port = ProfileString ( lt_INIFileName, lt_inifile_section, "Port",
"COM1:" )
CHOOSE CASE Upper ( lt_com_port )
 CASE "COM1:", "COM2:", "COM3:", "COM4:"
 lt_com_port = Upper ( lt_com_port )
 CASE ELSE
 //Default to COM1
 lt_com_port = "COM1:"
END CHOOSE

//Get the baud rate from the .INI file
ln_baud_rate = ProfileInt ( lt_INIFileName, lt_inifile_section, "BaudRate",
9600 )
CHOOSE CASE ln_baud_rate
 CASE 110, 300, 600, 1200, 2400, 4800, 9600, 19200
 //baud rate is OK
```

```
  CASE ELSE
  //Default to 9600 baud
  ln_baud_rate = 9600
 END CHOOSE

 //Get the flow control from the .INI file
 lt_flow_control = ProfileString ( lt_INIFileName, lt_inifile_section, "FlowCon-
trol", "None" )
 CHOOSE CASE Upper ( lt_flow_control )
  CASE "NONE"
  lc_flow_control = Char ( 0 )
  CASE ELSE
  //Default is NONE
  lc_flow_control = Char ( 0 )
 END CHOOSE

 //Get the number of data bits from the .INI file
 ln_data_bits = ProfileInt ( lt_INIFileName, lt_inifile_section, "DataBits", 8 )
 CHOOSE CASE ln_data_bits
  CASE 7, 8
  //Convert to char
  lc_data_bits = Char ( ln_data_bits )
  CASE ELSE
  //Default to 8 data bits
  lc_data_bits = Char ( 8 )
 END CHOOSE

 //Get the parity from the .INI file
 lt_parity = ProfileString ( lt_INIFileName, lt_inifile_section, "Parity", "None" )
 CHOOSE CASE Upper ( lt_parity )
  CASE "NONE"
  lc_parity = Char ( 0 )
  CASE "ODD"
  lc_parity = Char ( 1 )
  CASE "EVEN"
  lc_parity = Char ( 2 )
  CASE "MARK"
  lc_parity = Char ( 3 )
  CASE ELSE
  //Default is No Parity
  lc_parity = Char ( 0 )
 END CHOOSE

//Try to open the comm port
in_CommID = OpenComm ( lt_com_port, 1024, 1024 )
IF in_CommID < 0 THEN Return FALSE

//Enable communications notification to this window
ln_result = EnableCommNotification ( in_CommID, Handle ( this ), an_trigsize, -1 )
IF ln_result = 0 THEN
 fw_CloseComm ( )
 Return FALSE
END IF

//Trap communication events
ln_EventMask = 1
SetCommEventMask ( in_CommID, ln_EventMask )

//Get the current com port state
ln_result = GetCommState ( in_CommID, ls_dcb )
IF ln_result <> 0 THEN
```

```
 fw_CloseComm ( )
 Return FALSE
END IF

//Configure the com port
ls_dcb.BaudRate= ln_baud_rate
ls_dcb.bits2= lc_flow_control
ls_dcb.ByteSize= lc_data_bits
ls_dcb.Parity= lc_parity

ln_result = SetCommState ( ls_dcb )
IF ln_result <>0 THEN
 fw_CloseComm ( )
 Return FALSE
END IF

Return TRUE
```

The fw_readcomm function is used to read the data coming in the serial port. It is called by the commnotify event, which is triggered by the Windows environment when it senses data being delivered to the serial port.

fw_readcomm

```
//Returns:   boolean
//Arguments:
 string at_result reference
//Declare local variables
integer ln_result, ln_EventMask
ws_comstat ls_comstat

ln_EventMask = GetCommEventMask ( in_CommID, 0 )
ln_result = GetCommEventMask ( in_CommID, ln_EventMask )

//Read information about the event from the com port handler
ln_result = GetCommError ( in_CommID, ls_comstat )

//Padd the result string with empty spaces equal to the amount of
//characters waiting to be read in the comm port queue
at_result = Fill ( " ", ls_ComStat.cbInQue )

//Read the characters from the comm port queue
ln_result = ReadComm ( in_CommID, at_result, ls_ComStat.cbInQue )

Return TRUE
```

Serial communications often uses special characters to indicate the beginning and end of relevant sections of the data stream. The data stream may also contain characters that we want to remove or modify in order to make the data more useful to us. Therefore, we will include a function (fw_search_and_replace) in the window that can be used by descendants of this window to strip out or modify characters in the data stream.

fw_search_and_replace

```
//Returns: boolean
//Arguments:
string  at_string_to_search
string  at_char_to_find
string  at_char_to_replace
```

```
string  at_new_string reference
//Declare local variables
integerln_pos

//Find the first occurance of the character to replace
ln_pos = Pos ( at_string_to_search, at_char_to_find )

DO WHILE ln_pos > 0
//Replace the character with the new character
 at_string_to_search = Replace ( at_string_to_search, ln_pos, 1,
at_char_to_replace )
 ln_pos = Pos ( at_string_to_search, at_char_to_find )
LOOP

at_new_string = at_string_to_search

Return TRUE
```

We need to declare a few instance variables for the window as well. The first (it_serial_port_data) is used to buffer the data stream until we are ready to process it. The second (it_inifile_section) is used to indicate what section of the application INI file should be read and used to configure the serial port. This allows us to have a single INI file with multiple sections used to configure the different serial ports, or the same serial port at different times for different purposes. Finally, the last (in_commid) is used to track the reference to the serial port that was assigned by Windows when we initiated the link to the serial port. We will need this reference to read the data from the serial port and to close the link when we are done using this window.

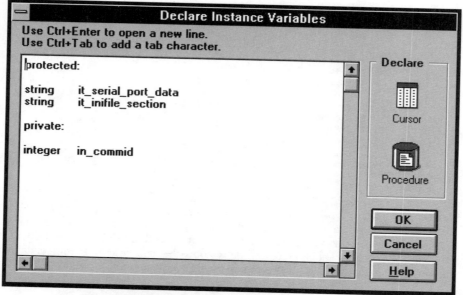

Figure 38-27: Instance variables for reading the serial port.

The functions that we will be using from the Windows API require, in some cases, arguments in the form of structures.

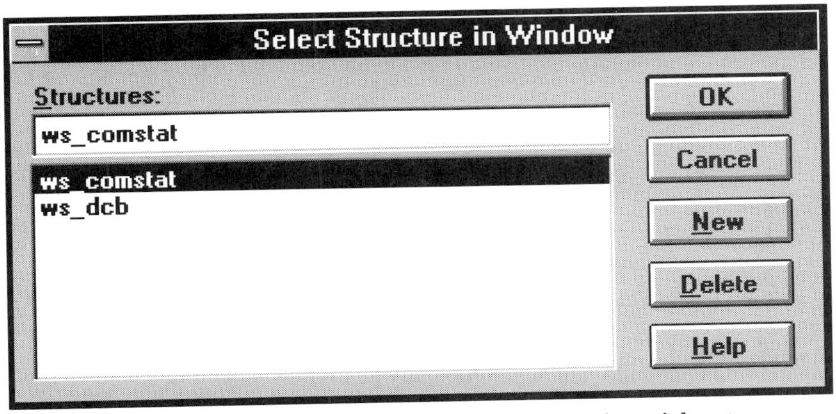

Figure 38-28: Object-level structures for reading the serial port.

The ws_commstat structure is used to determine the status of the serial port when Windows notifies us that there is data to process.

The ws_dcb (device control block) structure is used to read and set the configuration of the serial port when we establish the communications link.

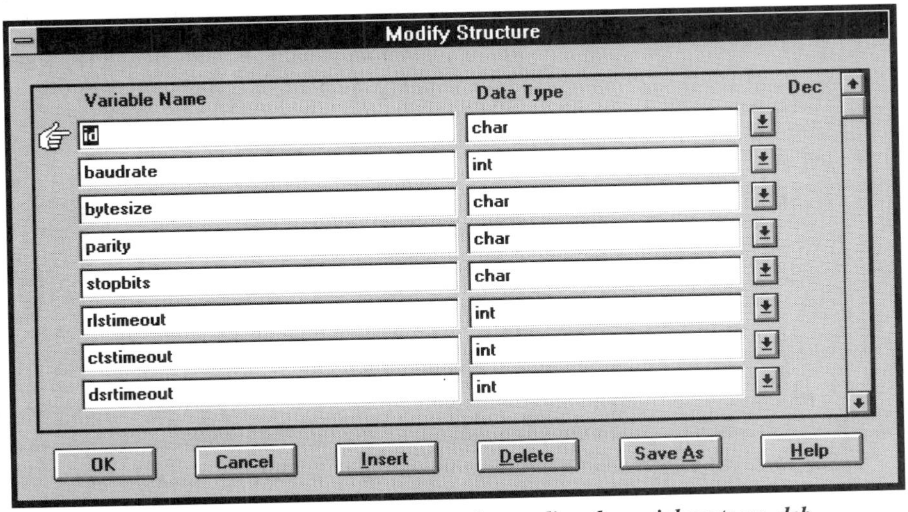

Figure 38-30: Object-level structures for reading the serial port: ws_dcb.

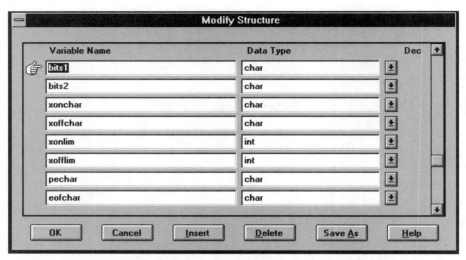

Figure 38-31: Object-level structures for reading the serial port: ws_dcb, continued.

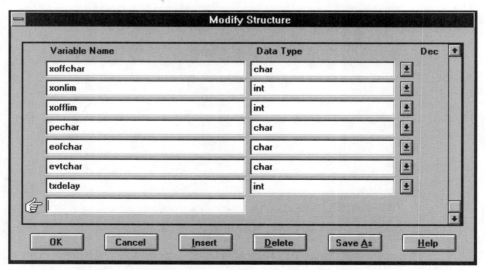

Figure 38-32: Object-level structures for reading the serial port: ws_dcb, continued.

In the close event for the window, we simply call the window-level function to terminate the link between this window and the serial port.

Close Event

```
//Close the comm port that was opened in the dofinishopen event
//if it hasn't been closed already
```

```
fw_CloseComm ( )
```

In the open event of the window, we call the window-level function that configures the serial port and links it to this window. If the window-level function fails (indicating a problem configuring the serial port) we display a MessageBox to inform the user.

Open Event

```
//Open the comm port specified in the .INI file and monitor
//it for incoming data streams
IF NOT fw_opencomm ( 1 ) THEN
 MessageBox ( this.title, "Problem Opening Serial Port" )
END IF
```

In the commnotify event, we call the window-level function that reads the pending data from the serial port into a local string. We then append that string to the instance variable string that holds the incoming data. In descendants of this object, we will also use this event to determine when or if the data in the instance variable is ready for processing. If so, we will call other window-level functions, declared in those descendants, to process the data. As the data is processed, we will remove it from the front of the instance variable.

CommNotify Event

```
//Declare local variables
string lt_serial_port_data
//Read the data from the comm port queue
IF NOT fw_readcomm ( lt_serial_port_data ) THEN
 MessageBox (this.title, "Problem Reading Serial Data")
END IF

//Append it to the instance variable that holds the
//entire result set
it_serial_port_data = it_serial_port_data + lt_serial_port_data
```

How it works

When the window opens, the fw_opencomm function is called. That function calls the GetWindowsDirectory function in the Windows API to determine where the user's personal Windows directory is at. By convention, that is where application-specific INI files are stored, so it's where we're going to search for our own application INI file. Using an application INI file means that we do not have to hard-code the configuration information for our serial communications into the application. This is important, because we don't want to force the users to employ a specific serial port in order to use the application. It also allows us to modify the communications protocol later without having to recompile our application.

The fw_opencomm looks for the section of the application INI file specified in an instance variable of the window (so that different windows can use different sections and so can be configured differently). It looks for the following keys:

Key	Use
Port	Which serial port to use (COM1 to COM4, defaults to COM1).
BaudRate	What speed the port should be configured to (110, 300, 600, 1200, 2400, 4800, 9600, or 19200, defaults to 9600).
FlowControl	What type of handshaking to use in the communications (defaults to NONE).
DataBits	The number of databits to use (7 or 8, defaults to 8).
Parity	What parity to use (NONE, ODD, EVEN or MARK, defaults to NONE)

The reference to i_application in this function is to an instance variable that is declared in the ancestor for all popup windows.(I pass a reference to the application object to all of the windows so that they can access or, if necessary, modify application-level attributes.)

This is a pop-up window because I want it to act like a nonvisual user object, but it has to be a window-type object to receive the commnotify event. Therefore, I make it a pop-up window, set its visible attribute to False, and simply open it when needed.

The function then tries to open the specified comm port and, if it succeeds, establishes a link between the comm port and this window. When the port is opened, the function establishes a 1024 byte buffer so that we don't have to constantly be processing the port.

When the link is established between the comm port and this window, we pass the argument that was passed to the function. That value determines how often the window will receive notifications that data is being received. The lower the value passed to the function, the more often that the window will process the data being collected. The function then reads the current configuration of the comm port and modifies that configuration to match that found in the application INI file.

Now, until the serial port actually receives data, the window won't do anything else. As the serial port receives data, Windows checks to see if the trigger size has been exceeded yet. If so, it sends a notification message to the window that is linked to the comm port. That's the message we trapped with the commnotify event–so when that event is triggered, we know we need to go read the comm port.

Therefore, the commnotify event calls our fw_readcomm. And that function calls the GetCommEventMask function to determine why the message occurred. It then calls the function again to clear the message.

Ideally, I would check this value to ensure that we're getting the message we want. (If we've got data to process, the value of ln_EventMask should be 1.) There are a number of other events that could occur from the serial port that might also cause this message. The possible return values for the GetCommEventMask function and their meanings are.

Value	Meaning
1	Data has been moved into the receiving queue
2	The event character has been placed in the receiving queue
4	The last character was send from the output queue
8	The clear-to-send signal changed status
16	The data-set-ready signal changed status
32	The receive-line-signal-detect signal changed status
64	A break was detected while receiving
128	A line status error occurred
256	The status of the ring indicator during the last interrupt
512	A printer error occurred
1024	Indicates the state of the CTS signal
2048	Indicates the state of the DSR signal
4096	Indicates the state of the RLSD signal
8912	Indicates the state of the ring indicator

One reason I'm not checking for those other values is because when I called the SetCommEventMask in the fw_opencomm function, I only enabled messaging for the first message. Again, a more ideal implementation would do more error checking and response than this.

The fw_readcomm then calls the GetCommError function and passes the ls_comstat structure. When that structure is returned, the cbInQue member will contain the number of characters in the input queue there are for processing. Therefore, we pad our result string with that many empty spaces (we need to pre-fill any string data that we pass by reference to a DLL or we won't be able to use the result). That result string is then passed to the ReadComm function of the Windows API in order to retrieve the pending data.

The fw_readcomm function then appends that data to the end of the instance variable we are using to buffer the incoming data within the window. In a descendant of this window, we would extend the commnotify event to call a window-level function to actually process that data.

If the data stream contains marker characters to indicate the beginning and end of valid data (which is common), we would want to parse out that data. One way to do that is to convert the marker characters into tabs and new-line characters. That's why we've included the fw_search_and_replace function in this ancestor object. Once we have done this, it is a simple matter to use the ImportString function to parse the string into a DataWindow.

Finally, we need to close the serial port before the user closes the window. To do this, we've included a call in the close event for the window to our window-level function fw_closecomm. This function simply calls the CloseComm function in the Windows API to close the comm port.

Working with the Printer

Background

One of the major "features" of programming within the Windows environment is that it provides a uniform interface for you to deal with the user's hardware. Specifically, unlike developing DOS applications, you shouldn't need to code specifically for special features of your user's printers. For that matter, you shouldn't even particularly care what kind of printer they might use. Instead, you communicate the information you want printed to the Windows API, and it (through a device driver specify to the user's printer) handle getting it printed.

Unfortunately, though it is now easier, it still isn't simple to work with printers. The functions provided in the Windows API are powerful, but they can also be complicated to use. For example, the DeviceCapabilities function (the big-brother of the earlier GetDeviceCaps function) only allows you to query on one device capability at a time, and the output of the function varies depending on the information you requested. This can make working with the function confusing for someone who doesn't use it frequently or hasn't used it before.

pprtr.dll

Fortunately, third party DLLs that simplify this interaction are becoming available. pprtr.dll is just such a shareware DLL. The device capabilities function within this DLL (PrtrCap) returns all of the device capabilities of the printer in a single function call in the form of a structure. Developers only need check the attribute(s) of the structure that they are interested in. The result is a consistent means of determining the printer's capabilities.

The DLL contains a number of other functions, which are demonstrated below.

Putting it together

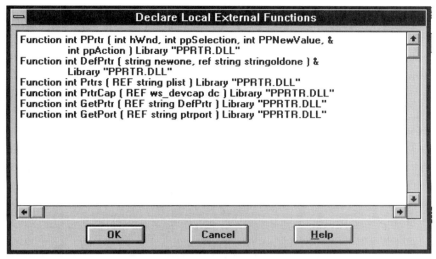

Figure 38-33: Local external functions for pprtr.dll.

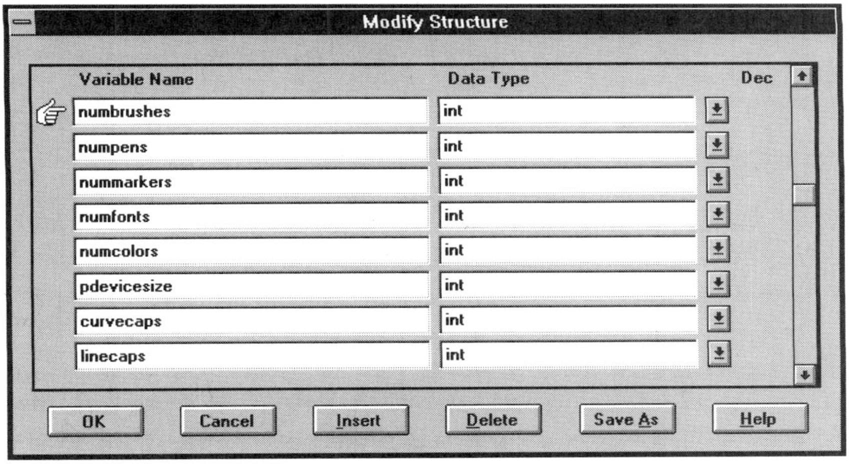

Figure 38-34: Local external functions for pprtr.dll: ws_devcaps.

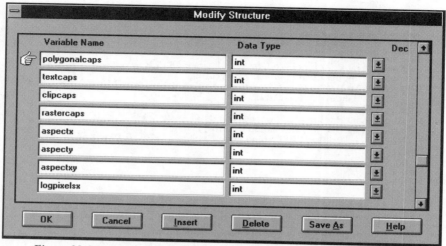

Figure 38-35: Local external functions for pprtr.dll: ws_devcaps, continued.

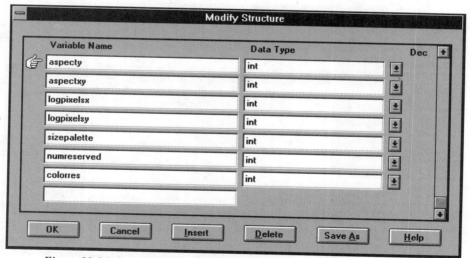

Figure 38-36: Local external functions for pprtr.dll: ws_devcaps, continued.

Individual function calls

Prtrs

```
//Declare local variables
intln_delimit_pos
stringlt_active_printers
```

```
//Prefill the string variable
lt_active_printers = fill ( " ", 255 )

//Get the list of active printers
prtrs ( lt_active_printers )

//Replace the ";" characters in the string with new line characters
ln_delimit_pos = Pos ( lt_active_printers, ";", 1 )
DO WHILE NOT ln_delimit_pos = 0
 lt_active_printers = Replace ( lt_active_printers, ln_delimit_pos, 1, "~r" )
 ln_delimit_pos = Pos ( lt_active_printers, ";", ln_delimit_pos )
LOOP

//Display the list of active printers
MessageBox ( "Active Printers", lt_active_printers )

PrtrCap
//Declare local variables
ws_devcap ls_devcap
//Get the printer capabilities
prtrcap ( ls_devcap )

//Display the version number of the printer driver
MessageBox ( "Printer Driver Version", String ( ls_devcap.driverver-
sion,"########" ) )
```

PPptr

```
//Declare local variables
integer ln_result
ln_result = pprtr ( handle(this), 1, 0, 0 )

CHOOSE CASE ln_result
 CASE 1
 MessageBox("Printer Orientation","Portrait")
 CASE 2
 MessageBox("Printer Orientation","Landscape")
END CHOOSE
```

GetPrtr

```
//Declare local variables
string lt_prtr
//Prefill the string
lt_prtr = fill ( " ", 255 )

//Get the current printer
getprtr ( lt_prtr )

//Display it to the user
MessageBox ( "Current Printer", lt_prtr )
```

GetPort

```
//Declare local variables
string lt_port
//Prefill the string
lt_port = fill ( " ", 255 )

//Get the current port
getport ( lt_port )
```

```
//Display it to the user
MessageBox ( "Current Printer Port", lt_port )
```

DefPrtr

```
//Declare local variables
string lt_newprinter, lt_oldprinter
//Prefill the variables
lt_newprinter = ""
lt_oldprinter = fill ( " ", 255 )

//Call the function that would normally change the default printer
defprtr ( newprinter, oldprinter )

//Display the current printer
MessageBox("Current Printer",oldprinter)
```

How it works

Prtrs is used to retrieve the list of available printers from the user's win.ini file. It takes a string as an argument by reference, since that is the way it will return the data. As with any other string passed by reference to a DLL, we need to fill it first with spaces to the greatest length that we might expect as a result. If we do not, the DLL will not be able to provide us with information beyond the point to which we prefilled the string.

The list of printers is returned as a string, with semicolons as delimiters between the printer names. In the example shown, we are using the PowerBuilder Replace function to convert the semicolons with new line character so that the printers will appear on separate lines when we display the string in a MessageBox. In a working application, we might replace the semicolons with tab characters prior to using ImportString to move the data into a DataWindow. Alternatively, we might also use a loop to convert the string into a string array, with one element in the array per printer.

PrtrCap is used to determine the capabilities of the printer. It takes a structure as an argument. Once again, since the data is being returned in the argument we pass it by reference. Structures, even if they contain strings, do not need to be prefilled before they are passed. They only need to be instantiated, as we have done in this example by declaring a local instance of the structure in this script.

PPptr is used to query and/or modify printer characteristics. It takes four arguments. The first is the handle of the window that called the function. The second argument is the feature that we want to query or modify. In the example, we are querying on the printer orientation. The possible values for the second argument to this function are:

Value	Feature
1	orientation
2	paper size
4	paper length
8	paper width
16	scale
256	copies
512	default paper source
1024	print quality
2048	color
4096	duplex mode
8192	y resolution
16384	true type setting

The third argument, if non-zero, indicates the new value we want to provide for that feature. The value depends on the feature we are modifying, and is fully explained in the documentation that comes with this shareware DLL.

The fourth argument indicates whether or not we are trying to modify the feature. If we pass 0, as we have done in our example, the function simply reports back on the current setting for the default printer. If we pass a 1 for this argument, the value passed as the third argument becomes the new value for the specified feature.

GetPrtr is used to determine the current printer. A string (prefilled with spaces of course) is passed by reference as the argument. The returned string contains the name of the current printer.

GetPort is used to determine the port that the current printer is pointed to. Once again, we pass a prefilled string by reference and the returned value contains the port.

DefPrtr is used to change the current printer. It takes two argument, both strings. The first argument is the name of the new printer, and the second argument is a string (prefilled and passed by reference) that will report back the name of the old printer. If the first string is an empty string, the function will simply report back the current printer. However, if we pass the name of another printer (obtained using the Prtrs function explained earlier) the passed name will be used as the new printer and the function will report back the printer that is no longer the current printer.

Functions Requiring Callbacks

Background

As mentioned previously, some of the Windows API functions require callbacks. A callback is a pointer to a user-defined function that the Windows API function should return information to. This requires a lower-level language. Products like PowerBuilder and others (i.e., Visual Basic) aren't capable of providing pointers to user-defined functions, largely because they don't compile into machine executable code. Basically, you can call a Windows API function or other DLL from your code, but a Windows API function or other DLL can't call your code.

In order for a higher-level language like PowerScript to interface with a Windows API function that requires callbacks, someone must develop a DLL that acts as a "wrapper" for the Windows API function. That is, the wrapper DLL sets up its own routine for the callback and then calls the Windows API function for you. It accepts parameters from you and will then give back the data returned from the Windows API function. One advantage of such "wrappers" is that they help mask the complexity of the function call. The disadvantage is that you don't always get all of the features that would be available if you could call the function directly.

A couple of examples that have already been developed are for the ChooseColor and ChooseFont functions in the Windows API.

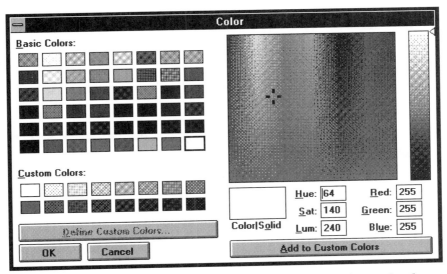

Figure 38-37: The ChooseColor function is used to display this dialog box, so that the user can select a custom color for some attribute of the application.

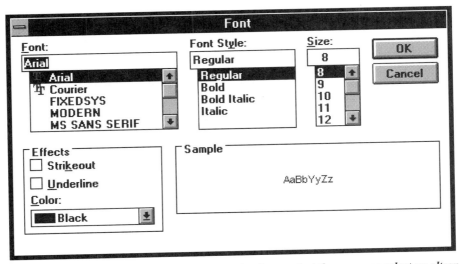

Figure 38-38: The ChooseFont shows a similar dialog box, so that the user may select an alternate font for some text in the application.

Now, at first glance, these functions don't seem to require callbacks. They both accept a structure passed by reference as an argument. A closer look shows that one element in the structures for those functions is a callback. There are a couple of wrapper DLLs available, though, for dealing with this.

ChooseColor

Putting it together

The first thing we're going to need to do is declare the function in the third party DLL as an external function within our PowerBuilder application. Just for demonstration purposes, we're just going to use a simple stand-alone window–so create a window and use the following as the local external function call. A copy of the third-party DLL is provided on the CD that accompanies this book.

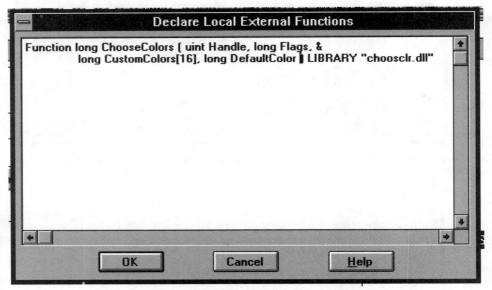

Figure 38-39: Local external functions for ChooseColor.

On the window you create, set up four checkboxes–cbx_default, cbx_full_dialog, cbx_custom_colors, and cbx_help–which will be used to set the value of flags that we will pass to the function. Create a window-level function for the window, and add the following script to that function:

fw_choosecolor

```
//Returns:   boolean
//Arguments: none
//Declare local variables
long ln_SelectedColor, ln_CustColors[16], ln_flags, ln_index

//Populate the default custom colors array
FOR ln_index = 1 to 16
 ln_CustColors[ln_index] = RGB(4*ln_index, 2*ln_index, 8*ln_index)
NEXT

IF cbx_default.checked THEN ln_flags = ln_flags + 1
IF cbx_full_dialog.checked THEN ln_flags = ln_flags + 2
```

```
IF cbx_custom_colors.checked THEN ln_flags = ln_flags + 4
IF cbx_help.checked THEN ln_flags = ln_flags + 8

ln_SelectedColor = ChooseColors ( Handle ( this ), ln_flags, &
 ln_CustColors, this.BackColor )

IF ln_SelectedColor <> -1 THEN
  this.BackColor = ln_SelectedColor
  Return TRUE
ELSE
  Return FALSE
END IF
```

Finally, put a call to the menu-level function in the script for the clicked event of the command button.

One of the options that we have when using this function is to provide a "Help" button on the dialog box. However, if we do, we need to process any request for help that the user makes. In order to do so, we're going to declare a custom use event as follows:

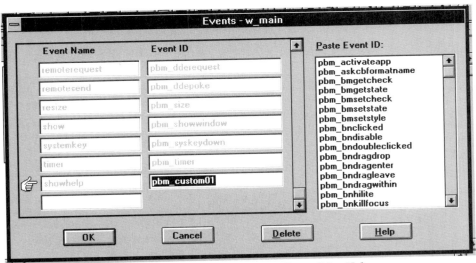

Figure 38-40:Custom user events for ChooseColor Help.

In the Other event of the window we're going to use the following script:

```
//See if the user requested help
IF message.number = 50236 THEN
 this.PostEvent ( "ShowHelp" )
END IF
```

And this script in our custom user event:

```
//Display help for the custom control dialog box
ShowHelp ( "c:\windows\winhelp.hlp", Index! )
```

How it works

If we compare the information we need to pass to this function with the information we need to provide in the structure we would need to pass if we were calling the ChooseColor function directly, we see how the use of this DLL has made using the function much simpler. The structure we would need to pass to the ChooseColor function looks like this:

Name	Data Type	Use
lStructSize	Long	Indicates size of this structure.
HwndOwner	Handle	Handle of window that is calling the function.
HInstance	Handle	Identifies a template if the Flags parameter indicates one should be used.
RGBResult	Long	The color selected by the user, and the color to show as the default if the Flags parameter indicates that a default is provided.
lpCustColors	16 element array of Long Pointers	The custom palette,, which the user may modify.
Flags	Long	Used to configure the dialog box that appears for user input.
lCustData	Long Pointer	Application defined data that is passed to the user defined function below.
lpfnHook	Uint Pointer	Pointer to a user defined function that processes messages intended for the dialog box.
lpTemplateName	Long Pointer	Name of the resource file that is used instead of the default if the Flags parameter indicates that this should be used instead.

To use the third-party DLL, we only need to specify a subset of these items. In particular, we still provide HwndOwner, Flags, lpCustColors, and RGBResult. In addition, this function separates the two purposes of the RGBResult element into two separate parameters (one for the default color and another for the user selected color). The third party DLL, however, does not require us to provide lStructSize, HInstance, lCustData, lpfnHoo, and lpTemplateName. Of course, we lose the ability to use those features of the ChooseColor function, but we don't have to deal with them when we don't want to use them, which is the majority of the time.

The function itself returns the color that the user selected, or a negative value if there was an error, or the user canceled instead of picking a color. The first parameter we pass to the function, as with many Windows API functions, is simply a handle that points to the window that called the function. The third parameter is the array of RGB values for the custom palette, and the fourth parameter is the RGB value we want shown to the user as a default (if any). The second value (flags) to the function takes a little more explanation. If we were calling the ChooseColor function directly, we could pass the following flags:

Name	Value	Meaning
cc_rgbinit	1	Use the passed value as the default
cc_fullopen	2	Show the custom colors portion of the dialog box when the dialog box is first opened
cc_preventfullopen	4	Disable custom colors
cc_showhelp	8	Show the help button on the dialog box.
cc_enablehook	16	Use the user defined function pointed to by the structure
cc_enabletemplate	32	Use the template from within the COMMDLG.DLL pointed to by the structure
cc_enabletemplate handle	64	Use a custom template pointed to by the structure

The actual value of the flags parameter is determined by combining the desired options. However, since the third-party DLL isolates us from dealing with user defined callback functions or the custom templates, only the first four values are of any concern to us. That's why we used four checkboxes in our window and why the script that processes this function combines the values for each parameter depending on the checked attribute of those checkboxes.

The dialog box automatically uses black as the default. The cc_rgbinit flag is used, therefore, to indicate that the value passed as the last parameter to the third-party DLL function will be used as the default color instead. The dialog box would normally open without the custom color palette modification portion shown, and the command button to open that section would be enabled.

The cc_fullopen portion of the flag indicates that the custom color palette should be open when the dialog box is open. The cc_preventfullopen portion of the flag disables the command button that would show the custom color palette modification portion of the window. As long as the cc_fullopen parameter was not set, that will prevent the user from modifying the custom color palette. Note that if the cc_fullopen parameter is set, the dialog box will automatically disable the command button used to open that portion of the window, so it is not necessary (though you can do it anyway) to set cc_preventfullopen when cc_fullopen is set.

Normally the dialog box shows without the "Help" command button. Setting the cc_showhelp portion of the flag will show the "Help" button on the dialog box. If the user clicks that button, the dialog box will send a commdlg_hlp message back to the window that the function was called from. This means you would have to trap that message and respond to it for the "Help" button to do anything.

That's what we've added the custom user event and the script in the Other event to handle. Many of the Windows messages are mapped to equivalent PowerBuilder events, and there is a PowerNote from powersoft that details that mapping. However, there is no PowerBuilder mapped event to the Windows commdlg_hlp message.

Fortunately, PowerBuilder provides the other event to trap the unmapped messages. All we need to do is check to see if the window received a message. In the other event, we check the message number, and if it is 50236–the number for the commdlg_hlp message–we do a PostEvent to the custom user event we will use to display the help for the dialog box.

I didn't find the commdlg_hlp message particularly well documented in the Windows API on-line help. I determined the message number using a "spy" utility that traces the messages received by a window. There are a number of such utilities available, including a good freeware one on CompuServe called SuperSpy.

In our custom user event, we simply use the PowerScript ShowHelp function to call our on-line help. You'll note, however, that the call I've included isn't to a help file that tells us anything about the ChooseColor dialog box. There isn't any such help provided with Windows that I could find, so we need to develop some of our own. The call I've included simply brings in the "Help on Help" file that is provided with Windows, and is enough to show how the function would work.

If you don't feel comfortable creating your own on-line help files, don't worry. In another chapter in this same book I'll show you how to do that as well.

ChooseFont

Putting it together

AS with the ChooseColor DLL wrapper, the first thing we need to do is declare the ChooseFont DLL wrapper function as an external function in our PowerBuilder application. Again, we're only doing a demo, so we'll just create a stand-alone window and declare the DLL function as a local external function in that window:

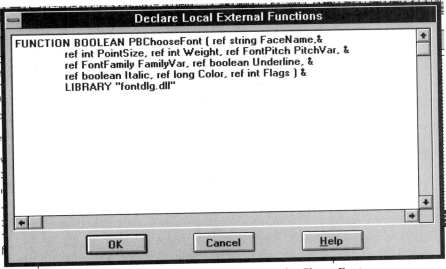

Figure 38-41: Local external functions for ChooseFont.

We need to do a little more work with the window, though, to prepare it to demonstrate the functions, as we did with ChooseColor. That's largely because fonts have more attributes than colors. You'll need to create four groups of radio buttons on the window: input flags, output flags, font family, and font pitch. (see below).

Group Name	Option
Input Flag	Only screen fonts
	Only printer fonts
	Both screen and printer fonts
Output Flag	Screen font
	Printer font
	Both screen and printer font
	Simulated screen font
	Simulated printer font
	Both simulated screen and printer
Font Family	Any

	Script
	Decorative
	Swiss
	Modern
	Roman
Font Pitch	Default
	Fixed
	Variable

We will also include static text that we will use to display the user-selected font, and a command button to call the window-level function that will in turn call the local external function. Below is one example of how to configure the controls on the window:

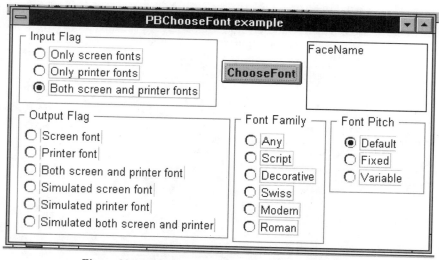

Figure 38-42: Configuring controls for ChooseFont.

We then declare our window-level function, and use the following script to set up our call to the DLL:

fw_choosefont

```
//Declare local variables
boolean lb_return, lb_italics, lb_underline
integer ln_PointSize, ln_Weight, ln_flags
```

```
string  lt_FaceName
fontpitch  lfp_1
fontfamily lff_1
long  ln_color
lt_FaceName = space(32)

//Get the input flag
IF rb_input_screen.checked THEN ln_flags = 1
IF rb_input_printer.checked THEN ln_flags = 2
IF rb_input_both.checked THEN ln_flags = 3

//Call the function
lb_return = PBChooseFont ( lt_FaceName, ln_PointSize, ln_Weight, &
 lfp_1, lff_1, lb_underline, lb_italics, ln_color, ln_flags)

IF lb_return THEN

 //Show some example text in the selected font
 st_facename.text = lt_FaceName + " " + string(-1 * ln_PointSize) + "pt"
 st_facename.facename = lt_FaceName
 st_facename.TextSize = ln_PointSize
 st_facename.Weight = ln_Weight
 st_facename.Italic = lb_italics
 st_facename.UnderLine = lb_underline
 st_facename.Textcolor = ln_color

 //Show the type of font selected
 CHOOSE CASE ln_flags
 CASE 1
 rb_output_screen.checked = TRUE
 CASE 2
 rb_output_printer.checked = TRUE
 CASE 3
 rb_output_both.checked = TRUE
 CASE 5
 rb_output_simul_screen.checked = TRUE
 CASE 6
 rb_output_simul_printer.checked = TRUE
 CASE 7
 rb_output_simul_both.checked = TRUE
 CASE ELSE
 //These are the only valid returns
 Return FALSE
 END CHOOSE

 //Show the font pitch selected
 CHOOSE CASE lfp_1
 CASE Default!
 rb_default.checked = true
 CASE Fixed!
 rb_fixed.checked = true
 CASE Variable!
 rb_variable.checked = true
 CASE ELSE
 //These are the only valid values
 Return FALSE
 END CHOOSE
 CHOOSE CASE lff_1
 CASE AnyFont!
 rb_anyfont.checked = true
 CASE Decorative!
 rb_decorative.checked = true
```

```
CASE Modern!
rb_modern.checked = true
CASE Roman!
rb_roman.checked = true
CASE Script!
rb_script.checked = true
CASE Swiss!
rb_swiss.checked = true
CASE ELSE
//These are the only valid values
Return FALSE
END CHOOSE

Return TRUE

ELSE
//User canceled the dialog box
Return FALSE
END IF
```

How it works

The structure that we would need to pass the ChooseFont if we were to call it directly looks similar to the ChooseColor structure, with a few extra elements:

Name	Data Type	Use
lStructSize	long	Indicates size of this structure.
HwndOwner	handle	Handle of window that is calling the function.
HDC	handle	A pointer to the device context for the printer that will be used if printer fonts are selected.
lpLOGFONT	logfont structure	A structure used to identify the attributes of the selected font.
iPointSize	integer	Indicates the point size of the selected font, in tenths of a point.
Flags	long	Used to configure the dialog box that appears for user input.
RGBColors	long	Color of selected font
lCustData	long pointer	Application defined data that is passed to the user defined function below.
lpfnHook	uint pointer	Pointer to a user defined function that processes messages intended for the dialog box.
lpTemplateName	long pointer	Name of the resource file that is used instead of the default if the Flags parameter indicates that this should be used instead.
hInstance	handle	Identifies a template if the Flags parameter indicates one should be used.
lpszStyle	long pointer	Pointer to style data. If set in the flags parameter, is used to set the style in the dialog box. Is also used to return the selected style.
nFontType	integer	Specifies the type of the selected font.
n/a	word	dummy element, isn't used

nSizeMin	integer	Indicates the minimum font size the user may select, if the option to set that has been set in the flags parameter.
nSizeMax	integer	Indicates the maximum font size the user many select, if the option to set that has be set in the flags parameter.

Note that we pre-populate the lt_FaceName variable with spaces before we pass it to the function. This is because DLLs called from PowerBuilder can't increase the size of any string variables we pass to them. If we didn't pre-populate the variable, it would have no length when passed, and then the DLL couldn't populate it on the return.

Once again, the third-party DLL simplifies the function call. All we need to provide are variables to store the selected font name, point size, weight, pitch, family, underline status, italics status and color. We also pass a flag to customize the dialog box. In fact, the last option is the only one we set before we call the function; all of the other parameters are populated and returned to us by the function.

The function is rather simple to use. We pass our one input parameter to indicate whether the fonts that appear in the DropDownListBox on the dialog box should be just the screen fonts, just the printer fonts, or both. The function returns an integer in the same parameter that indicates what font type the user actually selected, and we use that value in a CHOOSE CASE statement to set the radio button indicating the user's response.

The function actually returns an integer, either 0 or 1, but we can also designate that return as Boolean (False or True respectively). Similarly, the function returns the italics and underline status for the selected font as an integer 0 or 1, but we also treat that as a Boolean.

A related technique is used to treat the returned information about the font pitch and family. Once again the function returns integers for those two parameters. However, PowerBuilder has a couple of built-in enumerated datatypes (Fontpitch and Fontfamily) that map directly to the values that are returned by the function. That's why we declared those parameters as the enumerated datatypes, rather than as integers. We will eventually use those enumerated datatypes to set the appropriate radio button to indicate the font pitch and family selected.

Since the other return values also correspond to the datatypes used by PowerBuilder, we simply apply them directly to the attributes of our sample static text in order to display the text in the selected font. The one minor exception is the point size. Within the Windows API, the size of a font, (particularly its height) can be expressed in either a positive or a negative number. If it is expressed in a positive number, it usually indicates that the application works with fixed pitch fonts, and the size is indicated in appropriate units (i.e., characters per inch). If it is expressed as a negative number, it indicates that the application works with variable pitch fonts, and the size is indicated in points. Since the latter is the way that PowerBuilder works with fonts, the third-party DLL only returns negative numbers (ones that Power-Builder can use). Therefore, to display the text size correctly in the static text, it is multiplied by -1 first to convert it to a positive number.

Undocumented Calls

"Undocumented" means that the functions are not described in the standard Microsoft Windows API function references. The example below and many other "undocumented" functions are covered in some detail in a number of third-party books, such as *Undocumented Windows* (see the references at the end of the chapter).

ShellAbout

You've probably noticed that most of the applications that you have that run under Windows have a Help/About response window that provides information about the program. Perhaps you've even developed them for your applications. But did you know that there is a function built into the Windows API that will create one for you? It's one of a number of undocumented calls in the Windows API.

(Actually, ShellAbout is documented in the WinNT API references as a "new" function. However, it is present in the standard Windows API as well.)

You can use this function in your own applications to avoid having to develop your own Help/About windows. It is, however, rather limited. The function accepts two string arguments and a reference to the application icon. An example of the response window it produces follows. In this example, "Program Title" and "Program Information" were the two strings passed to the function, and the application icon just happens to be the PoweRsofT logo.

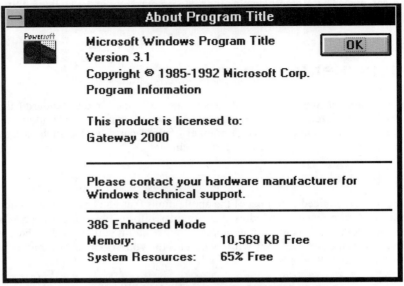

Figure 38-44: An example of ShellAbout.

Putting it together

In addition to the ShellAbout function, we are also going to declare the LoadIcon function of the Windows API as a local external function for the window. The LoadIcon function will be used to obtain the handle to the application icon, which is the ShellAbout function will need if it is to display the icon on the response window. If a valid handle to the application icon is not passed to the function, it will display the Windows icon instead.

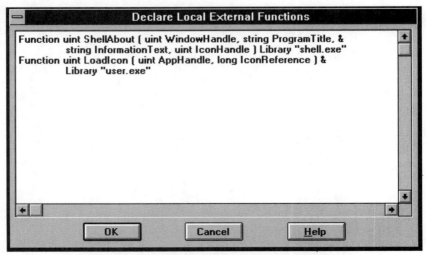

Figure 38-45: Local external functions for ShellAbout.

In order to reference the application icon, we need a reference to the application itself. Once the application open event completes, however, we normally don't have any way of referring to the application. To provide that capability, we're going to pass a reference to the application to our window in the application open event. We'll need to declare an instance variable of datatype Application to hold that reference after the window is opened.

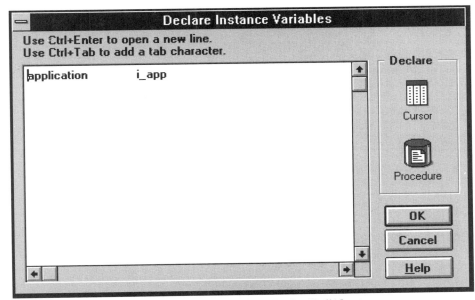

Figure 38-46: Instance variables for ShellAbout.

In the application open event, then, we simply pass a reference to itself as a PowerObject-Parm when we open our window.

Open Event for application

```
OpenWithParm ( w_shellabout_demo, this )
```

In the open event for our window, we immediately assign the PowerObjectParm portion of the Windows message object to our Application datatype instance variable. We need to do this in the open event before any other functions that might trigger other events, or we run a high risk of losing the information that was passed to the window.

Open event for our window

```
i_app = message.PowerObjectParm
```

Finally, we declare a window-level function that actually calls the LoadIcon and ShellAbout functions.

fw_help_about

```
//Declare local variables
uint ln_icon_han dle
//Get the handle of the application icon
ln_icon_handle = LoadIcon ( Handle ( i_app), Long ( 1000, 0 ) )

//Call the help about function in the Windows API
ShellAbout ( 0, "Program Title", "Program Information", ln_icon_handle )

Return TRUE
```

How it works

It actually fairly simple. The LoadIcon expects a handle for the application and a reference to the application icon as arguments and returns a handle to the application icon. The second argument is -expected as a Long, with the resource identifier for the application icon in the low-order word and a 0 in the high-order word. In a PowerBuilder application, the resource identifier for the application icon is always 1000. We use one of the forms of the Long function to convert that value into a Long in the format that the LoadIcon function expects.

We then pass the returned value to the ShellAbout function, along with the string information we want to show. The first argument is the handle for the window that calls the function, but you can pass 0 (i.e., a null reference) there as well. The second argument is used as part of the window title and the first line of the dialog after "Microsoft Windows." If the string contains a "#" character, the function displays the section preceding the "#" in the window title, and the part following the "#" in the first line of the dialog. Otherwise, the entire string is placed in both locations.

The third argument is the text that you want displayed in the dialog box after the version and copyright information for Windows. If you want to include more that one line of information in the third argument, you simply append the strings together with new-line characters (~n) between them and pass them as a single string. The fourth argument is the handle to the icon we want to display. We could either pass the icon reference we obtained through the LoadIcon call, or we could pass 0 (i.e., a null reference). If the handle is null or is invalid, the function will display the Windows icon; otherwise it will display the icon we provided the handle to.

For Further Information

Undocumented Windows

A Programmer's Guide to Reserved Microsoft Windows API Functions
Addison-Wesley Publishing Company
One Jacob Way
Reading, MA 01867

Contains the name and use (if determined) for the undocumented calls in the Windows API through Windows 3.1. Also contains a 3.5 inch disk of handy utilities.

Windows API Bible

Waite Group Press, Inc.
200 Tamal Plaza, Suite 101
Corte Madera, CA 94925

An earlier book, this covers all of the documented Windows API function through Windows version 3.0.

Windows Bible: The New Testament

Waite Group Press, Inc.
200 Tamal Plaza, Suite 101
Corte Madera, CA 94925

A more recent book, this covers the documented functions in the Windows API for Windows 3.1 that were added since *The Windows API Bible* was published. It also includes a CD-ROM that contains all of its own code samples, along with those from *The Windows API Bible*.

Windows SDK on-line help

The Windows SDK on-line help is provided as part of many of the Windows programming tools, such as Microsoft's Visual C/C++.

CHAPTER 39

Concurrency Control

By Michael Pflieger

Concurrency Control

by **Michael Pflieger**

Relational databases allow concurrent accesses to the same data at the same time. With this ability also comes danger. What would happen if two users access a bank customer's record for customer John Doe and both users attempt to change the balance at the same time? This depends on how we set up the DataWindow to control concurrency. Concurrency control is a method of insuring that one user's data doesn't get overwritten or modified while in the process of making a change. Following the example above, we will see what settings on the DataWindow we can use to control concurrent accesses. To illustrate, we will use a very simple banking system. We are maintaining a checking account for John & Jane Doe:

Acct_Number	Name	Address	Balance	Status
1234–56	John & Jane Doe	1212 Mockingbird Lane	$800	Active

John goes to a bank teller to cash a $200 check. The teller will retrieve the customer's account information to verify the balance, which shows as $800. At the same time across town, John's wife, Jane, is at an ATM machine making a $500 deposit. The machine retrieves the current balance as $800. Back at the bank, the teller sees the balance is higher than the check amount, cashes the check, and updates the balance to $600. An instant later, the teller machine accepts the deposit and attempts to save the balance as $1300. Will the DBMS accept this change? The following is a diagram of these events:

SEQ	Teller	ATM
1	Select – balance $800	
2		Select – balance $800
3	Update – balance $600	
4		Update – balance $1300

Using the Update Characteristics window in the DataWindow painter, we can determine the where clause that will be generated for the update. This means we can control what happens in this situation. We are given three options on the Update Characteristics window:

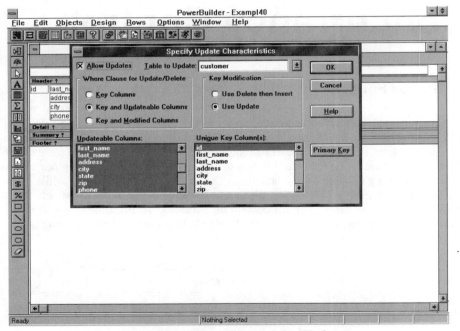

Figure 39-1: Update Characteristics Window

1) **Key Columns** – A **Where** clause will be generated which compares the key columns on the table to the values originally retrieved. In our example, the update made by the ATM would overwrite the update made by the teller, and the bank would be missing $200.

2) **Key and Updateable Columns** – A **Where** clause is generated which compares the key columns as well as updateable columns on the table to the values originally retrieved. In our

case, the balance originally received in both cases would have been $800. When the teller tried to save the account balance after the check was cashed, the balance would still have been $800, so the update would have been made. Then, when the ATM tried to update the balance, it is no longer $800, so the update will fail because the columns no longer match.

3) Key and Modified Columns – A **Where** clause is generated which compares key columns as well as columns that have been modified. In our example, this would have the same affect as the *Key and Updateable Columns option, since the balance was modified and was no longer equal to the value originally retrieved.*

Let's assume another scenario. Instead of the spouse depositing money at the ATM, let's assume at the same instant, the spouse is calling customer service to notify the bank of a stolen checkbook and ATM card. The customer service rep (CSR) has the same information as the teller, and changes the status to "Hold". This status flags the account to avoid further activity until appropriate stop payments and cancellations can be made. The CSR saves the status information and immediately afterwards, the teller saves the balance. What will happen this time?

SEQ	Teller	CSR
1	Select	
2		Select
3		Update – status HOLD
4	Update – balance $600	

1) Key Columns – A **Where** clause will be generated which compares the key columns on the table to the values originally retrieved. In our example, the update made by the CSR would change the status to HOLD, but since the key was the same for the teller, the balance would be updated, basically ignoring the hold status.

2) Key and Updateable Columns – A **Where** clause is generated which compares the key columns as well as updateable columns on the table to the values originally retrieved. In our example, the balance originally received in both cases would have been $800. But when the teller attempts to update the balance to $600, the original status, which was "Active", is now compared to the new status of "Hold". The change is rejected with an error message being returned from the DBMS.

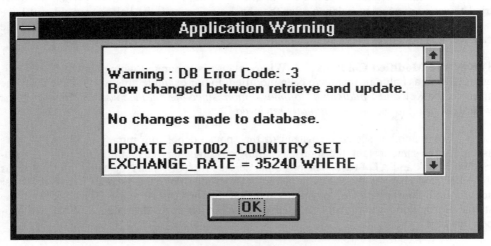

Figure 39-2: Update Error Message

3) Key and Modified Columns – A **Where** clause is generated which compares key columns as well as columns that have been modified. In our example, this would have the same affect as the Key Columns option, since the column being modified is equal to the value originally retrieved.

In our example, Key and Updateable Columns would prevent us from updating the row if the status has changed. It would also prevent other potentially 'allowable' concurrent changes, such as a teller changing the balance and a CSR changing the customer's address.

Depending on the DBMS you are using, there are other alternatives to controlling concurrent accesses and updates. One such alternative is to use locking. Locking is the ability to hold the row to keep anyone else from updating it until you release the lock by ending the transaction, i.e. executing a COMMIT, ROLLBACK, or DISCONNECT. PowerBuilder gives you the ability to have a WITH HOLDLOCK generated in the FROM clause of the Select statement in the DataWindow painter for those DBMSs which support the option. To select the WITH HOLDLOCK option; from the SQL window in the DataWindow painter, hold the right mouse button over the table window header. The last choice on the popup menu is **HOLDLOCK.**

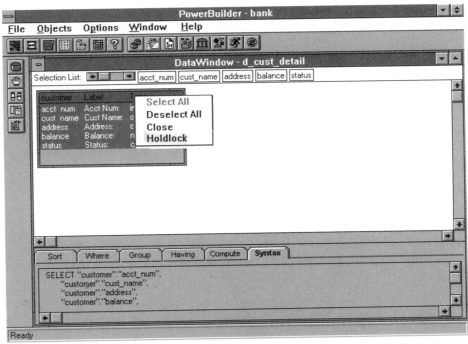

Figure 39-3: Displaying the Holdlock option

By selecting this option, an SQL statement is generated for the dw.Retrieve() event that locks the data you are retrieving. This prevents anyone from accessing the data. The problem with this approach is if the user then walks away from his PC while the data is displayed, no one else can update that data. Another problem is that most DBMSs do not currently support row level locking. This means that even though you only "want" to lock the one row you are retrieving, more rows are actually being locked (usually a "page" of data). This could cause a lot of time–outs in trying to access data, and severely limits concurrent access.

Some DBMSs support the use of special timestamp columns to control concurrency. Each row of every table would contain a timestamp column. This would be updated every time the row is updated with either INSERT or UPDATE SQL commands. When you attempt to do an update, the WHERE clause would verify that the timestamp retrieved was equal to the timestamp in the row at the instant before the update. This would insure you were not over-writing someone else's updates. In essence, this works much the same as the Key and Updateable Columns option, since even though two users might be trying to change different columns in the same row, the second update would be rejected. DBMSs such as SYBASE and Microsoft SQLServer support the use of the TIMESTAMP column. In fact, when using either DBMS, if a table has a column with the name of TIMESTAMP and a datetime datatype, PowerBuilder will ignore the Update Characteristics. The WHERE clause will be generated with keys and the TIMESTAMP.

PowerBuilder supports the options presented here. The correct option for your application depends on what level of assurance you need that 1) data will not be "accidentally" overwritten, and 2) "stale" data isn't being used (as was the case in our HOLD status example). PowerBuilder provides options to cover all needs involved with concurrency control.

PowerBuilder Install Disk Builder

By Michael Griffith

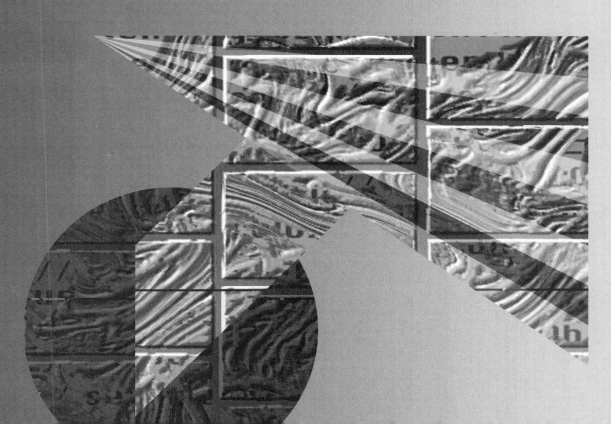

PowerBuilder Install Disk Builder

by **Michael Griffith**

An Overview

One of the most used new features of PowerBuilder 4.0 is bound to be the Install Disk Builder that Powersoft has bundled with the PowerBuilder Developer's Toolkit. Being able to package your work with a clean and seamless installation utility conveys to your clients the level of quality that you've built into your application, and helps reduce the hassle of deploying it.

Building a set of Install disks for your application is relatively easy. You tell PowerBuilder the different components to be included in the installation, and it builds an image of the diskettes in a directory on your hard drive or network. Once the diskette image has been built, a menu selection allows you to copy the image to diskettes, and you are ready to install.

Getting Started

The Install Disk Builder is installed as c:\pb4\pbsetup.exe as part of the Developer's Toolkit.

The Disk Builder is a single document interface style of application. Its main interface is shown in Figure 40-1:

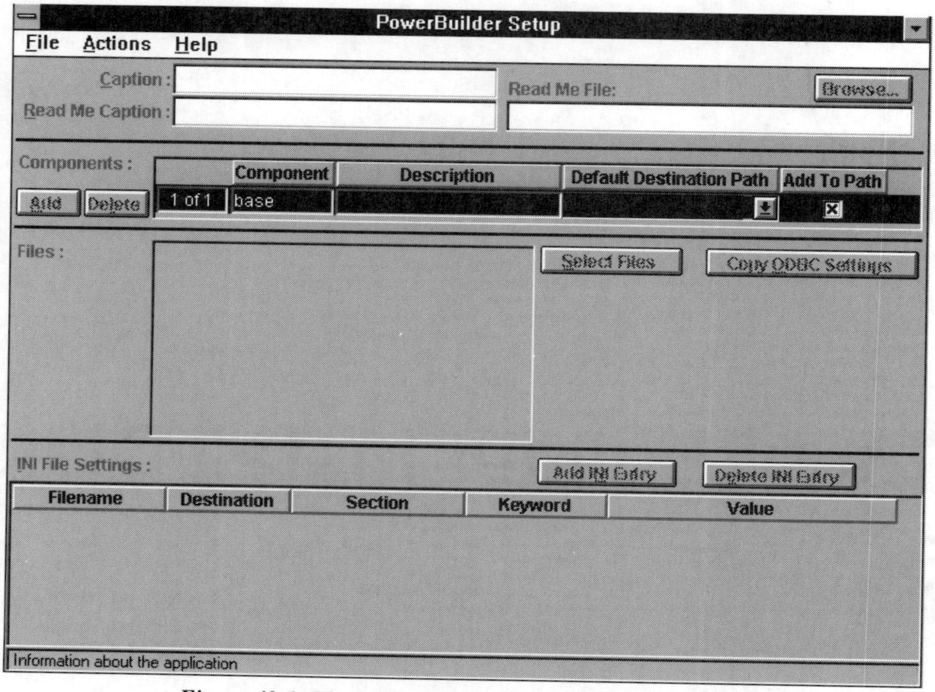

Figure 40-1: The main window of the Install Disk Builder.

All information for creating a set of diskettes is stored in a configuration file (.cfg). Every application for which you want to create Install diskettes will have a separate configuration defining its particular components. Each of these files contains information used by the Setup executable when you run your Install program. This information includes:

Headings used by the Windows Setup program.

A file to be displayed as the Read Me file while the Windows Setup is installing your application.

The installation components.

The files within each component.

Default path and directory names for each component.

Whether to add a component's directory to the user's autoexec.bat file.

.ini file settings, including odbc.ini settings for ODBC data sources.

Each application component contains settings, specifications, and a list of related files to install. Each component that you define is accessed by the Install Disk Builder, and copied to the diskette image directory that you specify when it comes time to build the diskettes.

The first step to creating your installation diskettes is to create the configuration file for the application, as in Listing 1:

Listing 1: *Creating a new configuration.*

```
1 Select File...New from the main menu bar.
  The New File Name common dialog box displays.

2 Change the drive and directory as needed, and
  specify a name for the
  configuration file in the dialog box.

3 Click "OK".
```

There, now you are ready to start defining the individual components of the installation. The single-line edit labeled "Caption" specifies the title that the Setup program displays at the top of the screen as your application is installed.

While your application is installing, you can display a ReadMe file for the user to browse, showing pertinent information about your application, errata in documentation, or application-specific information.

One small gripe about the ReadMe file: the Install process always displays the ReadMe window while copying files. If no file is provided, Setup still shows the window that *would* have been used to display the file. Since this is a standard behavior of the Setup program, you'll always want to provide a ReadMe file that contains, at minimum, a greeting, and how to contact your organization for upgrades or technical support. This will prevent your users from being confused by the existence of an empty ReadMe window. Define the ReadMe file as shown in Listing 2.

Listing 2: *Defining the ReadMe titles and file.*

```
1.Specify a title for the ReadMe window in the
  Read Me caption box.

2.Specify the name of the text file to be displayed
  in  the ReadMe window. If you don't know the full
  path and name of the ReadMe file, click "Browse",
  which displays the Select ReadMe File common dialog
  box.

  Change the drive and directory as needed, and select
  the text file to be displayed in the ReadMe window
  during installation. Then click "OK".
```

Once you have defined this information, save your configuration: choose File...Save from the main menu. Now you are ready to define the components that you would like to install.

Defining Application Components

Application components define what you are actually going to install. A large application may be comprised of many small pieces, of which the user may install only sections. An example of that would be an accounting package that is broken down into modules. One user may choose to install only the General Ledger and Accounts Receivable modules, while another user may choose all components.

Additionally, there are often many components that are duplicated across all PowerBuilder application installations. Examples are the PowerBuilder Deployment kit or the Watcom DB engine. If your users have already installed these components for another PowerBuilder application, there is no need to install them again. As you define components for the Install Disk Builder, these components will show up as optional parts of the installation that the user can either include or exclude by clicking on the checkboxes provided for each component.

Component details

The definition of each application component must include the files that comprise that component. Other information, enumerated below, is optional.

To add or delete components, click on the "Add"/"Delete" command buttons in the component section. As you scroll through the list of defined components for this configuration, each component shows the options set for it.

Once you have added a component, you define the following information:

> A description of that component (i.e. Order Entry System).

> The default destination (path) for the component to be installed into.

> Whether to update the autoexec.bat file with the path information for this component.

The files that comprise that component.

.ini file settings to be updated for that component.

Specify the name of the component by typing a short description in the Component Description

Edit box. Once you have the description, click in the Default Destination Path box and type a default pathname for the component's files.

Each component can be installed in a directory suggested by the Setup program, or alternatively configured by the user. When adding components, specify one of the following options:

A directory suggested by you, the developer. (Example: C:\SIGNATUR\CALL-TRACK)

The base directory, or a subdirectory from the base.

A separate directory for this component.

To specify the component path, click on the down arrow in the Default Destination Path DropDownListBox to choose one of the predefined directories, (windows, windows\system) or type in the suggested relative path name.

The Setup application allows you to install components into subdirectories of the base or Windows directories by using variables. A variable is defined by substituting the @(<**variablename**>) expression for the relative path. This variable name can be @(**base**), @(**windows**), @(**system**), or even @(**component**). At install time, the installation program replaces @(<**variablename**>) with the pathname the user specifies for the base component.

For each component you define, the Setup program can update the autoexec.bat file to include the path selected by the user at Install time. To use this feature, click the "Add to Path" checkbox to add the component path to the autoexec.bat path statement.

Each component installed will copy the files that you have specified as constituting that component. Define these files by using the procedure given in Listing 3.

Listing 3: Defining the files for a component.

```
1 Click the "Select Files" command button.

  The Select Files for Base Component dialog box
  displays.

2 Select the appropriate drive or directory to
  display the files desired for this component. Use
  the DropDownListBox List Files of Type, and the
  File Name box, to select any files displayed.

3 Include a file by doing one of the following:
    • Double-click the filename of one of the
      available files.
    • Drag the file from the top box to the Selected
      Files box.

  The Install Diskette Builder moves the file
  from the Available Files list box to the Selected
  Files list box.
```

```
    4 Remove a file from the Selected Files list by doing
      one of the following:
      • Click the filename to deselect, then click
        "Deselect Selected File" command button.
      • Drag the file from the Selected Files list
        box to the Available Files list box.
    5 When you have selected all files for the
      component, click "OK" to close the dialog.

      The Install Diskette Builder main workspace
      displays with the selected files for that component.
```

You can define the .ini file settings for each individual component to be updated by the Install process. This is very useful when distributing a Watcom database, as the Install Disk Builder can read your odbc.ini file and include the settings to be updated on the target machine. To copy odbc.ini settings to the .ini File Settings box, follow the procedure in Listing 4.

Listing 4: Adding the odbc.ini file settings.

```
    1 Click "Copy ODBC Settings" command button.
      The ODBC Choices dialog box displays.

    2 Click on the data source to be included with this
      component.

      The data source's individual odbc.ini line
      entries display in the Entry box.

    3 Review the Entry lines to ensure the correct choice.
    4 Click "OK".
```

When your user installs this particular component, the Install process will update the *odbc.ini* file settings. You can specify other .ini files to be updated as well; applications frequently store information in the win.ini file or the system.ini file, since they are always in the execution path.

Choose the level that you wish to add the entry for. You can add multiple entries for the same .ini file by adding additional line entries. If you want to add an entry to another file, click an entry in the Filename column; if you want to add an entry to another section within a file that already has .ini file settings, click an entry in the Section column.

Click the "Add .ini Entry": command button, and a blank line appears in the .ini file section. For each blank line, specify the name of the .ini file, the installed directory of the .ini file, the section and keyword to search for, and the value to set.

Specifying the Program Manager group

Once you have defined each component, select Actions...Define Program Group from the main menu. When the dialog box displays, specify the name of the group to be added and the components for that group. For each component, specify directory and file. These attributes become the item's description and properties. During Setup, users will be prompted to set up a group in the Program Manager for this application. If they so choose, each component specified here will be added to the appropriate program group. This dialog is shown in Figure 40-2 below.

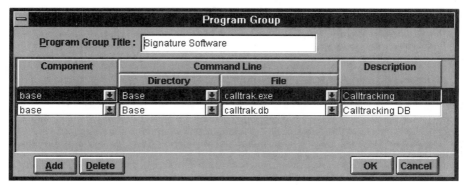

Figure 40-2: specifying the Program Manager group.

Defining reusable components

PowerBuilder applications often share many components. These components may be database interface files, third party controls, libraries, or other programs that you may choose to install with your application. Rather than having to configure them each time that you build a new configuration file, you can build them as reusable components. Then when you build the diskette images, PowerBuilder will allow you to choose these optional components to be part of this installation routine.

To create a reusable component, select Action...Define Reusable Components from the main menu. You will see the dialog pictured in Figure 40-3.

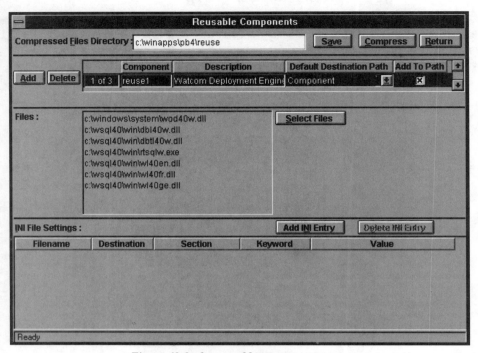

Figure 40-3: the reusable component screen.

Define the files to be included, odbc.ini, and other .ini file settings, as well as whether to update the autoexec.bat file, just as you did with the previous components. One option you'll notice on this screen is the "Compress" command button. This option allows PowerBuilder to compress the reusable components to conserve disk space. To create compressed versions of reusable modules, click on "Compress." The Install Diskette Builder will save compressed versions of the files in your reusable components list into a directory, which you can specify in the Compressed Files Directory single-line edit. When the Install Builder creates the diskette images, it uses these files as specified in the FOR EACH BUILD.

Building the Diskette Images

Now you are ready to build the diskette images. In order to proceed to this step, you must first save the configuration file from the File...Save menu selection. Saving the configuration forces the Install Disk Builder to validate all of the components that you have defined to ensure that any needed information has been supplied. If the save is successful, the Actions...Create Diskette Images menu selection will become active. Choosing this menu selection will display the Create Diskette Images dialog box shown in Figure 40-4.

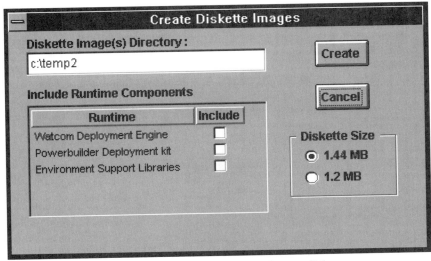

Figure 40-4: The Create Diskette Images dialog.

In order to build the diskette images, you specify a directory for PowerBuilder to use as its workspace by filling in the Diskette Images Directory single-line edit. Each time you rebuild a diskette image, PowerBuilder will ask you to confirm that the entire directory will be over-written. Be careful here, it really means it: the entire diskette image directory will be recreated each time you build the images for the diskettes.

Additionally, you can include any of the reusable components by checking on the checkbox for each one.

Once you have specified the directory and the reusable components and have clicked "OK", the Install Diskette Builder creates the directories, compresses files, and populates the directories with component and reusable files.

During this image building process, PowerBuilder will use a DOS compression utility to arrange files in the correct directory structure. The process looks like what you see in Figure 40-5.

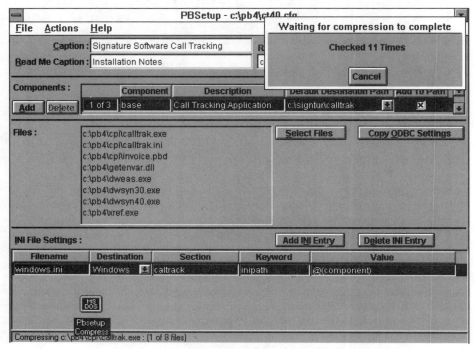

Figure 40-5: Creating the diskette image directories.

On completion, the Diskette Builder creates subdirectories named disk1, disk2, disk3...one for each disk that will be needed.

Creating Master Diskettes

If the image of the diskettes is successfully created, the Actions...Create Diskettes menu selection will be enabled from the main menu. This is a simple and straightforward process whereby PowerBuilder allows you to copy the contents of each subdirectory created in the image directory to a diskette. A nice feature included here is that the Install Disk Builder will tell you how many diskettes it will need to get the entire application copied. You can also control how many copies of the diskettes to make, and which drive to use as the target drive for the copy. A sample of the dialog appears in Figure 40-6.

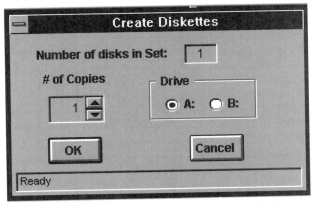

Figure 40-6: Creating the Install diskettes from the image.

Clicking "OK" will begin the copy. If you provide a diskette that has files already on it, the Install Disk Builder will inform you, and allow you to cancel the copy or to overwrite the entire diskette with its new contents.

After the copy is complete, you will be informed that the installation diskettes have been successfully created. You are now ready to install your application from the diskettes. A sample Install screen is shown below in Figure 40-7.

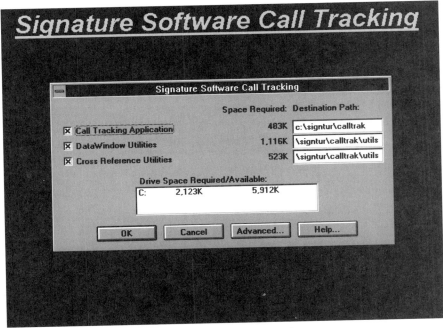

Figure 40-7: The finished product.

Final Analysis

I found a few things in the Install Disk Builder that are non-standard, or against my personal preferences. For the most part these can go into the nit-picky category, since they don't really affect the final result–an installable version of your application. Some of these things are:

> Non-standard colors for editable fields. This is something that is common in many Powersoft demo applications or utilities. If a field is editable, make it white like a single-line edit, otherwise slate gray to show that I cannot edit the field.

> Additional drives don't show up when I use the Create Diskette dialog box.

> Some accelerator keys are duplicated. For instance, <Alt>-<A> to add a component is also the accelerator key for the Actions menu. These should be unique.

> No separate file, other than the ReadMe file, can be provided for installation notes. If you click on the "Help" button while the Setup program is running, your ReadMe file displays. It would be nice to be able to define a separate Help file to appear when this button is clicked.

> Powersoft splashes its name in here and there. They can, it is their product–however, when I buy a car, I make sure the dealers remove any tag that displays their name. Similarly, since I am the one distributing the setup program to my users, I don't necessarily want them to know what tool was used to develop the application or the setup program.

> There is no way that I could find to have Setup add DOS environment variables. This is not a requirement, just something that I think would be a nice feature for the next release.

Again, most of these issues are small, insignificant items that I feel would enhance the professionalism of this product. Overall, the Install Disk Builder is a terrific addition to Power-Builder, and I'm sure that it is a facility that will be used often.

The Project Painter

By Henry Cortinas

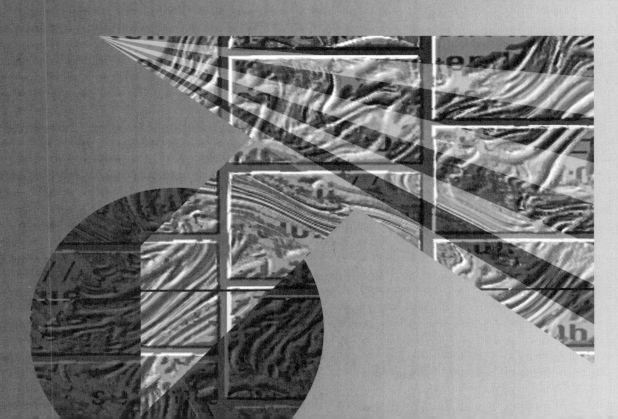

The Project Painter

by **Henry Cortinas**

The Project painter simplifies the generation of executable files and PowerBuilder dynamic libraries. If you are working on a large project that includes several .PBDs you expect to build and rebuild many times, using the Project painter to create a project object will save you considerable time. New to PowerBuilder 4.0, the Project painter can be used to create and maintain PowerBuilder project objects. Project objects contain required information for building the executable file and .PBDs, including:

```
(a)   the name of the executable file (.EXE file)
(b)   the PowerBuilder libraries to be deployed as dynamic
      libraries (.PBD files)
(c)   any needed PowerBuilder resource files (.PBR files)
```

Once a project object has been defined for your current application, you can rebuild your application from the Project painter by clicking a single button on the PainterBar or by selecting Build Project from the Project painter File menu. Building a project object for your application can greatly reduce the amount of time spent creating an executable, .PBDs, and .PBRs for every build you want to generate.

Launching the Project Painter

To start or open the Project painter, click the "Project" button in the PowerBar. The Select Project dialog box appears.

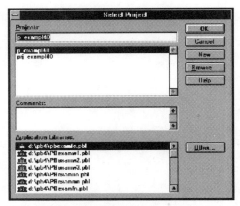

Figure 41-1: The Select Project dialog box

Creating a Project Object

To create a project object, follow these steps:

Select a project object or click "New" to create a new project object. The Select Executable File dialog box appears.

Figure 41-2: The Select Executable File dialog box

Enter executable and resource file names

Enter a file name for the executable file you want to create and click "OK". The Project painter workspace appears with the executable file name you specified appearing in the Executable File Name text entry box.

When the Project painter workspace appears, you can enter information to define how PowerBuilder will create the executable file and check which .PBLs you want to deploy as .PBDs.

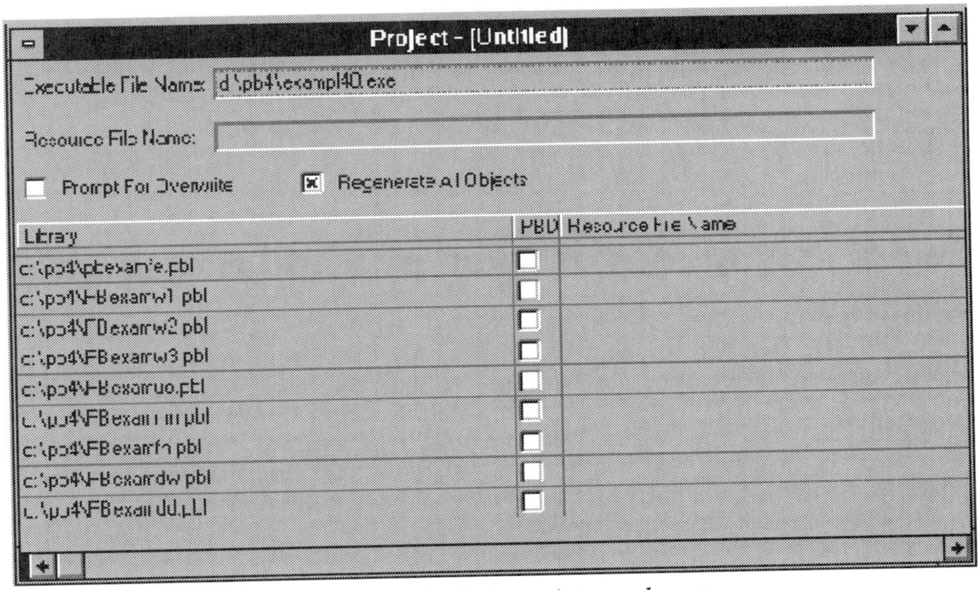

Figure 41-3: The Project painter workspace

You can enter a resource file name for the Executable file as well as for each of the .PBDs you specify. In the first Resource File Name text entry box, enter the .PBR file you would like to use for building the .EXE. Or select Paste ExecutableÕs Resource... from the Options menu to browse your directories for the resource file name you want to include for the .EXE in the project object definition.

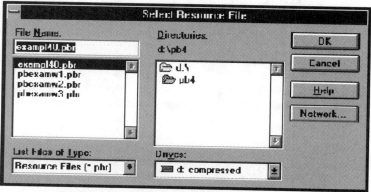

Figure 41-4: The Select Resource File dialog box

Select Prompting for Overwrite and Regenerate Options

Select Prompt for Overwrite if you want PowerBuilder to prompt you before overwriting any .EXE or .PBD files it creates during the build process. Generally, you will want to regenerate your application objects before rebuilding .EXEs and .PBDs. You can select Regenerate All Objects if you want PowerBuilder to always regenerate all objects in the application libraries before the .EXEs and .PBDs are built. If this CheckBox is not selected, PowerBuilder does not regenerate the objects.

Figure 41-5: The Project Painter CheckBoxes

Choose which libraries to include as PowerBuilder dynamic libraries (.PBDs)

The Library column in the Project painter workspace lists the libraries defined in the library search path for the current application. To flag a library as a PowerBuilder dynamic library (.PBD) to be included in the build, you can select the .PBD CheckBox next to the specified .PBL.

You can add resource file names as necessary for each library name. In the Resource File

Name text entry box, you can enter the .PBR file you would like to use for building the, .PBD, or you can paste these resource file names into the Resource File Name column's text entry field by selecting Paste Dynamic Library's Resource from the Options menu. Pasting through the menu allows you to browse your directories for the resource file (.PBR) you want to associate with a particular PowerBuilder dynamic library (.PBD).

Saving the Project Object and Exiting the Project Painter

When you have finished defining the project object or are satisfied with the project object definition you have created, save the object by selecting Save or Save As from the File menu.

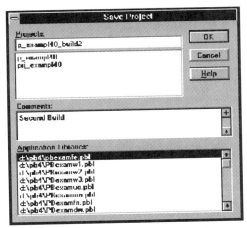

Figure 41-6: The Save Project dialog box

Close the Project painter by selecting Close from the File menu or the Control menu.

To build the application executable and its .PBDs, click the "Build" button on the Project PainterBar or select Build Project from the Project painter File menu.

Creating Executables and .PBDs Using the Project Painter

Currently, there are two ways to produce executables in PowerBuilder. You can use the Project painter to create a project object that defines the executable file name, .PBDs, and .PBRs. This first way allows you to create a new executable and .PBDs with all required resource referencing without having to redefine the executable each time you want to create it. The other way is to use the "Create EXE button" in the Application painter to define how

PowerBuilder will search for application objects at execution time as it creates an executable. This approach requires that you create .PBDs by using the Build Dynamic Library option in the Utilities menu of the Library painter.

Using the Project painter to create an executable

Open the Project painter by clicking on the "Project Painter" button in the PowerBar. The Select Project dialog box appears. Select a project.

To build the executable file and any .PBDs you have specified, click the "Build" button in the Project painter PainterBar or select Build Project from the File menu. PowerBuilder will then compile the executable file and .PBDs. If specified, it will regenerate all application objects. Any error messages will appear in a message box.

Once the process is complete, you can close the Project painter. If you have not saved changes in your project object, PowerBuilder prompts you to save the object.

Maintaining Project Objects

To modify an existing Project object or change the information contained in a project object, you first open the Project painter.

Select the project object you want to edit, and click "OK". The project painter opens with the settings defined for the executable (.EXE) file name, dynamic library (.PBDs) file names, resource (PBRs) file names, and library (.PBLs) names.

Modify the project object settings as necessary. When you have finished making changes to the project object, save the object definition by selecting Save from the File menu. Note, you do not have to build the project after defining or editing a project object.

To save the object under a new name, select Save As from the File menu.

To close the Project painter without saving any changes you may have made, select Close from the File menu, doubleÐclick the Control box, or select Close from the Control menu. When PowerBuilder prompts you to save the object, select "No" and no changes will be saved.

Deleting Project Objects

You can delete project objects from the Library painter. Project objects appear beneath the library in which the application object has been defined. To delete a project object:

Click the "Delete" button from the toolbar or select Delete from the Entry menu. Before PowerBuilder deletes an entry, it displays a message box asking if you are sure you want to delete the entry.
You can click:

>   (a)"Yes", to delete the entry.

>   (b)"No", to cancel deletion of the current entry, but continue deleting other selected entries not yet deleted.

>   (c)"Cancel", to cancel deletion of the current entry and the deletion of selected entries not yet deleted. Entries already deleted are not restored to the library.

The Project painter simplifies building and rebuilding executables and dynamic libraries for your projects by allowing you to define all the necessary files included in the project at one time. This added functionality to PowerBuilder 4.0 is sure to be a valuable tool in helping you manage and build your projects.

CHAPTER **42**

Grab Bag of
PowerBuilder Functions

By Michael MacDonald

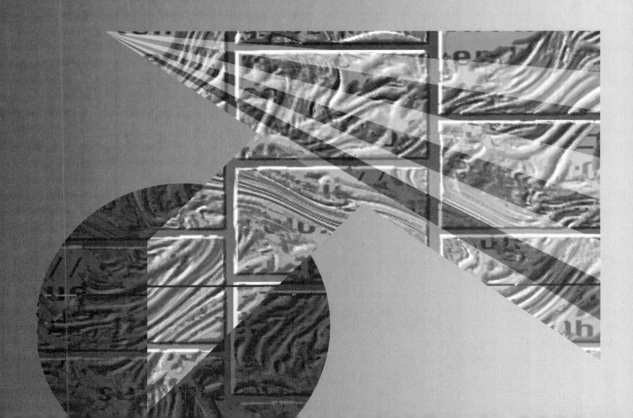

Grab Bag of PowerBuilder Functions

by **Michael MacDonald**

This chapter provides a grab bag of functions you will find useful in your day-to-day programming. These functions are also available to you as three .pbls: mdm.pbl includes a demonstration applet; dates.pbl includes date and financial functions; and mci_test.pbl includes a bonus multimedia set of routines.

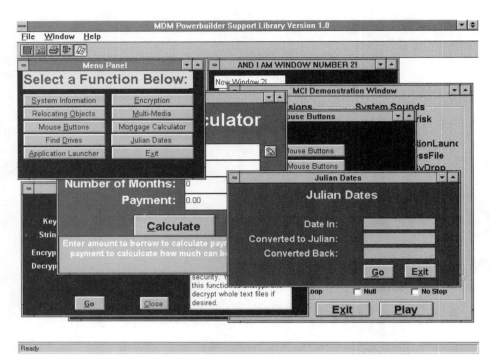

Figure 42-1: The main menu in the function demonstration applet with several sheets opened.

Some of these functions have been published in the pages of *PowerBuilder Developer's Journal* and have been collected here for your convenience. Also included in this chapter as well as published previously in the pages of *PBDJ* is a string encryption utility and a working multimedia applet for your use. However, most of these functions are original and appear here for the first time.

Many of these functions rely on interfacing with an outside DLL. Some make calls to util.dll. This dynamic link library has been written especially for this book and includes many useful functions. To use any function listed below that requires util.dll, you will need to copy that file from the CD-ROM to your Windows\System directory.

ChangeCurrentDir (string lpszDir)

RETURNS: Integer

PROTOTYPE: Function **Int ChangeCurrentDir (string lpszDir)** Library util.dll

This function accepts a fully qualified path string, changing the directory, and if necessary, the drive. The function returns 0 for success and -1 for error. **ChangeCurrentDir** effectively combines the **ChDrv** and **ChDir** functions located elsewhere in this library. Use this function for programmatic changes of the current directory where doing so via the common dialog interface would not be appropriate.

EXAMPLE:

```
string lpszDir
int i_rtn

lpszDir = "C:\PB4"

i_rtn = ChangeCurrentDir (lpszDir)
```

DEPENDENCIES: None

SEE ALSO: **ChDir, ChDrv**

ChDir (string lpszPath)

RETURNS: Integer

PROTOTYPE: Function **Int ChDir (String lpszPath)** Library util.dll

his function accepts a new directory as a string argument, and attempts to change to that directory. The function will not change drives (see **ChDrv** to change the drive; **ChangeCurrentDir** to perform both operations at once). The function returns 0 for success and -1 for failure. Use this function to change directories programmatically where doing so via the common dialog user interface would be inappropriate.

EXAMPLE:

```
int i_rtn
string s_path

s_path = "\Windows\System"

if ChDir (s_path) then
MessageBox ("Change Directory","Could not change. Possibly " + &
 s_path + " is an invalid directory!")
else
MessageBox ("Change Directory","Success!")
end if
```

DEPENDENCIES: None

SEE ALSO: **ChangeCurrentDir, ChDrv**

ChDrv (int Drive)

RETURNS: Integer

PROTOTYPE: Function **Int ChDrv(Int Drive)** Library util.dll

This function accepts an integer argument where 1 = Drive A, 2 = Drive B, etc., and attempts to change to that drive. The current directory is not changed. This function returns 0 for success and -1 for failure. Use this function to change drives programmatically where doing so by the common user interface dialog would be inappropriate.

EXAMPLE:

```
int i_drive
int i_rtn

i_drive = 3\\ Drive C

i_rtn = ChDrv (i_drive)
if i_rtn = -1 then
MessageBox ("Error","Could Not Change to Drive " + char(i_drive))
end if
```

DEPENDENCIES: None

SEE ALSO: **ChangeCurrentDir**, **ChDir**

EncryptString (string lpszString, string lpszKey)

EncryptString2 (string lpszString, string lpszKey)

RETURNS: Boolean

PROTOTYPE: Function Boolean **EncryptString (Ref String lpszString, String lpszKey)**
Library util.dll

Function Boolean **EncryptString2 (Ref String lpszString, String lpszKey)**
Library util.dll

These functions take two arguments: lpszString and lpszKey. LpszString is the string to be encrypted (or decrypted) and lpszKey is the password. The functions change lpszString directly and return TRUE for success and FALSE if an error was encountered.

While the two versions of the encryption algorithm work the same cosmetically, the second version is actually much more secure and is recommended.

To encrypt a string, pass it as the lpszString argument as shown below. Depending on the nature of what the program is doing, either the user or the program will provide a password. After returning from the function call, lpszString will contain the encrypted string. To unencrypt it, repeat the function call using the same password. Do NOT call the function using the wrong password–you may encrypt the string beyond recovery!

Please note that if you pass the text from a single-line edit box, what is shown on the screen will not change automatically, though its value in memory will. This is clearly shown in the example code snippet below.

The size of the input string or the key (see the caveat below) may be up to 32k.

The first version of the routine is a simple algorithm. The supplied password is boiled down to a one-character key and can be easily hacked by someone able to try 256 times. The second routine also uses a one character password, but changes it for every character in the file.

> **Note:** Federal law prohibits the export of any algorithm utilizing a key of more than thirty-one characters. The author distributes a full-featured encryption package–CCRYPT–which allows a key of up to twenty-four characters and limitless data size. CCRYPT can be found on most BBSes as shareware. The most recent release was 2.1 (ccrypt21.zip).

EXAMPLE:

```
If EncryptString (sle_password.text, "ABCDEF") then
sle_encrypted.text = sle_password.text
If EncryptString(sle_encrypted.text,"ABCDEF") then
sle_unencrypted.text = sle_encrypted.text
end if
else
MessageBox ("Error","String was not encrypted")
End If
```

DEPENDENCIES: None

SEE ALSO: f_EncryptString

f_2int_2long (integer, integer)

RETURNS: Long

This function takes two integer arguments and converts them into a long integer. The first argument forms the lower 16 bits while the second argument forms the high order 16 bits. The formula used is $(Arg1 + (65536 * Arg2)) * 65536$. This is useful in passing parameters, for example, to Windows API functions.

EXAMPLE:

```
Int i_XPos, i_YPos
Long l_rslt

i_XPos = 100
i_YPos = 100

l_rslt = f_ 2int_2long (i_Xpos, i_YPos)
```

SOURCE CODE:

```
// this function accepts two integer arguments and creates
// a 32-bit long integer out of them, placing the first
// argument into the lower 16 bits and placing the second
// argument into the high order 16 bits

Return (int1 + (65536 * int2) ) * 65536
```

DEPENDENCIES: None

f_8087()

RETURNS: String

This function returns Yes if a math coprocessor is present in the system, No if there is not, and Unknown if an error is encountered. This is useful in performing an inventory of system resources.

EXAMPLE:

```
String Rtn

Rtn = f_8087 ()

Choose Case Rtn
Case "Yes"
sle_1.text = "Yes, there is a math coprocessor present."
Case "No"
sle_1.text = "Nope - it ain't there."
Case Else
sle_1.text = "Uh-oh. Something doesn't compute."
End Choose
```

SOURCE CODE:

```
// this function checks for the existence of a math coprocessor
// returning yes or no
// set up the call

Long Rtn

Rtn =  f_win_flags ( 2 )

Choose Case Rtn
Case 1
return "Yes"
Case 0
return "No"
Case else
return "Unknown"
End Choose
```

DEPENDENCIES: None

SEE ALSO: f_win_flags

f_cpu ()

RETURNS: string

Function returns a string containing the type of CPU located in the system. Presently, the function returns one of the following values:

```
8086
80186
```

```
80286
80386
80486
Unknown
```

EXAMPLE:

```
sle_1.text = "The CPU on this system is a " + f_cpu()
```

SOURCE CODE:

```
// this function determines the CPU in the system
// the function works by passing the selected service to the
// WinFlags routine. Note that that routine could be called
// by itself

Long Rtn// CPU Type

Rtn = f_win_flags ( 1 )

Choose Case Rtn
Case 86
Return "8086"
Case 186
Return "80186"
Case 286
Return "80286"
Case 386
Return "80386"
Case 486
Return "80486"
Case else
Return "Unknown"
End Choose
```

DEPENDENCIES: None

SEE ALSO: f_win_flags

f_date_2_julian (date)

RETURNS: Long

This function takes a variable of type date and converts it to a julian format in the form yyyyddd.

EXAMPLE:

```
// convert date in sle_1 to julian and
// then back again

sle_2.text = string (f_date_2_julian (date(sle_1.text)))

sle_3.text = string (f_julian_2_date (long(sle_2.text)))
```

SOURCE CODE:

```
// this function takes a date, makes it into a julian,
// and accepts the argument:
// date_inof type date

long rtn
int temp, i
int days[12] = {31,28,31,30,31,30,31,31,30,31,30,31}

// first, determine if this a leap year

if f_is_leap (Year(date_in)) then
rtn++
end if

// now, figure the month portion

temp = month(date_in) - 1
for i = 1 to temp
rtn = rtn + days[i]
next

// now, figure the day portion

rtn = rtn + day(date_in)

// now, correct for possibly 2/29

if month(date_in) = 2 and day(date_in) = 29 then
rtn --
end if

// now, add on the year

rtn = rtn + (Year(date_in) * 1000)

return rtn
```

DEPENDENCIES: None

SEE ALSO: f_julian_2_date

f_day_of_year (date)

RETURNS: Integer

This function takes the date provided and returns the number of the day of the year such as 32 for February 1st.

EXAMPLE:

```
int i_day_no

i_day_no = f_day_of_year (12/25/94)
```

SOURCE CODE:

```
// this function accepts a date and returns the
```

```
// day of the year that it falls on
// date_in of type date

long temp

temp = f_date_2_julian ( date_in )

return mod (temp, 1000)
```

DEPENDENCIES: f_date_2_julian

SEE ALSO: f_date_2_julian

f_dos_ver()
RETURNS: Decimal

This function determines the current version of DOS running on the system and returns it as a decimal.

EXAMPLE:

```
sle_1.text = "The current version of DOS is " + string (f_ dos_ver (), "#.##")
```

SOURCE CODE:

```
// this function returns the current DOS version

Decimal d_rtn
Integer i_HiVer, i_LoVer ,i_wver
Long l_RecValue

l_RecValue = GetVersion ()

i_wver = IntHigh (l_RecValue )
i_HiVer = MOD(i_wVer,256)
i_lover = i_wver / 256

d_rtn = i_HiVer + (i_LoVer / 100)

Return d_rtn
```

DEPENDENCIES: None

SEE ALSO: f_win_ver

f_EncryptString (string lpszString, string lpszKey)
RETURNS: Boolean

PROTOTYPE: Function Boolean EncryptString(ref string lpszString, string lpszKey) Library util.dll

This function accepts two arguments: lpszString and lpszKey. LpszString is the string to be encrypted (or decrypted), and lpszKey is the password. The function changes lpszString directly, and returns True for success and False if an error was encountered.

To encrypt a string, pass it as the lpszString argument as shown below. Depending on the nature of what the program is doing, either the user or the program will provide a password. After returning from the function call, lpszString will contain the encrypted string. To unencrypt it, repeat the function call using the same password. Do NOT call the function using the wrong password–you may encrypt the string beyond recovery!

Please note that if you pass the text from a single-line edit box, what is shown on the screen will not automatically change, even though its value in memory will. This is clearly shown in the example code snippet below. A strategy for encrypting a string and then displaying the result would be to use a temporary string variable, e.g.:

```
string s_temp
s_temp = sle_1.text
if f_EncryptString (s_temp, sle_password)
sle_1.text = s_temp
end if
```

The size of the input string and the key (see the caveat below) may be up to 32k.

Please note that this a simple encryption algorithm. The supplied "password" is boiled down to a one-character key; thus, a hacker would have a one in 256 chance of breaking the code. However, this should provide adequate protection for password storage on the database, etc. If there is interest in a more sophisticated scheme, please let me know.

Note: Federal law prohibits the export of any algorithm utilizing a key of more than thirty-one characters. The author distributes a full-featured encryption package–CCRYPT– which allows a key of up to twenty-four characters and limitless data size. CCRYPT can be found on most BBSes as shareware. The most recent release was 2.1 (ccrypt21.zip).

EXAMPLE:

```
If f_EncryptString (sle_password.text, "ABCDEF") then
sle_encrypted.text = sle_password.text
If f_EncryptString(sle_encrypted.text,"ABCDEF") then
sle_unencrypted.text = sle_encrypted.text
end if
else
MessageBox ("Error","String was not encrypted")
End If
```

DEPENDENCIES: None

SEE ALSO: EncryptString

f_exit_windows (long, integer)

RETURNS: Integer

PROTOTYPE: Function Int ExitWindows(Long dwReturnCode, Int reserved) Library User This function attempts to exit Windows. If any application, such as a DOS window, refuses to terminate, then this function will return 0 to the application. At that point the programmer should send a MessageBox to the user indicating what has happened. Please note that this function will also cause your application to terminate, and should only be used under carefully selected circumstances.

This function accepts two arguments. DwReturnCode is a numeric return code to be passed to DOS. Normally, this can be filled with a zero, unless you wish to specifically pass a certain code. For instance, a DOS batch file might launch a Windows application and then evaluate the error code on return. Also, passing a value of 1 will cause the system to reboot.

> **Tip:** Passing a value of 67 will do the same thing, since this equates to the Hex 43 that Windows uses to signal DOS to reboot the system.

The second argument is an integer that is reserved for use by future versions of Windows, and is provided here for upward compatibility.

EXAMPLE:

```
// the following code will reboot the system unless one or
// more applications refuse to terminate

Int dummy

dummy = f_ Exit_Windows (1,0)

// if we have come this far, then Windows did not shut down!
// Normally, dummy will have a value of zero. However, this
// code does make that assumption.

MessageBox ("Exit Windows","One or more apps refused to close!",Exclamation!)
```

SOURCE CODE:

```
// this function causes windows to end. If a program
// refuses to end, then this routine returns with a zero

// the dwreturncode controls how this happens:
// a value of 1 causes the system to reboot
// any other value causes dwreturncode to be sent to DOS
// as a return value

Int i_rtn
long l_rtnval

If dwreturncode = 1 then
l_rtnval = 67
else
l_rtnval = dwreturncode
end if

i_rtn = ExitWindows (l_rtnval,1)

return 0
```

DEPENDENCIES: None

f_exit_windows_exec (string lpszEXE, string lpszParams)

RETURNS: Integer

This function will exit Windows and run a DOS application, where lpszExe is the full path name of the DOS program to run. LpszParams is an optional command line argument to the DOS program. Windows will restart after the DOS program terminates.

EXAMPLE:

```
// need to run this COM program before proceeding

f_exit_window_exec ("c:\comm\procomm.exe","-support.scr")
```

SOURCE CODE:

```
// this function will terminate Windows, run the DOS
// application specified in the lpszExe argument
// (must be a full path name) and then restart windows.
// Use the lpszParams argument to pass any parameters or
// command line arguments to the DOS application

return ExitWindowsExec (lpszExe, lpszParams)
```

DEPENDENCIES: None

f_file_extension (string)

RETURNS: String

This function will return the extension of the filename provided.

EXAMPLE:

```
string s_file_name = "c:\windows\win.ini"
string s_ext

s_ext = f_file_extension (s_file_name)
```

SOURCE CODE:

```
// this function accepts a string as an argument and
// returns the x characters to the right of the period.

return  right(fname, (len(fname)-pos(fname,".")))
```

DEPENDENCIES: None

f_free_gdi()

RETURNS: Integer

This function returns an integer of 0 to 100, which is the percentage of free space for GDI objects. This includes such items as fonts and drawing objects.

EXAMPLE:

```
Int PctFree

PctFree = f_free_gdi()
```

SOURCE CODE:

```
// This function returns as an integer from 0 to 100
// the percentage of free space for GDI objects

Return GetFreeSystemResources (1)
```

DEPENDENCIES: None

SEE ALSO: f_free_sys, f_free_user

f_free_sys ()

RETURNS: Integer

This function returns an integer of 0 to 100, which is the percentage of free system resources.

EXAMPLE:

```
Int PctFree

PctFree = f_free_sys()
```

SOURCE CODE:

```
// This function returns as an integer from 0 to 100
// the percentage of free system resources

Return GetFreeSystemResources (0)
```

DEPENDENCIES: None

SEE ALSO: f_free_gdi, f_free_user

f_free_user ()

RETURNS: Integer

This function returns an integer of 0 to 100, which is the percentage of free space for user objects, such as windows and menus.

EXAMPLE:

```
Int PctFree
```

```
PctFree = f_free_user()
```

SOURCE CODE:

// This function returns as an integer from 0 to 100
// the percentage of free system resources

Return GetFreeSystemResources (0)

DEPENDENCIES: None

SEE ALSO: f_free_gdi, f_free_sys

f_fut_value (decimal principal, decimal intrate, integer periods)
RETURNS: Decimal

This financial function will return the result of investment principal invested at intrate interest rate, compounded for the periods provided.

EXAMPLE:

```
// Calculate the return on 1000 invested for 24 months
// at 12% per year compounded monthly

decimal return

return = f_fut_val (1000, .01, 24)
```

SOURCE CODE:

```
// This function will calculate the total
// amount of principal and interest on
// an investment given an interest rate
// and a number of compound periods
// The function takes the arguments:
//  Principal  Amount Invested
//  IntRate    Interest Rate per Period
//  Periods    Number of Periods Invested

Return Principal * ((1 + IntRate)^ Periods)
```

DEPENDENCIES: None

SEE ALSO: f_periods, f_pmt, f_pmt_beg, f_periods, f_periods_beg

f_Get_Disk_Free (int Drive)
RETURNS: Unsigned Long

This function returns the amount of free space available on the drive indicated in the argument. Use an integer for the argument: A=1, B=2, C=3, and so on. Use this function to determine if there is enough free space for adding data to a database, writing out a large file, etc.

EXAMPLE:

```
// find the amount of free space on C drive

sle_3.text = string (f_Get_Disk_Free(3),"#,##0")
```

SOURCE CODE:

```
// returns the amount of free space on the drive specified
// where drive 1 = A, 2 = B, etc.

if drive > 0 then
if drive < 27 then
Return GetDiskFree(Drive)
end if
end if

MessageBox ("f_get_disk_free","Drive"&
 + string(drive) + "is out of range",StopSign!)
Return -1
```

DEPENDENCIES: None

f_get_drive_type (int DriveNo)

RETURNS: Integer

This function searches for the drive specified and determines the type of drive. To use, specify the drive (see below). The function then returns one of the following values:

0 = Drive does not exist or could not determine type
2 = Removable media (i.e. floppy diskette)
3 = Fixed media (i.e. hard drive)
4 = Remote media (i.e. network drive)

Drive is specified as an integer using A = 0, B = 1, ... Z = 25.
This function might be useful when trying to determine where to write a temporary file (fixed drives are faster than removable).

EXAMPLE:

```
integer i_counter
For i_counter = 64 to 89

// ASCII values A through Z minus 1

s_drive = "Drive " + char (i_counter + 1)

Choose Case f_get_drive_type (i_counter )

Case 0
sle_1.text = " not present"
Case 2
sle_1.text = " is a removable drive"
Case 3
sle_1.text = " is a fixed drive"
```

```
Case 4
sle_1.text = " is a remote drive"

End Choose
```

Next

SOURCE CODE:

```
// this function returns the type of the drive specified
// and is also called to determine if the drive exists
// Function returns:
// 0-Drive not found or could not determine type
// 2-Removable (ie floppy)
// 3-Fixed (hard disk)
// 4-Remote (network)

Return GetDriveType (nDrive)
```

DEPENDENCIES: None

SEE ALSO: Demo the program window, w_find_drives, which uses this function in a loop to find all of the connected disk drives.

f_get_sys_color (integer)

RETURNS: Long

This is an interesting function that returns the RGB color of the control, indicated in the comments section of the function (see source code below). For instance, to get the color of the button face, call f_get_sys_color (15).

EXAMPLE:

```
long l_rgb_color

// get system color of caption text

l_rgb_color = f_get_sys_color (9)
```

SOURCE CODE:

```
// this function accepts an argument specifying the Windows
// system object and returns it's color. This applies to
// all windows system-wide objects.
// to access a specific object, its value must be supplied:
//    Object          Value
// -------------    ------------
// Scroll Bar        0
// Background        1
// Active Caption    2
// Inactive Caption  3
// Menu              4
// Window            5
// Window Frame      6
// Menu Text         7
```

```
// Window Text             8
// Caption Text            9
// Active Border          10
// Inactive Border        11
// App Work Space         12
// Highlight              13
// Highlight Text         14
// Button Face            15
// Button Shadow          16
// Gray Text              17
// Button Text            18
// Inactive Caption Text  19
// Button Highlight       20

Return GetSysColor (nIndex)
```

DEPENDENCIES: None

f_get_sys_dir ()

RETURNS: String

This function returns the fully qualified path of the Windows system directory as a string. This directory, normally c:\windows\system, is where drivers and dynamic link libraries (DLLs) should be installed. The function is useful if your application either installs these DLLs or needs to access them directly.

Note that the native windows function for this has two limitations that the library circumvents. First, the path is returned without the trailing "\" character, unless the system directory is also the root directory. This function always ensures that the path is returned with a trailing backslash. Second, the Windows function requires a preallocated string. This function allocates a 128-character string, and then passes a trimmed version of that string back to the application.

EXAMPLE:

```
string s_path_name = f_get_sys_dir ()
```

SOURCE CODE:

```
// this function adds onto the GetWindowsDirectory
// function to return the System directory.

string s_path
s_path = space (128)
GetWindowsDirectory (s_path, 128)
s_path = trim(s_path) + "\System\"

Return s_path
```

DEPENDENCIES: None

SEE ALSO : f_get_win_dir

f_get_win_dir ()

RETURNS: String

This function returns the Windows directory, ensuring that the trailing slash has been added so the programmer doesn't have to add it. This function would be used if the win.ini, system.ini, or other .ini files needed to be examined.

EXAMPLE:

```
string s_path_name

s_file_name = f_get_win_dir + "Win.Ini"
```

SOURCE CODE:

```
// this function returns the windows
// directory adding the "\" if needed

string s_path
s_path = space (128)
GetWindowsDirectory (s_path, 128)

s_path = trim(s_path)

if right(s_path,1) <> "\" then
s_path = s_path + "\"
end if

Return s_path
```

DEPENDENCIES: None

f_GetMem()

RETURNS: Long

This function returns the amount of free memory, in bytes, from the global heap.

EXAMPLE:

```
Long AmtFree

AmtFree = GetMem()

If GetMem() < 500000 then
MessageBox ("Memory","Insufficient Memory for Operation)
End If

SLE_1.Text = String (GetMem())
```

SOURCE CODE:

```
// this function returns the number of bytes of memory
// in the global heap
```

```
Long NoBytes

NoBytes = GetFreeSpace (0)

Return NoBytes
```

DEPENDENCIES: None

f_is_leap(integer year)

RETURNS: Boolean

This function returns true, if the supplied year is a leap year.

EXAMPLE:

```
int i_year = 1996

If f_is_leap (i_year) then
// do something
else
// do something else
end if
```

SOURCE CODE:

```
// Function RETURNS True if it is a leap year
// and accepts as an argument:
//   Year_In as Long

If IsDate("Feb 29, " + string(Year_in)) then
RETURN TRUE
ELSE
RETURN FALSE
END IF
```

DEPENDENCIES: None

f_julian_2_date (long)

RETURNS: Date

This function is the complement to f_date_2_julian. It converts a julian date, in the format of yymmdd or yymmdd, to a date variable.

EXAMPLE: see f_date_2_julian

SOURCE CODE:

```
// this function takes in a julian date and coverts it to
// a regular date. It accepts:
//   julian_in  of type long

int year_temp
string temp
```

```
// first, get the year

year_temp = julian_in / 1000
julian_in = MOD (julian_in, 1000)
year_temp --

// now, work forward from 12/31 of prior year

temp = "12/31/" + string(year_temp)
return RelativeDate (date(temp), julian_in)
```

DEPENDENCIES: None

SEE ALSO: f_date_2_julian

f_launch_file (string filename)

RETURNS: Integer

This function will "launch" a filename provided to it in one of two ways. If it is an executable such as an .exe, .com, .pif, or .bat file, the program will be launched directly. Otherwise, the win.ini file will be examined for the application association of the filename provided, and the function will then launch the application with the filename as an argument.

EXAMPLE:

```
int i_rtn
string s_title

i_rtn = f_launch_file ("*.*")

if i_rtn < 0 then
MessageBox(s_title,"An error was encountered")
end if
```

SOURCE CODE:

```
// this function displays a list of files of matching 'type'
// and attempts to launch the one selected using
// the win.ini file extensions

string s_filename, s_extension, s_app, s_path
integer i_rtn

if filetype = "" then filetype = "*.*"

s_extension = f_file_extension (filetype)

i_rtn = GetFileOpenName ("Launch File",s_path,s_filename,s_extension, &
s_extension + "files, *." + s_extension)

Choose Case i_rtn
case -1 /* error */
return -1
case 0  /* cancel */
return 0
case 1  /* file selected */
```

```
s_extension = f_file_extension (s_filename)
choose case upper(s_extension)
case "BAT","COM","EXE","PIF"
run (s_path)
case else
s_app = profilestring & ("win.ini","Extensions",s_extension,"none")
If s_app = "none" then
MessageBox("Launch File",&"
There is no application associated~n~rwith "+s_extension&
+" in the WIN.INI")
Return -2
End If

// now, peel the '^.aaa' off of the end

s_app = left(s_app, pos(s_app, "^.", len(s_app) - 6) - 1 )

Run (s_app + " " + s_path)
end choose
End Choose

Return 1
```

DEPENDENCIES: None

f_mci (string)
RETURNS: Integer

This is a simple function to play a .wav file. See the mci.pbl in the sample application for more sophisticated routines.

EXAMPLE:
```
string s_wav = "C:\Windows\Tada.Wav"

f_mci (s_wav)
```

SOURCE CODE:
```
// this function passes a command to the mci device
// As a test, play TADA!

int rtn
Long TempZ = 0

rtn = mciSendString ("Open " + cmd, TempZ, 0, 0)
rtn = mciSendString ("Play " + cmd, TempZ, 0, 0)
rtn = mciSendString ("Close " + cmd, TempZ, 0, 0)

return 1
```

DEPENDENCIES: None

f_mode ( )
RETURNS: String

This function determines the current operating mode (386 Enhanced or Standard) that Windows is operating in.

EXAMPLE:

```
string s_cur_mode:

s_cur_mode = f_mode ( )
if s_cur_mode = "Enhanced" then

// do something

end if
```

SOURCE CODE:

```
// this function determines the Windows Mode
// the function works by passing the selected service to the
// WinFlags routine. Note that that routine could be called
// by itself

Long Rtn // Mode

Rtn = f_win_flags ( 3 ) // first, is this enhanced mode?

If Rtn = 1 then Return "Enhanced"

Rtn = f_win_flags ( 6 ) // Then, is this standard mode?

If Rtn = 1 then Return "Standard"

Return "Unknown"
```

DEPENDENCIES: None

f_pmt (decimal principal, decimal intrate, integer periods)

RETURNS: Decimal (payment amount)

This financial function works the same as the payment calculation function in Excel, Lotus 1-2-3 and Quattro Pro. You provide the amount to be borrowed, the yearly interest rate, and the length of the loan in months and the function will calculate the monthly payment as shown in the illustration.

EXAMPLE:

```
sle_4.text = string (f_pmt ( dec(sle_1.text), (dec(sle_2.text) / 12),  & inte-
ger(sle_3.text)),"#,###.00")
```

SOURCE CODE:

```
// this function will calculate the payment amount for
// a loan of the specified length at the specified
// interest rate for a loan paid at end of
```

```
// the payment period. Input is:
//      Principal of loan
//      IntRate of loan
//      Periods Length of Loan

Decimal Temp1, Temp2

Temp1 = IntRate * ((1+IntRate)^Periods)
Temp2 = ((1 + IntRate)^Periods) - 1

Return Principal * (Temp1 / Temp2)
```

DEPENDENCIES: None

SEE ALSO: f_pmt_beg, f_periods

f_pmt_beg (decimal principal, decimal intrate, integer periods)

RETURNS: Decimal (payment amount)

This function is the same as f_pmt, except that the payment is calculated as though each payment were made at the beginning of each loan period (instead of the more typical end of each period), thus reducing the payment amount somewhat.

EXAMPLE:

```
// 30 year loan of $100,000 at 8% interest

decimal payment

payment = f_pmt_beg (100000, .08, 360)
```

SOURCE CODE:

```
// this function will calculate the payment amount for
// a loan of the specified length at the specified
// interest rate for a loan paid at end of
// the payment period. Input is:
//      Principal of loan
//      IntRate of loan
//      Periods Length of Loan

Decimal Temp1, Temp2

Temp1 = IntRate * ((1+IntRate)^Periods)
Temp2 = ((1 + IntRate)^Periods) - 1

Return Principal * (Temp1 / Temp2)
```

DEPENDENCIES: None

SEE ALSO: f_pmt, f_periods_beg

f_principal (decimal payment, decimal intrate, integer periods)

f_principal_beg (decimal payment, decimal intrate, integer periods)

RETURNS: Decimal (amount that can be borrowed)

These two functions are the complements to f_pmt and f_pmt_beg, respectively. Each function calculates how much can be borrowed using a given payment amount, interest rate, and loan length. F_principal_beg assumes that each payment will be made at the beginning of the period, instead of the end, thus increasing the amount somewhat.

EXAMPLE:

```
// how much can be borrowed for a loan of 30 years at 8% if
// the payment amount is $750 per month?

decimal amount

amount = f_principal (750, .08, 360)
```

SOURCE CODE:

```
f_principal

// this function determines how much principal
// could be borrowed given a certain payment,
// interest rate, and repayment period. Payment
// is assumed to be at the end of the payment
// period. Function takes three arguments:
//   Payment   Amount of Payment
//   IntRate   Interest Rate
//   Periods   Number of Payment Periods

Decimal Temp1, Temp2

Temp1 = ((1 + IntRate)^Periods) -1
Temp2 = IntRate * ((1 + IntRate)^Periods)

Return Payment * (Temp1 / Temp2)

f_principal_beg

// this function determines how much principal
// could be borrowed given a certain payment,
// interest rate, and repayment period. Payment
// is assumed to be at the beginning of the payment
// period. Function takes three arguments:
//   Payment   Amount of Payment
//   IntRate   Interest Rate
//   Periods   Number of Payment Periods

Decimal Temp1, Temp2

Temp1 = Payment * (IntRate + 1)
Temp2 = (1 - ((1 + IntRate)^(Periods * -1))) / IntRate
```

```
Return Temp1 * Temp2
```

DEPENDENCIES: None

SEE ALSO: f_pmt, f_pmt_beg

f_set_parent_any (integer i_obj, window w_new_parent)

RETURNS: Integer

This is an interesting function which can move any control from one window to another. The programmer needs to determine the handle of the object to be moved (see the source code example and the f_set_paren_ddlb following as examples), and then pass the new window. The object will then be moved to that new window.

EXAMPLE:

```
int i_obj
string s_title

if cb_1.enabled = false then
return
else
cb_1.enabled = false
end if

s_title = "Move ListBox Demo"

MessageBox (s_title, "About to Open 2nd Window")

opensheet (w_list2,w_mdi_frame,2,ORIGINAL!)

MessageBox (s_title, "Now about to move listbox~n~rand Who Am I button to the
other window!")

ddlb_1.text = "Now Window 2!"
i_obj = Handle(ddlb_1)

If f_set_Parent_any (i_obj, w_list2) < 1 then
MessageBox (s_title, "Move of drop down list box failed.")
else
MessageBox (s_title, "It worked! Will now move Who AM I button...")
End If

i_obj = Handle(cb_2)

If f_set_Parent_any (i_obj, w_list2) < 1 then
MessageBox (s_title, "Move of command button failed.")
else
MessageBox (s_title, "It worked! Ain't life just grand?")
End If
```

SOURCE CODE:

```
// This function moves the object referenced as 'obj' and
// moves it to the window specified as par.
// It is the user's responsibility to determine the handle number
// of the object. The function looks it up for the window. This
```

```
// allows this routine to be used by any object. Object specific
// functions are also located as part of this library and these
// take care of both handle lookups
// The function returns the handle of the previous window. Thus, if
// zero is returned, an error has occurred.

int i_hnd

i_hnd = HANDLE(w_par)

Return SetParent(i_obj, i_hnd)
```

DEPENDENCIES: None

f_set_parent_ddlb (dropdownlistbox dl_obj, window w_par)

RETURNS: Integer

This function is similar to the previous one, except that it takes care of finding the handle of the object being moved.

SOURCE CODE:

```
// This function moves the drop down list box specified
// to the window specified as w_par.
// The function returns the handle of the previous window. Thus, if
// zero is returned, an error has occurred.

int i_hnd, i_obj

i_hnd = HANDLE(w_par)
i_obj = Handle(dl_obj)

Return SetParent(i_obj, i_hnd)
```

DEPENDENCIES: None

f_set_sys_color (integer nchanges, integer syscolor, long color)

RETURNS: None

This function is the complement of the f_get_sys_color, and changes the system color of the specified object (see the source code below). Nchanges indicates the number of colors that will be changed in the event that syscolor is an array. Just use 1 for nchanges and change one color at a time, as shown in the example.

EXAMPLE:

```
// make the system color for text white

f_set_sys_color (1, 9, 65280)
```

SOURCE CODE:

```
// this function sets the color value specified by
```

```
// lpColorValues for the object specified by lpSysColor.

// This object may be one of the following:
//    Object              Value
// -------------        ------------
// Scroll Bar               0
// Background               1
// Active Caption           2
// Inactive Caption         3
// Menu                     4
// Window                   5
// Window Frame             6
// Menu Text                7
// Window Text              8
// Caption Text             9
// Active Border           10
// Inactive Border         11
// App Work Space          13
// Highlight Text          14
// Button Face             15
// Button Shadow           16
// Gray Text               17
// Button Text             18
// Inactive Caption Text   19
// Button Highlight        20

// Note that while the Windows function allows the
// changing of multiple items at one time, this one only
// does one at a time. Variable naming conventions are
// consistent with the Windows API; however, for future
// enhancement considerations.

SetSysColors (1, lpSysColor, lpColorValue)

Return
```

DEPENDENCIES: None

f_Swap_Mouse (Int)

RETURNS: Integer

This function swaps the functionality of the left and right mouse buttons. To use, pass a 1 to swap and pass a 0 to restore default functionality. The function will return one of the following values:

```
         0 = Buttons swapped OK.
 -1 or 1 = Left and Right were already swapped.
    -100 = Illegal Swap value passed. No action taken.
```

This function accepts one argument, Swap. Pass a 1 to swap the buttons or a 0 to restore default functionality.

EXAMPLE:

```
Int i_Swap, i_Rtn

i_Swap = 1 \\ swap left and right buttons
```

```
Rtn = f_swap_mouse (i_Swap)

\\ If Rtn is now equal to 1 or -1, then  the buttons have
\\ already been swapped.
\\ If Rtn equals 0, then the function swapped the buttons.
\\ -100 indicates that the i_Swap argument had an illegal
\\ value.
```

SOURCE CODE:

```
// this function will swap the left and right mouse buttons
// when passed 1 as a parameter. Passing 0 restores
// normal functionality.
// If an illegal argument (non 0 or 1) is passed, then the
// function immediately returns a -100
// Function returns -1 if the mouse buttons
// were reversed prior to this call. Otherwise, 0 is returned.

If (bSwap < 0) or (bswap > 1) then
return -100
end if

Int i_Rtn

i_Rtn = SwapMouseButton (bSwap)

If i_rtn = 0 then
return 0
else
return -1
end if
```

DEPENDENCIES: None

f_win_flags (integer request)

RETURNS: Long

This function is used by numerous other system functions. Win_flags contains coded (at bit level) information, such as the current DOS and Windows versions. Because PowerBuilder does not contain bit-wise operators, we are forced to do successive divisions by two to "strip off" each bit in succession. This function is not meant to be called directly.

SOURCE CODE:

```
// this routine is called by various other routines or can be
// called directly. The Request parameter is used as follows:

//     Request        Description
//     -------        ------------------------------------------------
//        1           CPU type. RETURNS 86, 186, 286, 386, 486,
//                       or 0 = Unknown
//        2           CoProcessor. RETURNS 1 = Yes, 0 = No
//        3           Enhanced Mode. RETURNS 1 or 0
//        4           Paging Active. RETURNS 1 or 0
//        5           Protected Mode. RETURNS 1 or 0
```

```
//      6            Standard Mode. RETURNS 1 or 0
//      7            Windows Emulated. RETURNS 1 or 0
//      99           RETURNS long win_flags for program evaluation
//      Other        RETURNS -1 error

// Note that this is coded very awkwardly because I
// cannot figure out how to get at the bit level of a byte

Long Flags
Boolean LFrame, SFrame, MChip, Prot, Std, Enh
Int CType

Flags = GetWinFlags ()

If Request = 99 then return Flags

If Flags >= 32768 then Flags = Flags - 32768

If Flags >= 16384 then Flags = Flags - 16384

If Flags >= 8192 then Flags = Flags - 8192

If Flags >= 4096 then Flags = Flags - 4096

If Flags >= 2048 then Flags = Flags - 2048

If Flags >= 1024 then
MChip = True
FLags = Flags - 1024
End If

If Flags >= 512 then
SFrame = True
FLags = Flags - 512
End If

If Flags >= 256 then
LFrame = True
Flags = Flags - 256
End If

If Flags >= 128 then
CType = 186
Flags = Flags - 128
End If

IF Flags >= 64 then
CType = 86
Flags = Flags - 64
End If

If Flags >= 32 then
Enh = True
Flags = Flags - 32
End If

If Flags >=16 then
Std = True
Flags = Flags - 16
End If

If Flags >= 8 then
```

```
CType = 486
Flags = Flags - 8
End If

If Flags >= 4 then
CType = 386
Flags = Flags - 4
End If

If Flags >= 2 then
CType = 286
Flags = Flags - 2
End If

If Flags >=1 then
Prot = True
End If

Choose Case Request

Case 1
Return CType
Case 2
If MChip then
Return 1
else
return 0
End If
Case 3
If Enh then
Return 1
else
Return 0
End If

// Case 4
// Not implemented
// Case 5
// Not Implemented
// Case 6
// Not implemented
// Case 7
// Not Implemented

Case Else
Return -1
End Choose
```

f_Window_2_Top (Window)

RETURNS: Integer

```
 0 = No Error
-1 = Window Not Found
```

This function brings the named window to the top, regardless of the window's current location.

EXAMPLE:

```
Int Rtn

Rtn = f_window_2_top (This)

Rtn =f_window_2_top (w_customer_update)

If f_window_2_top (w_display_customer_popup) < 0 then
MessageBox ("Error","Could Not Locate Window!")
End If
```

SOURCE CODE:

```
// function brings the specified object/window to the top
// to bring the prior window to the top, set prior to true
//
// Function returns:
//
//    0 = Success
//   -1 = Object Not Found

Integer i_HandleNum, i_rtn
Boolean b_Dummy

i_HandleNum = Handle (ObjectName)

// add true or false to get prior object

IF i_HandleNum = 0 then
  Rtn = 1
Else
b_Dummy = BringWindowToTop (HandleNum)
i_Rtn = 0
End If

Return i_Rtn
```

DEPENDENCIES: None

RevString(string lpszString)

RETURNS: None

PROTOTYPE: SubRoutine String RevString(string lpszString) Library util.dll

This function takes a string as an argument and reverses it. This may be useful to facilitate searching backward through a string, etc.

EXAMPLE:

```
string s_temp

s_temp = sle_1.text
RevString(s_temp)
sle_1.text = s_temp
```

DEPENDENCIES: None

CHAPTER 43

Creating Reusable DataWindow Functionality

By Steve Benfield

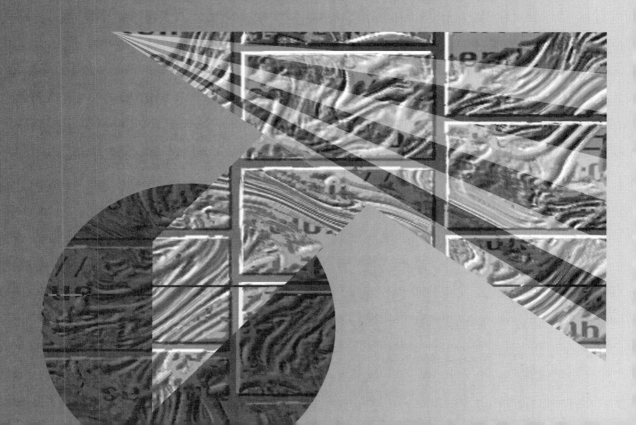

Creating Reusable DataWindow Functionality

By **Steve Benfield**

Most people don't start using inheritance in their PowerBuilder applications until they've written a few small ones. They eventually dig into the manual and start learning how to inherit windows. A large number of PowerBuilder programmers may stop there believing that they are using inheritance to its fullest. However, if you stop at just inheriting windows, you are selling yourself, and PowerBuilder, short. The flexibility and power of a reusable ancestor DataWindow control is amazing. Not only is the DataWindow control powerful in its own right, by customizing it and extending it, you can make the DataWindow downright amazing. To really understand and use this chapter, you'll need to know some prerequisites:

Understand the DataWindow Control and DataWindow Object
Have a least a cursory knowledge of Modify
Understand how user objects work

> *[Note: For the remainder of this chapter, we'll refer to the ancestor DataWindow control user object as dwa_main. You may name your control whatever you want however.]*

Using Inheritable DataWindow Controls

So lets begin by looking at some benefits of an inheritable DataWindow control and how to reengineer your system if you haven't been using one. Also, we'll learn a technique to almost force our programmers to use the new inheritable DataWindow user object.

Why should you use a user object DataWindow instead of PowerBuilder's?

When you place a DataWindow control on a window what you are doing is creating a new DataWindow based on the system defined DataWindow. What this means is that the only way to add functionality to your DataWindow is to add code to the event scripts. Can you declare your own functions for that DataWindow? No, you can't. Can you add attributes or instance variables to that DataWindow? No, you can't. (You can only add them to the Window itself at this point.) If you wanted to duplicate behavior on two different DataWindows what would you have to do? Well, the only way would be to rewrite code. So, is this a good use of Object-Oriented programming? No way.

The answer is to define a DataWindow user object. This is very easy to do. Just go into the User Object Painter and select New and then Standard Visual user object. Then select DataWindow as the type. You'll now see a little white box. This is your DataWindow control. Save it and name it dwa_main. This will become your highest level ancestor DataWindow.

Now, instead of placing PowerBuilder's internal DataWindow on your windows, you'll place the user object. Placing the user object is easy too; just select the user object toolbar button. (It is just to the right of the GroupBox button on the Window painter.) You'll be given a list of objects you can place, select dwa_main. Now, double click on the new DataWindow you've placed. What is it named? If you started with a brand new window, this control should be called dw_1. As far as the window is concerned, all you did was place a DataWindow control on the window. You can use all of the normal functions, attributes, and events of the DataWindow like you've always done. However, you can now add instance & shared variables, events, and functions to your ancestor DataWindow. All of these new things you add will be available on each of your DataWindows from now on because you'll be inheriting from dwa_main—not PowerBuilder's built-in DataWindow control.

What if you haven't been using a DataWindow user object?

One problem with trying to use a new reusable object is that none of your old code will use that object. However, there is a technique that will allow you to change the ancestor DataWindow that your windows are using from DataWindow to dwa_main.

To perform this surgery, export the windows or user objects that have DataWindows on them, change a few references, and then reimport your objects back into your library. Before doing any of this, please make sure you backup.

When you export your windows (or Custom Visual user objects) you'll see some code like the following:

```
type dw_1 from datawindow within w_anc
```

What this tells the PowerBuilder compiler is that you are declaring a DataWindow named dw_1 inherited from datawindow. Well, to make dw_1 inherit from dwa_main, just change datawindow to dwa_main. You'll have to make this change one more time in the exported file because the line shown above is repeated twice in the window source code. For more information on changing your ancestor objects, read the November issue of the *Power-Builder Developer's Journal*.

Getting Rid of the default DataWindow Icon and substituting yours

If you'd like your programmers begin placing your dwa_main user object on the screen, you'll want to customize the window toolbar. What you want to do is add a new icon to represent the DataWindow control. Place it directly to the right of the original PowerBuilder DataWindow icon. A dialog box will popup asking for information on the user object you want. Select dwa_main, set any microhelp or toolbar text that you'd like. After you've determined that your new button really works, go back to the toolbar and remove PowerBuilder's built in toolbar.

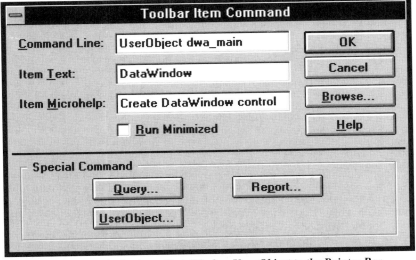

Figure 43-1: Assigning a DataWindow User Object to the Painter Bar

Figure 43-2: Revised PainterBar

The toolbar in Figure 1 looks very similar to the one PowerBuilder provides but you'll notice that the DataWindow button is different. Many of your programmers may never notice!

The DataWindow Constructor Event

If you need to write code that only executes when your application is first run, you'd put it in the open event of the application. If you needed to write code that only executes the first time a window is opened, you'd put it in the open event of the window. Now, time for the test. If you wanted to write code that executed when a DataWindow was "opened", which event would you use? You'd use the constructor event. The constructor event fires when the DataWindow is created. Each control on a window will fire its constructor event before the window even begins its open sequence. Assume you have three controls on a window: cb_ok (which has a tab order of 1), sle_1, and dw_1. If you open this window as a sheet using the OpenSheet() function, you'd get the following event sequence:

```
cb_ok::constructor
sle_1::constructor
dw_1::constructor
window::open
window::show
window::resize
window::activate
cb_ok::getfocus
```

If you opened an SDI window using the Open() function you'd get the following:

```
cb_ok::constructor
sle_1::constructor
dw_1::constructor
window::open
window::activate
cb_ok::getfocus
window::show
window::resize
```

One caveat is that none of the window initialization code that you normally put in your open event will have been executed when the constructor events fire. If you pass data to your window with OpenSheetWithParm() or OpenWithParm() then you need to take care in using the message object in your constructor events. If any of your constructor events change the StringParm, DoubleParm, or PowerObjectParm attributes of the message object, your open event may get invalid information in the message object.

Working with the Transaction Object

Automatically Setting the Transaction Object

If you are like me, you hate keying dw_1.SetTransObject(SQLCA) all the time. What a pain. 99% of the time, we're going to use SQLCA. So why not create some default behavior on our DataWindow to set itself to SQLCA. To do this, we'll need to use an event that will fire when the DataWindow is created. As we've just seen, that event is the constructor event.

Event: Constructor

To have your DataWindow automatically use SQLCA, put the following line of code in the ancestor event for dwa_main.

Object: dwa_main

```
SetTransObject( SQLCA )
```

Now that was hard wasn't it! Don't worry if you are using an external DataWindow, Power-Builder won't ever try to use the transaction object anyway! If you always use dwa_main then you'll never have to code SetTransObject(SQLCA) again. However, just remember to call SetTransObject() if you need to use a different transaction object. If you need to use a different transaction object, you can just call SetTransObject() again in your descendant window or DataWindow.

Keeping Track of the Transaction Object

Have you ever written embedded SQL in the itemchanged event of a DataWindow? If so, you probably used SQLCA as your transaction object. Perhaps you have an instance variable on your window that holds the current window's transaction object. What happens when you have the need to have one DataWindow on a window get data from one source, say SYBASE, and the other DataWindow get data from WATCOM? Well, you may have had to add another instance variable for the specific window that needs this functionality. However, there is a better, more object-oriented way of doing this. The way we can do that is to have the DataWindow tell us the transaction object that it is using. However, PowerBuilder doesn't give us that functionality. Once you call SetTransObject(), there isn't a way to do a corresponding GetTransObject().

Hold on you may say! What about GetTrans(). Well, GetTrans() returns to us something call the internal transaction object. This gets set when we call SetTrans(). However, the internal transaction object has nothing to do with the transaction object we use when we call Set-TransObject().

Well if PowerBuilder won't let us get that information we'll have to use an array of instance variables to keep track of each transaction object for each DataWindow right? Wrong. We'll let the DataWindow give us that information by overriding some of PowerBuilder's built-in behavior.

You can override any of PowerBuilder's built-in object functions through inheritance. What we can do is create an instance variable to hold the transaction object, override the SetTransObject() function to populate our instance variable, and then create a function to return that instance variable.

The first step is to declare the following instance variable:

```
protected    transaction   SQLTrans
```

After declaring the instance variable, declare the following function:

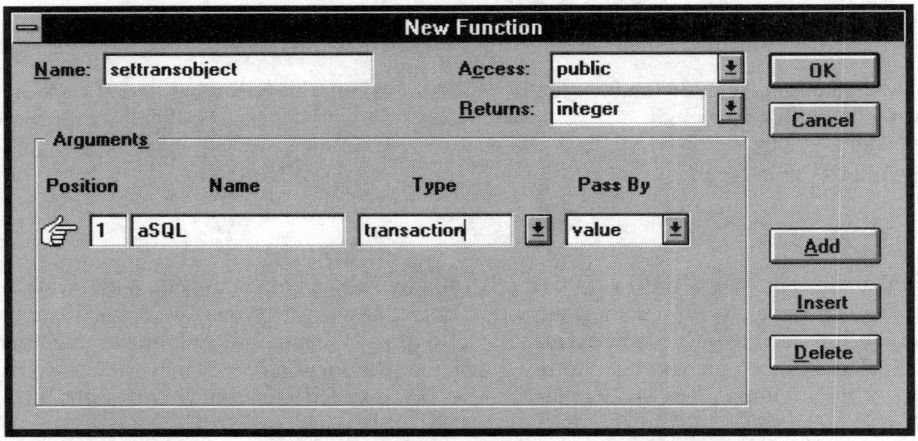

Figure 43-3: Declaration of our SetTransObject function.

This is the code for the new SetTransObject Function:

Function: SetTransObject(transaction)

Object: dwa_main

```
Function: public integer SetTransObject( transaction aSQL)
integer  rc
rc = Super::SetTransObject( aSQL )
if rc > 0 then
 SQLTrans = aSQL
end if
return rc
```

What our new SetTransObject() function does is call the ancestor SetTransObject. What is the ancestor of dwa_main? Well, its the built-in PowerBuilder SetTransObject. Therefore, we're just calling the default SetTransObject function. If the SetTransObject is successful then we're making SQLTrans point to the new transaction object.

Function: GetTransObject()

Now, if you'll notice, we declared SQLTrans as a protected variable. This means that if someone tries to write code in a window like dw_1.SQLTrans = SQLCA, it won't compile. What I prefer to do in this case is create a function to return the transaction object. Let's name this function GetTransObject. Here's the simple function:

Object: dwa_main

```
Function: public transaction GetTransObject( )
return SQLTrans
```

To get the transaction object from a DataWindow now, we'll just issue a dw_1.GetTransOb-ject() function. I suspect that Powersoft may eventually add this function as a system level function. If so, you can just delete this function declaration at that time.

Now when you need to write embedded SQL in a DataWindow, you'll do something like the following:

```
SELECT sum(balance)
FROM invoice
WHERE customer_id = :cust_id
USING   SQLTrans ;
```

[Note: You may want to add the SQLTrans instance variable to your main window ancestor also. This way you can pass a transaction object to a window as a default. Any embedded SQL you write in any window will use SQLTrans instead of SQLCA. This allows you to have a window use any login or transaction needed. Remember, if at all possible, don't hard code object references which is what we are doing when we use SQLCA.]

Selecting Rows

We generally select rows in DataWindows. The user has to select a row to change or a row to see more detail on. Perhaps we are going to allow the user to delete or modify a group of rows and we need to allow them to select multiple rows. This all relatively easy in Power-Builder. However, if you don't have standard functions to handle this in a DataWindow ancestor, it can become cumbersome. Let's take a look at various ways we can select rows.

No row highlighting at all

The normal behavior of a DataWindow is to not highlight any rows at all. This is, of course, pretty easy to program. It means you do nothing. This type of behavior is good for lists of data the user can only scroll through and view or for single row DataWindows.

No row highlighting, use focus indicator

One thing we can do is use the SetRowFocusIndicator function to highlight the current row. A focus indicator shows a graphic on the screen pointing to the current row. A common use of this is to have a little hand pointing to the current row. There will only be one focus indicator per DataWindow because there is only one current row at a time. The focus indicator is generally used in a multi-row updateable DataWindow. To set the focus indicator to a pointing hand, issue the following function call:

```
SetRowFocusIndicator( Hand! )
```

You can also specify Off! to turn on the indicator, FocusRect! to specify a dotted line focus rectangle that covers the borders of the whole row. Finally, you can specify a picture control to use.

The reason I generally don't highlight rows in an editable DataWindow is you get some really ugly looking "reverse" highlighting going on if the user has text selected in a column. The following two figures show this behavior:

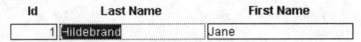

Figure 43-4: User has Last Name Column Selected

Now, if we issue a SelectRow(1, TRUE), the first row will highlighted and the screen will look like:

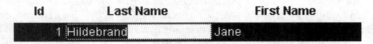

This "reverse" highlighting doesn't look so good.

Single Row Selection

Single row selection means that the user can only have one row selected at a time. This is useful for situations when the user is going to select one row to perform some sort of action upon such as show detail or delete. The following code in the RowFocusChanged event will allow single row selection:

Event: RowFocusChanged

Object: Any DataWindow

```
if GetRow() > 0 then
 SelectRow( 0, FALSE )
 SelectRow( GetRow(), TRUE )
end if
```

Automatic Selection of Multiple Rows

Auto selection of multiple rows means that as the user clicks on an unhighlighted row, that row will become highlighted—and vice-versa. If the user clicks on a highlighted row, then the row will become unhighlighted.

To make such behavior work, put the following code in your RowFocusChanged event:

Event: RowFocusChanged

Object: Any DataWindow

```
if GetRow() > 0 then
 if IsSelected( GetRow() ) then
 SelectRow( GetRow(), FALSE )
 else
 SelectRow( GetRow(), TRUE )
 end if
end if
```

A shorter version of this is:

```
if GetRow() > 0 then SelectRow( GetRow(), NOT IsSelected( GetRow()))
```

Use of Shift-Click, Control-Click, and Control-Shift-Click

When you use program manager, or almost any other windows program, you can use keyboard to alter the select behavior of your mouse AND keyboard actions. PowerBuilder doesn't give the DataWindow any of this capability, we've got to program it ourselves.

To create this type of functionality we need to keep track of an anchor row. When you use the shift or control-shift key, the rows selected are between the anchor row and the current row the user is clicking or keying onto. So the DataWindow will have to keep track of its current anchor row. To do so, we'll create an instance variable:

```
protected  long il_anchor_row
```

Now when the user clicks or makes a keyboard action, we're going to test whether the user has the Shift or Control key down using the KeyDown() function and checking for KeyShift! and KeyControl!. Here's a table with the functionality we're talking about:

Keys Down	Action
None	Highlight current row only
Only Control	Toggle current row highlight
Only Shift	Clear highlight and select from anchor to current row
Control-Shift	Add rows between anchor and current row to selection

Creating Select Functions

To make this behavior work from when the user clicks and when the user uses the keyboard, we'll have to call our functionality that selects the rows from the clicked event and a custom user event mapped to the pbm_dwnkey event. This way the select behavior is called regardless of whether the user uses the mouse or keyboard. You could put this functionality into the RowFocusChanged event also. However, I like to be able to do a SetRow() and not have various rows highlighted and unhighlighted.

Also, to make this row selection functionality reusable, we're going to create some function. Two actually. One to set the type of select behavior we want and one to actually run that select behavior.

How will the DataWindow know which type of select behavior to perform? An instance variable:

```
protected  integer  ii_select_behavior
```

This variable will hold the following values:

Value	Description
0	No Select Allowed
1	One Row Selected at all times
2	Automatic Multiple Select
3	Full Keyboard Select with Click/Shift-Click
99	No Select Allowed; Use Hand Indicator

Whenever you have a protected or private variable, you need functions to all programmers to set the value and to get the value. In addition, you need functions to perform processing based on that variable.

Function: f_SetSelect(Select_behavior)

So the first function we'll write will allow the programmer to set the select behavior.

```
Function: public integer f_SetSelect( integer ai_select_behavior)
/*

 This function sets the select behavior of the DataWindow
 These are the valid select behaviors:
   0 = No Select
   1 = Single Select Only
   2 = Automatic Multiple Select
   3 = Full Select with Shift/Control-Shift ala Faxback
  99 = No Select with Hand Focus indicator
*/

CHOOSE CASE ai_select_behavior
 CASE 0, 1, 2, 3, 99
 ii_select_behavior = ai_select_behavior

 // At least one row must be selected
 if ai_select_behavior = 1 then
 f_process_select( GetRow(), "Keyboard" )
```

```
   end if

   if ai_select_behavior = 99 then
   SetRowFocusIndicator(Hand!)
    else
   SetRowFocusIndicator(OFF!)
   end if

    return 0
   CASE ELSE
    return -1
END CHOOSE
```

Function: f_ProcessSelect(long al_row, string as_input_type)

Once the selection type is set, each row has to be processed. I put this code into a function
called f_ProcessSelect. This function processes the select behavior. You tell the function the
row you want to process and whether processing coming via the keyboard or the mouse.
Here's the function:

```
long   l_row
boolean  b_reset_anchor
boolean  b_keyboard, b_mouse

// Is this keyboard or mouse action?
if Upper(left(as_input_type,1)) = "K" then
 b_keyboard = TRUE
else
 b_mouse = TRUE
end if

/*
 Make sure the user clicked on row, not a footer/header, etc.
*/

IF al_row < 1 THEN Return -1

/*
 Sometimes we may not want to reset the anchor_row variable
 So create a boolean to hold that fact.
*/
b_reset_anchor = TRUE

// Things go faster with Redraw false!
SetRedraw(FALSE)

/*
 Valid Select Behaviors:
    0 = No Select
    1 = Single Select Only
    2 = Automatic Multiple Select
    3 = Full Select with Shift/Control-Shift ala Faxback
   99 = No Select with Hand Focus indicator
*/

CHOOSE CASE ii_select_behavior
 CASE 0, 99
 // Do nothing.
```

```
CASE 1 // Single Select
SelectRow(0,FALSE)
SelectRow(al_row,TRUE)

CASE 2 // Automatic Multiple Select
// This only runs if the user clicks. Kinda strange to
// Do with the keyboard
if b_mouse then
SelectRow(al_row, NOT IsSelected( al_row ))
end if

CASE 3
IF keydown(KeyShift!) AND KeyDown(KeyControl!) THEN
/* Shift & Control: Add to current selection */
IF il_anchor_row > al_row then
FOR l_row = il_anchor_row TO al_row STEP -1
this.selectrow(l_row,TRUE)
NEXT
ELSE
FOR l_row = il_anchor_row TO al_row
this.selectrow(l_row,TRUE)
NEXT
END IF
ELSEIF KeyDown(KeyShift!) Then
/* Clear current selection then add new rows */
SelectRow(0,FALSE)
IF il_anchor_row > al_row then
FOR l_row = il_anchor_row TO al_row STEP -1
this.selectrow(l_row,TRUE)
NEXT
ELSE
FOR l_row = il_anchor_row TO al_row
this.selectrow(l_row,TRUE)
NEXT
END IF
b_reset_anchor = FALSE
ELSEIF Keydown(KeyControl!) THEN
/* Toggle selected on and off */
SelectRow( al_row, NOT IsSelected( al_row ) )
ELSE
/* For a normal click, clear out existing selection */
 SelectRow(0,FALSE)
 SelectRow(al_row,TRUE)
 END IF
END CHOOSE

SetRedraw(TRUE)
if b_reset_anchor then il_anchor_Row = al_row
return 0
```

Now, all we need to do now is call f_ProcessSelect() when we want to process a row selection. This function should be called when the user clicks on a row or when the user hits the up or down arrow on a DataWindow. In addition, I've got code here that traps the home and end keys as well. So here's the code that goes into the user event we_keydown event (mapped to pbm_dwnkey).

Event: we_keydown (pbm_dwnkey)

```
Object: Any DataWindow
if KeyDown(KeyDownArrow!) and GetRow() <> RowCount() then
 f_processSelect( GetRow() + 1 , "Keyboard")
elseif KeyDown(KeyUpArrow!) and GetRow() <> 1 then
 f_processSelect( GetRow() - 1 , "Keyboard")
elseif KeyDown(KeyHome!) and RowCount() > 0 then
 f_processSelect( 1, "KeyBoard")
elseif KeyDown(KeyEnd!) and RowCount() > 0 then
 f_processSelect( RowCount(), "Keyboard")
end if
```

Event: clicked

Object: Any DataWindow

And finally, we need code in the clicked event:

```
f_processSelect(GetClickedRow(), "Mouse")
```

Concept: Controllers

There as many ways of selecting various rows as you could possibly imagine. Because of this, your functions to select rows might get quite complicated and spaghetti like. Here's an idea: Create a non-visual object (Custom Class object in PowerBuilder 4.0 Terminology) that processes the selected rows. You'd have to pass this non-visual object the row you want to work with and what type of action initiated the function call. You could then instantiate the proper non-visual object at runtime to control your DataWindow. In addition, this select behavior would not be reusable and could be attached to any DataWindow you have. This is how the ObjectStart class library from Greenbrier and Russel implements their select behavior. Its worth looking into and very Object-Oriented.

Inserting & Deleting Rows

The Phantom Save

When we insert rows in a DataWindow, we usually do more than just call the InsertRow(). There's a ScrolltoRow(), a SetColumn(), and usually a few SetItems() to do some initialization. If you do a SetItem() on a new DataWindow, you'll find that you'll run into what I call a "phantom" save. The DataWindow will attempt to execute an INSERT statement for your new row because it thinks some data has changed (your SetItems made that happen.) Had you not done a SetItem, the row would be initialized with a row status of New!. PowerBuilder doesn't do any SQL with a row status New! because it knows you haven't actually typed any data. Now, if you insert a row, let's say a detail row in an order entry system, you're going to execute a SetItem() to set the order id of the detail row. When you do that, your row status will change to NewModified!. When the DataWindow is updated, an INSERT statement will be executed on that row. Has the user typed anything? No. Will the user understand when the INSERT fails with a NULL column error. No the user won't. What the user will say is that they inserted a row but didn't type anything into it. Why can't your program take care of that?

The way to overcome this problem is to change the row's status from NewModified! back to New!. The way to do this is with the SetItemStatus() function. The following line of code will change the row status to New! for us:

```
SetItemStatus( rownumber, 0, Primary!, NotModified! )
```

Now it may seem strange to set the status to NotModified, why not just change it to New? The reason we're changing it to NotModified is that ItemStatus really contains two different pieces of information: Modified or not modified and New or not new. So when you change the status to NotModified! what you are really telling the DataWindow to do is to "reset" the Modified bit. Therefore the modified bit goes off and the status goes from NewModified! to New!.

Now do we want all of our programmers to remember to do this each time? Probably not. Why don't we just do it for them? And the place we can do that is the InsertRow() function. In fact, what we can do is create a place for programmers to put the row initialization code. This will not only aid in development but also in maintenance. You'll always know where the initialization code goes. Now you come to a choice: event or function. Either way I advise you to go will draw criticism from certain circles. Object-oriented purists will tell you to go functions all the way (I tend to lean that way), but others will tell you to use events because they are easier to work with in PowerBuilder. In the end, its your call. You know how your organization works, you know the skills of your programmers, you know how O-O you want to be. In any event, the technique I use will work with both events or functions.

What we're going to do is override the built-in InsertRow() functionality of our DataWindow. We're going to add functionality to go call out to another function (or event if you like.) This function will hold the code to actually initialize your row—your SetItems. After calling your initialization functions, the InsertRow() function will then perform a SetItemStatus returning the rowstatus to New!. Once you set it up and begin using it, you'll never have to worry about phantom saves again.

Before continuing, let me introduce the concept of callouts. Let's say you inherit the following code:

```
long l_row
l_row = InsertRow()
ScrollToRow( l_row )
SetItem( l_row, "cust_id", is_customer_id )
SetItem( l_row, "order_id", ii_order_id )
SetItemStatus( l_row, 0, Primary!, NotModified! )
```

Well, if you wanted to make this generic, you'd probably want to keep track of the first three lines and the last one. The two SetItems in the middle will change based on each descendant. If you write your ancestor like the code above, you're into override city. You'll wind up making a copy of the InsertRow() and SetItemStatus code for each descendant. Definitely not cool. Nor reusable. The way you get ride of code like that is to code the SetItems elsewhere in a function or an event. In addition, what we'd like is to have the code shown above always execute whenever a programmer calls InsertRow(). What we're going to do is create our own InsertRow() function an override PowerBuilder's built-in one.

Function: InsertRow(row_number)

Object: dwa_main

```
public long InsertRow( long al_row )
long l_row
if al_row < 0 then return -1
l_row = Super::InsertRow( al_row )
// If you want to automatically ScrollToRow, include this line:
ScrollToRow( l_row )
f_initialize( l_row )
SetItemStatus( l_row, 0, Primary!, NotModified! )
```

In this example, we'll create a function called f_initialize in our ancestor DataWindow. There won't be any code in that function except a simple return 0. This is called a stub function or in C++ parlance it is similar to a virtual function.

If you wanted to use an event to do this, do the following:

Declare an event called ue_initialize in your DataWindow ancestor. Instead of calling ue_initialize() in the InsertRow() function, you'll use a TriggerEvent. Here's how:

```
long l_row
if al_row < 0 then return - 1
l_row = Super::InsertRow( al_row )
ScrollToRow( l_row )
Message.DoubleParm = l_row
TriggerEvent("ue_initialize")
SetItemStatus( l_row, 0, Primary!, NotModifed! )
```

So now you have an InsertRow that does a little bit extra and makes your programming life easier.

Deleting a Row

One thing I like to do when deleting a row is to as the user for confirmation. However, I believe the DataWindow should know whether it is supposed to ask for confirmation. Why is this? Because if you don't have the DataWindow do the work of asking, you have to write script like this all throughout your code:

```
rc = MessageBox("Confirm Delete", "Are you sure you want to delete?", &
    Question!, YesNo!)
if rc = 1 then DeleteRow(0)
```

I don't like to rewrite code like this over and over. I also don't like it to be in a global function since it isn't easy to then change the DeleteRow behavior on one given DataWindow. Putting things in global functions makes it harder to write reusable, encapsulated code.

So where can we put this code? We could create a function called f_deleterow() in our ancestor DataWindow. Then when we wanted to delete a row, we'd just call f_deleterow() instead of DeleteRow. Even this, to me, is not worth the effort. Why? Because then my programmers have to relearn how to Delete a row. Also, any other objects I might purchase from the outside won't use f_deleterow(). To me, its overkill because what I really should do is to Override the built-in PowerBuilder DeleteRow() function. I'll do this in my ancestor DataWindow control, dwa_main.

The way I'll implement this functionality is to use an instance variable on the DataWindow that describes the delete functionality. So, if the variable is 0 then I'll use PowerBuilder's delete functionality, otherwise if it is 1, I'll ask for a delete confirmation. The reason it isn't a boolean is because I may add cases in the future such as only to ask if the row is a pre-existing row.

Here's the code needed to override PowerBuilder's DeleteRow() function:

Instance Variable:

Object: dwa_main

```
protected integer ii_delete_behavior = 0
```

Function: f_ConfirmDelete(boolean)

Object: dwa_main

```
public boolean f_ConfirmDelete(boolean ab_confirm)
boolean  ab_original_delete
ab_original_delete = ii_delete_behavior
if ab_confirm then
 ii_delete_behavior = 1
else
 ii_delete_behavior = 0
end if
return ab_original_delete
```

Function: DeleteRow(row)

DeleteRow is a built in PowerBuilder function that we are going to override. This is why the function doesn't start with f_.

Object: dwa_main
```
public int DeleteRow( long a_row )
integer rc
if ii_delete_behavior = 1 then
 if MessageBox( title, "Confirm Deletion of this row", &
   Stop!, YesNo! ) = 2
 return -1
```

```
 end if
end if
rc = Super::DeleteRow( a_row )
return rc
```

Using Modify and Describe

As you probably know, the real power behind the DataWindow is in the use of Modify and Describe. As you probably know, the DataWindow Control and the DataWindow Object are separate entities. The object defines what goes to and from the RDBMS as well as the presentation style. The control acts as a viewport to the dataobject and contains events and Powerscript for processing logic. During runtime, you can't directly access the objects on your dataobject; you've got to use Modify or Describe to either set or retrieve information about an object on the DataWindow.

The Modify statement is covered elsewhere in this book so I won't go into how it works. But we will cover some useful techniques you can use with Modify and Describe to add good ancestor functionality to your windows.

Here are some useful attributes of the dataobject that you might want to use:

DataWindow Object Level Attributes:

DataWindow.Column.Count	# of columns in the DWO
DataWindow.Data	Gives data in tab delimited string
DataWindow.FirstRowOnPage	Row at the top of the visible DWC
DataWindow.LastRowOnPage	Row at the botton of the visible DWC
DataWindow.MessageTitle	Default message box title for DataWindow error messages
DataWindow.Nested	Whether the DataWindow has nested reports
DataWindow.Objects	Tab delimited list of objects on the DataWindow
DataWindow.Print.<attrib>	Printing Attributes

	Collate: Collate multiple copies or not
	Copies: How many copies to print
	Duplex: Simple, Verticle Duplexing, or Horizontal Duplexing
	DocumentName: Document name for your print spooler reference
	Filename: File to send print output to, blank means printer
	Orientation: Portrait or Landscape
	Page.Range: Specify "1, 5-10, 15", etc. Can be multiple ranges
	Page.RangeInclude: Odd, Even, or All
	Preview: Display DataWindow in preview mode or not
	Prompt: Prompt for cancellation of print before job begins
DataWindow.ReadOnly	Sets the DataWindow to be readonly or not
DataWindow.QueryMode	Set and reset QueryMode
DataWindow.QuerySort	Whether QueryMode has a sorting option
DataWindow.Syntax	Returns the complete syntax of the DataWindow
DataWindow.Syntax.Data	Returns the syntax and data of the DataWindow in parse format. With this you can issue a dw_1.Create(syntax, errorbuffer) to recreate the DataWindow with data.
DataWindow.Table.Update	Table which the DW is set to Update
DataWindow.Zoom	DataWindow Scaling

Column or Object Level Attributes:

Columns can be specified by Column Name or "#" and column number.

<column>.Border	0 = None, 5 = 3D Lowered
<column>.ColType	Returns type of column: Char(x), Numeric
<column>.dbName	Table and Column name in the form table.column
<column>.Font	Font Characteristics

	Escapement, Face, Family, Height, Italic, Weight
<column>.Format	What is the display format of the column?
<column>.Height	Height of the column
<column>.Height.Auto-size	Whether the column is autosized
<column>.Initial	What is the initial value of the column?
<column>.Key	Is the column part of Primary Key? yes/no
<column>.Name	What is the name of the column on DWO?
<column>.Protect	Can user enter data in column? 1/0)
<column>.TabSequence	What is the tab order of the column?
<column>.Tag	What is the tag value for the column?
<column>.Update	Is the column updateable to DBMS? yes/no
<column>.Validation	Validation expression
<column>.Valida-tionMsg	Validation error message
<column>.Width	Width of the column

Getting the Number of Columns

When writing generic functionality, one of the most common things you'll do is loop through the columns on the DataWindow. You'll loop through and the do some sort of test and if that test is true, you'll perform the function you want to on that particular column. Before doing this, you'll need to know how many columns are on the DataWindow. This functionality is pretty straightforward:

```
int i_columns
i_columns = Integer( Describe( "DataWindow.Column.Count" ))
```

If you plan to work a lot with columns on a DataWindow, you might want to create a function to return this value so you don't have to type this over and over. Here's the function:
Function: public int f_GetColumnCount()

```
Return Integer( Describe ( "DataWindow.Column.Count" ) )
```

Getting a Column Name

If you have a column number, such as 1. How do you get the name of the column? One way is to do a SetColumn(1) and then a GetColumnName(). However, this is a bit extreme and makes your programming life a real pain. The way to do it is to ask the DataWindow for the name using Describe(attribute.name). So here's how we do it:

```
string s_colname
integer i, i_count
i_count = f_GetColumnCount()
for i = 1 to i_count
 s_colname = Describe("#" + string(i) + ".Name")
 //... do something with the column using s_colname
next
```

If you do this a lot (and I do), you could create your own GetColumnName() function and overload PowerBuilder's built in one. I'd love to be able to call GetColumnName(column_number) and get the column's number. Well, since I inherit all my DataWindows from a common ancestor, dwa_main, I can have that functionality. Here it is:

Function: GetColumnName(column_number)

Object: dwa_main

```
Function: public string GetColumnName ( int ai_column_number )
string s_colname
s_colname = Describe("#" + string(i_col) + ".Name")
if s_colname = "!" or s_colname = "?" then s_colname = ""
return s_colname
```

Setting a Column Border

You can use the function SetBorderStyle(column, style) to set the border style of a DataWindow column. However, with the SetBorderStyle() function you are limited to the following styles: None, ShadowBox, 3D Lowered, and 3D Raised. You can't set the border to a line an underline or a resize box like you can in Modify.

Modify and Describe usually use the format "object.attribute" in the Modify string. However, if you don't know the column name, you can use the format "#<column number>.attribute". With this feature in mind, if you wanted to loop through each column on the DataWindow and give it a Resize border you could do the following:

```
int i_column, i
i_columns = Integer( Describe( "DataWindow.Column.Count" ))
for i = 1 to i_columns
 // Use the Modify(#<column#>.Attribute) Format
 Modify("#" + String(i) + ".Border=3")

next i
```

Use of Tag Value for MicroHelp

Every object in the DataWindow has a tag value. The tag value is just a string for programmer use. You can put anything into that string and process it accordingly. I use the tag value to flag certain columns that need specific behavior. For example, I have code that automatically protects key columns on a DataWindow from changes. However, there are times when I don't want a particular column protected. Well, instead of having to program a Modify statement each time, I just have my protection logic check for the string "[NOPROTECT]" in the column's tag value.

The most common use of the tag value is for MicroHelp. Since you can define default tag values in the comments in PowerBuilder's extended attributes, you can define help once in the Database painter extended attribute comments and each new DataWindow will have those comments in the tag values. In fact, if you use Erwin or S-Designor, you can define comments in those programs and have them transferred to the extended attribute repository in PowerBuilder.

Let's take a look at how to do automatic MicroHelp. I am assuming you have a global variable named gw_FRAME which points to the MDI frame. (In the open event of your MDI frame put the line gw_FRAME = this, declare gw_FRAME as a window object type.) If you don't like the idea of a global variable, you could try Parent.ParentWindow() since the parent of any MDI sheet is the MDI frame.

Events: ItemFocusChanged *and* GetFocus

Object: dwa_main

```
if GetRow() < 1 then return
string s_help
s_help = Describe( GetColumnName() + ".Tag" )
if s_help = "?" then    // No tag value
 gw_FRAME.SetMicroHelp("Enter " + GetColumnName() )
else
 if Pos( s_help, "[" ) > 0 then
 s_help = left( s_help, Pos( s_help, "[" ) - 1 )
 end if
 gw_FRAME.SetMicroHelp( s_help )
end if
```

In your DataWindow's losefocus event you need to set the microhelp back to your default.

Event:LoseFocus

Object: dwa_main

In PowerBuilder 3.0, you'd do the following:

```
gw_FRAME.SetMicroHelp( "Ready" )
```

In PowerBuilder 4.0, do this:

```
gw_FRAME.SetMicroHelp( GetApplication().MicroHelpDefault )
```

Checking for a Key Column

Now what if you wanted to set the border of each key column to underlined? (You can set unique or Primary Key column in the Rows --> Update menu of the DataWindow object painter. Well, just stick an IF statement in your code and you are off and running:

If a column is a key column on the DataWindow, then the describe string "column.key" will return yes, otherwise it returns no. Remember, the DataWindow returns yes/no in lower case so your string comparison should take that into account.

```
int i_column, i
i_columns = Integer( Describe( "DataWindow.Column.Count" ))
for i = 1 to i_columns
 // Remember to make yes in lower case on the next line
 if Describe("#" + String(i) + ".Key" ) = "yes" then
 Modify("#" + String(i) + ".Border=4")
 end if
next i
```

Protecting Columns From Changes

There are times when you don't want a user to make changes to a column. Perhaps the column doesn't need updating for your purposes; perhaps the user doesn't have security to change the column. Perhaps its Tuesday and you can't change a column on Tuesday—who knows. In PowerBuilder 3.0 the only way we could protect a column from user changes was to set the tab order to 0. When we wanted to unprotect the column we'd have to set the tab order back to its original value. This meant we needed to keep the tab order information around in an instance variable. One technique that I used was to read all the tab sequences into an array when the DataWindow was created. (This would be in the constructor event of the DataWindow.) If I change the tab order of column five to 0, all I had to do was look at array element five to set the tab order back.

PowerBuilder 4.0 now gives a much simpler way of doing this and that is the Protect attribute. If a column's protect attribute is 1 then the column can't be entered by the user. If protect = 0 then the user can make a change.

This is a much, much, much better way of doing things than in 3.0. In fact, some the techniques that I'm going to show replaced many lines of Powerscript that tested for various conditions. It made my code much more readable and simplified.

So here's the basic form of the protect. Assume we've got a table with id as a column. To make id unchangable by the user, we'd have the following line of code:

dw_1.Modify("id.protect=1")

If you want to completely protect the DataWindow from changes, there are at least five ways to go:

1) Set the DataWindow to Redraw(FALSE)
2) Set the enabled attribute of the DataWindow to FALSE
3) Set the Tab Sequence of each column to 0
4) Set the DataWindow to "Read Only" using Modify("DataWindow.ReadOnly = yes")
5) Protect all the columns from change (loop and set protect attribute = 1 for all columns)

The first two options completely disable the DataWindow from being changed. You can't event scroll down. At least in the second form you could programmatically change the display of the DataWindow. The third form is how we'd stop the user from making changes to column but we'd require the original tab sequences to change them back. The fourth was also available with PowerBuilder 3.0. The only effective difference between options four and five is that when the user clicks on a column, the itemfocus will not change. Also, in the fourth form, the user can still click on different columns. Finally, in the fourth form the user can hit the tab key to go from column to column. The fifth is more restrictive than the fourth and preferable when you only want to user to select columns instead of editing them.

Function: f_Protect(string as_colname, boolean ab_protect)

Because I protect columns quite often, I've come up with a function to do the protection. Its called f_protect (gee what innovative naming!) It sets the protect attribute to a 1 or 0 and returns what the protect attribute was before you just set it. If the column name you send is incorrect, it returns a NULL.

Object: dwa_main

```
public boolean f_Protect( string as_colname, boolean ab_protect )

boolean    ab_last
integer    i_colnumber, i_protect
SetNull( ab_last )

if IsNumber(as_colname) and Pos(as_colname, "#") = 0 then
 as_colname = "#" + as_colname
end if

if Describe(as_colname + ".ColType") <> "column" then
 return ab_last // Return a null
end if

ab_last = (Integer(Describe( as_colname + ".Protect")) = 1 )

if ab_protect then i_protect = 1 else i_protect = 0
Modify(as_colname + ".Protect=" + s )
return ab_last
```

Only Protecting Key Columns

This function works well if you just want to turn the protection on and off for a given column regardless of row. However, there are times we only want protection given for certain rows. For example, I've been asked on several occasions to provide the capability of disallowing changes if the user is trying to change a key column. This is a pretty good request since changing the primary key is something you usually want to control if possible. In 3.0, I'd have to change the tab order and remember that tab order in case the user wanted us to repro-gram it to allows maintenance on those columns later. In 4.0, the job is a bit easier. Remem-ber that Describe("column.KEY") will return a yes/no depending on whether the column is a key one.

There will be times when I also want columns other than the key to be protected. In addition, I may want certain key columns to be changeable. What I need is a way to either force a col-umn to be protected or to make sure it isn't protected. The mechanism must be transportable from window to window for the same DataWindow object. So, where in the DataWindow object can I store information like this for each column? How about the tag! To force a col-umn to be protected, I'll put the word "[PROTECT]" in my tag, otherwise if I want to keep it from being protected, I'll put the word "[NOPROTECT]" in the tag. The algorithm used to do the protection will need to check for these before doing its work.

Given these specs, here's the functionality you'll need to run to get the desired behavior: So the functionality to protect key columns is:

```
int    i_count, i
string  s_colname, s_tag

count = f_GetColumnCount()

FOR i = 1 to count
  s_colname = Describe("#" + string(i) + ".Name")
  s_Tag = Describe( s_colname + ".Tag")
  IF (( s_colname + ".key" = "yes" ) AND &
      POS( s_Tag, "[NOPROTECT]" = 0 )) OR &
      POS( s_Tag, "[PROTECT]" = 1 ) THEN
  f_protect( s_colname, TRUE )
  END IF
NEXT
```

Creating a DataWindow that Only Allows New Data

You may have come across the need to only allow changes on rows that are new. That means that the user can look at the old data but only change the new data. I can tell you from expe-rience that trying to do this in PowerBuilder 3.0 was not easy. It worked but the code needed to enforce that behavior was a pain to write and maintain since it required you to do lots of stuff in the RowFocusChanged event.

The solution to the problem in 4.0 is now trivial. The reason is that there are now two new DataWindow object level functions: IsRowNew() and IsRowModified().

IsRowNew() returns true if the row has been inserted using the InsertRow() function. It is false if the row was retrieved from the database.

IsRowModified() returns true if the current row has been changed by the user. It is false if no changes have been made.

Because of the IsRowNew() function, we can easily write code to only allow changes if the row is new. Here's how we'll do it:

Loop through each column.

Set the Protect Attribute to be equal to If(IsRowNew(), 0, 1) using the following attribute setting:

column.Protect='1~tIF(IsRowNew(), 0, 1)'

If you aren't familiar with this extended version of Modify where you can make an attribute equal to an expression, check out the on-line help for Modify. It explains it quite well.

Really hard wasn't it. NOT. In fact, if you use the new DataWindow --> Attribute right mouse button menu in the DataWindow painter, you could set the protect attribute manually for each column and have no need for PowerScript to execute!

Here's the code:

```
int i_column, i
string s_modstring
i_columns = Integer( Describe( "DataWindow.Column.Count" ))
for i = 1 to i_columns
 Modify( "#" + string(i) + ".Protect=`1~t" + &
 "IF( IsRowNew(), 0, 1 )'")
next i
```

You can apply this technique to change the previous example to only allow changes to primary key columns on new rows. Here's the code:

```
int   i_count, i
string  s_colname, s_tag

count = f_GetColumnCount()

FOR i = 1 to count
 s_colname = Describe("#" + string(i) + ".Name")
 s_Tag = Describe( s_colname + ".Tag")
 IF (( s_colname + ".key" = "yes" ) AND &
     POS( s_Tag, "[NOPROTECT]" = 0 )) OR &
     POS( s_Tag, "[PROTECT]" = 1 ) THEN
 Modify( s_colname + ".Protect=`1~t" + &
 "IF( IsRowNew(), 0, 1 )'")
 END IF
NEXT
```

Conclusions

If you haven't been doing much with DataWindows, I hope this chapter opened your eyes to some its amazing possibilities. We didn't talk about QueryMode, Sharing, dynamic DataWindow Creation, using Stored Procedures, dynamically changing the SQL Select statement, or a whole laundry list of things you can do with DataWindows. We've barely scratched the surface. Even so, what I've presented is considered advanced by many people. The Power-

Builder community hasn't been well educated on the real underlying power of the DataWindow. I encourage you to explore the DataWindow's possibilities and don't be intimidated by the Modify and Describe functions. They really are tamer than they seem.

There is one thing you must do, have to do, cannot live without. That thing is to always inherit from some ancestor DataWindow. If you aren't doing that, you'll lose out on a lost of advanced functionality you could give your systems in the future as you learn more about DataWindows.

CHAPTER 44

PowerBuilder
Version 5.0 and Beyond

By Michael MacDonald

PowerBuilder Version 5.0 and Beyond

by **Michael MacDonald**

This is the fun chapter. The one where I get to take educated guesses about what lies in store for us in future releases of PowerBuilder, as well as unabashedly mix in my own personal wish list. It is my hope that this list become somewhat self–fulfilling, in that the good folks in Concord, MA are certain to read this and maybe, just maybe, say, "Gee, why didn't we think of that?" Of course, it is just as likely one engineer will turn to the other and say, "Who does this guy think he is?"

It was also in this chapter that I had planned to predict a buy-out of Powersoft (Yes!). The only trouble is that the prediction came sooner than I or most anyone expected. And I didn't see the Sybase move coming at all. I suppose I was going to predict a Borland, or possibly even Microsoft merger, the year after next.

So what does the merger do to the other database? Watcom is a very capable server engine and with its new-found stored procedures and triggers, has considerable overlap in function-ality with SQL Server itself. For the time being, the two will develop in tandem, with Wat-com being positioned as a departmental server, and Sybase being touted as an enterprise solution.

Beyond that, all else should remain status quo with the good folks in Waterloo. They have C++ compiler technology that is second to none, and remain the only game in town when it comes to compiling Netware Loadable Modules. VX–Rexx is a great product for OS/2, and along with their other products, Watcom represents true technical excellence.

OS/2 for the masses but not for you

Speaking of OS/2, why isn't Powersoft developing a PowerBuilder for OS/2, and will it anytime soon? Don't expect it before 5.0, and possibly not even then. The problem lies in Powersoft's (wise) insistence on maintaining a single code base. Calls to the Windows API will execute correctly on the Macintosh and MOTIF through the use of libraries from Alture and Bristol Technologies. No such tool exists on the OS/2 platform, and until it does, I would not hold my breath for a native OS/2 PowerBuilder.

Compiled PowerBuilder? Yes!

And will PowerBuilder ever be a truly compiled language? The answer is yes, and probably in Version 5.0. David Dewan, Vice President for Technology at Powersoft, has already gone on record as saying, "Using Watcom technology, we'll go straight to compiled code on the most popular platforms, and most likely go to [generated] C, which can go to compiled code on all the other platforms." While they are at it, why not generate C code for Windows platforms too?

As exciting as that may be, there are more mundane improvements to PowerBuilder I anticipate that will also make the product much more enjoyable to use, and/or more powerful.

Editor! Editor!

Perhaps the most annoying aspect of PowerBuilder is having such a weak editor in so powerful a package. The first thing that you will see when you open PowerBuilder 5.0 (remember, I have no insider information) is a color-coded editor. Comments will be in green, reserved words in black, variables in blue, and so on. Just like every other good development environment!

Speaking of the editor, here's one that annoys me (and it will be fixed! – I think). Put the cursor on a line with forty characters in it and press the <END> key. The cursor goes to the end. All well and fine so far. Now, suppose the line below is four characters, and then the next line is forty characters again. Press the down arrow. The cursor goes to the end of the second line (the four character one). Press the down arrow again. The cursor stays at the fourth character. No! It should go to the end of the line like any other editor! Mass editing with the PowerBuilder editor is nigh to impossible. Who knows, perhaps you will see an intelligent indenter, such as with Visual Basic.

And let's really go for the gold. Now that we have an intelligent editor, let's be able to highlight a function or such, press <F5>, and go to that painter automatically. I think not.

Preferences for the Preferences Painter

The ugliest painter in PowerBuilder is the one for preferences. Mark my words–one day soon, David Litwack is gonna fire up PowerBuilder, open this particular painter, and say, "Nay, nay. This has got to go." The Preference Painter will be replaced by a tabbed dialog in Version 5. Or sooner.

Conditional compilation and compiler directives

You will also see conditional compilation in version 5.0:

```
#If debug then
Messagebox ("The value of X is",string(x))
#End If

#If ExeBuild then
....
#End If
```

Compiler directives:

```
#Include "Header.Fil"
```

Enough said. But I will really go out onto a limb and predict a new event for the Application object–the define event:

```
#define lbs_notify = 0x001
#define lbs_lb_sort = 0x002
```

Objects For hire
(Uncle! Uncle!)

Objects will become more ancestor-aware. Instead of just being able to display ancestor scripts, you will have a similar button available when you select; for example, declare window functions. An ancestor button will allow you to view the functions of the ancestor. The same will be true for objects. When you click on your inherited user object with the right mouse button, one of the options will be Object Functions. However, you will not see objects become descendant-aware, at least not in Version 5.

While we are talking about difficulty with ancestor objects, how about the annoyance of opening a window painter, only to be foiled because the painter for one of its components is open? Annoying! This is an inconsistency in the PowerBuilder interface from the word Go. Nowhere else does PowerBuilder protect me from myself when it comes to inheritance. Don't do it here. Give me a warning if you want, but allow me to do what I will. No more "Open of window failed, possible causes are ..." messages.

Arrays of controls
(or: the one thing I really like about Visual Basic)

Visual Basic has a nifty feature–arrays of controls. With this concept, instead of having say, cb_1, cb_2, . . . cb_100, you would have cb_1 [1 to 100]. Imagine, if you will, that you were programming the game Minesweeper in PowerBuilder (not that you would be likely do so). You might want to put ten rows of ten picture buttons on a window. You might find it necessary to write script behind each and every button to execute basically the same thing. With arrays of controls, all the picture buttons share the same script–you distinguish them by their index value: pb_button [1], pb_button [13], and so on. No more long IF THEN ELSEIF statements evaluating which of five different radio buttons is checked. While you can kind of simulate the same thing using the window's control array, it is really much less direct. I want arrays of controls, and if I have my way, will have them in Version 5. But, on this one I am not holding my breath.

DataWindow attributes revealed

DataWindows are not the easiest beasts to debug, and this is mostly because the debugger can't really see "inside" of them to their attributes. You will see major improvement here in Version 5. In fact, much of the debugger will see radical change.

Debugging the debugger

For those who are coming from a mainframe COBOL background, the PowerBuilder debugger is powerful indeed. However, it pales in comparison to those in Visual Basic, Borland's C++, and so on. This will change because it has to!

You will have the ability to "step over" functions in a script. You will have the ability to change code dynamically–while the application is running–and to specify the next line of code to execute. PowerBuilder will have, via the debugger, an "immediate mode," where you can type a function in a window and see the result immediately. You will see more flexible breaks. Instead of just breaking when a certain line of code is executed, you will see the ability to break when any of a variety of conditions is true, such as i_i_ctr > 10 or i_b_validated = FALSE. You will see a history stack–that is, the ability to see what the last "n" lines of code executed were. If you think this is all very aggressive, it is. But I don't have to write the debugger.

Since we're already commenting on debugging

The use of PBDEBUG and SQL Trace will be adequately documented and new options added. You will be able to monitor SQL access times, analyze inefficiencies in your code (to include blocks that are never executed), and generate opportune program dumps. You heard it here first.

Now, let's debug the comments

If an event has only comments scripted, it still fires. It's really ugly in the retrieverow event! Yes, I understand why, but I still want it fixed. And by fixed, I mean I don't want it to happen. A true compiler would take care of that of course, but it seems to me the interpreter could be a little smarter in the meantime.

Wizards and other geniuses

The option to generate an MDI application shell in Version 4 is just the beginning. The folks in Concord are already planning enough Wizards to make Bill Gates blush. There will even be a Wizard to format quotes and tildes. Just leave the spell checker out.

3—Dwithout special glasses

You will see one of the pet wants of my associate, Peter "Madman Pierre" Horwood: a 3–D tab object. And you won't have to wear special glasses to appreciate it. It will be based on the Windows95 object.

Call me back In the morning

And if all this isn't enough, PowerBuilder 5 will, I would hope, support Callbacks in DLLs. Right now it takes trickery and container .dlls to support libraries requiring callbacks. And wait, there's more.

Shhh! We're in the library

Powersoft will resist the much clamored for request for global search and replace across multiple objects. But they will cave in by Version 6 when several thousand programmers send in for free evaluation copies of Delphi. You will soon be able to perform searches across multiple .pbls. Not that any reader of this book would lose an object and not know what .pbl it was in.

The Library Painter will also sport a hierarchical regen facility in Version 5, and significant improvements in version control.

Check It out!

Version 5 would be a fine place to introduce a convenience in the Library Painter–to open an object at the same time that you check it out. You could call it, let's see, "Check Out and Open." Yes, I like it.

And lock it up

Ouch! How many times have I aligned my objects just so and placed them exactly where I want them, only to accidentally move them just a smidgen? Too many, and it's annoying. Version 5 will see an Align and Lock option, whereby the only way to move an object again will be from the Align menu with an Unlock Position command.

Pointed, dynamic personalities

Some PowerBuilder "variables" such as transaction objects are actually pointers. More traditional variables such as integers and strings are not pointers. However, as in C and C++, pointers to memory locations, as opposed to the actual values themselves, can and would be enormously helpful. Look for pointers around Version 6 or so as Watcom compiler technology makes itself felt ever more.

While we (and Powersoft) are at it, how about dynamically created variables?

```
pointer integer p_myinteger

p_myinteger = create integer
....
destroy p_myinteger
```

Structure, structure, how big art thou?

Team Powersoft Guru Bruce Armstrong wants a SizeOf (str) function in his Christmas stocking.

Object repositories

I suppose this one belongs more in the Library Painter section. But what I would like to be able to do is to cross-reference an object by all of the scripts that call or reference it. Imagine, I highlight function f_xyz and up pops a window displaying everywhere that I called that f_xyz function from. Now, that's a repository!
And an easy one:

How about built-in support for key search for dddw and ddlb, instead of coding it? What do you think–Version 5?

Ooo la la!

This is an international marketplace we work in, and English is not the only language on the face of this globe. PowerBuilder will make strides not only in internationalizing the product, but also in helping the programmer internationalize the application. A separation of the presentation and data layers in DataWindows will go a long way toward accomplishing this.

Modify dwModify

And not by renaming it to Modify (as Powersoft did in PowerBuilder 4.0)! I would like to be able to modify DataWindows by changing the attributes directly. Imagine a line of script dw_1.color = 255.

Lastly, the competition

Powersoft handily won the battle of the OOP, GUI, and database development tools by beginning work on a product before the demand existed. In other words, by seeing the future. Powersoft has been extremely nimble in this respect, even jumping from OS/2 to Windows when the first Win 3.0 betas shipped. Few of us remember now that previous versions of Windows were an abomination—it wasn't until 3.0 that sales hit the roof. In the past couple of years, PowerBuilder has been duking it out primarily with Gupta's SQL Windows. The latter is a very capable product, but it is the former that has won the sales battle and achieved the market presence. That is not to say that no battles lie ahead: ninety percent of the potential market lies untapped. The product those people and companies buy will determine the future of Powersoft and PowerBuilder.

So, who is the competition? Certainly SQL Windows remains a sticky competitor, continuing to produce an excellent set of development tools. Borland is introducing Delphi. And others certainly exist. The true future nemesis of PowerBuilder is; however, a product from the Pacific Northwest–none other than Visual Basic. Said an insider at PowerBuilder last year, "The only product set that we worry about for the next three years is Visual Basic."

At the same time that Sybase and Powersoft merged, another merger went relatively unnoticed. You will see a Concord–Cambridge courtship bloom between Powersoft and Lotus that will hit paydirt for both companies when Notes finally catches fire and sales go through the roof.

And those are my predictions. Thank you for reading and for buying this book, *PowerBuilder 4.0: Secrets of the PowerBuilder Masters*.

Products &
Services Directory

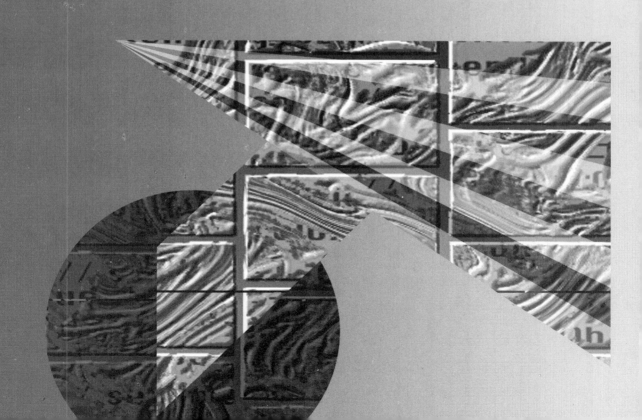

SPECIAL BOOK INSERT
PowerBuilder 4.0: Secrets of the Masters   Page 35

U.S. $12.00 (CANADA $15.00)

PowerBuilder Developer's Journal

APRIL 1995 - Volume: 2 Issue: 3

A SYS-CON Publication

SYS-CON
PUBLICATIONS

PowerBuilder Developer's Journal

PowerBuilder Developer's Journal is the only monthly technical source of quality PowerBuilder information. The PBDJ editorial team is packed with the world's top PowerBuilder experts, including nine members of Team Powersoft, a group of PowerBuilder developers hand-picked by Powersoft for their in-depth knowledge and ability to communicate that knowledge. Each monthly issue brings 50-80 pages of critical PowerBuilder information to advanced PowerBuilder developers.

SPECIAL BOOK INSERT PowerBuilder 4.0: Secrets of the Masters Pg 37

PowerProgrammer
M A G A Z I N E

APRIL/MAY 1995   A POWERBUILDER™ MAGAZINE FOR ex xBASE ex COBOL & ex VISUAL-BASIC PROGRAMMERS

POWERBUILDER STRING HANDLING:
An in depth look

IMPLEMENTING A TABBED DIALOG BOX

POWERBUILDER'S MOST DANGEROUS PROPERTY

BUILDER'S BLOCK:
What's In a Name

An Alternative to the DwShareData Function

DATAWINDOW TECHNIQUES:
Connecting PowerBuilder to the Database

A SYS-CON Publication

U.S. $6.95	Canada $9
U.K. £7	Germany DM 15
Japan ¥1,500	Switzerland SF 12

ISBN 1-886141-00-2

NEW COLUMN
Accessing COBOL from PowerBuilder

ADVANCED QUERY TECHNIQUES:
Using Self-Joins

PowerProgrammer

PowerProgrammer, a PowerBuilder
Magazine for ex-xBase, ex-COBOL and
ex-Visual Basic developers is devoted to
developers still in the process of learning
PowerBuilder, event-driven programming, graphical user interfaces, and
object-oriented techniques. A special
focus is also given to programmers who
are migrating from other relational databases to PowerBuilder. With the same in-
depth coverage and editorial quality of
PowerBuilder Developer's Journal,
PowerProgrammer Magazine will help
you make a successful transition to
PowerBuilder.

SPECIAL PREVIEW ISSUE

U.S. $15 (Canada $18)

SYBASE Developer's Journal

Special Preview Edition

A SYS-CON Publication

EDITORIAL BOARD

Derek Ball, Rey Bango, Steve Benfield,
Breck Carter, Tom Flynn, Ed Gaudet,
Randy Hompesch, Michael MacDonald,
Jeff Roberts, John Sirano

Executive Editor: Scott Davison
Managing Editor: Michael Griffith
Senior Editor: Ed Gaudet
Technical Editor: Rey Bango
API Editor: Ira Krakow
Microsoft SQL Server Editor: Joe Celko
Product Review Editor: Michael MacDonald
Tips & Techniques Editor: Breck Carter
PowerBuilder Editor: Randy Hompesch
Copy Editors: Jane Roseen, Alix Lowenthal

SUBSCRIPTIONS

For subscriptions and requests for bulk
orders,please send your letters to
Subscription Department

Subscription Hotline: 800-825-0061

Cover Price: $15/issue.
Domestic: $78/yr. (6 issues)
Canada/Mexico: $98/yr.
Overseas: Basic subscription price plus air-
mail postage (U.S. Banks or Money Orders).

Back Issues: $15 each

Chief Executive Officer: Fuat A. Kircaali
Vice President, Production: Jim Morgan
Vice President, Marketing: Carmen Gonzalez
Chief Financial Officer: Zack Ackerman
Circulation Manager: Shelley Ulyak

EDITORIAL OFFICES

SYS-CON Publications, Inc.
46 Holly Street, Jersey City, NJ 07305
Telephone: 201 332-1515
Fax: 201 333-7361
CompuServe: 73611,756
Postmaster: Second class postage is paid in
Jersey City, NJ and other USP locations.
Send address changes to Editorial Offices.

ISSN # 1078-1889

DISTRIBUTED in USA by International Periodical Distributors,
674 Via De La Valle, Suite 204, Solana Beach, CA 92075 (619) 481-7928

SYBASE Developer's Journal

SYBASE Developer's Journal is the newest title from SYS-CON Publications for SYBASE developers who are seeking quality SYBASE development and programming techniques written by the top SYBASE developers in the world. With real-life application development issues in mind, SYBASE Developer's Journal delivers invaluable knowledge to professional client/server programmers.

Index

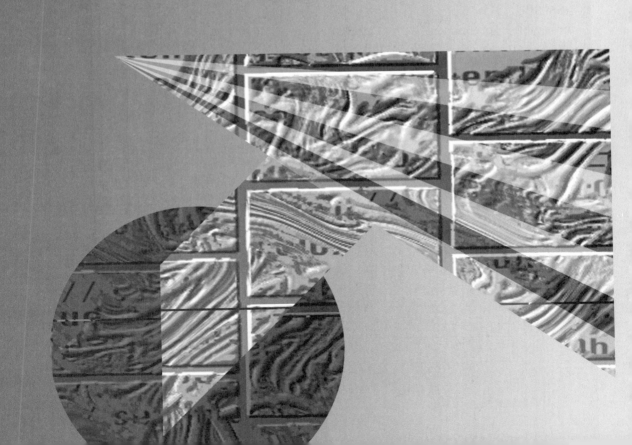

Price: $59.95 USD
(Price includes the CD-Rom)